Do Think Tanks Matter?

Do Think Tanks Matter?
Assessing the Impact of Public Policy Institutes

DONALD E. ABELSON

Third Edition, Revised and Expanded

McGill-Queen's University Press
Montreal & Kingston · London · Chicago

ISBN 978-0-7735-5324-8 (cloth)
ISBN 978-0-7735-5325-5 (paper)
ISBN 978-0-7735-5385-9 (ePDF)
ISBN 978-0-7735-5386-6 (ePUB)

Legal deposit fourth quarter 2018
Bibliothèque nationale du Québec

Printed in Canada on acid-free paper that is 100% ancient forest free (100% post-consumer recycled), processed chlorine free

This book has been published with the help of a grant from the J.B. Smallman Publication Fund, Faculty of Social Science, University of Western Ontario.

Funded by the Government of Canada | Financé par le gouvernement du Canada | Canada | Canada Council for the Arts | Conseil des arts du Canada

We acknowledge the support of the Canada Council for the Arts, which last year invested $153 million to bring the arts to Canadians throughout the country.

Nous remercions le Conseil des arts du Canada de son soutien. L'an dernier, le Conseil a investi 153 millions de dollars pour mettre de l'art dans la vie des Canadiennes et des Canadiens de tout le pays.

The author and publisher are grateful to the following for permission to draw on previously published material: Donald E. Abelson, "Do Think Tanks Matter? Opportunities, Constraints and Incentives for Think Tanks in Canada and the United States," *Global Society* 14, no. 2 (2000): 213–36; Donald E. Abelson, "Public Visibility and Policy Relevance: Assessing the Impact and Influence of Canadian Policy Institutes," *Canadian Public Administration* 42, no. 2 (summer 1999): 240–70; and Donald E. Abelson and Christine M. Carberry, "Following Suit or Falling Behind? A Comparative Analysis of Think Tanks in Canada and the United States," *Canadian Journal of Political Science* 31, no. 3 (1998): 525–55.

Library and Archives Canada Cataloguing in Publication

Abelson, Donald E., author
Do think tanks matter?: assessing the impact of public policy institutes/ Donald E. Abelson. – Third edition, revised and expanded.

Includes bibliographical references and index.
Issued in print and electronic formats.

ISBN 978-0-7735-5324-8 (cloth). – ISBN 978-0-7735-5325-5 (paper). – ISBN 978-0-7735-5385-9 (ePDF). – ISBN 978-0-7735-5386-6 (ePUB)

1. Policy sciences. 2. Research institutes. 3. Research institutes – Canada. 4. Research institutes – United States. I. Title.

H97.A24 2018 320.6 C2018-900333-2
C2018-900334-0

This book was typeset by Marquis Interscript in 10/12 Sabon.

To four dear friends, Adrian and Susan Hoad-Reddick
and Ralph and Mary Germaine

Contents

Tables and Figures ix

Acknowledgments xix

Acronyms xxi

Introduction 3

1 Surveying the Think Tank Landscape in the United States and Canada 21

2 Thinking about Think Tanks: A Conceptual Framework 58

3 In the Arena: Opportunities, Constraints, and Incentives for Think Tanks in the United States and Canada 73

4 Competing in the Marketplace of Ideas: The Strategies of Think Tanks 89

5 Public Visibility and Policy Relevance: Assessing the Influence of Think Tanks 105

6 On the Road to the White House: Presidential Candidates and the Think Tanks That Advised Them 150

7 Policy Experts or Policy Instruments? Think Tanks and the Debate over Constitutional Reform in Canada 180

8 In the Pipeline: Think Tanks and the Debate over Keystone XL 197

9 Conclusion: The More Things Change … Policy Influence, Policy Relevance, and the Future of Think Tanks in Canada, the United States, and Beyond 226

Appendix One: A Profile of Selected American Think Tanks 241

Appendix Two: A Profile of Selected Canadian Think Tanks 251

Appendix Three: Media Citations for Selected American Think Tanks, 1998–2008; 2009–16 267

Appendix Four: Media Citations for Selected Canadian Think Tanks, 2000–2008; 2009–16 311

Appendix Five: References to Selected American Think Tanks in the US Congress, 1999–2008; 2009–16 347

Appendix Six: References to Selected Think Tanks in Parliamentary Committees, 1999–2008; 2009–16 377

Appendix Seven: Documents Related to Keystone XL Pipeline 405

Notes 417

Bibliography 451

Index 531

Tables and Figures

TABLES

1.1 Selected Profiles of American Think Tanks 30
1.2 Selected Profiles of Canadian Think Tanks 31
5.1 Newspaper Citations for Selected American Think Tanks, 1991–97 110
5.1.1 Newspaper Citations for Selected American Think Tanks, 1998–2016 111
5.2 ABC, NBC, CBS, and CNN Evening News Citations for Selected American Think Tanks, 1991–97 112
5.2.1 ABC, NBC, CBS, and CNN Evening News Citations for Selected American Think Tanks, 1998–2016 113
5.3 References to Selected Canadian Think Tanks on CBC Radio, 1988–96 118
5.3.1 References to Selected Canadian Think Tanks in CBC Radio, 1997–2016 119
5.4 Media Citations for Selected Canadian Think Tanks, 1985–99 120
5.4.1 Media Citations for Selected Canadian Think Tanks, 2000–16 121
5.5 Newspaper Citations for Selected Canadian Think Tanks, 1985–99 124
5.5.1 Newspaper Citations for Selected Canadian Think Tanks, 2000–16 125
5.6 *Globe and Mail* Citations for Selected Canadian Think Tanks, 1985–99 126
5.6.1 *Globe and Mail* Citations for Selected Canadian Think Tanks, 2000–16 127

5.7 CTV National Evening News Citations for Selected Canadian Think Tanks, 1998–99 128
5.7.1 CTV National Evening News Citations for Selected Canadian Think Tanks, 2000–16 129
5.8 CBC TV National Evening News Citations for Selected Canadian Think Tanks, 1988–99 130
5.8.1 CBC TV National Evening News Citations for Selected Canadian Think Tanks, 2000–16 131
5.9 Ranking Research Institute Consultations 133
5.10 Federal Government Departments Consulting with Selected Canadian Think Tanks 134
5.11 Parliamentary Committee Reports Consulted for Think Tank Testimony 137
5.12 Appearances by Selected Think Tanks before Parliamentary Committees, 1980–99 139
5.12.1 Appearances by Selected Think Tanks before Parliamentary Committees, 2000–16 140
5.13 Appearances of Institutes for House Committee Testimony, 1980–99 141
5.13.1 Appearances of Institutes for House Committee Testimony, 2000–16 142
5.14 Appearances of Institutes for Senate Committee Testimony, 1980–99 144
5.14.1 Appearances of Institutes for Senate Committee Testimony, 2000–16 146
5.15 Appearances of Institutes for Joint Committee Testimony, 1980–99 148
5.16 Spearman's Rank Correlation Coefficient Results 148
A3.1 References to Selected American Think Tanks in National Media (television, newspapers, and magazines), 1998–2008 268
A3.1.1 References to Selected American Think Tanks in National American Media (television, newspapers and magazines), 2000–16 269
A.3.2 References to Selected American Think Tanks on American Television News, 1998–2008 270
A3.2.1 References to Selected American Think Tanks on American Television News, 2009–16 272
A3.3 References to Selected American Think Tanks on American Television News by Network, 1998–2008 273
A3.3.1 References to Selected American Think Tanks on American Television News by Network, 2009–16 274
A3.4 References to Selected American Think Tanks on ABC News, 1998–2008 275

A3.4.1 References to Selected American Think Tanks on ABC News, 1999–2016 277
A3.5 References to Selected American Think Tanks on NBC News, 1998–2008 278
A3.5.1 References to Selected American Think Tanks on NBC News, 2009–16 280
A3.6 References to Selected American Think Tanks on CBS News, 1998–2008 281
A3.6.1 References to Selected American Think Tanks on CBS News, 2009–16 283
A3.7 References to Selected American Think Tanks on CNN, 1998–2008 284
A3.7.1 References to Selected American Think Tanks on CNN, 2009–16 286
A3.8 References to Selected American Think Tanks on FOX News, 1998–2008 287
A3.8.1 References to Selected American Think Tanks on FOX News, 2009–16 288
A3.9 References to Selected American Think Tanks in National Newspapers, 1998–2008 289
A3.9.1 References to Selected American Think Tanks in National Newspapers, 2009–16 291
A3.10 References to Selected American Think Tanks in National Magazines, 1998–2008 293
A3.10.1 References to Selected American Think Tanks in National Magazines, 2009–16 294
A3.11 References to Selected American Think Tanks in Canadian and International Newspapers, 1998–2008 295
A3.11.1 References to Selected American Think Tanks in Canadian and International Newspapers, 2009–16 296
A3.12 References to Selected American Think Tanks in Canadian Newspapers, 1998–2008 297
A3.12.1 References to Selected American Think Tanks in Canadian Newspapers, 2009–16 298
A3.13 References to Selected American Think Tanks in International Newspapers, 1998–2008 299
A3.13.1 References to Selected American Think Tanks in International Newspapers, 2009–16 301
A3.14 Comparison of Annual Budget to Number of National Media References for Selected American Think Tanks, 1999–2008 303
A3.14.1 Comparison of Annual Budget to Number of National Media References for Selected American Think Tanks, 2009–16 305

A3.15 Comparison of Annual Budget to Number of International Media References for Selected American Think Tanks, 1999–2008 308
A3.15.1 Comparison of Annual Budget to Number of International Media References for Selected American Think Tanks, 2009–16 309
A4.1 Media Citations for Selected Canadian Think Tanks (radio, television, and newspaper), 2000–08 312
A4.1.1 Media Citations for Selected Canadian Think Tanks (radio, television and newspaper), 2009–16 314
A4.2 Television Citations for Selected Canadian Think Tanks, 2000–08 317
A4.2.1 Television Citations for Selected Canadian Think Tanks, 2009–16 318
A4.3 CBC TV National Evening News Citations for Selected Canadian Think Tanks, 2000–08 320
A4.3.1 CBC TV National Evening News Citations for Selected Canadian Think Tanks, 2009–16 322
A4.4 CTV National Evening News Citations for Selected Canadian Think Tanks, 2000–08 324
A4.4.1 CTV National Evening News Citations for Selected Canadian Think Tanks, 2009–16 326
A4.5 References to Selected Canadian Think Tanks on CBC Radio, Oct. 2004–08 328
A4.5.1 References to Selected Canadian Think Tanks on CBC Radio, 2009–16 330
A4.6 Newspaper Citations for Selected Canadian Think Tanks, 2000–08 332
A4.6.1 Newspaper Citations for Selected Canadian Think Tanks, 2009–16 335
A4.7 References to Selected Canadian Think Tanks in American Newspapers, 1998–2008 338
A4.7.1 References to Selected Canadian Think Tanks in American Newspapers, 2009–16 340
A4.8 Comparison of Annual Budget to Number of National Media References for Selected Canadian Think Tanks, 1999–2008 342
A4.8.1 Comparisons of Annual Budget to Number of National Media References for Selected Canadian Think Tanks, 2009–16 344
A5.1 Total References to Selected American Think Tanks in the US Congress (Senate, House of Representatives, *Extension of Remarks*, and *Daily Digest*), 1999–2008 348

A5.1.1 Total References to Selected American Think Tanks in the US Congress (Senate, House of Representatives, *Extension of Remarks* and *Daily Digest*), 2000–16 349
A5.2 References to Selected American Think Tanks in the US Senate, 1999–2008 352
A5.2.1 References to Selected American Think Tanks in the US Senate, 2009–16 354
A5.3 References to Selected American Think Tanks in the US House of Representatives, 1999–2008 356
A5.3.1 References to Selected American Think Tanks in the US House of Representatives, 2009–16 358
A5.4 References to Selected American Think Tanks in the US Congress (*Extension of Remarks*), 1999–2008 360
A5.4.1 References to Selected American Think Tanks in the US Congress (*Extension of Remarks*), 2009–16 361
A5.5 References to Selected American Think Tanks in the US Congress (*Daily Digest*), 1999–2008 364
A5.5.1 References to Selected American Think Tanks in the US Congress (*Daily Digest*), 2009–16 365
A5.6 Comparison of Annual Budget to Number of References in the US Congress for Selected American Think Tanks, 1999–2008 368
A5.6.1 Comparison of Annual Budget to Number of References in the US Congress for Selected American Think Tanks, 2009–16 370
A5.7 Appearances by Selected American Think Tanks before Congressional Committees, 1999–2008 372
A5.7.1 Appearances by Selected American Think Tanks before Congressional Committees, 2009–16 374
A5.8 Committees, United States Senate and House of Representatives 376
A6.1 Appearances by Selected Canadian Think Tanks before Parliamentary Committees, 1999–2008 378
A6.1.1 Appearances by Selected Canadian Think Tanks before Parliamentary Committees, 2009–16 379
A6.2 Appearances by Selected Canadian Think Tanks before Senate Committees, 1999–2008 382
A6.2.1 Appearances by Selected Canadian Think Tanks before Senate Committees, 2009–16 383
A6.3 Appearances by Selected Canadian Think Tanks before the House of Commons, 1999–2008 386
A6.3.1 Appearances by Selected Canadian Think Tanks before House of Commons, 2009–16 388

A6.4 References to Selected Canadian Think Tanks during Debates in the House of Commons, 1994–2008 390
A6.4.1 References to Selected Canadian Think Tanks during Debates in the House of Commons, 2009–16 393
A6.5 References to Selected Canadian Think Tanks during Debates in the Senate, 1994–2008 396
A6.5.1 References to Selected Canadian Think Tanks during Debates in the Senate, 2009–16 399
A6.6 Comparison of Annual Budget to Number of Appearances before Parliamentary Committees for Selected Canadian Think Tanks, 1994–2008 401
A6.6.1 Comparison of Annual Budget to Number of Appearances before Parliamentary Committees for Selected Canadian Think Tanks, 2009–16 403
A.7.1 Public Exposure of Selected US Think Tanks in Relation to Keystone XL 406
A.7.2 Newspaper Coverage of Selected Canadian Think Tanks in Relation to Keystone XL 414

FIGURES

A3.1 References to Selected American Think Tanks in National Media (television, newspapers, and magazines), 1998–2008 268
A3.1.1 References to Selected American Think Tanks in National American Media, 2009–2016 269
A3.2 References to Selected American Think Tanks on American Television News, 1998–2008 271
A3.2.1 References to Selected American Think Tanks on American Television News, 2009–2016 272
A3.3 References to Selected American Think Tanks on American Television News by Network, 1998–2008 273
A3.3.1 References to Selected American Think Tanks on American Television News by Network, 2009–2016 274
A3.4 References to Selected American Think Tanks on ABC News, 1998–2008 276
A3.4.1 References to Selected American Think Tanks on ABC News, 2009–2016 277
A3.5 References to Selected American Think Tanks on NBC News, 1998–2008 279
A3.5.1 References to Selected American Think Tanks on NBC News, 2009–2016 280

A3.6 References to Selected American Think Tanks on CBS News, 1998–2008 282

A3.6.1 References to Selected American Think Tanks on CBS News, 2009–2016 283

A3.7 References to Selected American Think Tanks on CNN, 1998–2008 285

A3.7.1 References to Selected American Think Tanks on CNN News, 2009–2016 286

A3.8 References to Selected American Think Tanks on FOX News, 1998–2008 287

A3.9 References to Selected American Think Tanks in National Newspapers, 1998–2008 290

A3.9.1 References to Selected American Think Tanks in National Newspapers, 2009–2016 292

A3.10 References to Selected American Think Tanks in National Magazines, 1998–2008 293

A3.10.1 References to Selected American Think Tanks in National Magazines, 2009–2016 294

A3.11 References to Selected American Think Tanks in Canadian and International Newspapers, 1998–2008 295

A3.11.1 References to Selected American Think Tanks in Canadian and International Newspapers, 2009–2016 296

A3.12 References to Selected American Think Tanks in Canadian Newspapers, 1998–2008 297

A3.12.1 References to Selected American Think Tanks in Canadian Newspapers, 2009–2016 298

A3.13 References to Selected American Think Tanks in International Newspapers, 1998–2008 300

A3.13.1 References to Selected American Think Tanks in International Newspapers, 2009–2016 302

A3.14 Comparison of Annual Budget to Number of National Media References for Selected American Think Tanks, 1999–2008 304

A3.14.1 Comparison of Annual Budget to Number of National Media References for Selected American Think Tanks, 2009–2016 306

A3.15 Comparison of Annual Budget to Number of International Media References for Selected American Think Tanks, 1999–2008 308

A3.15.1 Comparison of Annual Budget to Number of International Media References for Selected American Think Tanks, 1999–2016 310

A4.1 Media Citations for Selected Canadian Think Tanks (radio, television, and newspaper), 2000–2008 313
A4.1.1 Media Citations for Selected Canadian Think Tanks (radio, television, and newspaper), 2009–2016 315
A4.2 Television Citations for Selected Canadian Think Tanks, 2000–2008 317
A4.2.1 Television Citations for Selected Canadian Think Tanks, 2009–2016 319
A4.3 CBC TV National Evening News Citations for Selected Canadian Think Tanks, 2000–2008 321
A4.3.1 CBC TV National Evening News Citations for Selected Canadian Think Tanks, 2009–2016 323
A4.4 ctv National Evening News Citations for Selected Canadian Think Tanks, 2000–2008 325
A4.4.1 CTV National Evening News Citations for Selected Canadian Think Tanks, 2009–2016 327
A4.5 References to Selected Canadian Think Tanks on CBC Radio, Oct. 2004–2008 329
A4.5.1 References to Selected Canadian Think Tanks on CBC Radio, 2009–2016 331
A4.6 Newspaper Citations for Selected Canadian Think Tanks, 2000–2008 334
A4.6.1 Newspaper Citations for Selected Canadian Think Tanks, 2009–2016 337
A4.7 References to Selected Canadian Think Tanks in American Newspapers, 1998–2008 339
A4.7.1 References to Selected Canadian Think Tanks in American Newspapers, 2009–2016 341
A4.8 Comparison of Annual Budget to Number of National Media References for Selected Canadian Think Tanks 343
A4.8.1 Comparison of Annual Budget to Number of National Media References for Selected Canadian Think Tanks, 2009–2016 345
A5.1 Total References to Selected American Think Tanks in the US Congress (Senate, House of Representatives, Extension of Remarks, and Daily Digest), 1999–2008 349
A5.1.1 Total References to Selected American Think Tanks in the US Congress (Senate, House of Representatives, Extension of Remarks, and Daily Digest, 2009–2016 349
A5.2 References to Selected American Think Tanks in the US Senate, 1999–2008 353

A5.2.1 References to Selected American Think Tanks in the US Senate, 2009–2016 353
A5.3 References to Selected American Think Tanks in the US House of Representatives, 1999–2008 357
A5.3.1 References to Selected American Think Tanks in the US House of Representatives, 2009–2016 357
A5.4 References to Selected American Think Tanks in the US Congress (Extension of Remarks), 1999–2008 361
A5.4.1 References to Selected American Think Tanks in the US Congress (Extension of Remarks), 2009–2016 361
A5.5 References to Selected American Think Tanks in the US Congress (Daily Digest), 1999–2008 365
A5.5.1 References to Selected American Think Tanks in the US Congress (Daily Digest), 2009–2016 365
A5.6 Comparison of Annual Budget to Number of References in the US Congress for Selected American Think Tanks 369
A5.6.1 Comparison of Annual Budget to Number of References in the US Congress for Selected American Think Tanks, 2009–2016 371
A5.7 Appearances by Selected American Think Tanks before Congressional Committees, 1999–2008 373
A5.7.1 Appearances by Selected American Think Tanks before Congressional Committees, 2009–2016 375
A6.1 Appearance by Selected Canadian Think Tanks before Parliamentary Committees, 1999–2008 379
A6.1.1 Appearances by Selected Canadian Think Tanks before Senate Committees, 2008–2016 379
A6.2 Appearances by Selected Canadian Think Tanks before Senate Committees, 1999–2008 383
A6.2.1 Appearances by Selected Canadian Think Tanks before Senate Committees, 2009–2016 383
A6.3 Appearances by Selected Canadian Think Tanks before the House of Commons, 1999–2008 388
A6.3.1 Appearances by Selected Canadian Think Tanks before the House of Commons, 2009–2016 388
A6.4 References to Selected Think Tanks during Debates in the House of Commons, 1994–2008 392
A6.4.1 References to Selected Think Tanks during Debates in the House of Commons, 2009–2016 393
A6.5 References to Selected Think Tanks during Debates in the Senate, 1994–2008 398

A6.5.1 References to Selected Think Tanks during Debates in the Senate, 2009–2016 400
A6.6 Comparison of Annual Budget to Number of Appearances before Parliamentary Committees for Selected Canadian Think Tanks, 1994–2008 402
A6.6.1 Comparison of Annual Budget to Number of Appearances before Parliamentary Committees for Selected Canadian Think Tanks, 2009–2016 404
A7.1 Newspaper Coverage of Selected Canadian Think Tanks in Relation to Keystone XL 413
A7.2 Newspaper Coverage of Selected Canadian Think Tanks in Relation to Keystone XL 413

Acknowledgments

Since the first edition of *Do Think Tanks Matter?* appeared in 2002, I have been able to rely on a dedicated team of students and staff to help gather, consolidate, and organize information for many of the projects I have undertaken. In writing the third edition of this text, I have once again benefited from their professionalism and commitment to academic research. I am grateful to Tom Cooke and Christine Wall for helping me update and format many of the tables, graphs, and charts in this book, and to Hannah Guiang, Ryan Park, and Kaitlyn Tyschenko for devoting countless hours to tracking down new information for several of the appendices. I would also like to thank Anna Zuschlag for her meticulous attention to detail in preparing the index. Over the past few decades, I have been able to reach out, and receive feedback from, several scholars who share my interest and passion for the study of think tanks, and for this, I am eternally grateful. They are Stephen Brooks (University of Windsor/University of Michigan), Kent Calder (Johns Hopkins University), Evert Lindquist (University of Victoria), Mark Garnett (University of Lancaster), James McGann (University of Pennsylvania), Inderjeet Parmar (City University London), Diane Stone (University of Warwick), and R. Kent Weaver (Georgetown University).

As my fascination and preoccupation with the study of think tanks have grown, my family and friends have exhibited far more patience and understanding than I deserve. I would like to thank my father, Alan Abelson, for his encouragement and guidance, and my three sisters, Lynn, Joan, and Karen, for their love and support. My mother, Estelle Abelson, who passed away in the fall of 2004, continues to be a great source of inspiration. I think of her often. Rebecca and Seth, my two wonderful children, should also be recognized. I have had the great privilege of watching them grow and mature over the years, and take such pleasure in observing the things in life they most value. I could not be more proud.

In my first year as an undergraduate at the University of Toronto, I had the good fortune of meeting three amazing people – Adrian Hoad-Reddick, Susan Hoad-Reddick (née Munn), and Ralph Germaine. We met in the Sir Daniel Wilson Residence at University College and it did not take long for us to strike up a friendship, one that has spanned over thirty-five years. This book is dedicated to them and to Mary Germaine, Ralph's wife, for always being there for me.

Monda Halpern, a professor in the Department of History at the University of Western Ontario and the person with whom I share my life, continues to be my strongest and most vocal ally. Her warmth, intelligence, tremendous wit, and beauty stop me cold in my tracks. And if for some unknown reason I neglect to acknowledge all she has done, her twin sister, Sonia, will not hesitate to remind me. I would like to express my sincere thanks and gratitude to Sonia and to her terrific partner, Lawrence Burden, for their love and friendship.

My sincere thanks to Gillian Scobie for her superb copy editing. I was fortunate to have Gillian copy edit my 2016 book, *Northern Lights*, and was thrilled to have her on board for this project. My work could not be placed in more capable hands. Finally, I would like to thank Philip Cercone, executive director of McGill-Queen's University Press (MQUP) and his incredible staff for their advice and assistance over the years. When I was considering a publisher for the first edition of *Do Think Tanks Matter?* Richard Vernon, my distinguished colleague and friend, suggested that I contact Philip at MQUP. Rarely have I received better advice.

Acronyms

AEI	American Enterprise Institute for Public Policy Research
AIMS	Atlantic Institute for Market Studies
APEC	Atlantic Provinces Economic Council
CAP	Center for American Progress
CCACD	Canadian Centre for Arms Control and Disarmament
CCFPD	Canadian Centre for Foreign Policy Development
CCIPS	Canadian Council for International Peace and Security
CCMD	Canadian Centre for Management and Development
CCPA	Canadian Centre for Policy Alternatives
CCSD	Canadian Council on Social Development
CIC	Canadian International Council
CEIP	Carnegie Endowment for International Peace
CFR	Council on Foreign Relations
CIIA	Canadian Institute of International Affairs
CIIPS	Canadian Institute for International Peace and Security
CIGI	Centre for International Governance Innovation
CIPE	Center for International Private Enterprise
CISS	Canadian Institute of Strategic Studies
CNAS	Center for a New American Security
CPRN	Canadian Policy Research Networks, Inc.
CSE	Citizens for a Sound Economy Foundation
CSIS	Center for Strategic and International Studies
CTF	Canadian Tax Foundation
CWF	Canada West Foundation
ECC	Economic Council of Canada
GDN	Global Development Network
IPS	Institute for Policy Studies
IRPP	Institute for Research on Public Policy
NIRA	National Institute for Research Advancement

NPA	National Planning Association
NSI	North-South Institute
PPAC	Private Planning Association of Canada
PNAC	Project for the New American Century
PPF	Public Policy Forum
PPI	Progressive Policy Institute
PRI	Policy Research Initiative
RIIA	Royal Institute of International Affairs
SCC	Science Council of Canada

Do Think Tanks Matter?

Introduction

According to the *2017 Global Go To Think Tank Index Report*, an annual publication compiled by James McGann and his associates at the University of Pennsylvania, close to 8,000 public policy institutes, or think tanks, as they are more commonly called, exist worldwide.[1] Of these, slightly more than 1,870 are headquartered in the United States, with the largest concentration located inside Washington: think tanks such as the world-renowned Brookings Institution, the Carnegie Endowment for International Peace, the Heritage Foundation, and the American Enterprise Institute, which recently moved into its brand new multimillion-dollar headquarters on Think Tank Row, a stone's throw from Washington, DC's Dupont Circle. For many scholars and journalists studying the so-called think tank phenomenon, the explosion of policy institutes since the latter part of the twentieth century and in the first decades of the twenty-first reflects their growing importance, stature, and influence, both in the political arena and in the policy-making process. This perception is reinforced by directors of think tanks, who often credit their institutes with shaping the discourse around major policy debates as well as the language in key pieces of legislation. Yet, despite the more visible presence of think tanks in many advanced and developing countries, few studies have engaged in serious discussions about how to assess or evaluate their impact. Acknowledging that such an assessment is notoriously difficult, many scholars have consciously avoided conversations about how best to measure their effectiveness; others have simply asserted that think tanks exercise influence, without demonstrating how they actually achieve it.

Fortunately, in recent years, as scholarly interest in the role of think tanks has grown, more attention has been devoted to exploring ways to evaluate think tank performance. Although few definitive answers have been offered, scholars are at least beginning to think more critically about the complex nature of the policy-making process and the efforts of think tanks to mold the policy preferences and choices of policy-makers. They are also beginning to think more methodically and systematically about how, and under what circumstances, think tanks may, through various governmental and non-governmental channels, influence public opinion around a host of domestic and foreign policy issues. In 2002, the title of the first edition of this book posed what to most readers was a seemingly straightforward and unambiguous question – *Do Think Tanks Matter?* Yet, as my research at the time concluded, there are no simple answers when it comes to revealing the extent to which think tanks make a difference in the policy-making process. However, as more data have become available about the visibility of think tanks in the political arena and their efforts to more effectively market ideas to multiple stakeholders, it is possible to offer a more nuanced argument, along with more informed observations about their involvement at different stages of the policy cycle. Making this information available and accessible to readers was the motivation for a second edition of *Do Think Tanks Matter?*, which appeared in 2009. In that edition, and in this, the third edition, I look again at the experiences of think tanks in the United States, a country where these organizations have become an integral feature of the political landscape, and in Canada, where think tanks have become increasingly visible in recent years but, compared with their American counterparts, enjoy less prominence in policy-making. My central argument, which builds on the thesis I unveiled in the first edition, is that think tanks in both countries have at times played an important role in shaping the political dialogue and the policy preferences and choices of policy-makers, but often in different ways and during different stages of the policy cycle. For instance, several American think tanks, including the American Enterprise Institute, the Hoover Institution, the Heritage Foundation, and the Brookings Institution, have undertaken active roles in several presidential campaigns and in the transition periods that followed. Indeed, several scholars from these and other institutes provided advice to Donald Trump, Barack Obama, George W. Bush, and other presidential candidates during the hotly contested primaries in which they were engaged, and made a concerted effort to pass along policy recommendations to them and to those in their administration. Conversely, think tanks in Canada are rarely important repositories of policy expertise during federal and provincial elections. They tend to maintain a modest presence during a new government's transition to power. Nonetheless, a handful of Canadian think tanks, including the Fraser Institute, the C.D. Howe Institute, the Caledon Institute, and the Canadian Centre for Policy Alternatives, among others, are often active at other stages of the policy cycle, particularly when the parameters of policy debates are being framed. To market their ideas, these and other think tanks pursue a range of strategies, including relying on print, broadcast, and social media, distributing a range of publications to policy-makers and journalists, inviting presidents and members of their administration to unveil new policy proposals at their institutes, and testifying before various legislative committees. As will become clear in the chapters that follow, while think tanks in the United States and Canada share a common desire to influence public opinion and public policy, how and under what circumstances they seek to do so ultimately depends on a wide range of internal and external factors, ranging from the priorities they assign to engaging key stakeholders at various stages of policy-making, and the financial resources available at their disposal, to the policy direction set by boards of directors and trustees.

Much of the literature that compares think tanks in the United States with those in parliamentary systems such as Canada and Great Britain, sparse as it is,[2] suggests that the "distinctive characteristic of think tanks in the United States is not their size or, for that matter, the considerable funding of some institutions ... What makes think tanks in the United States unique, besides their sheer number, is the extent to which they have become involved actively in various stages of the policy-making process."[3] Implicit in this observation is the idea that think tanks, by virtue of the multiple channels of access they are afforded, tend to play a more significant role in the United States. That country's political system is more decentralized and fragmented than Canada's, where the principles of strong party unity and cabinet solidarity are enforced and where the presence of a permanent senior civil service entrusted with advising policy-makers is thought to limit opportunities for think tanks and other non-governmental organizations to influence policy-making. Significant disparities in the financial resources available to top-tier think tanks in the US and in Canada may also account for why Canadian think tanks generally engage less actively in policy-making than their counterparts in the United States. The perception that think tanks in the United States have had a more discernible impact on policy-making and in shaping specific policy issues than think tanks in Canada has, for the most part, been supported by scholars in the field. Indeed, the few case studies on the subject have concluded that while several US think tanks have played a decisive role advising leading policy-makers, shaping key policy debates, and contributing to the formulation of government legislation by offering detailed blueprints on how to implement important policy initiatives, Canadian think tanks, with few exceptions,[4] have made only modest contributions to public discussions on issues ranging from pension reform and tax policy to how to enhance Canada's role on the world stage.[5]

Think tanks in the United States may indeed have more opportunities, or access points and channels, than Canadian think tanks, to directly and indirectly influence public policy and may face fewer constraints in conveying ideas to policy-makers.[6] However, it would simply be wrong to ignore the contributions several Canadian think tanks have made both to policy-making and to shaping the policy- or decision-making environment.[7] The importance of distinguishing between influencing policy-making and the policy-making environment will become clearer in the case studies included here. It will also become clear that although some institutional constraints or political structures, as well as a host of other factors, have limited the potential impact of Canadian think tanks at some stages of the policy cycle, it would be naive to suggest that their presence in the political arena goes unnoticed.[8] Parliamentary systems, parliamentarians, and public servants do not pose an insurmountable barrier to think tanks or to their leaders, as some have suggested.[9] The ability of think tanks in parliamentary systems to convey their ideas effectively is constrained less by the political environment they inhabit and more by the challenges many think tanks face in remaining afloat. Interestingly enough, although American think tanks have more opportunities to influence public policy, modest institutional resources also plague the majority, who do not have the luxury of drawing on massive budgets. Unlike the RAND Corporation, the Brookings Institution, the Heritage Foundation, and a handful of other well-heeled institutes that have annual budgets approaching, or vastly exceeding, $100 million, most US think tanks face similar financial constraints as those in Canada.

Scholars continue to struggle with the question of how much impact or influence think tanks wield in policy-making and in shaping the policy-making environment. And despite some progress that has been made in identifying the conditions under which think tanks can position themselves to affect policy change, scholars still resist offering definitive conclusions about the influence of think tanks. But in all fairness, rather than stating categorically that think tanks, by their very nature, exercise considerable influence, those who study these institutions would be on stronger footing if they pointed out that the amount of influence think tanks wield varies enormously across the think tank population, and even more across the various stages of the policy cycle. It also depends on a host of political factors, many of which are beyond the control of think tanks competing in the marketplace of ideas. These findings may continue to fuel frustration among those looking for more concrete answers, but providing a measured and qualified response is entirely appropriate. Having studied think tanks for over two decades, I too struggle to determine how these organizations leave their mark on policy-makers and on public policy. But the alternative – making unfounded and unsubstantiated assertions about how much or little influence think tanks enjoy – is even more disconcerting for those seeking to provide a more nuanced and subtle understanding of their behaviour in the policy-making process.

One major methodological problem in assessing influence is that think tanks and policy-makers, not to mention the scholars who study them, have different perceptions of what constitutes influence and how it can best be evaluated.[10] Moreover, as the policy-making community becomes increasingly crowded, tracing the origin of a policy to a particular individual or organization can prove futile in all but the most exceptional cases. As many have claimed, every successful policy idea has a hundred mothers and fathers; every bad policy idea is an orphan.

Some efforts, including those taken in this study, have been made to track how often think tanks in Canada and the United States are referred to in the media, as well as the frequency with which their staff testify before parliamentary and congressional committees. But despite the large data sets that have been compiled on these and other indicators that often speak to the level and intensity of think tank engagement around different policy issues, scholars have reached few hard and fast conclusions on their impact in policy-making.[11] The extent of media coverage think tanks generate may speak to how adept they are at placing issues on the political agenda, not to mention the priority and resources they assign to media outreach; several journalists and directors of think tanks in both countries have made such claims. Yet, as will be discussed, media exposure cannot, and should not, be used as the sole indicator, or, indeed, even a reliable indicator, of policy influence, even at the most preliminary stages of the policy-making process. Several factors explain why some think tanks in Canada and in the United States appear to have more impact on the policy-making community than others. As Monique Jérôme-Forget, former president of the Montreal-based Institute for Research on Public Policy observes, "quantitative measures, such as the number of media citations, show only that ideas are being talked about, as opposed to genuinely influencing the thinking of observers of an issue."[12]

This book will follow two central paths of inquiry to explain how and to what extent think tanks shape the policy-making environment and the policy-making process. First, it must consider the stage or stages in the policy cycle at which think tanks are most actively engaged. While think tanks in both Canada and the United States rely on similar strategies to convey their ideas to policy-makers and to the general public, they often take advantage of different opportunities to achieve their goals. As noted, providing advice to US presidential candidates or to an incoming president and his or her staff is an opportunity they cannot afford to miss. Chapter 6 notes that it is not uncommon for American think tanks to devote considerable resources to providing presidential candidates and new administrations with detailed blueprints revealing the various ways to manage the nation's affairs. During the riveting and mind-boggling 2016 US presidential election, which saw Donald Trump, the billionaire real estate mogul and reality TV star, defeat Hillary Clinton to become the 45th president of the United States,[13] Trump, the self-proclaimed Washington outsider and political neophyte, dipped into a gift basket of ideas painstakingly prepared by the Heritage Foundation to help him move the country far more to the right. From proposing concrete ways to repeal and replace the Affordable Care Act (a shortened version of the Patient Protection and Affordable Care Act), widely known as Obamacare, to assembling a list of potential conservative appointees to the US Supreme Court (a list that included Judge Neil Gorsuch, who was confirmed as a US Supreme Court Justice by the Senate during Donald Trump's first 100 days in office), the Heritage Foundation emerged as the darling of the Trump administration. Several of these studies have hit the bestseller list. Ironically, despite the widespread exposure that Heritage's latest blueprint on how to reform the federal government generated, and the extent to which the organization established close ties to the Trump transition team and to key figures in the Oval Office, Heritage president Jim DeMint was forced to resign his post in April 2017. His term was cut short by Heritage's board of trustees, which had become increasingly concerned with the direction the former South Carolina senator (2005–13) was taking, that DeMint was far more invested in having Heritage engage in political advocacy than in policy research. A call from the board of trustees for DeMint's resignation passed unanimously, and Edwin Feulner, co-founder and president of Heritage for over thirty years, was reinstated as president until DeMint's successor, Kay Coles James.[14]

Other US think tanks and the people who staff them have made their presence felt during the first months of the Trump administration. In fact, some have gone to great lengths to ensure that the president fulfills many of the commitments he made on the campaign trail. These included: supporting the construction of the Keystone XL pipeline, a bilateral initiative embraced by the Harper government but rejected by the Obama administration; and withdrawing from the Paris Climate Agreement, for which, under President Obama, the US became a signatory. As will be discussed in more detail in chapter 6, the Competitive Enterprise Institute (CEI), a Washington, DC-based think tank with strong libertarian leanings, employed several tactics to pressure Trump to make good on both promises. Already predisposed to moving forward with Keystone and withdrawing from the Paris accord, Trump's controversial decision, particularly on the latter, has generated considerable opposition from all but a handful of world leaders. When Trump announced from the Rose Garden on 1 June 2017 that the US would withdraw from the historic agreement, Myron Ebell, director of Global Warming and International Environmental Policy at the Competitive Enterprise Institute, and several of his colleagues, applauded the president's actions. Ebell, a supporter of global climate deniers Scott Pruitt, head of the Environmental Protection Agency, and Steve Bannon, Trump's controversial former White House chief strategist, rarely concealed his contempt for the Paris Climate Agreement. Still, while Ebell and his colleagues at CEI and in the broader anti-climate-change-agreement community celebrated Trump's announcement, closer scrutiny is required to determine how much credit they could legitimately take for the president's decision. Although CNN reported that CEI exercised enormous influence on Trump's vitriolic stance on the Paris Climate Agreement, an important question remains: did policy experts at CEI convince Trump to move in this direction or did they simply reinforce what the president intended to do if he assumed the reins of power? How much influence did CEI truly exercise? Did it provide the intellectual ammunition to Trump about the "science" of climate change so that he could justify his decision, or did it simply offer him some political reinforcement? Perhaps both. How crucial a role did CEI play in informing Trump's decision and his efforts, albeit limited, to sell his position to world leaders and to the American public?

Questions regarding how much policy influence think tanks wield, and the kind of drama that has unfolded in recent months among the leadership at several top-tier US think tanks is not unique to US think tanks; it simply plays out on a larger stage, which creates the impression that think tanks in the US often find themselves embroiled in internal and external political squabbles. Indeed, during the formative years of the Centre for International Governance Innovation (CIGI), one of Canada's largest think tanks, based in Waterloo, Ontario, co-founder Jim Balsillie came under fire for his role in replacing key figures in CIGI's leadership team.[15] Although the internal squabbles at think tanks and their efforts to influence public policy occasionally grab the headlines, what is even more pressing is how these organizations navigate their way through the policy-making process. Unlike in the US, think tanks in Canada rarely regard elections and transition periods as the most opportune time to convey their ideas to policy-makers. Many Canadian think tanks place a higher priority on identifying key issues in policy debates and on working closely with senior and middle-level public servants and members of the cabinet on an ongoing or ad hoc basis to advance their interests. This strategy is pursued by such think tanks as the Caledon Institute, the Public Policy Forum, and the more advocacy-oriented Canada 2020, a think tank with close ties to the Washington-based Center for American Progress (CAP). As noted, Canadian think tanks may not enjoy the stature and visibility of some think tanks in the United States, but their less noticeable presence does not necessarily translate into limited policy influence. As Judith Maxwell, founding president of the now defunct

Canadian Policy Research Networks, Inc. (CPRN), stated, "the most important type of influence is never documented."[16]

By determining where in the policy cycle think tanks in the two countries are most actively engaged, we can explore several factors that may help to explain why think tanks in the United States are thought to play a more significant role in the policy-making process than those in Canada. As this study will reveal, while think tanks in Canada and the United States function in very different political systems, their ability or inability to establish and maintain a strong presence in the policy-making community may have as much to do with how they define their missions and with the directors who lead them, and the resources and strategies they employ to achieve their stated goals, as with the political environments they inhabit and seek to shape.

In addition to considering how various institutional, political, economic, and cultural factors facilitate or constrain think tank development, it is important to think more critically about how to measure their relative performance in what has become, particularly in the United States, an increasingly competitive space where think tanks compete intensely for the attention of key stakeholders. Should their influence be measured by media citations; number of appearances before legislative committees; followers on Facebook, Twitter, and Instagram; and total number of publications released in a given year or downloaded from their websites? Or should other performance indicators be taken into consideration? This second and more difficult avenue of inquiry may not necessarily allow us to confirm how much influence think tanks wield or whether they deserve to be ranked higher or lower in global rankings and surveys of think tanks, but it will, nonetheless, provide tangible and some intangible indicators to consider in evaluating the strengths, limitations, and priorities of policy institutes.

CLASSIFYING THINK TANKS

Several scholars who have studied think tanks have made important contributions to our understanding of how these institutions have evolved and the many political, economic, and social factors that have influenced their development. James Smith's exploration of American think tanks, *The Idea Brokers: Think Tanks and the Rise of the New Policy Elite*; Thomas Medvetz's recent study of American think tanks, *Think Tanks in America*; and a co-edited volume, *Think Tanks, Foreign Policy and Geo-Politics,* that I produced with my colleagues Stephen Brooks and Xin Hua that focuses on think tanks in several different countries, are but three examples of studies that have assisted both students and practitioners of public policy and public administration to better understand the role of think tanks in the policy-making process.[17] But some basic questions remain unanswered. To begin with, what are the defining characteristics of think tanks? How do they differ from the multitude of other organizations, including interest groups, that populate the policy-making community? What is their primary function? And what conceptual frameworks have been constructed to study their involvement in policy-making?

Defining a think tank has long posed problems for those seeking to accurately describe what has become an increasingly diverse set of organizations. As R. Kent Weaver and James McGann acknowledge, although the term think tank was originally employed in the United States during the Second World War to refer to a secure room or environment where defence scientists and military planners could meet to discuss strategy, it has since been used to describe several different types of organizations engaged in policy analysis. Consequently, several classifications of think tanks have been developed.

These organizations elude simple definition, in large part because there is no consensus about what constitutes a think tank. While it is not difficult to identify universities and trade unions, organizations that also engage actively in research and analysis, trying to agree on what a think tank is and what its primary goals are results in more questions than answers. For some, the term "think tank" should be reserved only for a handful of large well-funded organizations populated with dozens of high-powered intellectuals committed to studying critical political, social, and economic issues. In the United States, the Brookings Institution, a Washington icon long heralded as the quintessential think tank; the RAND corporation; the National Bureau of Economic Research; the Peterson Institute for International Economics; and the Urban Institute would likely be among the special class of institutes satisfying these rather restrictive conditions. In Canada, the list would be even shorter: the Conference Board of Canada, the Centre for International Governance Innovation, and possibly one or two others. If this use of the term was adopted, a large cohort of less visible institutes that also engage in serious research and analysis would be overlooked or identified as something other than what they are. By contrast, if the term think tank is too inclusive, it could capture organizations with more nefarious objectives, such as the National Policy Institute (NPI), headed by Richard Spencer, the poster child for the alt-right, who, along with his associates and followers, remains committed to preserving a white America. The NPI attracted considerable attention during the 2016 US presidential campaign for its vocal support of Donald Trump. In March 2017, the Internal Revenue Service revoked the NPI's tax-exempt status as a 501 c. 3 charitable organization, a designation held by a majority of think tanks in the US. We will return to this subject later in this study.[18]

After struggling to define what a think tank is, most scholars have concluded that there *is* no typical think tank. As McGann concedes, "I know one when I see one."[19] Think tanks may range in size from entities with as few as one or two people to ones with several hundred staff and researchers. They may possess budgets as low as one to two hundred thousand dollars or as high as several million dollars. A think tank could look like RAND, one of America's premier foreign and defence policy institutes, with an annual budget exceeding $300 million and an impressive complex on prime oceanfront property in Santa Monica, California, or the Toronto-based Mackenzie Institute, which has less than a handful of staff and a budget barely topping $200,000.

Think tanks also vary tremendously in areas of specialization, research output, ideological orientation, and in their institutional independence. Some are affiliated with university departments and must rely on their resources to sustain them. The various defence and foreign policy centres established at over a dozen Canadian universities under the Department of National Defence's Military and Strategic Studies Program (MSSP), now called the Strategic Defence Forum (SDF), is a case in point. There are also think tanks that function inside government, including the Congressional Research Service and the Congressional Budget Office in the US.[20] Of particular interest to this study, though, are independent public policy think tanks. These organizations function much like private corporations but their bottom lines are measured not by profit margins but by their impact on policy ideas. We will emphasize these types of think tanks, in large part because their survival depends less on the willingness of legislators to sustain their operations (although some rely heavily on government funding) or on academic departments prepared to support their activities, than on how effective their directors and staff are in marketing and promoting their ideas.

Despite their considerable diversity, think tanks do share some characteristics: they are generally non-profit, nonpartisan organizations engaged in the study of public policy. The majority in Canada and the United States are registered as non-profit, tax-exempt organizations under the Income Tax Act and the Internal Revenue Code, respectively. They qualify for non-profit status by applying as educational organizations committed to increasing public awareness about a host of policy issues. To obtain tax-exempt status, they must also remain nonpartisan. In other words, while think tanks in Canada and the United States are not prohibited from taking positions on various policy issues, as many frequently do, and are not required by law to disclose the names of the individuals and organizations who fund them (although some think tanks in both countries are becoming more transparent about the sources of their funding), they cannot publicly endorse or oppose any political party or devote more than a legally prescribed percentage of their budget to lobbying government.[21] Think tanks can embrace whatever ideological orientation they desire and provide their expertise to any political candidate or office holder willing to take advantage of their advice. However, by law they must refrain from engaging in certain overt political activities.

What has traditionally distinguished think tanks from the multitude of other organizations in the policy-making community is the emphasis they place on research and analysis. Not all think tanks share the same commitment to scholarly research or devote comparable resources to performing this function, yet it remains, for many, their raison d'être. However, any contemporary study must reconsider the nostalgic vision of think tanks as idea factories, or brain trusts, created to address society's most pressing social, economic, and political problems.

THE ROLE OF THINK TANKS

During the progressive era of the early 1900s, leading industrialists and philanthropists in the United States, including the Scottish-American steel baron Andrew Carnegie; Robert Brookings, a St Louis businessman; and Herbert Hoover, the 31st president of the United States, recognized the importance of creating institutions composed of prominent economists, statisticians, mathematicians, political scientists, and historians capable of bringing their scientific expertise to bear on important public policy issues. Carnegie, Brookings, and Hoover believed, as did Jane Addams, the founder of Chicago's Hull House,[22] that by establishing an environment where academics would not be distracted by teaching responsibilities, but could focus entirely on research relevant to public policy, think tanks could play an important and much-needed role in policy-making. Several institutional features of the American political system, including the vacancies left by thousands of senior civil servants following a presidential election, have given rise to ample opportunities for think tanks to provide their insights and expertise.

The Carnegie Endowment for International Peace, the Brookings Institution, and a handful of other think tanks created during the first decades of the twentieth century to improve government decision-making, have contributed largely to the widely held perception of think tanks as objective and politically neutral organizations devoted to research and analysis. In recent years, however, as many policy institutes have placed a higher premium on marketing and recycling ideas than on generating them, this view of think tanks has come under closer scrutiny. In fact, as several think tanks, including the Heritage Foundation, the American Enterprise Institute, the Fraser Institute, and the Canadian Centre for

Policy Alternatives, to name a few, have placed a higher premium on political advocacy than policy research, it has become increasingly difficult to differentiate between think tanks and other types of non-governmental organizations like interest groups, advocacy coalitions, and lobbyists, which are also committed to shaping public policy.

The comparison often drawn between think tanks, particularly those that are more advocacy-oriented, and interest or pressure groups, is not entirely unwarranted. After all, many of the tactics that interest groups use to convey their concerns to governments, including preparing and distributing studies, publishing articles in newspapers, giving interviews on television and on radio, reaching their large constituencies through social media, arranging meetings with policy-makers and inviting them to speak at their conferences and workshops, and testifying before various legislative committees, are also frequently employed by think tanks. As charitable organizations, think tanks, like interest groups, also try to recruit high-profile individuals to their organizations in an effort to attract more funding. The Hoover Institution, located on the picturesque campus of Stanford University, is but one think tank that has done this. Included on its roster are Condoleezza Rice, former national security advisor and secretary of state to President George W. Bush; George Shultz, former secretary of state; Newt Gingrich, former speaker of the House of Representatives; and, for a brief period after he left his post at the Pentagon, Donald Rumsfeld, former secretary of defense during the Bush administration.

Still, despite the many similarities between think tanks and interest groups, there are some notable differences. To begin with, although some think tanks try to appeal to as large a segment of the electorate as possible, like most interest groups, they do not speak on behalf of a particular constituency. For instance, although the conservative-leaning Heritage Foundation may in principle support the right of Americans to bear arms, a constitutional right protected by the second amendment, it does not speak directly on behalf of gun owners in the United States. This function is performed by the National Rifle Association (NRA), one of America's most vocal interest groups and a staunch and vigorous opponent of gun control legislation. Second, the main purpose of interest groups is not to advance social science research (although some do devote considerable resources to it), but to ensure that elected leaders pursue policies compatible with their interests. To this end, interest groups, political action committees (PACs), and super PACs donate to the campaign chests of political parties, incumbents, and challengers most likely to support their wishes. Think tanks, by contrast, are prohibited by law from endorsing or opposing candidates for office and are not allowed to make donations to political parties or to candidates. They can, however, contribute in other valuable ways, including discussing various domestic and foreign policy issues with incumbents and aspiring office holders.

As think tanks place greater emphasis on marketing their ideas and as interest groups continue to invest more resources in building a stronger research capacity to enhance their credibility and legitimacy, the characteristics distinguishing the two will become increasingly blurred. Nevertheless, it is important to keep in mind that think tanks do perform a range of functions that in many ways make them unique. It is to this that I now turn.

There has been much debate over what the motivations and priorities of think tanks are, but one of their primary functions is clearly to help educate policy-makers and the public – not to mention the private and non-profit, or third, sectors – on pressing social, economic, and political issues. As educators, think tanks draw on various sources of information and expertise to communicate their views and concerns to multiple target audiences. Just as teachers attempt to shape the minds of their students, think tanks actively seek to mold public opinion and leaders' policy preferences and choices, some far more effective and engaging than others.

Think tanks perform their educational tasks frequently. At times they serve as research brokers by acting as a conduit between the scholarly community and policy-makers.[23] In this role think tanks communicate their findings to government officials and their staff in a clear and easily digestible form. At other times they provide a forum for policy-makers, academics, and representatives of the private and non-profit sector to discuss issues of common concern. A handful of think tanks perform this function well, including two Ottawa-based organizations, the Public Policy Forum and Canada 2020. Outreach and consultation are other important, related functions performed by think tanks. To share their ideas with the public and with policy-makers and to discover more about the concerns of particular stakeholders, think tanks frequently sponsor conferences and workshops. Several also undertake contract research for government and for the private sector.

For many think tanks, serving in an educational or research capacity does not mean that they should, or must, avoid taking positions on policy issues or advocate a particular set of values, beliefs, or principles. On the contrary, as outlined in their mission statements, all are committed to carrying out a set of goals and objectives. These may range from supporting the preservation of free market principles – a goal embraced by the Heritage Foundation, the American Enterprise Institute, the Fraser Institute, the Montreal Economic Institute, the Atlantic Institute for Market Studies, and the C.D. Howe Institute, among others – to stimulating public discussion on poverty and social policy, the mandate of the Ottawa-based Caledon Institute. The question for scholars studying think tanks is not whether they are committed to policy research or to political advocacy but how much emphasis they place on each. By better understanding the priorities of think tanks, which can often be assessed by looking at how their budgets are allocated, it is possible to provide more informed insights into the strategies they rely on to convey their ideas.

STUDYING THINK TANKS

In a 1987 study, Joseph Peschek remarked correctly that little research had been conducted on think tanks and their role in the policy-making process. At the time, only a handful of institutional histories of prominent American think tanks and a few academic articles had been written. Acknowledging this lack of scholarship, Peschek claimed that unless political scientists began to focus more on the "subtle levels of [policy-making where] identifying and defining problems, shaping public understanding of issues, and constructing a political agenda" occurred, the significance of think tanks and their impact would be overlooked.[24] Peschek's admonition has not been ignored. Since the publication of his study of elite policy planning organizations, several books, articles, and book chapters, not to mention hundreds of newspaper articles and blogs, have been written detailing the role of think tanks in various advanced and developing countries and their efforts to shape public opinion and public policy.[25] Directories have even been produced to keep track of the hundreds of policy institutes established worldwide, and several organizations in North America, Europe, and Asia have taken it upon themselves to issue global rankings of think tanks.[26] But as diverse as these publications are, so too are the various theoretical or conceptual approaches, or frameworks, employed to study think tanks.

As will be discussed in more detail in chapter 2, think tanks have been regarded by some, including Peschek, William Domhoff, Thomas Dye, and John Saloma, as organizations that often serve the economic and political interests of the corporate elite. The several-million-dollar endowments enjoyed by a select group in the United States, the number of prominent business leaders who serve on their boards of directors and trustees, and the steady pool of former and future high-level policy-makers working at these organizations, provide elite theorists with evidence to support their theories.[27]

However, since the think tank population is so ideologically and economically diverse, some theorists prefer to treat them not as instruments of the ruling elite but simply as one type of organization competing for attention in a pluralist political system. Like interest groups and trade unions, think tanks are seen as non-governmental organizations that employ a wide range of resources to influence the content and outcome of public policy. Influenced to some extent by elite theory, however, even proponents of the pluralist approach acknowledge that some think tanks are better positioned to engage in policy-making than others.

Drawing on the literature on elite and pluralist theories of democracy, a handful of scholars have studied think tanks from a different perspective. For instance, Hugh Heclo and Evert Lindquist treat think tanks as part of larger epistemic or policy communities, whose researchers are often called upon to help advise on particular policy matters.[28] In this sense, think tanks are regarded as sources of expertise that at times can help supplement the research capacity of government departments.

Many of these approaches are useful and can help to shed light on think tank development; this study of Canadian and American think tanks, however, will adopt a rather different perspective. Since the purpose of this book is to determine where and how think tanks have an impact on policy-making, more emphasis will be placed on trying to understand why some are far more effective at gaining access to some stages of the policy cycle than others. On this question the literature on think tanks and on other types of non-governmental organizations has been noticeably silent. As previously mentioned, the differences in the institutional or political structures of the two countries may help in part to explain why think tanks in the United States appear to have more access to policy-makers than those in Canada.[29] Nonetheless, differences in institutional structures tell us very little about why some think tanks in the same country are more visible at certain stages of policy-making than others. Explanations for different access to the executive, legislature, bureaucracy, and the media can be provided only by looking more closely at the priorities, resources, and strategies of think tanks.

Chapter 1 will provide an overview of the think tank population in Canada and the United States. The chapter will trace their evolution in the two countries and will discuss some of the many factors that have contributed to their increasingly diverse nature. Among other things, it will become apparent that think tanks in Canada and in the United States have followed a similar path of development, albeit in Canada's case at a more staggered pace. In the process of tracing the evolution of think tanks, the chapter will highlight some of the more prominent institutes in both countries.

Chapter 2 will shift from a discussion of the think tank population in the two countries to an assessment of the competing conceptual approaches that have been employed to study think tanks. As noted, scholars have tended to treat think tanks as elite organizations with close and lasting ties to policy-makers, as one of many non-governmental organizations that seek to influence public policy, or as institutes composed of experts who frequently participate in policy or epistemic communities.

While each of these approaches can yield and has yielded important insights about the behaviour of think tanks, this chapter argues that a different conceptual framework is needed to better assess the impact of think tanks, one more deeply rooted in the literature on agenda setting and policy formulation. Rather than trying to determine how much or how little influence think tanks have in shaping the policy-making environment and the policy-making process, an endeavour that, in most cases, proves futile, I suggest that scholars more closely scrutinize how think tanks become engaged at different stages of the policy cycle to ascertain the value they add to key policy discussions. By focusing on how think tanks attempt to shape the political agenda, contribute to policy formulation, and assist in policy implementation, a clearer picture emerges of which think tanks may or may not have played an important role during critical stages of the policy-making process.

Building on the conceptual framework set out in chapter 2, chapter 3 will explain why think tanks in the United States appear to be more actively engaged at some stages of the policy cycle than their Canadian counterparts. By comparing the different political systems, we can begin to explain not only why think tanks in the United States appear to be in greater demand but where in the policy cycle think tanks make their presence strongly felt. We will emphasize the importance of evaluating the various internal and external constraints that might limit the involvement of Canadian and American think tanks in policy-making, as well as the incentives decision-makers in the two countries might have to turn to think tanks for policy advice.

In chapter 4 I will discuss the various governmental and non-governmental channels that think tanks rely on to convey their ideas to policy-makers and to the public, distinguishing between the public and private uses of influence. The chapter will place particular emphasis on how think tanks in both Canada and the United States are relying increasingly on the media to shape the political dialogue and some of the implications of this strategy.

Documenting how think tanks attempt to influence policy is a reasonably straightforward exercise, but determining how to assess their impact at various stages of policy-making is not. In chapter 5 I will also explore how scholars use various indicators such as media citations, parliamentary and congressional testimony, and consultations with government departments and agencies to evaluate the impact or relevance of think tanks at particular stages of the policy-making process. I will also discuss the many methodological obstacles that must be overcome before any useful conclusions about think tank performance can be reached.

The amount of media exposure think tanks generate and the number of appearances they make before legislative committees may provide some insight into how visible particular organizations are. Such indicators, however, tell us little about what impact think tanks have had either on specific policy issues or in assisting policy-makers to formulate policy ideas. To acquire better insight into the relevance of think tanks, one must go beyond simple data sets. To this end, the chapter will employ three case studies that highlight some of the many functions think tanks perform in the policy-making process: an analysis of the involvement of a select group of American think tanks in several recent US presidential campaigns (chapter 6); an evaluation of the role of Canadian think tanks in the constitutional conferences leading up to the Charlottetown Accord (chapter 7); and a discussion of how a select group of think tanks on both sides of the Canada-US border attempted to shape the policy discourse around the construction of the Keystone XL Pipeline (chapter 8).

I have selected these case studies for several reasons. To begin with, by placing think tanks under a microscope, it is possible to ascertain how and to what extent these organizations engaged directly and indirectly in the policy-making process. Second, identifying the key think tanks involved does not require monitoring the activities of dozens of organizations, a problem frequently encountered in studying US think tanks. From various media accounts, government documents, and material from various presidential and think tank archives, a clear picture emerges of which think tanks played a critical role in advising various presidential candidates. Identifying the think tanks involved in the constitutional conferences is even easier: the federal government selected five think tanks in 1991–92 to organize a series of conferences on constitutional reform. And, finally, over a several-year period during which a handful of think tanks in Canada and the US weighed in on the potential benefits and costs of building a pipeline from Alberta to Nebraska, think tanks occupied centre stage in a battle that has re-emerged during the early days of the Trump administration. Although these case studies provide valuable insights into how think tanks in Canada and in the United States can contribute to policy development in different ways, an obvious disadvantage is the temptation to draw general conclusions about the effectiveness or ineffectiveness of think tanks from such limited studies. As a result, these cases are simply offered as probes or snapshots of how think tanks have become involved in policy-making at specific times. They are not intended to serve as the basis for making sweeping judgments about the behaviour of these or other institutes.[30] In chapter 9, I will present more recent data on the public exposure of a select group of think tanks in Canada and in the United States. These data reveal that over the last decades similar patterns in the various think tanks have emerged in both countries which capture the attention of journalists and policy-makers. Among other things, we will explore why some think tanks continue to attract far more exposure and notoriety than others.

In addition to discussing the many challenges confronting think tanks in Canada and in the United States in the future, including funding and recruitment, the concluding chapter will examine how policy institutes have come to play an increasingly active role in domestic and international politics. As will become apparent, think tanks, not unlike other non-governmental organizations committed to influencing public policy, clearly believe in the power of ideas.

CHAPTER ONE

Surveying the Think Tank Landscape in the United States and Canada

In the early 1900s, policy-makers in the United States and Canada did not need a directory to keep track of think tanks conducting research and analysis on domestic and foreign policy. Until the outbreak of the Second World War, fewer than two dozen policy institutes existed in the United States, and only a handful had been established in Canada. However, by the mid- to late 1970s and early 1980s, the think tank community in both countries had grown considerably. In his 1991 study on the rise of American think tanks, James Smith estimated that more than 1,200 private and university-based think tanks had sprung up throughout the United States, most notably in and around Washington, DC.[1] By 2017, this number exceeded 1,870, with approximately 400 policy institutes inside the Washington Beltway.[2]

Although much of the literature on think tanks has focused almost exclusively on the largest and most visible of the institutes in the United States, a typical American think tank more closely resembles the Climate Institute of Washington, DC, with fewer than ten full-time staff and a budget that has yet to reach $700,000, than the world-renowned Brookings Institution. Indeed, the majority of American think tanks have little in common with the Brookings Institution, the Hoover Institution, the Heritage Foundation, and a select group of other prominent institutes that have budgets greater than $40 to $100 million.[3] Most think tanks in the United States have even less in common with RAND, which has 1,875 staff and a budget exceeding $300 million. Interestingly enough, in size and resources, the majority of think tanks in the United States resemble those in Canada, where in recent years there has also been an increase in the think tank population.

The purpose of this chapter is not to chronicle the origin of the several hundred think tanks created over the last several decades but to illustrate their evolution and diversity in Canada and the United States. This will be done by focusing on four distinct periods, or waves, of think tank development: 1900–46, 1947–70, 1971–89, and 1990–2017. I begin by setting out a typology, or classification, of think tanks that can be used to describe the different types of policy institutes in the two countries. This will help to identify the major types of think tanks associated with the four time periods outlined above. To further highlight the significant differences among think tanks, I provide a brief profile of some of the most prominent institutes in both countries. For comparison, think tanks from the United States and from Canada, established during each of the periods under consideration, are profiled.

CLASSIFYING THINK TANKS IN THE UNITED STATES AND CANADA

Since there is no consensus about what constitutes a think tank, several scholars have constructed various typologies to account for the diversity among policy institutes that comprise the policy research community.[4] They have also attempted to identify the key motivations and institutional traits associated with each generation, or wave, of think tanks. For instance, in studying the evolution of American think tanks, Weaver identifies three types of think tanks in the policy-making community: universities without students, government contractors, and advocacy tanks. McGann, on the other hand, has indicated that at least seven types of think tanks may account for the entire spectrum in the United States: academic diversified, academic specialized, contract/consulting, advocacy, policy enterprise, literary agent/publishing house, and state-based. Additional typologies have surfaced as well.

These and other typologies were originally intended to help identify the different types of think tanks in the United States, but they can, with appropriate modifications, also provide a useful framework for comparing American and Canadian think tanks. Before chronicling the different kinds of policy institutes associated with the four major waves of think tank development, I will highlight some of the similarities and differences between the major types of think tanks in the two countries.

Universities without Students

Universities without students, the first category of think tanks identified by Weaver, are composed of dozens of academics hired to write scholarly studies, rather than assume teaching and administrative responsibilities. They function like universities in the sense that their principal mission is to adhere to rigorous academic standards in promoting a greater understanding of important social, economic, and political issues confronting society. Unlike universities, however, the seminars and workshops they offer and the studies they produce are generally intended for policy-makers, not students. Supported in large part "by funding from the private sector (with varying mixtures of foundation, corporate and individual funding)," scholars working at these institutions regard book-length studies as their primary research product.[5] The Brookings Institution and the Hoover Institution, two of the largest private research institutions in the United States, are among the few think tanks that would fall into this category, although even these institutes devote considerable resources to advocacy.

The Brookings Institution, the Hoover Institution, and other research-driven institutes have long been permanent fixtures in the United States, but these types of think tanks are noticeably absent in Canada. Despite recommendations made to the federal government in the late 1960s to create an independent interdisciplinary think tank on the scale of the Brookings Institution, Canada has yet to become home to a university without students. There are several think tanks that regard academic or policy-relevant research as one of their principal functions, including the Centre for International Governance Innovation (CIGI) based in Waterloo, Ontario, and the Mowat Centre, housed in the School of Public Policy & Governance at the University of Toronto. But none come close to resembling the largest and most distinguished research-oriented think tanks in the United States. In the Canadian context, then, it might be more appropriate to refer to these types of think tanks simply as policy research institutions than as "universities without students." Institutions in this category are staffed by economists, political scientists, and other trained academics who conduct research on a diverse range of policy issues. The majority of their resources are devoted to research, although book-length studies are not necessarily regarded as their primary outputs. The Ottawa-based Conference Board of Canada, well known for its expertise in providing economic forecasting to policy-makers and business leaders, is one think tank that would warrant this classification.

Government Contractors

What distinguishes government contractors from the preceding category is not so much the type of research they conduct (although some of what government contractors do is confidential) but their principal client and primary source of funding. Think tanks like RAND and the Urban Institute, two of the leading government contractors in the United States, rely primarily on government departments and agencies to sustain their operations. Similarly, there are several examples of think tanks in Canada whose work is, or was, almost entirely funded by government sources. In fact, during the 1960s the federal government created a handful of think tanks or "government councils" to provide advice in specific policy areas. Many of these institutes, including the Economic Council of Canada, and the Science Council of Canada, were disbanded in the early 1990s. Others, including the North-South Institute, which relied for much of its funding on the Canadian International Development Agency (CIDA), and the National Council of Welfare and the Canadian Policy Research Networks, Inc., both of which received the bulk of their funding from the federal government, were forced to close their doors in recent years because of budget cuts.

Advocacy Think Tanks

Since the early 1970s, the most common type of think tank to emerge in both Canada and the United States has been what Weaver refers to as the advocacy think tank. Advocacy think tanks, as the name implies, "combine a strong policy, partisan or ideological bent with aggressive salesmanship [in] an effort to influence current policy debates."[6] Known more for marketing and repackaging or recycling ideas than for generating them, advocacy think tanks have played a critical role in transforming the complexion of the policy research community, a subject that will be explored in more detail in chapter 4. Advocacy think tanks tend to place greater emphasis on producing brief reports for policy-makers than on producing book-length studies. Moreover, to influence public opinion and public policy, these types of institutes also place a high premium on gaining access to the media. Their staff frequently appear on network newscasts and political talk shows to share their insights on a wide range of topical policy issues, and take advantage of various social media to attract even greater exposure.

It is useful for comparative purposes to add a fourth and possibly fifth and sixth category – vanity, or legacy-based, think tanks, policy clubs, and think-and-do tanks. Legacy-based think tanks are created by aspiring office-holders (or their supporters) and by former leaders intent on advancing their political and ideological beliefs well after leaving office. Although at one time these institutes were far more numerous in the United States (the Jimmy Carter Center, the Center for the National Interest [formerly the Nixon Center for Peace and Freedom], etc.) several examples of Canadian think tanks now fall into this category. These include: the Calgary-based Manning Centre for Building Democracy and the Manning Foundation, established by former Reform party leader Preston Manning; the Broadbent Institute, founded by former federal

NDP leader Ed Broadbent; the Allan MacEachen Institute for Public Policy and Governance at Dalhousie University launched by the former federal Liberal cabinet minister; and the Brian Mulroney Institute of Government, which will open its doors at Nova Scotia's St Francis Xavier University in 2018. A 1959 graduate of St FX, the eighteenth prime minister has raised $60 million for the institute that bears his name.

The fifth category – policy clubs – may, according to Evert Lindquist, best describe the majority of think tanks in Canada. In his assessment of the impact of Canadian policy institutes, Lindquist suggests that it may be more appropriate to portray several think tanks in Canada as policy clubs (where academics, policy analysts, and, occasionally, policy-makers meet to discuss public policy issues) than as policy research institutions capable of providing long-term strategic analysis.[7] Since they are unable to compete with the institutional resources available in several bureaucratic departments and large trade associations, Lindquist contends that the nostalgic vision of think tanks as creators of new and innovative ideas simply does not conform to the experience of Canadian policy institutes. He bases his observations on the work of several policy institutes created in the early 1970s, but his insights about think tanks as policy clubs can also account for the activities of a handful of relatively small policy shops created in the first decades of the twentieth century.

Finally, we could add a new category of think tanks commonly referred to as think-and-do tanks. These are organizations that make a concerted effort to translate their policy proposals into concrete action. This may include, for example, developing a more effective system of wells in countries suffering from drought. Among the handful of think-and-do tanks that perform these dual roles is the Washington, DC-based Center for Global Development.[8]

PROCEEDING WITH CAUTION: THE LIMITS OF THINK TANK TYPOLOGIES

Classifying generations, or waves, of think tanks according to specific institutional criteria may allow scholars to distinguish one type of think tank from another, and typologies can be useful in comparing think tanks in different countries. Nonetheless, problems can arise in making such classifications. To begin with, since some organizations possess characteristics common to more than one type of think tank, they could conceivably fall into several categories. For instance, while few observers are likely to encounter difficulty distinguishing between the work of the Conference Board of Canada and the Fraser Institute or between the Brookings Institution and the Heritage Foundation, these institutions engage in similar activities: they all conduct research and, to varying degrees, market their findings. The main difference is in the emphasis they place on pure research and political advocacy. To argue, then, that the Conference Board of Canada and the Brookings Institution are policy research institutions and that the Fraser Institute and Heritage Foundation are advocacy think tanks, would, on the surface, be misleading. Each could conceivably be classified as both a policy research institution and an advocacy think tank.

This potential problem cannot be understated. How scholars and journalists classify institutes can have a profound impact on the way different think tanks are perceived in the media and by the public. Referring to the Brookings Institution as a world-renowned policy research institution provides the organization with instant credibility, legitimacy, and notoriety. Indeed, it creates the impression, rightly or wrongly, that Brookings produces objective, balanced, and scientifically rigorous research. Conversely, labelling the Heritage Foundation and the Fraser Institute as well-known advocacy think tanks may imply that they are more committed to advancing their ideological agenda than to pursuing scholarly research. The implication is that the views and recommendations of "research institutions" should be taken more seriously than those of "advocacy think tanks."

The problem of classifying think tanks incorrectly may become more pronounced as these organizations adopt similar strategies to convey their ideas. Like chameleons constantly changing their complexion to suit new environments, think tanks frequently alter their behaviour to become more competitive in the marketplace of ideas. To enhance their profile, some think tanks that were created in the early decades of the twentieth century now rely on tactics employed by the newer generations of institutes. Moreover, some newly created institutes have looked to older generations of think tanks for ideas on how to manage their operations. In short, despite the diverse and eclectic nature of think tanks, it is becoming increasingly difficult to isolate their unique institutional traits.

In distinguishing between different types of think tanks, scholars may describe some institutes incorrectly. Unfortunately, given the methodological problems often encountered in classifying them, this problem might be unavoidable; nevertheless, typologies can still be useful in identifying the kinds of think tanks that emerged during particular periods. As the section below illustrates, think tanks in each of the four waves of think tank development possessed certain defining characteristics. It is these characteristics that allow a new generation of think tanks to be identified.

THE EVOLUTION OF THINK TANKS IN THE UNITED STATES AND CANADA

The First Wave, 1900–45

The first decades of the twentieth century were a formidable period for think tank development in the United States. Although there were several prominent universities at the time, including Harvard University, Johns Hopkins University, and the University of Chicago, a handful of philanthropists and policy-makers believed that what was needed were institutions whose primary focus was not teaching but research and analysis. Guided by the belief that modern science could be used to solve social, economic, and political problems, a philosophy that was widely embraced during the Progressive Era,[9] a small group of philanthropists and social reformers set out to establish privately funded research institutes ostensibly dedicated to serving the public interest.[10] With generous funding from Robert Brookings, Andrew Carnegie, Herbert Hoover, John D. Rockefeller Sr, and Margaret Olivia Sage, among others, several of America's most venerable institutions were created. These included the Russell Sage Foundation (1907), the Carnegie Endowment for International Peace (1910), the Conference Board (1916), the Institute for Government Research (1916; it merged with the Institute of Economics and the Robert Brookings Graduate School of Economics and Government to form the Brookings Institution in 1927), the Hoover Institution on War, Revolution and Peace (1919), the National Bureau of Economic Research (1920), and the Council on Foreign Relations (1921).[11] Founded under different and often unusual circumstances, these institutions shared a commitment to debating and investigating a wide range of domestic and foreign policy issues in the hope of improving governmental decision making (for selected profiles, see table 1.1). Composed of scholars recruited primarily from the social sciences, the think tanks created during this era placed a premium on producing objective and neutral policy research. However, as previous studies have revealed, their goals were not always entirely altruistic, nor were those of their generous benefactors.[12]

While many of the studies produced by these institutes meet the highest scholarly standards, the institutes themselves can rarely be regarded as value-neutral research bodies. The Brookings Institution is a case in point. One of America's oldest and most revered think tanks, Brookings has cultivated a reputation as an independent institute that assigns the highest priority to providing objective research and analysis. Preventing its board of directors from interfering in the research agendas of its scholars is just one way the institute has attempted to maintain its intellectual independence. Nonetheless, being independent and producing objective research are two different things. Until recently, few scholars studying think tanks have questioned Brookings institutional independence, but this is beginning to change. As a result of a series of high-profile newspaper articles by Brooke Williams and a team of investigative journalists exploring the relationship between prominent US think tanks and funding from foreign governments, the extent to which policy institutes are able to remain insulated from donors is being questioned.[13] Allegations that many think tanks, including Brookings, are being seen increasingly as lobbyists paid to extract concessions from lawmakers, has created a hypersensitivity around the issue of funding in the think tank community. While think tank presidents, including Strobe Talbott, formerly of the Brookings Institution, have adamantly denied that donors are able to undermine the integrity of research conducted by his institute, rumours about pay for play at top-tier think tanks persist.[14] What is clear, however, is that think tank researchers, whether they are employed at Brookings or Heritage, are expected, and, in fact, encouraged, to make their policy preferences known. As early as 1920, a handful of scholars at the Institute for Government Research, one of the institutes from which Brookings evolved, engaged in an aggressive lobbying campaign to convince the federal government to adopt a national budget system. The result was the passage of the Budget and Accounting Act of 1921.[15]

Since then, Brookings has been at the forefront of many other major policy debates. What distinguishes Brookings and other early-twentieth-century policy institutes from more contemporary think tanks is not their reluctance to become involved in the political arena but the emphasis they continue to place on engaging in medium- and long-term research. In short, unlike such think tanks as the Heritage Foundation, which concentrates on providing policy-makers with what it would like them to know now, many first-generation think tanks focus on issues policy-makers may want to consider in years to come.

Despite gaining national prominence in the United States, major research-oriented think tanks were noticeably absent in Canada during the early 1900s.[16] There were a handful of relatively small organizations concerned about Canadian foreign policy, including the Round Table Movement; the Canadian Association for International Conciliation; the Institute of Pacific Relations, which enjoyed strong Canadian representation; and the Canadian Institute of International Affairs (CIIA), established in 1928 as the first offshoot of the British Institute of International Affairs (BIIA, later the Royal Institute of International Affairs (RIIA), known as Chatham House). Yet even the CIIA was created more as a "club" of influential Canadians interested in the study of international affairs and Canada's role in it,[17] than as a policy research institution composed of scholars preparing detailed analyses of world events. Some organizations were committed to the study of domestic policy as well. The National Council on Child and Family Welfare, which eventually led to the creation of the Canadian Council on Social Development (CCSD), was formed in 1920.[18] These organizations, as associations of interested individuals and groups, may not have looked like "policy" think tanks when compared with those south of the border. Nevertheless, they undertook important networking functions, and they did commission some research outside the government. Still, with few exceptions, the think tank landscape in Canada remained relatively barren until the early 1960s (for selected profiles see table 1.2).

The Second Wave, 1946–70

By the end of the Second World War, a new wave of think tanks was emerging in the United States, largely in response to the growing international and domestic pressures confronting American policy-makers. Acknowledging the invaluable contribution that defence scientists had made during the war, the Truman administration considered the enormous benefits that could be derived by continuing to fund private and university-based research and development centres. By tapping into the expertise of engineers, physicists, biologists, statisticians, and social scientists, policy-makers hoped to meet the many new challenges they had inherited as the United States assumed its role as a hegemonic power in the atomic age. It was in this environment that the idea for creating the most prominent government contractor, the RAND Corporation (RAND is an acronym for research and development) was born (1948).[19] In addition to making many important contributions to American defence policy, RAND was a prototype for other government contractors, including the Hudson Institute, founded by Herman Kahn, and the domestic-policy-oriented Urban Institute, whose creation was strongly endorsed by President Lyndon Johnson.[20]

In the post–Second World War era, policy-makers in Washington, like the philanthropists during the early part of the twentieth century, recognized the important role think tanks could play in several crucial policy areas. They also recognized the potential benefits of drawing on the expertise of independent research institutes that had the luxury of engaging in medium- and long-term strategic research, instead of relying on government officials and their staff, who were often besieged by daily paper work. Particularly in the area of defence policy, it was crucial for the government to be able to turn to think tanks that had assembled some of the best defence scientists in the country and that, unlike policy-makers and bureaucrats in Washington, were unlikely to be influenced by partisan interests.

Table 1.1
Selected Profiles of American Think Tanks, in Chronological Order

Institution	*Location*	*Date Founded*	*Budget Category ($ Millions)*	*Staff*
Russell Sage Foundation	New York, NY	1907	~13.5	10
Carnegie Endowment for International Peace	Washington, DC	1910	~42	>200
The Brookings Institution	Washington, DC	1916	>100	>300
Hoover Institution on War, Revolution and Peace	Stanford, CA	1919	>60	>150
National Bureau of Economic Research	Cambridge, MA	1920	~30	~40
Council on Foreign Relations	New York, NY	1921	~70	>200
American Enterprise Institute for Public Policy Research	Washington, DC	1943	>50	225
RAND	Santa Monica, CA	1946	>300	1,875
Foreign Policy Research Institute	Philadelphia, PA	1955	~2	~30
Hudson Institute	Indianapolis, IN	1961	>12	~80
Centre for Strategic and International Studies	Washington, DC	1962	>40	>220
Institute for Policy Studies	Washington, DC	1963	~4	45
Urban Institute	Washington, DC	1968	>95	~450
Heritage Foundation	Washington, DC	1973	>90	>250
Worldwatch Institute	Washington, DC	1974	2–5	~25
Ethics and Public Policy Center	Washington, DC	1976	4	~30
Rockford Institute	Rockford, IL	1976	1	9
Cato Institute	Washington, DC	1977	~30	~150
Northeast-Midwest Institute	Washington, DC	1977	~5	~10
Manhattan Institute for Policy Research	New York, NY	1978	16	~55
The Carter Center	Atlanta, GA	1982	~200	~1200
United States Institute of Peace	Washington, DC	1984	25	~85
Economic Policy Institute	Washington, DC	1986	5.5	47
Progressive Policy Institute	Washington, DC	1989	1–2	14
Center for the National Interest	Washington, DC	1994	1–2	12
Center for American Progress	Washington, DC	2003	~30	~100
Center for a New American Security	Washington, DC	2007	8.5	27

Source: Data for American Think Tanks obtained from various think tank websites, annual reports, and from Charity Navigator.

Table 1.2
Selected Profiles of Canadian Think Tanks, in Chronological Order

Institution	*Location*	*Date Founded*	*Budget Category ($ Millions)*	*Staff*
Canadian Council on Social Development	Ottawa, ON	1920	1.5–2	6
Canadian International Council	Toronto, ON	1928	1.5–2	1.5–2
Canadian Tax Foundation	Toronto, ON	1945	5–5.5	15
Atlantic Provinces Economic Council	Halifax, NS	1954	1–2	8
Conference Board of Canada	Ottawa, ON	1954	~40	200
Vanier Institute of the Family	Nepean, ON	1965	1–2	8
Canada West Foundation	Calgary, AB	1971	2.5–3	19
Institute for Research on Public Policy	Montreal, QB	1972	2–3	15
C.D. Howe Institute	Toronto, ON	1973	3.5–4	25
The Fraser Institute	Vancouver, BC	1974	~10	55
Canadian Institute of Strategic Studies*	Toronto, ON	1976	<1	2
Canadian Centre for Policy Alternatives	Ottawa, ON	1980	5–6	40
Canadian Centre for Philanthropy**	Toronto, ON	1981	4–4.5	37
Mackenzie Institute	Toronto, ON	1987	<1	3
Public Policy Forum	Ottawa, ON	1987	3.5–4	22
Institute on Governance	Ottawa, ON	1990	1.5–2	22
Caledon Institute of Social Policy	Ottawa, ON	1992	<1	8
Atlantic Institute for Market Studies	Halifax, NS	1994	1–2	10
Canadian Centre for Foreign Policy Development	Ottawa, ON	1996	2–5 (2002)	6 (2002)
Parkland Institute	Edmonton, AB	1996	<1	6
Frontier Centre for Public Policy	Winnipeg, MB	1997	1	8
Canadian Institute for Advanced Research	Toronto, ON	1982	16	36
Canadian Urban Institute	Toronto, ON	1990	3–5	19
Couchiching Institute on Public Affairs	Toronto, ON	1932	<1	2–5
Montreal Economic Institute	Montreal, QB	1999	2.25	13
Pembina Institute	Calgary, AB	1985	4–5	50

Notes: * The CISS was folded into the Canadian International Council as of 5 May 2008.
** part of Imagine Canada Umbrella; facts are for Imagine as a whole

Source: Data for Canadian think tanks obtained from their websites, annual reports, and through personal correspondence.

The United States had entered an era in which its defence and foreign policy would have a profound impact on shaping world affairs. What it required was sound, informative policy advice. For much of it, it looked to RAND and the Hudson Institute. But just as the federal government drew on these and other think tanks for advice on defence and security issues, President Johnson looked to the Urban Institute to suggest ways to alleviate the many economic, social, and political problems that were contributing to urban unrest throughout the turbulent 1960s. For Johnson, the war waging inside the United States deserved as much, if not more, attention at times as the conflicts taking place beyond America's borders. The onset of the Cold War and the war on poverty placed new demands on the United States government and provided new opportunities for think tanks to make their presence felt. Like the generation of think tanks before them, government contractors began to fill a void in the policy research community.

The postwar period in the United States also witnessed the emergence of several other think tanks, including the Center for Strategic and International Studies (CSIS) and the Institute for Policy Studies (IPS), which were not established as government contractors, but quickly became immersed in Washington's policy-making community nonetheless. Founded in 1962 by David Abshire, former assistant secretary of state for congressional affairs, and by Arleigh Burke, former chief of naval operations, CSIS has been home to several luminaries such as the late Zbigniew Brzezinski, national security adviser to President Carter; Admiral William Crowe, former chair of the Joint Chiefs of Staff; and James Schlesinger, former secretary of defense. From its new $100 million state of the art headquarters near Dupont Circle, CSIS often works closely with incoming administrations to outline foreign and defence policy issues. In many respects CSIS functions both as a research institution and as an advocacy think tank.[21] It has established an impressive research program but has also undertaken considerable efforts to market its ideas. The IPS, created in 1963 by Marcus Raskin and Richard Barnett, is another Washington-based think tank known for its interest in American foreign policy. However, unlike the more mainstream CSIS, the IPS has developed a reputation as Washington's think tank of the left for its Marxist/radical approach US foreign policy. Few would dispute it is ideologically driven.[22]

Several think tanks also emerged in Canada in the postwar period. The Toronto-based Canadian Tax Foundation (CTF) was founded in 1946 by representatives of the national law and accounting societies to conduct and sponsor research on taxation. Eight years later, a branch office of the New York–based Conference Board was established in Montreal to serve its Canadian members. The Conference Board of Canada has since evolved into Canada's largest policy institute, with 200 staff and a budget exceeding $40 million. In 1954, the Atlantic Provinces Economic Council (APEC) was formed to promote economic development in the Atlantic region. And in 1958 the Private Planning Association of Canada (PPAC) was founded as a counterpart to the National Planning Association (NPA) in the United States. PPAC was created by "business and labour leaders to undertake research and educational activities on economic policy issues." It was also intended to support the Canadian-American Committee and two other committees of the NPA, in an effort to help foster dialogue among business, labour, and government representatives.[23]

The growth of think tanks in postwar Canada did not end there. The Vanier Institute of the Family was established in 1965 by Governor General Georges P. Vanier and Madame Pauline Vanier to study "the demographic, economic, social and health influences on contemporary family life."[24] In 1968 the Parliamentary Centre for Foreign Affairs was created to provide research support to parliamentary committees and government departments examining various foreign policy issues.

By the early 1960s the Canadian government had also begun to show interest in creating research institutes. Although the federal government had traditionally relied either on bureaucratic departments or on royal commissions and task forces to advise it on key policy matters, it began to consider other ways to enhance its policy capacity.[25] But unlike the American government, which relied heavily on several private think tanks for research and analysis, the Canadian government decided to establish its own network of policy research institutes. It created several government councils, including the Economic Council of Canada (1963),[26] the Science Council of Canada (1966), the National Council of Welfare (1968), and the Law Reform Commission of Canada (1970) to advise it on a host of policy issues. As Abelson and Lindquist point out,

> These organizations received government funding in amounts that most non-governmental think tanks could only dream about, but operated at an arm's length relationship inside the government (full-time staff were public sector employees). Research activities, including work undertaken on contract by academics and other researchers outside government, were overseen by councils consisting of representatives from the private and non-profit sectors reflecting different constituencies and elements of society. The councils identified new research initiatives, oversaw a rolling portfolio of projects, and produced consensus reports informed by commissioned research studies. Although the councils were independent, members were appointed for fixed terms by the prime

minister and governments could request that new research initiatives be undertaken by the councils.[27]

Although they operated at arm's length from their employers, tensions between the councils and various governments eventually began to surface. The system of parliamentary and responsible government was simply not conducive to allowing organs of the state, no matter how independent, to express views on public policy that were at variance with government priorities and policies.[28] In its budget of February 1992, the government took drastic measures to sever its institutional ties with the various councils: in that year's budget, the Mulroney government disbanded close to two dozen policy institutes, including the Economic Council of Canada, the Science Council of Canada, the Law Reform Commission, and the Canadian Institute for International Peace and Security.[29] The Chrétien government took steps to remedy some of the damage caused by the 1992 budget, including supporting the Privy Council Office's Policy Research Initiative (PRI).[30] The PRI was intended to rectify the diminished policy capacity of government by strengthening the ties between several federal departments and agencies and the external research community. As part of this initiative, a number of think tanks were called upon to help the government think more strategically about the long-term impact of various economic and social policies, a subject that we will return to later.

The Third Wave, 1971–89

The second wave of think tank development – the emergence of government contractors and government councils – hit the United States and Canada at approximately the same time. However, by the time the third wave was making its presence felt in the United States, multiple waves were simultaneously hitting Canada. In the United States in the mid-1970s and 1980s, a new breed of policy institute – the so-called advocacy think tank – was beginning to attract considerable exposure. What distinguished advocacy think tanks from the earlier types of think tanks already established in the United States was not their desire to study public policy issues but their profound determination to market their ideas to various target audiences. Rather than reflecting on important policy issues from the comfort of their book-lined offices, founders of advocacy think tanks understood the importance of immersing themselves in the political arena. Ideas in hand, they began to think strategically and methodically about how to most effectively influence policy-makers, the public, the media, and other key stakeholders. Borrowing from some of the tactics adopted by the American Enterprise Institute (1943), the Heritage Foundation, founded in 1973, was at the forefront of this new wave, elevating political advocacy to new heights.[31] Specializing in quick-response policy research, Heritage emphasized the need to provide members of Congress and the executive with hand-delivered one-to-two-page briefing notes on key domestic and foreign policy issues. It also stressed the importance of marketing its ideas to the media.[32] Encouraged by the critical role Heritage played during the Reagan transition of 1980,[33] dozens of think tanks combining elements of scholarship with aggressive marketing techniques began to take root throughout this period.[34] These included the Rockford Institute (1976), which has enjoyed close ties to Reform presidential candidate Pat Buchanan, the libertarian Cato Institute (1977), and the Economic Policy Institute (1986).

As this new wave of think tanks was hitting the United States, three distinct waves of think tank development were emerging in Canada. First, by the late 1960s the federal government came to realize the potential benefits of having a large independent research institute in Canada similar to ones created in the United States during the early 1900s. Prime Minister Pierre Trudeau was familiar with the work of the Brookings Institution and painfully aware of the absence of such an institution in Canada. In 1968, he commissioned Ronald Ritchie to consider the feasibility of creating an independent interdisciplinary policy institute. The resulting report, submitted the following year, led to the creation of the non-profit Institute for Research on Public Policy in 1972, with endowment funding from the federal government and plans to receive additional support from the private sector and provincial governments.[35]

Second, four established organizations underwent significant transformations into modern think tanks during this period, and several new ones were created: the Canadian Welfare Council, established in 1920, was transformed into a social policy institute called the Canadian Council on Social Development; the small Montreal office of the New York-based Conference Board relocated to Ottawa, which contributed to its growing expertise in developing economic forecasting models for both the public and private sectors; and the C.D. Howe Research Institute was formed in 1973 (following a merger of the PPAC and the C.D. Howe Memorial Foundation) to become a centre for short-term economic policy analysis.[36] Finally, the profile of the Canadian Tax Foundation increased significantly during the early 1970s, due to a national debate stimulated by the Royal Commission on Taxation.

Several new think tanks in Canada were created as well. Two new foreign policy think tanks were established in 1976: the Ottawa-based North-South Institute, which, until it was forced to close its doors because of budget cuts in 2014, received the bulk of its funding from CIDA, to examine development issues, and the Canadian Institute of Strategic Studies in Toronto (CISS), which, as of 2008, has been part of the

Canadian International Council (CIC), the successor to the Canadian Institute of International Affairs. Moreover, the Canadian Centre for Philanthropy (now called Imagine Canada, which grew out of a merger between the Canadian Centre for Philanthropy and the Coalition of National Voluntary Organizations in 2005) was formed in 1981 to advance "the role and interests of the charitable sector for the benefit of Canadian communities."[37] The following year witnessed the creation of the Toronto-based Canadian Institute for Advanced Research (CIFAR), which supports global networks of researchers in their quest for answers to some of the world's most pressing scientific, environmental, and social problems. And, with an eye to resolving several other issues that were plaguing the international community at the time, the federal government agreed to establish and fund the Canadian Institute for International Peace and Security (CIIPS) in 1984. (CIIPS was neither a government council, nor, as it discovered after being dismantled in 1992, was it as independent as the Institute for Research on Public Policy.) In 1985, the Calgary-based Pembina Institute was established to study clean energy, among other things. And in the following year, the Mackenzie Institute opened its doors in Toronto. Notwithstanding its modest resources, the Mackenzie Institute has generated exposure for its research interests in terrorism and radical ideologies, a research area that has, since the events of 9/11 and the rise of al Qaeda and ISIS, continued to generate widespread interest. In 1987, the Public Policy Forum was established to improve public-policy-making by providing a forum for representatives from the public, private, and non-profit sectors to consider a wide range of policy initiatives. And in 1990 the Institute on Governance, currently located in Ottawa's historic Byward Market, was formed to promote effective governance. Among other things, it advises the Canadian government and governments of developing nations on how to better manage public services and train executives, and it often serves as a broker for Canadian agencies seeking to assist developing governments.

In the third, several institutions devoted to the advocacy of particular points of view, reflecting the latest wave of US think tank growth, were also created in this period. The Canada West Foundation, established in Calgary in 1971, was committed to injecting western perspectives on national policy debates. The Fraser Institute was created in 1974 to promote the virtues of free-market economics. And finally, the Canadian Institute for Economic Policy was formed in 1979 by Walter Gordon, a former Liberal finance minister, to sponsor a five-year research program working on the themes of economic nationalism. In 1980 the Canadian Centre for Policy Alternatives (CCPA) was established by supporters of social democratic principles to counter the influence of the Fraser Institute.[38] Not surprisingly, the CCPA has worked closely with the leadership of the New Democratic Party and several public advocacy coalitions, including the Council of Canadians, to convey its concerns on issues ranging from the growing disparity between rich and poor to protecting the environment. The trend toward more advocacy-driven think tanks also appealed to the Progressive Conservative party. Following its defeat in 1980, several party members supported the creation of a think tank on economic, social, and international issues, but the initiative foundered when the party chose a new leader. However, conservatives looking for fresh ideas have not been left out in the cold. Since 2005, former Reform leader Preston Manning has welcomed conservatives, both new and old, including those who support the presidency of Donald Trump, to participate in activities sponsored by the Manning Centre for Building Democracy (which, unlike its sister organization, the Manning Foundation, is more of an advocacy body than a think tank). Once a year, the Manning Centre hosts the Manning Networking Conference in Ottawa, which attracts over 1,000 participants.

The think tank population in the United States and Canada grew considerably during the 1970s and 1980s as both policy-makers and policy entrepreneurs began not only to identify the need for independent policy advice but to discover how effective think tanks could be in influencing public opinion and public policy. The growth of conservative advocacy institutions, in particular, was largely driven by generous benefactors who believed that with sufficient funding think tanks could have a significant impact in shaping the political dialogue, a subject that will be explored further in chapter 3. Think tanks continued to spring up in both countries in the 1990s, although at a much slower pace than in the previous decades. While many recent think tanks have much in common with earlier generations of policy institutes, there are, as the final wave of think tank development reveals, some notable differences.

The Fourth Wave? 1990–2017

Vanity, or legacy-based, think tanks represent another type of think tank that has emerged in the United States. Although they may not constitute a new wave, they nonetheless represent an innovative and interesting development. While legacy-based think tanks such as the (Jimmy) Carter Center (1982) and the (Richard) Nixon Center for Peace and Freedom (1994), now called the Center for the National Interest, have developed a wide range of research programs to help advance the legacies of their founders, some vanity think tanks appear more concerned with engaging in political advocacy.[39] Vanity think tanks are particularly interested in generating, or at the very least repackaging, ideas that will help lend intellectual credibility to the political platforms of politicians, a function no longer performed adequately by mainstream political parties. Vanity think tanks are also established, some have claimed, to circumvent spending limits imposed on presidential candidates by federal campaign finance laws.[40] Examples of these types of think tanks include Senator Bob Dole's short-lived institute, Better America;[41] the Progress and Freedom Foundation (1993), an organization that enjoyed close links to former Speaker of the House Newt Gingrich;[42] United We Stand, established by Ross Perot; and Empower America, founded in 1993 by an impressive band of neoconservatives, including the late Jeane Kirkpatrick, William Bennett, and former Republican vice-presidential candidate, the late Jack Kemp. In July 2004, Empower America joined forces with Citizens for a Sound Economy to form FreedomWorks.

As noted, several legacy think tanks and advocacy organizations have also taken root in Canada. In addition to the Manning Foundation and Manning Centre, the country is home to the Broadbent Institute, the Allan MacEachen Institute for Public Policy and Governance at Dalhousie, and the Mulroney Institute of Government at St Francis Xavier. To this list can be added the C.D. Howe Institute, named after its founder, a former Liberal cabinet minister, and the Pearson-Shoyama Institute (created in Ottawa in 1993 to examine issues related to citizenship and multiculturalism and named after former prime minister Lester Pearson and former federal deputy finance minister Thomas Shoyama). Room in this category could also be made for the Canadian Institute for Economic Policy, formed, as noted, by a former finance minister to further his ideas on economic nationalism.

An even more significant trend in Canada at the end of the twentieth century was the privatization of existing government research. In 1992 the Caledon Institute of Social Policy was created in Ottawa, with support from the Maytree Foundation, to enable Ken Battle, a former executive director of the National Council of Welfare, to develop a research agenda without the constraints of serving a government council. In 1994, CPRN, Inc, was created by Judith Maxwell, former head of the Economic Council of Canada, to sponsor longer-term, interdisciplinary policy research programs on social and economic policy issues and to leverage research capabilities from across Canada. Unable to remain financially viable, CPRN was disbanded in December 2009. Several other institutes were created in the 1990s: the Atlantic Institute for Market Studies (AIMS, 1994); the Canadian Council for International Peace and Security (CCIPS, 1995), which evolved from the Canadian Centre for Arms Control and Disarmament and the Canadian Centre for Global Security; the Centre for the Study of Living Standards (1995); and the Canadian Centre for Foreign Policy Development (1996),[43] housed until recently in the Department of Foreign Affairs and International Trade (DFAIT) and now called Global Affairs Canada, one of the many federal government name changes instituted by Prime Minister Justin Trudeau when he took office in the fall of 2015.

The growth of think tanks did not end there. In 1997, the Winnipeg-based Frontier Centre for Public Policy was established, and in the following year in neighbouring Saskatchewan, the Saskatchewan Institute of Public Policy (SIPP) was born. As of 2008, SIPP has operated under the auspices of the Johnson-Shoyama Graduate School of Public Policy at the University of Regina. In 1999, the Montreal Economic Institute (MEI) was founded, offering Quebec an alternative voice to the policy recommendations of Montreal's Institute for Research on Public Policy. Although several of the organizations created in the early 1990s no longer exist, those that remain have continued to maintain active research programs.

As we entered the new millennium, the proliferation of think tanks in the United States and Canada showed few signs of slowing down. In the United States, a handful of newcomers, including the Center for a New American Security (2007), a think tank with close ties to the Obama administration, was making an impression. But ironically, it was in Canada where much of the buzz about several new think tanks on the block was being heard, with good reason. In 2001, Jim Balsillie and Mike Lazaridis, then co-CEOs of the Waterloo-based company Research in Motion, creators of Blackberry, provided a $30 million endowment to launch the Centre for International Governance Innovation. In the same year, two other think tanks with considerably fewer resources at their disposal were founded: the Parkland Institute at the University of Alberta in Edmonton, the provincial capital; and the Canadian Defence and Foreign Affairs Institute (CDFAI), in Calgary. With a second office in Ottawa, the CDFAI (now named the Canadian Global Affairs Institute) boasts several distinguished scholars on its roster of research fellows, including Jack Granatstein, David Bercuson, and Colin Robertson, a former Canadian diplomat with considerable expertise in Canada-US relations. No sooner did these think tanks begin to gain momentum than four other organizations joined the policy research community: the Wellesley Institute (2006), dedicated to addressing "urban health disparities" in southeast Toronto, a think tank that, ironically, owes its existence to the closure of the Wellesley Central Hospital in 1998; Canada 2020, an advocacy think tank with strong ties to the Liberal party and to a handful of progressive think tanks in the US; the Mowat Centre, housed at the University of Toronto (2009); and the Macdonald-Laurier Institute (2010), led by Brian Lee Crowley, a well-known figure in the think tank community and founding president of the Atlantic Institute for Market Studies.

The emergence of some of the aforementioned think tanks was influenced by important and telling developments in public sector think tanks.

As noted, the federal government, as part of the first wave of serious budget cutting in 1992, eliminated the Economic Council of Canada, the Science Council of Canada, the Law Reform Commission of Canada, and the Canadian Institute for International Peace and Security – only the tiny National Council of Welfare was left untouched.

Its fate was determined several years later when Stephen Harper decided to cut its funding. The creation of the Caledon Institute and the Canadian Policy Research Networks, Inc. were direct reactions to these eliminations. The irony was that the government justified its decision not simply in terms of savings but also because of the great number of non-profit think tanks that had emerged in Canada since the 1960s. In the 1990s, Prime Minister Mulroney and his colleagues had argued that there was sufficient policy capacity outside government to supplement the research needs of federal departments and agencies, a claim widely disputed in the media and in some academic circles.[44]

In reviewing these waves, or periods, of think tank growth, it is important to keep in mind that each new wave has not supplanted the institutions that preceded it but rather has added new patches to an already complex and colourful tapestry. Moreover, the older types of think tanks have continued to be created in recent years in both countries. For example, the Peterson Institute for International Economics, established in Washington, DC, in 1981, is just one of many think tanks conceived of as a "university without students," an academic think tank similar to those of the first wave. At the same time, however, a more crowded marketplace of ideas has increased competition for funding and modified the practices of the older institutions, creating a greater awareness of the need to make findings accessible to and easily digested by policy-makers.[45] This lesson has not been lost on several new members of the think tank community in Canada and the United States, including the Frontier Centre for Public Policy (1997); the Saskatchewan Institute of Public Policy (1998); the MEI (1998); the Center for American Progress (2003), headed by John Podesta, former White House chief of staff to President Clinton, co-chair of President Obama's transition team, and chair of Hillary Clinton's 2016 presidential campaign; and the Center for a New American Security (2007). In short, the institutes that comprise the think tank community in the United States and Canada may have been created at different times and with different goals in mind, but they recognize the importance of adopting the most effective strategies to convey their ideas.

To provide additional insights into how some of the more visible think tanks evolved in the United States and Canada and into what resources they have at their disposal to market their ideas, the following section will profile a select group of prominent think tanks that were established in the United States and Canada during each of the four waves of development discussed above. The profiles are intended not to provide a detailed examination of the origins and activities of a select group of think tanks but simply to help further illustrate the considerable diversity of think tanks in the two countries. Among other things, these profiles will demonstrate that while think tanks may have much in common, each seeks to establish its own niche in the policy-making community, a subject that will be further explored in assessing the impact of think tanks.

A PROFILE OF SELECTED THINK TANKS IN THE UNITED STATES AND CANADA

The Brookings Institution

The Brookings Institution, which claims to be guided by "Quality, Independence, Impact" is one of the oldest and most prominent think tanks in the United States. Located on Washington's Massachusetts Avenue, a popular location for several DC-based think tanks, the Brookings Institution was formed when three separate institutions merged in 1927: the Institute for Government Research (1916), the Institute of Economics (1922), and the Robert Brookings Graduate School of Economics and Government (1924).[46] Recognizing the achievements of the founding institutes, while contemplating an even more significant role for his new institute, Robert Somers Brookings (1850–1932), a St Louis businessman, philanthropist, and social philosopher, was convinced that a nonpartisan interdisciplinary research institute could serve both the needs of policy-makers and the greater public interest. His determination to see the institute accomplish these goals was reflected in the organization's charter. It states that the Brookings Institution was established "to promote, carry on, conduct and foster scientific research, education, training and publication in the broad fields of economics, government administration and the political and social sciences generally, involving the study, determination, interpretation and publication of economic, political and social facts and principles relating to questions of local, national or international significance, to promote and carry out these objects, purposes and principles without regard to and independently of the special interests of any group in the body politic, either political, social, or economic."[47]

With about 300 resident and visiting scholars and support staff and an annual budget exceeding $100 million, the Brookings Institution is one of the largest think tanks in the United States. The majority of its revenues come from philanthropic foundations, corporate and private donations, including those from foreign governments (which as noted, has generated some controversy), and its over $200 million endowment. According to its *Annual Report 2016*, only 2 per cent of its revenues come from government sources.[48]

Brookings, like most universities, maintains separate research departments or what it refers to as programs. Its eleven main programs include: business and industry, cities and regions, defence and security, education, and global development economic studies. It also covers off most geographic regions of the world. Each program is headed by a director who is responsible both for overseeing the department's research activities and for generating sufficient funds to cover much of the department's direct costs. In addition, Brookings maintains several policy centers that focus on specific policy areas or themes. These include the Center for Health Policy, the Center for Middle East Policy, the Center on Social and Dynamics and Policy, and the Tax Policy Center.

Few think tanks in the United States have established a more impressive research record than Brookings. The institute publishes approximately two dozen books each year, as well as a wide range of other publications geared to different target audiences. Its scholars also take advantage of various media outlets (including social media) and opportunities to testify before congressional committees and subcommittees to convey their ideas on a wide range of issues. Its impressive roster of scholars includes or has included several former high-level policy advisers among its ranks, such as Alice Rivlin, former director of the White House Office of Management and Budget (1994–96), Charles Schultze, former chair of the President's Council of Economic Advisers (1977–80); former Brookings president Michael Armacost, who served in the US Department of State (1984–89); and Strobe Talbott, who occupied the Brookings presidency until November 2017 and served as deputy secretary of state during the Clinton administration. Talbott was succeeded by General John Allen, a retired US Marine Corps four-star general. This calibre of adviser also helps to enhance Brookings reputation as a prestigious policy research institution.

RAND

Unlike the Brookings Institution, RAND does not owe its existence to a philanthropist who believed in the power of ideas but to a small group of engineers and military leaders who understood how the development of intercontinental missiles could both threaten and enhance America's national security. In late 1945, General H.H. Arnold, commanding general of the Army Air Forces (the Department of the Air Force was established in September 1947), acting on the initiative of two engineers from the Douglas Aircraft Company, Arthur Raymond and Frank Collbohm, proposed a $10 million contract with Douglas to fund Project RAND, "for the study of V-1 and V-2 rocket techniques and other intercontinental air techniques of the future."[49] However, despite the government's initial enthusiasm for the project, relations between the air force and Douglas soured over the next two years. Concerned that Douglas was more preoccupied with making profits than advancing US security interests, the air force removed Project RAND from the aircraft company and proposed that an independent non-profit organization be created to undertake the initiative.[50]

With an initial capital investment of $1 million and close to $5 million in remaining funds from Project RAND, the RAND Corporation was chartered in May 1948, "to further and promote scientific, educational, and charitable purposes, all for the public welfare and security of the US of America."[51] Under the leadership of Collbohm, who left Douglas to become RAND's first president, a talented group of scientists, including Bernard Brodie and Herman Kahn, gathered at the Santa Monica think tank to consider how to protect and promote US security interests during the nuclear age. Using systems analysis, game theory, and various simulation exercises, RAND scientists devoted themselves in the immediate postwar years to serving the needs of the air force.[52]

RAND continues to receive the bulk of its $300 million budget from the US Air Force, the US Army, and the Office of the Secretary of Defense, but its research interests are not confined to defence and national security issues.[53] As members of the largest think tank in the United States, RAND's approximately 1,875 researchers and staff carry out research in over a dozen major policy areas, including health care, education, science and technology, energy and the environment, national security, and population and aging. The majority of RAND's staff work at its Santa Monica headquarters or its office in Washington, DC. Others are based at RAND's Council for Aid to Education in New York City, RAND Europe in the Netherlands, or at one of its smaller sites.

In addition to overseeing an extensive research program that has resulted in the publication of hundreds of books, policy briefs, reports, and academic journals, RAND established its own graduate school in 1970 to help train future policy analysts. The Frederick S. Pardee RAND Graduate School stresses the importance of educating students to examine complex policy issues from a multidisciplinary perspective. It is home to the largest PhD program in public policy in the United States.

The American Enterprise Institute for Public Policy Research

Established in 1943 by Lewis H. Brown, president of the Johns-Mansville Corporation, to promote the virtues of "free-market economics in the face of a rising tide of Keynesianism,"[54] the American Enterprise Association (AEA) existed in relative obscurity for over a decade. Although Brown hoped his organization would effectively challenge the growing influence of the Brookings Institution, by 1954 the AEA only had four full-time employees and an annual budget barely exceeding $80,000. In an attempt to transform his organization from a small business association that analyzed economic policies for corporate clients into an influential policy research institution, Brown turned to the AEA's executive vice president, William J. Baroody Sr. Baroody, who had formerly served with the US Chamber of Commerce, shared Brown's vision of a research institution committed to promoting free-market economics. After becoming president in 1962, Baroody took the first step toward restructuring and revitalizing the AEA by changing its name to the American Enterprise Institute "so that it sounded less like a trade association and more like an intellectual centre."[55] Committed to promoting conservatism as the "dominant strain of thought,"[56] Baroody invented a new role for policy entrepreneurs – that of impresario of intellectuals.[57] As Sidney Blumenthal, a journalist and former adviser to President Clinton points out, "AEI was his stage. Conservative thinkers would rehearse ideas there, and then present them to political leaders."[58]

Combining the skills of an advertising executive, a corporate fundraiser, and a political strategist, Baroody turned AEI from an insignificant business association into the "MGM of Washington think tanks."[59] By recruiting some of America's most prominent economists, political scientists, and former government officials, including Milton Friedman, Jeane Kirkpatrick, and the late Herbert Stein, Baroody created a strong platform from which to promote the organization's conservative beliefs. However, unlike Robert Brookings and Andrew Carnegie, who sought to insulate their research institutions from partisan interests, Baroody took pride in publicizing AEI's mission. Guided by the belief that the competition of ideas is fundamental to the survival of a free and democratic society, Baroody undertook several measures to ensure that AEI's conservative message would be heard. By inviting government leaders to participate in seminars, publishing books and periodicals, and encouraging resident scholars to solidify their ties to corporate leaders and public officials, Baroody carved out an important niche for AEI in the policy-making community.

AEI's rise to prominence can be largely attributed to Baroody's vision and guidance, but it may also have been facilitated by the changing direction of political winds in the United States during the late 1970s. According to Patricia Linden:

> It was the right idea at the right time, a period when the insistent voice of the neo-conservative think tanks began to invade

> opinion- and decision-makers' consciousness, and present formidable rivalry for research dollars as well. AEI's glittering lineup not only invigorated the organization with fresh ideas, it all but guaranteed lineage, attention, credibility and funding. The institute rocketed to prominence: a world-class organization peopled with multi-disciplinary star analysts whose wide-ranging views ... gave conservatism an intellectual depth.[60]

In 1978, after devoting more than twenty years to transforming AEI into one of Washington's leading think tanks, William Baroody Sr stepped down as president and invited his son, William Baroody Jr, to guide the organization into the 1980s. A former press secretary to Melvin Laird, secretary of defense in the Nixon administration[61] and the principal architect of the Ford administration's Office of Public Liaison, Baroody Jr was well qualified to market AEI's basic philosophy. Under his leadership, AEI's research program was expanded to encompass governmental, social, and international affairs and several former officials of the Ford administration, including the president himself, who became a distinguished fellow at AEI after leaving public office, were hired to further enhance the prestige and visibility of the organization. But like his father, Baroody Jr realized that unless AEI's ideas were properly marketed, the institution would be unable to exercise influence on Capitol Hill and in the White House. Consequently, in the ensuing years, he relied on his extensive experience in media relations to increase AEI's exposure in Washington. With the confidence of a prize fighter standing over his defeated opponent, Baroody extolled the virtues of marketing AEI's research products:

> I make no bones about marketing ... We pay as much attention to the dissemination of product as to the content. We're probably the first major think tank to get into the electronic media. We hire ghost writers for scholars to produce op-ed articles that are sent out to one hundred and one cooperating newspapers – three pieces every two weeks. And we have a press luncheon monthly. [AEI also produces a monthly television show on public policy shown on more than four hundred stations, a weekly radio talk show on more than 180 stations, and publishes four magazines (*Regulation*, *Public Opinion*, *The* AEI *Economist*, *Foreign Policy and Defense Review*), legislative analyses and books.] ... It's important for them [AEI scholars and government officials] to deal with public issues that permeate the environment in which they have to do business ... That's become clear to them.[62]

Baroody's preoccupation with marketing AEI and its products to policymakers and to the public began to generate concern among the organization's board members in the mid-1980s. Although the appointment of close to three dozen AEI scholars to government posts, boards, or commissions in the Reagan administration reflected the organization's growing visibility, Baroody's inability to properly manage AEI's research program began to cause major setbacks. In addition to blaming Baroody for mismanaging funds,[63] conservative critics argued that while the United States was moving comfortably to the right, AEI was drifting too far toward the centre of the political spectrum.

As the rising tide of conservatism swept across the United States in the mid-1980s, conservative foundations began to look to think tanks that were willing and able to promote ideas consistent with their mandate. For example, in 1986, fearing that AEI was not playing a leading role in the conservative revolution, two prominent foundations, the Olin Foundation and the Reader's Digest Association, withdrew their financial support from AEI and gave it to the Heritage Foundation, claiming that the former had strayed too far from its rightward course.[64] Faced with increasing criticism from board members and corporate sponsors, Baroody was fired and eventually replaced by Christopher DeMuth, a former official in the Reagan administration.[65] After leaving AEI, Baroody admitted that "he created too rich a feast and served it too fast."[66] DeMuth, who resigned from AEI in 2008, learned from his predecessors' mistakes. Commenting on the primary goal of AEI, DeMuth stated, "We will continue to be a research institution rather than a marketing institution."[67] With 225 staff and an annual budget in excess of $50 million, AEI's president Arthur C. Brooks oversees a major research institute that has expertise in seven main areas: economics, foreign and defence policy, health care, education, politics and public opinion, poverty studies, and society and culture. Each area is further subdivided into several program and policy areas. In addition to pursuing active research in these areas which accounts for over 50 per cent of its budget,[68] AEI has not lost sight of the importance of marketing its ideas. As Jeffrey Gedmin, a former research fellow at AEI points out, AEI "falls between two worlds,"[69] the secluded world of academic research and the real world of Washington politics.

AEI understands the importance of increasing its visibility, which may explain why it recently purchased and renovated one of Dupont Circle's most historic buildings. At a cost of $50 million (a pittance compared to the $100 million CSIS spent on its new building), AEI's new headquarters, which for years was occupied by the National Trust for Historic Preservation, is attached to the Carnegie Endowment for International Peace. AEI has also raised its profile over the years by hiring several former government officials and advisers, including Richard Perle, a member of the Pentagon's Defense Policy Board; former speaker of the House Newt Gingrich; Lawrence Lindsey, former chair of the National Economic Council; Senator Fred Thompson; David Frum, a former speech writer in the George W. Bush administration; John Bolton, former US ambassador to the United Nations; and Paul Wolfowitz, former US deputy secretary of defense and the tenth president of the World Bank.

Notwithstanding the many obstacles AEI has faced in its seventy-five-year history, it has left a lasting imprint on many important policy initiatives, from fighting the war on terror and recommending the surge in Iraq, to advising the executive branch on how to further deregulate key policy sectors.[70] From its early beginnings as a proponent of free-market economics, the American Enterprise Institute has paved the way for the creation of other advocacy think tanks in the United States. By transforming the role of think tanks from traditional nonpartisan research institutions to vehicles for the expression of political beliefs, AEI is to a large extent responsible for paving the way for third-generation think tanks. As Burton Yale Pines, former senior vice president and director of Research at the Heritage Foundation pointed out, "AEI is like a big gun on an offshore battleship. We are the landing party. If they hadn't softened it up, we wouldn't have landed."[71] Building on AEI's achievements in marketing its research findings, the Heritage Foundation has taken political advocacy to new heights. In fact, for many observers of Washington politics, the Heritage Foundation remains Washington's quintessential advocacy think tank.

The Heritage Foundation

Just as RAND served as a prototype for other government contractors, the Heritage Foundation has become the type of policy institute other advocacy-oriented think tanks have sought to emulate. Heritage was established in 1973 by two congressional aides, the late Paul Weyrich and Edwin Feulner, with $250,000 in seed money from Colorado brewer Joseph Coors. The idea of creating a think tank that could provide policy-makers with timely and policy-relevant information came to Weyrich and Feulner when the two sat down for lunch one day in the Senate Office building. As Feulner recalls,

> Weyrich and I were having lunch together and he showed me a study that had the pros and cons on the SST (Supersonic Transport). It was a good analysis, but it arrived on his desk the day after the vote took place. We both kicked that around and said, "Wouldn't it be great if there were an institution that

> delivered the kind of timely, usable policy analysis so that those of us working on the Hill could really make use of it?" I immediately called up the President of the organization to praise him for this thorough piece of research and asked why we did not receive it until after the debate and the vote. His answer: they did not want to influence the vote. That was when the idea for the Heritage Foundation was born.[72]

Operating from a small office space over a grocery store in one of the less desirable neighbourhoods of Washington, DC, Heritage rocketed from relative obscurity in the early 1970s to become America's most visible think tank during the Reagan years. Now located in an impressive office building only blocks from the Capitol Building, Heritage's profile in Washington's policy-making circles has continued to rise. "Committed to rolling back the liberal welfare state and building an America where freedom, opportunity, prosperity, and civil society flourish," Heritage's main goal is to persuade policy-makers, the public, and the media to embrace "the principles of free enterprise, limited government, individual freedom, traditional American values, and a strong national defense."[73]

Like most advocacy-oriented think tanks, Heritage does not try to conceal its mission. As Edwin Feulner, president of Heritage for over thirty years admits, "Our role is trying to influence the Washington public policy community ... most specifically the Hill, secondly the executive branch, thirdly the national news media."[74] In his second stint as president of Heritage, Feulner is unlikely to change his strategy. However, it is unlikely that he will depart drastically from a strategy that served Heritage well for so many years. Although Heritage publishes several books each year, its main focus is not on long-term studies but on what Feulner often referred to as quick-response policy research. Aware that policy-makers rarely have the time or inclination to sift through a report of several hundred pages, Heritage has built its research program around providing members of Congress and the executive with concise and timely reports on important domestic and foreign policy issues. At Heritage, marketing ideas is considered as important as, if not more important than, generating them. According to Heritage's executive vice president and chief operating officer, Phillip Truluck, "We certainly spend as much money on marketing our ideas as we do on research. We keep these two functions in balance because we believe that the process doesn't end when a paper is published ... Our aim is to change public policy – not merely to comment on it – so we have to give marketing a key role in our total mission. We cannot just put out a study and hope that it gets in the right people's hands."[75]

Heritage's formula for balancing policy research with political advocacy has clearly paid off, and the creation of its sister organization, Heritage

Action for America, founded in 2010 as an advocacy body with 501 c. 4 status under the Internal Revenue Code, has certainly helped raise the profile of key conservative issues. The Heritage Foundation's budget has more than quintupled in the past thirty years, rising from $17.9 million in 1989 to over 90 million in 2017. Heritage has been particularly successful in marketing its message to large numbers of conservative supporters throughout the United States. Three-quarters of its revenue is generated by more than a half–million individuals who make annual contributions to the organization.[76] Heritage has also received several generous donations from philanthropists and foundations who look to the organization to promote their conservative beliefs. Its largest contributor has been Pittsburgh billionaire Richard Mellon Scaife, who has donated over $20 million to the organization since its inception. In 1976, three years after Heritage opened its doors, Scaife donated $420,000, or 42 per cent of the organization's revenue at the time. Comparing the generosity of Joseph Coors to Scaife's, officials at Heritage have said jokingly, "Coors gives six-packs; Scaife gives cases."[77]

With over 250 staff who conduct research in both domestic and foreign policy, Heritage maintains a visible presence inside the Beltway. Often contacted by journalists to comment on policy issues confronting Congress, Heritage scholars rarely pass up an opportunity to convey their views. At times, some of these views, including those on health care reform, which became the foundation for President Trump's campaign to repeal and replace Obamacare, have generated considerable animosity. During Trump's first 100 days in office, a group of protesters stormed the lobby of the Heritage Foundation expressing their anger at how the organization had supported Trump's efforts.[78]

The Project for the New American Century (PNAC)

Despite closing in 2006 and being replaced by the Foreign Policy Initiative (closed in 2017 due to funding cuts) in 2009, PNAC continues to generate interest among scholars looking to better understand the role and impact of public policy think tanks. At the height of its notoriety in 2001, one might expect that, like the Heritage Foundation, PNAC occupied a large luxurious office space close to the main centers of political power. After all, where else would the think tank apparently responsible for creating a blueprint for the Bush administration's invasion of Afghanistan and Iraq be located? How about in a small suite of rented offices in a downtown building that at the time housed the American Enterprise Institute and *The Weekly Standard*, a conservative magazine edited by William Kristol, the chair of PNAC. With a budget of $600,000, PNAC could hardly afford an office building in Heritage's pricey neighbourhood.

Established in the spring of 1997 "to promote global leadership," PNAC employed four full-time staff and a handful of interns who, among other things, helped to write and disseminate policy papers and issue briefs (2 to 4 pages long) to approximately 2,000 journalists, academics, members of Congress, editorial writers, and think tanks every six weeks. This strategy, according to PNAC's president Gary Schmitt, a political scientist with a PhD from the University of Chicago, allowed us "to make a case that is well-reasoned and brief. We have a much bigger voice than our size because we offer a vision that is clear and articulate."[79]

PNAC's vision and creation, which was shaped by a 1996 *Foreign Affairs* article co-authored by William Kristol and Robert Kagan,[80] the best-selling author of *Of Paradise and Power*, was clearly articulated in its Statement of Principles released in June 1997. It states in part:

> American foreign and defense policy is adrift. Conservatives have criticized the incoherent policies of the Clinton Administration. They have also resisted isolationist impulses from within their own ranks. But conservatives have not confidently advanced a strategic vision of America's role in the world. They have not set forth guiding principles for American foreign policy. They have allowed differences over tactics to obscure potential agreement on strategic objectives. And they have not fought for a defense budget that would maintain American security and advance American interests in the new century. We aim to change this. We aim to make the case and rally support for American global leadership.[81]

What caught the eye of most journalists scanning PNAC's Statement of Principles was not the organization's desire to advance what amounted to a "Reaganite policy of military strength and moral clarity," but the list of high-profile policy-makers who offered their endorsement. As noted in the Introduction, among the original signatories to PNAC's principles were: Donald Rumsfeld, secretary of defense; Paul Wolfowitz, deputy secretary of defense; Lewis "Scooter" Libby, chief of staff to Vice President Dick Cheney; and Vice President Dick Cheney.

When President Bush's strategy to promote and protect American security interests began to take shape in the months following the tragic events of 11 September 2001, the small and relatively obscure conservative think tank with powerful connections in the Bush White House was propelled into the national spotlight. Its September 2000 report, entitled *Rebuilding America's Defenses,* outlined a series of policy recommendations strikingly similar to the actions President Bush was in the process of pursuing. Indeed, it appeared to several journalists, even those weary of conspiracy theories, that PNAC had laid the foundation for what became known as the Bush Doctrine. While there is no doubt that PNAC played an important role in contributing to the debate on global terror, its influence in shaping Bush's post-9/11 strategy has, by its own admission, been greatly exaggerated. This observation has been confirmed by further investigative reports.[82]

A VIEW FROM CANADA

The Conference Board of Canada

In many respects, the Conference Board of Canada is unique among Canadian think tanks. With a staff of over 200 and an annual budget over $40 million, it is by far the largest research institution in the country. But despite its visible presence in Canada, the Conference Board originated in the United States. In 1916 the Conference Board was established in New York to "facilitate a cross-fertilization of facts and ideas in industry as a way of identifying and solving its problems and enhancing the public's understanding of these problems."[83] Like many other think tanks created during the Progressive Era, the founder of the Conference Board insisted that the organization engage in "unbiased fact finding" and "refrain from all political activity."[84]

During the decades following its founding, the Conference Board established itself as a highly credible and competent research organization that proved capable of addressing the needs of both American and Canadian companies. Indeed, as Lindquist points out, "With 40 large Canadian companies alone participating in the US-based organization, the creation of a Canadian office seemed a natural step."[85]

In 1954 the Conference Board opened a small office in Montreal to respond to an expanding number of Canadian companies, Canadian-based US subsidiaries, and US companies interested in obtaining more information about Canada. The Conference Board of Canada has created a well-defined niche in the policy-making community. Unlike many smaller think tanks that attempt to influence public debates through their various publications and exchanges with policy-makers and journalists, the Conference Board specializes in providing knowledge in key areas to its members in the public and private sectors. In exchange for a membership fee, the Conference Board "[helps its] members anticipate and respond to the increasingly changing global economy … through the exchange of knowledge about organizational strategies and practices, emerging economic and social trends and key public policy issues."[86] Its primary goal is to help its members become better prepared to adapt to changes in the marketplace.

As well as providing members with access to its publications and conferences, the Conference Board undertakes contract research. Known for its expertise in economic forecasting and analysis, the board also specializes in several other areas, including economics, organizational performance, public policy, and leadership and human resources.

Given its size and the breadth of its research expertise, it is not surprising that the Conference Board attracts more media attention than any other policy institute in Canada, a finding that will be explored further in chapter 5. Its commitment to producing independent and unbiased research may also help explain why it has developed a reputation as one of the most credible institutes in Canada, despite the occasional slip-up that has proved embarrassing to the organization.[87]

The Vanier Institute of the Family

Established under the patronage of Their Excellencies, Canada's Governor General Georges P. Vanier (1959–67) and Madame Pauline Vanier, the "Vanier Institute of the Family began its work in 1965 immediately following the Canadian Conference on the Family the two patrons convened at Government House."[88] As the Vanier Institute observes in its brief history of the organization, "That founding conference brought together distinguished men and women from all walks of life, each of whom knew that the contribution of families is vitally important and ultimately shapes the world in which we live."[89] Governor General Vanier's "vision to create an enduring organization dedicated to the cause of our society through the family was supported by the leadership of renowned Canadian neuroscientist, Dr. Wilder Penfield."[90]

The Vanier Institute's vision to promote "the well-being of Canadian families" is anchored by a four-pronged strategy to:

- Build public understanding of important issues and trends affecting the healthy functioning of Canadian families;
- Foster a society that identifies and provides for the needs and aspirations of families;
- Encourage a family perspective among policy-makers, service providers, employers, educators and others whose work affects the lives of families; and
- Promote the inherent capacity of families to help themselves.[91]

To convey its ideas to multiple stakeholders, the Vanier Institute relies on its robust research program, its commitment to public education and traditional family values, and its willingness to form "strategic partnerships with public and private institutions, corporations, the media and the non-profit sector."[92] The Vanier Institute pays close attention to its public profile. Its annual reports state how often its publications, including its magazine, *Transition*, have been downloaded, the various media outlets with which its researchers have interacted, and the number of people who have attended the many conferences, seminars, and workshops it has organized.[93] With more than $16 million in investments, the Vanier Institute is well-positioned to continue the mandate it carved out over fifty years ago with assistance from one of English Canada's most popular governor generals.

The Fraser Institute

Well before Prime Minister Pierre Trudeau announced in his Christmas message in 1974 that "the marketplace was not a reliable economic institution and would increasingly have to be replaced by government action in order to sustain the economic well-being of Canadians," the seeds for creating the Vancouver-based Fraser Institute had already been planted.[94] Increasingly concerned by the federal government's Keynesian economic policies and the election of the first NDP government in British Columbia in 1972, T. Patrick Boyle, a senior industrial executive and then vice president of planning at MacMillan Bloedel, began considering how best to inform Canadians about the crucial role that markets play in economic development. After meetings with several business leaders and economists, including Csaba Hajdú and Michael Walker, Boyle "conceived the establishment of an economic and social research institution which he felt had to be unlike any other in existence in Canada."[95]

In early 1974, Boyle enlisted the support of the Honourable J.V. Clyne to raise seed money for the institute and managed to generate $75,000. Boyle also began working closely with Walker, Hajdú, and several other individuals, including John Raybould and Sally Pipes, to draft the institute's mission statement and operating plan. On 21 October 1974, the charter of the Fraser Institute, "so named for the mighty Fraser River, thereby giving this new institute a geographical, rather than ideological reference point," was granted by the Canadian government.[96]

The Fraser Institute experienced little difficulty locating its geographical or its ideological reference point during its first year, but, like most think tanks in Canada and the United States, it became preoccupied with staying afloat. With meagre resources during its first year of operation, fundraising became the greatest challenge confronting the newly created organization. Sir Antony Fisher, Fraser's acting director and founder of several other policy institutes, including the Institute of Economic Affairs in London, coordinated Fraser's fundraising efforts in 1975. A year later Fisher left the staff of the Fraser Institute, and Sally Pipes, who had worked in the

British Columbia government's statistical agency and the Council of Forest Industries in the province, assumed fundraising and membership responsibilities. Michael Walker, who had worked in the Department of Finance and at the Bank of Canada before joining Fraser, became the Institute's research and editorial director, a position he held until the fall of 2005 when he was replaced by Mark Mullins.[97]

The Fraser Institute's operating revenue and media profile steadily increased in the last quarter of the twentieth century and into the first decades of the new millennium. With a full-time staff of fifty-five and a budget hovering around $10 million, Fraser has become one of Canada's most talked about and written about think tanks.[98]

Fraser's current president, Niels Veldhuis, oversees an active research program that focuses on over a dozen policy issues and has resulted in the publication of a blog, *The Fraser Forum*, and dozens of books, conference reports, and bulletins. Fraser also recognizes the importance of encouraging and training future generations of conservative thinkers, the institute sponsors a university student internship program and an annual student essay competition. The institute generates considerable attention for its studies that examine school rankings, as well as the date each year when Canadians can actually keep their earnings instead of turning them over to the government. They call it Tax Freedom day.

The Fraser Institute, like the Heritage Foundation, has cultivated a reputation, deservedly so, as a free-market advocacy-oriented think tank that places considerable emphasis on shaping public opinion and public policy. Indeed, its obvious bias toward relying on market solutions to economic problems has often made it an easy target for critics. Still, it is important to keep in mind that think tanks from the entire political spectrum engage in some form of political advocacy.

As the final think tank profiles illustrate, even more liberal think tanks with far more modest resources than the Fraser Institute recognize the importance of conveying their ideas to policy-makers and the public.

The Caledon Institute of Social Policy

It is difficult to discuss the Ottawa-based Caledon Institute without immediately invoking the name of its director Ken Battle. In fact, few other think tank directors in Canada, perhaps with the exception of Michael Walker when he held that position,[99] have become so closely identified with a policy institute. Battle's reputation as one of the country's most astute thinkers on social policy is well known in Ottawa's key policy-making circles. Often invited to advise senior policy-makers on a range of social and tax policies, including old age security and child welfare benefits, Battle served as director of the National Council of

Welfare, a citizen's advisory body to the minister of national health and welfare, before founding Caledon in 1992.

After spending close to fifteen years at the National Council of Welfare, Battle became increasingly sensitive to how critical a publicly funded policy institute could be of government policies. As one of the Mulroney government's most vociferous critics, Battle was convinced that both his position and the future of the National Council of Welfare could be in jeopardy as long as he remained in charge. "At the time, I began looking around for other positions," Battle stated. "I thought for a while that I would try to become director of the Canadian Council on Social Development [CCSD], but then something else came up."[100]

What came up was a meeting with Toronto businessman and philanthropist Alan Broadbent, who wanted to fund a public policy organization that would have an impact. Although Battle initially approached Broadbent for funds to help rebuild the CCSD, Broadbent was more interested in creating a new organization that would study social and welfare policies than in revitalizing an existing institution: "Alan is one of those capitalists with a social conscience who clearly wanted to fund an organization that would make a difference ... When he made me an offer to head up a new institute, I accepted."[101]

Following a handful of meetings with Broadbent, Battle developed the Caledon Institute's mission statement, which reads: "The Caledon Institute of Social Policy is a leading private, non-profit social policy think tank that conducts social policy research and analysis. As an independent and critical voice that does not depend on government funding, Caledon seeks to inform and influence public and expert opinion and to foster public discussion on poverty and social policy. Caledon develops and promotes concrete, practicable proposals for the reform of social programs at all levels of government and of social benefits provided by employers and the voluntary sector."[102]

With roughly $300,000 from Broadbent's Maytree Foundation, Caledon opened its doors in February 1992. It currently has a budget of less than $1 million that is generated from the Maytree Foundation and from other sources for project-specific funding. From its inception, Caledon has purposely maintained a lean operation; its board of directors, which meets once a year, barely satisfies the minimum legal requirement of three people. In addition to Battle, the board consists of Broadbent, a lawyer, and a financial analyst. "The advantage of having a lean operation is that we can change direction fast if we have to," Battle notes. "This allows us to move ahead of the government and influence substantive policies and the political agenda."[103]

Caledon maintains a tiny research staff. Assisting Battle are Sherri Torjman, vice president of Caledon, who has written extensively on several issues, including social spending, health care, and fiscal arrangements; and senior scholar Michael Mendelson, a former deputy secretary of the cabinet in Ontario, who has several publications on social and fiscal policy to his credit, as well as a handful of policy associates.

With a small research staff, Caledon has managed to establish an impressive publication program. Its commentaries on various social policy issues, "Caledon's most useful product," according to Battle, are widely circulated to policy-makers, social advocacy organizations, and the media. Caledon's media profile is modest compared with several other think tanks such as the Fraser Institute and the C.D. Howe Institute, but, as chapter 5 will demonstrate, its contribution to policy formulation is well recognized by directors of party research offices and senior policy-makers.[104]

Parkland Institute

Located in the Faculty of Arts at the University of Alberta, with a second office in Calgary, "Alberta's left-leaning" Parkland Institute, as its critics often label it, "studies economic, social, cultural and political issues facing Albertans and Canadians using the perspective of political economy."[105] According to its 2008 "Self-Study," Parkland's values "include being open, critical, innovative, transformative, and solutions oriented."[106] Its mission rests on five pillars:

- "To [provide] top quality policy research focussing on Canadian energy security and environmental sustainability, social justice, and social equity.
- To lead and expand the policy and political debate through research and outreach programming that changes the framing of issues in Alberta and Canada.
- To [provide] policy research that is transformative, proposing positive policy solutions that lead to systematic and structural changes that improve the quality of life and social justice.
- To help inform an engaged public by publishing our research in accessible language, disseminating our work widely, and by creating spaces (colloquia, conferences, symposia, web dialogues) where academics and citizens can actively engage with each other on current issues; and
- To foster provincial, national and international research networks and synergies."[107]

The Parkland Institute began its life with "three years of seed funding from the Faculty of Arts,"[108] and, despite its small staff and modest resources, has been able to establish a strong foothold in Western Canada. Its stature has been enhanced in recent years by the launch of an endowment program propelled by a million-dollar donation. In addition to its many research studies on health care, environmental sustainability, and energy, the Parkland Institute has relied on several other channels to communicate its findings and policy recommendations to multiple audiences. The Institute hosts several workshops and conferences throughout the year and its staff and research fellows regularly interact with the media. Parkland is well aware of the importance of demonstrating to potential donors how much of an impact its work has on shaping public opinion and public policy. It also recognizes that it may have a greater impact at some stages of the policy cycle than others. To this end, it has compiled a body of data to assess its reach and impact relative to some of its competitors.[109] Although the Parkland Institute may not enjoy the same level of public visibility and notoriety as the Fraser Institute, the C.D. Howe Institute, and other public policy research organizations, it occupies an important position on the Canadian think tank landscape.

This chapter has explored in some detail the evolution and growing diversity of the think tank community in Canada and the United States. In the process, it has helped confirm why it is so difficult to define what a think tank is. The think tank landscape does not consist of organizations with similar profiles. Rather, it resembles an ever-expanding patchwork that consists of institutes of all shapes and sizes. Although think tanks are far more numerous in the United States than in Canada, it is clear that the same types of policy institutes have taken root in both countries.

CHAPTER TWO

Thinking about Think Tanks: A Conceptual Framework

As think tanks have come to have a more visible presence in both advanced and developing countries, scholars have employed various theoretical approaches to explain their role and significance in the policy-making community. In this chapter, we explore what these approaches are and what steps can be taken to provide more informed insights about their impact in shaping public policy. As we will discover, it is important to both build on and move beyond the existing literature in the field to develop a more useful conceptual framework to evaluate their involvement in policy-making.

When academics began thinking and writing about think tanks in the late 1960s and early 1970s, many of their observations about how policy institutes interacted with state and non-state actors were deeply rooted in liberal theories of the state: elite theory, pluralism, and statism. Although admittedly dated, these theories continue to find their way into the literature that seeks to evaluate the role, significance, and impact of think tanks in the policy-making community. In the pages that follow, we consider the strengths and limitations of these theories, and what steps can be taken to provide more informed insights about how think tanks attempt to influence public opinion and public policy. In the process, we will offer suggestions as to how to examine these organizations in a more systematic and comprehensive manner. We will come to the realization that what has changed is not simply the terminology political scientists and sociologists use to describe how think tanks engage different communities. The continued growth and increased presence of think tanks on the political landscape, and their desire to become more advocacy-oriented, compels us to re-evaluate what they do, how their role has changed, and the extent to which they have become more entrenched in policy-making.

As noted, several of the earliest studies of think tanks, which focused predominantly on policy institutes in the United States, discussions about how and why these organizations enjoyed privileged status, and were rewarded with preferential access to powerful members of the bureaucracy, Congress, and the White House, were linked to liberal theories of the state. For example, elite theorists posited that many of those who occupied key positions in think tanks, or donated large gifts to sustain their operations, travelled in the same social and financial circles, attended many of the same Ivy League institutions, and belonged to social clubs where the country's leading political figures congregated. Moreover, they argued that these strong and overlapping ties provided think tanks with the access and opportunities they required to advance both their institutional interests and those of their corporate and philanthropic donors. Several American scholars, including C. Wright Mills, relied heavily on elite theory to analyze the US military-industrial complex in the mid-1950s. Indeed, his seminal 1956 work on the topic, *The Power Elite*,[1] caused quite a stir in both academic and policy-making circles when it first appeared. His growing concerns about how the US Congress, the Pentagon, and defence contractors worked together to fuel the Cold War was not lost on President Dwight Eisenhower. In his farewell address on 17 January 1961, Eisenhower warned the American people about the dangers of the military-industrial complex.[2] Over a half a century later, journalists and scholars all too familiar with what and whom are driving US foreign policy are expressing similar concerns.[3] Studies on elite theory may not generate the scholarly attention they once did, but much of what Mills and his contemporaries revealed deserves our consideration. Although some of the terms used to describe elites might be outdated, the assumptions underlying this theory have remained largely intact. In fact, elite theory, which holds that nearly all political power is held by a relatively small and wealthy group of people sharing similar values and interests has helped to fuel other theories, some fanciful, others not, about how think tanks, with other key stakeholders, assist governments in convincing the public to embrace controversial domestic and foreign policies.

As tempting as it is to assume that think tanks are an elite set of actors that enjoy unlimited and unfettered access to the corridors of power, and as much as directors of think tanks would like to be treated as royalty in the White House and on Capitol Hill, some observers are not convinced that they should be perceived differently from other groups competing for attention in the policy-making community. Rather than elevating think tanks to a status generally reserved for a handful of organizations at the highest levels of government, those embracing the tenets of pluralism[4] argue that policy institutes, like interest groups, trade unions, human rights organizations, environmental associations, and a host of other institutions committed to influencing public policy, face similar hurdles as they try to navigate their way through the policy-making process. That some organizations are more effective than others in capturing the attention of policy-makers does not concern pluralists, as long as everyone follows the rules established by government to oversee the participation of non-governmental organizations in the policy process.

For pluralists, what matters is not that non-governmental organizations have different resources at their disposal, but that they have the opportunity to compete on a level playing field. By imposing restrictions on political and partisan activities, legislative bodies, with the support of government departments and regulatory agencies, attempt to exercise control over policy inputs (who contributes to public policy), not policy outcomes (the actual decisions of government). In other words, pluralists contend that policy-makers simply want to ensure that the guidelines non-governmental organizations must follow to participate in the policy-making process are fair and transparent. They also claim that policy-makers are less invested in who ultimately succeeds in influencing policy decisions, an assertion disputed by elite theorists, who recognize that how governments control policy inputs influences policy outcomes.

Third, there are a handful of scholars who, although they acknowledge the presence of think tanks and other non-governmental organizations in the policy-making community, suggest that relative to the state's authority and autonomy, they play a very modest role in shaping public policy. Contrary to the assertions of scholars who argue that public policy is controlled and manipulated by elites and/or by special interest groups, those embracing the "statist paradigm" maintain that the state can and does act independently of various societal and bureaucratic pressures,[5] that the fate of the nation rests in the hands of presidents, prime ministers, and their cabinets, not external groups seeking to impose their agenda on the state. And, finally, there are scholars who focus less on the elite, pluralist, or statist nature of think tanks and the policy environment they inhabit and more on the institutional structure and orientation of the organizations themselves. Scholars influenced by the "institutionalist" tradition pay close attention to the mandate and resources of think tanks, and to the many factors that influence the strategic choices they make to become involved at different stages of policy-making.[6] It is to these particular approaches that we now turn.

THINK TANKS AS POLICY ELITES

For some scholars, including Joseph Peschek, Thomas Dye, William Domhoff, John Saloma, and William Minter,[7] think tanks not only regularly interact with policy elites, they help comprise part of the nation's power structure. For example, in the United States, where think tanks frequently serve as talent pools or holding tanks for incoming presidential administrations and as retirement homes for former high-level policy-makers, think tanks are considered elite organizations that are both able and willing to influence public policy. The multimillion-dollar budgets at the disposal of a handful of American think tanks, and the many prominent and distinguished business leaders and former policy-makers who serve on their boards of directors and trustees help reinforce this image. The close and intimate ties between think tanks and the corporate and philanthropic donors and foreign governments who fund them[8] suggest to Marxists and elite theorists[9] that think tanks are indeed instruments of the ruling class. They argue that by virtue of the unique space they occupy at the intersection of the academic and policy-making worlds, think tanks are more than capable of advancing the interests of those with economic and political power over individuals and organizations that are marginalized in and by the political system they inhabit. The argument scholars in this field advance is straightforward: in exchange for large donations, think tanks use their policy expertise and connections with key policy-makers to advance the political agendas of their generous benefactors. On the surface, this seems entirely plausible. After all, it is unlikely that corporations and philanthropic foundations would donate thousands, and sometimes millions, of dollars to think tanks that are acting contrary to their interest. They fund think tanks that share similar ideals and concerns about the nation, and those they believe are capable of affecting policy change. As David Roodman, formerly of the Washington, DC-based Center for Global Development observes, "Every funder has motives. Every funder of a policy-influencing think tank can therefore be described as "buying influence."[10] However, it is important to question the type of return donors expect on their investment. To quote Enrique Mendizabal, founder of the blog *On Think Tanks*, "Domestic or foreign, nobody hands over money to think tanks without wanting [something] in return. They may want to influence certain policy decisions or they may just want to see their name outside an office in the think tank's new building. They all want something."[11]

While it makes sense for philanthropic foundations, corporations, and leaders of foreign governments to fund think tanks that can frame issues in ways that will help advance their core interests, it is less important for these and other donors to rely on them to help establish contact with senior-level policy-makers. Through their sizeable donations to congressional and presidential candidates, not to mention their personal friendships and social ties to dozen of politicians, it is unlikely that donors with this kind of cachet would require think tanks to introduce them to government officials. This is not to say that think tanks are unwilling to make introductions – they often do. The point is whether it is necessary for them to do so. Moreover, since corporations and foreign governments can and do hire lobbyists to represent their interests on Capitol Hill and on Parliament Hill, it is unlikely they would turn to institutions like think tanks that are prohibited under the Internal Revenue Code and the Income Tax Act from engaging in overt political lobbying. And since professional lobbyists have an incentive to work tirelessly on behalf of their clients, what can think tanks offer corporate America and Canada that lobbyists cannot? The answer is simple: credibility and respectability, or, what Joseph Sandler, an American lawyer with expertise on statutes governing lobbying, refers to as a "patina of academic neutrality and objectivity."[12]

Corporations and philanthropic foundations turn to "elite" think tanks such as Brookings, the Carnegie Endowment, and the Hoover Institution, not so they can take advantage of their political connections (although this could help periodically), but so they can benefit from the relationships these and other think tanks have to the media, to universities, and to other power centres in Canada and in the United States. But even more important, corporations and philanthropic foundations can take advantage of the reputation think tanks have cultivated as scientific, neutral, and scholarly organizations to more effectively influence public opinion and public policy. Writing large cheques to political campaigns may provide corporations with access and political capital, but it does not necessarily buy them credibility. Credibility, like valuable information, can prove to be a commodity more precious than money. On the other hand, supporting think tanks that supply the media and policy-makers with a steady stream of information, expertise, and policy recommendations might allow donors to secure both. This could explain in part why corporations and philanthropic foundations also lend a helping hand to other types of research organizations and university departments who can draw on their reputation as scholarly institutions to influence both the policy-making environment and actual policy decisions.

By closely examining the interaction between the largest think tanks in the United States and Canada and key officials in government, scholars may be justified in concluding, as some have, that think tanks play a critical role in influencing public policy. However, since few institutes in Canada or in the United States have resources comparable to the

Brookings Institution, the Heritage Foundation, or the RAND Corporation, we must question the utility of employing an approach that assumes that think tanks, by their very nature and purpose, are capable of promoting the interests of the ruling elite. We must also question whether think tanks, as charitable organizations engaged in policy analysis, should be treated as elites.

Think tanks are in the business of shaping public opinion and public policy, but, as noted, have very different ideas of how various domestic and foreign policies should be formulated and implemented. Several think tanks, for example, embrace the views of some elites that free market solutions to economic problems should be pursued. The C.D. Howe Institute, the Fraser Institute, the Montreal Economics Institute, and the Washington-DC-based American Enterprise Institute, among others, would certainly favour such an approach. But there are many other think tanks, including the more progressive Canadian Centre for Policy Alternatives (CCPA), the Parkland Institute at the University of Alberta, and the Washington-based Institute for Policy Studies that have profoundly different views of how governments should resolve economic and social problems, and go to great lengths to address widespread inequality. Should think tanks that regularly oppose the interests of the ruling elite and work tirelessly on behalf of those marginalized in our country be considered part of the elite?

Despite some limitations that will be explored in more detail below, adopting an elite approach to the study of think tanks has some advantages. As Domhoff and others have discovered,[13] examining the close and interlocking ties between members of think tanks and leaders in business and government can provide interesting and useful insights into why some policy institutes may enjoy far more visibility and notoriety than others. Moreover, by keeping track of who sits on the boards of directors of think tanks, we may be able to explain why some institutes generate more funding than their competitors. Nonetheless, it is important to keep in mind that while members of think tanks frequently interact with high-level business leaders and policy-makers, their connections to key figures does not necessarily allow them to exercise policy influence. The networks they have established may facilitate access to important officials on Capitol Hill and Parliament Hill, but their ability to influence public policy depends on a wide range of factors.

By portraying think tanks as policy elites, scholars can make sweeping assertions about who controls public policy. But as appealing as this might be, it is also problematic because it tells us little about the ability or inability of think tanks to exercise influence at different stages of the policy cycle. It tells us even less about how to assess or evaluate the impact of think tanks in policy-making. In short, an elite approach assumes that with the right connections think tanks can and will be able to influence public policy. Unfortunately, it offers little insight into how this will be achieved.

THE PLURALIST TRADITION: ONE VOICE AMONG MANY

Members of think tanks may occasionally travel in elite policy circles, but according to some political scientists, including David Newsom,[14] they represent but one of many types of organizations that populate the policy-making community. According to this perspective, which is deeply rooted in the American pluralist tradition,[15] think tanks compete among themselves and other non-governmental organizations for limited resources. The gains achieved by one group or organization are frequently offset by costs incurred by others.[16] Since policy-makers, and the governments they represent, are assumed to behave as moderators or referees monitoring the competition among groups, pluralists devote little attention to assessing government priorities. They view public policy not as a reflection of a specific government mandate, but rather as an outcome of the struggle between competing interests.

Studying think tanks within a pluralist framework has its advantages. For one thing, it compels scholars to acknowledge that, despite the widely held view that think tanks enjoy preferential access to policy-makers and to other key stakeholders, they constitute only one of many organizations intent on leaving a mark on public policy. This approach also serves as a reminder that think tanks, like interest groups and other non-governmental organizations, rely on similar strategies to shape public policy, a subject that will be explored further in chapter 4.

The pluralist approach, however, has serious weaknesses. To begin with, although disciples of pluralism assume that, in the final analysis, decisions on domestic and foreign policy matters reflect the outcome of an ongoing struggle among groups to advance their respective interests, pluralism sheds little light onto why some organizations may be better positioned than others to influence public attitudes and the policy preferences and choices of decision-makers. Is it simply a matter of which groups have the largest budgets, staff resources, and most extensive research programs that determines who does and does not have influence? Or, do other factors such as access to the media, policy-makers, and affluent donors offer better clues as to which group or groups are destined to succeed or fail in the political arena?

The major deficiency of pluralism is not that it assumes that all groups are able to influence public policy. On the contrary, pluralists acknowledge that non-governmental organizations vary enormously in terms of size, resources, and expertise, important factors that can account for how successful organizations are in achieving their desired goals. The problem with pluralism is that it exaggerates the virtues of a level playing field, while ignoring how groups with vastly superior resources at their disposal can easily outrun or outmanoeuvre their opponents. For pluralists, process matters far more than outcomes. They are so concerned with following the rules of the policy game that they pay little attention to why some organizations always seem to cross the finish line first. By the same token, if pluralists treat think tanks as simply one of many voices in the policy-making community without recognizing what makes them unique, they will overlook why, at times, some policy institutes have more opportunities to influence public policy than interest groups and other non-governmental organizations. Think tanks may indeed be part of the chorus, but they possess certain attributes that allow them to stand out. By virtue of their expertise and close ties to policy-makers, think tanks may compete among themselves for prestige and status, but they do not necessarily compete with the hundreds of other participants in the policy-making community. In fact, in some policy areas, think tanks may face little competition at all.

Pluralists also need to acknowledge that as committed as policy-makers might be to ensuring that the policy-making process is fair and transparent, they often have a vested interest in influencing the outcome of group competition. Instead of behaving as referees, policy-makers representing various government branches and departments can and do rely heavily on select organizations to achieve their goals. Many of these organizations are also closely aligned with large voting blocs in congressional districts and/or parliamentary ridings that elected officials cannot afford to ignore. As we will discuss in the case studies included in this study, at critical stages of the policy-making process members of the US Congress and the Executive, and their counterparts in the Canadian Parliament, regularly turn to specific think tanks for advice on how to tackle thorny policy issues. At other times, they rely on think tanks to help frame the parameters of important policy debates.

Marxists and pluralists disagree about the extent to which think tanks are entrenched in the policy-making process and the willingness of the state to embrace their ideas. However, both acknowledge that think tanks have the ability to play a vital, and, at times, decisive role in public policy, a position that has been questioned by proponents of state theory. While scholars employing the first two approaches focus on various societal and bureaucratic pressures to reveal how public policy is shaped and molded, those advancing the statist paradigm look no further than the state to explain who makes policy decisions.

IN THE NATIONAL INTEREST: A STATIST APPROACH

As multinational corporations, media conglomerates, and powerful special interest groups have established a strong foothold in the western world, it is not surprising that we have lost sight of who ultimately is entrusted with protecting the national interest, a concern raised most recently by several scholars in the United States.[17] But despite their global reach and visibility, it is not Bill Gates, Warren Buffett, or leaders of other blue chip companies who speak on behalf of the United States and take steps to promote its economic, political, and security interests. It is the president and the people who surround him or her who make decisions that are intended to serve the needs of the nation. To remind us of this, a handful of scholars, including Theda Skocpol and Stephen Krasner, have emphasized the relative autonomy of the state in making difficult policy decisions.[18] State theory, according to Aaron Steelman, advances the argument "that while the public can indeed impose some restraint on the actions of the bureaucracy and elected officials, the state retains a degree of autonomy and works according to its own logic."[19]

In his book, *Defending the National Interest*, Stephen Krasner elaborates on the theory of statism. He notes: "[Statism] is premised upon an intellectual vision that sees the state autonomously formulating goals that it then attempts to implement against resistance from international and domestic actors. The ability of the state to overcome domestic resistance depends upon the instruments of control that it can exercise over groups within its own society."[20] For Krasner, it is the central state actors – the president and the secretary of state – and the most important institutions – the White House and the State Department – that control foreign policy.

If Krasner, Skocpol, and other proponents of state theory are correct, what impact could think tanks possibly have in influencing state behaviour? Although one might assume that think tanks would be relegated to the sidelines, Steelman suggests that state theory leaves ample room for think tanks to make their presence felt: "State theory can help explain the seeming anomalous cases of former think-tank staffers who enter government pledging to work for a certain set of ideas and then enacting policies that are quite different. In some cases, these individuals have been co-opted by the system; in others, they are generally doing their best to reach their goal, however slowly or circuitously. But either way, the state itself is an important actor."[21]

There are several advantages to incorporating state theory into studies of think tanks. First, it helps to explain how think tank staffers can become directly involved in making key policy decisions. If we accept

Krasner's argument that the president and the secretary of state, and the two institutions they represent – the White House and the State Department – are the most important participants in the foreign policy-making process, it becomes very clear which think tanks have or do not have access to the highest levels of government. Rather than trying to monitor the efforts of think tanks to influence Congress and the media, scholars could simply explore the relationship between the president, the secretary of state, and their closest advisers. If it appears that members from think tanks have been advisers, or recruited to serve in the White House or in the State Department, we could assume that they have had direct access to the policy-making process. After all, if the president and secretary of state (along with the secretary of defense, Joint Chiefs of Staff, and national security adviser) are the most influential participants in foreign and defence policy-making and often rely on think tank experts for advice, it would be logical to conclude that think tanks are in a position to influence policy decisions. Conversely, if there is little evidence to suggest that think tanks have gained access to the upper echelons of government, scholars could, according to state theory, conclude that they have had little impact in influencing state conduct. In short, state theory, whether it is applied to domestic or foreign policy decision-making in the United States, Canada, or in other democracies, can explain when think tanks have or have not been influential.

However, state theory is not without its limitations. It may be useful in explaining why some presidents, such as Richard Nixon, were able to insulate themselves from Congress and the American people.[22] But by the same token, it is less helpful in explaining why many recent presidents have gone to great lengths to consult with the public, members of Congress, foreign governments, international organizations, and a host of non-governmental organizations before making important policy decisions. President George H.W. Bush's efforts in 1990–91 to secure an international coalition to deter Iraqi aggression is a case in point. Before deploying US armed forces to the Persian Gulf, President Bush made sure he had the support of the United Nations and several of its member states, a strategy that his son considered, but later abandoned, before invading Iraq.[23] As the foreign policy-making process has become more transparent over time and as more governmental and non-governmental organizations have sought to become involved in shaping world affairs, proponents of state theory have had a more difficult time defending the relative autonomy of the state. They certainly have had difficulty explaining why the US Congress appears to have taken a more active interest in foreign policy.[24] In the final analysis, both advocates and critics of state theory acknowledge that the president makes decisions that can profoundly influence America's conduct in the international community. Yet, as we have witnessed in recent years, how presidents make policy decisions ultimately depends on their management style and willingness to listen to their inner circle of advisers. State theory might help to account for the management of US foreign policy under President George W. Bush, but might do little to shed light on how Presidents Clinton and Obama governed the nation.[25]

Thus far, we have looked at three different theoretical approaches and how they can be employed to study think tanks. Before considering how it might be possible to integrate them more effectively, it is important to consider a fourth approach that has attracted considerable attention: focusing on think tanks as a diverse set of organizations that have very different priorities and concerns, rather than as members of the policy elite, the state, or the broader policy-making community. This approach appears more promising. As we will discover below, a more informed understanding of how think tanks function at various stages of the policy-making process can allow scholars to identify where these institutions have the greatest impact.

DIFFERENT THINK TANKS, DIFFERENT PRIORITIES: AN INSTITUTIONAL APPROACH

Three distinct institutional approaches to the study of think tanks have surfaced in the literature in recent years. The most common approach focuses either on the history of particular think tanks or on the evolution and transformation in particular countries. Several scholars have written institutional histories of the Brookings Institution, the Council on Foreign Relations, the Heritage Foundation, and RAND.[26]

A number of studies have also detailed the rise of think tanks in the United States, Canada, and other advanced and developing countries.[27] The obvious advantage of providing detailed histories of think tanks is that they offer a wealth of information on the nature and mandate of organizations, the research projects they have conducted over time, and the various institutional changes they have undergone. The main disadvantage, however, is that many of these studies are simply histories and offer little concrete data to support or deny claims that particular think tanks have played a major role in shaping public policies.

The second and more systematic institutional approach has concentrated on the involvement of think tanks in what students of public policy commonly refer to as epistemic or policy communities.[28] These communities consist of individuals and organizations that, by virtue of their policy expertise, are invited to participate in policy discussions with government decision-makers. The formation of policy or epistemic communities is often seen as a critical stage in policy formulation and regime formation. This approach has been undertaken by a handful of political scientists, including Hugh Heclo, Evert Lindquist, and Diane Stone, who regard think tanks as important participants in these communities.[29]

By examining think tanks within a policy or epistemic community framework, scholars can make several important observations. To begin with, by focusing on policy issues such as the campaign to repeal and replace Obamacare or the considerable domestic and international fallout from President Trump's executive order restricting travel to the US, scholars can more accurately identify the key organizations and individuals who have been invited to share their thoughts with policy-makers. In addition to determining which groups and individuals participate in the "sub-government," a term used to describe the various non-governmental and governmental policy experts who coalesce around particular policy issues, this approach offers better insight into the nature of the policy-making process itself. Among other things, a policy or epistemic community framework compels scholars to delve far deeper into the mechanics of policy-making. Rather than treating policy decisions as an outcome of interest group competition or as a reflection of elite interests, this approach requires scholars to think seriously about how policy decisions can be influenced through discussions between non-governmental and governmental policy experts.

There are other advantages to adopting this approach as well. Once the actors participating in the sub-government have been identified, it is possible to compare the recommendations made by participants to the actual policy decisions that were made. Access to minutes of meetings, personal correspondence, testimony before legislative committees, published recommendations, and other information may not enable scholars to make definitive conclusions about which participants in a policy community were the most influential. Nonetheless, these and other materials can offer useful insights into whose views generated the most support.

Given the involvement of policy experts from think tanks in different policy communities, it is not surprising that this framework is being used more often. It is important to keep in mind, however, that while this approach may be better suited to the study of think tanks than either an elite or a pluralist framework, it too has its shortcomings. Examining think tanks within a policy community is useful in identifying which institutes are called upon to offer their expertise at an important stage in policy formulation. Unfortunately, it does not tell us what impact, if any, think tanks inside policy communities or those operating outside the sub-government have in shaping public attitudes and the policy preferences and choices of policy-makers. In short, this approach may tell us who is sitting at the table when key issues are being discussed, but it does not tell us whose voices have struck a responsive chord with those in a position to influence policy decisions. Since we cannot assume that all, or any, important policy decisions are made inside specific policy communities – after all, it is politicians, not policy experts, who cast votes in the legislature – a third group of scholars has begun to consider using a more inclusive approach in studying the involvement of non-governmental organizations in policy-making.

Recognizing that the mandates, resources, and priorities of non-governmental organizations vary enormously, John Kingdon and Denis Stairs, among others, suggest that rather than trying to make general observations about how much or how little impact societal groups have on shaping policy-making and the policy-making environment, scholars should examine how groups committed to influencing public policy focus their efforts at different stages of the policy cycle.[30] Although Kingdon and Stairs do not write specifically about think tanks, their approach to studying how groups seek to place issues on the political agenda and how they try to convey their ideas to policy-makers throughout the policy-making process is well-suited to the study of think tanks.

POLICY CYCLES AND POLICY INFLUENCE: A HOLISTIC APPROACH

For Kingdon and Stairs, trying to determine which domestic and external forces shape public policy constitutes an enormous, and, at times, overwhelming undertaking. In fact, as the policy-making community in the United States and in Canada has become increasingly crowded, it has become difficult, if not impossible, to identify those groups that have had a direct impact on policy issues. As a result, instead of making generalizations about which groups influence public policy, Kingdon and Stairs, among others, recognize that not all organizations have the desire or the necessary resources to participate at each stage of the policy cycle: issue articulation, policy formulation, and policy implementation. While some organizations may have an interest in placing issues on the political agenda by articulating their concerns through a number of channels (issue articulation), others may be more inclined to enter the policy-making process at a later stage (policy formulation or policy implementation). In other words, some organizations may be more interested in sharing their ideas with the public than in working closely with policy-makers to formulate or implement policy.

By acknowledging that think tanks do have different priorities and mandates, it is possible to construct a conceptual framework that allows scholars to make more concrete observations about the role and impact of think tanks in policy-making. At the very least, a framework that recognizes the diversity of think tanks and their distinct missions will discourage scholars from making sweeping and often unfounded observations about their impact.

The conceptual framework employed in this book, which will be expanded upon in the chapters to follow, is based on a simple premise: think tanks in Canada, in the United States, and in much of Europe, represent a diverse set of organizations that share a common desire to influence public policy. However, because of their unique institutional characteristics, each think tank must make strategic decisions about how and where in the policy cycle to make their presence felt. In other words, since think tanks possess different resources, which, not surprisingly, affect the nature and extent of activities they undertake, they naturally assign different priorities to participating at various stages of the policy cycle. This becomes particularly important in interpreting data such as media citations and testimony before legislative committees that can be used to evaluate think tank performance.

After considering the four approaches that have been employed to study think tanks and their involvement in policy-making, one central question remains: which approach or conceptual framework best explains their role and function? Unfortunately, there is no simple answer. As we have discussed, each approach encourages scholars to move in a certain direction and to ask a unique set of questions. Therefore, the question that should be posed is not which theory best explains how the functional role of think tanks has changed, but which framework helps scholars to better understand a particular feature or characteristic of their behaviour. For instance, those concerned about the relationship between think tanks and corporations could benefit far more from drawing on the assumptions underlying elite theory than from tapping into pluralist theories of democracy. On the other hand, scholars interested in explaining why some think tanks seem more preoccupied with working on various policy initiatives than with grabbing headlines would learn a great deal from Kingdon and other students of public policy who have written extensively about how institutions set priorities.

Examining the efforts of think tanks to influence key domestic and foreign policy debates requires an integrated approach. This approach would draw on the observations showcased by each of the theories outlined in this chapter, but would not adhere exclusively to any particular one. The advantage of relying on multiple theories to explain the involvement of think tanks in public policy is that it offers scholars some breathing space to test different hypotheses about when and under what conditions think tanks can have the greatest impact. The alternative is to select a theoretical framework that offers but one perspective on the nature of think tanks and their relationship to policy-makers. For example, one could adopt Krasner's statist paradigm to explain why think tanks and interest groups have had marginal success in constructing and implementing the Obama administration's war on terror. Given the relatively small group of advisers to whom Obama listened, and the president's decision to continue the war on terror with limited support from the international community, state theory might offer scholars the answers they need. However, the same theory would offer little insight into the debate over national missile defence that has been kept alive for over three decades by a handful of think tanks, including the Heritage Foundation and the Center for Security Policy. Contrary to the central assumptions underlying state theory, successive administrations have succumbed to pressure from interest groups, think tanks, and corporate and bureaucratic interests to construct and deploy a missile defence. Rather than looking to Krasner for answers as to why this has occurred, scholars would likely benefit more by reading the work of C. Wright Mills and others who have provided valuable insights about the military-industrial complex.

In the final analysis, scholars must select a theory or theories that will help them to understand the information they have uncovered. They should not rush to find a theory and then hope to gather empirical and statistical evidence to make it more credible. Such an approach may be of little comfort to those looking for a grand theory to explain what think tanks do and how they achieve influence. Still, as many experts of American foreign policy and international relations have learned, as tempting as it is to construct one theory that will reveal the complexity of world affairs, such efforts often amount to little more than an exercise in futility. But before we rush to judgment about which theory or theories best explain how and to what extent think tanks engage in the policy-making process, it is necessary to more fully explore how think tanks function in very different political environments. Only then can we determine how the various approaches included in this chapter enhance or obscure our understanding of these unique organizations.

CHAPTER THREE

In the Arena: Opportunities, Constraints, and Incentives for Think Tanks in the United States and Canada

In an ideal world, think tanks would have few, if any, financial concerns, conduct research on a wide range of timely and policy-relevant issues, and, from the comfort of their book-lined offices, would observe their ideas translated into concrete policy decisions. The world of think tanks and the reality of the policy-making process, however, is far from ideal. The vast majority of think tanks in the United States, like those in Canada, lack the resources they require to examine the many complex policy questions confronting government. Many also lack the resources to convey their ideas effectively to decision-makers. Moreover, since policy-makers must usually juggle competing political interests, think tanks often have to struggle to capture their attention.

Aware of the complexity of the policy-making process, as well as the demands placed on their limited resources, think tanks must make a number of strategic decisions, not the least of which is where in the policy cycle they will seek to have the greatest impact. As I will discuss in this chapter, although think tanks in both countries make similar choices, those in the United States have far more opportunities to become involved in policy-making than their Canadian counterparts. But why is this the case? Does the highly fragmented and decentralized nature of the US government, combined with a weak party system, provide think tanks and other non-governmental organizations with more opportunities to influence policy-making?[1] Conversely, do the principles of strong party unity and cabinet solidarity, reinforced by effective party leadership control over the rank and file, the increasingly important role played by backroom strategists in shaping party platforms,[2] and the presence of a permanent civil service entrusted with advising senior officials, limit opportunities for think tanks in Canada to engage at critical stages of policy-making?

Comparing the institutional environments in which think tanks in the two countries function offers some insight into why US policy institutes have established a more visible presence than those in Canada.

Several features of the US political system have indeed facilitated think tanks' access to various stages of the policy-making process. However, differences in political structures cannot entirely account for American think tanks appearing to play a more significant role in policy-making than those in Canada, nor can they explain why some institutes in both countries are more influential than others. In fact, as some heads of Canadian think tanks have argued, including David Zussman, former president of the Public Policy Forum, the structure of the Canadian government may have very little to do with whether think tanks are effective or ineffective at conveying their ideas. The political structure of a country may influence the types of strategies non-governmental organizations use to reach policy-makers, but according to Zussman, it is the modest resources available to most policy institutes that have limited their impact far more than the political system they inhabit. Gaining access to policy-makers in Canada is not a problem, Zussman claims. Rather, it is obtaining sufficient funds to conduct long-term research and analysis.[3]

If Zussman is correct, then it is important to draw a distinction between opportunities for think tanks to participate in policy-making and the constraints that may undermine their effectiveness. In doing so, it can be demonstrated, as Diane Stone has done in a study comparing think tanks in Great Britain with those in the United States, that parliamentary democracies and their structures may not pose as much of a barrier to think tank access as previously thought.[4]

This chapter examines the opportunities for think tanks in both countries to participate in policy-making, as well as some of the internal and external constraints that might undermine their efforts to influence policy formulation and the policy-making environment. It also looks more closely at the incentives decision-makers in both countries may have to turn to think tanks for policy expertise. The central argument here is that while think tanks in the United States and Canada function in very different political systems, this factor alone cannot account for their success or failure.[5] Their ability or inability to market their ideas effectively may have as much to do with how they define their missions; the talent, skill, and political savviness of the directors who lead them; the resources they have at their disposal; and the strategies they employ to achieve their stated goals. The amount of funding they have and the quality of their staff, not to mention the timing of the issues they hope to advance, may be more important in determining how influential they become.

OPPORTUNITIES FOR THINK TANKS IN THE UNITED STATES AND CANADA

There are few parts of the policy-making process or a branch or department of the US government where think tanks have not made their presence felt.[6] Think tanks specializing in a wide range of domestic and foreign policy areas have conveyed their ideas to key policy-makers in Congress, the executive, the bureaucracy, and, more recently, the judiciary.[7] There are also think tanks at the state level, including the New York-based Manhattan Institute, which has established strong ties to local government leaders.[8] As will be discussed later in this section, dozens of staff from think tanks have become policy-makers themselves.

Among the many factors that have contributed to the proliferation of think tanks in the United States is the structure of the political system. As several scholars have observed, few countries provide an environment more conducive to the development of think tanks.[9] With a government based on separate branches sharing power, a party system in which members of Congress are free to vote as they wish, and a growing number of presidential candidates trying to develop new ideas, think tanks have multiple opportunities to shape public opinion and public policy. In Congress (the US House of Representatives and the US Senate) alone there are 535 elected officials (in addition to three non-voting members from the District of Columbia), not to mention dozens of staff and committee aides, whom think tanks can approach to consider their policy ideas.[10] Recognizing this, think tanks have employed several strategies to attract attention, ranging from testifying before congressional committees and distributing concise summaries of key policy issues to members of Congress and the executive to inviting representatives and senators, White House staffers, bureaucrats, and their staff to participate in seminars and workshops.[11] For a brief period, a select group of policy experts from some of America's leading think tanks could rely on another channel to share their expertise regularly with members of Congress: in March 1998 the Congressional Policy Advisory Board was formed to allow policy experts from outside government to discuss several policy issues with the House leadership. Of the twenty-eight policy experts who comprised the board, twenty-one were affiliated with US think tanks, including the board's chair, the late Martin Anderson, who spent much of his distinguished career as a senior fellow at the Hoover Institution.[12] However, the board was disbanded in 2000 with little notice or explanation. A more detailed assessment of these and other channels think tanks rely on to influence policy-making will be discussed in the next chapter.

Since members of Congress are not bound by party unity, but are free to vote according to their conscience and the wishes of their constituents, they need not be concerned that their association with particular think tanks, or their endorsement of some of their policy ideas, would undermine party cohesion. Rather than evaluating ideas from think tanks in terms of their compatibility with party preferences and policies, members of Congress can evaluate them on their own merits, and whether they will serve their personal goals. Moreover, as Weaver and others have argued, the weak party system in the United States not only provides opportunities for think tanks to influence policy-making but has in some ways increased the demand for them.[13] In Germany, political parties have created their own think tanks or foundations, supported by the state, to conduct research and analysis; political parties in the United States have not.[14] There are a handful of congressional research institutes or public think tanks, including the Congressional Research Service and the General Accounting Office, from which members of Congress can request information.[15] However, these bodies cannot be expected to provide timely and policy-relevant research, as many independent think tanks do.

A number of think tanks, including the Heritage Foundation and its advocacy arm, Heritage Action for America, assign the highest priority to influencing Congress. Nonetheless, they also recognize the importance of solidifying ties to the bureaucracy, the executive, and the many agencies that advise the president. The Executive Office of the President (EOP), which comprises several important agencies, including the National Security Council and the Office of Management and Budget, provides think tanks with further opportunities to influence government. During several recent administrations, for instance, presidents have appointed senior staff from think tanks to serve in cabinet- and subcabinet-level positions and on advisory boards and executive agencies.[16] Many of these appointees have previously served on policy task forces and on transition teams in presidential elections, a subject that will be discussed in more detail in chapter 6.[17]

It is not uncommon for presidential candidates to establish task forces during the primaries and the general election to investigate policy concerns. These groups are particularly important for challengers who lack the resources available to an incumbent president or who lack experience in federal politics. For instance, during the presidential election campaign of 2000, Governor George W. Bush enlisted the support of scholars and policy analysts from a handful of think tanks, including the Hoover Institution and the American Enterprise Institute.[18] Twenty years earlier, during the 1980 election, Martin Anderson and Richard Allen of the Hoover Institution were responsible for organizing close to fifty task forces on domestic and foreign policy to advise Governor Ronald Reagan on a host of issues.[19] And in his historic run for the presidency in 2008, Barack Obama turned to several researchers from top DC think tanks to advise him on a host of domestic and foreign policy issues.[20] Although Donald Trump had limited interaction with think tanks during his 2016 run for the presidency, experts from some institutes, including the Heritage Foundation, contributed ideas during his transition to power, a subject that will be examined more closely in chapter 6.

It is rare, however, for Canadian federal party leaders to organize task forces, or to establish close ties to think tanks during campaigns. Part of the problem is logistical: the election period is far shorter in Canada – it typically lasts thirty-six days, from the time the prime minister advises the governor general of his or her intention to call an election to the day Canadians vote – compared with the lengthy primary season and general election in the United States.[21]

And until the passage of the fixed election law in 2007, the electoral cycle in Canada has also been more unpredictable, though some scholars remain convinced that the government can still call an election at any time during its mandate, up to a maximum of five years after taking office.[22] This element of uncertainty poses further problems for think tanks contemplating a more active role during elections. In addition, most Canadian party leaders do not turn to the broader policy community for advice but rely on their own staff, party research caucus, and party strategists and pollsters instead.[23] The prime minister may have even less need for policy task forces during campaigns, for in addition to his or her own staff, the prime minister enjoys the support of the Prime Minister's Office (PMO), which serves as a "practical policy think-tank charged with an advisory capacity on the political fortunes of the prime minister and his cabinet."[24] With a staff of over one hundred, including about a dozen researchers, the prime minister has little incentive to seek the advice of think tanks during campaigns. Staff from think tanks are more likely to be called on when the prime minister establishes a royal commission or commission of inquiry to study a particular policy issue, such as free trade or the creation of a security intelligence agency.[25]

While there is little to prevent think tanks in Canada from releasing studies before or during elections or discussing ideas with party members, they do not, for the reasons given above, engage as actively in electoral politics as some of their US counterparts. Yet it is important to point out that while institutional and logistical constraints may limit the involvement of think tanks during elections, so too does the desire of some think tanks, primarily for legal and political reasons, to maintain an arm's-length relationship with political parties.[26] The Vancouver-based Fraser Institute is a case in point. Although Fraser rarely concealed its conservative leanings or support for several policies advanced by the Harper government[27] or by the former Canadian Alliance, it has been reluctant to become too closely associated, and justifiably so, with the Conservative Party of Canada. According to Paul Wilson, who served as director of research for the Canadian Alliance, while there has been some interaction between members of his party and the Fraser Institute, "Fraser is concerned about being too close to us. They do not want to be seen as a Reform [or an Alliance] mouthpiece. We, on the other hand, are less choosey about the [think tanks] we talk to. Parties are like intellectual prostitutes. We will take good ideas from any source."[28] Other think tanks, however, appear less concerned about their ties to political parties; for instance, the Canadian Centre for Policy Alternatives (CCPA), headquartered in Ottawa with several regional offices, maintains very close links to the New Democratic Party (NDP). As Judy Randall, a former senior researcher with the NDP Caucus Research Office acknowledged, "our strongest link to a think tank is the CCPA, although we also use a lot of the work done by the Canadian Council on Social Development, the National Council of Welfare (now defunct), the National Anti-Poverty Organization and other organizations ... Several of our members have served on [the CCPA's] Board of Directors and their executive director Bruce Campbell worked for us."[29]

There appear to be both external and internal limits to how much direct access think tanks have to party leaders during campaigns. There also appear to be limits to how much impact think tanks have during government transition periods. As previously mentioned, a handful of think tanks, including the Heritage Foundation, the Hoover Institution, and CSIS, have played key roles in assisting incoming presidential administrations make the transition to power. In addition to serving on the transition staff, several think tank scholars have helped by identifying topical issues and have advised on placing appropriate people in the thousands of vacant positions that become available when governments change. These functions provide think tanks that are close to transitions with further opportunities to expand and grow their networks and influence policy.

By contrast, think tanks in Canada rarely offer or are called upon to assist in transition planning, although some, including the Ottawa-based Public Policy Forum (PPF) have in the past undertaken major projects on managing transitions.[30] Again, there are several reasons for this. First, unlike in the United States, the transition period before a new government assumes power in Canada does not take three months but is completed in less than two weeks. This short time frame makes it extremely difficult for think tanks to communicate their ideas to transition leaders. Second, few Canadian think tanks have the resources or expertise to arrange the types of transition planning seminars organized by the Heritage

Foundation, Brookings, CSIS, and other US top-tier think tanks.[31] Third, and perhaps more important, the federal transition process is overseen and orchestrated by the Privy Council Office (PCO), which is "staffed by career civil servants [and serves as] a major policy-advising agency of the federal government."[32] Furthermore, unlike US think tanks, which take advantage of transition periods to fill vacant positions in the bureaucracy, either with their own staff or like-minded colleagues, Canadian think tanks have little incentive to closely monitor job vacancies after an election. An incoming US president must identify and recruit thousands of people to fill vacant positions in a new administration, but a Canadian prime minister has the power to fill only a limited number of senior bureaucratic posts after an election, usually at the level of deputy minister. The majority of individuals who obtain these positions are career civil servants, not think-tank staffers.

If think tanks in Canada do not make their presence felt during elections and transitions, when and where do they have an impact? Canadian think tanks, like many in the United States, do not always select the same target audiences or stages in the policy cycle to become most actively involved. When, where, and how they exercise policy influence ultimately depends on several factors, including their mandate and resources, which, as the previous chapter demonstrated, vary enormously.

The priority for some think tanks in Canada, including the Fraser Institute and the C.D. Howe Institute, is to influence both the policy-making environment and the policy-making process. As a result, both institutions welcome opportunities to enhance their visibility by submitting articles to newspapers, relying heavily on social media to reach multiple audiences, and by giving interviews on radio, television, and through podcasts. Moreover, these and other think tanks acknowledge how critical it is to secure access to the cabinet and senior levels of the bureaucracy, where political power in Canada is concentrated. Although think tanks frequently testify before parliamentary committees and provide party research offices, middle and senior-level policy analysts in government departments, and MPs with their publications, they devote less attention to influencing the fate of bills being considered by Parliament.[33]

They are reluctant to devote resources to influencing debates in the House of Commons, particularly after a bill has passed first reading, largely because of the strong party system. This system encourages party leaders to exercise a virtual stranglehold over party members who are forced to accept their role as spectators rather than active participants in parliamentary discussions. Although all Westminster parliamentary systems are not as suffocating for party members as Canada's (Britain's is far more relaxed), the limited opportunities for MPs, particularly those occupying the backbenches, to ask questions and highlight concerns during question period is reason enough why parliamentarians generally do not attract the sustained attention of think tanks. Put simply, unlike high-profile members of Congress and key figures in the administration, who are in a position to bring considerable attention to bear on various issues of concern to the public and to think tanks and other NGOs, what takes place among MPs, and even the prime minister on the floor of the House of Commons, rarely captivates the daily work of think tanks. Think tanks in Canada understand all too well that the time to influence the content and direction of a proposed bill is before it reaches the floor of the House. Once the government (assuming it has a majority of seats) has endorsed a bill, there is little that opposition parties can do to prevent its passage.

Publishing op-ed articles in newspapers, writing blogs, providing commentary on the radio and on TV, and testifying before parliamentary committees (which appear to be operating more smoothly since Prime Minister Justin Trudeau came to power) might be useful ways to reach policy-makers, but to have a real impact, think tanks must get further inside the policy-making process. Ken Battle, president of the Caledon Institute, realized this shortly after he published an article in *The Globe and Mail* in late 1993 on the ill-fated seniors' benefits. As a result of his article, Battle was approached by several provincial premiers for advice, and, later, by some senior cabinet ministers interested in drawing on his expertise in these and related areas.[34] According to Battle, "I recall getting a call at home one afternoon from Paul Martin [the Liberal finance minister], who proceeded to grill me for the better part of an hour on a piece I wrote on the social security review. It was worse than the grilling I took during oral exams at Oxford."[35]

Judith Maxwell, founding president of the now defunct CPRN, Inc., acknowledges that to have an impact in policy-making, think tanks must rely on diverse, and, at times, less visible forms of policy influence. Although Maxwell does not downplay the importance of media exposure, she maintains, like Battle and Zussman, that think tanks exercise the most influence working with key stakeholders behind the scenes, not by discussing policy issues with reporters.[36] Maxwell believes that part of the CPRN's role was to bring together senior bureaucrats, academics, and representatives from the private and non-profit sector in closed door meetings to discuss social and economic policy issues: "We are interested in creating new mental maps for policy-makers. Our research [and workshops] are not intended to simply summarize issues, but to generate new thinking. We want to help start conversations between people that would have never taken place before."[37]

Canadian think tanks may not have as many channels to influence policy-making as those in the United States, but the political structure in

Canada does not hinder their access to policy-makers as much as some have suggested. What may restrict their influence more than the political environment they function in are the limited resources most Canadian, and, indeed, American think tanks have at their disposal.

CONSTRAINING IDEAS: DO CANADIAN AND AMERICAN THINK TANKS FACE SIMILAR CONSTRAINTS?

Different types of political systems impose different types of constraints on non-governmental organizations seeking access to power. Clearly, the political system in the United States is more permeable than the system in Canada and in some other parliamentary systems. Nonetheless, to better understand why US think tanks appear to be more firmly entrenched in the policy-making community than those in Canada, several factors unrelated to the institutional structure of the Canadian and American governments must be considered.

In Canada, as in the United States, most think tanks have modest financial and human resources. The Brookings Institution, with its sizeable endowment, multimillion-dollar operating budget, and over 300 staff and researchers is sometimes mistakenly regarded as a typical US think tank. However, as noted, Brookings and the handful of other institutes with comparable resources are anything but typical. The typical think tank in Canada and the United States has approximately a dozen staff and a budget between $1 and $2 million, fewer resources in fact than several trade associations, including the Ontario Federation of Labour and Canadian Manfacturers & Exporters (CME), which in 2014–15 posted revenues of more than $17 million.[38]

The major difference between think tanks in the two countries is that while the United States has such prominent repositories of policy expertise as Brookings, the Hoover Institution, the Heritage Foundation, and RAND, think tanks that generate considerable attention in the media and in some scholarly circles, Canada has few if any of comparable size and stature. Even its largest institute, the Conference Board of Canada, functions more as a business-oriented planning organization than as a traditional interdisciplinary policy research institute like Brookings.[39]

The absence of a think tank of this scale in Canada cannot be attributed to the lack of qualified individuals to staff it; for decades Canada has had a surplus of PhDs in the social sciences – the degree most policy research institutes require of applicants. The pool of graduating PhDs in the social sciences in the United States and in Canada has remained relatively strong over the past several years, with increases in the number of students completing PhDs in science and engineering. In 2005, for instance, the last year for which Statistics Canada kept data on the number of people who have earned doctorates, 774 PhDs in the social sciences were awarded, compared with slightly over 3,000 in the United States.[40] In 2014, more than 15,000 doctorates in the social sciences were awarded by American universities.[41] Given the tremendous difficulty PhD graduates face in securing academic positions (assuming this is their preferred career path), they may very well consider seeking employment at a think tank.

While finding qualified people to staff a large think tank in Canada is not a problem, it is becoming increasingly difficult to secure sufficient sources of revenue. As in the United States, the majority of think tanks in Canada do not have endowments on which to draw to ensure financial security and independence, and those that do, with few exceptions, continue to face financial challenges. The Centre for International Governance Innovation (CIGI), the Institute for Research on Public Policy (IRPP), and the Caledon Institute are among the handful of policy institutes in Canada whose core funding is secured through endowments.

Without endowments on which to draw, think tanks in Canada have no alternative but to consider how to secure adequate revenue. For some, including the various defence and foreign policy institutes at over a dozen Canadian universities, this has meant relying heavily on government funds, often in the form of specific contracts, and on support from private foundations. This dependence places think tanks in a vulnerable position; Roy Culpeper, former president of the North-South Institute (NSI), observed years before NSI was forced to close its doors that receiving large sums of money from only a few sources can be "both a blessing and a curse."[42] Since government agencies and philanthropic foundations often have vested interests in ensuring that their recipients express views consistent with theirs, think tanks might be reluctant to be overly critical of policies supported by their donors. As several government-funded institutes experienced first-hand following the 1992 Canadian federal budget, and more recently during the Harper years, as long as governments have the power to change their priorities, there is little think tanks can do to ensure their survival.

The financial security of think tanks that receive little or no government funding is also precarious. These organizations must turn to the private sector, to the public, and to foundations and private donors, for support. In the United States, the Koch, Ford, Rockefeller, and Carnegie Foundations, among others, have long supported social science research, much of which has been at think tanks.[43] This generous tradition of philanthropic support in the United States, however, has not taken root to the same extent in Canada, where the majority of think tanks struggle to keep afloat.

Relying too heavily on philanthropic foundations and corporations can also be risky, of course. As mentioned, like governments that require foreign aid recipients to make certain concessions, philanthropic foundations and large corporate donors must be satisfied that the organizations they are making grants to act in a manner consistent with their institutional missions. Failing to appease the political agenda of philanthropic and corporate donors can, as the American Enterprise Institute (AEI) discovered in the mid-1980s, have serious repercussions. When the AEI president, William Baroody Jr, was unable to convince several right-wing foundations, including the Olin Foundation and the Reader's Digest Foundation, that AEI was committed to pursuing a truly conservative agenda, these and other like-minded donors withdrew their significant financial support, bringing the AEI to the verge of bankruptcy.[44]

As noted, several think tanks in Canada, including the NSI and the National Council of Welfare, were not as fortunate. Conversely, acting in the interests of affluent donors can pay handsome dividends for some think tanks, as the Washington-based conservative think tank Citizens for a Sound Economy (CSE) discovered after it began its campaign to derail a multibillion-dollar federal plan to restore the Florida Everglades in 1998. For its efforts, CSE received $700,000 in contributions from Florida's three largest sugar enterprises, "which stand to lose thousands of acres of cane-growing land to reclamation if the Army Corps of Engineers plan goes into effect."[45]

For most think tanks in Canada, and in the United States for that matter, achieving financial independence is the most significant obstacle they must overcome to ensure a strong presence in the policy-making community. Without a sustainable budget, think tanks will not be able to mount the extensive research and media relations program necessary to attract the attention of policy-makers. More important, without ample resources think tanks will not be able to recruit the type of people most qualified to produce policy-relevant research, as will be discussed in more detail shortly.

Some consideration should also be given to important cultural differences between Canada and the United States, which could also affect the prominence of think tanks in the policy-making process. One significant cultural factor that may account for their playing a less visible role in Canada is the relative absence of a strong, vocal entrepreneurial class in the private sector. As Abelson and Carberry point out, "In the US, independent policy entrepreneurs have provided important leadership in the formation of think tanks dedicated to providing information and advice to government. In Canada, on the other hand, such leadership is likely to come from the government itself or from senior public servants.

This difference reflects both the incentives created by the institutional structure of each form of government as well as cultural understandings of the appropriate repositories of policy expertise."[46]

John Kingdon's work on policy entrepreneurs, defined as "advocates for proposals or for the prominence of an idea," demonstrates how these individuals can have an important impact on policy issues: "their defining characteristic, much as in the case of a business entrepreneur, is their willingness to invest their resources – time, energy, reputation, and sometimes money – in the hope of a future return."[47] Why do policy entrepreneurs undertake these investments? They do so, according to Kingdon, "to promote their values, or affect the shape of public policy."[48]

Without effective and meaningful government initiatives to establish policy institutes like the IRPP and the various strategic and defence studies institutes at various Canadian universities, leadership must come from one or more policy entrepreneurs. According to the limited research conducted in this area, there is some evidence to suggest that, with respect to the private sector, these entrepreneurs are likely to be more prominent in the United States than in Canada. In their study of the environmental agenda in the two countries, Kathryn Harrison and George Hoberg observed a difference in policy entrepreneurship.[49] Among other things, they discovered that policy entrepreneurs in the United States played an important role in promoting certain environmental issues, particularly the effects of radon, and were able to facilitate their discussion on the political agenda. They also noticed that there was an absence of similar activity in Canada. Harrison and Hoberg note how the presence of policy entrepreneurship is, in a certain sense, tied to the institutional arrangements of each political system.[50] The highly fragmented American political system, combined with an absence of strong party unity, provides incentives to private policy entrepreneurs to shape the political agenda. By contrast, the relatively closed and party-driven system in Canada offers few allurements to such entrepreneurs.

As discussed in chapter 1, several think tanks in the United States owe their existence, and, indeed, their success to the efforts of policy entrepreneurs committed to injecting their political and ideological views into the policy-making process. Robert Brookings, Andrew Carnegie, and the Heritage Foundation's Edwin Feulner and Paul Weyrich represent but a handful of such entrepreneurs who have created think tanks as institutional vehicles to promote their beliefs. This entrepreneurial spirit is also evident in the vanity and legacy-based think tanks in the United States.

By way of comparison, Canada has few examples of think tanks that are the direct creation of *private* sector policy entrepreneurship.[51] The Fraser Institute, under the initial guidance of Sir Antony Fisher, Patrick Boyle, and economists Sally Pipes and Michael Walker; the Manning

Centre and Foundation; and a handful of others are notable exceptions.[52] On the other hand, the *public* sector has been a viable source of leadership. Senior public servants, including Michael Pitfield and Michael Kirby,[53] played important roles in creating the IRPP, the Economic Council of Canada, the Science Council of Canada, and other governmental advisory bodies.[54]

The fact that major initiatives for creating Canadian centres of policy expertise tend to come from inside the government and not from the private sector, as in the United States, is not surprising. In part, it reflects both countries' cultural understanding of the relationship between government and the provision of policy expertise. This role for governmental leadership in Canada is not unexpected, given the importance granted to bureaucratic and party policy advice in the parliamentary process.[55] Colin Gray, former chair of the Virginia-based National Institute for Public Policy, has suggested that the culture of "officialdom" in the Canadian and British bureaucracies discriminates against external groups seeking to provide advice to government. This ethos of officialdom contrasts with the relatively open access of the US system, in which the role of the bureaucracy in providing policy advice is often overshadowed by the presence of "independent" advisors operating in the private sector.[56]

The difference in think tank development in the two countries, particularly in the source of their creation and growth, may reflect broader societal trends: sociological analyses of Canadian and American societies provide an interesting comparison. Canada's political structure has long been viewed as more "conservative, traditional ... statist, and elitist" than the United States.[57] By contrast, American attitudes about individualism and the limited role of the state have supported a culture encouraging private entrepreneurship. As Seymour Martin Lipset argues, "If one society leans toward communitarianism – the public mobilization of resources to fulfill group objectives – the other sees individualism – private endeavor – as the way an 'unseen hand' produces optimum, socially beneficial results."[58]

In sum, think tank development in the United States is supported by cultural influences: a value system stressing individual effort, a tradition of philanthropy, and the presence of independent advisors operating alongside the bureaucracy. This has encouraged policy entrepreneurship from the private sector, with think tanks originating from society. The Canadian cultural context provides a different environment for think tanks, particularly its bureaucratic ethos, which, at times, discourages external advice. Governments in Canada have taken, and continue to take, an active role in creating and maintaining think tanks, as evidenced by the recent creation of a handful of institutes, including the Saskatchewan

Institute of Public Policy in June 1998.[59] This does not mean that private entrepreneurship is unwelcome, but it means that it may face substantial challenges to overcome both the cultural climate and institutional arrangements to secure a meaningful role in policy debates.

The opportunities for think tanks to convey their ideas to policy-makers and the constraints that may undermine their efforts helps to shed light on some of the differences between them in Canada and the United States. Still, it is also important to consider another issue – the incentives for government officials to turn to think tanks for advice. A closer look at this factor may help to better explain why think tanks in the United States appear to be more relevant in policy-making than the majority in Canada.

EXPLORING INCENTIVES: WHY POLICY-MAKERS TURN TO THINK TANKS

There are several reasons why policy-makers in the United States would turn to think tanks for information and advice. To begin with, a number of US think tanks have established impressive research programs in domestic and foreign policy by recruiting not only first-rate academics but many former high-level policy-makers to their institutions. The presence of former cabinet secretaries and other seasoned policy-makers also provides an incentive for members of Congress, the executive, and presidential candidates to solicit their advice. Access to think tank luminaries, including Brent Scowcroft, Henry Kissinger, Condoleezza Rice, and George Shultz, may help to open other doors for office-holders or for those aspiring to become policy-makers. In short, members of Congress, the executive, and the bureaucracy can benefit from the wealth of expertise and the extensive network of contacts available at several US think tanks. Moreover, unlike most university professors, who have little incentive to produce timely and policy-relevant research, scholars at think tanks are more sensitive to the policy needs of office-holders. They can provide decision-makers with what they need – clear and concise summaries of the costs and benefits associated with particular policy proposals.

There are other incentives to turn to think tanks. As previously mentioned, several think tanks have been able to assemble talent pools of scholars for incoming administrations to access to fill important positions in government. For instance, during the Carter, Reagan, Clinton, Bush, and Obama administrations, many think tanks, including the Brookings Institution, the Hoover Institution, the AEI, and the Center for a New American Security, contributed key staff.[60] Politicians and aspiring office-holders can also turn to think tanks for ideological support: advocacy-oriented think tanks like the Heritage Foundation often help to validate or reinforce the ideological views of incumbents and challengers.[61]

It is less clear why policy-makers in Canada would turn to think tanks for advice. To begin with, some preliminary data reveal that the majority of researchers at most private think tanks in Canada, unlike their colleagues at equivalent institutions in the United States, do not possess doctorates (although several think tank directors do), despite the availability of individuals with PhDs in Canada. Most have an undergraduate or a masters' degree in the social sciences.[62] Furthermore, with few exceptions, the majority of think tank analysts have little or no government experience. This is not to suggest that previous government experience is necessary to provide informed observations about government or the issues confronting elected officials, but it does suggest that policy-makers may be more inclined to rely on think tank personnel who have worked in government in some capacity and who have some direct experience working with stakeholders. Their extensive government experience may in fact explain why Judith Maxwell, when she was in charge of CPRN, Inc., and Ken Battle have been approached by cabinet ministers and senior officials for advice. It may also explain why, compared with several other think tanks, the Caledon Institute has become so firmly entrenched in the policy-making process. Second, unlike in the United States, where there appears to be a revolving door between think tanks and government, it is rare for think tank scholars in Canada to be recruited into senior positions in the bureaucracy, or for former cabinet ministers, bureaucrats, and experienced parliamentarians to go to think tanks after leaving public office.[63]

Some directors of Canadian think tanks have, as noted, held important government positions. However, few think tanks have been able to hire leading policy experts, in large part because of limited financial resources. Others, like the Public Policy Forum, elect not to actively recruit high-profile policy analysts, preferring instead to hire individuals with an array of talents.[64] Regardless of the importance think tank directors place on hiring prominent academics or policy-makers, the absence of high-profile experts may discourage some government officials from using think tanks. The uneven quality of research being produced at some institutes may also discourage them. As Lindquist has noted, to be relevant think tanks must produce work that contributes to a better understanding of the intricacies of important policy issues. But as Lindquist discovered in his detailed examination of Canadian policy institutes, it is questionable how much some think tanks have added to major policy debates, a subject that will be addressed in chapters 7 and 8.[65] Finally, while many think tanks in the United States may lend intellectual credibility to the ideological agenda of policy-makers or aspiring office-holders, this function is less critical for policy-makers in Canada. Members of Parliament may benefit from, and, indeed, welcome ideological support from think tanks, but it is the party leadership and backroom strategists, not independent think tanks, that dictate the party line.

Policy-makers in Canada appear to have fewer incentives to rely on think tanks for expertise, but this could be changing. As the internal policy capacity of government diminishes, a subject that will be examined in the concluding chapter, public servants are beginning to strengthen their ties to the external policy research community. In this environment, Canadian think tanks may be able to overcome some important obstacles and constraints and play a more decisive role in the policy-making community.

Comparing think tanks across nations and understanding how political structures can promote or impede their access to policy-makers is invaluable in explaining why, for instance, think tanks in the United States and in other democracies enjoy more opportunity to shape public opinion and public policy than independent institutes operating in countries with totalitarian and authoritarian regimes. Yet, as this chapter has illustrated by comparing two countries, it is important not to exaggerate the extent to which institutional differences are responsible for elevating or diminishing the profile of think tanks. In other words, the significant differences in the governmental systems of the United States, and, say, China, helps explain why, compared with US think tanks, those in China enjoy far less visibility, although even this is beginning to change as China's population of think tanks continues to rise.[66]

Gray has noted that "American-style think-tanks could not function in Canada or Great Britain ... because of the differences in political culture and government structure."[67] But, as this chapter and chapter 1 have demonstrated, the same types of think tanks that exist in the United States have not only emerged in Canada but have contributed in some instances both to policy-making and to shaping the policy-making environment. They have accomplished this in many ways: by advising cabinet ministers, as Ken Battle and others have done; and by helping to increase public awareness about the costs and benefits of introducing different pieces of legislation by sharing their ideas with the media, as the Fraser Institute, the C.D. Howe Institute, and others frequently do. Moreover, as the next chapter reveals, contrary to Gray's assertions, not only have American-style think tanks taken root in Canada, but they have adopted many of the strategies employed by US think tanks to influence policy-makers, the public, and other important stakeholders.

CHAPTER FOUR

Competing in the Marketplace of Ideas: The Strategies of Think Tanks

Think tanks are in the business of developing and promoting ideas and, like corporations in the private sector, they devote considerable attention to marketing their product. Unlike corporations, however, think tanks measure success not by profit margins but by how much influence they have in shaping public opinion and the policy preferences and choices of leaders. Unfortunately, for think tank directors and those who study these institutions, it is far simpler to read their annual reports than to measure their performance. In this chapter, I lay the foundation for assessing the impact of think tanks by exploring the many channels policy research institutes use to market their ideas. It is important to keep in mind that while think tanks in Canada and the United States have very different missions, resources, and priorities, they tend to rely on similar strategies to influence policy. Where they differ is in the emphasis they place on pursuing each strategy. In other words, while generating media exposure is a preferred tactic for more advocacy-oriented think tanks, including the Heritage Foundation and the Fraser Institute, to name a few, it is not considered a priority for some institutes, like the Public Policy Forum and the Caledon Institute, which pay little attention to the media exposure they generate, preferring instead to commit their resources to strengthening ties to key policy-makers and other key stakeholders.

The chapter begins by highlighting the strategies think tanks usually employ to generate attention in the public arena and in important policy circles. Particular emphasis is placed on what has become the most visible method think tanks pursue to attract exposure – gaining access to the media. Finally, the chapter will discuss some of the many methodological problems that arise in assessing think tank influence and what steps can be taken to provide more informed judgments about the impact of think tanks.

PUBLIC INFLUENCE

Though often portrayed as elite organizations composed of scholars pursuing research in relative isolation, think tanks have become increasingly visible. As more think tanks have entered the marketplace of ideas, there has been a growing awareness among both newer and older generations of policy institutes that they must compete for the attention of policy-makers and the public, not to mention the financial support of government agencies, individuals, and corporate and philanthropic donors.[1] While some of the strategies think tanks rely on to exercise influence are concealed from the public, many can be easily identified. In fact, to varying degrees, think tanks in the United States and Canada employ some or all of the following strategies to influence policy-makers, academics, business leaders, journalists, and the public:

- holding public forums and conferences to discuss various domestic and foreign policy issues. Several of these events are podcast live;
- encouraging scholars to give public lectures and addresses;
- testifying before committees and subcommittees of Congress and Parliament;
- publishing books, opinion magazines, newsletters, policy briefs, and journals that are widely distributed;
- creating email distribution lists to facilitate the transmission of new publications; and posting key information about the work of their institute on websites;
- targeting the public during annual fundraising campaigns; and
- enhancing their exposure through the use of various social media.

Holding public forums or conferences is among the most common strategies think tanks employ to increase awareness about a particular domestic or foreign policy issue. Policy-makers, journalists, academics, and representatives from the private and non-profit sectors are regularly invited to discuss timely and often controversial issues before public audiences. At times conferences are also arranged to generate exposure for a newly released study. A well-publicized and well-attended conference on important topics such as stabilizing world markets, enhancing border security, and promoting a greener economy, several of which have been organized by Canadian and US think tanks or a conference on the impact of US presidential and congressional elections on domestic and foreign policy, which several Washington-based think tanks have sponsored, can benefit these organizations in many ways. In addition to taking credit for encouraging opinion-makers to discuss issues they have helped identify, think tanks use conferences to educate those in attendance about the role of their institute and the work in which they are engaged. To reach even more individuals who might be interested in the type of research they conduct, think tanks in both countries encourage their resident scholars to give lectures at universities, Rotary associations, and other organizations interested in contemporary political affairs. Once again, high-profile speakers from think tanks can serve as ambassadors for their institutes as they travel across the country, sharing their thoughts on a host of policy issues. Several scholars at think tanks regularly perform this role, and in the process remind their audience of the efforts their organizations are undertaking to convince policy-makers to follow the right path.

Several think tanks also recognize the importance of conveying ideas to policy-makers and the public more formally. Some policy institutes in Canada and the United States accomplish this by testifying before legislative committees – although some, including the Brookings Institution, the Heritage Foundation, the Canadian Council on Social Development, and the Conference Board of Canada, clearly assign a higher priority to performing this function than others. Providing testimony, particularly to a prominent committee, can attract considerable attention. The oral presentations and written briefs policy experts provide are included as part of the official record and are often cited by journalists and academics. Agreeing to appear before legislative committees can also serve to enhance the credibility of think tanks in the eyes of some policy-makers and help think tank directors convince potential donors of the widespread influence of their institutes. This may explain why several think tanks in the United States and Canada prominently display the testimonies given by staff on their website.

Think tanks employ several other strategies to market their message. Many, particularly those with well-established research programs, such as the Brookings Institution, the Heritage Foundation, the AEI, and the IRPP, rely on blogs, journals, newsletters, and books to reach their various target audiences. For example, from 1977 to 2013, the Heritage Foundation published *Policy Review*, an opinion magazine that contained brief articles by many leading conservatives on various policy issues. The Foundation now relies on issue briefs, factsheets, and other electronic and print publications to reach out to the media and to other intended audiences. But Heritage has taken its media outreach even further. In 2014, it created *The Daily Signal*, a multimedia news organization designed to combat what it believes is liberal bias in the media. Investigative reporters with *The Daily Signal* examine and report on a host of policy issues inside and beyond the Beltway through a conservative lens. Not to be outdone by Heritage, the free-market-oriented Kansas Policy Institute, with the backing of the Koch brothers, launched its own news service called *The Sentinel* in 2016 to help infuse public policy discussions with a more conservative edge. Although there appears to be a trend among some US think tanks to augment the conservative media by creating their own news services, some continue to rely on more academic research outlets to convey their views. For example, the *Brookings Review*, published by the Brookings Institution, *The American Enterprise Institute Economics Working Paper Series*, produced by the AEI, and *American Outlook*, published by the Sagamore Institute, are examples of opinion magazines distributed US think tanks. Several think tanks in Canada also publish online opinion magazines and blogs, including *Policy Options* and *The Fraser Forum*, published by the Institute for Research on Public Policy and the Fraser Institute, respectively. For many think tanks, these types of publications are their most effective product, because, unlike books, which are often outdated by the time they are released, opinion magazines and concise online commentaries provide policy-makers with insights into current policy problems. These publications, often on a particular theme, help to frame the parameters of important and relevant policy debates, and, more important for policy-makers' hectic schedules, they can be read in a matter of minutes.

Think tanks produce publications for other consumers as well. Several, for example, publish refereed scholarly journals that are intended to be read by university students and academics. Among these are *Foreign Affairs*, the flagship journal of the New York-based Council on Foreign Relations; Orbis, produced by the Philadelphia-based Foreign Policy Research Institute; and *International Journal*, published by the Canadian International Council, formerly the Canadian Institute of International Affairs. In addition to scholarly journals and opinion magazines, dozens of think tanks produce books and monthly newsletters that are intended to keep readers informed about the most important developments at their institutes.

A number of think tanks also reach potential consumers through other forms of communication. In the past, for instance, the Heritage Foundation produced *Monthly Briefing Tapes*, which included interviews with some of their policy experts, as well as speeches given by prominent (mostly conservative) opinion-makers. To market this product, Heritage often sought the endorsement of high-profile policy-makers. Among those who helped sell the monthly briefing tapes was former speaker of the house Newt Gingrich. In his endorsement, which appeared in various Heritage publications, Gingrich referred to the tapes as "A monthly dose of conservative common sense. You'll wonder how you ever got along without it."

As new technologies were developed, audio tapes were replaced with video clips, podcasts, chat rooms, live interviews, and various forms of social media, including Facebook, Twitter, Instagram, etc., linked to websites maintained by think tanks. Virtually every think tank in the United States and Canada relies extensively on the internet to publicize its work. Their websites provide a wealth of information, ranging from an institute's most current publications and staff directory to upcoming conferences and seminars. Some sites also provide links to important data bases. The Urban Institute, for instance, provides a link to the National Center for Charitable Statistics, a repository of data on the non-profit sector in the United States that includes information on the budgets of thousands of non-profit organizations throughout the US. Others – such as the one maintained by the Heritage Foundation, one of the more sophisticated websites constructed by US think tanks, have gone so far as to advise young conservatives on how to find policy jobs in Washington. Think tanks also regularly update their email distribution lists to ensure that academics, policy-makers, journalists, and others interested in their work are kept informed about key issues and events. Many think tanks also track the number of website hits they generate as well as the number and kinds of documents that are downloaded from their sites. These figures are posted along with other performance indicators think tanks like to showcase in their annual reports. These and other data may help think tanks make a stronger case to potential donors that their work is attracting larger audiences.

Fundraising is yet another way think tanks in both countries can market themselves to the public and to policy-makers. Again, some think tanks, particularly in the United States, have enlisted the support of high-profile policy-makers to convince the American public to make donations. For instance, in 1982, at the request of Heritage Foundation president Edwin Feulner, Edwin Meese III, a special adviser to President Reagan and later US attorney general, wrote a letter to potential Heritage donors telling them that in exchange for a tax-deductible donation of $1,000, they would be allowed to join the president's club. The club, according to Meese, who for several years has held a fellowship at Heritage, would entitle them to "a series of meetings with the most senior members of the administration and Congress."[2] In an accompanying fundraising letter, Feulner added, "You will be provided with an access to Washington policy-makers which cannot be had at any price. I have no doubt that you will find your membership fee returned to you many times over." Dismissing claims that he was directly asking people to give money to the Heritage Foundation, Meese remarked, "I am enthusiastic about the establishment of the Heritage Foundation President's Club ... [It is] a vital communications link [between the White House and those who support President Reagan and] this administration will fully cooperate with your efforts."[3]

Years later, Jim DeMint, in his role as president of the Heritage Foundation, and his staff, would regularly send emails to members requesting funds to support the organization's activities. In exchange for donations, DeMint would more than imply that donors would be rewarded with access to top officials. It is this kind of gesture, along with the ties many top-tier think tanks have with foreign governments, that led Ken Silverstein, Brooke Williams, and other investigative journalists in the US to make a strong case that think tanks are becoming more like lobbyists, a subject that we will return to later in the study.

Still, of all the public uses of think tank influence, none are more visible than the efforts of think tanks to secure access to the media. As will be discussed in more detail later in this chapter, since several directors of think tanks often equate media exposure with policy influence, many devote considerable resources to enhancing their public profile. By ensuring that they are regularly quoted in the print and broadcast media, think tanks seek to create the perception that they play a critical role in shaping public policy. However, as we will discover, while it is important for think tanks to communicate their views to the public on television broadcasts or on the op-ed pages (opposite the editorial page) of Canadian and American newspapers, media exposure (including social media) does not seamlessly translate into policy influence. Generating media attention may enable some think tanks to influence public opinion, but it does not necessarily guarantee access to other critical stages of the policy-making process.

PRIVATE INFLUENCE

The many channels upon which think tanks rely to exercise public influence are relatively easy to observe and document. However, it is often difficult to monitor how think tanks seek to influence policy-makers privately. The following list provides examples of how think tanks and the scholars affiliated with them have attempted to exercise private influence. As will become apparent, most of these strategies are unique to US think tanks. Among the many private uses of influence are

- accepting cabinet, subcabinet, or bureaucratic positions in administrations;
- serving on policy task forces and transition teams during presidential elections and on presidential advisory boards;
- maintaining liaison offices with the House of Representatives and the Senate;

- inviting selected policy-makers to participate in conferences, seminars, and workshops;
- allowing bureaucrats to work at think tanks on a limited-term basis;
- offering former policy-makers positions at think tanks; and
- preparing studies and policy briefs for policy-makers.

There are few ways experts from think tanks can get closer to the policy-making process than by becoming policy-makers themselves. As previously noted, in several presidential administrations dozens of staff from think tanks have been recruited into senior-level positions in the government. Many, including the late Jeane Kirkpatrick (AEI) and the late Zbigniew Brzezinski (CSIS), have served in cabinet and subcabinet positions, while others have been appointed to important positions in the bureaucracy. More recently, as will be discussed in chapter 6, a handful of prominent policy experts, including Lawrence Lindsey and Robert Zoellick, left their positions at think tanks to join the administration of President George W. Bush, and many others found their way into the Obama administration and to the Trump transition team. There are several potential benefits to think tanks of having staff members appointed to an incoming administration, not the least of which is the publicity surrounding the appointment itself. By assembling a talent pool of scholars upon which administrations may draw, not only do think tanks enhance their prestige and visibility, they can foster even stronger ties to those making critical policy decisions. This may explain why some think tanks, like the Heritage Foundation, closely monitor vacancies in the bureaucracy in the hope of placing like-minded colleagues in important positions.

Think tanks can establish and strengthen ties to key decision-makers through other channels as well. Presidential campaigns, for example, provide think tanks, particularly those that are ideologically in tune with certain candidates, with a tremendous opportunity to help shape the political platform and agenda of aspiring office-holders. As chapter 6 illustrates, several presidential candidates have turned to experts from think tanks for information and advice on how to address a wide range of domestic and foreign policy issues. In the process, a number of experts have been invited to serve on policy task forces or on transition teams to assist both presidential candidates and presidents-elect to assume power. Furthermore, during some administrations several think tank scholars have been appointed to important presidential advisory boards, including the President's Foreign Intelligence Advisory Board (PFIAB), the President's Intelligence Oversight Board (PIOB), and the President's Economic Policy Advisory Board (PEPAB).[4] Since political power in the United States, unlike in Canada, is not concentrated in the executive but is largely shared with the legislative branch, US think tanks also develop strategies to strengthen their ties to members of Congress. Several, including Heritage, have done this by establishing liaison offices with the House of Representatives and the Senate. Maintaining close contact with the legislature enables think tanks to meet regularly with members to discuss their concerns and policy needs. It also allows them to monitor and track the most important issues on the floor of the House and Senate, which, in turn, helps them prepare the type of research policy-makers require to make critical choices. Some think tanks, including Brookings, have also held focus groups with congressional staffers to better assess how useful they find their research products. This type of input can prove extremely valuable when think tanks consider the best ways to tackle complex issues, not to mention the most effective channels through which to communicate their findings. By contrast, think tanks in Canada, as noted, rarely devote considerable resources to establishing strong ties to the legislature, other than the time some experts invest in preparing testimony to deliver before parliamentary committees. As noted, unlike in the US Congress, Parliament is not home to hundreds of elected officials with the luxury or freedom to automatically embrace the ideas espoused by outside policy experts, especially if the policy recommendations being made are at variance with the wishes of their party. Indeed, the limited freedom MPs have to express their concerns or to challenge the direction of their party is one of the many features of parliamentary democracy in Canada that several seasoned parliamentarians are seeking to change.[5] While think tanks routinely distribute their publications to members of Parliament, there is less incentive for think tanks in Canada to try to persuade individual MPs to endorse their studies; more can be gained by working closely with cabinet members and senior officials in the bureaucracy, who are in a position to implement policy changes.

To discuss certain policy issues in more detail, some think tanks regularly invite members of Congress to attend private seminars, conferences, and workshops. Once again, this strategy enables policy experts at think tanks to share their insights with policy-makers who are in a position to influence the content of legislation. Think tanks like the Heritage Foundation, CSIS, and the Hoover Institution also realize that many newly elected members of Congress, as well as some seasoned policy-makers, could benefit from acquiring more knowledge of particular policy issues. They also realize the importance of establishing good communications with congressional staff and legislative assistants who regularly advise members of Congress.

Established in 1980, the Hoover Institution's two-day Washington Seminars (as they were then called), held on the picturesque campus of Stanford University in Palo Alto, have played an important role in facilitating the exchange of ideas between Hoover scholars and congressional aides. Renamed the Stuart Family Congressional Fellowship Program, the seminars, held twice a year, have been attended by Democratic and Republican congressional staffers from the House and Senate Committees on International Relations/Foreign Relations, Appropriations, the Budget, Armed Services, Finance, Ways and Means, and Intelligence and by the offices of the senate majority leader and the house speaker, the minority leader, and the majority whip. The seminars are often followed by meetings in Washington to bring together individuals who have participated in the program, Hoover scholars, and other government officials. According to the Hoover Institution, "these meetings and seminars are now playing a critical role in the ongoing dialogue between scholars and policy-makers, which is so important to the effective development and implementation of legislative and executive department policies and programs."[6]

The Hoover Institution also sponsors seminars for journalists and recent college graduates (known as the Hoover Policy Boot Camp) to help inform and educate them about a range of policy issues. Some think tanks also maintain close contact with bureaucratic departments and agencies. For instance, through the State Department's Diplomat in Residence Program, diplomats can, between assignments, take up residence at think tanks and universities to write, conduct research, and deliver lectures. Diplomats have been sent to several think tanks, including the American Enterprise Institute, the Hoover Institution, RAND, the Council on Foreign Relations, the Carnegie Endowment for International Peace, and the Heritage Foundation.

Some policy-makers, particularly in the United States, are so impressed with think tanks that they decide to make them their permanent home after completing their public service. However, it is important to point out that many former high-profile policy-makers are not recruited to think tanks because of their potential as researchers but because of their ability to attract funds, which is likely why think tanks have often approached former presidents and cabinet secretaries to join their ranks.

Finally, think tanks in both countries often hold informal meetings with key policy-makers to discuss studies that their institutes have produced or simply to outline a range of policy options elected officials have at their disposal. Most of these meetings are rarely publicized or talked about, but they nonetheless can help shape public policy. Indeed, for many think tanks, working quietly behind closed doors might be the most effective channel they have to influence policy-making.

The strategies think tanks use and the emphasis they place on each is influenced not only by the political environment they inhabit but by their mandate and resources. In other words, for advocacy-oriented think tanks such as the Heritage Foundation and the Fraser Institute, which are committed to influencing public dialogue and which have the resources to market their ideas effectively, producing opinion magazines, securing access to the media, and holding public forums will be a top priority. On the other hand, as previously noted, institutes like the Public Policy Forum and the Caledon Institute, which prefer to exchange ideas with policy-makers in meeting rooms instead of in public, will devote less consideration and fewer resources to marketing their message. To sum up, think tanks develop strategies that allow them to reach their specific target audience or audiences most effectively.

MARKETING THE MESSAGE: THINK TANKS AND THE MEDIA

For most policy experts at think tanks, testifying before a high-profile congressional or parliamentary committee or publishing a study on a controversial domestic or foreign policy issue may attract attention in some policy-making circles. However, it is unlikely to generate the exposure that an appearance on the CBS or CBC evening news would, or reach the sizeable readership that an op-ed article in the *New York Times* or *The Globe and Mail* would. This may explain why some think tanks devote considerable time and resources to gaining access to the print and broadcast media, and why, in recent years, they have paid far more attention to social media. It might also explain why the competition between think tanks for media exposure is so intense. As Patricia Linden explains, for think tanks to compete, "their ideas must be communicated; otherwise the oracles of tankdom wind up talking to themselves. The upshot is an endless forest of communiques, reports, journals, newsletters, op-ed articles, press releases, books, and educational materials. The rivalry for attention is fierce; so much so that the analysts have come out of their think tanks to express opinions on lecture and TV circuits, at seminars and conferences, press briefings and Congressional hearings."[7]

Securing access to the media on a regular basis provides think tanks with a valuable opportunity to shape public opinion and public policy. At the very least, media exposure allows think tanks to plant seeds in the mind of the electorate that may develop into a full-scale public policy debate. There was certainly no shortage of think tank commentaries on President Trump's first 100 days in office, and on virtually every important domestic and foreign policy issue confronting policy-makers in Canada and the US, the presence of think tanks has been felt, a subject that we will return to later in this study.

In addition to contributing to the public dialogue, think tanks understand that media exposure helps foster the illusion of policy influence, a currency they have a vested interest in accumulating. At the very least, constructing a narrative that suggests media exposure translates seamlessly into policy influence is a message that think tank directors are only too willing to convey and reinforce. The Fraser Institute is just one of many think tanks that has employed this strategy. Although former Fraser Institute chair Alan F. Campney acknowledged in the Institute's 1976 annual report that it "is almost as difficult to measure the effects of the Institute's work as it is to ascertain what Canada's economic problems are," Fraser has consistently relied on media coverage to assess its impact. According to its twenty-five-year retrospective, "One of the indicators the Institute has used from its inception [to measure performance] is media coverage. How many mentions does an Institute book receive in daily newspapers? How many minutes of airtime do Institute authors and researchers receive during interviews?"[8] Such data, as the next chapter will reveal, may tell us which think tanks attract the most attention, but it provides little insight into how much impact institutes have in the policy-making process.

Few think tanks have devoted more time and resources to securing access to the media than the Heritage Foundation. In 2015, Heritage spent over $11 million of its close to $100 million budget on media and government relations. By contrast, in the same year, AEI spent 13 per cent or approximately $5 million of its budget on communications, and Brookings allocated 3 per cent of its $95 million budget to performing this function. To put this in context, Heritage's media relations budget line exceeds the operating revenue of the Fraser Institute.[9]

Heritage's public relations program is based on a simple premise: "provide journalists, opinion leaders and the general public with the positive message of responsible conservatism and conservatism will remain competitive, and even triumph, in the marketplace of ideas." Its goal is even simpler: "Make sure journalists never have a reason for not quoting at least one conservative expert – or for not giving the conservative 'spin' in their stories."[10]

The Heritage Foundation has clearly accomplished its goal: the mainstream media in the United States relies disproportionately on Heritage and a handful of other conservative think tanks inside the Beltway for their expertise and political commentary. In Canada, the media appears to rely heavily on a handful of free-market institutes as well.

To make sure journalists do not overlook the views of their scholars, the Heritage Foundation and several other think tanks, including the Hoover Institution and the AEI, have developed programs designed to flood the mainstream print media with hundreds of op-ed articles each year. For example, between 1998 and 2008, well over 1,000 op-ed articles penned by Heritage scholars appeared in some of America's leading newspapers, including the *Chicago Tribune*, the *Christian Science Monitor*, the *Los Angeles Times*, the *New York Times*, *USA Today*, the *Wall Street Journal*, the *Washington Times*, and the *Washington Post*. In 2015 alone, close to 1,500 commentaries by Heritage experts were published in a wide range of print outlets.[11] Several think tanks have also given considerable thought to how to increase their exposure on the air. While some American institutes have created their own television programs or have had documentaries or conferences broadcast on cable TV, most viewers recognize think tank scholars from their regular appearances on network newscasts (CBS, ABC, NBC, CNN, and Fox News), *PBS NewsHour*, or a host of political talk shows, including *Meet the Press* and *This Week* (with George Stephanopoulos). Scholars from Canadian think tanks regularly appear on the CBC and CTV evening news.

Establishing personal relationships with journalists is also critical for think tanks trying to enhance their media profile. As Brian Lee Crowley, president of the Ottawa-based MacDonald-Laurier Institute and founding president of the Halifax-based Atlantic Institute for Market Studies observed, to secure access to the media, think tanks should ensure that their institutional interests coincide with those of journalists. According to Crowley, "having sound ideas and doing the research to back them up are only one-half of your job. The other half is putting a lot of energy into strategic communications, and putting that strategy into effect. The place to start is not with ideas, but with personal relationships. Journalists are moved much more by personal contact than by the best ideas in the world. One way that they economize on scarce time is by having a stable of people, experts in their field, in whom they can have confidence, knowing that if they are told something by these people, they can put a great deal of weight on it without running the risk of looking stupid and foolish."[12]

The potential benefits of being a guest commentator on a national newscast or radio program or of publishing op-ed articles on a regular basis are great. Not only do these activities bode well for think tank scholars looking for a broader audience to convey their ideas, but they can also promote the goals of the institutions they represent. As the late William J. Taylor Jr, a senior adviser in the International Security Program at the Center for Strategic and International Studies (CSIS) for many years noted, to raise the visibility of CSIS, "he [took] advantage of every opportunity to appear on television, not so much for personal reasons "but for the glory of CSIS and its mission of informing the public. When we're on television, we're up there as individuals, but it says CSIS under our name."[13] Yet, as Howard Kurtz, a former reporter with the *Washington Post* and currently host of *Fox News Channel's* MediaBuzz says, what the viewer fails to learn from the title flashing under Taylor's name – "CSIS Military Analyst" – is that "CSIS is a markedly conservative organization that forms a sort of interlocking directorate with the Washington establishment … That it has received $50,000 to $250,000 from such defense contractors as Boeing, General Dynamics, Rockwell, Honeywell and Westinghouse. [And that its annual report boasts: 'we network in Washington with the Congress, the executive branch, the scholarly community, the corporate and labor communities and the media.']"[14]

It is not difficult to understand why think tanks covet media attention. After all, as the Heritage Foundation, the AEI, the Brookings Institution, the Fraser Institute, the C.D. Howe Institute, and others have discovered, media coverage can and does play a critical role in allowing institutes to effectively market their message. But what makes some think tanks more media friendly than others? Although the next chapter will examine this topic more fully, a few factors are worth noting. First, think tanks that have large and diverse research programs supported by dozens of staff are likely better positioned to attract more media exposure than institutes offering only a narrow range of expertise. Think tanks such as many of those mentioned above appeal to journalists because they can comment, on very short notice, on a range of domestic and foreign policy issues. In a sense, the AEI, the Heritage Foundation, and the Brookings Institution function as one-stop policy shops. They also appeal to journalists who are looking for a particular political perspective on an issue. When reporters call the Heritage Foundation or the Fraser Institute, which are well known for their commitment to free market principles, they can be assured that any proposal by the president or Congress or by the prime minister to increase taxes to pay for social welfare programs will be criticized. It is no coincidence that scholars from the Heritage Foundation, a strong advocate for many of the policy positions advocated by Donald Trump, regularly appear on network newscasts and talk shows to bolster the president's agenda. Knowing what positions think tanks will generally take may also account for the media's reliance on the same group of think tank scholars. The reliability of policy experts is also a consideration, as Crowley noted, particularly when journalists are under tight deadlines. Sam Donaldson, who served as a reporter and news anchor with ABC news for over forty years, agrees:

> Clearly there are problems with going to the same people … [But] to sit down while you're facing a deadline and say, "Gee, there must be some other experts we haven't thought of. Let's beat the bushes and launch a search of the city or the country for them." Well, that takes a lot of time and energy because for TV it involves a lot more than flipping a card on the Rolodex. A second reason is

> that we know [some guys] provide a succinct response. You can't come to me and say, "Sam, I know you're on a deadline, you need to comment on such and such, go out and take a chance on Mr X." No, I'm sorry folks, I don't have the time to take a chance with Mr X ... I know Mr Y ... is going to deliver the goods.[15]

As Donaldson implies, how effective pundits are at communicating their ideas to the public is also important. Possessing the ability to explain complex issues in a simple, straightforward, and engaging way is also a highly marketable and sought after skill that think tanks look for when they hire policy experts. Tammy Haddad, a media entrepreneur, and a former executive producer of several shows, including *Larry King Live*, and *Hardball with Chris Matthews*, agrees, observing that "there are so many people out there who know so much, but they're lousy guests. They have to be able to explain [issues] in such a way that my mother in Pittsburgh understands what they're talking about."[16] During newscasts it becomes even more crucial for guests to be succinct – they do not have the time to offer long exposés on the state of the world. Those scholars who realize what the broadcast media requires will continue to find their names at the top of smartphone contact lists.

STUDYING THINK TANK INFLUENCE

Think tanks frequently boast about their influence in the policy-making community, and go to great lengths to publicize how much attention they generate. In their annual reports, they regularly include a section entitled "Think Tank by the Numbers," which highlights, among other things, how many media citations their institute has received in the past year; the number of visitors to their website, the volume of publications downloaded, the number of times their staff have testified before legislative committees, and the number of followers they have on Facebook, Twitter, and other social media, along with a smattering of other so-called indicators of influence. These data are intended to convince donors how much influence they have in shaping public policy. Think tanks also pay very close attention to how they shape the narrative around their policy impact. For example, a few months after Ronald Reagan entered the Oval Office, Heritage Foundation president Edwin Feulner claimed that over 60 per cent of the policy recommendations included in his institute's mammoth study, *Mandate for Leadership*, had been or were in the process of being implemented by the Reagan administration. To Feulner's delight, his remarks appeared in several newspapers throughout the United States. What most journalists failed to point out, however, was that many of the recommendations Feulner was taking credit for had been proposed by other individuals and institutes years before. Indeed, not a single journalist bothered to inventory the various policy recommendations Feulner claimed had influenced Reagan's domestic and foreign policy. The illusion of the Heritage Foundation's newly acquired policy influence, fostered in part by the media, had become reality. Similarly, when asked to consider what federal government programs or policies his institute had helped shape in the previous ten years, Michael Walker of the Fraser Institute remarked, "the Fraser Institute has played a central role in most policy developments during the last decade and it is simply too onerous a task to specify."[17]

The Fraser Institute's current president, Niels Veldhuis, has made similar claims about how extensive a reach his organization has in Canada's policy-making process. But Veldhuis should not be singled out. Most think tank presidents understand how important it is to portray their institute in the most favourable light, and go to great lengths to do this.[18] They are not shy when it comes to flaunting their organization's achievements, nor are they modest in seeking the praise and endorsement of high-profile policy-makers and scholars. For years, the Fraser Institute would quote the late Nobel-prize-winning economist Milton Friedman, who stated that "the Fraser Institute has become a remarkably influential think tank: one of the most influential in the world," or former British prime minister Margaret Thatcher, who acknowledged that "the great work [Fraser has done] has had a tremendous influence."[19]

These and other testimonials intended to raise the profile of think tanks often appear in promotional material and on think tank websites, and in some cases, they may even hold a kernel of truth. But whether or not the praise heaped on think tanks is warranted, it is incumbent on scholars and journalists to delve more deeply into how and to what extent think tanks have shaped the discourse around key policy issues. Think tank directors and presidents have good reason to showcase their accomplishments, which, in many cases, continue to pay handsome dividends; on the other hand, scholars interested in assessing policy influence have good reason to be skeptical.

Evaluating think tank influence, a topic that we will return to in the next few chapters, is inherently difficult because directors of policy institutes, not to mention those who study them, have different perceptions of what constitutes influence and the circumstances under which it can best be achieved. As noted, for some think tank directors and presidents, the amount of media exposure their institute generates or the number of publications they produce reflects how much influence they wield. Conversely, some think tank leaders rely on other performance indicators, such as how many staff have been appointed to senior government positions or the size of their budget, to assess their impact. What makes evaluating their influence even more difficult is that the policy-makers, academics, and journalists who subscribe to think tank publications or attend their conferences and workshops invariably have different impressions of how useful or relevant they find their work. Scholars thus cannot assume that think tanks measure influence in the same way, nor can they take for granted that policy-makers and other consumers of their products use similar criteria to evaluate their work. This is one of the many problems of publishing global rankings of think tanks, which tend to be highly arbitrary, ad hoc, and impressionistic.[20]

Even if think tanks used the same performance indicators and assigned the same priority to becoming involved at each stage of the policy-making process, numerous methodological obstacles would still have to be overcome to accurately measure their influence on public policy. Since dozens of individuals and organizations seek to influence policy debates through various channels, tracing the origin of a policy idea becomes problematic. In an increasingly crowded political arena, it is often difficult to isolate the voice or voices that made a difference. Moreover, it can take months, if not years, before an idea proposed by a think tank or any other non-governmental organization for that matter, has any discernible impact. Indeed, by the time a policy initiative is introduced, it may not resemble a think tank's initial proposal at all.

Directors of think tanks can, and often do, provide anecdotal evidence to reveal how much influence their institutes wield, but such pronouncements offer little insight into how relevant think tanks are in the policy-making process; claiming to have influence is far simpler than documenting how it was achieved. In the following chapter we will examine one approach that can be used to make more informed judgments about the relevance of think tanks at different stages. Rather than assuming that think tanks in general have influence or that some think tanks have more influence than others, we will evaluate which think tanks in Canada and the United States appear to be most actively involved at key stages of the policy-making process. Drawing on extensive empirical data for a handful of performance indicators, including media citations, parliamentary and congressional testimony, and consultations with bureaucratic departments, the chapter will show that it is possible to demonstrate, particularly in Canada, that policy-makers do not always rely on the most visible think tanks for information and advice. Several think tanks that generate little media attention are also invited to participate in various stages of policy-making, and in doing so, make their presence felt.

CHAPTER FIVE

Public Visibility and Policy Relevance: Assessing the Influence of Think Tanks

Much has been written in recent years about the growing influence of the Heritage Foundation, the Fraser Institute, and several other think tanks in the United States and Canada. Those who study the burgeoning think tank population in these countries point to their ever-expanding output of publications, their appearances before congressional and parliamentary committees, and their considerable media exposure as evidence of their heightened importance in the policy-making community. This perception, as noted, is reinforced by directors of think tanks who often credit their institutes with, among other things, influencing major policy debates, executive orders, and government legislation. While it is not surprising that think tanks exaggerate their impact in policy-making, it is surprising that few journalists, or scholars for that matter, have considered whether the increased media visibility of policy institutes reflects how relevant or active they are in shaping public opinion and public policy. Indeed, rather than acknowledging that think tanks exercise different types of influence at different stages of the policy-making cycle, it is assumed that the most talked-about and written-about think tanks are those best suited, equipped, and positioned to influence the discourse around key policy issues.

As funding agencies and philanthropists continue to place more pressure on think tanks to provide evidence of policy impact, and as scholars struggle to assess direct and indirect policy influence, it is important to consider ways in which we can provide more informed observations about think tanks and their involvement, or level of engagement, as I prefer to call it, in the policy-making process. One approach is to undertake a quantitative assessment of think tank performance by measuring, for instance, how much media exposure think tanks have generated and how often staff from various think tanks have testified before legislative committees. Keeping track of other performance indicators, such as the number of publications think tanks produce and the volume of studies that are downloaded from their website, the number of followers they have on Facebook and Twitter, and how many conferences and seminars they hold, might also be worth considering.[1]

Although there are potential pitfalls in relying too heavily on a quantitative assessment of think tank performance, there are also some important benefits, as will become clear. At the very least, by monitoring how much media exposure think tanks generate and how often they appear before legislative committees, we can determine more easily how active or inactive think tanks are on particular policy issues. These kinds of indicators or metrics may thus provide useful insights into how engaged some think tanks are, and why their activities may warrant closer scrutiny. However, it is important to keep in mind that some think tanks do not relish or covet public exposure, and indeed find it advantageous to avoid attracting media attention. Preferring instead to work behind the scenes by meeting and discussing policy issues with elected officials and other key stakeholders in private, their limited visibility does not necessarily translate into a lack of policy impact. On the contrary, flying below the radar might be exactly what some policy institutes strive to achieve.

The purpose of this chapter, in undertaking a quantitative assessment of think tank influence, is to challenge the widely held perception that the most visible think tanks must also, by implication, be the most influential. To do so, I will address one important and frequently ignored question: Do policy institutes that generate high media exposure (hereafter referred to as public visibility) also engage actively in other important phases of the federal government's policy formulation process – consultation with government departments and testimony before congressional and parliamentary committees (two indicators of policy relevance)? Can we expect think tanks that are effective at capturing media attention to be as effective at, or interested in, participating in other stages of policy-making? Interestingly enough, in comparing the media visibility and policy relevance of think tanks in Canada and the United States, two very different patterns emerge.

As R. Kent Weaver and Andrew Rich discovered in examining the visibility of fifty-one US think tanks, institutes that attract considerable media exposure are more likely to be called upon to testify before congressional committees than those with modest media profiles.[2] Moreover, as Rich observed in a separate study, there appears to be a relationship between think tanks that enjoy high media exposure and those that policy-makers and other opinion leaders consider the most influential.[3]

By contrast, when the public visibility and policy relevance of a select group of Canadian policy institutes is measured, a different set of observations comes to light.[4] As in Weaver and Rich's study, the data on the public visibility of Canadian think tanks reveal that, with few exceptions, the print and broadcast media in Canada rely disproportionately on the same group of policy institutes: the Conference Board of Canada, the Fraser Institute, and the C.D. Howe Institute, which rank among the think tanks most often cited by the media. Several factors that will be discussed could account for the media's reliance on these institutes. However, in Canada high media exposure does not appear to be a precondition for advising senior public servants and policymakers. In fact, two institutes that advise several government departments, the now defunct Canadian Policy Research Networks, Inc. (CPRN), and the Caledon Institute of Social Policy, have, relative to other institutes in Canada, limited public visibility. A simple ranking test that focuses on the period between 1991–97, when CPRN was still active, confirms that there is no correlation between public visibility and the number of departments with whom institutes consult. Unfortunately, the Canadian government has not issued a revised study documenting the interaction of public policy institutes with government departments. As a result, although reference will be made to the initial findings showcased in the previous edition of *Do Think Tanks Matter?* additional data cannot be presented. More recent data (1998–2016) on the amount of media exposure a select group of American and Canadian think tanks generate, as well as the frequency with which experts from many of these institutes testify before various legislative committees, will instead be highlighted. In comparing results between the first set of data (1991–97) with our more up to date findings (1998–2016), it will become clear that despite some variations in the rankings among American and Canadian think tanks in media exposure and legislative testimony during the two time periods, a strong relationship continues to exist between these variables. In other words, think tanks that attract high media exposure also tend to have their experts appear more regularly before legislative committees. It stands to reason that the more familiar elected officials and staff serving on committees are with the work and policy direction of particular think tanks, the more likely they are to consider inviting some of those experts to share their insights on proposed changes to legislation. Just as scholars garner attention from their peers by publishing their findings in highly respected academic journals and scholarly presses, think tank experts often enhance their credibility and legitimacy with elected officials and other stakeholders by being quoted in print, broadcast, and social media. Effective and sustained media exposure for policy experts at think tanks can help to create other opportunities for them to market and promote their ideas. Recognizing the vitally important role many high-profile congressional and parliamentary committees play in supporting or stalling legislation, the efforts of scholars from think tanks to shape the conversation or discourse around proposed laws simply cannot be ignored.

This chapter begins by evaluating Weaver and Rich's work on the visibility and impact of American think tanks and the many lessons that can be drawn from their analyses. The chapter will then discuss the public visibility of a cross-section of Canadian think tanks and offer several reasons to explain why some think tanks in Canada have generated considerably more media exposure than others. Following this, the relevance of Canadian policy institutes during the phases of policy formulation mentioned above will be examined. Think tanks will be ranked according to the number of departments that list them as consultants and the number of appearances they have made before parliamentary committees. A Spearman's rho, a statistical test to measure the correlation between two sets of ranked variables, will be used to assess the relationship between media visibility and policy relevance. The final section will briefly discuss what additional steps scholars can take to assess the influence of think tanks.

THINK TANKS AND THE AMERICAN MEDIA

As the previous chapter discussed, gaining access to the media has become one of the most common and important methods think tanks employ to convey their ideas to policy-makers and to the public. For think tanks committed to advocating a particular point of view, achieving widespread media exposure is critical: "Without a mass constituency backing their efforts, the influence of expertise-providing organizations often depends on the visibility their research obtains. Moreover, media visibility is often assessed as a measure of the organizational viability and success of research organizations by those who might fund their activities."[5]

To determine which think tanks in the United States generate the most media exposure, Weaver and Rich analyzed references to fifty-one national and regionally focused think tanks in six national newspapers (the *Washington Post*, the *New York Times*, the *Christian Science Monitor*, USA *Today*, the *Wall Street Journal*, and the *Washington Times*) between 1991 and 1996.[6] A sample of their findings is given in table 5.1.

Weaver and Rich discovered that among the many factors that could explain why some think tanks generated considerably more media exposure than others, two important variables stood out – funding and location. First, as the authors observe, "Money is critical for a think tank to gain visibility and get its message out ... Our analysis suggests that this funding translates into media visibility, which, in turn, may encourage additional financing for visible organizations." With some notable exceptions, including RAND, which boasts the largest budget of all US think tanks, and the well-heeled Urban Institute and Hoover Institution, think tanks with significant financial resources generated the most media attention.[7] Of the top five institutes ranked by media visibility, none had budgets of less than $10 million. By contrast, think tanks with budgets below $1 million received very little exposure.

Second, being located in Washington clearly provides think tanks with an advantage over institutes based outside the Beltway. Indeed, despite the ease with which think tank experts spread out across the country can communicate with journalists stationed in DC, having a physical presence in the nation's capital clearly pays handsome dividends. Weaver and Rich's data confirm that think tanks headquartered in Washington attract considerably more media attention: "Washington-based think tanks remain the overwhelmingly dominant players relative to think tanks based outside the Beltway, not just as a function of size, but also of proximity, which promotes the development of personal relationships and networks among social scientists, journalists, and policymakers' staffs."[8] Think tanks with a Washington address have the added benefit of cultivating ties to journalists who cover national politics. As the previous chapter demonstrated, once journalists have assembled a stable of local experts willing and able to offer their insights at a moment's notice, there may be little need to expand their list of contacts.

Weaver and Rich did not examine the amount of exposure think tanks generated in the broadcast media during the same period, but it appears from table 5.2 that they would likely have arrived at similar conclusions. All those that ranked high in print media exposure also attracted the attention of television journalists. Ranked first in the number of citations it received in the print media, the Brookings Institution topped the list of institutes that received the most attention on America's four major television networks (ABC, NBC, CBS, and CNN). Between 1991 and 1997, staff from Brookings appeared on evening news broadcasts 171 times, more than twice as often as staff from the Carnegie Endowment for International Peace (69 times) and the American Enterprise Institute (61 times), and more than three times as often as spokespersons from the Heritage Foundation (47 times). With the exception of RAND, think tanks located outside the Beltway received little, if any, television exposure.

For the most part, the data revealed in tables 5.1.1 and 5.2.1 (which cover the same media outlets) confirms the pattern observed by Weaver and Rich. Over an eighteen-year period (1998–2016), the Brookings Institution continued to generate the most print media references with a total of 19,977 mentions. AEI remained in second place with 11,782 mentions. The Carnegie Endowment moved from its third-place ranking to seventh, losing ground to several think tanks, including the

Table 5.1
Newspaper Citations for Selected American Think Tanks, 1991–97

	Washington Post DC	*New York Times*	*Christian Science Monitor*	*USA Today*	*Wall Street Journal*	*Washington Times* DC	*Total*
Brookings Institution	1,205	881	416	493	526	699	4,220
American Enterprise Institute	602	487	239	171	487	737	2,723
Carnegie Endowment for International Peace	647	317	153	335	384	236	2,072
Cato Institute	320	165	57	132	332	831	1,837
Center for Strategic and International Studies	240	123	150	139	146	780	1,578
Heritage Foundation	105	142	39	46	255	731	1,318
Institute for Policy Studies	306	339	101	74	227	151	1,198
Progressive Policy Institute	315	261	155	62	127	236	1,156
Urban Institute	418	246	76	94	155	119	1,108
Worldwatch Institute	114	81	41	40	176	271	723
Hoover Institution	208	68	44	36	114	167	637
Hudson Institute	69	192	21	24	141	95	542
Manhattan Institute	67	49	74	24	21	38	273
RAND	74	35	11	9	6	53	188
Rockford Institute	3	7	2	0	8	50	70

Source: Data set compiled by R. Kent Weaver and Andrew Rich.

Heritage Foundation which catapulted from sixth to third. The considerable investment Heritage has made in media and government relations has clearly paid off. Although it is not surprising that Brookings' more centrist leanings make it more appealing to liberal media outlets such as the *New York Times* and the *Washington Post*, Heritage also managed

Table 5.1.1
Newspaper Citations for Selected American Think Tanks, 1998–2016

Institute	*Washington Post* DC	*New York Times*	*Christian Science Monitor*	USA *Today*	*Wall Street Journal*	*Washington Times*	*Totals*
Brookings Institution	7,366	5,138	1,425	1,430	4,618	0	19,977
American Enterprise Institute	3,607	2,269	643	663	4,598	2	11,782
Heritage Foundation	3,246	1,677	727	681	2,222	28	8,581
Cato Institute	1,958	990	481	522	1,709	7	5,667
Center for Strategic and International Studies	2,212	1,718	920	497	1,549	3	6,899
Urban Institute	1,856	1,078	227	272	965	2	4,400
Carnegie Endowment for International Peace	1,254	950	386	149	718	1	3,458
Hoover Institution	625	629	135	110	2,235	5	3,739
Manhattan Institute	410	916	80	82	1,714	0	3,202
RAND Corporation	243	1,270	133	49	193	0	1,888
Hudson Institute	406	246	142	70	1,017	1	1,882
Institute for Policy Studies	279	229	87	47	231	0	873
Progressive Policy Institute	225	139	58	50	143	1	616
Worldwatch Institute	84	47	42	48	38	0	259

Source: Factiva.com

to generate hundreds of mentions from these two newspapers. Because large and well-funded DC-based think tanks with extensive research programs overseen by dozens of scholars can comment on contemporary domestic and foreign policy issues through very different ideological lenses, journalists will in all likelihood continue to turn to them regularly for analysis. Indeed, as long as these and other top-tier think tanks regard

Table 5.2
ABC, NBC, CBS, and CNN Evening News Citations for Selected American Think Tanks, 1991–97

Institute	*1991*	*1992*	*1993*	*1994*	*1995*	*1996*	*1997*	*Total*
Brookings Institution	47	40	26	12	15	13	18	171
Carnegie Endowment for International Peace	15	8	12	19	7	7	1	69
American Enterprise Institute	10	9	14	9	8	6	5	61
Heritage Foundation	8	11	7	1	8	4	8	47
Center for Strategic and International Studies	7	5	8	15	2	1	4	42
RAND	2	4	3	3	1	5	6	24
Progressive Policy Institute	1	5	0	1	5	0	1	13
Worldwatch Institute	2	3	2	2	0	0	3	12
Urban Institute	0	0	0	0	0	1	1	2
Cato Institute	0	0	0	0	0	1	0	1
Hoover Institution	0	0	0	1	0	0	0	1
Rockford Institute	0	0	0	0	0	0	0	0
Manhattan Institute	0	0	0	0	0	0	0	0
Institute for Policy Studies	0	0	0	0	0	0	0	0
Hudson Institute	0	0	0	0	0	0	0	0

Source: Vanderbilt University Television News Archive.

media visibility as a priority, they will remain among the most cited policy institutes in the United States.

As to the frequency with which think tanks and their scholars are cited by the broadcast media, there has been a noticeable change in rankings among the top five thinks over the two time periods covered in this chapter. Once again, Brookings remains the most cited think tank during evening news programs produced by ABC, NBC, CBS, and CNN. CSIS is ranked second according to the Vanderbilt Television News Archive, a considerable improvement over its fifth-place ranking close to two decades ago. CSIS has clearly made a long-term commitment to, and investment in, strengthening its ties to the media. With state of the art communications facilities, including access to its own satellite, CSIS understands the power of ideas and how critical it is for think tanks to shape the narrative around key policy issues. This lesson has not been lost on RAND which has also made significant headway in improving its media visibility. Moving from a sixth-place ranking eighteen years ago to third represents a considerable improvement. Rounding off the top five think tanks in broadcast exposure on four of the major networks is Heritage in fourth place and the Carnegie Endowment in fifth.

The data in tables 5.1.1 and 5.2.1 present a general picture of the extent to which a group of top-tier US think tanks have attracted print

Table 5.2.1

ABC, NBC, CBS, and CNN Evening News Citations 1998–2016

	1998	*1999*	*2000*	*2001*	*2002*	*2003*	*2004*	*2005*	*2006*	*2007*	*2008*	*2009*	*2010*	*2011*	*2012*	*2013*	*2014*	*2015*	*2016*	*Totals*
Brookings Institution	55	57	61	52	41	29	28	20	36	30	12	19	8	14	7	5	2	1	0	477
Center for Strategic and International Studies	6	13	12	21	21	36	24	13	33	39	13	15	20	12	0	4	4	1	2	289
RAND	1	1	6	8	3	7	3	1	0	1	0	0	0	0	0	0	0	0	0	31
Heritage Foundation	4	9	23	11	12	19	24	23	21	19	7	11	5	5	5	2	6	3	1	210
Carnegie Endowment for International Peace	5	12	8	9	20	14	21	6	9	4	5	8	3	11	2	1	0	1	0	139
American Enterprise Institute	15	4	6	5	11	7	17	11	11	6	7	6	6	1	1	1	0	2	0	117
Cato Institute	3	3	8	1	2	6	5	5	1	4	2	8	3	0	1	2	0	1	0	55
Institute for Policy Studies	0	0	0	3	3	3	2	1	0	1	0	1	0	1	0	0	0	0	0	15
Urban Institute	0	0	4	0	1	2	3	0	0	2	0	1	0	0	2	0	0	0	0	15
Hudson Institute	0	4	2	4	1	1	0	1	0	0	2	0	0	0	0	0	0	0	0	15
Manhattan Institute	0	0	5	2	2	0	0	1	1	1	0	0	0	0	0	0	0	0	1	13
Hoover Institute	0	0	0	1	0	2	1	0	1	0	0	2	0	0	0	0	0	0	0	7
Progressive Policy Institute	0	0	1	0	1	0	0	0	0	0	0	0	0	0	0	0	0	0	0	2
Worldwatch Institute	0	0	2	0	0	0	0	0	0	0	0	0	0	0	0	0	0	0	0	2
Rockford Institute	0	0	1	0	0	0	0	0	0	1	0	0	0	0	0	0	0	0	0	2
Totals	89	103	139	117	118	126	128	82	113	108	48	71	45	44	18	15	12	9	4	1,389

Source: Vanderbilt University Television News Archive

and broadcast exposure (in selected media outlets) over a twenty-year period. Scholars who are intent in delving more deeply into these data sets could also examine why some think tanks generate more attention in some newspapers or on television networks than others, and why, for instance, media exposure peaks for some institutes during specific periods of time. Is it because of a particular news event that falls into a think tank's area of expertise, a controversial report that has been released, or possibly both? Several factors could account for why some think tanks attract more attention than others, but despite arriving at a compelling explanation, the question remains – what does media exposure tell us about the nature and influence of think tanks?

Is Media Exposure a Reliable Indicator of Policy Relevance?

Think tanks that attract considerable media exposure in the United States are also effective at relying on other channels to shape public opinion and public policy. Indeed, many of the think tanks that dominate the airwaves and the op-ed pages of newspapers also make regular appearances before congressional committees. And just as bias in certain news organizations may account for why some think tanks are quoted more often than others, the ideological preferences of committee members appear to influence the frequency with which scholars from some policy institutes appear before Congress.[9] As Weaver and Rich note in a separate study, "data on congressional testimony demonstrate the powerful effects of 'gatekeeping' by the majority parties in Congress." They state, "Prior to the Republican takeover of Congress in 1994, staff members from the Brookings Institution were the most frequent think tank testifiers at congressional hearings in most years, often followed by witnesses from the more conservative American Enterprise Institute. In 1995, with Republican legislators and staff controlling the bulk of witness slots, the Heritage Foundation became the most frequently represented think tank, followed by the AEI, the libertarian Cato Institute, and Brookings, in that order (see Appendix 5). Testimony by liberal think tanks lagged far behind."[10]

A similar pattern can be observed between 1999–2008, a period in which the Republicans not only controlled the White House, but also, with the exception of the 110th Congress, both the House and the Senate (see Appendix 5). Between the 107th and 109th Congress, scholars from the American Enterprise Institute testified before congressional committees more than any of their counterparts. Below AEI's first-place ranking, other conservative and libertarian think tanks were well represented, including the Heritage Foundation (ranked third) and the Cato Institute (ranked fourth). CSIS placed third overall, and Brookings received an eighth place ranking. However, by the time the Democrats retook the White House in 2009, and took control of both Houses of Congress (2009–11), the appearances by scholars at Brookings increased dramatically. Even when the Republicans regained a majority of seats in the house in 2011, the Democrats, with majority support in the Senate, created opportunities for scholars from Brookings and other more liberal think tanks to testify. It is also worth noting that with a change in party leadership in the house between 2001–17, Heritage Foundation scholars began to appear before congressional committees with greater frequency (see Appendix 5), findings consistent with Weaver and Rich's earlier results.

Many of the conservative think tanks that frequently testify before Congress are perceived to have the most influence in the political process. In a 1997 survey conducted for the global consulting firm Burson-Marstellar, Rich noted that of the 110 congressional staff and Washington-based journalists surveyed, "68 per cent of respondents identified conservative think tanks as having a greater impact on policy-making than liberal think tanks: only five per cent named liberal think tanks as being most influential."[11] The Heritage Foundation was considered by 42 per cent of respondents as the single most influential think tank; Brookings was ranked second by 28 per cent of respondents. However, when asked to rank institutes according to their credibility, think tanks with no identifiable ideology ranked considerably higher than either the liberal or the conservative think tanks.

Weaver and Rich's study on the media visibility and policy relevance of US think tanks offers an interesting contrast when undertaking a similar analysis in Canada. While the size and funding of institutes are important in attracting media exposure, being located in Ottawa does not offer policy institutes a decisive advantage. Indeed, many of Canada's most prominent think tanks, including C.D. Howe, CIGI, Fraser, and IRPP are headquartered in other Ontario cities or in other provinces. An Ottawa address may explain why some think tanks appear before parliamentary committees and consult with federal government departments more often than those located outside the nation's capital. Yet, with few exceptions, the institutes that receive the most media attention are based elsewhere. The amount of media exposure think tanks in Canada generate may thus have more to do with the type of expertise they offer, and the priority they assign to media outreach, than with their proximity to policy-makers.

In addition, unlike the gatekeeper phenomenon observed in the US Congress by Weaver and Rich, the frequency with which think tanks testify before parliamentary committees does not appear to be heavily influenced by the party in power. Finally, while there is a moderately strong correlation between think tanks that generate high media exposure in Canada and those that are invited to testify before legislative committees, the most visible think tanks are not necessarily those that policymakers always consider the most relevant. If consultations with federal government departments can be considered an indicator of policy relevance, some of the least visible think tanks in Canada may be having the greatest impact at the most critical stages of the policy cycle, a subject that we will return to later in the chapter.

THINK TANKS AND THE CANADIAN MEDIA

Although references to think tanks in newspapers and on radio and television tell us little about their impact in shaping public opinion or about the quality of their commentaries, data on media exposure can offer some insight into which institutes are actively attempting to influence specific policy debates. It can also reveal in which parts of the country think tanks generate the most attention and whether the age, size, and financial resources of institutes influence the amount of exposure they receive.

Between 1985 and 1999, four think tanks – the Conference Board of Canada, the C.D. Howe Institute, the Fraser Institute, and the now defunct Economic Council of Canada – generated 60 per cent of all media citations. The Conference Board alone, which ranks first in public visibility, received close to 25 per cent of all media coverage. Indeed, it is only on CBC Radio that the Conference Board does not rank first in citations – it shares a sixth-place ranking with the Mackenzie Institute (table 5.3), which places nineteenth in overall visibility. The Canadian Tax Foundation (CTF), well known for its commentary on tax reform and budgetary matters, rounds off the top five institutes in the media visibility category, despite securing a fifth-place ranking in only one category, newspaper citations (including *The Globe and Mail*). Beyond the top four think tanks there is tremendous fluctuation in media rankings. The former Science Council of Canada received more citations than the CTF in *The Globe and Mail*. On CBC Radio, the CTF was outranked by eleven institutes, including the Science Council, the National Council of Welfare, the Canadian Council on Social Development, and the Canadian Centre for Policy Alternatives (CCPA). On the CBC and CTV national evening news, the Toronto-based Canadian Institute of Strategic Studies generated more coverage than the CTF. On CTV, three other institutes, the National Council of Welfare, the Mackenzie Institute, and the Canada West Foundation, had slightly more onscreen appearances or text references than the CTF. Of the twenty-two policy institutes for which data on media citations were collected, only half generated more than

1,000 references. The eleventh-ranked institute, the Canadian Institute of Strategic Studies, received 1,007 citations, 915 more than the lowest-ranked institute, the Parliamentary Centre, at 92 (table 5.4).

How do these data compare to results collected over a more recent time period (2000–08 and 2009–17)? Between 2000–08, the Fraser Institute squeezed by the Conference Board of Canada to secure a first-place ranking, with a total of 5,547 media mentions, 316 more than the second-ranked Conference Board. These organizations were followed by C.D. Howe and the Canada West Foundation, which received third and fourth place rankings respectively. Other institutes that fared well in media exposure were the Calgary-based Pembina Institute, the CCPA, and the IRPP (see Appendix 4). From 2009–17, the rankings among the top Canadian think tanks reveal some movement, but overall, the pattern remains unchanged (see Appendix 4). The Conference Board of Canada returned to a first-place ranking with 7,549 media mentions, followed by the Fraser Institute (5,175), C.D. Howe (4,716), the CCPA (2,378), and the Canada West Foundation (948). On the CBC and CTV national evening newscasts during this period, the Conference Board ranked first, followed by the Fraser Institute, and the CCPA. And on CBC Radio, it was the Fraser Institute (with 39 mentions) barely edging out the Conference Board (with 37 mentions). Not surprisingly, the same group of think tanks received the lion's share of references in the various newspapers and other media included in the study.

What factors could account for these rankings? Why do the media rely disproportionately on four or five policy institutes? A number of possible explanations are worth exploring. A useful point of departure is to consider when the institutes generating the most media attention were created, since one might expect the more established think tanks to attract more exposure. Of the five institutes registering the highest media ranking between 1985 and 1999, the oldest is the CTF, established in 1945, followed by the Conference Board (1954), the Economic Council (1963), the C.D. Howe Institute (1973), and the Fraser Institute (1974). Only Fraser, C.D. Howe, and the Conference Board are ranked among the top five think tanks in the two more recent time periods studied (table 5.4).

The longevity of an institute may go some way to establishing its legitimacy and credibility in the policy-making community, but even possessing this valuable currency does not appear to be a crucial factor in attracting media attention, a finding consistent with Weaver and Rich's study of US think tanks. Several policy institutes, including the Canadian Council on Social Development (CCSD, 1920) and the Canadian Institute of International Affairs (CIIA, 1928, now the Canadian International Council), with considerably lower media rankings, predate C.D. Howe, Fraser, and the Conference Board by decades.

Table 5.3
References to Selected Canadian Think Tanks on CBC Radio, 1988–96

Institute	*Total*
C.D. Howe Institute	110
Fraser Institute	58
Economic Council of Canada	43
Canadian Institute of Strategic Studies	27
Caledon Institute of Social Policy	21
Canadian Centre for Policy Alternatives	21
Conference Board of Canada	18
Mackenzie Institute	18
Canada West Foundation	14
Science Council of Canada	14
National Council of Welfare	13
North-South Institute	12
Canadian Council on Social Development	10
Institute for Research on Public Policy	10
Pearson-Shoyama Institute	10
Canadian Tax Foundation	8
Canadian Institute for International Peace and Security	7
Canadian Council for International Peace and Security[1]	7
Canadian Institute of International Affairs	2
Parliamentary Centre	2
Public Policy Forum	2
Canadian Policy Research Networks, Inc.[2]	–

Source: These data were obtained from the CBC Radio Archives, Toronto. In 1994, the CBC introduced a new computer system (Prolog) for logging citations on newscasts and radio talk shows. Though more comprehensive in scope than the previous database, the majority of institutes in this table could not be accessed by Prolog. As a result, this table underestimates citations. The trends that can be observed, however, provide an indication of think tank visibility on radio programs.

1 Includes data for its two predecessors, Canadian Centre for Arms Control and Disarmament (CCACD) and Centre for Global Security.

2 Data not included.

The size of an institute's budget, which in turn influences how many staff it employs and the range of expertise it offers, may provide a more compelling explanation. The Conference Board, the largest policy institute in Canada, with 200 employees, ranks first, with an annual budget of more than $40 million, close to ten times that of the majority of Canadian think tanks. With the exception of CIGI, which boasts a comparable budget, but far fewer staff, and the Winnipeg-based International Institute for Sustainable Development, which has a comparable number of staff, but less than half the financial resources, only a handful of other institutes

Table 5.3.1
References to Selected Canadian Think Tanks on CBC Radio, 1997–2016

Institute	*Total*
Fraser Institute	39
Conference Board of Canada	37
Canadian Centre for Policy Alternatives	30
C.D. Howe Institute	22
Canada West Foundation	22
Institute for Research on Public Policy	16
Public Policy Forum	15
Canadian Council for Int'l Peace & Security	9
Canadian Policy Research Networks	5
Mackenzie Institute	5
North-South Institute	4
Parliamentary Centre	2
Caledon Institute of Social Policy	1
Canadian Institute of Strategic Studies	1
Canadian Tax Foundation	1
National Council on Welfare	1
Canadian Council on Social Development	0
Canadian Council for Int'l Peace & Security	0
Canadian Institute of International Affairs	0
Pearson-Shoyama Institute	0
Economic Council of Canada	0
Science Council of Canada	0
Total	210

Source: Eureka.cc (formerly Newscan), via York Library.

have budgets larger than $5 million, a paltry amount when compared with high-profile US think tanks. These include: the Asia-Pacific Foundation, the CTF, the Fraser Institute, the CCPA, and the Canadian Institute for Advanced Research.

There appears to be a strong relationship between high media visibility and the amount of funding upon which think tanks draw; however, there are some notable anomalies. The C.D. Howe Institute, which ranked third overall in visibility between 2009–17, has a budget of $3.5–4 million, comparable to that of several less visible institutes, including the Parliamentary Centre, the Canadian International Council, and the now defunct North-South Institute.

Closely related to the budgets of institutes is the number of staff they employ. Again, the Conference Board ranks first. It employs over 200 people, who provide research and analysis on economic and social issues.[12] The Conference Board's ability to construct economic forecasting models is particularly attractive to government and to the large number

Table 5.4
Media Citations for Selected Canadian Think Tanks, 1985–99

	Newspaper Total[1]	*Globe and Mail*[2]	CBC *Radio*[3]	CBC TV *News*[4]	CTV *News*[4]	*Total*	*Rank*
Conference Board of Canada	6,289	2,204	18	57	59	8,627	1
Fraser Institute	3,790	761	58	47	27	4,683	2
C.D. Howe Institute	3,053	1,290	110	55	45	4,553	3
Economic Council of Canada	2,033	1,318	43	40	17	3,451	4
Canadian Tax Foundation	999	473	8	22	4	1,506	5
Science Council of Canada	714	618	14	12	4	1,362	6
National Council of Welfare	952	286	13	13	9	1,273	7
Canadian Council on Social Development	885	354	10	19	4	1,272	8
Institute for Research on Public Policy	747	347	10	3	2	1,109	9
Canada West Foundation	824	210	14	16	5	1,069	10
Canadian Institute of Strategic Studies	770	162	27	33	15	1,007	11
North-South Institute	497	279	12	3	0	791	12
Canadian Centre for Policy Alternatives	629	118	21	13	4	785	13
Canadian Institute for International Peace and Security	558	119	7	10	3	697	14
Canadian Council for International Peace and Security[5]	479	173	7	0	0	659	15
Public Policy Forum	490	91	2	1	0	584	16
Caledon Institute of Social Policy	381	124	21	5	0	531	17
Canadian Institute of International Affairs	360	159	2	5	3	529	18
Mackenzie Institute	291	42	18	7	8	366	19
Canadian Policy Research Networks, Inc.	136	60	0	2	1	199	20
Pearson-Shoyama Institute	154	21	10	0	0	185	21
Parliamentary Centre	60	30	2	0	0	92	22

1 *Source*: Infomart, includes citations from January 1985 to December 1999 for papers as described in Appendix 1.

2 *Source*: Info Globe, includes citations from January 1985 to December 1999.

3 *Source*: CBC Radio Archives; includes citations from January 1988 to December 1996.

4 *Source*: National Media Archive, Fraser Institute; includes citations and appearances from January 1988 to December 1999.

5 Includes references to its two predecessors, CCACD and Canadian Centre for Global Security, for all media citations, with the exception of CBC and CTV National News.

Table 5.4.1
Media Citations for Selected Canadian Think Tanks, 2000–2016

Institute	*Newspapers Total***	*Globe and Mail***	CBC *Radio**	CBC TV *News**	CTV *News**	*Total*	*Rank*
Conference Board of Canada	5,586	1,565	19	66	118	7,354	1
Fraser Institute	5,904	486	11	36	71	6,508	2
C.D. Howe Institute	4,736	1,145	14	24	18	5,937	3
Canada West Foundation	3,870	146	3	6	16	4,041	4
Canadian Centre for Policy Alternatives	3,104	328	17	28	36	3,513	5
Institute for Research on Public Policy	1,708	218	7	2	7	1,942	6
Public Policy Forum	1,419	111	7	11	20	1,568	7
Canadian Policy Research Networks	876	9	0	0	0	885	8
Mackenzie Institute	265	14	0	5	18	302	9
Caledon Institute of Social Policy	262	36	1	0	0	299	10
Economic Council of Canada	186	91	0	0	4	281	11
Canadian Tax Foundation	190	40	0	0	0	230	12
North-South Institute	194	19	1	0	1	215	13
Parliamentary Centre	164	7	0	0	0	171	14
Canadian Council on Social Development	142	13	0	0	1	156	15
Science Council of Canada	46	4	0	0	0	50	16
National Council of Welfare	40	2	0	0	0	42	17
Pearson-Shoyama Institute	12	0	0	0	0	12	18
Canadian Institute of International Affairs	7	4	0	0	0	11	19
Canadian Institute of Strategic Studies/ Canadian International Council	6	1	0	0	0	7	20
Canadian Council for International Peace and Security	4	1	0	0	0	5	21
Canadian Institute for International Peace and Security	3	0	0	0	0	3	22

**Source:* Eureka.cc.

***Source:* Factiva.com.

of corporations who form part of its extensive client list. The Conference Board's size may help to explain why, at times, it has attracted almost twice the amount of media exposure as the Fraser Institute. It might also explain why several other institutes considered large by Canadian standards often find themselves in the media spotlight – organizations such as the Fraser Institute, which employs 55 staff, the CCPA (40), C.D. Howe (25), the Public Policy Forum (22), and IRPP (15). However, size cannot explain, for instance, why the International Institute for Sustainable Development which, as noted, is as large as the Conference Board, with a healthy budget, receives a fraction of the media attention paid to the Conference Board, nor can it explain why CIGI, an organization with more than 80 people and a budget hovering around $40 million, also garners only modest media exposure.[13] With some exceptions then, the size of an institute's budget and the number of staff it employs may explain why some generate more exposure than others.[14]

At the risk of stating the obvious, with limited funding and few staff resources on which to draw, the ability of think tanks to undertake extensive long-range research projects and/or organize regular conferences and seminars will be compromised, which in turn will likely affect the amount of media attention they attract. Moreover, with limited funds, it is unlikely that think tanks will have the luxury of employing communications or media/public relations specialists who have the experience to effectively market the products institutes produce; by contrast, well-heeled think tanks can and often do hire individuals with these backgrounds to enhance their profile. The Heritage Foundation, the Brookings Institution, the Hoover Institution, and the American Enterprise Institute, to name a few, have well-established public relations departments. With few exceptions, however, this does not appear to be the pattern in Canadian think tanks; even policy institutes with reasonably high budgets by Canadian standards rarely assign more than a fraction of it for marketing purposes, although this may be changing.[15]

A related and perhaps more important consideration in discussing media exposure is the diversity of an institute's research; think tanks that offer expertise in a wide range of policy areas are likely to capture more media exposure than those that focus on only one or two. For example, the Ottawa-based Vanier Institute of the Family and the Caledon Institute may be asked to comment on how proposed legislation on child or seniors' benefits will affect Canadian families, but they are unlikely to be invited to comment on constitutional reform, political scandals, or the general state of Canadian parliamentary democracy, issues likely to find broader interest in the media. The extent to which think tanks tap into their areas of expertise in novel ways to engage the public and other stakeholders is also a consideration in explaining their success in courting the media. For instance, the Fraser Institute's annual pronouncement of Tax Freedom Day, the day Canadians can hold onto their hard-earned money instead of turning it over to the Canada Revenue Agency, results in dozens of media citations for the free-market-oriented institute each year.

The mandate of institutes may go a step further in accounting for why some organizations receive more exposure than others and why some institutes receive more media attention in specific regions of the country. The Calgary-based Canada West Foundation is a case in point. Established to study the social and economic characteristics of the western and northern regions of Canada and to assess the West's economic and social contributions, the Canada West Foundation, not surprisingly, receives the majority of its media exposure in western newspapers, such as the *Calgary Herald* (309) and the *Edmonton Journal* (225) (table 5.5).These two papers combined account for close to 65 per cent of Canada West's exposure in Canadian newspapers (*The Globe and Mail* excluded). In *The Globe and Mail* (table 5.6), which, until recently, was regarded as Canada's only national newspaper, the Canada West Foundation received just over 2 per cent of all references to think tanks. The Canada West Foundation's emphasis on regional issues may also explain its limited exposure relative to other think tanks on the CTV (2.4 per cent) and CBC (4.4 per cent) national evening news (tables 5.7 and 5.8).

The Canada West Foundation continues to generate considerable exposure in western-based newspapers. Indeed, between 2000 and 2017, 33.6 per cent of its print media mentions came from the *Edmonton Journal* and *Calgary Herald,* but as table 5.5.1 reveals, compared with two decades ago, the foundation is attracting a great deal of media interest in other provinces, including Ontario (*Toronto Sun*) and Nova Scotia (*Halifax Daily News*). Still, its exposure in *The Globe and Mail* and on CTV and CBC television evening news remains modest (see tables 5.6.1, 5.7.1, and 5.8.1).

Despite these findings, being located outside the nation's capital need not be a disadvantage for think tanks seeking media visibility. A very different pattern emerges in Canada than in the US; ranked second in overall visibility, Vancouver's Fraser Institute is close to 3,000 miles from Ottawa; the C.D. Howe Institute, the third-ranked institute, is in downtown Toronto. Meanwhile, several think tanks based in Ottawa, including the Parliamentary Centre, the Caledon Institute, and the Pearson-Shoyama Institute, have limited public visibility. Thus, it may be that a determining factor in generating media exposure for Canadian think tanks is not their location but their mandate and resources.

Think tank resources are important when considering their media visibility, but so too are other, less tangible, factors. The priorities think

Table 5.5
Newspaper Citations for Selected Canadian Think Tanks, 1985–99

	Ottawa Citizen	*Toronto Star*	*Montreal Gazette*	*Vancouver Sun*	*Edmonton Journal*	*Calgary Herald*	*Halifax Daily News*	*Toronto Sun*	*Total*
Conference Board of Canada	1,261	984	961	780	787	801	436	279	6,289
Fraser Institute	549	455	366	1,007	480	482	187	264	3,790
C.D. Howe Institute	619	652	581	346	332	275	155	93	3,053
Economic Council of Canada	473	534	341	216	177	162	76	54	2,033
Canadian Tax Foundation	219	165	164	115	115	128	50	43	999
National Council of Welfare	177	214	129	118	133	119	31	31	952
Canadian Council on Social Development	208	193	138	92	94	115	31	14	885
Canada West Foundation	70	51	67	76	225	309	17	9	824
Canadian Institute of Strategic Studies	161	150	70	104	90	99	60	36	770
Institute for Research on Public Policy	216	116	170	90	69	54	24	8	747
Science Council of Canada	234	184	94	85	60	38	16	3	714
Canadian Centre for Policy Alternatives	136	97	65	153	64	58	46	10	629
Canadian Institute for International Peace and Security	183	123	59	65	59	55	11	3	558
North-South Institute	173	123	98	37	32	24	7	3	497
Public Policy Forum	228	34	56	20	73	56	9	14	490
Canadian Council for International Peace and Security[1]	127	170	48	55	38	26	11	4	479
Caledon Institute of Social Policy	105	74	37	38	42	44	29	12	381
Canadian Institute of International Affairs	93	71	103	28	30	19	10	6	360
Mackenzie Institute	41	58	19	67	35	21	10	40	291
Pearson-Shoyama Institute	20	56	2	6	3	66	1	0	154
Canadian Policy Research	29	28	10	12	37	12	6	2	136
Parliamentary Centre	24	9	3	6	9	6	2	1	60
Total	5,346	4,541	3,581	3,516	2,984	2,969	1,225	929	25,091

Source: Infomart.

1 Includes references to its two predecessors, the Canadian Centre for Arms Control and the Disarmament and Canadian Centre for Global Security.

Table 5.5.1
Newspaper Citations for Selected Canadian Think Tanks, 2000–2017

Institute	*Globe and Mail*	*Toronto Star*	*Toronto Sun***	*Montreal Gazette*	*Vancouver Sun*	*Edmonton Journal*	*Calgary Herald*	*Halifax Daily News***	*Ottawa Citizen*	*National Post*	*Total*
Conference Board of Canada	2,499	1,075	976	830	1,119	843	1,346	97	1,030	1,288	11,103
Fraser Institute	950	455	991	484	1,324	435	1,393	992	671	2,049	9,744
C.D. Howe Institute	1,724	651	982	349	506	339	418	995	507	1,763	8,234
Institute for Research on Public Policy	352	174	2,165	109	131	94	121	2,220	197	356	5,919
Canadian Centre for Policy Alternatives	491	775	1,000	155	598	172	207	1,000	284	218	4,900
Canada West Foundation	377	87	998	53	230	476	1,107	999	134	238	4,699
Public Policy Forum	173	100	1,839	47	46	48	31	998	257	102	3,641
Canadian Policy Research Networks	103	50	647	14	27	18	21	1,485	75	29	2,469
Mackenzie Institute	48	34	754	15	48	36	51	767	123	134	2,010
Canadian Institute of Strategic Studies	57	20	589	27	31	38	29	598	127	87	1,603
Canadian Tax Foundation	105	32	552	10	27	15	16	621	48	70	1,496
Canadian Council on Social Development	48	68	567	18	24	15	29	599	59	33	1,460
Canadian Council for Int'l Peace & Security	84	87	550	19	21	21	11	588	0	0	1,381
Caledon Institute of Social Policy	73	67	362	8	21	15	12	382	24	17	981
North-South Institute	53	41	311	6	6	7	1	343	42	9	819
Canadian Institute of International Affairs	40	15	267	10	8	6	13	276	30	37	702
Economic Council of Canada	62	14	201	1	7	5	9	222	12	26	559
Parliamentary Centre	18	5	232	0	1	5	1	247	24	21	554
National Council on Welfare	6	13	100	0	3	2	5	110	1	5	245
Science Council of Canada	5	4	69	0	1	3	1	74	3	11	171
Canadian Institute for Int'l Peace & Security	11	4	69	1	2	1	1	20	3	11	123
Pearson-Shoyama Institute	0	1	16	0	0	0	0	17	7	0	41
Total	7,279	3,772	14,237	2,156	4,181	2,594	4,823	13,650	3,658	6,504	62,854

Source: Factiva.

***Source:* LexisNexis.

Table 5.6
Globe and Mail Citations for Selected Canadian Think Tanks, 1985–99

Institute	*Total*
Conference Board of Canada	2,204
Economic Council of Canada	1,318
C.D. Howe Institute	1,290
Fraser Institute	761
Science Council of Canada	618
Canadian Tax Foundation	473
Canadian Council on Social Development	354
Institute for Research on Public Policy	347
National Council of Welfare	286
North-South Institute	279
Canada West Foundation	210
Canadian Council for International Peace and Security[1]	173
Canadian Institute of Strategic Studies	162
Canadian Institute of International Affairs	159
Caledon Institute of Social Policy	124
Canadian Institute for International Peace and Security	119
Canadian Centre for Policy Alternatives	118
Public Policy Forum	91
Canadian Policy Research Networks, Inc.	60
Mackenzie Institute	42
Parliamentary Centre	30
Pearson-Shoyama Institute	21

Source: Info Globe.

1 Includes references to its two predecessors, CCACD and CGS.

tanks assign to attracting media attention may also help explain why some think tanks receive more exposure than others. For instance, for institutes committed to shaping the parameters of national public debates, gaining access to the media will undoubtedly be a high priority. It would, after all, be difficult for think tanks to influence public opinion without publicizing their ideas in print or on the air. As a result, individuals from some think tanks, including the Fraser Institute and the Canadian Institute of Strategic Studies, like their counterparts in the Heritage Foundation and CSIS, welcome opportunities to appear on network newscasts. These and other think tanks also regularly submit op-ed articles to newspapers, in the hope of stimulating public debate.

A less tangible factor, but one that nevertheless deserves consideration, is how the political environment in Canada can enhance or diminish the profile of some think tanks. For instance, as Prime Minister Brian Mulroney moved closer to adopting the type of neoconservative agenda that his close friends and allies Ronald Reagan and George H.W. Bush

Table 5.6.1
Globe and Mail Citations for Selected Canadian Think Tanks, 2000–2016

Institute	*Total*
Conference Board of Canada	2,400
C.D. Howe Institute	1,724
Fraser Institute	950
Canadian Centre for Policy Alternatives	491
Canada West Foundation	377
Institute for Research on Public Policy	352
Public Policy Forum	173
Canadian Tax Foundation	105
Canadian Policy Research Networks	103
Canadian Council for Int'l Peace & Security	84
Caledon Institute of Social Policy	73
Economic Council of Canada	62
Canadian Institute of Strategic Studies	57
North-South Institute	53
Canadian Council on Social Development	48
Mackenzie Institute	48
Canadian Institute of International Affairs	40
Parliamentary Centre	18
Canadian Institute for Int'l Peace & Security	11
National Council on Welfare	6
Science Council of Canada	5
Pearson-Shoyama Institute	0
Total	7,180

Source: Factiva.
Search parameters: 1 January 2000–1 January 2017.

were adopting south of the border, the policy recommendations of the free-market-oriented Fraser Institute also began to receive more public attention. The amount of coverage an institute receives can thus also be influenced by the political climate of the day.

Numerous other factors can influence the media ranking of policy institutes. Although only passing reference has been made to media bias (whether regional, ideological, or both), it may also be an important consideration when interpreting the data on public visibility. While many factors, such as an institute's diversity of size and research, may also explain why some are called upon to advise government departments or to testify before parliamentary committees, other factors, which will be explored below, might account for why think tanks with limited media visibility nonetheless appear to be actively engaged in critical stages of the policy-making process.

Table 5.7
CTV National Evening News Citations for Selected Canadian Think Tanks, 1988–99

Institute	*1988*	*1989*	*1990*	*1991*	*1992*	*1993*	*1994*	*1995*	*1996*	*1997*	*1998*	*1999*	*Total*
Conference Board of Canada	1	5	7	9	7	7	5	4	5	3	3	3	59
C.D. Howe Institute	1	0	2	6	2	3	3	0	1	15	11	1	45
Fraser Institute	0	1	0	2	4	2	6	5	2	1	2	2	27
Economic Council of Canada	3	2	4	2	4	0	0	1	1	0	0	0	17
Canadian Institute of Strategic Studies	0	2	5	3	3	0	2	0	0	0	0	0	15
National Council of Welfare	0	0	2	1	0	1	0	1	1	0	2	1	9
Mackenzie Institute	0	0	0	1	0	0	0	2	0	3	2	0	8
Canada West Foundation	0	0	0	3	2	0	0	0	0	0	0	0	5
Canadian Tax Foundation	0	0	1	0	0	1	0	2	0	0	0	0	4
Science Council of Canada	0	0	0	0	2	0	0	0	0	0	2	0	4
Canadian Centre for Policy Alternatives	0	0	0	0	0	1	0	2	0	0	0	1	4
Canadian Council of Social Development	0	1	0	0	0	2	0	0	0	0	0	1	4
Canadian Institute for International Peace and Security	0	0	2	1	0	0	0	0	0	0	0	0	3
Institute for Research on Public Policy	0	0	2	0	0	0	0	0	0	0	0	0	2
Canadian Institute of International Affairs	0	0	0	0	0	0	0	0	1	0	0	2	3
Canadian Policy Research Networks, Inc.	0	0	0	0	0	0	0	0	0	0	1	0	1
Canadian Council for International Peace and Security[1]	0	0	0	0	0	0	0	0	0	0	0	0	0
Caledon Institute of Social Policy	0	0	0	0	0	0	0	0	0	0	0	0	0
North-South Institute	0	0	0	0	0	0	0	0	0	0	0	0	0
Parliamentary Centre	0	0	0	0	0	0	0	0	0	0	0	0	0
Pearson-Shoyama Institute	0	0	0	0	0	0	0	0	0	0	0	0	0
Public Policy Forum[2]	0	0	0	0	0	0	0	0	0	0	0	0	0
Total	5	11	25	28	24	17	16	17	11	22	23	11	210

Source: The National Media Archive, Fraser Institute.

1 Data do not include information on its two predecessors, the Canadian Centre for Arms Control and the Disarmament and Canadian Centre for Global Security.

2 Data not included.

Table 5.7.1

CTV National Evening News Citations for Selected Canadian Think Tanks, 2000–2016

Institute	*2000*	*2001*	*2002*	*2003*	*2004*	*2005*	*2006*	*2007*	*2008*	*2009*	*2010*	*2011*	*2012*	*2013*	*2014*	*2015*	*2016*	*Totals*
Conference Board of Canada	2	7	0	3	1	1	6	2	11	11	3	10	3	4	7	8	8	87
Fraser Institute	1	1	2	4	3	1	0	0	2	0	0	0		3	1	21	2	41
Canadian Centre for Policy Alternatives	1	0	0	0	0	0	1	1	0	1	1	1	1	3	5	2	2	19
Mackenzie Institute	0	0	1	0	1	0	2	3	0	1	0	1	1	0	0	0	0	10
Canadian Institute of Strategic Studies	0	2	2	2	0	2	0	0	0	0	0	0	0	0	0	0	0	8
Canada West Foundation	1	0	1	0	0	1	0	0	0	0	0	0	0	1	1	0	2	7
Canadian Council for Int'l Peace & Security	0	0	1	0	0	0	0	1	0	0	1	0	0	0	1	0	1	5
C.D. Howe Institute	0	0	2	0	0	0	0	1	0	0	0	0	0	0	0	0	2	5
Canadian Council on Social Development	2	0	0	2	0	0	0	0	0	0	0	0	0	0	0	0	0	4
Institute for Research on Public Policy	0	0	0	0	1	0	0	0	0	0	0	0	0	0	0	1	0	2
North-South Institute	2	0	0	0	0	0	0	0	0	0	0	0	0	0	0	0	0	2
Canadian Institute for Int'l Peace & Security	0	1	0	0	0	0	0	0	0	0	0	0	0	0	0	0	0	1
Canadian Policy Research Networks	0	0	0	0	1	0	0	0	0	0	0	0	0	0	0	0	0	1
National Council on Welfare	0	1	0	0	0	0	0	0	0	0	0	0	0	0	0	0	0	1
Caledon Institute of Social Policy	0	0	0	0	0	0	0	0	0	0	0	0	0	0	0	0	0	0
Canadian Institute of International Affairs	0	0	0	0	0	0	0	0	0	0	0	0	0	0	0	0	0	0
Canadian Tax Foundation	0	0	0	0	0	0	0	0	0	0	0	0	0	0	0	0	0	0
Economic Council of Canada	0	0	0	0	0	0	0	0	0	0	0	0	0	0	0	0	0	0
Parliamentary Centre	0	0	0	0	0	0	0	0	0	0	0	0	0	0	0	0	0	0
Pearson-Shoyama Institute	0	0	0	0	0	0	0	0	0	0	0	0	0	0	0	0	0	0
Public Policy Forum	0	0	0	0	0	0	0	0	0	0	0	0	0	0	0	0	0	0
Science Council of Canada	0	0	0	0	0	0	0	0	0	0	0	0	0	0	0	0	0	0
Total	9	12	9	11	7	5	9	8	13	13	5	12	5	11	15	32	17	193

Source: Eureka.cc (formerly Newscan), via York Library.

Table 5.8

CBC TV National Evening News Citations for Selected Canadian Think Tanks, 1988–99

Institute	*1988*	*1989*	*1990*	*1991*	*1992*	*1993*	*1994*	*1995*	*1996*	*1997*	*1998*	*1999*	*Total*
Conference Board of Canada	5	7	7	7	9	6	1	3	3	4	3	2	57
C.D. Howe Institute	2	3	4	5	2	4	7	4	4	11	7	2	55
Fraser Institute	0	2	0	5	3	8	4	9	6	2	4	4	47
Economic Council of Canada	9	1	4	12	7	2	1	2	1	0	0	1	40
Canadian Institute of Strategic Studies	1	1	5	12	5	4	2	1	1	0	0	1	33
Canadian Tax Foundation	0	2	0	1	0	5	3	4	1	3	1	2	22
Canada West Foundation	0	0	2	5	5	1	0	0	2	0	1	0	16
Canadian Council on Social Development	1	1	0	1	5	3	2	0	2	0	1	3	19
Canadian Centre for Policy Alternatives	0	2	0	4	1	1	0	2	2	0	1	0	13
National Council of Welfare	2	2	1	1	1	1	0	0	1	1	3	0	13
Science Council of Canada	1	0	0	4	2	0	0	0	0	2	3	0	12
Canadian Institute for International Peace and Security	0	2	4	3	1	0	0	0	0	0	0	0	10
Mackenzie Institute	0	0	0	0	1	0	1	1	1	1	1	1	7
Canadian Institute of International Affairs	1	0	0	0	1	0	0	0	2	1	0	0	5
Caledon Institute of Social Policy	0	0	0	0	0	0	2	0	1	0	1	1	5
Institute for Research on Public Policy	1	0	2	0	0	0	0	0	0	0	0	0	3
North-South Institute	0	0	0	0	0	1	0	1	1	0	0	0	3
Canadian Council for International Peace and Security[1]	0	0	0	0	0	0	0	0	0	0	0	0	0
Canadian Policy Research Networks, Inc.	0	0	0	0	0	0	0	0	0	0	0	2	2
Parliamentary Centre	0	0	0	0	0	0	0	0	0	0	0	0	0
Pearson-Shoyama Institute	0	0	0	0	0	0	0	0	0	0	0	0	0
Public Policy Forum[2]	0	0	0	0	0	0	0	0	0	0	0	1	1
Total	23	23	29	60	43	36	23	27	28	25	26	20	363

Source: The National Media Archive, Fraser Institute.

1 Data for CCACD and Centre for Global Security, the two predecessors of the Canadian Council for International Peace and Security (CCIPS), not included.

2 Data not included.

Table 5.8.1

CBC TV National Evening News Citations for Selected Canadian Think Tanks, 2000–2016

Institute	*2000*	*2001*	*2002*	*2003*	*2004*	*2005*	*2006*	*2007*	*2008*	*2009*	*2010*	*2011*	*2012*	*2013*	*2014*	*2015*	*2016*	*Total*
Conference Board of Canada	2	7	3	2	1	1	13	6	18	16	6	23	8	7	13	20	28	174
Fraser Institute	0	0	3	3	4	5	4	3	1	9	4	4	1	2	3	4	9	59
Canadian Centre for Policy Alternatives	0	0	3	1	0	2	1	2	4	2	2	1	3	2	7	5	6	41
C.D. Howe Institute	0	0	1	0	1	0	3	0	2	2	2	2	2	2	5	9	4	35
Canada West Foundation	0	0	3	2	6	1	6	2	0	0	0	0	0	1	2	0	3	26
Mackenzie Institute	0	0	4	4	1	2	6	2	0	2	2	1	0	0	0	0	0	24
Canadian Institute of Strategic Studies	0	0	1	6	2	2	4	0	0	0	0	0	0	0	0	0	0	15
Public Policy Forum	0	0	0	1	1	0	1	0	0	4	1	0	2	0	0	1	3	14
Institute for Research on Public Policy	0	0	0	0	2	1	0	0	0	1	0	0	0	0	0	1	0	5
Canadian Policy Research Networks	0	0	1	0	0	0	2	1	0	0	0	0	0	0	0	0	0	4
Canadian Council on Social Development	0	0	1	0	1	0	0	0	0	0	0	0	0	0	0	0	0	2
Canadian Institute of International Affairs	0	0	0	1	0	0	0	0	0	0	0	0	0	0	0	0	0	1
Canadian Tax Foundation	0	0	1	0	0	0	0	0	0	0	0	0	0	0	0	0	0	1
North-South Institute	0	0	1	0	0	0	0	0	0	0	0	0	0	0	0	0	0	1
Caledon Institute of Social Policy	0	0	0	0	0	0	0	0	0	0	0	0	0	0	0	0	0	0
Canadian Council for Int'l Peace & Security	0	0	0	0	0	0	0	0	0	0	0	0	0	0	0	0	0	0
Canadian Institute for Int'l Peace & Security	0	0	0	0	0	0	0	0	0	0	0	0	0	0	0	0	0	0
Economic Council of Canada	0	0	0	0	0	0	0	0	0	0	0	0	0	0	0	0	0	0
National Council on Welfare	0	0	0	0	0	0	0	0	0	0	0	0	0	0	0	0	0	0
Parliamentary Centre	0	0	0	0	0	0	0	0	0	0	0	0	0	0	0	0	0	0
Pearson-Shoyama Institute	0	0	0	0	0	0	0	0	0	0	0	0	0	0	0	0	0	0
Science Council of Canada	0	0	0	0	0	0	0	0	0	0	0	0	0	0	0	0	0	0
Total	2	7	22	20	19	14	40	16	25	36	17	31	16	14	30	40	53	402

Source: Eureka.cc (formerly Newscan), via York Library.

Assessing Policy Relevance

The policy-making process consists of several stages, or cycles, including agenda setting, policy formulation, and policy implementation.[16] This section focuses on the involvement of think tanks during two stages of policy formulation – consultations with government departments and parliamentary testimony. Although it is difficult to weigh the relative importance of different stages of policy-making, it is still possible to make more informed judgments about the relevance of institutes during particular phases.

Think tanks may become involved in policy formulation in several ways. They may, for instance, distribute copies of their reports on an issue to policy-makers and bureaucrats, in the hope that their findings will have an impact. They may invite members of Parliament and the public service to participate in conferences and workshops or hold private meetings with government officials. Depending on their area and level of expertise, they may be called upon to consult with government departments or to testify before a parliamentary committee. At times, the federal government might also enlist the support of think tanks to organize public hearings on policy issues, a subject that we will return to in chapter 7. The data on think tank involvement during these particular stages of policy formulation may tell us little about the quality of their advice, or the frequency or intensity of their interaction, but it does show how active institutes have been in using these channels to convey their ideas.

As part of ongoing efforts to assess the policy capacity of the federal government, a task force, headed by Ivan Fellegi, chief statistician of Canada, and Ole Ingstrup, then principal of the Canadian Centre for Management and Development, was created in late 1994 to investigate the state of the external policy research community.[17] An umbrella group composed of assistant deputy ministers was then formed to recommend how to strengthen policy development and practices. The report, released in July 1997, made several recommendations on how to enhance the ability of government departments to generate their own policy research, including strengthening ties between federal departments and policy institutes. This recommendation was based in part on responses from a survey distributed to government departments that asked senior civil servants to provide the names of research institutes that assist them in policy development. This list, summarized in table 5.9, sheds some light on which think tanks have been called upon to consult with government departments. At the time of writing, an updated study on think tank consultations with government departments and agencies had yet to be released.

Some of the methodological weaknesses in how the data were gathered must be pointed out before discussing the ranking of institutes in

Table 5.9
Ranking Research Institute Consultations

Institute	*Number of Department Consulting Think Tanks*	*Departments*
Conference Board of Canada	9	Environment Canada, Department of Foreign Affairs and International Trade, Human Resources Development Canada, Industry Canada, National Defence, Natural Resources Canada, Canada Mortgage and Housing Corporation, Department of Finance, Canadian Heritage
Canadian Policy Research Networks, Inc.	6	Environment Canada, Human Resources Development Canada, Industry Canada, Citizenship and Immigration Canada, Health Canada, Department of Justice
Canadian Council on Social Development	5	Human Resources Development Canada, Citizenship and Immigration Canada, Indian Affairs and Northern Development, Canada Mortgage and Housing Corporation, Department of Finance
Caledon Institute of Social Policy	3	Human Resources Development Canada, Canada Mortgage and Housing Corporation, Department of Finance
C.D. Howe Institute	3	Environment Canada, Industry Canada, Department of Finance
Public Policy Forum	2	Environment Canada, Natural Resources Canada
Canadian Institute of Strategic Studies	2	Department of Foreign Affairs and International Trade, National Defence
Institute for Research on Public Policy	2	Industry Canada, Department of Finance
Fraser Institute	2	Industry Canada, Department of Finance
CIIA	1	Department of Foreign Affairs and International Trade

Source: Department of Finance, Umbrella Group on Policy Management, *Report.*

government consultations. Many of these weaknesses reflect the tremendous difficulty that policy-makers, not to mention scholars, encounter in trying to isolate the influence of think tanks from the influence of the multitude of other organizations that have vested interests in influencing policy-making. Thus, despite some apparent gaps in the questionnaire distributed to government departments, these data should not be considered unreliable, but suggestive and preliminary.

Table 5.10
Federal Government Departments Consulting with Selected Canadian Think Tanks

	Number of Departments	*Rank*
Conference Board of Canada	9	1
Canadian Policy Research Networks, Inc.	6	2
Canadian Council on Social Development	5	3
C.D. Howe Institute	3	4
Caledon Institute of Social Policy	3	4
Fraser Institute	2	5
Institute for Research on Public Policy	2	5
Canadian Institute of Strategic Studies	2	5
Public Policy Forum	2	5
Canada West Foundation	1	6
Canadian Institute of International Affairs	1	6
Economic Council of Canada	0	7
Canadian Tax Foundation	0	7
Science Council of Canada	0	7
National Council of Welfare	0	7
North-South Institute	0	7
Canadian Institute for International Peace and Security	0	7
Canadian Council for International Peace and Security	0	7
Canadian Centre for Policy Alternatives	0	7
Mackenzie Institute	0	7
Pearson-Shoyama Institute	0	7
Parliamentary Centre	0	7

Source: Department of Finance, Umbrella Group on Policy Management, *Report*.

While government departments were asked to provide a list of policy research organizations they turn to for advice and guidance (table 5.10), they were not asked several related questions critical for arriving at conclusions about the potential relevance of think tanks in policy-making. For instance, respondents were not asked what criteria they used to differentiate policy research organizations from other types of nongovernmental organizations, including interest groups, and advocacy bodies, that are also committed to influencing public opinion and public policy. In other words, did all the respondents agree what constituted a think tank or policy research organization? In the absence of a consensus among those who filled out the questionnaire, it is conceivable that senior bureaucratic officials consulted with institutions that are not widely regarded as think tanks. As a result, the lists that departments provided may not be entirely accurate. Furthermore, officials were not asked to comment on the frequency of consultations with institutes or the period over which the consultations took place. We are not told, for example, if Environment

Canada consulted with the Caledon Institute once or one hundred times during a particular period. We are not even told what policy issues these institutes were consulting on or the nature and products generated from these consultations. Did institutes submit extensive reports, policy briefs, or other kinds of publications? Were they widely circulated and discussed? More important, were their analyses and recommendations, assuming some were made, found to be very useful, moderately useful, or not useful at all? Responses to the last question would be particularly revealing in relation to the size and prominence of departments. Thus, having moderate influence in high-profile departments such as Finance or Global Affairs Canada may be more important for some think tanks than exercising considerable influence in a less visible department. Answers to these and other questions would provide a better sense of the data. In the absence of such information, however, we are left with only one indicator of relevance – the number of government departments that list policy research organizations as consultants.

On the basis of these data, problematic and preliminary as they are, we can again provide a simple ranking. As in many other categories, the Conference Board ranks first in government consultations (9), a reflection no doubt of its wide-ranging expertise. The Canadian Policy Research Networks, Inc., according to the survey, consulted with at least six departments, one consultation more than the Canadian Council on Social Development.[18] Of the remaining institutes in the study, the Caledon Institute of Social Policy and the C.D. Howe Institute had three consultations, one more than the Canadian Institute of Strategic Studies, the Institute for Research on Public Policy, the Public Policy Forum, and the Fraser Institute.

The number of departments that turn to particular policy institutes for assistance can be attributed to several factors. First and foremost, the think tanks' areas of expertise will determine a department's decision about which one to consult. It is unlikely that the Canada Mortgage and Housing Corporation would seek policy input from CISS (now housed at Canadian International Council [CIC]), which studies defence and foreign policy issues. A related factor is a department's perception of the quality of expertise offered by institutes. This in turn can be influenced by a host of other factors, including the personal and professional contacts think tank staff have established with senior public servants. Directors or staff of think tanks who previously served in government may thus be better positioned to foster close ties to the public service than those with limited knowledge or experience with, or in, the bureaucracy.

A more reliable set of data on the relevance of policy institutes could be obtained by tracking the number of appearances think tanks make before parliamentary committees. Providing testimony to a committee as it considers implementing or revising legislation affords think tanks an important opportunity to convey their recommendations directly to policy-makers. Extending invitations to members of think tanks to provide testimony can also be an indication of how useful or damaging policy-makers believe their input could be. After all, it would be naive to suggest that members sitting on legislative committees do not have political agendas when it comes to arriving at a witness list. Indeed, some members may go out of their way to ensure that policy experts from think tanks with well-known views on particular matters are either invited or intentionally ignored.

Individuals testifying before parliamentary committees (table 5.11) have either received a formal invitation to appear from the committee or have requested the opportunity to share their expertise. Committee members make the decision about who will be invited to appear, often in consultation with staff members and public servants.[19] Between 1980 and 1999, no policy institute appeared more often before parliamentary committees than the Economic Council of Canada, which registered 117 appearances (table 5.12), more than twice as many as the second-ranked institute, the Canadian Council on Social Development (57). It was followed by the Conference Board (44), the Fraser Institute (43), the North-South Institute (42), the Science Council of Canada (40), the C.D. Howe Institute and the Institute for Research on Public Policy (both had 38), and the National Council of Welfare (37). Eight other institutes registered ten or more appearances.

Over the past eighteen years (2000–17), a reshuffling in the rankings of think tanks testifying before parliamentary committees has occurred. Moreover, several think tank staffers are appearing in Parliament with greater regularity. During this period, experts from the Conference Board of Canada registered the largest number of parliamentary committee appearances with 785, over twice as many as the second-ranked Fraser Institute (369). Ironically, the third-place ranking went to the Economic Council of Canada (342), which was dissolved in 1993. Clearly, many experts who once worked at the ECC were identified in committee reports by their earlier affiliation. Staff from CISS also appeared over 300 times (310), and the now defunct National Council of Welfare had experts testify on 222 occasions. Eight other institutes in the table registered over 100 appearances, with the remaining organizations testifying between 1 and 99 times. Unlike the data on government consultants, the figures on parliamentary testimony reveal that far more policy institutes were represented at this stage of policy-making.

What factors influence how often think tanks appear before parliamentary committees? Again, the nature of their expertise, as well as their willingness and ability to invest the time and resources necessary to

Table 5.11
Parliamentary Committee Reports Consulted for Think Tank Testimony

HOUSE COMMITTEES

Aboriginal Affairs and International Development
Acid Rain (Sub-Committee for Fisheries and Forestry)
Agriculture
Alternative Energy and Oil Substitution
Arms Exports
Bill C–17 (Sub-Committee for Finance Committee)
Bill C–29: Public Sector Compensation Act
Business of Supply (Sub-Committee for Procedure and House Affairs)
Canadian Heritage
Canadian Institute for International Peace and Security
Canadian Security Intelligence Service Act and Security Offenses Act Review
Communication and Culture
Consumer and Corporate Affairs
Electoral Reform
Employment Opportunities for the 1980s
Energy, Mines and Resources Environment
Equality Rights (Sub-Committee for Justice and Legal Affairs)
Expenditure Priorities (Sub-Committee for Finance Committee)
External Affairs and International Trade
External Affairs and National Defence
Federal-Provincial Fiscal Arrangements
Finance, Trade and Economic Affairs
Government Operations
Health and Welfare
Human Resources and Development
Human Rights (Foreign Affairs and International Trade Committee)
Human Rights and Status of Disabled Persons
Immigration Consultants and Diminishing Returns (Citizenship and Immigration Committee)
Indian Affairs and Northern Development
Industry, Science and Technology, Regional and Northern Development
International Debt
International Development (Sub-Committee of Committee on External Affairs and National Defence)
International Financial Institutions (Sub-Committee for Finance Committee)
International Human Rights
International Trade (External Affairs and International Trade Committee)
Justice and Legal Affairs
Labour, Manpower and Immigration
Meech Lake Accord Proposed Companion Resolution
National Resources and Public Works
National Trading Corporation
North-South Relations
Peace Process in Central America
Pension Reform
Procedure and House Affairs

Table 5.11
Parliamentary Committee Reports Consulted for Think Tank Testimony *(continued)*

HOUSE COMMITTEES
Public Accounts
Reform of the House of Commons
Regional Development
Regulations and Competitiveness (Sub-committee for Finance Committee)
Regulatory Reform
Research, Science and Technology
Review of Employment Equity Act
Transport
Veterans Afairs
SENATE COMMITTEES
Agriculture and Forestry
Banking, Trade and Commerce
Bill C-21
Bill C-22
Canadian Security Intelligence Service
Energy and Natural Resources – Environment and Natural Resources
Fisheries
Foreign Affairs
Health, Welfare and Science
Mass Media
Meech Lake Constitutional Accord (Senate Submissions Group)
National Defence
National Finance
Northern Pipeline Poverty
Retirement Age Policies
Science Policy
Social Affairs, Science and Technology
Training and Employment (Sub-Committee of Social Affairs, Science and Technology Committee)
Transport and Communications
Veterans Affairs (Sub-Committee of Social Affairs, Science and Technology)
Youth
JOINT COMMITTEES
Canada's Defence Policies
Canada's International Relations
Regulations and Other Statutory Instruments
The 1987 Constitutional Accord

prepare testimony would have to be considered; proximity to Ottawa may be advantageous. The ideological orientation of committee members and their desire to invite like-minded think tanks to testify may also be

Table 5.12
Appearances by Selected Think Tanks before Parliamentary Committees, 1980–99

	Number of Appearances	*Rank*
Economic Council of Canada	117	1
Canadian Council on Social Development	57	2
Conference Board of Canada	44	3
Fraser Institute	43	4
North-South Institute	42	5
Science Council of Canada	40	6
C.D. Howe Institute	38	7
Institute for Research on Public Policy	38	7
National Council of Welfare	37	8
Parliamentary Centre	34	9
Canadian Centre for Policy Alternatives	26	10
Caledon Institute of Social Policy	23	11
Canadian Council for International Peace and Security[1]	20	12
Canadian Institute for International Peace and Security	19	13
Canadian Institute of Strategic Studies	15	14
Canada West Foundation	14	15
Canadian Policy Research Networks, Inc.	10	16
Canadian Institute of International Affairs	9	17
Canadian Tax Foundation	8	18
Mackenzie Institute	6	19
Public Policy Forum	4	20
Pearson-Shoyama Institute	4	20
Total	648	

Source: Parliamentary Committee Reports, Thirty-Second to Thirty-Sixth Parliament, First Session, 1980–99.

1 Includes references to its two predecessors, the Canadian Centre for Arms Control and Disarmament and the Canadian Centre for Global Security.

worth taking into account. In the United States, as noted, there has been a marked increase in the number of appearances before congressional committees by conservative think tanks since the Republicans assumed control of both Houses of Congress.[20] As gatekeepers, they have clearly made an effort to fill congressional hearings with analysts from avowedly conservative think tanks, including the Heritage Foundation, the American Enterprise Institute, and the libertarian Cato Institute. In Canada, however, there does not appear to be any relationship between the party in power and the ideological orientation of think tanks invited to testify. For instance, the Fraser Institute, not known for concealing its conservative leanings, appeared before parliamentary committees more often under the Liberal government of Jean Chrétien than under Prime Minister Mulroney's Conservatives (see tables 5.13, 5.14, and 5.15).

Table 5.12.1
Appearances by Selected Canadian Think Tanks before Parliametary Committees, 2000–2017

Institute	*Number of Appearances*	*Rank*
Conference Board of Canada	785	1
Fraser Institute	369	2
Economic Council of Canada	342	3
Canadian Institute of Strategic Studies	310	4
National Council on Welfare	222	5
Parliamentary Centre	195	6
Canadian Council on Social Development	185	7
Canadian Centre for Policy Alternatives	177	8
Canadian Tax Foundation	169	9
Science Council of Canada	163	10
Public Policy Forum	135	11
Institute for Research on Public Policy	134	12
Canada West Foundation	132	13
C.D. Howe Institute	99	14
Canadian Policy Research Networks	92	15
Canadian Institute of International Affairs	65	16
Canadian Council for Int'l Peace & Security	60	17
North-South Institute	35	18
Caledon Institute of Social Policy	27	19
Mackenzie Institute	13	20
Canadian Institute for Int'l Peace & Security	12	21
Pearson-Shoyama Institute	1	22

Source: Parliamentary Committee Reports.

Indeed, in the six years before the Harper Conservatives gained power (1999–2005), the Fraser Institute continued to appear on a regular basis before parliamentary committees. During this period, experts from Fraser testified seventy-six times (table 5.13.1), far more often than any other think tank that does not accept government funding. Ranked second in parliamentary testimony behind the Conference Board of Canada, and ahead of the now defunct National Council of Welfare, the Fraser Institute continued to be active before parliamentary committees during the Harper years (2006–15).

While the ideological orientation of political parties and think tanks may not help to determine why some policy institutes are invited to testify more regularly than others, some consideration should be given to the range of committees think tanks are qualified to appear before. The number of committees before which think tanks that have a narrow range of expertise could make presentations, such as the Canadian Global Affairs Institute (formerly the Canadian Defence and Foreign Affairs Institute) and the Mackenzie Institute, are rather limited. Nonetheless,

Table 5.13
Appearances of Institutes for House Committee Testimony, 1980–99, by Parliamentary Session

	Session				
	32 (14/4/80– 9/7/84)	*33 (5/11/84– 1/10/88)*	*34 (12/12/88– 8/9/93)*	*35 (17/1/94– 27/4/97)*	*36 (22/9/97– 18/9/99)*
Institute	*Liberal*	PC	PC	*Liberal*	*Liberal*
C.D. Howe Institute	1	3	8	7	6
Caledon Institute				10	7
Canada West Foundation			1	6	
Canadian Tax Foundation					5
CCIPS	1	3	5	1	
CCPA			3	7	11
CCSD	10	1	6	7	6
CIIA	2				1
CIIPS			12		
CISS	1	1	7		
Conference Board of Canada		3	7	4	3
CPRN			1	1	5
Economic Council of Canada	8	12	16		
Fraser Institute	1	3	8	10	9
IRPP	2	1	7		
Mackenzie Institute			1		
National Council of Welfare		3	6	2	4
North-South Institute	3	2	13	6	6
Parliamentary Centre	1			3	
Pearson-Shoyama Institute				2	
Public Policy Forum					1
Science Council of Canada	3	8	7		

Source: Parliamentary Committee Reports, 1980–99.

while they might appear before only a few committees, they may do so far more regularly than those institutes sharing their expertise with several committees. Much insight can be gained by focusing on the participation of think tanks before parliamentary committees, particularly high-profile committees; however, we cannot assume that all think tanks assign the same importance to using this channel to reach policy-makers: briefing members of Parliament may be a priority for some institutes, but it could also be a channel deliberately avoided by others. For instance, concerned about being perceived as a policy advocate, for many years the highly visible CTF made a conscious decision not to give testimony on a regular basis.[21] Between 1980–99, it made only eight appearances before committees. Interestingly enough, over the past two decades, CTF has clearly

Table 5.13.1
Appearances of Institutes for House Committee Testimony, 1999–2016, by Parliamentary Session

	36th Parliament 2nd Session 04/99–10/00	*37th Parliament 1st Session 01/01–09/02*	*37th Parliament 2nd Session 09/02–11/03*	*37th Parliament 3rd Session 02/04–05/04*	*38th Parliament 1st Session 10/04–11/05*	*39th Parliament 1st Session 04/06–09/07*
Institute	*Liberal*	*Liberal*	*Liberal*	*Liberal*	*Liberal*	*Conservative*
Conference Board of Canada	32	34	14	6	40	26
Fraser Institute	14	18	19	4	21	15
National Council on Welfare	15	6	6	2	5	4
Canadian Centre for Policy Alternatives	0	4	6	1	15	19
C.D. Howe Institute	7	8	6	4	11	14
Canadian Council on Social Development	2	4	9	4	6	3
Canada West Foundation	0	4	1	2	0	2
Canadian Tax Foundation	0	1	0	0	1	8
Public Policy Forum	4	5	2	1	5	3
Institute for Research on Public Policy	2	2	2	1	0	4
North-South Institute	0	3	0	0	0	0
Caledon Institute of Social Policy	0	2	0	0	0	4
Mackenzie Institute	0	7	0	0	0	0
Canadian Policy Research Networks	0	1	1	0	2	1
Parliamentary Centre	0	0	1	0	1	0
Economic Council of Canada	0	0	0	0	2	0
Canadian Council for International Peace and Security	0	0	0	0	0	0
Canadian Institute for International Peace and Security	0	0	1	0	1	0
Pearson-Shoyama Institute	0	1	0	0	0	0
Canadian Institute of International Affairs	0	0	0	0	0	0
Canadian Institute of Strategic Studies	0	0	0	0	0	0
Science Council of Canada	0	0	0	0	0	0
Totals	76	100	68	25	110	103

Source: Library of Parliament.

Note: No data for 36th Parliament session avaialble on Parliamentary database.

39th Parliament 2nd Session 10/07–09/08	*40th Parliament 1st Session 11/08–12/08*	*40th Parliament 2nd Session 01/09–12/09*	*40th Parliament 3rd Session 03/10–03/11*	*41st Parliament 1st Session 06/11–09/13*	*41st Parliament 2nd Session 10/13–08/15*	*42nd Parliament 1st Session 12/15–*	*Totals*
Conservative	*Conservative*	*Conservative*	*Conservative*	*Conservative*	*Conservative*	*Liberal*	
21	121	10	21	121	88	29	563
13	28	4	17	28	23	33	237
9	59	2	1	59	4	0	172
11	44	0	26	19	44	24	100
16	20	0	31	15	20	3	86
2	2	1	3	2	2	0	40
2	7	3	4	7	3	1	36
1	10	0	0	10	0	0	31
0	0	0	1	0	1	2	24
0	6	2	1	6	0	3	17
0	0	1	0	0	6	1	11
3	4	4	6	4	0	0	9
0	0	0	0	0	0	0	7
0	0	0	0	0	0	0	5
0	0	0	1	0	1	1	5
0	0	0	1	0	0	1	4
0	0	0	1	0	1	0	2
0	0	0	0	0	0	0	2
0	0	0	0	0	0	0	1
0	0	0	0	0	0	0	0
0	0	0	0	0	0	0	0
0	0	0	0	0	0	0	0
78	301	27	114	271	193	98	1,352

Table 5.14
Appearances of Institutes for Senate Committee Testimony, 1980–99, by Parliamentary Session

	Session				
	32 (14/4/80– 9/7/84)	*33 (5/11/84– 1/10/88)*	*34 (12/12/88– 8/9/93)*	*35 (17/1/94– 27/4/97)*	*36 (22/9/97– 18/9/99)*
Institution	*Liberal*	*PC*	*PC*	*Liberal*	*Liberal*
C.D. Howe Institute	3	3	4		1
Caledon Institute			5	1	
Canada West Foundation					
Canadian Tax Foundation	1		2		
CCIPS	1	3			1
CCPA			3		
CCSD		8	16		
CIIA			1		
CIIPS		4	2		
CISS	1		1		
Conference Board of Canada	5	4	15	2	
CPRN				2	1
Economic Council of Canada	22	18	37	2	
Fraser Institute	1	1	3	3	3
IRPP	4	3	19		
Mackenzie Institute		1	1		2
National Council of Welfare	2	7	12	1	
North-South Institute		3		3	
Parliamentary Centre	3	4	21		
Pearson-Shoyama Institute				2	
Public Policy Forum			2	1	
Science Council of Canada	9	5	7		

Source: Parliamentary Committee Reports, 1980–99.

had a change of heart, perhaps recognizing the importance of increasing its public profile in a more competitive market of ideas. From 1999 to 2017, the organization registered thirty-one appearances before committees in the House of Commons, and 138 in the Senate (tables 5.13.1 and 5.14.1).

Interpreting the Results: Comparing Public Visibility to Policy Relevance

To compare the public visibility and policy relevance of think tanks between 1989 and 2008, three Spearman's rank correlation coefficients were used to test the correlation between the following pairs of variables:

media ranking and parliamentary testimony, media ranking and government consultations, and government consultations and parliamentary testimony.[22] The results of the tests are shown in table 5.16. According to the tests, there is a strong correlation between media visibility and parliamentary testimony, but there is no correlation between media visibility and government consultations and between parliamentary testimony and government consultations.

What do the results of the tests tell us about the nature of think tank influence? Perhaps most important, they tell us that it should not be assumed that the most visible think tanks are necessarily the most influential and credible institutes in the policy-making process. It is important to recognize, as this chapter has shown, that the relevance or impact of think tanks varies at different stages of the policy cycle. Think tanks like the Cato Institute, the Fraser Institute, and the Public Policy Forum might be effective in shaping the national agenda or enlarging "the terms of political discourse," as Les Pal observes,[23] but they might be less influential in contributing to policy development at more formal stages, while, on the other hand, think tanks with more modest media profiles, such as RAND, the Caledon Institute of Social Policy, and the Canadian Council on Social Development, might play a more active role in more formal stages of policy formulation.

Monitoring how often think tanks are quoted in the media or provide testimony may not allow scholars to ascertain which think tanks are the most or least influential; indeed, such data may tell us very little about their impact. Nonetheless, collecting data on these and other indicators helps to shed light on where in the policy cycle think tanks appear to be most actively engaged, if they are engaged at all. If some think tanks devote little time and energy to conveying their views to the media, one could argue with some degree of confidence that their influence on public opinion is limited. After all, how can think tanks influence the way people think if the public is unaware of their views? Similarly, how can think tanks claim to have policy influence if they do not convey their ideas directly to policy-makers? However, by tracking which think tanks rely most heavily on the media to promote their views and which depend on other channels to market their ideas, we can look more closely at their involvement at different stages of the policy-making process.

In the following three chapters, I will take a closer look at how a select group of think tanks in the United States and Canada has sought to influence the policy-making environment and specific policy debates. Beginning with a detailed examination of the involvement of several American think tanks in presidential campaigns in chapter 6, I will explore how they have taken advantage of a critical opportunity to influence the policy direction of incoming presidents. In addition to identifying which

Table 5.14.1
Appearances of Institutes for Senate Committee Testimony, 1999–2016, by Parliamentary Session

	36th Parliament 2nd Session 04/99–10/00	*37th Parliament 1st Session 01/01–09/02*	*37th Parliament 2nd Session 09/02–11/03*	*37th Parliament 3rd Session 02/04–05/04*	*38th Parliament 1st Session 10/04–11/05*	*39th Parliament 1st Session 04/06–09/07*
Institute	*Liberal*	*Liberal*	*Liberal*	*Liberal*	*Liberal*	*Conservative*
C.D. Howe Institute	N/A	N/A	N/A	N/A	N/A	N/A
Caledon Institute of Social Policy	0	1	0	0	0	10
Canada West Foundation	6	0	2	2	0	12
Canadian Centre for Policy Alternatives	1	0	0	0	0	2
Canadian Council for International Peace and Security	0	0	0	0	0	0
Canadian Council on Social Development	N/A	N/A	N/A	N/A	N/A	N/A
Canadian Institute for International Peace and Security	N/A	N/A	N/A	N/A	N/A	N/A
Canadian Institute of International Affairs	1	0	3	1	0	0
Canadian Institute of Strategic Studies	1	2	0	0	0	0
Canadian Policy Research Networks	1	0	1	0	0	4
Canadian Tax Foundation	0	1	0	0	0	10
Conference Board of Canada	10	8	16	8	24	18
Economic Council of Canada	N/A	N/A	N/A	N/A	N/A	N/A
Fraser Institute	1	1	0	0	6	16
Institute for Research on Public Policy	3	2	1	1	4	8
Mackenzie Institute	0	0	2	0	0	0
National Council on Welfare	2	1	0	0	1	0
North-South Institute	0	0	1	0	1	0
Parliamentary Centre	1	2	1	0	2	1
Pearson-Shoyama Institute	0	0	0	0	0	0
Public Policy Forum	1	3	1	0	1	0
Science Council of Canada	N/A	N/A	N/A	N/A	N/A	N/A
Totals	28	21	28	12	39	81

Source: Library of Parliament.

Note: No data for 36th Parliament session avaialble on Parliamentary database.

Note: Senate of Canada website database no longer offers data prior to 40th Parliament, 3rd session – existing data above is a reflection of previous research on select institutes. https://sencanada.ca/en/In-The-Chamber/Debates/Search.

39th Parliament 2nd Session 10/07–09/08	*40th Parliament 1st Session 11/08–12/08*	*40th Parliament 2nd Session 01/09–12/09*	*40th Parliament 3rd Session 03/10–03/11*	*41st Parliament 1st Session 06/11–09/13*	*41st Parliament 2nd Session 10/13–08/15*	*42nd Parliament 1st Session 12/15–*	*Totals*
Conservative	*Conservative*	*Conservative*	*Conservative*	*Conservative*	*Conservative*	*Liberal*	
N/A	N/A	N/A	1	5	4	3	13
0	N/A	N/A	0	1	3	3	18
2	N/A	N/A	13	34	17	8	96
2	N/A	N/A	9	36	16	11	77
0	N/A	N/A	9	31	9	9	58
N/A	N/A	N/A	33	55	32	25	145
N/A	N/A	N/A	1	9	0	0	10
0	N/A	N/A	11	30	14	5	65
0	N/A	N/A	83	131	90	3	310
0	N/A	N/A	14	37	21	9	87
0	N/A	N/A	20	61	26	20	138
9	N/A	N/A	29	53	24	24	223
N/A	N/A	N/A	65	129	100	45	339
6	N/A	N/A	20	35	33	14	132
0	N/A	N/A	25	38	20	15	117
0	N/A	N/A	2	2	0	0	6
0	N/A	N/A	5	19	11	11	50
0	N/A	N/A	5	8	6	3	24
0	N/A	N/A	27	66	60	30	190
0	N/A	N/A	0	0	0	0	0
0	N/A	N/A	24	37	30	14	111
N/A	N/A	N/A	29	66	49	19	163
19	0	0	425	883	565	271	2,372

Table 5.15
Appearances of Institutes for Joint Committee Testimony, 1980–99, by Parliamentary Session

	Session				
	32 (14/4/80– 9/7/84)	*33 (5/11/84– 1/10/88)*	*34 (12/12/88– 8/9/93)*	*35 (17/1/94– 27/4/97)*	*36 (22/9/97– 18/9/99)*
Institute	*Liberal*	*PC*	*PC*	*Liberal*	*Liberal*
C.D. Howe Institute		2			
Caledon Institute					
Canada West Foundation	3	2		2	
Canadian Tax Foundation					
CCIPS		3		2	
CCPA		1		1	
CCSD	1	1	1		
CIIA		3		2	
CIIPS		1			
CISS		2		2	
Conference Board of Canada				1	
CPRN					
Economic Council of Canada	1		1		
Fraser Institute				1	
IRPP		2			
Mackenzie Institute				1	
National Council of Welfare					
North-South Institute		2		4	
Parliamentary Centre	1	1			
Pearson-Shoyama Institute					
Public Policy Forum					
Science Council of Canada			1		

Source: Parliamentary Committee Reports, 1980–99.
Data on testimony before joint committees of parliament not available for the period 2000–17.

Table 5.16
Spearman's Rank Correlation Coefficient Results

Pairs of variables	*Correlation coefficient*	*P*
Media citations vs. parliamentary testimony	0.664	<.0010
Media citations vs. government consultations	0.207	<.356
Parliamentary testimony vs. government consultations	0.169	<.451

Significant at p <.01.

think tanks have contributed ideas to presidential candidates, some consideration will also be given to why some candidates actively seek the advice of think tanks. Chapter 7 will focus on how a small group of Canadian think tanks became involved in a major policy debate in Canada – the Renewal of Canada Initiative – which was intended to generate public discussion about the future of constitutional reform. And chapter 8 will provide an overview of how a select group of think tanks on both sides of the border weighed in on discussions surrounding Keystone XL. Although one must be careful not to generalize about the impact of think tanks by relying on a handful of case studies, the following chapters will highlight the many different ways think tanks can make their presence felt.

CHAPTER SIX

On the Road to the White House: Presidential Candidates and the Think Tanks That Advised Them

In April 1998, Republican presidential candidate George W. Bush interrupted a fundraising trip for a gubernatorial candidate in Northern California to meet with several scholars from the Hoover Institution. The purpose of the meeting, which took place at the home of former secretary of state and Hoover fellow George Shultz, was to allow the governor of Texas to get acquainted with some of the nation's leading policy experts. Although Bush had little knowledge of the Hoover Institution or the work many of its scholars engaged in before accepting Shultz's invitation, his friendship with Hoover fellow and economist Michael Boskin may explain why Bush gravitated toward the California think tank.[1] As a result of the close to four-hour meeting, Bush "engaged twelve or so Hoover fellows to advise his presidential campaign on issues from taxation to welfare to foreign affairs."[2] In addition to relying heavily on scholars from the Hoover Institution to help educate him on the intricacies of domestic and foreign policy issues, Bush enlisted the support of several other policy experts, including his top economic adviser, Lawrence Lindsey, former Federal Reserve governor and fellow at the American Enterprise Institute, and Robert Zoellick, who stepped down as president of the Center for Strategic and International Studies after only four months to advise Bush.[3]

Bush's decision to turn to some of the nation's most prominent think tanks for policy advice is not surprising. Indeed, it has become common for presidential candidates, particularly those who lack experience in federal politics, to establish close ties to think tanks. Eager to find candidates who can help translate their ideas into concrete policy decisions, it has also become common for think tanks to provide much of the intellectual ammunition presidential contenders require to sell their message to the electorate. As the late Martin Anderson, a senior fellow at the Hoover Institution for many years and a close adviser to Ronald Reagan, observed, "it is during this period that presidential candidates solicit the advice of a vast number of intellectuals in order to establish policy positions on a host of domestic and foreign policy issues. Presidential candidates exchange ideas with policy experts and test them out on the campaign trail. It's like a national test marketing strategy."[4]

This chapter provides a snapshot of how some think tanks in the United States seek to influence public policy. I explore how a select group of think tanks have capitalized on presidential elections to share their ideas with candidates and incoming administrations to demonstrate one way policy institutes in the United States have tried to make a difference. The chapter begins by examining the various factors that motivate presidential candidates to turn to think tanks for policy advice and the general willingness of institutes to assist in their endeavours. As will be discussed, both presidential candidates and the think tanks that advise them recognize the enormous benefits that can be derived from a successful partnership. Following this, the close ties that were established between think tanks and six presidential candidates who would go on to win the presidency – Jimmy Carter (1976), Ronald Reagan (1980 and 1984), Bill Clinton (1992 and 1996), George W. Bush (2000 and 2004), and Barack Obama (2008 and 2012) – will be examined. The chapter will also make some preliminary observations about the various think tanks Donald Trump tapped into during the hotly contested Republican presidential primaries, and in the general election and transition period that followed. These candidates and their elections have been selected for a number of practical and empirical reasons: first, it enables scholars to identify the close ties that the leading presidential candidates have established with a select group of think tanks in each election. Materials obtained from presidential archives and from other primary sources, including newspapers and speeches, enable scholars to make some preliminary observations about the participation of think tanks in these elections. Of course, considerable gaps will remain unfilled until the remaining records from the Reagan years and the complete records of the Clinton, Bush, and Obama presidencies become available. Second, by focusing on these elections, scholars can demonstrate that the think tanks that became involved in these important events in America's history mattered in different ways and at different times. For instance, unlike several scholars from the Hoover Institution who provided their expertise to Ronald Reagan during the 1980 campaign, the Heritage Foundation's contribution to the candidate's policy education was modest. Nonetheless, by providing Reagan's closest advisers with a detailed blueprint on how to reform government, Heritage played a decisive role during Reagan's transition to power. Close to forty years later, Heritage developed another blueprint for reforming government that clearly spoke to many of Donald

Trump's priorities and ambitions. As will be revealed, Heritage and other think tanks inside the Beltway made their presence felt, but not always in the same way. The final section of the chapter will consider some of the many lessons to be drawn from the involvement of think tanks in presidential campaigns and transitions: among other things, why think tanks may find it difficult to resist the temptation to enter the political arena in such a highly visible way, and some of the potential repercussions of their engagement.

A PERFECT UNION: THINK TANKS AND PRESIDENTIAL CANDIDATES

To launch a successful presidential bid, candidates require not only sufficient cash flow but a steady stream of policy ideas that they can share and test out with the American public. Although the former is often in short supply, particularly during the presidential primaries when candidates must raise their own funds, rarely do those seeking the nation's highest office face a shortage of policy ideas.[5] Surrounded by political strategists, pollsters, media consultants, party loyalists, and lobbyists for various causes, candidates are inundated with policy advice, some helpful and informative, some very damaging and divisive. Yet, despite this, several presidential candidates have, often with the encouragement of their closest advisers, turned to think tanks. But why do candidates try to forge close ties to think tanks? And why are so many think tanks, in all but a handful of cases, willing to offer their services?

To begin with, candidates, especially those with little or no exposure to politics at the national level, can, if they are so inclined, tap into the wealth of knowledge available at some of America's most distinguished think tanks.[6] Jimmy Carter, Ronald Reagan, Bill Clinton, and George W. Bush had all been governors, but none had served in any federal government capacity. The current occupant of the White House, Donald J. Trump, had no political experience at any level of government before assuming the presidency. Committed to "draining the swamp" in Washington, Trump came to office with a limited and often misguided understanding of domestic and foreign policy, but plenty of contempt for career politicians, a subject that we will explore later in the chapter.

Presidential candidates also recognize the enormous benefits of relying on think tanks that are populated with many former high-profile policy-makers and leading policy experts willing to share their intimate knowledge and sophisticated understanding of how Washington works. They understand how helpful think tanks can be in providing tips on how best to navigate their way through the policy-making process, and what they need to do to nurture and strengthen their ties to the media and other key stakeholders. Moreover, by attending meetings organized by the Council on Foreign Relations, the Brookings Institution, RAND, CSIS, Heritage, and others, where several former policy-makers and prominent business leaders are often in attendance, candidates can develop additional contacts in the private and public sectors that may prove invaluable as they travel the country soliciting support. However, even more important than the network of contacts think tanks can offer is the credibility and legitimacy they can give to a candidate's ideas, a currency often more valuable than money. Receiving the endorsement of leading public intellectuals and world leaders, or, better yet, having academics of such a high calibre providing advice can significantly enhance the intellectual depth of a candidate's platform. Candidates can also benefit from their visible association with think tanks that are in a position to reinforce the ideological underpinnings of their policy ideas.

The support of think tank staff generally costs candidates very little. Unless policy experts from think tanks take a leave of absence from their institute to work on a campaign, they generally offer their services free.[7] In sum, for candidates there are few costs and potentially enormous benefits in relying on think tanks that can help them strike a responsive chord with the electorate; for think tanks, there can be considerable benefits that stem from aligning themselves with a winning presidential candidate. Not only does an election victory bring prestige, notoriety, and, at times, job offers, but a higher profile can translate into more funds from affluent donors.

Although some candidates have relied more heavily on think tanks than others, a clear pattern is emerging. When candidates need policy advice from seasoned policy experts, they are turning to these organizations with great regularity. And to the delight of many think tanks, candidates appear willing to court them as they embark on the long and often difficult road to the White House.

JIMMY CARTER AND THE SEARCH FOR POLICY ADVICE

When President Gerald Ford granted Richard Nixon "a full, free and absolute pardon" for "any and all crimes" committed during the Watergate scandal, it seemed even more probable that a Democrat would become the next president. Tainted by widespread corruption and unable to bring about an expeditious conclusion to the Vietnam War, the Republican Party failed to convince the American electorate that it could provide effective and responsible leadership. In fact, well before President Nixon resigned in August 1974, several political commentators were convinced that a Democrat would win the 1976 presidential campaign.[8] Yet, while a number of prominent Democrats entered the presidential race, including Henry "Scoop" Jackson and George Wallace, it was Jimmy Carter, a relatively unknown one-term governor of Georgia who was sworn into office in January 1977.

While Jimmy Carter's rapid rise to power continues to baffle some political analysts, his ties to prestigious policy research institutions in New York and Washington, DC, may in part explain his ability to gain national exposure. Analyzing Carter's dependence on think tanks for policy advice makes it possible to identify the organizations that played a major role during and after his bid for the presidency. A closer examination of his association with a handful of prominent northeastern think tanks also reveals how research institutions seek to expand their networks of influence throughout the policy-making community.

Shortly after Jimmy Carter became governor of Georgia in 1970, he began to set his sights on the nation's highest office. However, it soon became apparent to Carter and his political and financial supporters that if he was to launch a successful presidential campaign, he would have to attract the attention of several prominent Democrats. Although Carter enjoyed the backing of many prominent leaders in Atlanta's business and policy-making circles, it was the support of leading academics, financiers, and journalists in the Northeast that he dearly coveted. According to Laurence Shoup, by gaining access to the eastern establishment, Carter hoped to become part of the national power structure in the United States.[9]

As early as 1971, Carter had become preoccupied with gaining national exposure. Through some of his close personal advisers, such as former secretary of state Dean Rusk, he met a number of individuals who were in a position to broaden his base of political support. Among the most influential contacts were David Rockefeller, chair of the Chase Manhattan Bank, and Hedley Donovan, editor-in-chief of *Time* magazine. Following a *Time* cover story on Carter and the New South in May 1971, Carter met with Donovan, who introduced him to George S. Franklin, a Rockefeller in-law and executive director of the Council on Foreign Relations.[10] It was through one or more of these connections that Carter became known to David Rockefeller, who invited the governor to lunch with him at the Chase Manhattan Bank in November 1971.

Carter's southern disposition and Kennedy-style approach to state politics must have impressed Rockefeller, because when the latter decided to establish the Trilateral Commission in 1973, Carter was invited to become a member.[11] Zbigniew Brzezinski, who helped Rockefeller select individuals for the Trilateral Commission, maintained that Carter was asked to join because he seemed to share the organization's commitment to improving international economic relations: "We were very impressed that Carter had opened up trade offices for the state of Georgia in Brussels and Tokyo. That seemed to fit perfectly into the concept of the Trilateral."[12]

While Carter's international economic initiatives appeared to coincide with the Trilateral Commission's mandate, the possibility of having one of their members occupy the Oval Office also appears to have influenced Rockefeller and Brzezinski's decision. As Barry Goldwater points out, Carter's invitation to join the Trilateral Commission was motivated by political as well as institutional interests. "David Rockefeller and Zbigniew Brzezinski found Jimmy Carter to be their ideal candidate. They helped him win the nomination and the presidency. To accomplish this purpose, they mobilized the money power of the Wall Street bankers, the intellectual influence of the academic community – which is subservient to the wealth of the great tax-free foundations – and the media controllers represented in the membership of the CFR [Council on Foreign Relations] and the Trilateral."[13]

Goldwater and other conservative spokespersons recognized that a Carter election victory would pay handsome dividends for the Trilateral Commission, but Carter also derived many benefits from participating in this organization. According to Laurence Shoup, "By becoming a member of the Trilateral Commission, Carter met and became friends with powerful upper class individuals who had contacts and influence where it mattered – in business, the mass communications media, in governments at home and abroad, in universities, in the associations and foundations. Jimmy Carter ... whom few people outside Georgia had even heard of in 1973, had become part of a group which could help him become President of the US"[14]

Few political commentators identified the close connection between Carter and the Trilateral Commission during the early 1970s, but by 1976 it had become increasingly apparent that the Democratic presidential candidate was relying heavily on his Trilateral colleagues for policy advice. For instance, in June 1976 the *Los Angeles Times* described a "task force" that helped the candidate prepare his first foreign policy speech, which began, "The time has come for us to seek a partnership between North America, Western Europe and Japan."[15] With several of his Trilateral advisers leading the applause, Carter emphasized the importance of encouraging closer cooperation between advanced industrial nations. In the ensuing months, the Democratic candidate continued to espouse other foreign policy recommendations proposed by the Trilateral Commission. In fact, Carter's growing dependence on an elite group of Trilateral advisers, including Brzezinski and Cyrus Vance, convinced some campaign observers that "Carter's entire foreign policy, much of his election strategy, and at least some of his domestic policy [came] directly from the Commission and its leading members."[16]

It is difficult to determine the extent to which various Trilateral advisers influenced Carter's views on foreign and domestic policy, but there is little doubt that membership on the commission left a lasting impression on him. As Carter noted, "In order to insure the continuing opportunity for penetrating analyses of complicated, important, and timely foreign policy questions, there is an organization known as the Trilateral Commission. A group of leaders from the three democratic developed areas of the world meet every six months to discuss ideas of current interest to Japan, North America and Europe ... Membership on this commission has provided me with a splendid learning opportunity, and many of the other members helped me in my study of foreign affairs."[17]

Zbigniew Brzezinski, the Trilateral Commission's first director and later national security adviser to President Carter, agrees that the commission offered Carter an invaluable learning experience but denies that it advised him on domestic and foreign affairs:[18]

> The Commission did not play any role in advising [Carter] whatsoever. But I think the commission was of importance to him in two ways. One, it provided the framework for his generally first extensive exposure to international affairs. Prior to his membership on the commission, he had no exposure to international affairs. It was through the commission that he really became exposed to foreign affairs. Secondly, on the commission, he met a number of people interested in foreign affairs, some of whom he recruited to work for him when he was making the appointments for his administration. I believe that someone once counted, I don't remember the exact number, but I sort of vaguely remember that up to eighteen senior appointees in his administration were from members of the commission.[19]

Brzezinski, who passed away in May 2017, could not recall the exact number of Trilateral commissioners who were appointed by President Carter,[20] but in an earlier interview with the author stated that "all the key foreign policy decision makers of the Carter administration had served in the Trilateral Commission."[21] Other than Brzezinski, several Trilateral members received appointments in the Carter administration, including Walter Mondale, Paul Volcker, and Paul Warnke.

Carter depended heavily on several Trilateral commissioners to fill key posts in his administration, yet his search for policy advice did not end there. The Trilateral Commission quickly established a reputation as one of the premier policy research institutions in the United States. However, the president-elect could not afford to ignore the elite group of policy specialists at other distinguished think tanks, such as the Council on

Foreign Relations. Moreover, since many Trilateral commissioners were also members of the CFR, Carter's access to some of the nation's most prominent decision makers was greatly facilitated.[22]

At Carter's invitation, at least fifty-four members of the CFR joined his new administration. Among them were P.R. Harris, secretary of Housing and Urban Development (HUD) and Health, Education and Welfare (HEW); Philip Habib, undersecretary of state; Stansfield Turner, director of the CIA; D. Aaron, deputy to the national security adviser; A. Solomon, undersecretary of the Treasury; and Donald McHenry, ambassador to the United Nations. Having assembled an impressive team of policy advisers from the Trilateral Commission and the Council on Foreign Relations, Carter finally turned to the Brookings Institution to complete his "brain trust."

Recognizing the invaluable contribution that several Brookings scholars had made in formulating various governmental policies during previous Democratic administrations, Carter first approached the institution in July 1975 for advice. During his brief visit, he attended two informal luncheons on foreign policy and economics and began to establish ties to many of Brooking's most distinguished residents. Following his election victory, Carter invited several Brookings scholars to join his staff. In addition to Stephen Hess, who advised him on how to restructure his White House staff, Carter appointed over a dozen other members of the Brookings Institution to administrative posts, including Charles L. Schultz, chair of the Council of Economic Advisors; C. Fred Bergsten, assistant secretary of the treasury for international economic affairs; Henry Aaron, assistant secretary of Health, Education and Welfare for planning and evaluation; Karen Davis, deputy assistant secretary of Health, Education and Welfare; Emil Sunley Jr, deputy assistant secretary of the Treasury; Barry Blechman, assistant director of the Arms Control and Disarmament Agency (ACDA); Barry Bosworth, director of the Council on Wage and Price Stability; Henry D. Owen, special White House representative for economic summits; L.N. Cutler, White House counsel; L.W. Benson, undersecretary of state; Gerard C. Smith, ambassador at large; and Nancy H. Teeters, Federal Reserve Board.

With the support and advice of over 100 policy analysts from three of America's most prestigious think tanks, Carter rose from relative obscurity to occupy the Oval Office. Although several factors contributed to his election victory, the vital role think tanks played during his campaign cannot be overlooked. Carter's dependence on think tank specialists did not end when he entered the White House. On the contrary, as the newly installed president sought to chart a new course for America in the latter half of the decade, he began to rely even more on his advisers for direction and guidance. While Carter solicited the advice of his top economic advisers to enhance America's position in the international economy, his preoccupation with resolving tensions in Latin America and the Middle East provided foreign policy analysts, both in and out of government, with unique opportunities to capture the president's attention. In fact, on several occasions Carter's policies toward these particular regions appeared to be shaped and moulded by prominent members of Washington's think tank community.[23]

RONALD REAGAN AND THE THINK TANKS THAT ADVISED HIM

Carter depended on several prestigious northeastern think tanks to gain national exposure, but his successor turned to other policy research institutions to transform his set of conservative beliefs into a winning election platform. Ronald Reagan had occasionally solicited the advice of policy analysts from prominent think tanks and universities during his tenure as governor of California, but it was not until he launched his bid for the presidency in 1980 that he began to surround himself with some of the nation's most respected conservative policy intellectuals.[24]

Despite finishing second to Gerald Ford at the 1976 Republican National Convention in Kansas City, Missouri, Ronald Reagan wasted little time preparing for the 1980 presidential campaign. As one of his campaign advisers observed during the candidate's return flight to California, Reagan stared out the plane's window for a few seconds and then proceeded to write the following note on the back of a ticket to the national convention, "We dreamed – we fought & the dream is still with us."[25]

In those few words, Reagan expressed his commitment to return to the campaign trail in the hope of securing the 1980 presidential nomination. And on 17 July 1980 in Detroit, Michigan, Reagan won the Republican nomination by an overwhelming majority. One hundred and eleven days later, he won the general election. On 20 January 1981, Ronald Wilson Reagan became the fortieth president of the United States.

Reagan's sweeping victory over an increasingly despondent and frustrated President Carter is often attributed to the Carter administration's failure to safeguard US economic and political interests in the international community. Carter's inability to prevent the overthrow of the Shah of Iran, the installation of the Sandinista government in Nicaragua, the seizure of the US embassy in Tehran, and the Soviet invasion of Afghanistan did little to instill confidence in the electorate. Nonetheless, Carter's foreign policy failures alone did not ensure a Republican victory. The ability of Reagan's advisers to translate a set of conservative beliefs into an appealing political agenda also contributed to the outcome of the 1980 campaign.

Before Reagan's plane had even landed in Southern California following his acceptance speech in Detroit, some of his campaign advisers began to map out a new strategy to promote their candidate's views on domestic and foreign policy. And just as Reagan had undergone a political conversion by leaving the Democratic Party to join the Republican cause following Kennedy's narrow election victory over Nixon in 1960, his campaign advisers now had to determine how to expedite the American electorate's conversion to conservatism.[26]

For the late Martin Anderson, a senior fellow at the Hoover Institution and a key member of Reagan's inner circle of policy advisers, the most effective way to communicate his candidate's political agenda to the American public was to attract the support of some of the nation's leading intellectuals. Convinced that "ideas move nations"[27] and that policy ideas arise primarily in universities and think tanks, Anderson set out to assemble an impressive team of academics who could promote Reagan's vision of America.[28] As Anderson points out in his memoirs of the Reagan years, "[A]s early as 1975, after I agreed to join his presidential campaign, I started a systematic effort to introduce the nation's best economists to Reagan. Most of them were selected from my personal file of leading policy experts I began collecting during Nixon's campaign in 1967. This was part of a more general effort to recruit an army of intellectuals to advise and counsel Reagan on the entire range of policy issues."[29]

After inviting such prominent economists as Milton Friedman, William Niskanen, and Murray Weidenbaum to join Reagan's campaign team, Anderson began to set his sights on creating several policy task forces to advise Reagan on domestic and foreign policy.[30] Anderson first recognized the importance of establishing policy task forces to advise presidential candidates when he was in charge of policy research for Nixon in 1968. He notes, "I learned that policy advisers from the intellectual world could be a tremendous asset to a campaign ... the very existence of a large group of distinguished intellectuals gave a powerful boost to the credibility of the candidate. In effect, those intellectuals were co-signing the ideas of the candidate."[31]

Anderson was in charge of organizing the domestic and economic policy task forces, and Richard Allen, a fellow Hoover colleague, was entrusted with overseeing the foreign and defence policy groups.[32] Reflecting on how his policy groups channelled information to Reagan, Allen stated,

> I had a total of 120 people; 80 foreign policy advisers and 40 defence and national security advisers. These people were typically specialists in the field, either academic specialists or retired or departed specialists from government, including people from the Pentagon and the Department of State, former diplomats and

> the like. [They] produced information, opinions, parts of speeches that would be included in the speeches of the candidate ... That's the way that part of the system worked. [The policy groups] were extremely useful in providing background information and general data.[33]

A press release issued by Reagan on 23 October 1980 documented the scope and function of the policy task forces: "Governor Reagan today announced the completion of 23 domestic and economic policy task forces with 329 advisers who have been asked to address the important issues that will have to be faced by a new administration... These task forces join 25 foreign policy and defence working groups with 132 advisers that are examining, in detail, the major questions that relate to these two important areas."[34]

Transition team director Edwin Meese III commented on the active involvement of policy task forces during the Reagan campaign: "Reagan's 1980 campaign had been served by policy task forces that comprised 'the largest and most distinguished group of intellectuals ever assembled for an American political campaign.' Nearly fifty groups, with over 450 advisers, studied numerous areas of foreign, defence, domestic, and economic policy and provided hundreds of recommendations."[35] By producing detailed studies on topics ranging from welfare reform to missile defence, and by outlining several policy recommendations, the policy task forces had, in effect, established a blueprint for the incoming administration. As Martin Anderson points out, "[w]hen Reagan took power in 1981, the battle plan for what to do with that power was largely written."[36]

Two weeks before president-elect Reagan took the oath of office, at a dinner in honour of the Hoover Institution's Board of Overseers, Meese elaborated on the important contribution the policy development teams made in assembling information for the new administration. "We have already had a series of meetings ... with [the] Heritage [Foundation] and others to make recommendations to the new president-elect as to the course his administration should follow. By the time January twentieth comes around, there will already be an agenda of initial action projects which will carry the administration through its first year of operation and which will set major and intermediate goals so that there will always be an eye on the blueprint of what the administration seeks to accomplish."[37]

The president-elect wasted little time rewarding advisers who had made important contributions to his campaign. Among those participating on Reagan's policy task forces who received high-level government appointments were Alan Greenspan, chair of the board of governors of the Federal Reserve; Antonin Scalia, appointed to the Supreme Court; George Shultz, secretary of state; Caspar Weinberger, secretary of defense; William Howard Taft IV, deputy secretary of defense; Richard Allen, national security adviser; James Miller, chair of the Federal Trade Commission and later director of the Office of Management and Budget (OMB); Edwin Harper, deputy director of the OMB; Murray Weidenbaum and Beryl Sprinkel, chairs of the Council of Economic Advisers (CEA); William Niskanen and Thomas Moore, CEA; Norman Ture and Paul Craig Roberts, undersecretary and assistant secretary for economic policy in the Department of the Treasury; Arthur F. Burns, ambassador to Germany; Darrell Trent, deputy secretary of Transportation; Rudolph Penner, head of the Congressional Budget Office; and Martin Anderson, chief domestic and economic policy adviser.[38]

Of these, more than half had been members of think tanks before joining the Reagan administration. Their institutional affiliations were as follows: Richard Allen: the Center for Strategic and International Studies, the Heritage Foundation, and the Hoover Institution; Martin Anderson, Thomas Moore, and Darrell Trent: the Hoover Institution; Norman Ture: the Heritage Foundation; Caspar Weinberger: the Institute for Contemporary Studies;[39] Murray Weidenbaum, James Miller, and Arthur Burns: the American Enterprise Institute; and William Niskanen: RAND and the Institute for Defence Analyses.[40]

The number of individuals belonging to think tanks who decided to join the Reagan crusade is far more extensive. Between 1981 and 1988, close to 200 members from America's leading conservative think tanks participated in the Reagan administration in a full-time consulting or advisory capacity.[41] Five think tanks in particular were well represented during the Reagan years; fifty-five scholars came from the Hoover Institution, thirty-six from the Heritage Foundation, thirty-four from the American Enterprise Institute, thirty-two from the Committee on the Present Danger,[42] and eighteen from the Center for Strategic and International Studies.[43]

Until the 1980 campaign records at the Reagan Presidential Library become available, it will be difficult to provide a more detailed examination of the relationship between think tanks and the Reagan administration. Nonetheless, a preliminary search of available materials indicates that some think tanks played a crucial role in the transition period following the 1980 election. Although several think tanks were actively involved in the campaign, few assumed more importance during the transition than the Heritage Foundation.

In the fall of 1979, in anticipation of a Republican presidential victory, Heritage president Edwin Feulner began to consider how his organization could assist in the transition to a conservative administration. After consulting several of his colleagues in the policy research community,

Feulner decided to launch an extensive research project to produce a study that could, in effect, serve as a manual for conservatives to follow in implementing domestic and foreign policy initiatives. According to Feulner, "our strong feeling was that people who came into the administration should have some source of information and guidance other than what you get from the incumbents that you replace."[44]

With the assistance of over 300 academics, consultants, lawyers, and former government officials divided into twenty project teams, the Heritage Foundation produced a 1,100-page "blueprint for the construction of a conservative government."[45] In its *Mandate for Leadership: Policy Management in a Conservative Administration*, the Heritage Foundation outlined 2,000 proposals on issues ranging from how to streamline the government bureaucracy to ways to improve US national security.[46]

Delighted with the results of Heritage's year-long study, not to mention the outcome of the 1980 campaign, Feulner presented a copy of the manuscript to Edwin Meese III at the Hay-Adams Hotel in mid-November 1980.[47] After scanning the extensive report, Meese said that the *Mandate for Leadership* study was very impressive and that the Reagan team "will rely heavily on it."[48] It was "one of the most meaningful and best things that President Reagan and those associated with him will have to guide them in the next few years."[49] According to Meese, "President Reagan gave a copy of the book to each member of his cabinet and directed them to read it."[50]

In his memoirs of the Reagan years, Meese, former Ronald Reagan Distinguished Fellow Emeritus at the Heritage Foundation, stated that the *Mandate for Leadership* study was largely responsible for the growing influence of the Heritage Foundation: "This major accomplishment put Heritage 'on the map' as far as Washington decision makers were concerned. Indeed, many leaders in the federal government were appointed from among the Heritage staff and the contributors to *Mandate for Leadership*. [Moreover] Edwin Feulner provided expert advice to the new administration in varying capacities."[51] Meese's overwhelming endorsement of the Heritage study may explain in part why it appeared on the *Washington Post*'s bestseller list for three weeks in early 1981. It may also explain why observers of Washington politics began referring to the study as the bible of the Reagan administration – even a year after *Mandate for Leadership* was released, journalists and policy analysts were speculating on the extent to which President Reagan's domestic and foreign policies had been influenced by the publication.

However, few paid more attention to how closely government officials followed the policy recommendations outlined in the Heritage study than Edwin Feulner, who estimated in early 1982 that more than 60 per cent of Heritage's proposals had been adopted by the Reagan administration.[52]

In flaunting this statistic, Feulner neglected to explain that a number of the policy recommendations included in his organization's study did not originate there but had been developed and refined by other policy research institutions over several years. According to Glenn Campbell, former director of the Hoover Institution, many of Heritage's recommendations were extracted from an earlier Hoover publication, *The United States in the 1980s*.[53] Even former Soviet president Mikhail Gorbachev was convinced that several of the Reagan administration's policies were borrowed from the Hoover Institution's three-and-a-half-pound study. Waving a copy of the publication in front of Secretary of State George Shultz and Robert McFarlane, Reagan's third national security adviser,[54] Gorbachev shouted, "We have read this book and watched all its programs become adopted by the Reagan administration."[55]

Notwithstanding the disagreement over where the majority of policy recommendations outlined in the Heritage study originated, it is difficult to ignore the integral role this organization played during Reagan's transition to power. As journalist Bernard Weinraub points out, "Working from an out-of-the way, white brick building in north-east Washington that once housed a Korean grocery and a halfway house for drug addicts, a group of little-known academics and congressional aides ... emerged as a major force in Ronald Reagan's transition to the presidency."[56]

The *Mandate for Leadership* study had propelled the Heritage Foundation into the national spotlight, and from its new headquarters located just two blocks from the Capitol Building, the "feisty new kid on the conservative block" as President Reagan called it, continued to shape America's political agenda.[57] By 1984 Heritage's clout in Washington's policy-making community had grown to the point that New Republic columnist James Rosenthal, writing on the impact of *Mandate for Leadership II*, commented, "Heritage helps shape what people in Washington talk about after they read the morning paper. It helps set the agenda."[58]

Riding the new wave of conservatism that was quickly sweeping across the United States, the Heritage Foundation soon became immersed in Washington's decision-making establishment. While several liberal policy research institutions were simply concerned with remaining afloat during the Reagan years, the Heritage Foundation, with the financial support of a growing number of individuals and corporations, began to transform itself into one of Washington's leading think tanks. Yet, despite its increasing visibility and overt desire to shape the political agenda, the Heritage Foundation did not monopolize the attention of decision makers. By making their way through Washington's policy-making labyrinth, members of the Center for Strategic and International Studies, the Committee on the Present Danger, the Hoover Institution, and the American Enterprise Institute were also able to advise key government officials on a host of domestic and foreign policy issues in various capacities.

Like his predecessor, Reagan surrounded himself with some of the nation's most distinguished scholars. By doing so, he not only broadened his base of intellectual support throughout the academic community but, more important, attracted individuals who could translate his conservative beliefs into a set of viable policy options. In the process of advancing Reagan's political mandate, several think tanks that had previously observed the mechanics of government from the sidelines became firmly integrated into the decision-making network. As active participants in the political arena, many took advantage of new opportunities to shape governmental policies, though the extent to which various think tanks were ultimately responsible for directly influencing American domestic and foreign policy during Reagan's terms in office is difficult to measure. What is clear, however, is that during the 1980s think tanks assumed a more visible profile on America's political landscape. Indeed, it was not until George H.W. Bush assumed the presidency in 1989 that the presence of think tanks in key policy-making circles began to diminish.

Unlike Reagan, Bush did not invite dozens of academics from think tanks to participate in his 1988 or 1992 presidential campaigns, nor did he rely heavily on them to fill high-level positions in his administration. On the contrary, Bush made a concerted effort to distance himself from think tanks that had established and maintained close ties to his predecessor. As Annelise Anderson, a senior fellow at the Hoover Institution and former adviser to Vice President Bush points out, "President Bush wanted to climb out of Reagan's shadow and [therefore] distanced himself from most Republican experts attached to Reagan. He also treated neo-conservatives much like President Carter did. They both discounted their importance as intellectuals ... In doing so, they excluded a lot of intellectual firepower, people like Jeane Kirkpatrick, Norman Podhoretz, and Irving Kristol, who had inspired and invigorated the Reagan administration."[59]

When Bill Clinton announced his bid for the presidency in 1991, think tanks began to attract considerable attention once again. As Clinton's campaign gained momentum, journalists began to pay more attention to the individuals and organizations who were advising the Arkansas governor. What they discovered was that Clinton, like Carter and Reagan, had established close ties to a handful of think tanks.

BILL CLINTON AND A PLACE CALLED THE PROGRESSIVE POLICY INSTITUTE

In the winter of 1991, few Democrats on Capitol Hill or, for that matter, throughout the United States, could have predicted that the Republicans' decade-long reign in the White House would soon come to an end. Enjoying unprecedented popularity in the polls, largely as a result of the overwhelming support for the US-led coalition to "liberate Kuwait," President Bush appeared destined to win a second term in office.[60] As a former Washington insider and long-time resident at a think tank confidently remarked at the time, "Jesus Christ could run on the Democratic ticket and he still wouldn't beat George Bush."[61] Yet Bush's political future no longer seemed assured as American voters' growing frustration and concern over worsening economic conditions overshadowed their initial enthusiasm for Operation Desert Storm. In fact, in the ensuing months it became apparent that unless he could convince the US public that an economic recovery plan for America constituted an integral part of his vision for a New World Order, the Oval Office would soon have a new occupant.

Anxiously anticipating a Democratic victory on election day, several think tanks began preparing blueprints for the next administration. Modelling their ambitious research projects on the Heritage Foundation's *Mandate for Leadership*,[62] several think tanks outlined a series of recommendations for the next president to follow on issues ranging from health care and educational reform to international trade agreements and defence procurement programs.[63] By the spring of 1992, as Bill Clinton began to accumulate enough delegates to secure the presidential nomination, it appeared to many think tanks that if they were to have any impact on shaping Clinton's campaign platform, they would have to capture the governor's attention.

For Clinton, the five-term governor of Arkansas who easily secured his party's nomination at New York's Madison Square Garden in July 1992, there was little question about which think tanks and policy advisers he would turn to for advice throughout his campaign and during his transition to the presidency.[64] Dozens of academics, interest groups, business leaders, and representatives from a range of non-governmental organizations conveyed their ideas to Clinton in the months preceding the November election. However, it appeared to many journalists covering the campaign that Bill Clinton would rely predominantly on the Washington-based Democratic Leadership Council (DLC) and on its policy arm, the Progressive Policy Institute (PPI), to develop his election platform.[65]

Making this prediction hardly required a crystal ball. After all, in addition to being one of the forty founding members of the DLC, which was created in 1985 following Walter Mondale's humiliating defeat in the election of 1984, Clinton was its chair from 1990–91.[66] Throughout his association with the DLC, Clinton, along with approximately 3,000 other members, invested considerable time and energy to put the principal mandate of the DLC in place: to move the Democratic Party from the left to the centre of the political spectrum.[67] In an attempt to broaden the Democratic Party's base of political support by appealing to disillusioned voters, particularly in the southern and western regions of the United States, Clinton participated in the creation of the PPI in 1989 to convince Americans that Democrats, like Republicans, could successfully compete in the marketplace of political ideas. By the 1992 election, the PPI was prepared to spread its message across the country. Fortunately for the institute, it found the right messenger. According to Achenbach, "After creating the DLC, their next move was to create an idea arm, the PPI ... The solution was to come up with new ideas, and find someone to embody them – which happened when Clinton became chair of the DLC and then carried the group's agenda into the presidential campaign."[68]

Clinton did far more than just carry some of the PPI's policy ideas into the campaign, however. Once in office, he tried to translate several of the institute's suggestions into concrete public policies, often with the assistance of a handful of staff from the DLC and the PPI that had joined his administration.[69] Several administration policies, including reforming America's health care system, linking student aid to national service, helping communities cope more effectively with crime, demanding that welfare recipients perform a variety of community services, and injecting an entrepreneurial spirit into the federal government, are among the many program initiatives that bear a striking resemblance to the recommendations made by various contributors to the PPI's study *Mandate for Change*.[70] Some of these ideas had been advocated by other individuals and organizations, but few institutions in the 1992 campaign offered a more comprehensive guide to reforming government than the PPI.

In addition to drawing heavily on the recommendations made by the DLC and the PPI, Clinton also consulted formally and informally with several other individuals to solicit their advice on a wide range of policy initiatives before assuming office. For instance, during the Clinton-Gore economic conference held in Little Rock, Arkansas, on 14–15 December 1992, Clinton listened to 329 of the nation's leading economists, corporate executives, and labour leaders comment on how to address the economic problems confronting the United States.[71] In a less formal setting he also mingled with several hundred members of America's elite during the now famous Renaissance Weekend held at Hilton Head, South Carolina, over New Year's.[72]

The involvement of think tanks in the campaigns that propelled Carter, Reagan, and Clinton to office reveals one of the most visible channels think tanks rely on to shape the policy direction of incoming administrations. It also demonstrates how candidates can benefit from the considerable policy expertise available at some of America's leading policy institutes and the potential rewards those institutes can earn by being so closely linked to a winning campaign. This may explain why George W. Bush, unlike his father, enlisted the support of policy experts from several think tanks and why so many think tanks were willing to help shape his policy ideas.

PLANTING NEW IDEAS: GEORGE W. BUSH AND HIS QUEST FOR THE PRESIDENCY

As a US congressman, former director of the CIA, ambassador to the United Nations, and vice president and president of the United States, George H.W. Bush was the consummate Washington insider. By contrast his eldest son, George W. Bush, had little first-hand experience with the types of issues he had to confront as president. In the Texas state legislature in Austin, Bush became familiar with a host of local concerns, ranging from education and health care to the environment and transportation, but as president, he required insight into a multitude of domestic and international issues that until then he had demonstrated little knowledge of.[73] Like Carter, Reagan, and Clinton before they declared their intention to run for the presidency, Bush possessed only a limited understanding of foreign affairs, an observation not lost on several journalists and political opponents. In fact, his inability to pass a journalist's pop quiz on foreign policy in November 1999 raised serious concerns about his grasp of America's international priorities.[74]

In an attempt to allay concerns about his ability to lead the world's remaining superpower and to promote America's economic interests in the twenty-first century, Bush assembled a team of over 100 policy experts, many from the Hoover Institution,[75] to advise him on economic, foreign, and defence policy. During his campaign, he also set up policy advisory committees on issues such as education and technology to help deepen his knowledge of domestic policy issues. Bush's team of economic advisers was headed by Lawrence Lindsey of the American Enterprise Institute (AEI), who was appointed assistant to the president for economic policy.[76] Joining Lindsey were several prominent economists, including John Taylor, a Hoover fellow who served on President George H.W. Bush's Council of Economic Advisers; Harvard Economics professor Martin Feldstein; J.D. Foster, executive director of the Washington-based Tax Foundation; and R. Glenn Hubbard of Columbia University's Business School.[77]

Bush's thirteen-member education policy advisory committee was also well stocked with experts from several leading think tanks. Among those who agreed to take some time away from their institutes to assist Bush were Lynne Cheney, a senior fellow at the AEI and wife of former vice president Dick Cheney, and her colleague Lynne Munson; Williamson Evers, a senior fellow at the Hoover Institution; and Diane Ravitch, a well-known historian of education who has held research posts at the Brookings Institution and the New York-based Manhattan Institute for Policy Research.[78]

The foreign policy and defence policy teams Bush assembled were even more impressive, reading, as James Kitfield observed, "like a Who's Who of the Reagan and Bush foreign policy establishments."[79] Heading the foreign policy brain trust were Condoleezza Rice, Bush's national security adviser, who, in addition to being a fellow at the Hoover Institution, had also served in the National Security Council under President George H.W. Bush;[80] Rice's colleague at Hoover, former secretary of state George Shultz; and Vice President Dick Cheney, a former secretary of defense. Other prominent defence and foreign policy analysts included Paul Wolfowitz, Richard Perle, and Robert Zoellick, former Pentagon and State Department officials; Wolfowitz was dean of the Johns Hopkins School for Advanced International Studies (SAIS) and president of the World Bank; Perle was former assistant defence secretary and director of the AEI's Commission on Future Defenses; and Zoellick was former president of the Center for Strategic and International Studies and the US trade representative.[81]

Much has been written about the impact President Bush's inner circle of foreign and defense policy advisers – the so-called vulcans – had on shaping his foreign policy agenda, a subject that I explore in considerable detail in *A Capitol Idea*.[82] Although it will take years for historians and political scientists to paint an accurate picture of what and whom ultimately influenced President Bush's decision to wage war on Iraq, it is clear that several policy experts at a handful of Washington-based think tanks, including the Project for the New American Century (PNAC) and AEI, played an important role in helping the Bush administration market the war on terror to the American people.[83] Given Bush's lack of foreign policy experience before assuming the presidency, it is not surprising that several advisers close to him were able to shape his thinking. During his first presidential campaign, it became clear that Bush would rely heavily on his battle-hardened team of experts for advice. As Bush stated in an interview with the *New York Times* during the 2000 campaign, "I may not be able to tell you exactly the nuance of the East Timorian situation, but I'll ask people who've had experience, like Condi Rice, Paul Wolfowitz, or Dick Cheney. I am smart enough to know what I don't know, and I have good judgement about who will either be telling the truth, or has got some agenda that is not the right agenda."[84]

Unlike his brother Jeb Bush, former governor of Florida and a 2016 Republican presidential candidate, George W. Bush never saw himself as a "policy wonk," a phrase often used in the media to describe political leaders who enjoy immersing themselves in the intricacies of policy formulation.[85] And according to Tim Adams, a veteran of President George Bush's administration who organized a briefing for the Texas governor on technology, he did not want to be. As Adams observes, George W. Bush "believes a chief executive should set out principles, a vision of where you want to go, and then surround yourself with very smart people and listen to them and work with them."[86] In many respects, Bush's management style proved to be similar to Reagan's, who, unlike Carter, preferred to leave the details of policy development to his subordinates. In Reagan's case, the decision to rely heavily on his subordinates often paid handsome dividends, but as the Iran-Contra scandal demonstrated, it also led to some egregious foreign policy debacles. For Bush, his willingness to trust the defence and security of the United States and the stability of the international system to a small group of advisers motivated by ambition and self-interest proved disastrous. However, in the final analysis, as Daalder and Lindsay point out,[87] President Bush is ultimately responsible for the management and mismanagement of American foreign policy in the post-9/11 world. His decision to follow the advice of some key advisers, while ignoring dozens of policy recommendations made by academics and policy experts at think tanks, must fall on his shoulders. This may in part explain why, in the 2004 presidential campaign, Bush paid little attention to the advice of think tanks. He knew what his game plan was and therefore did not feel compelled to listen to policy experts shouting from the sidelines.

For Governor Bush, there was much to be gained and little to lose by developing an extensive network of policy experts. Although he was under no obligation to accept anyone's policy advice, Bush had at his disposal dozens of leading economists, political scientists, and former policy-makers who could give substance to his vision of how America should be governed. But Governor Bush forgot an important lesson when he became President Bush. Great leaders do not make critical policy decisions while wearing blinders. They make decisions only after reviewing the best possible options and considering the potential consequences of their actions. Think tanks, not unlike interest groups and other NGOs, are motivated by a profound desire to leave an indelible mark on public policy. But they also perform a valuable role by providing decision makers and the public with a range of options for addressing particular policy problems. Unfortunately, the Bush administration was simply not prepared to listen to anyone who offered a perspective that differed with theirs.

As noted, with few exceptions (PNAC, Heritage, AEI, etc.), think tanks had limited access to President Bush and his inner circle. However, policy experts in the think tank community were more than prepared to offer their advice to the long list of Democratic and Republican presidential candidates as they competed to elect the forty-forth president of the United States. While this may have been discouraging to the dozens of think tanks inside the Beltway and hundreds of others scattered around the US, during the 2008 presidential primaries, several candidates, including Barack Obama, Hillary Clinton, John McCain, Rudy Giuliani, and Mitt Romney, to name a few, shared and exchanged ideas on a multitude of domestic and foreign policy issues with leading think tanks. Over a period of several months, dozens of newspapers kept close tabs on which policy experts comprised the brain trusts of leading candidates. Once the party nominees were chosen, journalists and political pundits began to scrutinize more closely who Senator Obama and Senator McCain would likely turn to for advice during the general election and in the transition period. Senator Obama's roster of policy experts consisted of scholars from the Brookings Institution, the Council on Foreign Relations, CSIS, the Center for American Progress, and the Washington Institute for Near East Policy. Not surprisingly, Senator McCain gravitated more to the right of the political spectrum in search of policy experts willing to endorse and enhance his policy positions. Scholars from AEI, Heritage, and the Hoover Institution figured prominently in his discussion groups.[88]

In the weeks leading up to the beginning of Barack Obama's historic presidency, it was all but certain that several foreign policy experts from leading think tanks would receive high-level positions in the new administration. In December 2008, Susan Rice, a foreign policy expert from the Brookings Institution who had advised Senator John Kerry in 2004 and Senator Obama in 2008, was the first think tank resident to be catapulted into a high-profile position; she was confirmed by the Senate as US ambassador to the UN. But as the section below illustrates, Rice was not the only think tank staffer to attract Obama's attention.

CHANGING MINDS, CHANGING COURSE: OBAMA, THINK TANKS, AND HIS VISION FOR AMERICA AND THE WORLD

When Senator Obama announced his intention to seek the 2008 Democratic nomination for president on 10 February 2007, he understood what foreign policy challenges he would confront if elected. Speaking before thousands of people crammed into Springfield, Illinois' Town Square, he said that one of his priorities would be to bring US combat troops home from Iraq. But the Democratic presidential candidate also understood that ending an unpopular war would not, in and of itself, repair or restore America's position on the world stage. Before the United

States could realize its potential at home and abroad, Obama required a far more comprehensive foreign policy plan – one that would address global challenges to America's economic, political, and security interests. To do this, he reached out to a small, but well-connected core of international affairs experts, many of whom he had come to know when he served on the Senate Foreign Relations Committee.

As early as May 2007, journalists in the United States began to track whom Obama was turning to for foreign policy advice. Initially, his cadre of foreign policy experts included Mark Lippert, a former staff member on the Senate Appropriations Committee Foreign Operations Subcommittee; Gregory Craig, director of policy and planning at the State Department under Secretary of State Madeleine Albright; Anthony Lake, former national security adviser; and Susan Rice, assistant secretary of state for African affairs during the Clinton administration.[89] It did not take long for pundits to identify the number of people in the Obama camp who had worked in the Clinton administration, nor did it take long for other Democratic and Republican presidential candidates competing for their party's nomination to develop their own stable of experts. By the fall of 2007, comprehensive lists of foreign and defence policy advisers who had gravitated to various Democratic and Republican campaigns appeared in major US newspapers. In an article entitled, appropriately, "The War Over the Wonks,"[90] dozens of policy experts and their ties to the Clinton, Obama, Edwards, Giuliani, Romney, and McCain campaigns were duly noted. Some of these advisers had worked in government, taught at universities,[91] or consulted for the private sector. But overwhelmingly, these experts were recruited from leading American think tanks.

These individuals brought different experiences to the campaign, but what they had in common was a desire to associate themselves with a candidate who shared their convictions and possessed the ability to engage the public in important conversations about America's role in world affairs. It was not just about finding a messenger to communicate ideas they had developed and crafted over years. They needed the right messenger. For many of them, it was Barack Obama. The group of policy advisers who had lent their names and offered their expertise to the Obama campaign included: former ambassador Jeffrey Bader (Brookings Institution); Zbigniew Brzezinski (Center for Strategic and International Studies); Ivo H. Daalder (Brookings Institution); Richard Danzig (Center for Strategic and International Studies and later the Center for a New American Security); Philip Gordon (Brookings Institution); Lawrence Korb (Center for American Progress); Denis McDonough (Center for American Progress); Bruce Riedel (Brookings Institution); and Dennis Ross (Washington Institute for Near East Policy). Not surprisingly,

Republican candidates turned to more conservative think tanks for advice. Policy experts from the Heritage Foundation, Hoover Institution, AEI, and the Hudson Institution were well represented.

The policy experts who had agreed to participate in the Obama campaign in the weeks and months leading up to and during the presidential primaries were not simply looking to pad their resumes. Many had already established impressive credentials at think tanks and in previous government positions. They were there to inform, advise, and educate a candidate who could conceivably become the next president of the United States. They were also there to exchange ideas with a candidate who was committed to changing the nature and direction of US foreign policy. The information that experts communicated to Senator Obama took different forms, ranging from policy briefs and papers, to one or two sentences that could be used in a stump speech or in a more formal address. They covered topics ranging from counter-terrorism, how to deter Iran from acquiring a nuclear capability, to expanding trade in the Pacific Rim. Few topics were off limits. What Obama hoped to achieve by developing a network of policy experts was not only a wealth of knowledge, but a group of talented people who were prepared to defend their policy recommendations. He wasn't looking for consensus. What mattered more to Obama was engaging in difficult conversations with leading foreign policy experts who were prepared to outline the costs and benefits of moving the United States in a different direction. After all, the senator – a former law professor – was known for his willingness to encourage a lively exchange of views. By surrounding himself with people who were capable of providing thoughtful and penetrating insights about how the United States could navigate its way through troubled waters, the candidate felt he could make some headway. Obama's thirst for more knowledge and advice about the complex world of international affairs only increased when he finally captured enough delegates on 4 June 2008 to secure his party's nomination for president. After defeating Senator Hillary Clinton in the hotly contested Democratic primaries, Obama's foreign policy team went into full swing.

In mid-July 2008, *New York Times* reporter Elisabeth Bumiller noted that 300 foreign policy advisers "divided into 20 teams based on regions and issues" comprised what amounted to a "mini State Department" for Senator Obama. A thirteen-member "senior working group" was also established as part of the senator's foreign policy bureaucracy. According to Bumiller, "Every day around 8 a.m., foreign policy aides at Senator Barack Obama's Chicago campaign headquarters sent him two e-mails; a briefing on major world developments ... and a set of questions accompanied by suggested answers."[92] This process was overseen by Susan Rice and other members of the core foreign policy group, including

Lippert and Craig. As Bumiller noted, the foreign policy "infrastructure funnels hundreds of e-mail messages and reams of position papers and talking points each day to members of the core group, who in turn seek advice or make requests for more information to team members down the line." She added that "advisers often say they are unclear about what happens to all the policy paragraphs they churn out on request," but recognize the constant pressure to brief Senator Obama.

The hundreds of advisers assembled to help shape Obama's vision of America's role in the world clearly paid off. Despite facing Senator John McCain, a far more seasoned and knowledgeable expert on foreign affairs, Senator Obama was more than capable of holding his own in debates over foreign and defence policy. While several factors may explain Obama's historic win in the 2008 presidential election, presenting himself to the American public as a viable leader in international affairs may very well have had an impact. If Obama's competence on important global issues was indeed a factor in his election victory, think tanks deserve much of the credit.

President-elect Obama did not have to be reminded of the important contribution dozens of policy experts from think tanks had made throughout his campaign. Within seventy-two hours of giving his victory speech in Chicago's Grant Park, the Obama campaign announced that John D. Podesta, former chief of staff to President Clinton and president of the Center for American Progress (CAP), would co-chair the transition team along with Valerie Jarrett and Pete Rouse.[93] Founded in 1993 as a counterweight to the Heritage Foundation, CAP currently has over 100 staff and a budget in excess of $50 million. Well known for his progressive views on domestic and foreign policy, Podesta also played an important role in helping to launch the Center for a New American Security (CNAS) in 2007, a think tank co-founded by Kurt Campbell and Michèle Flournoy. Both Campbell and Flournoy had previously held positions with the Center for Strategic and International Studies (CSIS).[94] As part of their strategy to develop an effective transition for the incoming Obama administration, Podesta and his co-chairs established several groups that would be responsible for meeting with outgoing officials in the Bush administration to identify key domestic and foreign policy issues that would have to be addressed. According to Shailagh Murray and Carol Leonnig of *The Washington Post,* "135 people divided into 10 groups, along with a list of other advisers … will work until mid-December preparing reports to guide the White House, Cabinet members and other senior officials."[95]

Several prominent think tank staffers emerged as key figures in the Obama transition. But in the area of foreign policy, no think tank generated as much notoriety and media interest as the Center for a New

American Security. According to Yochi Dreazen of *The Wall Street Journal*, the CNAS, "a small think tank with generally middle-of-the-road policy views, is rapidly emerging as a top farm team for the incoming Obama administration."[96] CNAS co-founders Campbell and Flournoy,[97] along with Susan Rice, Richard Danzig, Wendy Sherman, and James Steinberg, members of the CNAS board of advisers, were singled out as leading contenders for senior positions in the Pentagon and the State Department. Other than Danzig, former Secretary of the Navy under President Clinton, the remaining four members of the CNAS board of advisers would serve in the Obama administration: Susan Rice, as US representative to the United Nations; Michèle Flournoy, as undersecretary of defense for policy; Kurt Campbell, as assistant secretary of state for East Asian and Pacific affairs; Wendy Sherman, as undersecretary of state for political affairs; and James Steinberg, as US deputy secretary of state.

As this section has revealed, from the time Barack Obama won his Senate seat in 2004, he had understood, and gained an appreciation for, the contribution think tanks could make to shaping public policy in the United States. He also understood, as did many of his colleagues in the Senate, that President Bush's efforts to advance US security interests in the post-9/11 era were not paying off. After involving the United States in two wars, spending trillions of dollars, and sacrificing thousands of lives, Obama argued that a different way of thinking about America's role in the world was required. To assist him in developing a new strategy for the United States, he enlisted the support of dozens of policy experts from leading think tanks. Scholars from think tanks shared their expertise with Senator Obama during the 2008 presidential primaries and in the general election, participated on his transition, and served in the first term of his administration. Many of these experts also contributed their time to helping President Obama secure a second term in office.

In his second term, a new foreign policy posture took root. Without compromising America's commitment to combatting global terror, President Obama managed, among other things, to remove troops from Iraq, impose a deadline for withdrawing US personnel from Afghanistan, orchestrated the capture and killing of Osama bin Laden, reset America's relationship with Russia, and to mend fences with several world leaders. Although it made several mistakes made along the way, the Obama administration embraced a far more pragmatic and less ideological approach to managing America's international relations than the Bush administration. Much of this changed, however, when Donald Trump, the self-proclaimed Washington outsider and political neophyte was sworn in as America's 45th president. Since taking the oath of office, Trump has confirmed in the minds of his critics what Hillary Clinton proclaimed on the campaign trail: that the real estate mogul and former TV reality star is temperamentally unfit and wholly unqualified to be commander-in-chief. Although some policy experts at the Heritage Foundation and other conservative think tanks took issue with Clinton's remarks, they too were reluctant to embrace Trump during the Republican presidential primaries. This has changed, however, since Trump assumed the presidency. As we will discuss below, a handful of DC-based think tanks have come out in support of the president's position on the travel ban on foreign nationals from mostly Muslim countries, his decision to withdraw from the Paris Climate Agreement, and his nomination of Neil Gorsuch to fill the vacancy left by Justice Antonin Scalia on the US Supreme Court. As noted, some think tanks, including Heritage, have been even more vocal in their support of Trump and have offered him a detailed blueprint on how to reform government. It is to the role that think tanks have played so far in the Trump administration that we now turn.

NOT A WHOLE LOTTA THINKING GOIN' ON: THINK TANKS AND THE PRESIDENCY OF DONALD TRUMP

According to a model of think tank recruitment constructed by Abelson and Carberry, Donald Trump, as a Washington outsider with strong ideological leanings, would be the ideal candidate to embrace think tanks.[98] He had never served in political office, possessed little more than a rudimentary understanding of domestic and foreign policy issues, and even less of an appreciation for how a political system based on separate branches sharing power was intended to function. He also infused many of his stump speeches with political rhetoric that resonated at times with some advocacy-oriented think tanks, including the racist National Policy Institute. But Trump was anything but a typical candidate. Unlike George W. Bush, who had the humility and good sense to acknowledge that he was smart enough to know what he didn't know, and, therefore, was inclined to turn to those with appropriate expertise for help, Trump was simply unwilling, or perhaps psychologically incapable of, recognizing his limitations. Not used to taking a back seat to anyone, or admitting that he could actually benefit from listening to those far wiser and more seasoned, the narcissistic Trump maintained that he had little to learn even from the nation's top national security experts. Indeed, on multiple occasions during the presidential primaries and in the general election that followed, Trump claimed that when it came to fighting ISIS, he knew more than America's top generals. This brazen attitude may explain why, even as president-elect, he refused daily intelligence briefings.

With no intellectual curiosity to speak of, and an aversion to reading books unless of course they bore his name, Trump demonstrated repeatedly that he was unwilling to listen to, or learn from, even his closest policy advisers. For Trump, a third-party candidate who happened to find a vacancy in the Republican tent, his primary concern was not to become educated in the ways of politics; rather, it was to hold onto his base. Since the majority of people who supported Trump shared his antipathy toward the Washington elite, what incentive was there for him to reach out to think tanks, organizations often regarded as key players in the DC establishment? Moreover, according to Josh Rogin of the *Washington Post*, two of Trump's closest advisers, former chief strategist Steve Bannon, and his son-in-law and senior adviser Jared Kushner, are also wary of think tanks. They see them, Rogin writes, "as part of the Washington culture that has failed to implement good governance, while becoming beholden to donors."[99] Quoting a Trump transition official, Rogin notes, "This is the death of think tanks as we know them in D.C. … The people around Trump view think tanks as for sale to the highest bidder. They have empowered whole other centres of gravity for staffing this administration."[100] This view is not shared by think tank presidents, nor by others in the Trump administration, including former secretary of state Rex Tillerson, a long-time trustee of CSIS, and defense secretary, retired general James Mattis, who has been affiliated with the Hoover Institution. Nonetheless, Trump's anti-intellectual orientation, combined with his narcissistic tendencies, has not exactly endeared him to policy experts at think tanks or to conservative intellectuals more generally. Indeed, the *National Review*, a leading conservative magazine in the US, devoted its entire February 2016 issue entitled, "Against Trump," denouncing the Republican candidate.[101] Although Trump did not tweet about this publication, he did mention think tanks on occasion. In fact, one of the few times he referenced policy institutes during the primaries was when he mentioned a poll conducted by the Center for Security Policy which, among other things noted that "25% of those polled agreed that violence against Americans here in the United States is justified as part of the global jihad."[102] Trump relied in part on this report to justify his controversial ban on foreign nationals travelling to the US from seven predominantly Muslim countries.[103]

Not widely regarded among conservative intellectuals as a viable candidate to lead the Republican Party, during the primaries most leading conservative think tanks turned their attention to other candidates. For instance, Florida senator Marco Rubio interacted with AEI scholars on several occasions in the months leading up to the Republican national convention, and was seen by many at the institute as someone who could become the torch bearer for a wide range of conservative ideas.[104] Meanwhile, his colleague and challenger, Texas senator Ted Cruz, was making his presence felt at the Heritage Foundation, where he found a receptive audience.[105]

Heritage Foundation scholars may have preferred a Cruz victory, but it did not take long for the leadership at the foundation to jump aboard the Trump train. By most accounts, Trump enjoyed and continues to enjoy their company.[106] Once it became a foregone conclusion that Trump would become the Republican presidential nominee, several Heritage staff, including former president Edwin Feulner, and James Carafano, vice president for foreign and defence policy studies, agreed to participate on the Trump transition team. Several other Heritage scholars contributed to a study filled with dozens of policy recommendations entitled *Blueprint for Reform*, reminiscent of its ground-breaking tome, *Mandate for Leadership*, which Trump has been briefed on.[107] In addition, since assuming office, the president has periodically engaged other think tank staffers, although his interaction with the think tank community has remained modest. He has established ties to AEI's John Bolton, former US representative to the UN; and Jim DeMint, former president of Heritage; to discuss various issues, including national security and potential nominees to the US Supreme Court. Indeed, amid reports that Jim DeMint would be forced to leave Heritage, Trump thanked him profusely for helping him navigate the Gorsuch nomination through Congress.[108] As noted in the Introduction, there is no doubt that Trump is also grateful to Myron Ebell and his colleagues at the Competitive Enterprise Institute (CEI) for their unwavering opposition to the Paris Climate Agreement. When Trump announced his intention to withdraw from the accord in the summer of 2017, Ebell and the CEI were able to check off another policy victory. As the president moves forward on the construction of Keystone XL, CEI will undoubtedly have more to celebrate.

Trump may not turn to think tanks to become better informed about key policy issues, as many of his predecessors have done, but that does not mean he will ignore them if he believes enlisting their support may prove useful in advancing his political agenda. For Trump, think tanks represent a means to an end, not a repository of expertise; if they can help him win some political battles he may pay closer attention to them. Alternatively, should the support he requires come from other centres of gravity, he will not hesitate to ignore the steady stream of information and ideas think tanks provide. Similarly, if think tanks are willing to do the president's bidding, and some have already shown they are more than prepared to, they may not languish in obscurity as some have predicted, nor will they likely face an untimely demise. As think tanks continue to adjust to a new reality in Washington, they will make whatever adjustments are necessary to ensure they have access to the stakeholders upon whom they have come to rely to ensure their voices are heard. This certainly wouldn't be the first time, nor will it be the last, that think tanks are compelled to re-evaluate the strategies they employ to reach key officials.

AN OFFER TOO TEMPTING TO RESIST

Establishing close ties to the White House is an opportunity few think tanks appear willing to pass up. Indeed, since they are organizations committed to shaping public opinion and public policy, being in a position to influence the policy direction of the president may be the best opportunity some have to market their ideas. Yet in the process of finding an appropriate messenger to translate their ideas into concrete policies, think tanks are becoming increasingly aware of the potential costs of becoming publicly involved in presidential campaigns.

Aside from the obvious concern of having their tax-exempt status under the Internal Revenue Code revoked for engaging in inappropriate political activities, think tank directors realize that their institute's credibility can be damaged in some academic and policy-making circles if they are perceived as leading spokespersons for a particular candidate. As a result, although several think tank staff have participated and will likely continue to participate in presidential campaigns in various capacities, former directors like John Raisian of the Hoover Institution acknowledge "that we have to be very careful about how we handle it."[109] How Raisian's predecessor, Thomas Gilligan, and other think tank directors and presidents, including Edwin Feulner of the Heritage Foundation, "handle it" is by making sure that their staff are willing to provide policy advice, not political advice, to any candidate willing to listen. In this way they attempt to create the impression that, contrary to the views of their critics, they are nonpartisan.

Reinforcing their image as nonpartisan research institutes is not only necessary to keep the Internal Revenue Service at bay; it is critical in cultivating their reputation as independent and objective centres for research and analysis. After all, unless think tanks can demonstrate that they produce sound and balanced policy-relevant research that resonates among large constituencies, few policy-makers, including aspiring presidential candidates, will need their services. As the 2016 presidential campaign confirmed, there are plenty of organizations that lobby on behalf of various causes. But what most policy-makers require is sound policy ideas, not more political lobbyists.

How think tanks balance the need to create a credible research program with the desire to influence public policy will inevitably determine which institutes are called upon to advise presidential candidates. For the think tanks that are able to achieve an effective balance, the rewards can be vast. Not only do close ties between think tanks and presidential candidates often translate into more funds from admiring donors, but such an association can result in high-level job offers for think tank staff. Alternatively, for think tanks that are more interested in the cachet that comes from advising a presidential candidate than in providing informative and well-balanced policy advice, the costs can be significant. Being associated with a winning presidential campaign may result in heightened media exposure, but the long-term damage to a think tank's credibility could prove far more significant. This was clearly a concern for the Economic Policy Institute, which took offence to candidate Trump referencing some of their reports during the 2016 election.[110]

In examining the involvement of think tanks in the six presidential elections discussed in this chapter, two observations come to mind. First, Jimmy Carter, Ronald Reagan, Bill Clinton, and George W. Bush had much in common before embarking on their road to the presidency: in addition to being governors, none of the candidates had any formal experience in foreign policy, which may explain why they all turned to think tanks for insights on defence and foreign policy issues. Second, and perhaps more important, the candidates were drawn to think tanks because they could provide the candidates with credible and independent policy advice. Probably the most significant function of think tanks for the presidential candidates was their ability to enhance the legitimacy of the candidates' policy ideas. This certainly accounts for why many presidential candidates in the 2008 and 2016 campaigns established close ties to the think tank community.

Much has been written about the extent to which think tanks in the United States and, to a lesser extent, in Canada, have become engaged in political advocacy, often at the expense of producing solid policy research. While it is difficult to ignore how think tanks have become more advocacy-oriented, we cannot assume that the institutes most adept at marketing their institutional mandate will necessarily be of the greatest assistance to policy-makers in the long run. As demonstrated in this chapter and in the chapter that follows, despite what we have learned in the first months of the Trump administration, policy-makers may at times be more inclined to enlist the support of think tanks that are known more for their policy expertise than for their desire to bask in the political limelight.

CHAPTER SEVEN

Policy Experts or Policy Instruments? Think Tanks and the Debate over Constitutional Reform in Canada

In their annual reports and promotional materials, think tanks in Canada, like their American counterparts, frequently highlight their achievements. Among other things, they list their recent publications, provide data on the amount of media attention they generate, outline the many research programs in which they are engaged, and summarize their contributions to various policy issues. To put it simply, think tanks, like corporations, have a vested interest in convincing their target audiences that the work they carry out is important, and that the ideas and commentaries they offer are making a difference. It is not surprising, therefore, that at times, think tanks exaggerate both their impact in shaping the discourse around policy issues, and their level of engagement in the policy-making process.

As noted, think tanks try to create the impression that they play a critical role in injecting new and innovative ideas into policy debates. However, the handful of scholars in Canada who have closely scrutinized their contributions to various public policies have been less willing to embrace their image as indispensable repositories of policy expertise. For instance, rather than portraying think tanks as organizations that have had a decisive impact on shaping policy decisions, Lindquist and Tupper claim that Canadian think tanks have made only modest contributions to important policy debates. In his comprehensive analysis of Canadian think tanks, Lindquist examines the contributions of several research institutes to three policy debates (energy policy, pension reform, and tax policy process reform) that took place from the early 1970s to the mid-1980s. He concludes that while some think tanks may have played important roles during the initial stages of these debates, policy-makers have not been impressed by their contributions. As Lindquist observes:

> The general finding … is that institute public inquiry was not of direct relevance to actors interviewed in the case studies; the

> institutes rarely appeared to challenge senior officials in their deliberations and preparation for their political masters. This finding is of considerable interest because institutes had significant early roles in the debates on pension reform and tax policy process reform. Each case study revealed different aspects of this more general finding. The energy policy case revealed that institute studies were monitored more for political considerations. Officials were hard put to recall any influential work by the institutes, although there is evidence that indicates some of the more technical activities were viewed as being somewhat useful. The pension reform case study showed that senior officials labeled the institutes as interest or advocacy groups, yet none of the institutes were considered to be particularly effective advocates. Nor were they repositories of technical expertise and data on pension issues. The tax policy process reform case study suggests that even when the institutes appeared to have had the ear of senior officials, their work failed to provide insightful analysis of the issues at hand.[1]

Lindquist's conclusions about the relevance of think tanks in the policy-making process have been supported by other scholars in the field, including Allan Tupper. Tupper agrees that think tanks are becoming more visible, but, like Lindquist, questions how much impact they have had in shaping major policy debates. Although he admits that some institutes, including C.D. Howe, may have played a critical role during the Canada-US free trade debate, he is less convinced that think tanks in general produce the type of research that is necessary to provide the basis for informed policy discussions on critical issues. In his study, which examines the research contribution of three Canadian think tanks – the C.D. Howe Institute, the Canadian Centre for Policy Alternatives, and the Western Centre for Economic Research – on the "vexing problem of the public debt," Tupper concludes that little of value was added to resolving this ongoing issue confronting policy-makers. He notes, "I am critical of think tanks' contribution to our understanding of the public debt. Their research is short-sighted, too polemical, and in the main too wedded to the perspectives of modern economics. It adds little to our understanding of a contentious issue."[2]

In this chapter, I explore the contribution of think tanks to yet another important policy issue, constitutional reform. The findings of this case study, which is intended simply to illustrate the involvement of think tanks in one policy area, are consistent with Lindquist's and Tupper's skepticism about the contribution of think tanks to policy development. However, as this case study reveals, I am skeptical, not because of the questionable quality of some think tank publications, but because of the willingness of a handful of think tanks to jeopardize their institutional autonomy by advancing the political interests of policy-makers and other stakeholders. However, it is important to remind ourselves that think tanks contribute to public policy formation in different ways and at different times in the policy cycle. Indeed, their inability to persuade government officials to embrace a particular set of policy recommendations does not mean that they have completely failed in their mission to influence public discussions around key policy debates. As we will discuss in chapter 9, there are many ways think tanks can make a difference.

During the winter of 1992, five think tanks – the C.D. Howe Institute, the Institute for Research on Public Policy (IRPP), the Canada West Foundation, the Niagara Institute, and the Atlantic Provinces Economic Council (APEC), were unexpectedly thrust into the public debate over the future of constitutional reform in Canada. Although some of these institutes had written extensively on various aspects of the Constitution, it was not a particular publication or a speech given by a staff member that propelled them into the national spotlight. It was, ironically, the collapse of a parliamentary committee established to consult with Canadians on the proposed changes to the Constitution leading up to the Charlottetown Accord.

When the committee proved incapable of carrying out its responsibilities, Prime Minister Brian Mulroney and Joe Clark, then minister of constitutional affairs, relied on these five institutes to help revive public interest in the Constitution. In what was dubbed the Renewal of Canada, the think tanks were contracted to organize a series of constitutional conferences focusing on specific themes and recommendations outlined by the federal government in its 1991 report *Shaping Canada's Future Together.* Interestingly enough, the institutes were expected not to contribute policy ideas, their raison d'être, but to help transmit the government's policy ideas to an increasingly disillusioned public. According to most accounts, they performed this function extraordinarily well.[3] By serving as conference organizers and facilitators, they not only established a legitimate forum for public discussion but played a critical role in preventing the constitutional reform process from being completely derailed. Unfortunately, in the process of providing this crucial public service, some of the think tanks involved may have compromised their own legitimacy as independent and credible centres for research and analysis. As this chapter will demonstrate, rather than promoting themselves as policy experts, the think tanks that participated in the constitutional conferences actually served as policy instruments of the government.

The involvement of think tanks in the constitutional conferences enables scholars to bypass some of the many obstacles they encounter in trying to assess the impact of these organizations. Unlike their behaviour during the vociferous debate over free trade and the goods and services tax (GST), when several think tanks and other non-governmental organizations sought to convey their views through government and non-government channels, only a handful of think tanks were responsible for organizing the Renewal of Canada initiative. Identifying them does not therefore pose a problem, nor does isolating the group of scholars who were seconded to the Federal-Provincial Relations Office (FPRO) in 1991 to draft the government's twenty-eight recommendations on constitutional reform. The participation of think tanks in the constitutional conferences thus provides a unique opportunity to evaluate the impact of several think tanks at the height of their public visibility.

This case study has been selected because in addition to avoiding some methodological hurdles, it provides insight into the role several think tanks played in what might be the most important public policy debate in Canada of the last quarter of the twentieth century. With the exception of the Canada-US Free Trade Agreement (FTA) and the North American Free Trade Agreement (NAFTA), it is difficult to think of another policy issue to which the Canadian government has assigned a higher priority. If think tanks with expertise in constitutional issues could not play an important role in shaping the outcome of this critical policy debate, when could they be expected to have an impact?

Although the temptation to base observations about the nature of think tank influence on one case study must be resisted, much can be gained by looking more closely at the primary role these organizations played during the constitutional conferences. In examining their involvement, this chapter will address three major questions. First, why did the federal government hire think tanks to facilitate public discussions on the Constitution? Are they uniquely qualified to perform this role, or were there other factors that motivated the government's decision? Second, why did the think tanks agree to serve as conference organizers and facilitators when it was clear from the outset that they would not enjoy complete independence in running the conferences? Did they become involved to enhance their public visibility (all the conferences were televised by the CBC's *Newsworld*), or was the appeal of receiving large sums of government money sufficient to entice them? Third, and perhaps most important, if the federal government was not asking think tanks to generate their own policy ideas but simply to transmit theirs, what does this tell us about the role of these organizations in policy-making?

The government's decision to enlist the help of think tanks, or what Clark referred to as "credible independent organizations," was clearly not influenced by their in-house resources.[4] A constitutional conference secretariat, headed by Arthur Kroeger, an experienced deputy minister, had to be established to handle most of the logistics related to the conferences.[5]

Rather, the decision to hire think tanks instead of professional consultants or public relations/government relations firms was motivated by the government's desire to ensure the integrity and legitimacy of the public conferences and of the constitutional reform process. Confronted by intense and often harsh media scrutiny, not to mention a public that had grown tired, increasingly skeptical, and suspicious of the government's handling of constitutional issues, Mulroney and Clark made a conscious and strategic decision to engage organizations generally perceived as operating at arm's length to government. Because it had lost much of its own credibility, the government hoped, by drawing upon the support and tacit endorsement of think tanks, to enhance, or at the very least to restore some of their own credibility. Tapping into the reservoir of think tanks gave the government the much-needed transfusion of legitimacy it required to revive the constitutional reform process.

On the other hand, the decision of the five think tanks to serve as conference organizers was likely motivated by several factors, including a desire to increase their cash flow. With the exception of the IRPP, which draws on interest generated from its hefty endowment, the other institutes have modest budgets. Securing access to funds that could help subsidize their research for a long period of time had to have been a consideration. In addition, the desire of many think tanks to increase their public exposure also influenced their decision, as well as the prospect of increased access to key policy-makers. However, even more important than the question of why think tanks agreed to participate are the implications of the role they willingly agreed to undertake.

While a handful of journalists and scholars still cling to the view that think tanks are, first and foremost, serious research institutions of high-powered intellectuals committed to addressing society's most pressing economic, political, and social issues, this image has long been challenged and rebuked by many think tank directors and political scientists who work in these organizations. For several think tanks, particularly those more advocacy-oriented, policy research is only one of their functions; for some it is not even the most important. Stimulating debate on domestic and foreign policy issues through public workshops and seminars and by giving interviews to the media is often seen as a main priority, rather than producing scholarly studies. If this view of think tanks is accepted, then the role of the five policy institutes in the constitutional conferences should not be regarded as unusual. After all, if think tanks are no longer perceived as repositories of policy expertise, why would we expect the government to turn to them for policy advice? Moreover, why would they refuse to serve as conference organizers for the government, a role that they are clearly qualified to assume and one that many are prepared to accept?

Had the government turned to think tanks like the Fraser Institute or the Canadian Centre for Policy Alternatives (CCPA), which are known for engaging in more sharply ideological advocacy and research, or to one of several others in Canada that perform contract work for departments and agencies, there would be little need to pursue this inquiry further. However, given that Mulroney and Clark were concerned with preserving the integrity and legitimacy of the conferences, they intentionally avoided selecting think tanks that were perceived as overtly partisan or too closely linked to government. Instead of inviting think tanks like the Fraser Institute, which has often been subjected to negative media coverage, the government turned to the Canada West Foundation and the C.D. Howe Institute, which are widely recognized as highly competent research institutes. Yet despite their expertise, the government did not ask them for independent policy advice but simply to help spark public interest in the Constitution – the government was interested not in the insights they could offer but in the public relations services they could provide.

As will be revealed, the five think tanks clearly played an important role for the government, but perhaps not the role one might have imagined. They did generate public debate over constitutional reform, something the government was clearly incapable of doing, and several of the conferences led both to support for, and opposition to, some of the recommendations of the federal government, a clear benefit to the provincial premiers negotiating the Charlottetown Accord. Nevertheless, despite these contributions, think tanks did not appear to have much impact in shaping the initial recommendations for constitutional change.

This chapter will discuss background information on the events leading up to the creation of the constitutional conferences, followed by a brief profile of the five think tanks that participated in the Renewal of Canada initiative and the factors that may have motivated their involvement. Finally, the chapter will evaluate the contribution of think tanks in the constitutional conferences.

PLAN B: THE CREATION OF THE CONSTITUTIONAL CONFERENCES

In September 1991, the federal government released *Shaping Canada's Future Together*, a blueprint of twenty-eight recommendations or proposals for constitutional reform that would, if implemented, "revise the rules that shape the country's political life."[6] To ensure that Canadians would have sufficient opportunity to react to the government's vision of a new constitutional framework, something the government had been harshly criticized for not doing before the Meech Lake negotiations, a

Special Joint Committee of the House of Commons and the Senate (the Castonguay-Dobbie Committee, later to become the Beaudoin-Dobbie Committee) was established.[7] The committee, as Kroeger points out, "was to hold hearings across the country and submit a report by February 28 [1992]. The government would then make decisions about constitutional changes, taking into account the Committee's findings."[8]

Shortly after the committee began its public hearings, however, it appeared that it might not be able to spark the interest of the Canadian electorate, which had grown tired of what seemed like a never-ending debate over the Constitution. Moreover, the government's desire to engage the public in a comprehensive and constructive dialogue on constitutional reform was threatened by the committee's "carnival of blunders." According to David Milne, "After an ill-prepared plunge into townhall meetings in several provinces that seemed to offer either empty halls or ready platforms for redneck comments damaging to national unity, after consequent demands for the resignation of co-chairperson Ms. Dobbie, and the departure of her counterpart, respected Quebec Senator Claude Castonguay, the parliamentary committee had literally sputtered to a complete stop."[9]

Peter Russell, recognized widely as one of Canada's leading constitutional experts, offers an equally scathing indictment of the constitutional hearings: "The trail of Canada's constitutional odyssey is littered with the wreckage of constitutional vehicles that went off the rails, but for sheer disaster nothing can top the miserable performance of the Castonguay-Dobbie Committee."[10] By early November 1991, the committee appeared to have come to a complete standstill when no one showed up at its hearings in Manitoba. According to Milne, at that stage "the government needed to reassert its control over the constitutional process, or face irreparable damage to the constitutional package and its own reputation. Politically, the question was not simply one of finding some other vehicle for testing public attitudes, but rather of finding a means of restoring public confidence in the constitutional process itself."[11]

The Mulroney government understood the important role the parliamentary committee was asked to play and the potential repercussions its implosion could bring. Public input into the constitutional reform process was vital for the Conservative government, which had been harshly criticized for excluding ordinary Canadians from discussions leading up to the Meech Lake Accord. Sensitive to these and similar criticisms, Mulroney recognized the importance of generating public interest and public views on constitutional reform. But equally critical for the government was arriving at an accord that was acceptable both to Quebec and to western provinces, key constituencies for Mulroney. Not only was the Meech Lake Accord unpopular with the West, but its failure spurred a growth in separatist sympathies in Quebec, where Mulroney's promise of constitutional reform had secured his electoral victories in 1984 and 1988.[12] Faced with these considerable pressures before an election, it was critical for Mulroney to arrive at a deal; the collapse of the Castonguay-Dobbie Committee was nothing short of a disaster because of poor organization and poor attendance.

While the government recognized the need to restore public confidence in the constitutional reform process, it also acknowledged that it had little time to reflect on what had gone wrong. With the parliamentary committee's 28 February deadline approaching, Mulroney had to quickly reconsider his options. Cancelling the public hearings would be suicidal for the government, but so too would allowing the parliamentary committee to continue playing to sparsely attended halls. By mid-November the government had decided that instead of terminating the faltering hearings, it would resuscitate them by organizing "five Constitutional Conferences on five consecutive weekends in five different major cities across the country."[13] The government hoped the constitutional conferences, also known as Plan B, would provide a more legitimate forum for public discussion on the Constitution.[14]

The cabinet invited Arthur Kroeger to assume responsibility for the initiative. The 2 December news release noted that a series of five conferences on constitutional renewal would be held, with each sponsored by an independent institute.[15]

Surprisingly, however, the news release made no reference to why the five had been selected, or for that matter, why the government had decided to enlist the support of think tanks. Why did the government select a group of think tanks to save the sinking constitutional ship? Were think tanks a logical choice, or could the government have turned to other public or private organizations instead? And why did it select the APEC and the Niagara Institute, organizations not generally known for their expertise on constitutional matters?

At first glance, the government's decision appears logical. Think tanks frequently organize conferences and invite policy-makers, academics, journalists, and representatives from the private sector to participate. In doing so, they decide on the format of the conference, arrange for speakers, and determine whether and in what form to publish the proceedings, although few had organized conferences on such a scale.

It is unlikely, however, that their ability to organize conferences was sufficient incentive for government to invite their participation. Since the think tanks lacked the resources to effectively run the conferences, the government had to create a constitutional affairs secretariat, at a cost of $8.96 million,[16] to provide "logistic and operational assistance ... and information on the policy substance of the proposals."[17] The secretariat was expected to ensure that the conferences ran smoothly, and to provide the participants with background papers on the proposals under consideration.[18] If the think tanks were not expected to assume full responsibility for running the conferences or even to supply participants with independent appraisals of the constitutional proposals (although some, including C.D. Howe, did), why did the government solicit their assistance?

The simple answer is that what the government desperately needed was something that public relations/media relations firms and a host of other organizations capable of organizing conferences could not provide – instant credibility and legitimacy with the public.[19] The think tanks recruited had reputations as institutions operating at arm's length to government. They were independent, non-profit, nonpartisan organizations. And they attempted, though not always successfully, to portray themselves as organizations committed to improving government decision-making, not to advancing a particular ideological agenda, the priorities of their funders, or the interests of one political party. It is this perception that Clark hoped would play particularly well to the media, which had seized on the total breakdown of the Castonguay-Dobbie Committee to predict the imminent failure of future constitutional negotiations. The government also hoped that selecting think tanks to help manage the conferences might not only reignite public interest in the constitutional reform process, but would, at least in the short term, provide a new distraction for the media. To their delight, it did both.

Once the decision to engage think tanks was made, deciding which ones would be invited to host the conferences did not likely create much difficulty. Unlike in the United States, where policy-makers must rely on directories to keep track of the hundreds of think tanks, in Canada fewer than three dozen major independent think tanks exist. Of these, only a handful that specialize in domestic policy have made their presence felt in policy-making circles.[20] According to Ron Watts, a constitutional adviser to Joe Clark during this period, two important criteria influenced the selection process: credibility and regional representation.[21] It is unclear what factors or criteria were taken into consideration in determining whether or not some think tanks were deemed credible. However, the decision makers involved in the process were intent on selecting organizations whose reputation for balanced and neutral policy research was beyond reproach. In choosing the C.D. Howe Institute (Toronto), the IRPP (Montreal), the Canada West Foundation (Calgary), APEC (Halifax), and the Niagara Institute (Niagara on the Lake), the government, for the most part, satisfied both criteria.

The government's decision to pursue Plan B proved to be an important one. Not only did organizing the constitutional conferences save the parliamentary hearings from imminent disaster, but it renewed public interest in the debate over constitutional reform. By hiring think tanks to serve as conference facilitators, the government achieved what it clearly set out to do. It was able to significantly influence the public consultation process, something the parliamentary committee was incapable of doing, while creating the impression that "independent institutes" were running the show. Ironically, in the process of making the conferences a more legitimate public relations exercise for the government, the think tanks sacrificed some of their own independence, as will be explored more fully in the sections below.

THE CHOSEN FEW

The Atlantic Provinces Economic Council

Of the five think tanks invited to help organize the constitutional conferences, the APEC is the oldest. Created in 1954 "as a partnership between the provincial governments and the private sector," APEC's objective is "to promote the Economic Development of the Atlantic Region of Canada."[22] With about ten staff at the time, APEC drew on its $1 to $2 million budget to analyze and evaluate current and emerging economic trends and policies. Before the constitutional conferences, APEC had published very few newsletters and background papers on how a new constitution could affect the Atlantic region.[23]

The Canada West Foundation

Although APEC is not generally known for its expertise in constitutional affairs, that is a claim the Canada West Foundation can legitimately make. From its offices in Calgary, the CWF has been a strong advocate for promoting and protecting western Canada's economic, political, and social interests in the Canadian federation. Founded in 1970, the CWF draws on support from various corporations, foundations, and government departments to maintain its active research program. In 1996 it received two endowments totalling $1.5 million.[24] By the time David Elton, former president of the CWF, had been invited to participate in the Renewal of Canada initiative, his institute had released close to two dozen publications on constitutional issues, ranging from how to reform the Canadian Senate to the possible repercussions of Quebec separation, as well as organizing a handful of major conferences on constitutional reform.

The Niagara Institute

Unlike the CWF, the Niagara Institute, established in 1971, does not claim to have expertise in constitutional affairs or in any specific policy area, for that matter. According to Garry Rawson, former director of business development at the Niagara Institute, before the 1992 conferences his institute had never focused on constitutional issues. Niagara became involved, Rawson stated, "because of their skill in managing search conferences."[25]

Although the institute has clearly benefited from the research programs undertaken by the Conference Board of Canada, with which it merged in 1994, it does not engage in public policy research. Rather, it seeks "to enhance the quality of Canadian leadership in business, government and non-governmental organizations [by offering] specialized programs designed to help leaders identify, understand and address the issues of our time."[26] Of the five think tanks, the Niagara Institute was clearly the anomaly.

The C.D. Howe Institute and the Institute for Research on Public Policy

At the time of their involvement in the constitutional conferences, the two remaining institutes, the C.D. Howe Institute (1973) and the IRPP (1972), had similar institutional profiles.[27] Both had about fifteen members and budgets in the range of $2 million or more, and both institutes were created to improve public policy in Canada by providing objective and sound analysis of policy issues. Since then, both institutes have grown. As of 2017, C.D. Howe employs twenty-five staff and has a budget between $3.5 and $4 million and IRPP, with a budget of $2 to $3 million, has fifteen staff. However, unlike C.D Howe, the IRPP has, as noted, a sizeable endowment to support its activities. Of the two, C.D. Howe enjoys greater public exposure, no doubt a result of its more extensive research program.[28] C.D. Howe had published no fewer than twenty studies on constitutional issues before becoming involved in the conferences, more than twice the number produced by the IRPP.

THE CONSTITUTIONAL CONFERENCES

When the federal government approached the five institutes to help organize the constitutional conferences, it clarified that it did not expect them to produce independent appraisals of the twenty-eight proposals on constitutional reform; nor did it expect them to assume full responsibility for running the conferences. Instead, the institutes were contracted to perform six specific functions: to define the conference agenda and format, identify chairs and co-chairs for conference sessions, select appropriate participants, prepare conference material, offer on-site supports, and submit a conference report.[29]

Initially, it appeared that the institutes would exercise considerable independence in organizing the conferences, something they had apparently demanded in exchange for agreeing to participate. A closer look at the government's criteria, however, reveals that in several instances the government dictated how it wanted the conferences run. In addition to determining which of its twenty-eight proposals in *Shaping Canada's Future Together* would be the "primary thematic focus of each conference" (the conference agenda), the government had considerable input into the individuals who would be invited to participate. According to the news release of 2 December 1991, "The institutes are to invite to the Conferences on an ex-officio basis:

- all members of the joint parliamentary committee,
- two individuals selected respectively by each of the caucuses of the three federal political parties with parliamentary status,
- two individuals from each province and territory, to be selected by the Premier/Head of Government, and
- one representative of each of the four national aboriginal organizations."[30]

The government also specified that although the "Institutes are responsible for determining the manner in which [members of the public] are selected ... individuals selected should have a demonstrated interest in, and some knowledge of constitutional matters, and should have a significant record of service to their communities." Furthermore, it indicated that "experts invited by the Institutes to participate in panels and workshops must, taken together, represent a broad and balanced cross-section of views."[31]

The government also went to great lengths to outline the format of the conferences. It stated that at each conference, institutes had to provide "an opportunity for a government spokesperson to outline the constitutional proposals and underlying rationale with particular reference to those which are the subject of each conference."[32] Apparently the government had little confidence in the ability of experts from independent think tanks to explain the nature of the constitutional proposals under discussion. Nor did government officials demonstrate much confidence in the think tanks' ability to prepare final reports on the conference proceedings. The Constitutional Conferences Secretariat arranged with the Privy Council and the Federal-Provincial Relations Office "to have a team of 'note-takers' available at each conference." As Peter Harrison notes, "in summarizing what had been the gist of discussion in the various forums, this assisted rapporteurs in providing summaries to plenary sessions, and report writers in pulling together the sense of the conferences."[33]

Judging by the arrangements agreed to before the conferences began, it was clear that the institutes would not be permitted to exercise complete independence, a price however, that most institutes were prepared to pay. Asked why their institute became involved in the 1992 conferences even though they would not be permitted to enjoy complete independence, a senior analyst from one think tank remarked, "We did not want to get involved in the conferences but figured we had to. It would have been perceived as bad PR to not want to save the country" (off-the-record telephone interview). On the other hand, some institutes did not believe that their institutional independence was compromised at all. Despite the amount of government intervention, they continued to insist that they, not Ottawa, were ultimately in charge. In a report on the constitutional conference it helped organize, the Canada West Foundation stated: "The Conference was organized and managed by the Canada West Foundation, with assistance from a Conference Secretariat set up by the Government of Canada to aid in logistics and media coverage. Canada West Foundation exercised complete independence in the selection of conference participants, the organization of the program, the setting of the agenda, the selection of co-chairs and speakers, the preparation of pre-conference materials, and the writing of final report. There was no interference or direction, direct or indirect, on the part of the government."[34]

While these and similar statements were no doubt comforting to the government, the institutes were deluding themselves if they believed they had complete independence.[35] But sacrificing some independence may have been a small price to pay in return for the potential benefits derived from their participation, including, of course, establishing greater credibility with the government. Becoming more firmly entrenched in policy-making circles could pay handsome dividends for think tanks committed to shaping public policy. In addition, by helping to organize the conferences, the institutes were able to attract considerable media exposure. The importance of generating media attention cannot be overstated – not only does increased media coverage help foster the illusion of policy influence, but directors of several think tanks can often parlay their organization's media visibility into corporate and private donations.[36]

Generating free publicity was only one of the factors that would have motivated their decision to participate. Being centre stage at what might be the most important public policy debate in a quarter-century was also a strong incentive. For organizations committed to influencing public policy and public opinion, the opportunity to help put the constitutional reform process back on track would be difficult to pass up. Although they ran the risk of participating in conferences that could become public relations disasters, it would probably have been the government, not the institutes, that would have been held accountable.[37] If, on the other hand, the conferences succeeded, the think tanks would forever be linked to a pivotal period in Canada's constitutional development.

The financial rewards of accepting a generous government contract may also have convinced several of the think tanks with modest financial resources to take on the task. For its efforts, the Atlantic Province Economic Council received $314,000;[38] the C.D. Howe Institute and the IRPP shared $200,00 for co-organizing a conference; and the Canada West Foundation received $315,000. These figures, however, pale in comparison to the $760,000 cheque the Niagara Institute received.[39] Perhaps even more lucrative than accepting the government's offer was the potential for additional contracts in the future, an enormous benefit, since the majority of Canada's think tanks constantly struggle to keep afloat.

Each institute may have been motivated to participate in the Renewal of Canada conferences for different reasons, but in the final analysis, they all shared the government's commitment to move the constitutional process forward. The chapter has outlined the potential benefits and some of the costs of this decision. What needs to be discussed now is what contribution the think tanks made to this critical issue. I will now evaluate the role the institutes played at critical stages leading up to and during the conferences.

SOME CAUSE FOR CONCERN: AN ASSESSMENT OF THE IMPACT OF THINK TANKS

Well before the federal government made its twenty-eight proposals on constitutional reform known, most of the think tanks that participated in the constitutional conferences had given considerable thought to the future of the Canadian federation. With the exception of the Niagara Institute, the institutes involved had published studies detailing the economic, social, and political issues associated with a changed constitution, ranging from the potential ramifications of introducing a Triple E Senate to granting Quebec distinct status within the Constitution. The "independent credible organizations" that the government was hoping would provide legitimacy to the public consultation process on constitutional reform had already staked out their positions. Nevertheless, when the government began considering how to reform the Constitution after the failure of the Meech Lake Accord, it did not turn to these think tanks to draft a new blueprint but to a small group of academics in universities.

Shortly after Professor Ron Watts was seconded from Queen's University to the FPRO in April 1991 to serve as a constitutional adviser to Joe Clark, a select group of constitutional experts consisting of Kathy Swinton (University of Toronto), Roger Gibbins (University of Calgary), Peter Leslie (Queen's University), and Doug Purvis (Queen's University) were called upon to assist him in drafting the government's constitutional reform proposals.[40] Watts was also asked to edit a series of background papers intended to explain in a clear and straightforward manner the government's proposals for reforming the Constitution. So, when the government was formulating its vision of a new federation, the views of a handful of academics were clearly heard; the recommendations of private think tanks, on the other hand, were barely noticed.

Directors of think tanks often credit their institutes with helping formulate government legislation and initiatives, but in this particular case they appear to have had little impact. It was not until the parliamentary hearings on the Constitution failed that they even became part of the consultation process, but not as transmitters of knowledge – as conference organizers and facilitators. So they could not legitimately claim that their ideas on how to reform the constitution mattered. Think tanks made a difference in this later phase of constitutional discussions, but not in the way one might imagine.

The absence of think tanks during this critical stage of policy-making raises important questions about their role in policy research. If policy-makers were aware of the institutes' research on various constitutional issues after Meech Lake, why were they not asked to help draft the government's proposals? Did policy-makers question the quality of their publications or the credentials of their staff? If so, why then did the government regard them as sufficiently credible to organize their conferences? Were they simply selected because they were perceived by the *media* as credible institutions? Alternatively, if the government was unaware of their research, what does this say about the ability of think tanks to convey their ideas?

For some of the think tanks, organizing the constitutional conferences was a mixed blessing: it may have increased their exposure, but it did little to advance their reputations as scholarly research organizations. It demonstrated that some of the country's most talked-about think tanks have less influence than assumed in shaping some policy issues. The role of the five think tanks in the constitutional conferences should encourage scholars to think more critically about the contribution research institutes make to public policy. If they are simply expected to serve as policy instruments of government and provide tantalizing morsels of information to the media, then there should be little cause for concern. On the other hand, if think tanks are expected to serve as sources of policy expertise, then the nature of their participation in the Renewal of Canada conferences should raise some eyebrows.

LESSONS LEARNED?

The federal government clearly learned some important lessons from soliciting the assistance of think tanks in the winter of 1992. Among other things, it realized the potential benefits of enlisting the support of independent policy research institutes to facilitate discussions on important issues, particularly when the government's handling of those issues was being called into question. Policy-makers also realized that the reputation think tanks have cultivated as independent centres of policy expertise could work to their advantage. By drawing on their credibility, the government could enhance its own.

The success of the constitutional conferences did not go unnoticed by the federal Liberal government that handily defeated the Conservatives in 1993. In preparation for the 1994 budget, Minister of Finance Paul Martin called for a more open process of budget consultations, which included four public conferences. They would be held in Halifax, Montreal, Toronto, and Calgary in January 1994 and would be hosted by four think tanks, all but one of which, the Public Policy Forum, had participated in the 1992 conferences. The other think tanks involved were APEC, the IRPP, and the Canada West Foundation.[41]

In accepting Martin's invitation, the four institutes requested and received more control over the selection of the approximately one hundred participants who attended each conference than they had enjoyed in 1992. Some institutes, including the IRPP and the Canada West Foundation, also distributed materials their institutes had prepared for the participants shortly before the conferences began.[42] However, even though the think tanks were more conscious of playing a hands-on role at the 1994 conferences, many of the same issues remained.

As in 1992, the think tanks that became involved in the 1994 prebudget consultations were looked to not for their policy expertise but as organizations that could make the public consultation process work more smoothly for the government. Once again they seemed to perform this function admirably. Nonetheless, in the wake of the 1994 conferences, it is important for think tanks to re-evaluate what their priorities are and how they can best be advanced. While think tanks can serve the government's interests by acting as facilitators, they may not necessarily be advancing the public's interests, or their own. Think tanks, according to their own promotional material, are in the business of developing and promoting ideas. They exist to think critically about important policy issues, not simply to advance or market the ideas of policy-makers.

The case study presented in this chapter, like the studies prepared by Lindquist and Tupper, offers some insight into how Canadian think tanks have become involved in particular policy areas. The picture that emerges may not be favourable, particularly for the think tanks singled out for examination. Nonetheless, the findings reinforce the central argument of this book: that think tanks cannot be expected to play a decisive role at each stage of the policy cycle or, for that matter, in every policy area.

While some think tanks may help to frame the parameters of key policy debates through their publications and media commentary, they may be less effective, as Lindquist and Tupper observe, in influencing specific policy decisions. Or as the constitutional conferences revealed, policy-makers may not even be aware of the publications think tanks have produced, preferring instead to rely on them as conference facilitators.

The advantage of developing case studies that examine the participation of think tanks in specific policy areas is that it enables scholars to go beyond simple data sets to more accurately assess their relevance. The disadvantage is that it is difficult to make general observations about their impact in the policy-making process by relying on a handful of cases. Indeed, by focusing on Ken Battle's contributions to the development of social welfare policy in Canada, one might conclude – and justifiably so – that the president of the Caledon Institute has had a profound impact in shaping public policy. A similar conclusion might be reached in examining the contribution of the C.D. Howe institute to the free trade debate and to the future of the Canada Pension Plan. Depending on the specific policy issue that is under consideration and the particular stage of the policy-making process that one is focusing on, scholars may walk away with the impression that think tanks are either extremely influential or entirely irrelevant. Both impressions would be right. In the following chapter, I build on these observations by exploring the involvement of a select group of think tanks in Canada and the US and their efforts to shape the discourse around the construction of the controversial Keystone XL pipeline. Although some think tanks took credit for either halting or advancing discussions on the pipeline, conclusions about how much or little impact they exercised cannot be made until we fully understand the nature and scope of their contribution.

CHAPTER EIGHT

In the Pipeline: Think Tanks and the Debate over Keystone XL

As Canada's twenty-second prime minister, Stephen Harper had to learn the most effective and expedient ways to manage bilateral relations with the US, Canada's leading trading partner. Indeed, for 150 years, Canadian prime ministers have faced similar challenges in dealing with their continental neighbour – finding a balance between representing the interests of the country, and holding onto the support of their caucus, without alienating or infuriating the United States. Walking this tightrope has often required considerable political acumen and diplomacy. It becomes particularly difficult when Canada, relegated as the junior partner in this asymmetrical power relationship, finds itself at odds with US administrations pursuing domestic and foreign policies deemed offensive, destabilizing, and wholly inappropriate by the vast majority of Canadians. As a member of NATO, NORAD, the UN, and other regional and international organizations, as well as a signatory to several bilateral treaties and conventions, including the North American Free Trade Agreement (NAFTA) and the Great Lakes Water Quality Agreement, it is difficult to overstate the number of policy initiatives requiring Canadian and American cooperation. It is also difficult to overstate that US officials have a general expectation that Canada, as America's most loyal and ardent ally, should simply fall into lockstep with the United States.

When the interests of Canada and the United States do not converge, Ottawa is compelled to think strategically about how best to advance its sovereign interests in Washington, where Canada must compete with hundreds of other countries struggling to make their voices heard. At times, this involves working closely with key members of Congress sympathetic to Canadian federal and provincial concerns and strengthening ties to various government departments at the federal and state level. It may also entail engaging senior officials in the US embassy in Ottawa to stress the importance of keeping the Canada-US relationship intact and on track. But what tends to set the tone for relations between the two countries is not the many discussions with lawmakers that take place in the corridors of Congress or state legislatures, or, for that matter, meetings held in their respective embassies. It is the relationship that forms and evolves between prime ministers and presidents – a relationship that unfolds in full view of the media and millions of onlookers – that helps the electorate and the media gauge the temperature of bilateral relations.[1] How well or poorly prime ministers and presidents relate to each other may not dictate the success or failure of various bilateral initiatives. After all, the range of issues that define Canada-US relations extends far beyond the offices of the president and prime minister. Nonetheless, the relationship they form is one of many factors scholars need to consider in evaluating the health of bilateral relations.

Official state visits present a valuable opportunity for the Canadian prime minister and the US president to lay the groundwork for broader policy discussions. When US president Barack Obama made his first official visit to Canada on 19 February 2009, the leaders had much to discuss, from bilateral trade and climate change to border security and fighting the war on terror. They discussed many of these issues further when Stephen Harper made his first official visit to the Obama White House on 16 September, over six months later. On the surface, Harper and Obama seemed to get along well during both visits, strolling through Parliament and posing for pictures in the Oval Office. However, it did not take long for their facial expressions to change from warm and welcoming smiles to what could best be described as a cold and distant gaze. In the months and years following Obama and Harper's trips to each other's capitals, it became painfully clear that it was unlikely that they would see eye to eye on some bilateral policy initiatives. Although Harper and Obama understood that the close economic, political, and security ties that had bound the two countries for over a century and a half would weather virtually any storm, it was the contentious and protracted debate over the construction of Keystone XL, a proposed pipeline that would carry oil from Alberta to the US Gulf Coast, that created a rift between the two leaders. This rift became even more pronounced as Harper and Obama, in an effort to assuage different constituencies, continued to invest considerable financial and political capital to facilitate, or in Obama's case, stall the pipeline's construction. Known for having a short fuse, Harper became increasingly frustrated with Obama's handling of Keystone, an issue over which he believed the president was being needlessly obstructionist. At times, Harper could barely conceal his disappointment in Obama, whom he felt was dragging his feet on Keystone.[2] As Harper's frustration with Obama reached new heights, pundits were reminded that despite the many interests Canada and the

US share, as sovereign countries they have their share of policy differences. The periodic tensions that surfaced between Obama and Harper over the proposed project resulted in some uncomfortable moments in Canada-US relations. However, those who have studied this complex and multifaceted relationship have come to expect some friction. Throughout the history of Canada's relationship with the United States,[3] several political conflicts between prime ministers and presidents have emerged, some more intense and serious than others. John Diefenbaker's frustration with President Kennedy over his management of the Cuban Missile Crisis, Lester Pearson's less than cordial exchanges with Lyndon Johnson during the height of the Vietnam War, Pierre Trudeau's expressions of animosity toward Richard Nixon and Ronald Reagan, and Jean Chrétien's opposition to the Iraq war waged by George W. Bush, serve as a reminder that although we share the same border and inhabit the same continent, our cultural and political differences often run deep. But there have also been plenty of times, especially when prime ministers and presidents have embraced similar ideological leanings, when the special relationship between the two countries has been strengthened and bolstered. Brian Mulroney's close personal ties to Ronald Reagan and George H.W. Bush, and Jean Chrétien's admiration for Bill Clinton represent such moments.[4] In the final analysis, the enduring and deep relationship between Canada and the US does not necessarily depend on whether prime ministers and presidents get along, but rather how they manage and nurture the relationship.

The purpose of this chapter, however, is not to summarize the long and intriguing history between Canada and the United States, nor, for that matter, is it to provide a detailed assessment of Stephen Harper's interactions with Barack Obama. Rather, it is to highlight the involvement of a select group of Canadian and American think tanks in discussions around the proposed construction of the Keystone XL pipeline, one of the most controversial policy issues to surface in Canada-US relations during Harper and Obama's terms in office. By examining how think tanks on both sides of the border interacted with key stakeholders to convey their support for, or opposition to, Keystone XL, we will be able to provide yet another example of the willingness and determination of think tanks to rely on multiple channels to shape the discourse around key policy issues. During different phases of this ongoing policy discussion, think tanks for and against Keystone XL have claimed victory. Think tanks in Canada and the United States adamantly opposed to the pipeline celebrated President Obama's 2015 decision to veto its construction; those in favour, including Harper's successor, Justin Trudeau, have applauded President Trump's decision to move this project forward, a project that could ultimately be decided by Nebraska.

Examining how various individuals and organizations attempt to sway policy discussions, particularly those that are already underway, presents a host of challenges for scholars trying to figure out who or what has made a difference. This case study is no exception. Recognizing that many things can change between the time of writing and the final decision that is made regarding the future of Keystone XL, this chapter presents some preliminary findings on think tanks' participation in this issue. What has become clear is that a select group of think tanks in Canada and the United States have taken an active interest in Keystone XL, and have relied on the media to convey their views, presented testimony to legislative committees, and published several studies to transmit their policy recommendations. Among the Canadian think tanks that have made their positions known about the pipeline are four policy institutes in Alberta – the Canada West Foundation, the Calgary office of the Fraser Institute, the Parkland Institute, the Pembina Institute – and the Canadian Centre for Policy Alternatives, headquartered in Ottawa. Of these, only the Canada West Foundation has supported its construction. In the United States, there has also been a flurry of think tank activity around Keystone XL with the Cato Institute, the Center for American Progress, the Bipartisan Policy Center, the Council on Foreign Relations, and the Competitive Enterprise Institute, a strong advocate of the pipeline weighing in on this debate.

While the efforts of several think tanks to shape the discourse around Keystone XL cannot be ignored, it is also important not to exaggerate or inflate their impact. Think tanks have played an important and meaningful role on both sides of the border to raise awareness about the economic benefits and potential political and environmental costs of proceeding with Keystone XL. In doing so, they have helped mobilize both support for and opposition to its completion. Think tanks have also gone to great lengths to reinforce and elaborate on the messages conveyed by two sets of prime ministers and presidents. Still, it is important to keep in mind that think tanks were not responsible for placing Keystone XL on the political agenda – this mammoth project was a private sector initiative. Moreover, it does not appear that the presence of think tanks was required to convince political leaders in either country to support or oppose the pipeline. Stephen Harper, an adopted son of Alberta with strong ties to the energy sector, would have embraced the potential economic benefits of Keystone without reading a single line from a pro-Keystone think tank report. By the same token, Barack Obama did not require think tanks to persuade him that this project could possibly damage the environment by releasing more greenhouse gases, and adversely affect lands populated by Indigenous Americans. Sensitive to both global environmental challenges and to the plight of

Indigenous peoples, Obama was politically and ideologically opposed to Keystone. Think tanks adopting a similar position simply helped to reinforce his concerns.

Although think tanks may not be able to take credit for influencing the decisions taken by Harper and Obama, which led to a stalemate, or those announced in recent months by Trudeau and Trump, which have resuscitated Keystone, it does not mean that the voices of policy institutes have fallen on deaf ears. Consistent with the argument advanced in this study, think tanks can and often do make a contribution to shaping both the policy-making process and the political environment in which key decisions are made; but they do so at different times and in different ways. Indeed, their involvement in policy-making can be sporadic; rather than maintaining a consistent presence at various stages of the policy cycle, some think tanks frequently enter or exit policy discussions. And as we will discover, while their presence might be felt at some stages of the policy cycle, at other points in the process they may be noticeably absent. In the case of the debate around Keystone, the impact of think tanks was far more noticeable once the decision to consider this initiative was made. Once the project found its way onto the political agenda, a handful of think tanks got to work. As they had done many times before, they mobilized the resources they required to advance a series of policy recommendations they hoped would gain significant political traction. In many respects, their efforts paid off.

The first section of the chapter will present a brief history of Keystone XL. Following this, a discussion of how think tanks engage different stakeholders, and the major Canadian and American think tanks actively involved in the debate over the construction of the pipeline will be highlighted. Finally, the chapter will discuss some preliminary information on the extent to which various Canadian and American think tanks were able to raise awareness about the many political, economic, and environmental issues pertaining to the pipeline.

AND BY EXTENSION: A BRIEF LOOK AT KEYSTONE XL

The debate over building the Keystone XL pipeline has taken more twists and turns than a John le Carré spy novel, and now that the Trump administration has weighed in, there is no telling where it could end (see Appendix 7 for a Keystone Pipeline timeline). Still, it is important to provide a brief history of how this project has unfolded before we launch into a broader discussion of the various ways in which think tanks on both sides of the Canada-US border attempted to influence the outcome of this controversial project.

On 19 September 2008, the Calgary-based TransCanada Corporation submitted an application to the US State Department to obtain a presidential permit to construct the Keystone XL pipeline. The 2,735 kilometre pipeline would cross the Canadian border into the United States and cost approximately US$5.3 billion. If permission was granted, the pipeline would carry hundreds of thousands of barrels of bitumen from oil sands from Alberta to Texas. As noted in TransCanada's request for arbitration on 24 June 2016, three and a half years passed before TransCanada was advised by the US State Department that its application for a permit had been denied. After a new application was submitted to the US State Department on 4 May 2012, TransCanada had to wait another three and a half years before being told that its second request for a permit had been turned down.[5]

During several speeches and engagements in Canada and in the United States, including a discussion moderated by former US Treasury Secretary Robert Reich at the New York-based Council on Foreign Relations on 16 May 2013,[6] Harper made a strong, and what his supporters believed was a compelling case, that an extension to Keystone would be in the national interests of Canada and the United States. Among other things, Harper claimed that the proposed project would further reduce oil dependence on the Middle East, generate billions of dollars in revenue, and lead to thousands of temporary jobs in both countries. Admittedly, the number of permanent positions created once the pipeline extension was completed would be minimal.[7] While Harper also went to some lengths to counter growing concerns among environmental groups that the Keystone extension would cause far higher greenhouse gas emissions, he knew as early as November 2011 that it was highly unlikely that Obama would approve the pipeline. Even with Harper's full and unqualified support and aggressive lobbying by other Canadian officials and industry representatives in Washington, it became painfully clear that TransCanada would not be able to convince the US State Department to approve the pipeline. In fact, despite Harper claiming that Keystone was "a complete no brainer,"[8] critics of Keystone, including several well-known environmental groups, could not be swayed, nor could President Obama, who repeatedly expressed reservations about the pipeline because of its potentially damaging environmental impact.[9] Obama's tough stance on Keystone became particularly acute in the weeks and months leading up to his 2012 re-election bid. Sensitive to the environmental lobby's opposition to Keystone, and by "California's cultural elite," who took issue with Canada's "dirty oil," Obama was unwilling to risk losing their political and financial support. Increasingly frustrated and disillusioned with the Obama administration for catering to interest groups, celebrities, and members of Congress opposed to the pipeline, Prime Minister Harper conceded in July 2015 that it would take a change in US leadership before Keystone could move forward.[10] He was proven right when President Trump issued a presidential memorandum on 24 January 2017, paving the way for a reconsideration of Keystone XL. Just as environmental concerns dominated many of the discussions between Canada, the United States, and Mexico leading to the passage and implementation of NAFTA,[11] similar issues were at the forefront of the debate around Keystone.

When it came to opposing or supporting Keystone XL, there was little confusion over where various stakeholders stood. Not surprisingly, those who advocated for an extension highlighted the economic benefits the new pipeline would bring, while those opposed focused on environmental concerns and the impact it could have on Indigenous territories in Montana, South Dakota, Nebraska, Kansas, and Oklahoma, states over (and under) which the proposed pipeline would travel, carrying approximately 800,000 barrels of oil a day to the US Gulf Coast. Assembly of First Nations national chief Perry Bellegarde addressed these concerns following Donald Trump's announcement, shortly after taking office, that Keystone was back on the table. Bellegarde stated, "This is an important moment to remind Canadians that First Nations hold inherent rights and treaty rights recognized in Canada's Constitution ... This includes the right to free, prior and informed consent over any activities that could affect our lands, our lives or our future."[12]

Encouraged by how effective groups and several prominent individuals were in mobilizing opposition to the pipeline during the Obama administration, including a handful of Hollywood notables, Bellegarde and representatives from other Indigenous organizations have once again vowed to protest the construction of the pipeline.[13] They will not be alone. Joining them on both sides of the Canada-US border will be environmental groups such as the Sierra Club and Friends of the Earth, members of Congress and Parliament who remain outspoken critics of Keystone XL, and of course, think tanks that have positioned themselves strategically in this ongoing debate. Before turning our attention to the various Canadian and American think tanks weighing in on Keystone, it is useful to consider the various stakeholders with whom they engage in an effort to shape public opinion and public policy.

THINK TANKS AT WORK

As institutions ostensibly committed to analyzing the many challenges associated with implementing a wide range of domestic and foreign policy initiatives, it is not surprising that think tanks spend much of their time and often the bulk of their resources on activities related to various research programs and projects. Finding solutions to complex policy problems does not occur by accident, and rarely do think tanks stumble across quick fixes. The ideas they generate often take years to refine and package in a form that is palatable to policy-makers and to the public. In short, for think tanks to achieve lasting policy influence, they must be prepared to make a long-term investment in both their researchers and in the research they undertake. But as we have also discovered, competing in the marketplace of ideas often requires think tanks to do what is expedient. Considering the importance of providing policy-makers and other key stakeholders with information that is timely and relevant, some think tanks are only too willing to compromise the integrity and quality of their research. To make their presence felt, think tanks, interest groups, lobbyists and other organizations jostle, butt heads, and try desperately to outmanoeuvre each other to leave a fingerprint on public policy. With no less than the future of key domestic and foreign policies at stake, think tanks cannot afford to be complacent when it comes to showcasing their findings. Communicating, marketing, and promoting their work to multiple stakeholders, constituencies, or target audiences is, to put it mildly, critical to their success.

STAKING A CLAIM: THINK TANKS AND THEIR STAKEHOLDERS

Policy-Makers

For most think tanks, conveying ideas and policy recommendations to elected officials and career bureaucrats remains a priority. Although the nature of the political system think tanks inhabit will dictate how and to what extent they reach out to office-holders, a subject we explored in chapter 3, organizations involved in the study of public policy must keep a close watch on what policy-makers are thinking about and the issues they will likely have to consider in the near and foreseeable future. Just as government relations firms monitor how the legislative agenda could affect their clients' interests, think tanks cannot lose sight of the issues that have come to preoccupy those in positions of power. Think tanks with the insight and good fortune to anticipate and project the challenges policy-makers will face in the ensuing months and years will likely enjoy a strategic advantage over their competitors. However, even if think tanks can manage to stay ahead of the curve, they cannot expect to make a splash if the issues they tackle have little bearing on matters weighing heavily on the minds of policy-makers. To ensure they are generating research that is timely and relevant, it only makes sense for think tanks to establish extensive contacts throughout government. In addition to strengthening lines of communication, this gives think tanks confidence in knowing that they are on the same page as policy-makers. Many government staff prove helpful to think tanks: elected officials and their staff, policy advisors in the Prime Minister's Office (PMO) and the Privy Council Office (PCO); in the United States, experts in various agencies that make up the Executive Office of the President (EOP), employees in government departments and agencies, those who staff important legislative committees, and directors of party research offices.

For many think tanks, establishing and nurturing contacts throughout government can, over time, pay handsome dividends. This explains why several high-profile think tanks in the United States allocate millions of dollars annually to government relations. The Heritage Foundation's success in extending its tentacles deep inside the corridors and conference rooms on Capitol Hill, the executive branch, and the bureaucracy sent a clear signal to other policy institutes that much could be gained by building an extensive and expanding network throughout government. As noted, Heritage accomplishes this through several channels that go well beyond simply providing policy-makers with a full range of their publications: they rely on liaison offices with both houses of Congress to more closely monitor issues that are on the legislative agenda; maintain a database similar to an online dating site that matches job vacancies in government with suitable young Conservatives looking to start their careers in the nation's capital; host seminars and workshops for newly elected members of Congress; invite seasoned politicians to participate in their conferences; and provide accommodations for their staff to serve on presidential campaigns.

Several of the strategies Heritage employs have been adopted by other think tanks in the United States, in Canada, albeit to a lesser extent, and around the globe. Even the Brookings Institution, the iconic think tank that continues to be revered in the academic community, occasionally holds focus groups on Capitol Hill with congressional staffers to find out if the research it produces is well-received. Brookings, like manufacturers of brand-name cereals, has a vested interest in making sure it is satisfying consumer demands.

From the vantage point of think tanks, it would be illogical, not to mention counterproductive, to avoid targeting policy-makers. After all, with the public's endorsement, they are entrusted with the responsibility to implement public policy, so why wouldn't think tanks devote the time, energy, and resources (assuming they are available) to ensure that their voices are heard. While think tanks clearly see policy-makers through their view-finders, policy-makers, interestingly enough, are looking directly back at them. As elected officials and aspiring office-holders have come to learn, policy experts at think tanks can prove to be enormously helpful on the campaign trail and once they have been elected or re-elected to office.

Yet, to maintain their independence and status as registered charities, it is important for think tanks not to align themselves too closely with political parties. Of course, there are exceptions in Canada[14] and in the United States, and in countries like Germany, where some think tanks receive funding from the state to serve the needs of political parties.[15] However, unlike in Germany, the majority of think tanks in Canada and the United States do not want to be perceived as mere appendages of political parties. This is not to suggest that policy experts from think tanks avoid interacting with party members. As discussed, as part of a broad-based and multi-tiered strategy, think tanks provide elected officials with a steady dose of policy advice. While this channel affords think tanks valuable opportunities to strengthen their ties to policy-makers, these interactions are often mutually beneficial. Not only can policy-makers benefit from the expertise that is being offered, both office-holders and those aspiring to replace them can tap into much larger constituencies and networks think tanks have developed over time. Think tanks and the interest groups and other civil society organizations with whom they associate can, among other things, help mobilize voters to support, or oppose, particular policy initiatives. Such was the case when the NDP government of Premier Bob Rae enlisted the help of several think tanks, including the Canadian Centre for Policy Alternatives, to galvanize Ontario's opposition to NAFTA.[16]

For both incumbents and challengers, there are other advantages to maintaining close ties to think tanks. As we observed in chapter 7, during the last several US presidential elections, dozens of policy experts from some of the country's most prominent think tanks have played a critically important role in advising candidates. But even when experts from think tanks have not taken a leave of absence from their employer to work on presidential campaigns, candidates from both parties have been able to rely on think tanks to help assess the public's reaction to various policy proposals. It goes without saying that on the campaign trail, presidential and congressional candidates can ill-afford to be linked to highly unpopular programs or initiatives. Therefore, rather than risk jumping into unfamiliar waters with both feet, candidates can sit back and watch think tanks test policy ideas with voters. It doesn't cost their campaign valuable resources, and, based on the public's reaction to the ideas marketed by think tanks, they can make strategic decisions about which issues to embrace and to avoid.

In these and other ways, think tanks can wittingly or unwittingly be a strategic asset for policy-makers. But as noted previously, they also provide policy-makers with a currency even more valuable than solicited or unsolicited advice: credibility and respectability. Although the golden age of think tanks during the progressive era, when policy institutes assigned the highest priority to helping government think its way through complex policy problems, has long passed, think tanks have still managed to preserve an element of credibility and respectability with the public. Realizing this, policy-makers often turn to them or seek their endorsement to garner more traction and support with the electorate. Yet, as important as policy-makers are to think tanks and think tanks to policy-makers, neither could function without the support and confidence of the public, a second key stakeholder to which we will now turn.

The Public

In the US mid-term elections on 5 November 2014, a meagre 36.4 per cent of eligible voters cast a ballot for their preferred congressional candidates. Two years later, 59.7 per cent of eligible voters turned out for the US presidential election that saw Donald Trump defeat Hillary Clinton to become the 45th president of the United States. In Canada, voter turnout in some recent provincial and federal elections was higher – 52.1 per cent in Ontario in 2014, and 68.49 per cent in the 2015 federal election. However, when half to two-thirds of the voting public neglects to exercise their democratic right to vote, how invested is the electorate in issues as important as health care, education, taxation, pensions, and peace and security? And if they are apathetic about the various initiatives policy-makers undertake, why should think tanks concern themselves with what the public cares or doesn't care about? Why should think tanks be more committed to shaping public policy than the individuals who will be directly affected by it?

While there is no doubt that growing public apathy has become a widespread phenomenon,[17] it has not discouraged think tanks from trying to engage the public in a dialogue over a myriad of policy issues. For think tanks, it is not about trying to reach half or more of the population that pays little to no attention to current affairs. It is about creating a conversation with the millions of people who do. And if think tanks are able to hit a nerve with the attentive public as they probe more deeply into the costs and benefits of embracing health care reform, or the advantages of introducing significant changes to how personal income is taxed, their efforts could be handsomely rewarded. To alter the political climate in ways that will advance both their institutional and ideological interests, as well as those shared by their corporate and philanthropic donors, think tanks need to tap into a wellspring of public support. Once the public is prepared to weigh in, or alternatively, to agree, it is only a matter of time before elected officials act accordingly. Such was the case following the events of 9/11 when the US Congress, at the urging of the Bush administration, voted the controversial Patriot Act into law. Playing on heightened fears and growing anxiety among the American public, policy-makers, with the encouragement and blessing of several conservative think tanks, elected to suspend civil liberties in pursuit of the war on terror. As intelligence and security services were granted more extensive powers to monitor, wire-tap and surveil, most Americans sat idly by and watched the government curtail their freedoms, a mistake Canadians tried to avoid when the Harper government passed its anti-terrorism legislation, Bill C-51, into law in the summer of 2015.[18] The Trudeau government has proposed amendments to this bill.

The decision of the Bush administration to ramp up its fight against terror was seen as a victory by the Project for the New American Century (PNAC), AEI, the Heritage Foundation, and other think tanks inside the Beltway who were calling upon policy-makers to send a clear message to America's adversaries.[19] But think tanks were not satisfied with winning periodic battles. Their goal was to once again claim victory in the war of ideas, something Heritage and the conservative movement celebrated as America moved further to the right during the Reagan-Bush years, and now into the Trump years.[20]

The importance of making a long-term investment in shoring up public support for their policy initiatives has not been lost on Canadian policy institutes. As noted, both the Broadbent Institute and the Manning Centre understand all too well how critical it is to train future generations of policy experts and policy entrepreneurs to involve the public in ongoing discussions about the future direction of the country. In doing so, think tanks realize that they cannot just focus on supplying ideas, but must assemble sizeable and vocal constituencies that will lend their voice and support to the proposals they hope to advance. But to do this, think tanks must introduce and maintain effective ways of communicating with the public.

As we have covered in previous chapters, think tanks rely on various channels to communicate ideas to the public and to other target audiences. In addition to maintaining websites that keep readers updated about their research projects and publications, think tanks highlight upcoming conferences and workshops, lectures, and any other new initiatives that may be of interest to those who monitor their activities. Think tanks also rely increasingly on social media to share their insights with select audiences, and, of course, take advantage of the print, broadcast, and electronic media to comment on various domestic and foreign policy issues. In short, think tanks recognize the importance of making their work accessible to the public. They also understand that when it comes to educating, informing, and mobilizing the electorate, it makes little sense to bombard them with reams of information they are unable or unwilling to process. The same can be said of policy-makers, who, given increasing demands on their time, simply cannot wade through the mountain of documents on their desks. If the purpose of think tanks is to generate and disseminate ideas that will influence public opinion and public policy, how can they ensure that the material they circulate is being read? While think tanks can never be entirely certain that their work is having the desired effect on their intended target audiences, they can all but guarantee how to discourage potential stakeholders from considering their findings. They must produce materials in a form that is specifically tailored to meet the needs and interests of their audiences. Otherwise, they will not make a positive impression on their intended audience.

When it comes to communicating with the public, think tanks have to be particularly sensitive: they need to strike an appropriate balance between informing the citizenry without overwhelming them with extraneous information. Achieving this balance is not always easy given the complex nature of many policy issues. Nonetheless it is essential. Think tanks cannot afford to alienate the public or, for that matter, any of their core constituencies. Determining how best to communicate with people who may know little about think tanks, but who wish to remain informed about current affairs, remains a priority for most policy institutes. However, for think tanks to gain notoriety, it is not imperative for the public to remember who they are, or what they do. Indeed, a telephone survey asking a cross-section of Canadians to list two or three think tanks in Canada would likely not generate positive results. What is more important for think tanks is to plant ideas in the minds of the electorate that may develop and grow over time. If and when this happens, think tanks will not have to look to the public to acknowledge the contribution they have made to generating discussions about pressing policy issues. On their own and/or with the assistance of the media, another key stakeholder with whom they target regularly, think tanks will be more than willing to seek out the adulation and recognition they so dearly covet from policy-makers, journalists, academics, and donors.

The Media

At any given time on any given day, policy experts from think tanks may be called upon to comment on breaking news stories. As journalists scrambled to make sense of why a Malaysian commercial airliner was shot down over the Ukraine, or why a lone gunman killed an unarmed Canadian soldier guarding Canada's National War Memorial and then went on a shooting rampage in the Parliament Buildings, they knew that help was only a few key strokes away. Within a matter of seconds, journalists could phone, text, and/or email experts at any one of dozens of think tanks in North America or around the world. And more often than not, experts at policy institutes are only too willing to oblige.[21] At some high-profile think tanks in the United States, scholars need only walk down the hall to access their institute's television and radio stations from where they can speak to the national and international media.[22] As noted in chapter 4, some think tanks, including Heritage and the Kansas Policy Institute, have created their own news services to disseminate political commentaries. But even the majority of policy experts at think tanks that do not have access to their own news outlets or communication facilities can and do make their way regularly to network news studios to be interviewed. Although disparagingly referred to as "talking heads," think tank experts perform a useful, and, at times, valuable public function by making themselves available to the media. However, even more important, in the process of building a stronger media profile, experts are helping themselves and the institutes they represent grow their stature in the policy-making community.

The creation of CNN and other twenty-four-hour news stations was a windfall for both the media and for think tanks. With plenty of air time to fill, the media welcomed policy experts from think tanks of all political persuasions who could summarize and explain why viewers should pay attention to unfolding political events at home and abroad. And with the launching of various political talk shows on Fox News, PBS, BBC, CBC, TVO, and other television networks, the opportunities for think tanks to gain access to the broadcast media multiplied exponentially. Think tanks, and the domestic and foreign policy specialists they employ, required little encouragement to strengthen their ties to the media. For years, policy experts have contributed op-ed articles to hundreds of newspapers around the globe, and, more recently, have started blogs on their employers' websites. But to further enhance their exposure, think tank scholars take full advantage of opportunities to either appear as guests on network newscasts, or as participants in conferences and seminars that are broadcast or live-streamed by their institute.[23]

Increasing media exposure is not only vital to think tanks as part of their ongoing efforts to affect policy change; it is critically important for attracting donor funding. To assess their policy impact, think tanks rely on different performance indicators or metrics, including media hits, testimony by staff before legislative committees, the total number of publications downloaded from their website, citations in academic studies, and government reports. In the absence of a bottom line that highlights losses or gains, think tanks, as not-for-profit organizations, are under heightened pressure by their boards of trustees and directors to evaluate their effectiveness. Think tanks thus need to demonstrate how they have made a difference. And since directors of think tanks have an incentive to equate public visibility with policy influence, no other indicator seems to preoccupy them more than how much media exposure they generate compared with their competitors.[24]

Chatham House, also known as the Royal Institute of International Affairs, is widely considered to be the leading think tank in the UK. According to some indices, it ranks among the world's best.[25] Yet, despite its sterling reputation and hefty coffers, the institute, housed in stately quarters overlooking London's St James's Square, does not take its status or financial future for granted. For several years, Chatham House has enlisted the services of a media consultant to track its exposure in newspapers in more than 190 countries. Several times a week, staff in charge of media relations receive a detailed breakdown of how many times the institute and/or one of its studies/scholars have been cited in what is now a massive database. These data are carefully maintained and monitored. But as with other high-profile think tanks around the globe, Chatham House does not collect this information so it can pat itself on the back but to remind both current and potential donors how far, and to what extent, its impact is felt.[26]

Directors of think tanks understand better than most that public visibility, often measured by media exposure, is hardly indicative of how much policy influence their organizations wield. But when funding dollars are on the line, that is not the kind of confession they are inclined to make. Rather than point to the innumerable variables that can influence public opinion and the policy preferences and choices of elected officials, they try to keep the message simple: the more exposure we generate, the more likely it is that the public and policy-makers will listen, and the more they heed our advice, the better the likelihood that through the studies and commentaries we generate, the more we will be able to shape the political climate and hence public policy. And then comes the pitch, "if you too are concerned about the direction our country is moving in, you may want to consider making a tax-deductible gift to …"

That think tanks have not fundamentally changed the narrative they have so adeptly constructed around the importance of media exposure suggests that their strategy is paying off. They are simply repeating a story that those considering investing in them want to hear. Developing and growing a profile that can enhance an institute's power and influence is something donors understand and appreciate. It makes sense, and, after all, it is how many of them achieved personal and professional success. As we will discuss below, donors do not need to be lectured about the intricacies of domestic and foreign policy, or how difficult it is to compete in the marketplace of ideas. They want to know what kinds of products think tanks provide and if they are in a position to grow their market.

Providing evidence that the media are interested in what they have to say can and does go a long way to help think tanks make claims of widespread influence.

The interest think tanks have in augmenting their media profile will only continue to grow, as evidenced by the sizeable investments some well-heeled institutes are making in their communications infrastructure. Indeed, if more newspapers close over the next several years, due to dwindling advertising revenues, it is entirely conceivable that some think tanks will step in to fill the void. Since they are already in the business of providing commentaries on current events, it might not be much of a stretch for think tanks to provide readers with a daily dose of news around the globe. This may entail providing news feeds from other media organizations, offering commentaries on various events from their unique ideological perspective, or even hosting panel discussions that would help to promote the policy recommendations of their institute. Taking on a more active role as a media outlet is clearly something the Fraser Institute and other think tanks are considering.[27] The union that has formed between think tanks and the media has clearly served both of their needs. The media depend on information, analysis of current affairs, and succinct commentaries, and think tanks, for the reasons outlined above, are well-positioned and equipped to meet their demands.

Donors

The Montreal-based Institute for Research on Public Policy (IRPP), CIGI, the Brookings Institution, the Hoover Institution, and a handful of other well-financed think tanks on both sides of the border have the luxury of drawing on interest generated from an endowment to help defray the costs of running their institutes.[28] Still, for most think tanks that do not have the security of endowments, there is no alternative but to compete for donor funding. The United States has several philanthropic foundations, including the Ford, Rockefeller, and Carnegie Foundations, that have donated billions of dollars to support America's leading think tanks. And with strong support from the corporate sector and affluent private donors, top-tier US think tanks enjoy multimillion-dollar budgets. However, the vast majority of think tanks in the United States and Canada have annual budgets hovering between $1 and $3 million. To just remain afloat, they must scrape together sufficient funds. To avoid the fate of the North-South Institute, think tanks must develop and maintain a diverse funding base.

Without strong donor support, it is unlikely, indeed improbable, that healthy populations of think tanks would have emerged in the United States and Europe over the past few decades. Think tanks need money, and fortunately they have been able to attract the funding they require to make their presence felt. But why, with so many causes to fund, from medical research to enhancing the quality of inner city schools, have donors invested so much and so often in the work of public policy institutes? One possible explanation is that donors, like the think tanks they fund, are committed to helping policy-makers make more informed decisions about public policy. What better way to do this than to support organizations that are well-equipped and positioned to exchange ideas with elected officials in the hope of bringing about more enlightened domestic and foreign policies? On the surface, this makes perfect sense. After all, philanthropy is about helping others, so why not use private funds to serve the public interest? Unfortunately, it is not that simple.

Whether they are providing funds to health care facilities, schools, think tanks, or other not-for-profit organizations, donors are astute investors looking to make solid investments. They may decide to allocate funds for more hospital beds and MRIs or state-of-the-art computers in digital labs. Donations might also be made to renovate conference rooms, build libraries, and possibly to construct entirely new buildings. Still, when donors make large gifts to think tanks, they are expecting far more in return than a charitable tax receipt and a plaque acknowledging their contribution. They are investing in institutions that straddle the academic and policy-making worlds, that have the wherewithal and political connections to shape the political climate for a long period of time. By supporting organizations that can alter the very complexion of the political landscape, as the Heritage Foundation and other conservative think tanks have done, donors can amass a currency far more valuable than money – political influence. As Inderjeet Parmar, an expert on think tanks and philanthropic foundations, has observed, donors are intent on creating and sustaining an extensive network of scholars and organizations that can promote and nurture their vision of the world, a world in which they can continue to reap enormous political and economic rewards.[29] They are certainly not investing in those who are intent on dismantling the society they have tried to build. If Parmar is correct, and I have every confidence he is, we need to consider what, if any, influence and control donors have over the kind of research findings disseminated by think tanks, the main weapon they employ in the war of ideas.

As mentioned, following the publication of a *New York Times* article in the fall of 2014 by investigative reporter Brooke Williams and her colleagues which claimed that in exchange for large donations to several prominent US think tanks, including the Brookings Institution, foreign governments expected donor recipients to lobby on their behalf,[30] former Brookings president Strobe Talbott wasted little time clarifying the relationship between donors and scholars at his institution. He stated unequivocally that donors have no say in what or how Brookings scholars undertake research. Brookings is, as its president pointed out, an independent think tank that produces independent research.[31] Talbott's forceful denunciation of the *New York Times* exposé was predictable. After all, the Brookings president could hardly remain silent when one of the leading newspapers on the planet had given such extensive coverage to the relationship between think tanks and donors. Perhaps he could have ignored the story if it had been buried in the *National Enquirer,* but this was not the case. And, in all fairness, what else could he have said? That with each cheque donors make payable to Brookings, they should expect the institution to do whatever it can to ensure their policy preferences are well received by policy-makers? From his vantage point, the only recourse was to do and say what he did.

Without being privy to Talbott's innermost thoughts and to the conversations in which he took part with donors and key personnel, we can only speculate on the role donors play in shaping the research agenda of his institute. Indeed, they may play no role at all, but we can never know for sure. The same can be said of what latitude, if any, donors are granted in providing input on the research projects at other think tanks. Nonetheless, in light of the increased importance think tanks, including Brookings, have assigned to political advocacy, the relationship that policy institutes have forged with donors cannot and should not be overlooked. We may not be able to eavesdrop on what is said between donors, think tank presidents, and their fundraisers behind closed doors, but we do know this: donors are not in the habit of continuing to invest in people and projects that don't pay off. The AEI learned this painful lesson when, in the mid-1970s, several conservative foundations decided to withdraw their funding, leaving the institute on the verge of bankruptcy.[32] As the competition for funding increases,[33] we also know that think tanks have an incentive to keep donors satisfied. Some think tanks may be able to do this by producing high-quality independent research that is reaching its intended audiences and having a discernible impact on the political climate. This should help keep donors at arm's length. Others, however, may have to be more accommodating of those who fund them. In the process, they may be required to compromise their autonomy.

The Academy

Policy experts who conduct research at think tanks are intimately familiar with the academic community. Not only have they received advanced degrees from some of the most prestigious universities in North America and Europe, but many of them have held, or continue to hold, joint appointments in the academy. Others, perhaps to keep a foot in the academic world, or simply to pursue their true passion, offer university-level courses on a part-time or sessional basis. But the links between think tanks and universities does not end there. In their capacity as coordinators of, and/or participants in, various think tank research projects, policy experts often rely on university faculty to contribute to their studies. As previously mentioned, IRPP and C.D. Howe, among others, contract out much of their research to faculty across the country. Academics may be asked to provide a chapter for an edited collection or an article for a journal or opinion magazine, participate in a seminar, workshop, or conference, or even be invited to become an adjunct or non-resident fellow at a think tank. Furthermore, some faculty may, as noted, decide to spend part, or all, of their sabbatical at a prestigious policy institute.

Scholars who study think tanks need not peer through a crystal ball to figure out why policy institutes have a vested interest in establishing and strengthening ties to the academic community. Indeed, just as policy-makers turn to think tanks in the hope that some of the credibility policy institutes enjoy will rub off on them, think tanks look to universities and to many of their more accomplished scholars to help bolster their stature in the policy-making community. In a similar vein, universities, to create the impression that the work they undertake is of direct relevance to the public and to policy-makers and therefore deserving of increased (not lower) government funding, have demonstrated a growing interest in think tanks and in the many marketing strategies they employ to enhance their visibility. At times, this has resulted in the creation of well-funded think tanks on university campuses such as CIGI, an organization made possible through significant private and public funding. Other times, universities have simply provided modest funding to support research centres and institutes that, at least on paper, may go some way to augment their public profile.

Thus far, we have identified four of the key stakeholders with whom think tanks interact, and if I gave the impression that policy institutes make a concerted effort to reach out to these constituencies in order to advance their core institutional interests, then I have accomplished what I set out to do in this chapter. To become even more entrenched in the policy-making community, think tanks need to build alliances, and they have done this with varying degrees of success with policy-makers, the public, donors, and the academic community. Yet, in recent years we have discovered that think tanks have cast their net even wider by becoming more integrated in social movements, policy networks, and other fora that give even more momentum and traction to the policy ideas they are attempting to advance.[34]

NGOS, THINK TANKS, AND FELLOW TRAVELLERS

Think tanks have a vested interest in protecting their intellectual turf and retaining whatever strategic advantage they enjoy over competitors. But as we discussed in the previous chapter, think tanks are also creatures of habit and remain committed to pursuing their goal to influence both the content and direction of public policy. To this end, they have established relations with domestic and foreign think tanks, interest groups, religious institutions, and a smattering of other NGOs who share a commitment to shaping the political discourse around a myriad of policy issues.

Building and expanding networks that comprise these and other organizations can, as several think tanks in Canada and the United States have discovered, help create the momentum they need to compel policy-makers to rethink how they intend to approach pressing domestic and foreign policy challenges. The cliché that there is strength in numbers is particularly appropriate when it comes to generating support for, or opposition to, government policies, and rarely do organizations engaged in civil society or in various social movements miss an opportunity to make their voices heard.

As part of these and other social and political movements, think tanks are often regarded as centres of intellectual innovation that can provide leadership and guidance in helping to frame the parameters of key policy debates. And with the assistance of interest groups and advocacy coalitions, they can play an important role in informing the public about the costs and benefits associated with various issues dominating the country's political agenda. For think tanks and the many organizations with whom they cooperate, the advantages of participating in common endeavours far outweigh the drawbacks. By contributing their insights into how to navigate the policy-making process and build coalitions that will lend strength to their efforts, think tanks, interest groups, and other NGOs might be able to achieve together what they could not possibly have achieved on their own. In the end, each of the key participants may take credit for swaying public opinion and public policy, but that is to be expected. For those engaged in these networks, what matters even more is attaining results that they can parlay into additional donor support.

Think tanks have not selected the various stakeholders they target by accident. In their own way, each serves a particular purpose. Policy-makers, donors, academics, NGOs, the public, and the media represent different pieces of a puzzle that need to fit together to help think tanks achieve their desired goals. On the surface, the pattern of cooperation and interaction described in this chapter may suggest that a conspiracy is afoot. However, it may be more accurate to interpret it as a well-conceived and multi-layered strategy employed by think tanks to enhance their visibility and project their influence in the policy-making community.

Think tanks often interact with similar stakeholders to affect policy change, but they do not necessarily engage them in the same way or to the same extent. Depending on the policy issue under consideration, think tanks must make strategic decisions as to how best to move public policy and public opinion in a direction that satisfies their institutional interests and those of their donors. But the first decision they must make is whether the policy issue in play is one in which they feel compelled to invest. This decision can be influenced by various considerations, including how much expertise they have on the subject (which speaks to their credibility), the resources they can afford to inject into it, and whether this particular policy concern, relative to the other issues they are exploring, will help augment the profile and stature of their organization.

In the case of Keystone XL, a handful of think tanks in Canada and the US deemed this issue sufficiently important to make their presence felt, and pursued various strategies to ensure their voices were heard. Given their location, mandate, and research focus, it is not surprising that four think tanks with Alberta addresses – the Canada West Foundation, the Fraser Institute (one of its regional offices is in Calgary), the Parkland Institute, and the Pembina Institute – played an active role in the pipeline debate. Given its interests in the impact of trade on the environment, it was also predictable that the Canadian Centre for Policy Alternatives would not remain on the sidelines while this hotly contested initiative was being explored. Similarly, in the United States, several well-known fixtures in the think tank community, with varying degrees of expertise in domestic and foreign policy, engaged key stakeholders in an effort to shape the discourse around Keystone XL. As noted, they included: the Cato Institute, the Council on Foreign Relations, the Bipartisan Policy Center, the Center for American Progress, and the Competitive Enterprise Institute. A brief background on each of these organizations, and the stance each adopted and advanced on the proposed construction of the pipeline is provided below.

THE PLAYERS – CANADA

The Canada West Foundation

With a mandate to promote the economic, political, and social interests of the four western provinces, the Calgary-based Canada West Foundation could hardly be expected to remain silent when TransCanada Corp proposed extending the Keystone pipeline from Alberta to refineries along the US Gulf Coast. Indeed, it did not take long for the CWF to issue a warning to the entire country that stalling the construction of the pipeline would cost Canada dearly. In a report commissioned by the Saskatchewan government, Dylan Jones, then CEO of CWF stated, "The loss to the Canadian economy will be devastating if we don't dramatically expand our pipeline capacity to multiple markets."[35] Michael Holden, author of the report and formerly the foundation's senior economist added, "If pipeline projects such as Trans Mountain, Keystone XL and Northern Gateway don't move forward, Canada will be foregoing $1.3 trillion in economic output, 7.4 million person-years of employment and $281 billion in tax revenue between now and 2035."[36] The CWF has continued to follow and engage in discussions around Keystone XL and other energy-related projects, and has collaborated with scholars at the University of Ottawa to identify local opposition to various energy projects. Its current president, Martha Hall Findlay, supports the pipeline.[37]

The Canadian Centre for Policy Alternatives (CCPA)

Few think tanks in Canada have played a more important role in raising awareness about the environmental impact of NAFTA than the CCPA.[38] The organization's concerns with how increased trade can and often does lead to a downward harmonization of both environmental and labour standards continues to strike a responsive chord with experts at the organization. Not surprisingly, the proposed construction of Keystone XL has come under close scrutiny at the CCPA. In addition to highlighting how the pipeline extension could affect climate change, the CCPA has publicly challenged reports promoting the economic benefits of Keystone. It has also brought attention to the impact of the pipeline on First Nations fishing and hunting rights.

Based in Ottawa with regional offices in several provinces, CCPA has been a major presence in the Canadian think tank community for decades. Often partnering with other think tanks and NGOs to affect policy change, CCPA, as we will discuss in the next section, relies on several channels to convey its ideas. In the case of Keystone XL, it has taken a very strong position against its construction.

The Fraser Institute

The free-market-oriented think tank, which has been discussed in some detail in this book, has not been shy in confronting Keystone's critics. In several of its publications, analysts at Fraser challenged the Obama administration's concerns about how Keystone could affect greenhouse gas emissions. They also argued that carrying oil through pipelines, despite recent oil spills in Alberta, may be a safer mode of transportation than relying on rail. Experts at Fraser have also suggested that, contrary to some reports, pipelines are "safer, cheaper and greener."[39] Consistent with its founding principles, the Fraser Institute, while recognizing some challenges posed by the pipeline's construction, remains a strong and vocal advocate.

The Parkland Institute

Located in the Faculty of Arts at the University of Alberta, with a second office in Calgary, "Alberta's left-leaning" Parkland Institute, as its critics often label it, "studies economic, social, cultural and political issues facing Albertans and Canadians using the perspective of political economy."[40] According to its 2008 "Self-Study," Parkland's values "include being open, critical, innovative, transformative, and solutions oriented."[41] In addition to its many research studies on health care, environmental sustainability, and energy, the Parkland Institute has relied on several other channels to communicate its findings and policy recommendations to multiple audiences. The Institute hosts several workshops and conferences throughout the year and its staff and research fellows regularly interact with the media. Although the Parkland Institute may not enjoy the same level of public visibility and notoriety as the Fraser Institute, the C.D. Howe Institute, and other public policy research organizations, it occupies an important position on the Canadian think tank landscape.

Unlike the CWF, scholars at Parkland have been outspoken critics of Keystone XL and have released several publications, including one co-authored with the CCPA, that question whether the pipeline would bring significant economic benefits to the West and to the rest of Canada, or would, in fact, send Canadian jobs to the US. Some scholars affiliated with Parkland, including Gordon Laxer, a well-known political economist, have gone so far as to work with the Alberta Federation of Labour to file a motion with the National Energy Board to delay construction of the pipeline.

The Pembina Institute

The Pembina Institute for Appropriate Development was incorporated in 1985 in response to a "major sour gas well" blowout near Lodgepole, Alberta on 17 October 1982. For nearly two months, the Amoco Canada well "spewed 200 million cubic feet per day of deadly hydrogen sulfide gas – or poisonous sulphur dioxide when it was on fire – along with toxic condensates."[42] According to the Pembina Institute, "the emergency response by the company and government was completely inadequate, characterized by the denial of responsibility, downplaying of human health and environmental impacts, and failure to protect the community. As a result, more than 200 residents joined together to form the Pembina Area Sour Gas Exposures Committee."[43]

In response to intense media exposure and growing public concern, the group was able to help launch a public inquiry into the Lodgepole blowout. The result was that many of the recommendations made by the group to prevent similar catastrophes were adopted. It was from this experience that a handful of individuals, including Rob Macintosh and Wally Heinrichs, decided to establish and incorporate the Pembina Institute.[44] The mission of the Institute is "to advance clean energy solutions through innovative research, education, consulting and advocacy." To this end, "it envisions a world in which our immediate and future needs are met in a manner that protects the earth's living systems; ensures clean air, land and water; prevents dangerous climate change; and provides for a safe and just global community."[45] Headquartered in Calgary with four branch offices, the Pembina Institute focuses on six main policy areas, including energy efficiency, liquefied natural gas, and the oil sands. Since its creation, it has released an impressive array of publications and media commentaries.

Pembina has remained a strong and vocal critic of the Keystone XL pipeline. Among other things, the institute is concerned that the extension would lead to a significant increase in greenhouse gas emissions, threatening Canada's ability to reach its 2020 emissions target reductions. As Pembina states in one of its blogs, "Until strong enough policies are in place to ensure that the cumulative impacts of current and future oilsands production remain below science-based limits, we see approving transportation infrastructure that enables expanded oilsands production as the wrong choice."

THE PLAYERS – UNITED STATES

When it comes to issues involving Canada, it is often difficult to grab the attention of policy-makers in Washington, DC, unless of course the country finds itself at the centre of a political storm. Such was the case when Donald Trump lambasted several trade agreements during the 2016 US presidential election, including the NAFTA, and the Softwood Lumber Agreement, which he felt privileged Canada at the expense of the US. It is also unusual for policy wonks outside the formal institutions of government to take an active interest in Canada and the various social, political, and economic issues affecting Canadians. Indeed, with the exception of a handful of think tanks such as the Hudson Institute, the Brookings Institution, the Canada Institute at the Woodrow Wilson Center for International Scholars, and CSIS, America's leading policy institutes have devoted little research to the study of Canada at. However, in the case of Keystone XL, a project that would directly affect the US, a number of American think tanks took it upon themselves to stake out positions. The think tanks that appear to be most active in policy discussions surrounding Keystone are referenced briefly below.

The Bipartisan Policy Center

Founded in 2007 by Bob Dole, George Mitchell, Tom Daschle, and Howard Baker, the Washington, DC-based Bipartisan Policy Center conducts research in nine major policy areas, including national security, immigration, finance, governance, health, infrastructure, and energy. Its current budget is approximately $25 million. The Bipartisan Policy Center has embraced an interesting approach to Keystone. At times, it has focused more on the efforts of Democrats and Republicans to come together on this issue, an approach consistent with, and encouraged by, the Center's mandate; at other times, it has extolled the virtues of both Keystone and the oil and gas industry, which has called into question its supposed bipartisan position.[46]

The Cato Institute

Widely regarded as a libertarian think tank that has enjoyed strong financial support from the Koch brothers, scholars from Cato have been very active in discussions around Keystone. A more detailed description of the institute can be found in Appendix 1. Generally supportive of the initiative, Cato was critical of the Obama administration's handling of the issue, and has aggressively challenged environmental groups and other critics who maintain that the extension to the pipeline will generate a significant increase in greenhouse gas emissions.

The Center for American Progress

As noted in chapter 6, the Center for American Progress (CAP) was established in 1993 to serve as a counterweight to the Heritage Foundation, much like Heritage was created as a counterweight to the Brookings Institution. The CAP has remained largely supportive of President Obama's domestic and foreign policy initiatives, including his decision to veto the construction of Keystone XL.[47] Analysts have been very vocal in their support for this position, citing environmental concerns as well as the impact Keystone could have on Indigenous people.

The Council on Foreign Relations

Scholars at the Council on Foreign Relations, one of America's most distinguished think tanks, have commented extensively on Keystone, and have, overall, maintained a measured, though at times critical stance on the role played by President Obama and the US State Department in delaying, and eventually vetoing, the permit required for TransCanada Corp to build the pipeline. Commentaries, blogs, studies, and testimonies are among the many outlets the CFR has tapped to convey their views about this ongoing project.

The Competitive Enterprise Institute

Established in 1984 by Fred L. Smith Jr, the Washington, DC–based think tank, with approximately $7.5 million in revenue, is dedicated to the protection of free markets and limited government. The CEI has been one of the most vocal advocates of Keystone XL, an endeavour consistent with the institute's desire to promote free market-environmentalism. Not surprisingly, the CEI also remains staunchly opposed to the Paris Climate Agreement and supports President Trump's decision to withdraw from the treaty.

SHAPING THE POLITICAL CLIMATE: THINK TANKS AND KEYSTONE XL

When it comes to assessing the impact of think tanks on public opinion and public policy, it is important to consider several factors, including the desired goals and objectives of policy institutes with respect to particular issues, their level or degree of engagement, and the extent to which they were able to achieve a preferred outcome. Although think tanks often assign different priorities to, and invest varying degrees of resources in affecting the content and direction of various policy initiatives, it is nonetheless possible to provide some preliminary observations about their involvement in policy discussions surrounding Keystone. As noted, if think tanks in Canada and in the United States set out to change Prime Minister Harper's and President Obama's minds on Keystone XL, their efforts were in vain. From the time the idea of constructing the trans-boundary pipeline made its way onto the bilateral political agenda, both leaders had carved out a position, one that remained intact throughout their respective terms in office. Similarly, both Justin Trudeau and Donald Trump have maintained consistent messaging around Keystone since assuming power. But what if altering the policy preferences and choices of successive prime ministers and presidents was not the ultimate goal of the various think tanks engaged in discussions involving Keystone? Indeed, what if their goal was to simply increase public awareness about the benefits and drawbacks of the pipeline, or to ensure that different stakeholders made their presence felt on this issue? Judged by these goals or objectives, several think tanks could claim victory.

Armed with both a nuanced and sophisticated knowledge of the policy-making process and an acute understanding of what it takes to compete successfully in the marketplace of ideas, think tanks are in the business of thinking strategically about how to make an impact. In the case of Keystone, the strategy think tanks embraced appeared to be less about bringing direct pressure to bear on the political leadership of both countries than mobilizing public support for, or opposition to, the construction of the pipeline. Recognizing that Harper and Obama were unlikely to change their stance on Keystone, think tanks had to ascertain the most expedient ways to endorse or undermine the respective positions advanced by the two governments. As they had in the past, think tanks placed considerable stock in framing the parameters around Keystone, highlighting how the pipeline would or would not result in significant economic benefits, and/or how it could undermine the environment and encroach upon the rights of Indigenous peoples.

On both sides of the border, think tanks relied on several channels to inform and educate the public and other stakeholders about Keystone XL. They published op-ed pieces in various newspapers, appeared before legislative committees, released a steady stream of analyses and reports, organized conferences, and networked with other think tanks and NGOs, all in an effort to bring greater attention to this controversial initiative. While some think tanks, such as the Cato Institute, the Council on Foreign Relations, the Bipartisan Policy Center, the Fraser Institute, and Parkland, may have generated more public exposure than others (see Appendix 7), their goal remained the same – to raise awareness about the pipeline by engaging the public, the private sector, and other interested parties. In short, in the case of Keystone, think tanks did what they were supposed to do. However, this rather simple observation remains problematic both for think tank directors and presidents, who are accountable to their boards of directors and donors, and for scholars, who continue to struggle with the most appropriate way to assess their influence.

It is not enough to maintain that think tanks routinely perform their assigned duties; those who represent think tanks in leadership positions are, as noted, under increased pressure to demonstrate how the work their institutes have undertaken has made a difference, whether in shaping actual policy decisions or legislation, or by informing broader public discussions around particular policies. This explains why think tanks closely monitor various performance indicators or metrics such as media exposure and legislative testimony, data that scholars who study think tanks continue to view with suspicion. So where does this leave us with respect to evaluating the impact of think tanks on the Keystone XL debate? On the one hand, we can compile metrics such as those included in Appendix 7, which reveal, over a specific period of time, how often a select group of US think tanks testified before Congress and were cited by various media outlets. Some preliminary data on the media exposure a small group of Canadian think tanks generated in relation to Keystone XL, which is included in the same appendix, might also be helpful in this regard. We could also expand this database by looking at how often interest groups or other NGOs concerned about the proposed pipeline were mentioned by different media sources, and whether some of their staff appeared before legislative committees. Yet, in the final analysis, we will likely end up where we started, desperately trying, albeit with little success, to establish a correlation between public exposure and policy relevance.

But why is it so difficult to assess the influence of think tanks and other NGOs, especially when we are aware of the activities in which they are involved? We know, for example, that on 7 May 2013, Paul C. "Chip" Knappenberger, assistant director of the Center for the Study of Science at the Cato Institute, presented prepared remarks to the US House of Representatives Committee on Science, Space, and Technology Subcommittee on Energy and Subcommittee on the Environment.[48] His comments focused primarily on the scientific and environmental issues around Keystone XL. Similarly, we are aware that on 26 March 2014 and on several other occasions, Michael A. Levi of the Council on Foreign Relations testified before various congressional committees on topics related to energy and the environment. But even if a complete list of experts from think tanks who were invited to testify before Congress was provided, scholars would still be left wondering whether the comments made by these and other policy experts left a lasting impression or even resonated with committee members. Although it would be helpful to scholars if committee members were required to fill out questionnaires indicating how useful or instructive they found the presentations made before them, such an undertaking would likely produce mixed results: for a variety of reasons, some committee members might find the comments informative and worthy of consideration, while others may be less than flattering in their assessment. Moreover, unless access to each committee member was granted though interviews or surveys, we could only speculate about the extent to which the remarks they heard altered their position on a particular issue. And even if a member found him- or herself swayed, an important question remains: what overall impression was the subcommittee or full committee left with, and what actions, if any, did they take as a result? The fact that an expert from a think tank testified before a congressional committee or subcommittee does not in and of itself mean that he or she was able to exercise influence. The same can be said for commentaries written by think tank scholars that appear in electronic and print newspapers and magazines, the remarks they make on television or in blogs, or books they have penned that make their way onto the desks or bookshelves of elected officials and/or their staff.

CONCLUSION

To better understand how and to what extent think tanks have or have not had an impact on shaping specific policy decisions or in affecting the policy-making environment, it is critically important, as this study has argued, to isolate their involvement at different stages of the policy cycle. The fact that some think tanks were active during the issue articulation phase of the policy-making process when the parameters around Keystone XL were being framed does not mean that they were as engaged when, for instance, US State Department officials were weighing the costs and benefits of approving a permit for the pipeline's construction. To more effectively determine the extent to which specific think tanks left a mark on Keystone, scholars must peel back multiple layers of the policy-making to expose what actually took place. Unfortunately, this becomes a difficult exercise, especially when issues such as Keystone are still in flux. A more appropriate time to conduct this investigation is when the matter has finally been resolved and scholars are able to determine what was said at meetings or in correspondence between think tank analysts and key decision makers. Of course, this assumes that material of this nature is made available for review.[49] An initial assessment, such as the one outlined in this chapter, confirms that think tanks have pursued multiple strategies to ensure their voices are heard. Although it is unlikely that any one policy institute will be able to convince Canada and the United States to adopt a different posture toward the pipeline, it does not mean that the investment that institutes have made in informing the public and other stakeholders about Keystone will be lost. On the contrary, as historians and political scientists have observed on countless occasions, it often takes years, if not decades or centuries, for ideas to gain traction. The inability of policy institutes to affect immediate policy change should not be interpreted as a failure; rather, the seeds they have planted in the minds of policy-makers, journalists, industrialists, and the public should be viewed as opportunities for further discussion and reflection. Viewed in this light, much of what think tanks have said and done with respect to Keystone may resurface when pipeline projects in the future are placed on the political agenda of Canada and the United States.

CHAPTER NINE

Conclusion: The More Things Change … Policy Influence, Policy Relevance, and the Future of Think Tanks in Canada, the United States, and Beyond

Among the advantages of writing a third edition is that you are provided with yet another opportunity to refine and clarify many of the observations made in the first two versions. In theory, as time passes and your knowledge of the subject matter increases, you should be able to shed further light on your research findings. The third edition should thus be more informative and instructive than the preceding ones. In an attempt to produce a more enlightened understanding of think tanks and their role in the policy-making process, I have updated and revised many sections of the book. But after many months and countless revisions, I am left once again to ponder the central question of the study: do think tanks matter? As in the first two editions, I can only conclude that, after surveying the think tank population in Canada and the United States and examining their involvement in the policy-making process, there does not appear to be a simple answer. Depending on whom the question is directed to, responses may range from yes or no, to more than you can possibly imagine. In some respects all these answers are accurate. Indeed, as this study has demonstrated, several conclusions can be drawn regarding the role and significance of think tanks in policy-making.

Notwithstanding the considerable differences in their political systems, think tanks in the United States and Canada have often played an important role in contributing to shaping the public dialogue and many continue to do so. Through their publications, interviews with the media, their growing reliance on social media, appearances before legislative committees, and participation in conferences and seminars, think tanks have clearly made their presence felt. Moreover, in both countries think tanks have relied on less visible channels to convey their views to policy-makers. However, largely due to differences in their political structures, think tanks in the United States and Canada often attempt to exercise policy influence at different times and at different stages of the policy cycle.

The highly decentralized and fragmented political system of the United States, combined with its weak party system, helps explain why American think tanks assign a high priority to sharing their ideas with members of Congress. Since members of Congress are not constrained by party unity, think tanks have an incentive to establish contact with as many Democrats, Republicans, and independents as possible. The nature of the electoral cycle in the United States, and the absence of party-based research institutes, also helps to explain why think tanks regard presidential elections and the transition periods that follow as opportune times to influence the policy direction of government. By contrast, the presence of strong party unity in Canada and the prime minister's long-standing tradition of relying on the Prime Minister's Office, the Privy Council Office, and senior bureaucrats for policy advice may account for why think tanks in Canada often rely on different channels to reach policy-makers.

Differences in the institutional structures of the two countries may explain why think tanks in the United States have more opportunities or access points to influence policy-makers than think tanks in Canada. However, they do not explain why some are far more effective at marketing their message than others. Several factors, including their financial resources, the number and quality of their staff, the strong connections some think tank directors have to policy-makers, and their ability to convey their ideas to multiple audiences may influence how much or how little impact think tanks have.

The willingness of office-holders to embrace the ideas of certain think tanks is also important in explaining why some enjoy tremendous visibility while others languish in obscurity. As chapter 6 revealed, several presidential candidates, particularly those regarded as Washington outsiders, have helped to elevate the profile of several think tanks. Similarly, in Canada, there have been periods when the visibility and prominence of some think tanks has either been significantly enhanced or greatly diminished. As chapter 7 demonstrated, at no other time have Canadian think tanks generated as much public attention as during the constitutional conferences in the winter of 1992. Ironically, less than two weeks after the last constitutional conference organized by a think tank ended, several other think tanks in the policy research community were forced to close their doors.

While it is not difficult to observe where in the policy cycle think tanks in the United States and Canada appear to be most active, determining how influential they are at different stages of policy-making remains problematic, since several methodological barriers must be overcome to do so. One major barrier is how to measure policy influence, a subject that is explored in considerable detail in my recent book, *Northern Lights*. Should influence be measured by recording media citations, tracking the number of website hits, monitoring appearances before legislative committees, the number of publications, or the number of staff appointed to high-level positions in the government? Or are there other tangible and intangible indicators that should be considered? Do some indicators provide a more accurate measurement of policy influence than others?

Although data on each indicator may provide insight into the amount of exposure think tanks and their staff generate, they cannot confirm how much or how little influence they have in shaping public opinion and the preferences and choices of policy-makers. For instance, several think tanks tally how often their organizations are referred to in the media and the number of times their staff are called on to testify before legislative committees. But what conclusions can be drawn from these data? Not surprisingly, think tanks that register the most media citations and appearances before committees conclude that they are the most influential. Those studying these institutions must, however, be a bit more circumspect. They should also be careful when considering global rankings of think tanks, which are also highly problematic. Data on media citations may tell us which institutes are effective at making the news, yet they tell us little about whether their views have helped shape, reinforce, clarify, or change the minds of policy-makers and the public. It cannot be assumed that policy-makers or members of the general public are even familiar with what certain think tanks have stated in the media. Similarly, when think tanks testify before legislative committees, we cannot be certain that their statements made a difference in how policy-makers approached particular issues. At times their testimony may influence the views of some policy-makers; at other times, however, their input may simply reinforce the views of policy-makers or, as is often the case, experts from think tanks might simply be ignored. Other indicators, such as the number of their publications or how many of their staff receive high-level appointments, may reveal even less about their influence in policy-making. It is thus virtually impossible to assign a numerical value to the amount of influence think tanks wield. We cannot, for instance, conclude that think tanks have influence 20 per cent or 50 per cent of the time. We cannot even say for certain how much impact specific think tanks have had at particular stages of policy debates or whom exactly they have influenced. At best, by assessing their involvement in specific policy areas, we can obtain a better sense of how relevant or irrelevant they were.

In addition to considering how to measure policy influence or whether, in fact, it can be measured at all, other obstacles must be overcome to *evaluate* the impact of think tanks: for instance, determining how to isolate the views of think tanks from dozens of other individuals and governmental and non-governmental organizations that actively seek to influence public policy. As the policy-making community becomes increasingly congested, tracing the origin of an idea to a particular individual or organization creates its own set of problems.

Examining the organizations and individuals who coalesce around particular policy issues or who congregate at a certain stage in the policy cycle can offer a useful point of departure for studying the interaction between policy-makers and representatives of non-governmental organizations in specific policy communities.[1] In addition to identifying the organizations and individuals most actively involved in discussing a particular policy concern with government officials, interviews and surveys can often be used to identify the views that generated the most attention more clearly. Yet, unless policy-makers acknowledge that their policy decisions were based primarily on recommendations from a particular individual or organization or heavily influenced by them, something they are rarely inclined to do, it is difficult to determine how much influence participants in the policy process were able to wield.

Since it is unlikely that these and other methodological obstacles will be overcome, it may be more appropriate to discuss the relevance of think tanks in the policy-making process than to speculate about how much policy influence they exercise. In other words, rather than trying to state categorically on the basis of a handful of indicators that some think tanks are more influential than others, it should be determined if, when, and under what conditions they can and have contributed to specific public policy discussions and to the broader policy-making environment. At the very least, scholars studying these institutions should acknowledge that, given their tremendous diversity, all think tanks do not possess the resources, expertise, or desire to become embroiled in every policy debate. They should also concede that think tanks assign different priorities to becoming involved at different stages of the policy-making process. Thus, while some think tanks may play an active role in discussing the implications of a specific government policy with the media, others may be trying to convey their views to policy-makers through less visible channels.

However, the organizations themselves will remain committed to relying on the most effective ways to distinguish themselves in the policy-making community. For some think tanks intent on convincing various stakeholders that their ideas do matter, this will mean generating as much media exposure as possible. For others, more subtle and less visible channels to communicate their ideas to policy-makers will remain a preferred strategy. This may help to explain why a select group of think tanks in Canada and in the United States continue to enjoy a disproportionate amount of media exposure, a subject to which we now turn.

TAKE THREE: THINK TANKS AT WORK

The patterns that were identified in think tank visibility in Canada and in the United States before 2000 have, with few exceptions, remained the same over the past several years. As discussed below, although more think tanks have entered the marketplace of ideas, for the most part the same institutions continue to attract the lion's share of media attention and are the ones most frequently called upon to testify before legislative committees. The many new tables and charts in Appendices 3 to 7 make it possible for readers to compare how much ground think tanks have made in raising their public profile. While the data sets can be subjected to various statistical tests, the findings on which think tanks attract the most public attention are clear.

In Canada, the Fraser Institute, the Conference Board of Canada, and the C.D. Howe Institute continue to generate the most visibility (see Appendix 4). During the period between 2009 and 2016, their scholars and publications were cited more often on national radio (CBC), on television (CBC and CTV), and in newspapers than most of their competitors. Indeed, with the exception of the Canada West Foundation, the Pembina Institute, the Canadian Centre for Policy Alternatives, and IRPP, the remaining think tanks included in this study have very modest public profiles. As indicated in Appendix 4, Table A4.1.1, which tracks the percentage of total media exposure of Canadian think tanks, the Fraser Institute (18 per cent), the Conference Board of Canada (17 per cent), and C.D. Howe (14 per cent) account for just under half the media exposure (49 per cent) paid to think tanks in the country. Interestingly, the Pembina Institute, which attracted 7 per cent of total media exposure, surpassed C.D. Howe in combined television exposure (CBC and CTV) and immediately followed the top-ranked Fraser Institute in the number of references made to it on selected CBC national radio programs. In table A4.1.1 in the ten Canadian newspapers for which data on think tank references were obtained, Fraser ranked first with 5,904 references, followed closely by the Conference Board (5,586), C.D. Howe (4,736), Canada West (3,870), and Pembina (2,213). Similar results were found in tracking the exposure of selected Canadian think tanks in five leading US newspapers (*The Washington Post*, *The New York Times*, *Christian Science Monitor*, *Wall Street Journal*, and *The Boston Globe*). Between 2009 and 2016, the Fraser Institute was referred to 74 times, followed by the Pembina Institute (67), the Conference Board of Canada (52),

C.D. Howe (17), and the Public Policy Forum (13). The vast majority of other Canadian think tanks were barely mentioned.

However, the results are very different when the annual budgets of think tanks are taken into consideration. Ranked first in total media exposure, Fraser's budget of approximately $10 to $11 million amounts to approximately 25 per cent of the money available to the Conference Board ($40 million) but is almost three times more than the operating budgets of C.D. Howe, Canada West, and Pembina. In other words, compared with the Conference Board of Canada, the amount of media exposure Fraser enjoys is staggering, but its public profile is less impressive when compared with C.D Howe, Canada West, and Pembina, which have far fewer financial resources on which to draw.

In the same period, a select group of Canadian think tanks also made their presence felt before several parliamentary committees and in various policy debates in the House of Commons and in the Senate. But unlike the initial findings presented in the first edition, which confirmed that between 1980 and 1999 the now defunct Economic Council of Canada ranked first in total number of appearances before parliamentary committees, in the last eighteen years (see chapter 5 and appendix 6) policy experts from the Conference Board have appeared more often than their competitors. In the absence of the Economic Council of Canada and other government-funded think tanks – casualties of the 1992 federal budget – it is conceivable that the Conference Board is being asked to provide expertise once offered by others. For example, between 1999 and 2008, experts from the Conference Board testified 143 times, followed by C.D. Howe (98), Fraser (73), the Canadian Council on Social Development (47), the Canadian Centre for Policy Alternatives (46), and the Caledon Institute (35). In the most recent period for which data have been collected (2009–2016), experts from the Conference Board testified 399 times, followed by individuals identified with a previous affiliation to the Economic Council of Canada (341), the Canadian Institute of Strategic Studies (307) which folded its operations into the Canadian International Council in 2008, and the Fraser Institute (207). The results also confirm an earlier observation that the ideological orientation of Canadian think tanks does not appear to be a decisive factor in determining whether experts from think tanks will be invited as witnesses before parliamentary committees. Conservative think tanks, including the Fraser Institute and C.D. Howe, have testified before committees during Liberal governments as often, and at times more often, than when the Conservatives are in power. The size of a think tank's budget can make a significant difference in the number of appearances think tanks make before parliamentary committees. Given the amount of time and resources that are invested in helping experts prepare testimony, it is not entirely surprising that, with few exceptions (Canadian International Council), think tanks with the largest budgets are also those that testify most often. This is not to suggest that this is the primary reason why some think tanks are invited to appear before legislative committees more than others, but it does help to explain the willingness of some institutes to employ their limited resources for these purposes.

A similar pattern emerges when tracking the number of references made to think tanks in debates taking place in the House of Commons and in the Senate (see Appendix 6). In the House of Commons between 1999 and 2008, the Conference Board was referred to 266 times, just slightly more than Fraser (259) and almost twice as often as C.D. Howe (136). In the upper chamber, the Conference Board also ranked first with 115 references. C.D. Howe followed with 48 and Fraser with 33. Not surprisingly, many of the references made to think tanks in House and Senate debates refer to remarks they made to parliamentary committees. In the most recent period (2009 to 2016) for which data in this category has been collected, the Conference Board of Canada once again held onto its first place ranking with 358 references, followed by the Canadian Centre for Policy Alternatives with 185 and Fraser 140.

In the United States, the storyline is virtually identical. Over the past ten years, the same group of think tanks have continued to receive tremendous exposure in American newspapers, current affairs magazines, and on mainstream television networks (see Appendix 3), although there has been some movement in the rankings. Topping the list in the last period (1998 to 2008) was the Brookings Institution, which was referred to more often than any of its competitors in every category. In this ten-year span, Brookings received a total of 9,184 citations. The American Enterprise Institute was a distant second with 4,936, and the Heritage Foundation collected 4,568. More recently, (2009 to 2016), RAND has taken top spot in media citations with 22,151 hits, almost twice as many as Brookings (12,310), and close to three times as many as AEI (7497).

As in Canada, three organizations (Brookings (26 per cent), AEI (14 per cent) and Heritage (13 per cent) accounted for approximately half (53 per cent) of the media attention paid to US think tanks (53 per cent). In the same period (2009 to 2016) RAND received the most coverage on television (215) from CNN (76 times), followed by ABC News (59), NBC News (48), and CBS News (32). Data on appearances by think tank experts or references to their work on Fox News were not available for this period. In most instances, these figures represent the number of on-air appearances made by experts affiliated with a particular think tank. However, periodically the data also include references to institute studies or to other news related to the work being conducted at think tanks.

According to the Vanderbilt University Television News Archive, which collects data on how often think tanks are referred to on network newscasts, the Center for Strategic and International Studies (CSIS) ranked second with 55 mentions, followed by Brookings (51), the Heritage Foundation (34), and the Carnegie Endowment on International Peace (26). As the tables detailing the number of references made to selected think tanks on network newscasts reveal, the think tanks included in the study generated far more coverage on some networks than others. For instance, RAND generated more than twice the amount of coverage on CNN than on CBS. Similarly, Heritage received over eight times as much exposure on CNN as on CBS. Similarly, CSIS and RAND enjoyed considerably more exposure than Brookings on ABC. A number of factors, including the ideological orientation of television networks, the personal contacts between network producers and think tank scholars, and the availability of scholars to respond quickly to media requests could account for these findings.

The number of references RAND received in several national newspapers in the US was even more impressive, a considerable improvement over where it found itself in the previous period (1998 to 2008). In the nine newspapers for which data were collected between 1998 and 2008, Brookings was cited 8,361 times. The American Enterprise Institute secured a second-place ranking with 4,591 references, followed by Heritage (4,223), the Cato Institute (3,023), and CSIS (2,983). Once again, the findings revealed significant variations in the amount of coverage think tanks received in each newspaper. Moreover, with few exceptions, this pattern was repeated in five national magazines and in a broad sample of Canadian and other international newspapers. In short, the same group of think tanks that ranked high in television coverage also found themselves at the top of the list in newspaper and magazine citations. In the most recent period (2009 to 2016), it was RAND, with few exceptions, that took top billing. In the same nine US newspapers for which data had been collected in the previous period, RAND generated 21,625 hits, almost twice as many as Brookings (12,154). These two powerhouses were followed by AEI (7,416), Heritage (5,258), CSIS (4,121), and Cato (3,260) There is little doubt that the budgets of US think tanks can significantly influence how much media exposure they generate. As discussed, for some think tanks, including Brookings, AEI, and Heritage, generating media exposure is a key priority. As a result they invest millions of dollars each year promoting their work. By contrast, several other think tanks with different priorities but comparable or larger budgets attract a fraction of the media attention Brookings and other media-savvy think tanks enjoy.

A slightly different picture unfolds when tracking the number of references made to selected American think tanks in the US Congress (see

Appendix 5). From 1999 to 2008, no think tank was referred to more often during debates in the US Senate and in the US House of Representatives than the Heritage Foundation. According to the *Congressional Record,* Heritage generated more references in Congress and in two congressional publications – *Extension of Remarks* and *The Daily Digest* – than any of its rivals. Heritage ranked first with 607 references, close to 200 more than Brookings (427) and twice as many as RAND (301). CSIS, which ranked first among citations in *The Daily Digest*, ranked fourth in total number of citations with 243, followed by the Urban Institute (234) and AEI (192). The three top-ranked think tanks (Heritage 22 per cent, Brookings 17 per cent, and RAND (12 per cent) accounted for slightly over half (51 per cent) of all references to think tanks in Congress. However, these rankings change when we look at how often policy experts from think tanks are invited to testify before congressional committees. During the same period, experts from AEI appeared before congressional committees more often than their colleagues at other Washington, DC-based think tanks (264 times). CSIS policy experts ranked second with 221 appearances, followed by Heritage (208), Cato (178), and RAND (152).

Brookings scholars ranked eighth with 42 appearances, just behind their colleagues from the Hoover Institution (46). Taken together, the top five ranked think tanks in this category accounted for 77 per cent of all appearances by think tank experts before Congress, a finding consistent with Rich and Weaver's earlier observation that conservative think tanks are more likely to be invited to testify before Congress when the Republicans are in power. How do these figures compare with data collected from 2009 to 2016? The data on media visibility and on think tank references/appearances in Congress thus confirm that an elite group of think tanks dominates the national media and in the federal legislature. The data sets also confirm that, with few exceptions, think tanks with the largest budgets are more likely to attract the lion's share of attention from journalists and policy-makers.

WHAT NEXT? THE FUTURE OF THINK TANKS: A VIEW FROM CANADA, THE UNITED STATES, AND THE GLOBAL COMMUNITY

Unlike elite think tanks in the United States, the majority of policy institutes in Canada cannot impress policy-makers with high-profile staffers or multimillion-dollar budgets, nor will they likely have the resources to do so in the foreseeable future. Nonetheless, as this study has shown, think tanks do not require millions of dollars or dozens of staff to convey their ideas. As Ken Battle of the Caledon Institute and Brian Lee Crowley of the Macdonald-Laurier Institute, among others, have demonstrated, using some ingenuity and creativity to communicate ideas to policy-makers and to other stakeholders can go a long way in helping think tanks become more relevant players in policy-making.

In the coming years, Canadian think tanks will face important challenges, not the least of which is securing access to sufficient funds to allow them to engage in rigorous research (should they elect to do so), and to strengthen their ties to multiple target audiences. To remain competitive, or indeed to become more competitive in the marketplace of ideas, some institutes may have to merge or occasionally pool their resources with other think tanks, as the Canadian Institute of Strategic Studies and the Canadian Centre for Philanthropy have done. This may be the only way a number of smaller think tanks can remain afloat, particularly during times of austerity. Others, like the Canadian Institute of International Affairs, may rebrand themselves to enhance their overall profile. Still, unless philanthropic foundations and affluent donors in Canada become as enamoured with think tanks as several leading philanthropists in the United States and Germany have, it is unlikely that many Canadian policy institutes will enjoy financial security.

Besides constant funding concerns, think tanks in Canada will have to give serious thought to what their mission is and how it can best be achieved. If think tanks are truly committed to improving public policy, as they often claim, they should provide policy-makers with what they require most – long-term strategic thinking about key domestic and foreign policy issues. On the other hand, if they are more interested in advancing a particular ideological agenda than in supplementing the policy needs of government, they should pay closer attention to the strategies pursued by more advocacy-oriented institutes in the United States. Although several think tanks in Canada have adopted this mode, there remains a glimmer of hope for some institutes that serious policy research can and should be pursued.

The tendency of think tanks in the United States and around the globe to become more advocacy-oriented will, in all likelihood, continue. After all, why would policy institutes forgo a strategy that often pays handsome dividends? As more institutes enter the already crowded policy-research community, they will rely on a wide range of strategies to capture the attention of the public, the media, policy-makers, and other interested parties. Moreover, if the Democratic and Republican parties, not to mention the country itself, become even more polarized in the coming years, members of Congress will likely be even more willing to listen to those think tanks whose views strike a responsive chord with their constituents. However, the ever watchful eye of the Internal Revenue Service could interfere with the efforts of advocacy think tanks to achieve their goals. If the IRS revoked the tax-exempt status of a high-profile think tank for engaging in inappropriate political activities, it would send a strong message to other think tanks to curtail some of their more aggressive marketing techniques.

Although the IRS will pay closer attention to the activities of think tanks, there is little to suggest that the growth rate of policy institutes in the United States will come to a halt. Think tanks have continued to spring up throughout the country and have continued to spawn throughout the international community. As long as there are policy entrepreneurs willing to create them, and philanthropists prepared to fund them, there is no reason to believe that the proliferation of policy institutes witnessed over the past three decades will fizzle out. The mortality rate among think tanks, other than those that have become casualties of government cutbacks, remains low. However, while a handful of think tanks in the United States will likely continue to dominate the headlines, it must be remembered that the majority of American think tanks closely resemble, in size and scope, those that populate the Canadian think tank landscape. As is the case with the majority of Canadian think tanks, those in the United States will have to think more strategically and methodically about how to carve out their niche in the policy research community, a challenge made even more difficult by the presence of several institutes with multimillion-dollar endowments.

The proliferation and evolution of think tanks in Canada and the United States will provide those engaged in the study of comparative political institutions and international relations with much to think about in the coming years. As they have over the past decade, scholars interested in think tanks will pay even closer attention to the role and impact of policy institutes on the world stage. Recently, the Shanghai Academy of Social Sciences, L'Observatoire des think tanks in Paris, and other organizations devoted to the study of think tanks have sponsored several conferences and workshops to help think tanks in both developing and advanced industrialized countries to consider the most effective ways to promote social, political, and economic change. Moreover, scholars who study think tanks are no longer confining their research to what takes place in the United States and in other western democracies. The explosion of think tanks in the global community, not to mention the willingness of various international and regional organizations to support their work, has convinced scholars to reflect more critically on how different political systems facilitate or impede the spread of ideas. This research is resulting in very interesting findings that will have profound implications on how political scientists, historians, sociologists, and economists study the impact of ideas on policy-making.

The growing involvement of think tanks in the policy-making process at the national and international levels will give rise to a new set of intriguing questions. Undoubtedly one that will be asked is, do think tanks matter? Judging by this analysis of Canadian and American think tanks, it is unlikely that a simple answer will be found. At the very least, as the literature on think tanks continues to grow, scholars must keep abreast of what ground has been covered and what still needs to be studied. While much has been written about the think tank landscape in many industrial and developing nations, we still need to know more about the internal workings of think tanks and how they assess their own impact in the policy-making community. These answers cannot be gleaned from global think tank rankings, which tend to be driven more by the reputations of top-tier think tanks than the value of work they produce. As difficult as it is for scholars to arrive at some consensus about how to measure policy influence, think tank directors and presidents continue to struggle over how to evaluate their performance. For those in administrative positions who must explain to their boards of directors and donor agencies how their resources are being spent and what results they have achieved, providing accurate and worthwhile performance indicators is not merely an academic exercise. Unfortunately, for these and other individuals, it has become a marketing exercise. In the absence of a more scientific way to measure influence, think tank leaders have resorted to constructing a narrative around the impact they believe their organizations have had in shaping both policy decisions and the policy-making environment.

The reality facing think tank directors and those who study their institutions is that there is no single performance indicator that will provide an accurate assessment of what they have achieved relative to other institutes in the policy-making community, an observation consistent with the findings in chapter 5. Under ideal conditions we could assume that all think tanks agree on the same set of indicators or metrics and allocate a roughly equal percentage of their budgets to enhancing their performance in each category. After adjusting for differences in revenues and expenditures, scholars could then provide an annual ranking of institutes, perhaps similar to the *Maclean's* ranking of Canadian universities and colleges, which could in turn be passed on to think tanks. The job of think tank directors would then be done. Or would it? What directors of think tanks would be left with is some indication of where they ranked relative to other institutes – for instance, in media citations generated or testimonies given. Unfortunately, while some think tanks might find comfort in these numbers, others would still be left with the lingering question of how much difference their institutes really made.

A potential solution to this nagging question would be for think tanks not to compare themselves with other policy institutes, despite external and internal pressures to do so, but to set out their own measurements of success. By reviewing their mission statements, think tanks could begin the process of identifying what policy issues they believed were important to study and the various channels they needed to rely on to convey their insights to selected target audiences. Once they had done this, they could then set out the performance indicators that would provide them with some insight into whether they were making progress toward achieving their specific objectives.

In examining the internal workings of think tanks, future researchers in this field will undoubtedly discover that policy institutes will rely on very different benchmarks for success. Some will continue to emphasize the importance of enhancing their media exposure and will closely monitor the number of media citations they receive. Others, however, will likely focus on less visible but potentially more influential channels, such as meetings and conferences with key policy-makers. What will be interesting to discover is how think tanks seek to implement their goals while constantly confronting the financial pressures of staying open.

Scholars should also pay more attention to what policy-makers think about the contribution think tanks have made at different stages of the policy-making process. They could do so either through interviews with, or through surveys distributed to policy-makers throughout government. A comprehensive survey of the attitudes of policy-makers and journalists toward US think tanks was conducted by Andrew Rich, but a similar survey has yet to be released in Canada.[2] Although some policy institutes have apparently commissioned private polling firms to survey Canadians about their views of think tanks, a more extensive survey of policy-makers is needed. The obvious benefit of a survey is that policy-makers can be asked specifically which think tanks have contributed to public policy and in what ways. They can also be asked to give examples of where think tanks may have made a difference. Among other things, those examples would allow scholars to develop more complete case studies.

In the case studies included in this book we are left with the impression that by virtue of participating in presidential campaigns some think tanks in the United States have become firmly entrenched in the policy-making process. While this is certainly true for a handful of institutes, the vast majority have not had the privilege of establishing such close ties to government. We are also left with the impression that unlike their American counterparts, think tanks in Canada have rarely played a critical role in policy development. Although this finding is consistent with the observations made in chapters 7 and 8, there are countless other policy issues in which Canadian policy institutes may have played a more decisive role. A survey of policy-makers would go a long way toward identifying these areas.

For those looking for a definitive answer to the question posed at the beginning of this book, the conclusion that I have reached may be disappointing, but I am convinced it is the right one. As in other avenues of scholarly inquiry, we are often left with far more questions than answers. That is why we engage in the pursuit of knowledge. Think tanks are interesting, incredibly diverse, and highly eclectic organizations worthy of further scholarly attention. As their visibility continues to grow, more people will question how much impact they have. I suspect this is a conversation that will continue for some time.

APPENDIX ONE

A Profile of Selected American Think Tanks

- The Carnegie Endowment for International Peace
- The Hoover Institution on War, Revolution and Peace
- The Council on Foreign Relations
- The Center for Strategic and International Studies
- The Institute for Policy Studies
- The Urban Institute
- The Cato Institute
- The Manhattan Institute for Policy Research
- The Progressive Policy Institute

THE CARNEGIE ENDOWMENT FOR INTERNATIONAL PEACE

Located adjacent to the Brookings Institution on Washington's Massachusetts Avenue, the Carnegie Endowment for International Peace (CEIP) has become one of America's premier foreign policy think tanks. With a $10 million endowment, the CEIP was established by Andrew Carnegie in 1910 as a nonpartisan institute to educate the public about peace, "to spread arbitral justice among nations and to promote the comity and commerce of the world without the dangers of war."[1] Acting on the advice of several leading pacifists, including then secretary of state Elihu Root, Carnegie stated that the annual income derived from the endowment should be used in any way "appropriate to hasten the abolition of war." Moreover, he directed that when "the establishment of peace is attained … the revenue shall be devoted to the banishment of the next most degrading evil or evils, the suppression of which would most advance the progress, elevation and happiness of man."[2]

In accordance with the wishes of its founder, over 200 researchers and staff, drawing upon a budget in excess of $40 million, examine a wide range of issues that fall under ten main programs, including: Asia, Europe, cyber policy, nuclear policy, and Russia/Eurasia. For many years (1970–2008), the institute was best known for its quarterly journal, *Foreign Policy,* which was purchased by the *Washington Post* in 2008. Along with dozens of other publications, and the many seminars and workshops the CEIP conducts, the organization is committed to stimulating debate among leading foreign-policy-makers. The Carnegie Endowment also relies on other channels to convey its ideas. Staff from the institute frequently submit articles to major newspapers and regularly appear as guests on American television networks.

In 1993 the Carnegie Endowment decided to expand its reach even further by creating a public policy research centre in Moscow. Designed "to promote intellectual collaboration among scholars and specialists in the United States, Russia, and other post-Soviet states," the Carnegie Moscow Center sponsors workshops, seminars, and study groups that bring together academics, journalists, and representatives from the private, public, and non-profit sectors to exchange views. The centre also provides a forum for international leaders to discuss various issues with audiences in Moscow. In 2006, Carnegie, which has branded itself the first global think tank, has opened four other research centres in New Delhi, Beijing, Beirut, and Brussels.

THE HOOVER INSTITUTION ON WAR, REVOLUTION AND PEACE

Known for its commitment to pursuing traditional conservative principles, the Hoover Institution at Stanford University has rarely strayed from the mission its founder laid out for the institute decades ago. Established in 1919 by Herbert Hoover to protect and house valuable historical records acquired during the First World War, the Hoover Institution's primary mission has been to reduce the role of government in economic and social affairs and to promote the national security interests of the United States.[3] As Herbert Hoover noted in founding the institute,

> The Institution supports the Constitution of the United States, its Bill of Rights and its method of representative government. Both our social and economic systems are based on private enterprise from which springs initiative and ingenuity ... Ours is a system where the Federal Government should undertake no

> governmental, social or economic action, except where local government, or the people, cannot undertake it for themselves … The overall mission of this Institution is, from its records, to recall the voice of experience against the making of war, and by the study of these records and their publication, to recall man's endeavors to make and preserve peace, and to sustain for America the safeguards of the American way of life. This institution is not, and must not be, a mere library. But with these purposes as its goal, the Institution itself must constantly and dynamically point the road to peace, to personal freedom, and to the safeguards of the American system.[4]

With an initial donation of $50,000 from Herbert Hoover, the institute has evolved into a leading centre for research and analysis on domestic and foreign policy. Scholars at Hoover focus their attention in nine major research areas, including: economic policy, education, health care, foreign affairs and national security, and values and social policy. The Hoover Institution's active research program results in the publication of several books and public policy essays each year.

Relying on a budget larger than $60 million, the Hoover Institution has assembled a talented staff consisting of over 150 scholars, including several former high-level policy-makers and Nobel prize-winners. However, despite the contributions many of its scholars have made to the fields of economics, history, and political science, the institute has had a stormy relationship with Stanford faculty and administrators for years. The turbulent relationship between Hoover and Stanford is in large part fueled by the active role Hoover scholars have played in assisting several Republican presidential candidates to win office, a subject that was explored in chapter 6. The presence of what has been perceived by several faculty at Stanford as an openly conservative think tank at a predominantly liberal university has resulted in several heated exchanges between the two bodies.

Like many think tanks based in Washington, Hoover relies on several strategies to communicate its research to policy-makers, including organizing workshops and seminars for elected officials and scholars to debate various policy issues. Yet, unlike some think tanks located outside the Beltway, including the Hudson Institute and RAND, Hoover has resisted the temptation to open a Washington office. Concerned that such a move would distract the institute from pursuing its research agenda, Hoover prefers to remain somewhat detached from the vicissitudes of Washington politics. Nonetheless, Hoover, like many think tanks, relishes the attention it receives in the media. It is particularly fond of quoting from a 1991 article in the *Economist*, which noted in its evaluation of think tanks that "The Hoover Institution on War, Revolution and Peace is hard to match for sheer intellectual firepower." Hoover might be less willing to acknowledge that in the *2016 Global Go To Think Tank Index Report*, it ranked 151st among US and non-US think tanks.[5]

THE COUNCIL ON FOREIGN RELATIONS

The origin of the New York–based Council of Foreign Relations (CFR) can be traced to an elite monthly dinner club that was established in the spring of 1918 to discuss various aspects of foreign affairs. Headed by Elihu Root, who had played an important role in convincing Andrew Carnegie to create the Carnegie Endowment for International Peace, the distinguished group of thirty participants created a forum in which leaders from finance, industry, education, government, and science could share their thoughts on pressing international issues. However, it was not until 1921 that the monthly dinner club was transformed into a permanent institution committed to the study of foreign affairs.

The idea of creating an organization dedicated to an "improved understanding of American foreign policy and international affairs" emerged when twenty-one members of a select group called the Inquiry were invited to accompany Woodrow Wilson to the Paris Peace Conference in 1919. Frustrated by Wilson's refusal to accept their advice and disillusioned with several of the provisions in the Treaty of Versailles, members of the American delegation began to discuss the prospects of creating a transatlantic research organization with their British counterparts. Despite their initial enthusiasm for the joint venture, however, the American and British delegates made little progress in achieving their goals over the next two years. Indeed, after it appeared that the venture would not move forward, two members of the American delegation approached Root and asked if he would be prepared to merge his Council of Foreign Relations with the body the American delegates had established at the Paris Peace Conference. With Root's consent, the two groups consolidated and incorporated the Council on Foreign Relations on 29 July 1921.[6]

The primary mission of the Council on Foreign Relations is "to foster America's understanding of other nations – their peoples, cultures, histories, hopes, quarrels, and ambitions – and thus to serve our nation through study and debate." It seeks to accomplish this mission by pursuing three goals: improving understanding of world affairs and providing new ideas for US foreign policy, transforming the council into a truly national organization, and finding and nurturing the next generation of foreign policy leaders and thinkers.[7]

The Council on Foreign Relations publishes the quarterly journal *Foreign Affairs*, as well as a wealth of studies on various aspects of world affairs. Yet it is perhaps best known for its distinguished and exclusive group of members. Among its 3,500 members nationwide (they must be nominated before they can join) are former presidents, secretaries of state, and other high-level policy-makers. At its headquarters in New York and at its several branches throughout the United States, prominent policy-makers and scholars are regularly invited to present lectures before members. Although the Council on Foreign Relations has cultivated a reputation as an elite club for policy-makers, throughout its distinguished history, it has developed a wide-ranging research program. Over 200 researchers and staff work at the CFR and conduct research in several areas, including Asia, Africa, peace and conflict, science and technology, trade, immigration, security, and international economics.

THE CENTER FOR STRATEGIC AND INTERNATIONAL STUDIES

The directory of scholars at the Center for Strategic and International Studies (CSIS) reads like a who's who in Washington's foreign-policy-making community. Home to several former ambassadors, secretaries of defense, and national security advisers, CSIS is among the most respected defence and foreign policy think tanks in the United States. Founded in 1962 by David Abshire, former assistant secretary of state for congressional affairs, and by Arleigh Burke, former chief of naval operations, CSIS's mission is "to inform and shape selected policy decisions in government and the private sector by providing long-range, anticipatory, and integrated thinking over a wide range of policy issues."[8]

With over 220 staff, including research fellows, administrative staff, directors, chairs, and advisers, and with a budget in excess of $40 million, CSIS, from its state of the art compound on Rhode Island Ave. NW, is well-placed to put its mission statement into action. Each year the organization convenes hundreds of meetings, seminars, and conferences with policy-makers and scholars in the United States and abroad and generates a steady stream of media appearances. CSIS also publishes several books, journals, and conference papers. Its marquee publication is the *Washington Quarterly*.

Over the years CSIS has developed an extensive research program that covers every region of the world and has established specific initiatives within regions that address issues of current relevance. Examples include or have included the Human Space Exploration Initiative, the International Security Program, Global Aging Initiative, Asia Maritime Transparency

Initiative, China Power, Defense Industrial Initiatives Group, and the Post-Conflict Reconstruction Project.

THE INSTITUTE FOR POLICY STUDIES

Often regarded as Washington's think tank of the left, the Institute for Policy Studies was founded by Marcus Raskin and Richard Barnett, two former staffers in the Kennedy administration. Convinced that steps had "to be taken to combat the over-militarized ways of thinking in foreign and national policy,"[9] Raskin and Barnett decided to establish their own institute, and with $200,000 in grants, the IPS opened its doors in October 1963.[10]

The fundamental purpose of the IPS is to provide the country's most important social movements with the intellectual ammunition they require to transform "their moral passion into a sensible public policy." To this end, the IPS has developed five principal programs that are intended to stimulate public debate and to help social movements succeed: global economic justice, sustainable communities, economic and social rights, real security, and culture.

The IPS, like other advocacy-oriented think tanks, relies on several channels to influence political change. In addition to conveying its ideas to policy-makers and the public through the media, the institute has established links to several members of Congress and individuals in the executive branch. It has also advised several presidential candidates, including George McGovern, Jesse Jackson, Bob Kerrey, and Tom Harkin.

The IPS relies on several strategies to extend its reach to various civil society actors, and over the years has maintained a strong and passionate commitment to issues of social justice. The IPS also works closely with dozens of national and transnational social organizations to mobilize opposition to various public policies, including many being advanced by the Trump administration. With a budget of $4 million and approximately forty-five staff members, the IPS does not enjoy the visibility of Washington's larger and better-funded think tanks. Nonetheless, because of its publications and networks with other non-governmental organizations, its views have not been ignored.

THE URBAN INSTITUTE

The Urban Institute, according to Paul Dickson, "had a typically long bureaucratic birth."[11] Although its conception can be traced to the Kennedy administration, it was not until President Johnson put his weight behind the initiative that the prospect of creating a think tank that could address the many domestic problems plaguing the United States during the 1960s gained momentum. As noted in its annual report of 1998, "the Urban Institute got its start in 1968 as the brainchild of a blue-ribbon panel set up by President Lyndon Johnson to monitor and evaluate the Great Society Initiatives that sprang from some 400 laws that had been passed since 1964."[12] President Johnson believed that the Urban Institute could bridge "the gulf between the scholar in search of truth and the decision-maker in search of progress."[13] Or as Sarah Rosen Wartell, president of the Urban Institute, noted in the organization's *2015 Annual Report*, "The Urban Institute's charge from President Johnson in 1968 was "to help solve the problem that weighs heavily on the hearts and minds of all of us: the American city and its people."[14]

Answering the need "for independent analysis of government performance and for data-driven research on America's cities and their residents in the wake of widespread urban unrest," the Urban Institute devoted its early years to examining persistent domestic problems such as poverty, education finance, unemployment, urban housing shortages and decay, urban transportation gaps, and the need for welfare reform.[15] Since then it has greatly expanded its research program. With over 450 staff members and a budget exceeding $95 million, the Urban Institute conducts research in several areas, including education, population, health, and human resources, housing and poverty. It is also home to eleven policy research centers, and engages in strategic research partnerships with organizations throughout the US and the international community. Although approximately 90 per cent of its research agenda is financed by public agencies and foundations, the Urban Institute has made a concerted effort to broaden its base of support over the years. It lists dozens of private supporters as contributors. Moreover, the Urban Institute's multimillion endowment provides added financial security.

The Urban Institute, like many think tanks created during the Progressive Era, jealously guards its institutional independence. Despite relying heavily on government support, the institute has been able to insulate itself from outside interference. According to its former president, William Gorham, the government has largely refrained from interfering in work that it has funded.[16] The Urban Institute continues to publish dozens of studies each year, and its staff members are often quoted in the mainstream media.

THE CATO INSTITUTE

Founded in 1977 by Edward Crane, former national chair of the Libertarian Party, who served as Cato's president until the fall of 2012, the Cato Institute has become something of an anomaly in Washington. Named for "*Cato's Letters*, libertarian pamphlets that helped lay the philosophical foundation for the American Revolution,"[17] the institute, which moved from San Francisco to Washington in 1981, promotes an odd mix of conservative and liberal ideas. On the one hand, Cato recommends scrapping the social-security system in favour of a private retirement program, a suggestion embraced by many Republicans. On the other hand, it supports gay rights and the legalization of marijuana, and it takes a liberal view of pornography, positions generally held by the Democratic left.[18] What Cato consistently opposes, however, is virtually all forms of government intervention.

Initially bankrolled by Kansas oil baron Charles Koch, a steadfast contributor to libertarian causes who has periodically found himself at odds with the organization,[19] Cato has since broadened its base of financial support to include many foundations, corporations and private donors. Although some of its donors withdrew their funding after Cato criticized the US role in the Gulf War, it has since found support among several powerful corporations, including Google, Facebook, Whole Foods Market, and the American Bankers Association.[19] In 2016 Cato's budget was approximately $30 million, all of which was raised from private sources. It does not accept any government funding.

Cato has grown considerably since its founding. It now has approximately 150 researchers and staff. Among its many publications are the *Cato Journal*, published three times a year, and several policy briefs, working papers and commentaries. In addition to holding conferences on a regular basis, Cato staff frequently convey their views to the media. Cato maintains detailed records of how often its staff generate media exposure.

THE MANHATTAN INSTITUTE FOR POLICY RESEARCH

Located on Vanderbilt Avenue near Grand Central Terminal in the heart of Manhattan, the Manhattan Institute was often referred to as former mayor Rudolph Giuliani's favourite think tank. Created in 1978 by the late William Casey, former director of the Central Intelligence Agency under President Reagan, the free-market institute had been credited with helping Giuliani sell his conservative agenda in a city known for its liberal leanings.[20]

The Manhattan Institute's conservative credentials are well deserved. In 1980 it helped launch George Gilder's *Wealth and Poverty*, "a paean to tax cuts and freewheeling capitalism," and four years later it aggressively promoted Charles Murray's study *Losing Ground*, "a tough-minded attack on social welfare programs."[21] Murray would attract even more attention later with his best-selling and controversial co-authored book, *The Bell Curve,* which examined the relationship between class and intelligence.

During its forty-year history, the Manhattan Institute has advocated a number of policies intended to move New York more to the right. Among other things it has supported the privatization of hospitals and actively promoted school choice. It has also spoken out against rent control. The institute uses several channels to market its ideas. In addition to its quarterly magazine, *City Journal*, it publishes books and articles and holds lavish lunches several times a month at the Harvard Club with journalists, politicians, bureaucrats, and business leaders.

The institute's staff of approximately fifty-five senior fellows and adjunct fellows draw upon the organization's $16 million budget to engage in a large number of research projects. Among other things, institute staff conduct research on a wide range of municipal issues of interest to officials both in New York and in other cities throughout the United States.

THE PROGRESSIVE POLICY INSTITUTE

Created as an offspring of the Democratic Leadership Council (DLC) in 1989, the Progressive Policy Institute (PPI) did not have to wait long to attract the attention of policy-makers in Washington. When Bill Clinton, former chair of the DLC, decided to run for the presidency in 1992, the PPI found the right messenger to deliver its progressive message. Indeed, when president-elect Clinton endorsed the PPI's blueprint, *Mandate for Change*, a comprehensive study of how to reform government, it became clear to many journalists covering Washington politics, that the PPI's views would be well received in key policy-making circles. As Thomas Friedman of the *New York Times* stated, "*Mandate for Change* is as good a crib sheet as any for Mr Clinton's first State of the Union Message, and the recommendations are expected to become standard-issue bedtime reading for the 'new kind of Democrats' about to take over Washington."[22]

Several ideas that the PPI helped to formulate made their way onto Clinton's political agenda, including national service in exchange for college loans. Moreover, several other issues that the PPI explored, including crime prevention, health care, educational excellence, and environmental safety, found a receptive audience in the Clinton White House, which had become home to a handful of former PPI staffers.[23]

The PPI's research continues to advocate a new progressive politics for the United States. Among other things, the PPI believes in restoring the American dream by accelerating economic growth, expanding opportunity, and enhancing financial and personal security. It also maintains that global order can be sustained by building new international structures based on economic and political freedom. With approximately one dozen staff members and a budget between $1 million and $2 million, the PPI has attempted to model its marketing strategy on the strategies employed by the Heritage Foundation and the Cato Institute.[24]

APPENDIX TWO

A Profile of Selected Canadian Think Tanks

- The Asia Pacific Foundation of Canada
- The Atlantic Institute for Market Studies
- The Canada West Foundation
- The Canadian Centre for Policy Alternatives
- The C.D. Howe Institute
- The Centre for International Governance Innovation (CIGI)
- The Conference Board of Canada
- The Institute for Research on Public Policy
- The Macdonald-Laurier Institute
- The Montreal Economic Institute
- The Mowat Centre
- The Public Policy Forum

THE ASIA PACIFIC FOUNDATION OF CANADA

Established by an Act of Parliament, the Asia Pacific Foundation of Canada Act, the Vancouver-based not-for-profit institute, is the country's premier think tank on Canada-Asia relations. With a mandate to "raise awareness and foster informed decision-making" about Canada's ties to this critically important region, the foundation works closely with public and private sector institutions on a wide range of policy issues. Drawing on the expertise of approximately thirty staff and a budget hovering around $6 million, the Asia Pacific Foundation seeks to develop and nurture networks among individuals and organizations committed to establishing a stronger Canadian presence in Asia.

According to the Act, which gave birth to the organization and defined its mission, the Asia Foundation is responsible for: (*a*) promoting mutual awareness and understanding of the cultures, histories, religions, philosophies, languages, life styles and aspirations in the Asia Pacific region and Canada and their effects on each other's societies;

- "(*a.1*) promoting dialogue on, and understanding of, foreign policy issues as they relate to Canada and the Asia-Pacific region, an additional goal articulated in 2005;
- (*b*) supporting development cooperation between organizations, institutions and associations in Canada and in the Asia-Pacific region;
- (*c*) promoting collaboration among organizations, institutions and associations in private and public sectors in Canada and in the Asia-Pacific region;
- (*d*) promoting closer economic and commercial ties between Canada and the Asia-Pacific region;
- (*e*) promoting, in Canada, scholarship in and expertise on economic, cultural, social and other subjects relating to the Asia-Pacific region, and in the Asia-Pacific region, scholarship in and expertise on economic, cultural, social and other subjects relating to Canada; and
- (*f*) collecting information and ideas relating to Canada and the Asia-Pacific region and disseminating such information and ideas within Canada and the Asia-Pacific region."[1]

In August 2014, Yuen Pau Woo, an authority on China who served as the Foundation's president and CEO for nine years and holds the title of Distinguished East Asia Fellow, was succeeded by Stewart Beck, Canada's former High Commissioner to India and Ambassador to Nepal and Bhutan. The Foundation is governed by a board of directors which includes the president and CEO, four other directors appointed by the Governor in Council and up to eighteen additional directors. The board is chaired by John H. McArthur, Dean Emeritus, Harvard Business School. Among its directors are: Colin Dodds, president, Saint Mary's University; Kevin Lynch, vice chair, BMO Financial Group; and Indira Samarasekera, president and vice-chancellor, University of Alberta.

The Asia Pacific Foundation's funding is drawn primarily from an endowment provided by the Government of Canada and by corporate and individual donors. In recent years, donors who have provided $100,000 or more included: BMO Financial Group, Shell Canada, Manulife Financial, and Teck Resources Limited. Sizeable donations in amounts up to $99,999 were also made by HSBC Canada, Port Metro Vancouver, Air China, Blake, Cassels & Graydon LLP, Canadian Association of Petroleum Producers, Canadian Pacific, Cathay Pacific

Airways, Deloitte, Fiera Capital, Husky Energy, Port of Halifax, TELUS, Vancouver Airport Authority, Westport Innovations Inc., Encana Corporation, Five Stars Travel Limited, Harvest Operations Corporation, The Japan Foundation, New Routes to the Future Ecological Foundation, POSCO Canada, Province of Alberta, Salley Bowes Harwardt LC, United Way of Canada, and The University of British Columbia.

The Foundation's current research focuses on four themes: promoting trade, investment, and innovation; building skills and competencies; mobilizing energy assets; and understanding Asia. It maintains an active publications program overseen by an editorial team, and experts, both at the Foundation and those contracted to undertake research on its behalf, publish a steady stream of research papers, blogs, surveys, and analyses for various audiences on a wide range of social, economic and political issues affecting Canada's relations in Asia. With extensive expertise on the countries of Asia and Canada's ties to them, experts from the Asia Pacific Foundation are called upon regularly to share their insights with the media. In addition, the Foundation offers post-graduate and research fellowships to academics to produce policy papers. Moreover, to further generate and disseminate its findings, the Foundation engages in the following activities:

- Forum of Discussion – "Disseminating knowledge and raising public awareness through roundtables, panel discussions and speaking engagements.
- Research and Analysis – "Promoting informed discussion on Canada-Asia relations through research reports, publications and opinion editorials."
- Special Research Projects – "Identifying and filling knowledge gaps on issues affecting Canada-Asia Relations."
- Track Two Diplomacy – "Supporting government-to-government processes to encourage and pave the way for new strategic developments."
- Grants and Fellowship Programs – "Providing new-generation researchers and journalists with the opportunity to engage in policy research and media coverage of Asia."[2]

THE ATLANTIC INSTITUTE FOR MARKET STUDIES

With a generous start-up grant from the Donner Foundation, a group of Atlantic Canadians set out to create an organization that would encourage policy analysts to address the unique challenges and opportunities facing the region. The result was the Atlantic Institute for Market Studies (AIMS), a think tank committed to broadening "the debate about realistic options available to build [the Atlantic]."[3] To fulfill its mandate, AIMS pursues four main objectives: initiating and conducting research that identifies current and emerging economic and social issues confronting Atlantic Canada; investigating a full range of options for public and private responses to these issues; communicating its research to regional and national audiences in a non-partisan manner; and sponsoring seminars, lectures, and training programs.

Reflecting on the need to create a think tank in Atlantic Canada that examines current and emerging policy issues in the region, Brian Lee Crowley, founding president of AIMS who, since 2010, has been managing director of the Ottawa-based Macdonald-Laurier Institute, remarked:

> There are other national think-tanks that aim to stimulate people to think in new and better ways about economic and social policy, to take the long strategic view, to speak out on controversial issues ... The C.D. Howe Institute, the Fraser Institute, the Institute for Research on Public Policy and the [Canadian] Centre for Policy Alternatives spring to mind. But these national organisations can devote little of their time and effort to the particular challenges and circumstances of Atlantic Canada ... regionally, there are other groups, like the Atlantic Provinces Economic Council, that gather and publish the most complete and up-to-date economic data on Regional Development, public academic treatises ... AIMS seeks to do more than provide useful factual information on what's going on in the economy today ... rather, AIMS exists to offer a platform for the best and brightest to put forward their own thoughts and analysis about what to do about our challenges and opportunities, about how we can think and act strategically, and for the long term, to build a more prosperous future for the region.[4]

AIMS relies on several channels to convey its ideas on how best to confront the many challenges in Atlantic Canada. In addition to producing a quarterly newsletter, the *Beacon*, and several other publications, including blogs that are targeted to university students, AIMS regularly holds conferences and seminars to promote exchanges between policy-makers, academics, and leaders from the private and non-profit sectors. Moreover, AIMS actively engages the media and encourages its scholars to share their insights with journalists. Funded by foundations, corporations, and individual donors, AIMS maintains an extensive research program that covers a wide range of topics: education, energy, healthcare, security and defence, regional development, and urban affairs. The president of AIMS, Marco Navarro-Génie, a scholar of Latin American politics, society, and culture, is supported by a large board of directors representing several large companies in Canada.

THE CANADA WEST FOUNDATION

The Canada West Foundation traces its origins to the One Prairie Conference held in Lethbridge in 1970. A consensus developed at the conference that research on Western Canadian concerns should not only continue, but be expanded. This decision led to the formation of the Canada West Council, which in turn developed the mandate for the Canada West Foundation. The Canada West Foundation is governed by the Canada West Council, "which provides direction on the current and future education and research activities of the Foundation."[5] The Foundation's budget of approximately $2 million is drawn from several sources, including the interest generated from an endowment created in 1996 which, in 2013, was valued in excess of $8.5 million.[6]

The Foundation pursues three main objectives: "to initiate and conduct research into the economic and social characteristics and potentials of the West and North within a national and international context; to educate individuals regarding the West's regional economic and social contributions to the Canadian federation; and to act as a catalyst for informed debate."[7] Its mandate is "to explore public policy issues of particular interest to western Canadians, to test national policies against regional aspirations and to ensure an effective regional voice in national policy discussions and the national political process."[8]

Canada West maintains an active research program, and in 2013, added three new policy research centres focusing on trade and investment; natural resources; and human capital.[9] Since its inception, the organization has published hundreds of studies on issues ranging from the effects of free trade on the western economy to the regulation of charities in Alberta to investment opportunities for the western provinces in Mexico. It also publishes a quarterly magazine, *Window on the West*, which explores a wide range of social, economic, environmental, and political issues of interest to Western Canada. A passionate advocate for greater western representation in Parliament, the Foundation has sponsored publications and conferences that have focused on the prospects for constitutional reform in Canada. However, in recent years, Canada West has diversified its research program by moving beyond the West's role in the Canadian federation. Supported by a large board of directors with representatives from Alberta, British Columbia, Manitoba, and Saskatchewan, Canada West actively engages key stakeholders to advance its mission. In addition to participating in workshops and conferences, researchers at Canada West interact regularly with the media.

THE CANADIAN CENTRE FOR POLICY ALTERNATIVES

The Canadian Centre for Policy Alternatives was founded by a group of academic and labour economists, including Steven Langdon, Peter Findlay, and Robert Clarke, who, along with a cross-section of representatives from labour unions and left-leaning political organizations, "saw the need for an independent progressive research agency to counterbalance the right-wing Fraser and C.D. Howe Institutes."[10] Unlike the free-market-oriented C.D. Howe and Fraser Institutes, the CCPA believes that "social and economic issues ... are not something to be left to the marketplace or for governments acting alone to decide." The Centre "is committed to putting forward research that reflects the concerns of women as well as men, labour as well as business, churches, cooperatives, and voluntary agencies as well as governments, minorities, and disadvantaged people as well as fortunate individuals."[11]

Since its inception in 1980, the CCPA has published hundreds of peer-reviewed reports, studies, and books on a wide range of social, political, and economic policy issues. Among the many topics it has examined are sexism and gender inequality, trade, poverty, and human rights. In 1994, it also launched a monthly journal, *The Monitor*, which may undergo significant change as the new editorial team looks to expand the journal's reach. Since 1995, it has released the *Alternative Federal Budget*, an edited collection of articles that, as the book's title implies, suggests different ways the government could spend its revenue. In addition to conveying its ideas through its many publications, the CCPA often works closely with policy-makers and representatives from unions and other non-governmental organizations to advance its agenda. It also recognizes the importance of maintaining strong ties to the media and, according to its own findings, ranks among the most widely cited think tanks in the country. CCPA closely tracks the exposure it generates in newspapers, on radio and television, and in social media.[12]

The CCPA's budget of slightly over $5.5 million is generated primarily from the contributions of its over 12,000 organizational and individual donors.[13] Close to half of its resources are allocated for research. The institute performs contract work for various governmental and non-governmental organizations as well. The CCPA's national headquarters is based in Ottawa, where it has more than dozen staff members. In 1997, it expanded its operations beyond the nation's capital by opening branch offices in Manitoba, British Columbia, Nova Scotia, and Saskatchewan. The CCPA also has a regional office in Toronto.

THE C.D. HOWE INSTITUTE

Few think tanks in Canada have attracted more attention in the media and in policy-making circles than the Toronto-based C.D. Howe Institute, an organization with a mandate to help improve living standards in Canada through sound economic and social policy.[14] Named after the Liberal cabinet minister Clarence Decatur Howe (1886–1960), who served in the governments of Prime Ministers William Lyon Mackenzie King and Louis St Laurent continuously from 1935–1957, the institute's origins can be traced to the Private Planning Association of Canada (PPAC), established in 1958 "by business and labor leaders to undertake research and educational activities on economic policy issues."[15] In 1973 the PPAC merged with the C.D. Howe Memorial Foundation (1961) to become the C.D. Howe Research Institute (HRI). Eight years later, when the HRI dissolved, the "Foundation again became a separate entity and the reconstituted PPAC was renamed the C.D. Howe Institute."[16]

Known for its expertise on Canadian economic, social, and trade policy, C.D. Howe has published hundreds of studies and sponsored countless conferences and workshops on virtually every major policy initiative upon which the federal and provincial governments have embarked. In 2013, the institute held "a record 60 policy events and publish[ed] a record of 55 research studies."[17] Many of these studies have been written by its small staff of in-house experts, including C.D. Howe's president William Robson and Wendy Dobson, and cover topics ranging from energy and transportation policy and healthcare to payment technology and governance and tax rates and credits.[18] Countless others have been contracted out to some of the country's leading economists and political scientists, including David Laidler, Judith Maxwell, and Thomas Courchene, Robert Young, Michael Hart, Sylvia Ostry, and Michael Trebilcock.[19] The institute, which devotes approximately 90 per cent of its budget to research and related expenses, and prides itself on publishing high quality, peer-reviewed studies, does not try to overwhelm readers with monographs of several hundred pages, but relies on brief studies or commentaries to highlight the implications of particular government policies.

The C.D. Howe Institute, unlike many other think tanks, does not assess its influence solely by the number of publications it produces or by the many prominent business leaders who serve on its board of directors. Rather, it evaluates its impact by the contribution it makes to stimulating informed public debate. According to one of its annual reports,

"The Institute monitors whether its output measures up to the high standards of its members, the media, policy-makers, and the public. Key indicators of success are strong attendance at Institute meetings, wide news coverage of Institute publications, an improved quality of public debate, and, ultimately, the willingness of policy-makers to listen."[20]

The C.D. Howe Institute follows a simple formula to ensure that policy-makers listen: it outfits "influential decision-makers with concrete research, [and] provide[s] a forum in which they can interact, and mix vigorously."[21] This formula seems to have paid off. Over the years, C.D. Howe has received dozens of endorsements from policy-makers, journalists, and business leaders who have acknowledged the valuable work of the institute. They also continue to enjoy the support of several major donors, including the Donner Foundation, Aurea Foundation, Max Bell Foundation, Lotte & John Hecht Memorial Foundation, and Pfizer Canada Inc. In addition, the Institute receives funding from several corporations and private donors.

Although the institute takes great pride in the research it generates, it pays close attention to how often its studies and conferences are quoted in the press, and how much traffic is generated on its website. According to its 2013 annual report, "C.D. Howe received a total of 1,466 citations across Canadian and international media in 2013 – a 46 percent increase since 2010 ... Online, cdhowe.org surpassed 15,000 monthly visits for the first time."[22] In its *2016 Annual Report*, C.D Howe provides even more detailed figures on its media exposure, and the various activities in which it has been engaged on Parliament Hill and in other important venues.

CENTRE FOR INTERNATIONAL GOVERNANCE INNOVATION (CIGI)

With a budget and endowment[23] that most think tanks in North America and Europe could only dream of, CIGI is, in many respects, in a class by itself. Founded by Jim Balsillie and Mike Lazaridis of the Waterloo-based telecommunications firm Research in Motion (RIM), the manufacturers of Blackberry, with a $30 million endowment ($20 million from Balsillie and $10 million from Lazaridis), and "with more or less matching grants from the Canadian and Ontario governments,"[24] CIGI was created as "an independent, non-partisan think tank on international governance."[25] In addition to CIGI, which Michael Valpy of *The Globe and Mail* describes as "the jewel of [Balsillie's] global endeavour,"[26] the Waterloo-based entrepreneur has invested millions of dollars to build the Balsillie School of International Affairs, the Balsillie Centre for Excellence, the Canadian International Council, and the International Governance

Leaders and Organizations Online (IGLOO). All told, Balsillie has spent over $100 million to secure a foothold in the international relations community. Allegations surround Balsillie's involvement in the academic affairs of CIGI and the Balsillie School of International Affairs, and his efforts to create programs jointly supported by CIGI and other universities in Canada have not been without controversy. Indeed, in 2012, York University faced a rare censure from the Canadian Association of University teachers (CAUT) for considering establishing a school in international law with CIGI.[27]

According to its website, "CIGI supports research, forms networks, advances policy debate and generates ideas for multilateral governance improvements. Conducting an active agenda of research, events and publications, CIGI's interdisciplinary work includes collaboration with policy, business and academic communities around the world."[28] Since 2001, CIGI has made a concerted effort to recruit many of the top international affairs scholars around the globe. Its extensive listing of research fellows, which currently exceeds eighty, boasts several distinguished experts, including David Welch, Thomas Homer-Dixon, Fen Osler Hampson, Simon Dalby, and James Blight. With considerable expertise upon which to draw and the financial resources to sustain its work, CIGI has established a number of important research programs. These include: global economy, global security, environment and energy, and global development. Many of these initiatives are supported by municipal, federal, and provincial government departments, ministries, and agencies. CIGI also receives funding from some international government agencies such as the Geneva Centre for the Public Control of Armed Forces and the United Kingdom Department for International Development.[29]

CIGI's research output of books, policy papers, briefs, and other publications has been impressive. Indeed, by 2010, the institute was generating over 100 publications annually, and the organization's output continues to increase. CIGI is conscious of raising its public profile; however, being situated in Waterloo, Ontario instead of in a major urban centre, has limited the amount of national exposure it generates.

THE CONFERENCE BOARD OF CANADA

The Conference Board of Canada is the largest policy research institution in Canada, but despite its visibility, the Board's origins can be traced to the United States. In 1916, the Conference Board was established in New York to "facilitate a cross-fertilization of facts and ideas in industry as a way of identifying and solving its problems and enhancing the public's understanding of these problems."[30] Like many other think tanks created during the Progressive Era, the founder of the Conference Board insisted that the organization engage in "unbiased fact finding" and "refrain from all political activity."[31]

During the decades following its founding, the Conference Board established itself as a highly credible and competent research organization that proved capable of addressing the needs of both American and Canadian companies. Indeed, as Lindquist points out, "With 40 large Canadian companies alone participating in the US-based organization, the creation of a Canadian office seemed a natural step."[32] In 1954, the Conference Board opened a small office in Montreal to respond to an expanding number of Canadian companies, Canadian-based US subsidiaries, and US companies interested in obtaining more information about Canada.[33]

The Conference Board of Canada has created a well-defined niche in the policy-making community. Unlike many smaller think tanks that attempt to influence public debates through their various publications and exchanges with policy-makers and journalists, the Conference Board specializes in providing knowledge in key areas to its members in the public and private sectors. In exchange for a membership fee, the Conference Board "[helps its] members anticipate and respond to the increasingly changing global economy ... through the exchange of knowledge about organizational strategies and practices, emerging economic and social trends and key public policy issues."[34] Its primary goal is to help its members become better prepared to adapt to changes in the marketplace.

As well as providing members with access to its publications and conferences, the Conference Board undertakes contract research. Known for its expertise in economic forecasting and analysis, the board also specializes in several other areas, including corporate social responsibility, human resource management, public sector management, and information and innovation and technology.[35]

Given its size and the breadth of its research expertise, it is not surprising that the Conference Board attracts more media attention than any other policy institute in Canada, a finding that the organization showcases in its annual reports.[36] To better assess its reach and impact, it also monitors, among other things, the hundreds of research reports it has published, the number of tweets it has posted, how many followers it has on Twitter, and the frequency with which it issues news releases and advisories.[37] When it comes to determining which performance indicators to consider in evaluating their impact, the Conference Board leaves few stones unturned.

THE INSTITUTE FOR RESEARCH ON PUBLIC POLICY

The Institute for Research on Public Policy (IRPP) is unique among Canadian think tanks. To begin with, with the exception of CIGI and a handful of other think tanks, it is one of the few policy institutes in the country whose financial security has been guaranteed by a sizeable endowment. With a current market value of close to $40 million, IRPP's "endowment fund was built up in the 1970s and 1980s by $10 million from the private sector and provincial governments, matched by $10 million from the federal government."[38] Since the interest earned from the endowment covers most of IRPP's operating expenses, the IRPP, unlike other think tanks in Canada, does not have to mount annual fund-raising campaigns. IRPP is also unique because it is among the few independent English-language public-policy research institutes in Quebec. After IRPP opened its doors in Montreal in 1972, its head office moved to several cities, including Ottawa, Halifax, and Victoria, before relocating to Montreal in 1991.

The IRPP's creation was inspired by the eminent Canadian economist Ronald Ritchie, who was commissioned by Prime Minister Trudeau in 1968 to examine the feasibility of creating an independent multidisciplinary research institute in Canada. After surveying the think tank landscape in several countries, including the United States, and after interviewing dozens of think tank directors and policy-makers, Ritchie recommended that an institute similar to the Brookings Institution be established in Canada to provide long-term strategic analysis. Although Ritchie's report did not result in the creation of a think tank on the scale of the Brookings Institution, it did lead to the founding of the IRPP and several other policy research institutes.

Remaining loyal to Ritchie's vision of an institute conducting independent policy analysis, IRPP has undertaken a "measured approach to public policy, which revolves around informing policy debates rather than advancing a particular ideological position."[39] It seeks to inform and educate policy-makers and the public, primarily through its magazine *Policy Options* and through its book-length studies. While staff members from the institute have also testified before parliamentary committees and submitted op-ed articles to Canadian newspapers, IRPP has claimed in the past that enhancing its media profile is not a priority. However, this position appears to have changed as the institute, mirroring other think tanks, pays close attention to its "impact" in the public arena. Indeed, on the first page of its 2014 annual report, IRPP summarizes its impact by highlighting in bold blue that in the past year, it recorded: 370,322 website page views, 111, 280 website visitors, 2,440 Twitter followers, 332 Facebook likes, 615 stories in the media, 17 publications, 16 events, and published 6 issues of *Policy Options*.[40] And according to its 2016 annual report, IRPP's exposure continues to grow. In that year it recorded: 1,045 references in the media, 14 op-ed articles, 763,891 website visitors, 21,366 downloads, 5,975 Twitter followers, and 676 Facebook likes.[41]

Despite allocating the bulk of its $2 to 2.5 million budget to research, the IRPP has not developed significant in-house expertise. Indeed, rather than hiring several researchers, the institute, like C.D. Howe, relies on its small staff to coordinate research projects that are undertaken largely by academics at various universities. IRPP's current research activity focuses on several areas, including: skills and labour market policy, international trade and global commerce, faces of aging, income inequality, and health and public policy.

THE MACDONALD-LAURIER INSTITUTE

Named in honour of two of Canada's most beloved prime ministers (a die-hard conservative and a passionate liberal) the Macdonald-Laurier Institute (MLI) burst onto the think tank scene in 2010 with a mission to "make poor quality public policy unacceptable in Ottawa."[42] To achieve this, the MLI is committed to "proposing thoughtful alternatives to Canadians and their political and opinion leaders through non-partisan and independent research and commentary."[43] Founded by Brian Lee Crowley, former founding president of the AIMS, the small but dynamic institute, with markedly conservative leanings, has made its presence felt in key policy-making circles. No stranger to the world of think tanks, Crowley has assembled an impressive cohort of research fellows to weigh in on several formidable policy challenges in several policy areas, including national defence and security, foreign affairs, Aboriginal issues, energy, justice, and immigration. He has also paid close attention to the many channels upon which the MLI can rely to convey its ideas to key stakeholders. In addition to showcasing several books and studies authored by scholars affiliated with the MLI, the institute publishes a magazine, *Inside Policy*, published six times a year. It also releases a steady stream of policy commentaries and a report entitled *The MLI Leading Indicator* which tracks recent trends in the economy. To further enhance its presence in the nation's capital and around the country and to highlight the importance of domestic and foreign policy challenges confronting Canadians, the Institute sponsors several conferences, seminars, and debates that have featured many prominent policy-makers, journalists, and academics.

Well aware of the difficulty think tanks have in measuring their impact, the MLI, like many of its competitors, relies on several performance indicators and rankings from the *Global Go To Think Tank Index Report* to assess its standing. In its *2013 Annual Report*, the MLI points out that, according to the 2013 edition of the think tank index, "it ranked third in the world in the category of best young institute," and indeed with "great policy products, it also managed to rank ahead of other older think tanks."[44] In the *2017 Global Go To Think Tank Index Report,* the MLI ranked 10th among the top think tanks in Canada and Mexico.[45] The MLI also keeps tabs of how often it is referenced by the national media and how many followers it has on Twitter and Facebook. In its annual report, it also references the number of visitors that access its website annually. However, unlike most think tanks that offer little more than statistics to convince readers how much influence they ostensibly wield, the MLI provides information about how and why it believes it was able to help shape policy discussions. Indeed, in the section devoted to "Impact and Public Policy" in its annual report, the MLI makes a concerted effort to demonstrate the similarities between its policy recommendations and legislation adopted by policy-makers.[46] Although far more research must be undertaken to confirm its findings, the MLI at least recognizes the importance of offering more than mere statistics about the influence it exercises.

MONTREAL ECONOMIC INSTITUTE

"When he launched the MEI's operations in 1999, our current President and CEO Michel Kelly-Gagnon, had at his disposal a staggering budget of $15,000, and his office equipment consisted of a telephone and a fax machine set up in one corner of his apartment," recalls Hélène Desmarais, chair of MEI's Board in the organization's 2014 annual report.[47] But a year later, with the backing of a small group of supporters, the free-market-oriented MEI was able to escape obscurity in its journey toward occupying a visible presence on Quebec's public policy landscape. Its goal is clear: "to stimulate debate on public policies in Quebec and across Canada by proposing wealth-creating reforms based on market mechanisms."[48] With a budget of little more than $2 million, raised primarily from individual donors, businesses, and foundations (no government money is accepted), the MEI has established itself as a strong and assertive voice on provincial and federal policy initiatives. Critical to MEI's success has been its ability to engage the media and other key stakeholders. As Michel Kelly-Gagnon acknowledges, "The evolution of the MEI's status to that of a privileged media partner was confirmed in 2014. Never worried about stirring things up and ruffling a few feathers, the MEI's researchers are still ready and willing to challenge preconceptions. But they are now increasingly cited for their original research, referenced as representative of one of the main positions in a debate, and invited to clarify a complex policy issue."[49]

MEI's research focus is wide-ranging and includes studies on agriculture, energy, health care, housing, labour, and taxation. In addition to the many studies and policy briefs it has published, the institute encourages its scholars to interact with the media. According to its findings in 2013–14, the MEI was referenced by the media over 4,387 times, had 2,307 followers on Facebook, 3,590 followers on Twitter, and 24,401 views on You Tube.[50] Two years later, its exposure had risen dramatically, with 8,073 media mentions, 4,326 Facebook followers, 4,064 followers on Twitter, and 53,540 views on You Tube.[51] And, like the MLI, the MEI has taken steps to explain how it has made a difference in various public policy debates. There is little doubt that it has made great strides since its humble beginnings.

MOWAT CENTRE

Housed in the School of Public Policy & Governance at the University of Toronto, the Mowat Centre, named in honour of Sir Oliver Mowat (1820–1903), Ontario's third and longest-serving premier (1872–96), has as its mission to "provide an independent Ontario voice on public policy by conducting and communicating analytically-rigorous, evidence-based public policy research that has meaningful impact, actionable recommendations and strengthens Ontario in a rapidly changing world."[52] With a grant of $900,000 from the Government of Ontario, the Mowat Centre conducts research in four main areas: intergovernmental economic and social policy, government transformation, the not-for-profit sector, and energy. In carrying out its research, the Centre sees itself as performing three main roles: as an idea generator capable of identifying and disseminating information on key policy issues; as a convenor that holds seminars, workshops, and conferences, and engages in informal conversations with various target audiences; and as a communicator who, through its research and gatherings, is constantly "developing and leveraging relationships among stakeholders, influencers (a term you won't find in the *Oxford Dictionary*), leaders, and decision-makers."[53]

Unlike many think tanks that take for granted that their ideas permeate key decision-making circles, the Mowat Centre pays close attention to the "impact" its research has on constituent groups. In its 2016 annual report, the Centre provides an "Impact-Performance Indicators Legend" which outlines the different kinds of impact and reach it could achieve. These include: references/citations in official government reports and documents and legislative debates; media mentions; published op-eds; references in research studies; and website activity. Alongside each publication listed in its annual reports, the Centre references these and other indicators to highlight the study's impact. Although keeping track of how often the Centre was cited in research studies or in the Ontario legislature may speak to how engaged Mowat researchers are in various public debates, and may go a long way in impressing potential donors, outputs are not outcomes. As noted, visibility does not guarantee policy influence, an observation not highlighted in its annual reports. Aware that these and similar indicators may not go far enough in documenting how much of an impact it has, the Centre goes one step further by tracking the level and frequency of access its staff have secured to policy-makers at different levels and branches of municipal, provincial, federal, and foreign governments.[54] While the nature and result of their interactions with policy-makers is difficult to quantify, the Mowat Centre is clearly aware of the importance of portraying itself as an active participant in the policy research community. How much of an impact the organization has had is debatable. Still, there is little doubt that in a short period of time, it has filled an important niche in the Canadian think tank community by becoming a leading voice on critical issues facing the province of Ontario.

PUBLIC POLICY FORUM

Located a few blocks from Parliament Hill, the roots of the Public Policy Forum (PPF) can be traced to "a formative meeting in Calgary [in 1987] with federal deputy ministers and private sector leaders."[55] At that meeting, "a strong consensus emerged regarding the need to create an independent space where leaders from the private and public sectors could meet regularly to discuss governance and public policy."[56] As the PPF points out in its brief history of the organization, "Since that time, the Forum's membership has grown to include more than 180 leading organizations from business, federal, provincial and territorial governments, academic institutions, unions, and the voluntary and not-for-profit sectors."[57] The PPF does not regard itself as an advocacy think tank that seeks to impose its agenda on policy-makers. Indeed, in its promotional literature, the institute emphasizes that it does not take positions on any policy issues. As noted, it was founded not to advance a particular set of ideological goals, but "to provide a neutral venue where the private sector and the public sector could meet to learn from one another."[58] According to the PPF, "In the 1980s, it became clear that, in the global arena where the quality of government directly affected the competitiveness of the nation, Canada suffered from the isolation of government from the private sector."[59] To remedy this problem, the PPF's former president David Zussman, noted, "we help to bridge the gap between the two solitudes – government and the private sector – in order to deal more effectively with issues of common concern."[60] For many years, the organization has also included representatives from the voluntary, or "third," sector in its policy forums.

The PPF's emphasis on organizing conferences and workshops for policy-makers and representatives from the private and non-profit sectors is reflected in the allocation of its resources. Approximately 60 per cent of the institute's operating budget of $3.5 to 4 million, raised almost entirely from membership donations, is set aside for this purpose. Among its more than 100 members are the Bank of Montreal, Bell Canada, Canada Post Corporation, and several provincial governments. Only 20 to 25 per cent of its budget is allocated for research, a function to which the PPF has begun to devote more attention. The Forum, which has done considerable work in economic, social and trade policy, has identified three themes in its *2013–16 Strategic Plan*, which fall under the broad categories of public service & governance, economy and competitiveness, and human capital.

APPENDIX THREE

Media Citations for Selected American Think Tanks, 1998–2008; 2009–2016

Table A3.1
References to Selected American Think Tanks in National Media (television, newspapers, and magazines), 1998–2008

Institute	*Television*	*Newspapers*	*Magazines*	*Totals*
Brookings Institution	392	8,361	431	9,184
American Enterprise Institute	83	4,591	262	4,936
Heritage Foundation	138	4,223	207	4,568
Center for Strategic and International Studies	221	2,983	138	3,342
Cato Institute	35	3,023	259	3,317
Urban Institute	12	1,978	97	2,075
Carnegie Endowment for International Peace	107	1,641	70	1,818
Hoover Institution	4	1,451	217	1,672
Manhattan Institute	7	1,417	128	1,552
Hudson Institute	12	1,033	94	1,139
RAND	206	768	18	992
Progressive Policy Institute	2	484	48	534
Institute for Policy Studies	17	389	11	417
Worldwatch Institute	2	254	41	297
Rockford Institute	2	0	0	2

Sources: Vanderbilt University Television News Archive / Factiva.com / LexisNexis.com.

Figure A3.1
References to Selected American Think Tanks in National Media (television, newspapers, and magazines), 1998–2008

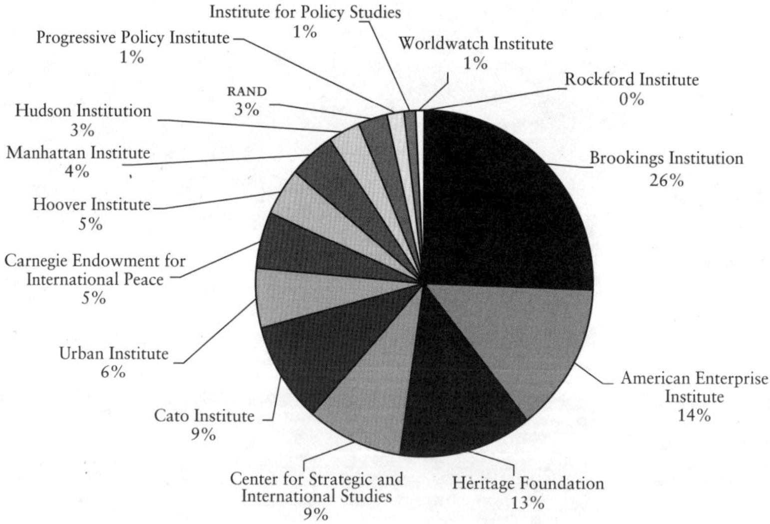

Table A3.1.1
References to Selected American Think Tanks in National American Media, 2009–2016

Institute	*Television*	*Newspapers*	*Magazines*	*Totals*
RAND	215	21,625	311	22,151
Brookings Institution	51	12,154	105	12,310
American Enterprise Institute	15	7,416	66	7,497
Heritage Foundation	34	5,258	61	5,353
Center for Strategic and International Studies	55	4,121	19	4,195
Cato Institute	11	3,260	86	3,357
Urban Institute	3	2,734	35	2,772
Hoover Institution	13	2,570	21	2,604
Manhattan Institute	0	1,780	50	1,830
Carnegie Endowment for International Peace	26	1,697	11	1,734
Hudson Institute	0	1,061	13	1,074
Institute for Policy Studies	1	564	8	573
Progressive Policy Institute	0	228	0	228
Worldwatch Institute	0	68	0	68
Rockford Institute	0	6	0	6
Totals	424	64,542	786	65,752

Source: Vanderbilt University Television News Archive.

Figure A3.1.1
References to Selected American Think Tanks in National American Media, 2009–2016

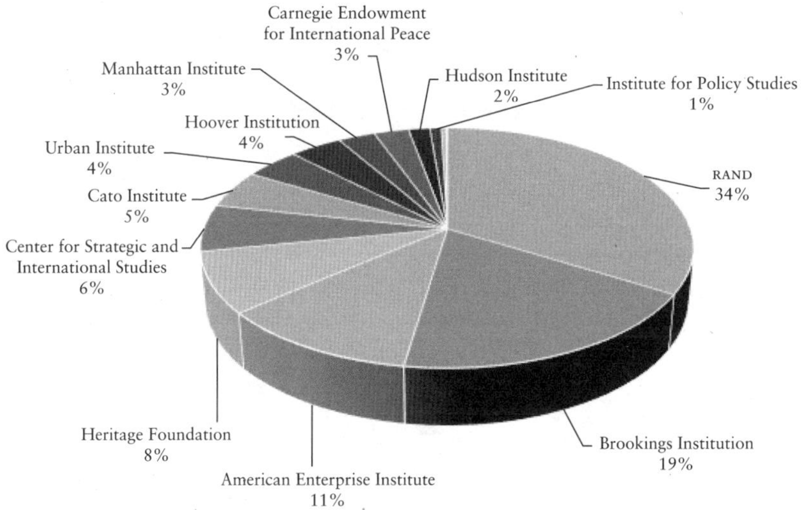

Table A3.2
References to Selected American Think Tanks on American Television News, 1998–2008

Institute	*1998*	*1999*	*2000*	*2001*	*2002*	*2003*	*2004*	*2005*	*2006*	*2007*	*2008*	*Totals*
Brookings Institution	52	53	59	51	40	26	27	20	30	34	0	392
Center for Strategic and International Studies	6	13	12	21	21	33	24	13	30	41	7	221
RAND	14	26	14	15	16	32	28	19	23	14	5	206
Heritage Foundation	4	9	10	10	12	16	22	23	19	10	3	138
Carnegie Endowment for International Peace	5	12	8	9	20	14	20	6	8	4	1	107
American Enterprise Institute	9	4	6	3	11	6	17	11	10	5	1	83
Cato Institute	2	3	8	1	2	5	5	5	1	3	0	35
Institute for Policy Studies	0	0	0	3	4	4	4	1	0	1	0	17
Urban Institute	0	0	4	0	1	2	3	0	0	2	0	12
Hudson Institute	0	1	2	4	1	1	0	1	0	1	1	12
Manhattan Institute	0	0	1	2	3	0	0	1	0	0	0	7
Hoover Institution	0	0	0	1	0	1	1	0	1	0	0	4
Progressive Policy Institute	0	0	1	0	1	0	0	0	0	0	0	2
Worldwatch Institute	0	0	2	0	0	0	0	0	0	0	0	2
Rockford Institute	0	0	1	0	0	0	0	0	0	1	0	2

Source: Vanderbilt University Television News Archive.

Figure A3.2
References to Selected American Think Tanks on American Television News, 1998–2008

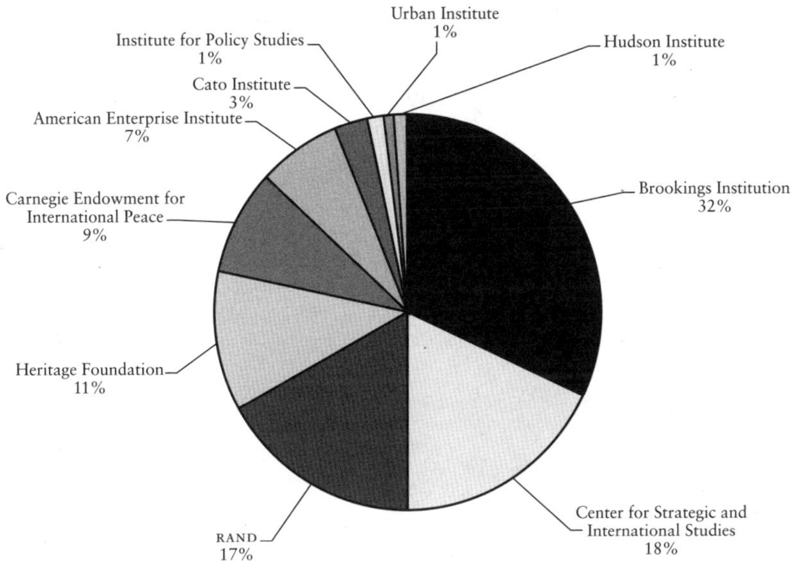

Table A3.2.1
References to Selected American Think Tanks on American Television News, 2009–2016

Institute	*2009*	*2010*	*2011*	*2012*	*2013*	*2014*	*2015*	*2016*	*Totals*
RAND	18	56	15	8	47	24	41	6	215
Center for Strategic and International Studies	17	16	12	1	4	4	1	0	55
Brookings Institution	18	8	12	7	3	2	1	0	51
Heritage Foundation	9	4	4	5	2	6	3	1	34
Carnegie Endowment for International Peace	7	4	10	3	1	0	1	0	26
American Enterprise Institute	6	4	1	1	1	0	1	0	14
Hoover Institution	0	0	1	0	11	1	0	0	14
Cato Institute	6	2	0	1	1	0	1	0	11
Urban Institute	1	2	0	0	0	0	0	0	3
Institute for Policy Studies	0	0	1	0	0	0	0	0	1
Hudson Institute	0	0	0	0	0	0	0	0	0
Manhattan Institute	0	0	0	0	0	0	0	0	0
Progressive Policy Institute	0	0	0	0	0	0	0	0	0
Rockford Institute	0	0	0	0	0	0	0	0	0
Worldwatch Institute	0	0	0	0	0	0	0	0	0
Totals	82	96	56	26	70	37	49	7	424

Source: Vanderbilt University Television News Archive.

Figure A3.2.1
References to Selected American Think Tanks on American Television News, 2009–2016

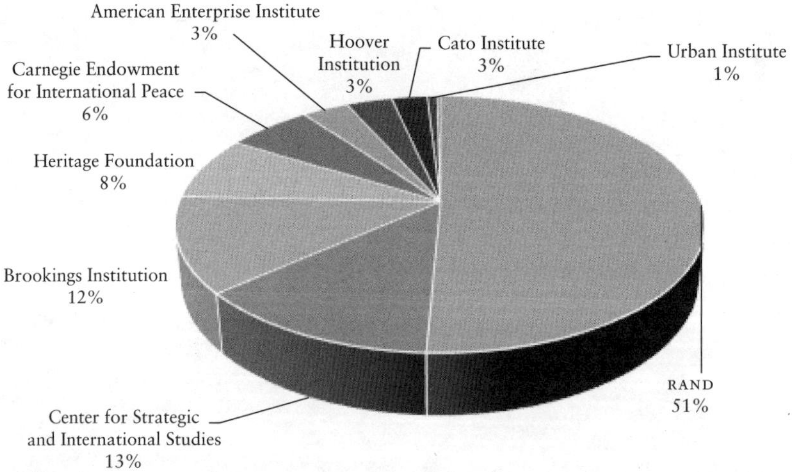

Table A3.3
References to Selected American Think Tanks on American Television News by Network, 1998–2008

Institute	*ABC News*	*NBC News*	*CNN*	*CBS News*	*FOX News*	*Totals*
Brookings Institution	79	200	70	37	6	392
Center for Strategic and International Studies	213	34	74	31	6	358
RAND	206	37	58	36	5	342
Heritage Foundation	23	34	44	24	11	136
Carnegie Endowment for International Peace	59	23	12	12	1	107
American Enterprise Institute	41	8	21	6	7	83
Cato Institute	6	12	9	4	4	35
Institute for Policy Studies	6	3	4	2	2	17
Urban Institute	0	6	1	5	1	13
Hudson Institute	1	6	1	1	0	9
Manhattan Institute	0	3	1	3	0	7
Hoover Institution	2	1	0	1	0	4
Progressive Policy Institute	0	2	0	0	0	2
Worldwatch Institute	1	0	1	0	0	2
Rockford Institute	2	1	1	0	0	4
Totals	639	370	297	162	43	

Source: Vanderbilt University Television News Archive.

Figure A3.3
References to Selected American Think Tanks on American Television News by Network, 1998–2008

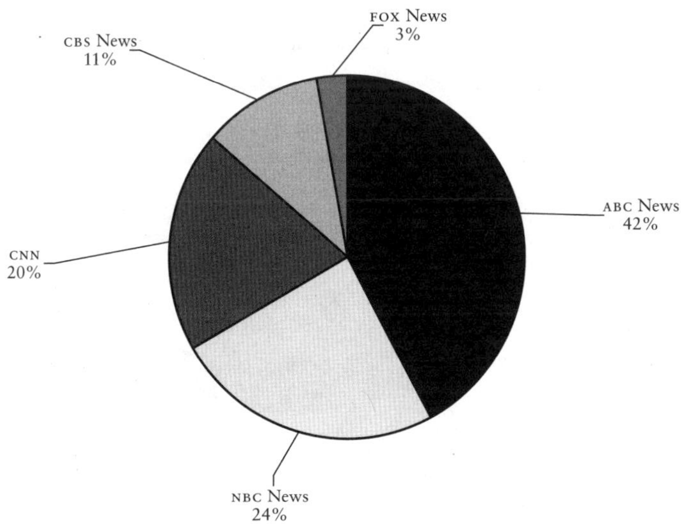

Table A3.3.1
References to Selected American Think Tanks on American Television News by Network, 2009–2016

Institute	ABC *News*	NBC *News*	CNN	CBS *News*	FOX *News*	*Totals*
RAND	59	48	76	32	0	215
Center for Strategic and International Studies	12	20	4	19	0	55
Brookings Institution	1	33	4	13	0	51
Heritage Foundation	8	7	17	2	0	34
Carnegie Endowment for International Peace	7	15	2	2	0	26
American Enterprise Institute	0	4	3	7	0	14
Hoover Institute	0	1	12	0	0	13
Cato Institute	0	5	1	5	0	11
Urban Institute	0	1	0	2	0	3
Institute for Policy Studies	0	1	0	0	0	1
Hudson Institute	0	0	0	0	0	0
Manhattan Institute	0	0	0	0	0	0
Progressive Policy Institute	0	0	0	0	0	0
Rockford Institute	0	0	0	0	0	0
Worldwatch Institute	0	0	0	0	0	0
Totals	87	135	119	82	0	423

Source: Vanderbilt University Television News Archive.

Figure A3.3.1
References to Selected American Think Tanks on American Television News by Network, 2009–2016

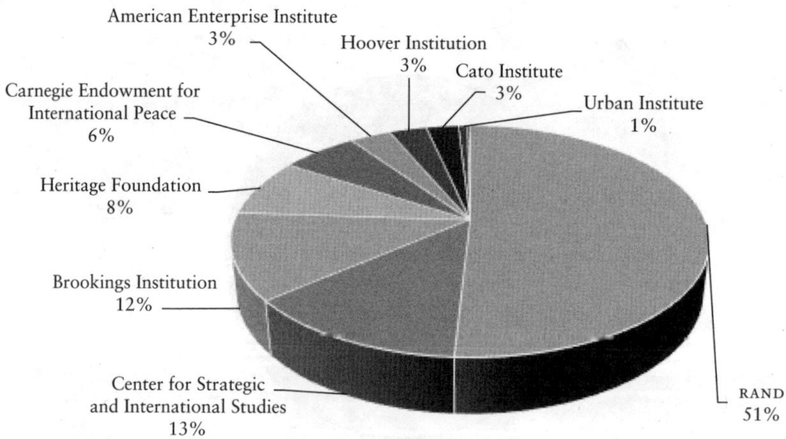

Table A3.4
References to Selected American Think Tanks on ABC News, 1998–2008

Institute	*1998*	*1999*	*2000*	*2001*	*2002*	*2003*	*2004*	*2005*	*2006*	*2007*	*2008*	*Totals*
Center for Strategic and International Studies	6	11	12	21	21	33	24	13	31	36	5	213
RAND	14	26	14	15	16	32	28	19	23	14	5	206
Brookings Institution	8	14	19	16	8	5	6	1	2	0	0	79
Carnegie Endowment for International Peace	4	9	2	6	13	10	5	5	4	1	0	59
American Enterprise Institution	6	4	4	2	6	5	5	4	3	2	0	41
Heritage Foundation	0	2	2	3	1	4	2	2	4	2	1	23
Cato Institute	0	0	1	0	1	3	0	0	0	1	0	6
Institute for Policy Studies	0	0	0	1	2	1	2	0	0	0	0	6
Hoover Institution	0	0	0	1	0	0	1	0	0	0	0	2
Rockford Institute	0	0	0	0	0	0	2	0	0	0	0	2
Worldwatch Institute	0	0	1	0	0	0	0	0	0	0	0	1
Hudson Institution	0	0	0	0	0	1	0	0	0	0	0	1
Progressive Policy Institute	0	0	0	0	0	0	0	0	0	0	0	0
Urban Institute	0	0	0	0	0	0	0	0	0	0	0	0
Manhattan Institute	0	0	0	0	0	0	0	0	0	0	0	0

Source: Vanderbilt University Television News Archive.

Figure A3.4
References to Selected American Think Tanks on ABC News, 1998–2008

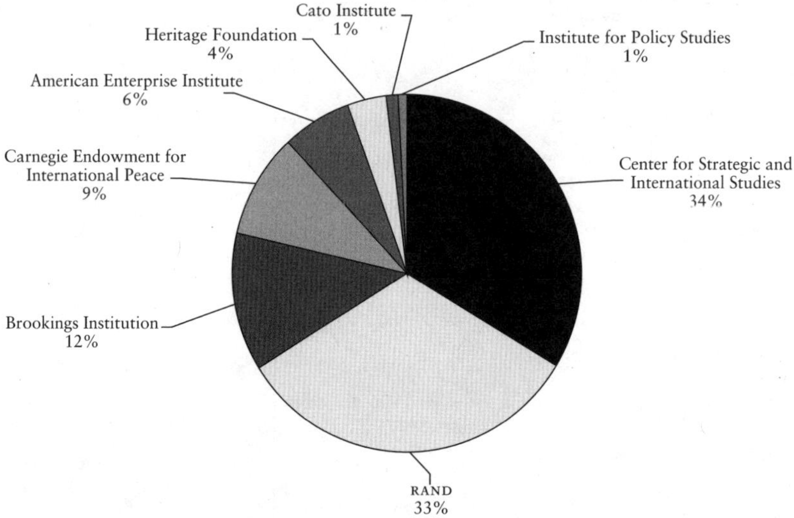

Table A3.4.1
References to Selected American Think Tanks on ABC News, 2009–2016

Institute	*2009*	*2010*	*2011*	*2012*	*2013*	*2014*	*2015*	*2016*	*Totals*
RAND	7	11	5	5	12	5	12	2	59
Center for Strategic and International Studies	1	6	2	2	1	0	0	0	12
Heritage Foundation	1	2	2	1	1	0	1	0	8
Carnegie Endowment for International Peace	4	0	3	0	0	0	0	0	7
Brookings Institution	0	0	1	0	0	0	0	0	1
Cato Institute	0	0	0	0	0	0	0	0	0
American Enterprise Institute	0	0	0	0	0	0	0	0	0
Urban Institute	0	0	0	0	0	0	0	0	0
Hudson Institute	0	0	0	0	0	0	0	0	0
Manhattan Institute	0	0	0	0	0	0	0	0	0
Institute for Policy Studies	0	0	0	0	0	0	0	0	0
Progressive Policy Institute	0	0	0	0	0	0	0	0	0
Hoover Institution	0	0	0	0	0	0	0	0	0
Rockford Institute	0	0	0	0	0	0	0	0	0
Worldwatch Institute	0	0	0	0	0	0	0	0	0

Source: Vanderbilt University Television News Archive.

Figure A3.4.1
References to Selected American Think Tanks on ABC News, 2009–2016

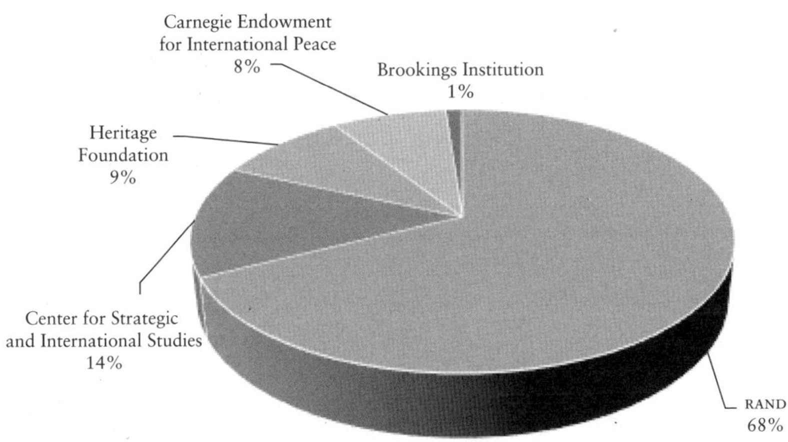

Table A3.5
References to Selected American Think Tanks on NBC News, 1998–2008

Institute	*1998*	*1999*	*2000*	*2001*	*2002*	*2003*	*2004*	*2005*	*2006*	*2007*	*2008*	*Totals*
Brookings Institution	26	26	23	20	25	9	10	15	20	26	0	200
RAND	3	0	3	4	4	4	5	7	6	1	0	37
Heritage Foundation	2	3	3	5	3	0	7	4	5	2	0	34
Center for Strategic and International Studies	1	1	2	5	5	6	4	4	1	3	2	34
Carnegie Endowment for International Peace	1	2	4	2	1	0	5	1	3	3	1	23
Cato Institute	1	1	3	1	0	1	2	2	0	1	0	12
American Enterprise Institute	1	0	1	1	3	0	1	0	1	0	0	8
Urban Institute	0	0	3	0	2	0	0	0	0	1	0	6
Hudson Institute	0	1	2	3	0	0	0	0	0	0	0	6
Manhattan Institute	0	0	1	1	1	0	0	0	0	0	0	3
Institute for Policy Studies	0	0	0	0	2	0	0	0	0	1	0	3
Progressive Policy Institute	0	0	1	0	1	0	0	0	0	0	0	2
Hoover Institution	0	0	0	0	0	0	0	0	1	0	0	1
Rockford Institute	0	0	0	0	0	0	0	0	0	1	0	1
Worldwatch Institute	0	0	0	0	0	0	0	0	0	0	0	0

Source: Vanderbilt University Television News Archive.

Figure A3.5
References to Selected American Think Tanks on NBC News, 1998–2008

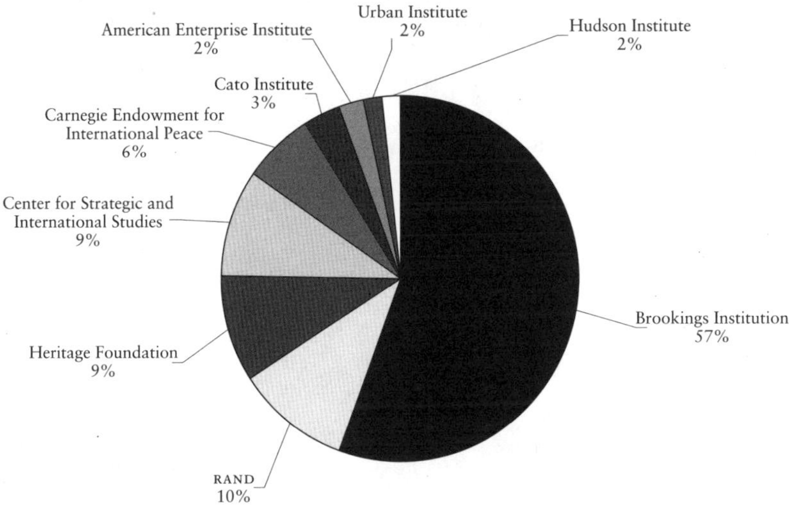

Table A3.5.1
References to Selected American Think Tanks on NBC News, 2009–2016

Institute	*2009*	*2010*	*2011*	*2012*	*2013*	*2014*	*2015*	*2016*	*Totals*
RAND	2	16	2	2	11	7	6	2	48
Brookings Institution	13	2	12	4	2	0	0	0	33
Center for Strategic and International Studies	6	6	3	0	2	1	1	1	20
Carnegie Endowment for International Peace	4	2	7	1	1	0	0	0	15
Heritage Foundation	2	2	1	2	0	0	0	0	7
Cato Institute	3	0	0	1	1	0	0	0	5
American Enterprise Institute	3	1	0	0	0	0	0	0	4
Urban Institute	0	0	0	0	0	0	0	1	1
Hoover Institution	0	0	1	0	0	0	0	0	1
Hudson Institute	0	0	0	0	0	0	0	0	0
Manhattan Institute	0	0	0	0	0	0	0	0	0
Institute for Policy Studies	0	0	1	0	0	0	0	0	0
Progressive Policy Institute	0	0	0	0	0	0	0	0	0
Rockford Institute	0	0	0	0	0	0	0	0	0
Worldwatch Institute	0	0	0	0	0	0	0	0	0

Source: Vanderbilt University Television News Archive.

Figure A3.5.1
References to Selected American Think Tanks on NBC News, 2009–2016

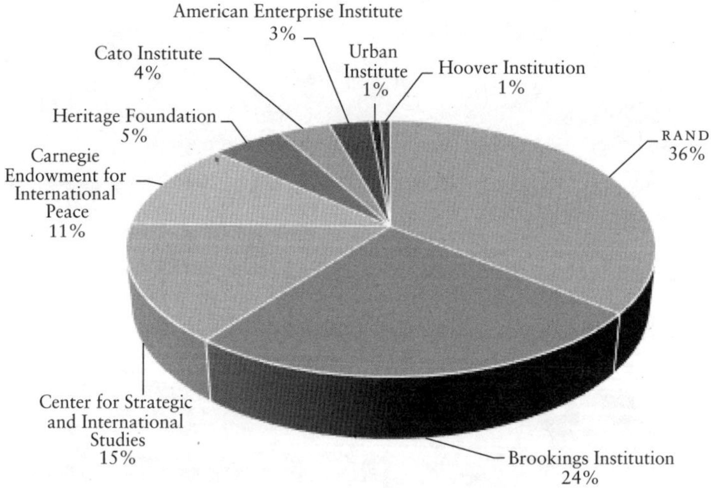

Table A3.6
References to Selected American Think Tanks on CBS News, 1998–2008

Institute	*1998*	*1999*	*2000*	*2001*	*2002*	*2003*	*2004*	*2005*	*2006*	*2007*	*2008*	*Totals*
Brookings Institution	1	2	5	7	2	5	5	1	1	8	0	37
RAND	2	0	6	3	2	11	4	2	0	3	3	36
Center for Strategic and International Studies	0	0	1	1	4	4	4	1	2	14	0	31
Heritage Foundation	1	4	2	0	2	6	5	2	1	1	0	24
Carnegie Endowment for International Peace	0	0	0	0	4	2	6	0	0	0	0	12
American Enterprise Institute	0	0	0	0	0	0	2	3	0	0	1	6
Urban Institute.	0	0	1	0	0	2	2	0	0	0	0	5
Cato Institute	0	0	2	0	0	0	2	0	0	0	0	4
Manhattan Institute	0	0	0	1	1	0	0	1	0	0	0	3
Institute for Policy Studies	0	0	0	1	0	1	0	0	0	0	0	2
Hudson Institute	0	0	0	0	1	0	0	1	0	0	0	2
Hoover Institution	0	0	0	0	0	1	0	0	0	0	0	1
Progressive Policy Institute	0	0	0	0	0	0	0	0	0	0	0	0
Worldwatch Institute	0	0	0	0	0	0	0	0	0	0	0	0
Rockford Institute	0	0	0	0	0	0	0	0	0	0	0	0

Source: Vanderbilt University Television News Archive.

Figure A3.6
References to Selected American Think Tanks on CBS News, 1998–2008

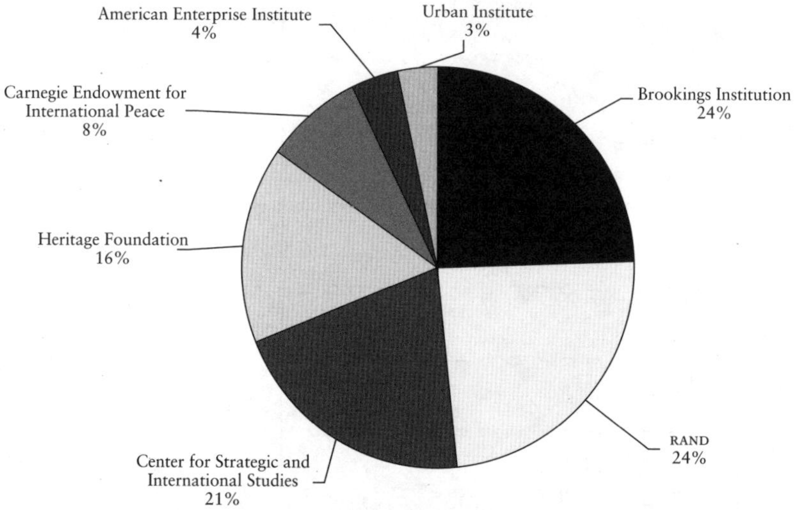

Table A3.6.1
References to Selected American Think Tanks on CBS News, 2009–2016

Institute	*2009*	*2010*	*2011*	*2012*	*2013*	*2014*	*2015*	*2016*	*Totals*
RAND	9	12	1	1	4	1	4	0	32
Center for Strategic and International Studies	5	7	7	0	0	0	0	0	19
Brookings Institution	3	6	2	1	1	0	0	0	13
American Enterprise Institute	1	5	1	0	0	0	0	0	7
Cato Institute	2	3	0	0	0	0	0	0	5
Heritage Foundation	0	0	1	1	0	0	0	0	2
Carnegie Endowment for International Peace	0	1	1	0	0	0	0	0	2
Urban Institute	1	0	0	1	0	0	0	0	2
Hudson Institute	0	0	0	0	0	0	0	0	0
Manhattan Institute	0	0	0	0	0	0	0	0	0
Institute for Policy Studies	0	0	0	0	0	0	0	0	0
Progressive Policy Institute	0	0	0	0	0	0	0	0	0
Hoover Institution	0	0	0	0	0	0	0	0	0
Rockford Institute	0	0	0	0	0	0	0	0	0
Worldwatch Institute	0	0	0	0	0	0	0	0	0

Source: Vanderbilt University Television News Archive.

Figure A3.6.1
References to Selected American Think Tanks on CBS News, 2009–2016

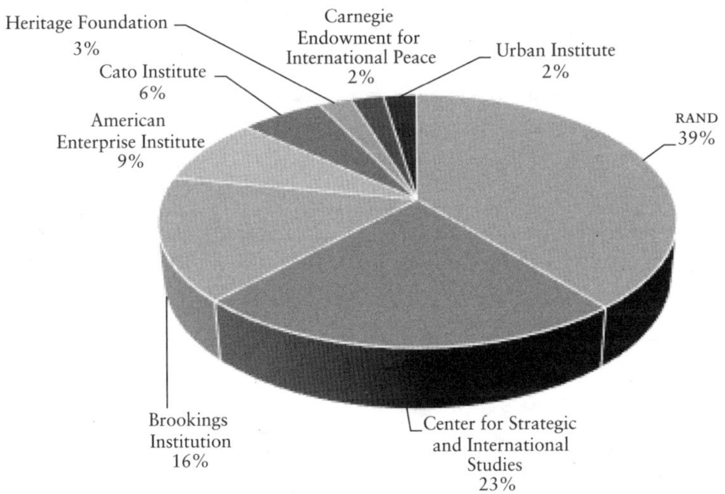

Table A3.7
References to Selected American Think Tanks on CNN, 1998–2008

Institute	*1998*	*1999*	*2000*	*2001*	*2002*	*2003*	*2004*	*2005*	*2006*	*2007*	*2008*	*Totals*
Center for Strategic and International Studies	4	9	5	2	4	7	9	4	9	20	1	74
Brookings Institution	17	11	12	8	5	7	4	2	4	0	0	70
RAND	3	19	2	3	4	4	8	6	7	2	0	58
Heritage Foundation	1	0	1	2	6	6	3	12	6	5	2	44
American Enterprise Institute	2	0	1	0	2	1	7	3	3	2	0	21
Carnegie Endowment for International Peace	0	1	2	1	2	2	3	0	1	0	0	12
Cato Institute	1	2	2	0	1	1	1	0	0	1	0	9
Institute for Policy Studies	0	0	0	1	0	2	0	1	0	0	0	4
Worldwatch Institute	0	0	1	0	0	0	0	0	0	0	0	1
Urban Institute	0	0	0	0	0	0	0	0	0	1	0	1
Rockford Institute	0	0	1	0	0	0	0	0	0	0	0	1
Manhattan Institute	0	0	0	0	1	0	0	0	0	0	0	1
Hudson Institute	0	0	0	1	0	0	0	0	0	0	0	1
Progressive Policy Institute	0	0	0	0	0	0	0	0	0	0	0	0
Hoover Institution	0	0	0	0	0	0	0	0	0	0	0	0

Source: Vanderbilt University Television News Archive.

Figure A3.7
References to Selected American Think Tanks on CNN, 1998–2008

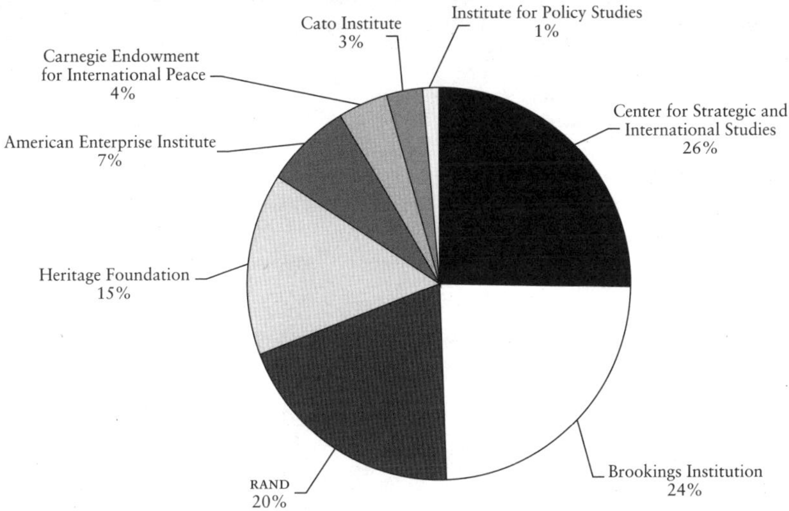

Table A3.7.1
References to Selected American Think Tanks on CNN, 2009–2016

Institute	*2009*	*2010*	*2011*	*2012*	*2013*	*2014*	*2015*	*2016*	*Totals*
RAND	6	14	6	3	17	9	18	3	76
Heritage Foundation	8	0	0	0	1	5	2	1	17
Hoover Institution	0	0	0	0	11	1	0	0	12
Brookings Institution	1	0	0	1	1	0	1	0	4
Center for Strategic and International Studies	1	1	0	0	0	1	0	1	4
American Enterprise Institute	1	0	0	1	0	0	1	0	3
Carnegie Endowment for International Peace	0	0	0	1	0	0	1	0	2
Cato Institute	1	0	0	0	0	0	0	0	1
Urban Institute	0	0	0	0	0	0	0	0	0
Hudson Institute	0	0	0	0	0	0	0	0	0
Manhattan Institute	0	0	0	0	0	0	0	0	0
Institute for Policy Studies	0	0	0	0	0	0	0	0	0
Progressive Policy Institute	0	0	0	0	0	0	0	0	0
Rockford Institute	0	0	0	0	0	0	0	0	0
Worldwatch Institute	0	0	0	0	0	0	0	0	0

Source: Vanderbilt University Television News Archive.

Figure A3.7.1
References to Selected American Think Tanks on CNN, 2009–2016

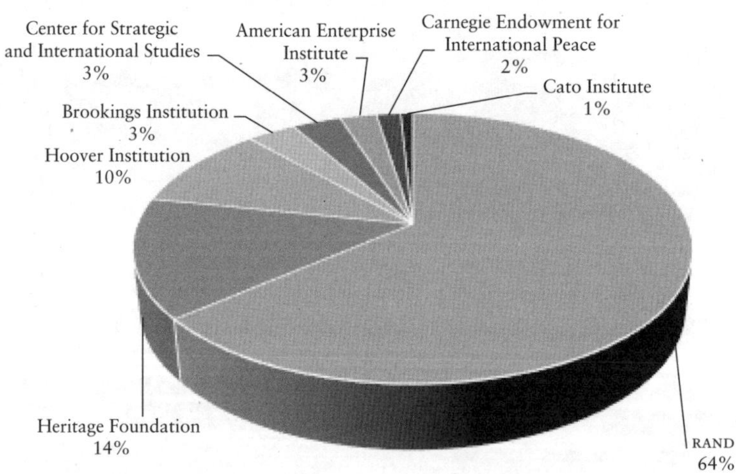

Table A3.8
References to Selected American Think Tanks on FOX News, 1998–2008

Institute	*2004**	*2005*	*2006*	*2007*	*2008*	*Totals*
Heritage Foundation	5	3	3	0	0	11
American Enterprise Institute	2	1	3	1	0	7
Brookings Institution	2	1	3	0	0	6
Center for Strategic and International Studies	0	1	4	0	1	6
RAND	1	1	3	0	0	5
Cato Institute	0	3	1	0	0	4
Institute for Policy Studies	2	0	0	0	0	2
Carnegie Endowment for International Peace	1	0	0	0	0	1
Urban Institute	1	0	0	0	0	1

* Data only available from 2004.
Source: Vanderbilt University Television News Archive.

Figure A3.8
References to Selected American Think Tanks on FOX News, 1998–2008

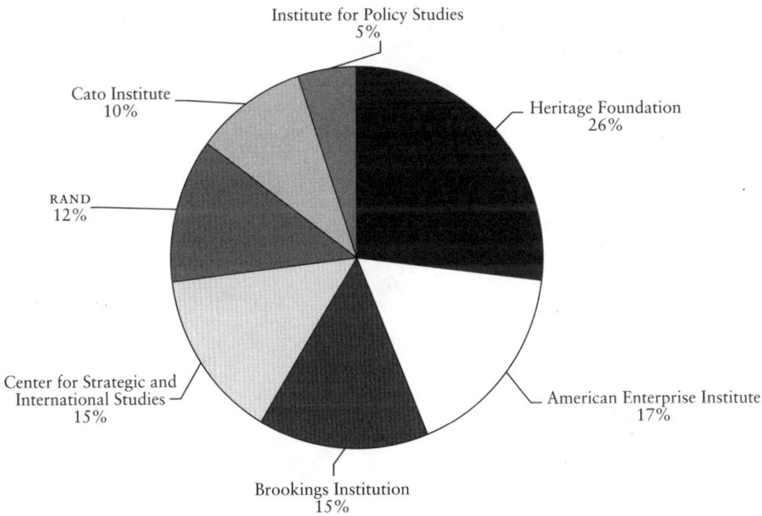

Table A3.8.1
References to Selected American Think Tanks on FOX News, 2009–2016

Institute	*2009*	*2010*	*2011*	*2012*	*2013*	*2014*	*2015*	*2016*	*Totals*
Brookings Institution	0	0	0	0	0	0	0	0	0
RAND	0	0	0	0	0	0	0	0	0
Heritage Foundation	0	0	0	0	0	0	0	0	0
Center for Strategic and International Studies	0	0	0	0	0	0	0	0	0
Carnegie Endowment for International Peace	0	0	0	0	0	0	0	0	0
Cato Institute	0	0	0	0	0	0	0	0	0
American Enterprise Institute	0	0	0	0	0	0	0	0	0
Urban Institute	0	0	0	0	0	0	0	0	0
Institute for Policy Studies	0	0	0	0	0	0	0	0	0

Source: Vanderbilt University Television News Archive.
NOTE: FOX no longer indexed on Vanderbilt TV News archive after 2008.

Table A3.9
References to Selected American Think Tanks in National Newspapers, 1998–2008

Institute	*Washington Post* DC	*New York Times*	*Christian Science Monitor*	USA *Today*	*Wall Street Journal*	*Boston Globe*	*Dallas Morning News*	*Atlanta Journal*	*Washington Times*	*Totals*
Brookings Institution	3,012	1,667	806	861	770	703	85	287	170	8,361
American Enterprise Institute	1,482	818	349	330	914	335	56	142	165	4,591
Heritage Foundation	1,234	601	422	370	445	459	158	267	267	4,223
Cato Institute	832	435	317	257	529	214	32	139	268	3,023
Center for Strategic and International Studies	890	569	461	338	286	270	36	133	0	2,983
Urban Institute	651	414	132	162	266	187	25	65	76	1,978
Carnegie Endowment for International Peace	632	328	222	108	103	113	13	25	97	1,641
Hoover Institution	248	279	93	70	477	61	8	34	181	1,451
Manhattan Institute	192	506	50	41	342	93	2	52	139	1,417
Hudson Institute	263	146	120	54	180	65	6	15	184	1,033
RAND	25	519	57	9	25	76	1	2	54	768
Progressive Policy Institute	162	84	53	40	47	47	4	13	34	484
Institute for Policy Studies	153	53	37	23	21	26	3	21	52	389
Worldwatch Institute	75	52	37	1	12	29	6	18	24	254

Source: Factiva.com and LexisNexis.com.

Figure A3.9
References to Selected American Think Tanks in National Newspapers, 1998–2008

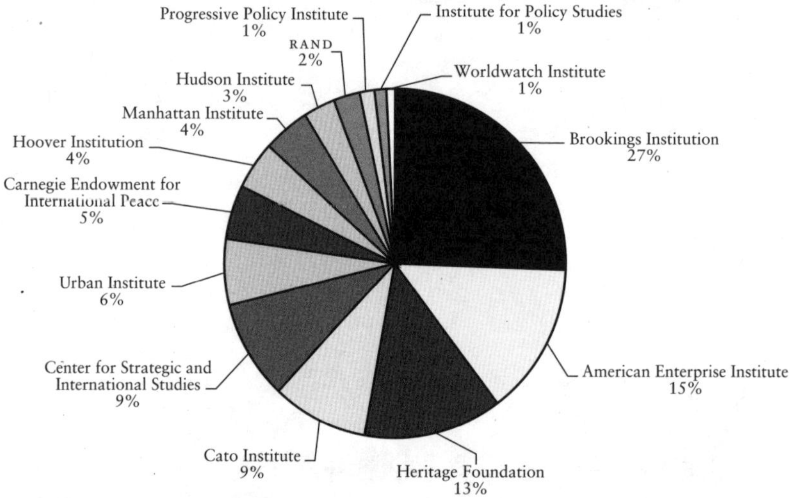

Table A3.9.1
References to Selected American Think Tanks in National Newspapers, 2009–2016

Institute	*Washington Post* DC	*New York Times*	*Christian Science Monitor*	USA *Today*	*Wall Street Journal*	*Boston Globe*	*Dallas Morning News**	*Atlanta Journal*	*Washington Times**	*Totals*
RAND	8,995	5,747	603	634	4,555	798	0	293	0	21,625
Brookings Institution	4,505	3,405	566	556	2,602	355	0	165	0	12,154
American Enterprise Institute	2,268	1,380	274	306	2,953	173	0	62	0	7,416
Heritage Foundation	2,106	1,061	291	299	1,130	176	0	195	0	5,258
Center for Strategic and International Studies	1,356	1,115	441	176	986	38	0	9	0	4,121
Cato Institute	1,278	542	152	179	915	110	0	84	0	3,260
Urban Institute	1,244	633	90	109	488	93	0	77	0	2,734
Hoover Institution	395	366	35	29	1,423	73	0	249	0	2,570
Carnegie Endowment for International Peace	633	618	159	40	488	24	0	5	0	1,967
Manhattan Institute	220	369	25	39	1,062	45	0	20	0	1,780
Hudson Institute	171	114	20	12	729	13	0	2	0	1,061
Institute for Policy Studies	156	177	46	21	154	9	0	1	0	564
Progressive Policy Institute	78	55	7	11	71	4	0	2	0	228
Worldwatch Institute	16	6	10	18	12	3	0	3	0	68
Rockford Institute	4	0	0	0	2	0	0	0	0	6

Source: Factiva.com and LexisNexis.com.

*NOTE: *Dallas Morning News* and *Washington Times* indexed, but not populating search results.

Figure A3.9.1
References to Selected American Think Tanks in National Newspapers, 2009–2016

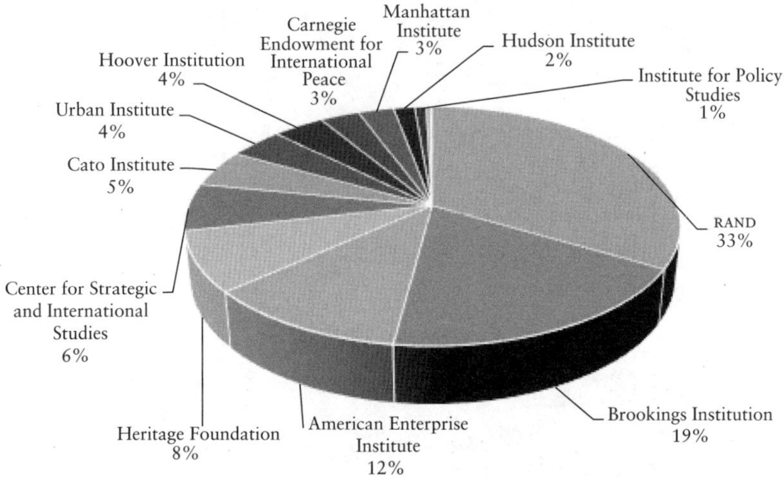

Table A3.10
References to Selected American Think Tanks in National Magazines, 1998–2008

Institute	*Time*	*Newsweek*	*Business Week*	*Forbes*	*Fortune*	*Totals*
Brookings Institution	92	70	200	21	48	431
American Enterprise Institute	36	49	90	63	24	262
Cato Institute	26	10	67	126	30	259
Hoover Institution	9	7	154	34	13	217
Heritage Foundation	25	22	61	77	22	207
Center for Strategic and International Studies	35	18	73	5	7	138
Manhattan Institute	10	9	11	95	3	128
Urban Institute	19	17	48	10	3	97
Hudson Institute	7	5	21	52	9	94
Carnegie Endowment for International Peace	25	4	39	0	2	70
Progressive Policy Institute	6	4	33	2	3	48
Worldwatch Institute	28	1	5	3	4	41
RAND	5	11	2	0	0	18
Institute for Policy Studies	2	2	4	1	2	11

Source: Factiva.com.

Figure A3.10
References to Selected American Think Tanks in National Magazines, 1998–2008

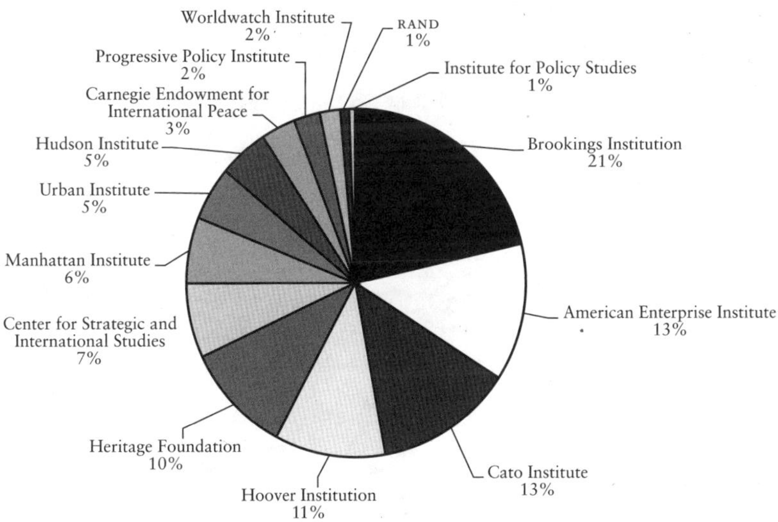

Table A3.10.1
References to Selected American Think Tanks in National Magazines, 2009–2016

Institute	Time	Newsweek*	Business Week	Forbes*	Fortune	Totals
RAND	N/A	101	N/A	210	N/A	311
Brookings Institution	N/A	67	N/A	38	N/A	105
Cato Institute	N/A	25	N/A	61	N/A	86
American Enterprise Institute	N/A	32	N/A	34	N/A	66
Heritage Foundation	N/A	22	N/A	39	N/A	61
Manhattan Institute	N/A	3	N/A	47	N/A	50
Urban Institute	N/A	7	N/A	28	N/A	35
Hoover Institution	N/A	14	N/A	6	N/A	20
Center for Strategic and International Studies	N/A	16	N/A	3	N/A	19
Hudson Institute	N/A	8	N/A	5	N/A	13
Carnegie Endowment for International Peace	N/A	11	N/A	0	N/A	11
Institute for Policy Studies	N/A	4	N/A	4	N/A	8
Progressive Policy Institute	N/A	0	N/A	0	N/A	0
Worldwatch Institute	N/A	0	N/A	0	N/A	0
Totals		310		475		785

NOTE: *Time Magazine* discontinued as of 01/2008; *Business Week* discontinued as of 07/2001; *Fortune* indexed as of 06/2016 on Factiva.com. None of these sources are available on LexisNexis.com.

**Source*: Factiva.com.

***Source*: LexisNexis.com.

Figure A3.10.1
References to Selected American Think Tanks in National Magazines, 2009–2016

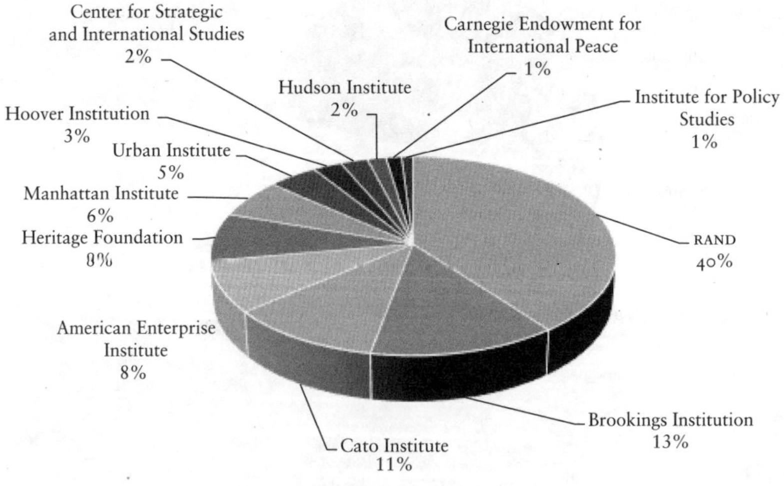

Table A3.11
References to Selected American Think Tanks in Canadian and International Newspapers, 1998–2008

Institute	*Canadian newspapers*	*International newspapers*	*Totals*
Brooking Institution	768	1,241	2,009
Heritage Foundation	611	676	1,287
Cato Institute	559	420	979
American Enterprise Institute	469	474	943
Center for Strategic and International Studies	603	53	656
Carnegie Endowment for International Peace	202	299	501
Hudson Institute	316	120	436
RAND	113	256	369
Urban Institute	291	46	337
Hoover Institution	156	116	272
Worldwatch Institute	102	99	201
Institute for Policy Studies	62	104	166
Manhattan Institute	58	74	132
Progressive Policy Institute	20	56	76

Source: Factiva.com.

Figure A3.11
References to Selected American Think Tanks in Canadian and International Newspapers, 1998–2008

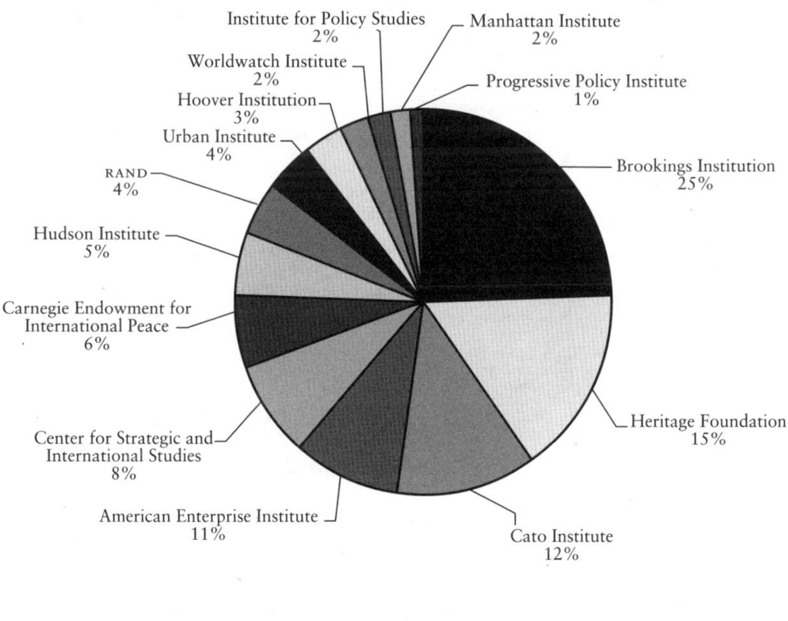

Table A3.11.1
References to Selected American Think Tanks in Canadian and International Newspapers, 2009–2016

Institute	*Canadian newspapers*	*International newspapers*	*Totals*
Brookings Institution	805	3,954	4,759
RAND	1,619	2,290	3,909
Heritage Foundation	239	618	857
Center for Strategic and International Studies	168	379	547
Carnegie Endowment for International Peace	140	365	505
Cato Institute	291	269	560
American Enterprise Institute	280	237	517
Urban Institute	160	136	296
Hudson Institute	132	81	213
Manhattan Institute	60	69	129
Institute for Policy Studies	31	45	76
Progressive Policy Institute	0	20	20
Hoover Institute	11	10	21
Worldwatch Institute	19	0	19
Totals	3,955	8,473	12,428

Source: Factiva.com.

Figure A3.11.1
References to Selected American Think Tanks in Canadian and International Newspapers, 2009–2016

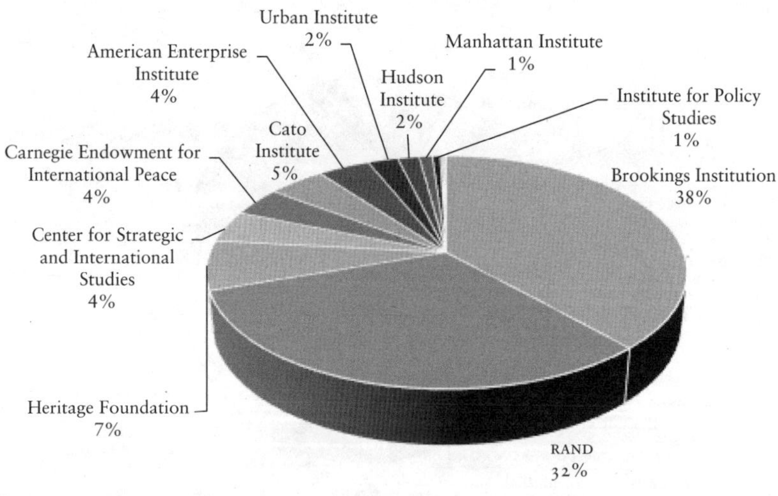

Table A3.12
References to Selected American Think Tanks in Canadian Newspapers, 1998–2008

Institute	*The Toronto Star*	*National Post*	*Winnipeg Free Press*	*The Globe and Mail*	*Totals*
Brookings Institution	181	256	63	268	768
Heritage Foundation	202	176	44	189	611
Center for Strategic and International Studies	75	204	58	266	603
Cato Institute	60	342	21	136	559
American Enterprise Institute	73	233	33	130	469
Hudson Institute	14	220	20	62	316
Urban Institute	131	43	15	102	291
Carnegie Endowment for International Peace	63	51	18	70	202
Hoover Institution	14	85	6	51	156
RAND	31	39	10	33	113
Worldwatch Institute	30	17	13	42	102
Institute for Policy Studies	15	28	5	14	62
Manhattan Institute	6	34	6	12	58
Progressive Policy Institute	2	4	4	10	20

Source: Factiva.com.

Figure A3.12
References to Selected American Think Tanks in Canadian Newspapers, 1998–2008

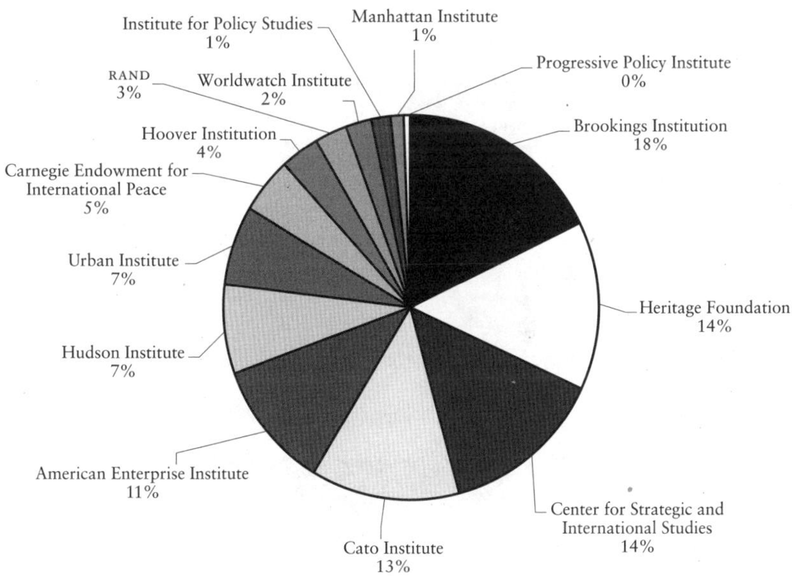

Table A3.12.1
References to Selected American Think Tanks in Canadian Newspapers, 2009–2016

Institute	*The Toronto Star*	*National Post*	*Winnipeg Free Press*	*The Globe and Mail*	*Totals*
RAND	502	347	95	675	1,619
American Enterprise Institute	34	83	15	148	280
Brookings Institution	177	140	30	458	805
Cato Institute	28	180	3	80	291
Heritage Foundation	46	74	11	108	239
Center for Strategic and International Studies	37	22	9	100	168
Urban Institute	55	28	8	69	160
Carnegie Endowment for International Peace	36	28	6	70	140
Hudson Institute	32	27	4	69	132
Manhattan Institute	15	15	2	28	60
Institute for Policy Studies	10	7	2	12	31
Worldwatch Institute	4	4	0	11	19
Hoover Institute	1	4	0	6	11
Progressive Policy Institute	0	0	0	0	0
Totals	475	612	90	1,159	2,336

Source: Factiva.com.

Figure A3.12.1
References to Selected American Think Tanks in Canadian Newspapers, 2009–2016

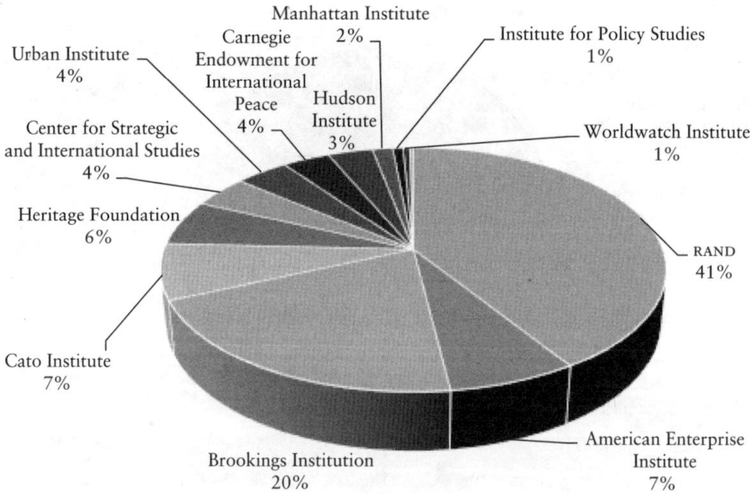

Table A3.13
References to Selected American Think Tanks in International Newspapers, 1998–2008

Institute	*El Pais*	*The Daily Telegraph*	*The Economist*	*Financial Mail (South Africa)*	*The Guardian*	*International Herald Tribune*	*The Straits Times Singapore*	*South China Morning Post*	*Totals*
Brookings Institution	4	27	339	4	367	17	311	172	1,241
Heritage Foundation	5	51	57	5	86	2	226	244	676
American Enterprise Institute	4	88	142	2	103	0	89	46	474
Cato Institute	1	15	92	2	58	0	127	125	420
Carnegie Endowment for International Peace	1	8	33	1	104	1	76	75	299
RAND	6	16	28	3	81	1	69	52	256
Hudson Institute	2	21	12	1	49	1	26	8	120
Hoover Institution	2	7	23	1	30	2	25	26	116
Institute for Policy Studies	0	8	5	1	41	27	21	1	104
Worldwatch Institute	1	1	5	0	66	1	8	17	99
Manhattan Institute	0	9	52	0	10	0	1	2	74
Progressive Policy Institute	0	0	20	0	3	0	30	3	56
Center for Strategic and International Studies	2	3	4	0	7	18	17	2	53
Urban Institute	0	0	25	1	14	0	4	2	46

Source: Factiva.com.

Figure A3.13
References to Selected American Think Tanks in International Newspapers, 1998–2008

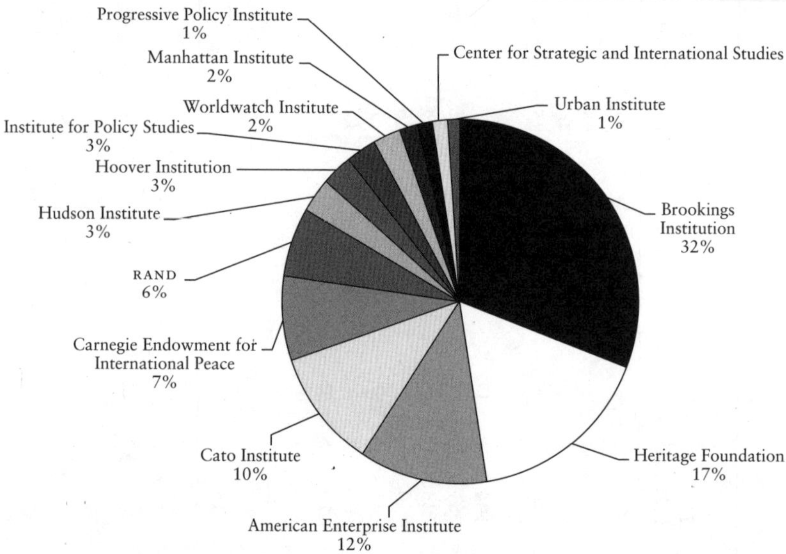

Table A3.13.1
References to Selected American Think Tanks in International Newspapers, 2009–2016

Institute	*El Pais*	*The Daily Telegraph*	*The Economist*	**Financial Mail (South Africa)*	*The Guardian*	*The New York Times International Edition (formerly the International Herald Tribune)*	*The Straits Times Signapore*	*South China Morning Post*	*Totals*
Brookings Institution	770	199	144	1	2,282	270	144	144	3,954
RAND	4	7	86	1,000	359	389	219	226	2,290
Heritage Foundation	2	6	31	8	192	87	113	179	618
Center for Strategic and International Studies	0	1	27	1	142	130	30	48	379
Carnegie Endowment for International Peace	3	4	13	1	106	119	46	73	365
Cato Institute	0	4	33	1	112	52	20	47	269
American Enterprise Institute	1	7	2	0	54	159	7	7	237
Urban Institute	0	1	4	0	31	25	48	27	136
Hudson Institute	0	0	14	1	31	30	2	3	81
Manhattan Institute	1	1	7	0	25	12	10	13	69
Institute for Policy Studies	0	2	5	0	16	20	1	1	45
Progressive Policy Institute	0	1	2	0	13	0	2	2	20
Hoover Institute	0	0	2	0	4	3	0	1	10
Worldwatch Institute	0	0	0	0	0	0	0	0	0
Totals	781	233	370	1,013	3,367	1,296	642	771	8,473

Source: Factiva.com.
**Source*: LexisNexis.com.

Figure A3.13.1
References to Selected American Think Tanks in International Newspapers, 2009–2016

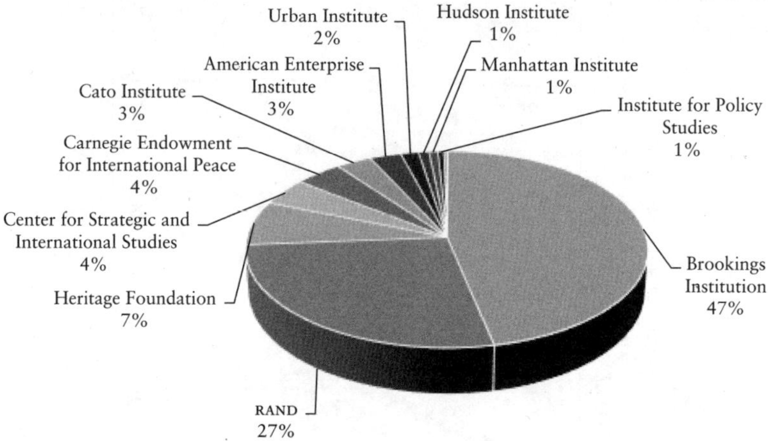

Table A3.14
Comparison of Annual Budget to Number of National Media References for Selected American Think Tanks, 1999–2008

Institutes	*Annual budget (millions of dollars)*	*Number of national references (television, newspapers and magazines)*
The Brookings Institution	30	9,184
American Enterprise Institute for Public Policy Research	20	4,936
Heritage Foundation	30	4,568
Centre for Strategic and International Studies	20	3,342
Cato Institute	20	3,317
Urban Institute	50	2,075
Carnegie Endowment for International Peace	20	1,818
Hoover Institution	30	1,672
Manhattan Institute for Policy Research	15	1,552
Hudson Institute	10	1,139
RAND	200	992
Progressive Policy Institute	2	534
Institute for Policy Studies	2	417
Worldwatch Institute	5	297
Russell Sage Foundation	5	0
The Twentieth Century Fund/ Century Foundation	5	0
National Bureau of Economic Research	10	0
Council on Foreign Relations	30	0
Foreign Policy Research Institute	3	0
Northeast-Midwest Institute	5	0
The Carter Center	30	0
Citizens for a Sound Economy Foundation	20	0
United States Institute of Peace	20	0
Economic Policy Institute	5	0
Empower America	10	0
The Progress and Freedom Foundation	5	0

Figure A3.14
Comparison of Annual Budget to Number of National Media References for Selected American Think Tanks, 1999–2008

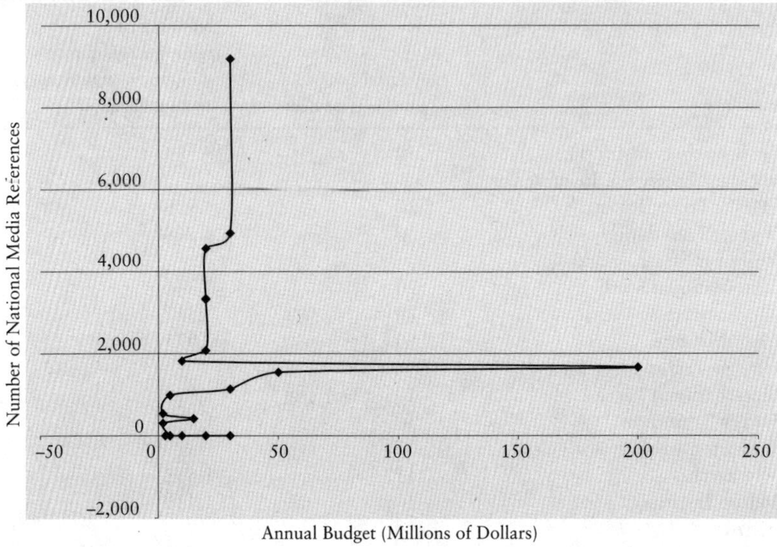

Table A3.14.1
Comparison of Annual Budget to Number of National Media References for Selected American Think Tanks, 2009–2016

Institute	*Annual Budgets (Millions of Dollars)*	*Number of National References (Televsion, Newspapers and Magazines)*
RAND	300	22,151
American Enterprise Institute	40	7,497
Council on Foreign Relations	70	6,444
Heritage Foundation	90	5,353
Center for Strategic and International Studies	40	4,195
Cato Institute	30	3,357
Urban Institute	85	2,772
Hoover Institution	60	2,604
Economic Policy Institute	6	2,267
The Carter Center	200	1,937
National Bureau of Economic Research	30	1,907
Manhattan Institute	16	1,830
Carnegie Endowment for International Peace	33	1,734
Brookings Institution	100	1,230
Hudson Institute	12	1,074
Institute for Policy Studies	4	573
United States Institute of Peace	25	246
Progressive Policy Institute	2	228
Empower America	10	94
Foreign Policy Research Institute	2	88
Worldwatch Institute	5	68
The Twentieth Century Foundation/ Century Foundation	62	21
The Progress and Freedom Foundation	5	14
Northeast-Midwest Institute	5	4
Citizens for a Sound Economy Foundation	20	0
Russell Sage Foundation	14	0

Source: Factiva.com.

Figure A3.14.1
Comparison of Annual Budget to Number of National Media References for Selected American Think Tanks, 2009–2016

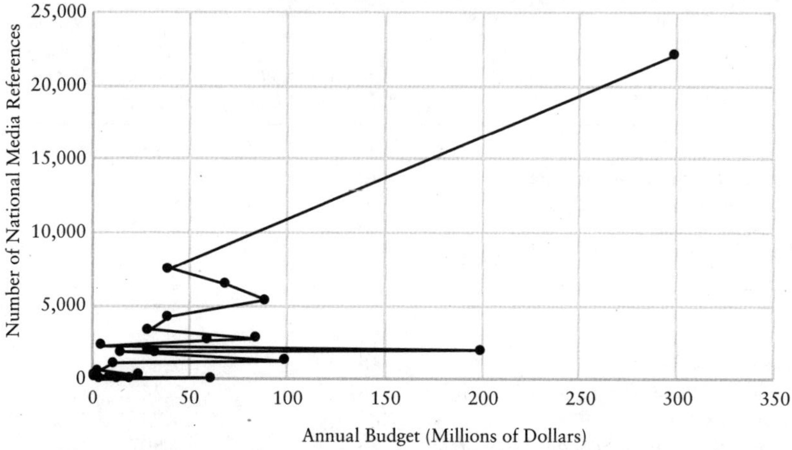

Table A3.15
Comparison of Annual Budget to Number of International Media References for Selected American Think Tanks, 1999–2008

Institutes	*Annual budget (millions of dollars)*	*Number of international media references (newspapers)*
The Brookings Institution	30	2,009
Heritage Foundation	30	1,287
Cato Institute	20	979
American Enterprise Institute for Public Policy Research	20	943
Centre for Strategic and International Studies	20	656
Carnegie Endowment for International Peace	20	501
Hudson Institute	10	436
RAND	200	369
Urban Institute	50	337
Hoover Institution	30	272
Worldwatch Institute	5	201
Institute for Policy Studies	2	166
Manhattan Institute for Policy Research	15	132
Progressive Policy Institute	2	76
Russell Sage Foundation	5	0
The Twentieth Century Fund/ Century Foundation	5	0
National Bureau of Economic Research	10	0
Council on Foreign Relations	30	0
Foreign Policy Research Institute	3	0
Northeast-Midwest Institute	5	0
The Carter Center	30	0
Citizens for a Sound Economy Foundation	20	0
United States Institute of Peace	20	0
Economic Policy Institute	5	0
Empower America	10	0
The Progress and Freedom Foundation	5	0

Figure A3.15
Comparison of Annual Budget to Number of International Media References for Selected American Think Tanks, 1999–2008

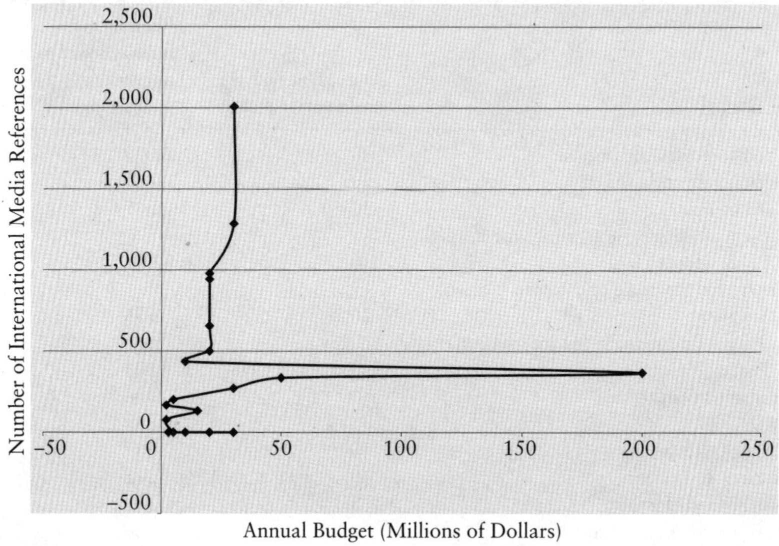

Table A3.15.1
Comparison of Annual Budget to Number of International Media References for Selected American Think Tanks, 2009-2016

Institute	*Annual budgets (millions of dollars)*	*Number of international media references (newspapers)*
Brookings Institution	100	3,954
RAND	300	2,290
Council on Foreign Relations	70	1,577
Heritage Foundation	90	618
Center for Strategic and International Studies	40	379
Carnegie Endowment for International Peace	33	365
Cato Institute	30	269
American Enterprise Institute	40	237
Economic Policy Institute	6	230
National Bureau of Economic Research	30	204
Urban Institute	85	136
The Twentieth Century Foundation/ Century Foundation	62	98
Hudson Institute	12	81
Manhattan Institute	16	69
The Carter Center	200	67
United States Institute of Peace	25	47
Institute for Policy Studies	4	45
Progressive Policy Institute	2	20
Foreign Policy Research Institute	2	15
Hoover Institution	60	10
Citizens for a Sound Economy	20	9
Empower America	10	6
Russel Sage Foundation	14	1
The Progress and Freedom Foundation	5	1
Northeast-Midwest Institute	5	0
Worldwatch Institute	5	0

Source: Factiva.com.

Figure A3.15.1
Comparison of Annual Budget to Number of International Media References for Selected American Think Tanks, 1999–2016

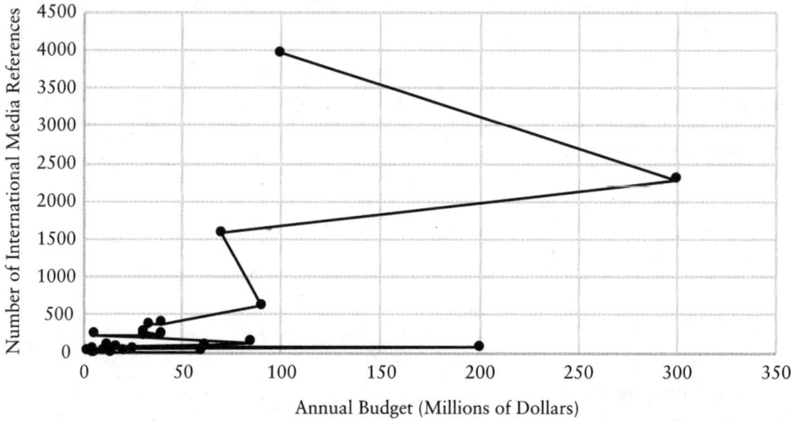

APPENDIX FOUR

Media Citations for Selected Canadian Think Tanks, 2000–2008; 2009–2016

Table A4.1
Media Citations for Selected Canadian Think Tanks (radio, television, and newspaper), 2000–2008

Institute	*Radio*	*Television*	*Newspapers*	*Total*
Fraser Institute	49	44	5,454	5,547
Conference Board of Canada	32	60	5,139	5,231
C.D. Howe Institute	15	14	3,026	3,055
Canada West Foundation	22	29	1,994	2,045
Pembina Institute	49	38	1,885	1,972
Canadian Centre for Policy Alternatives	36	19	1,331	1,386
Institute for Research on Public Policy	3	7	1,117	1,127
Canadian Institute of Strategic Studies	3	37	492	532
Mackenzie Institute	14	35	478	527
Canadian Policy Research Networks, Inc.	10	7	469	486
Public Policy Forum	3	3	447	453
Montreal Economic Institute	0	2	449	451
Parkland Institute	9	2	406	417
Canadian Council on Social Development	1	6	368	375
Canadian Tax Foundation	2	2	356	360
Canadian Urban Institute	0	5	258	263
Canadian Institute for Advanced Research	0	1	223	224
Frontier Centre for Public Policy	4	1	187	192
Canadian Institute of International Affairs	2	2	183	187
Caledon Institute of Social Policy	1	0	163	164
North-South Institute	2	1	148	151
Economic Council of Canada	0	0	121	121
Parliamentary Centre	0	0	71	71
National Council of Welfare	4	0	50	54
Couchiching Institute on Public Affairs	0	1	33	34
Science Council of Canada	0	0	29	29
Saskatchewan Institute of Public Policy	0	0	28	28
Canadian Institute for Int'l Peace & Security	0	0	15	15
Pearson-Shoyama Institute	0	0	13	13
Canadian Council for Int'l Peace & Security	1	0	1	2
Quebec Institute of Advanced Int'l Studies	0	0	0	0

Sources: Proquest / Lexis Nexis / CBC Radio Archives / Virtual News Library (CBC and CTV National Evening News).

Figure A4.1
Media Citations for Selected Canadian Think Tanks (radio, television, and newspaper), 2000–2008

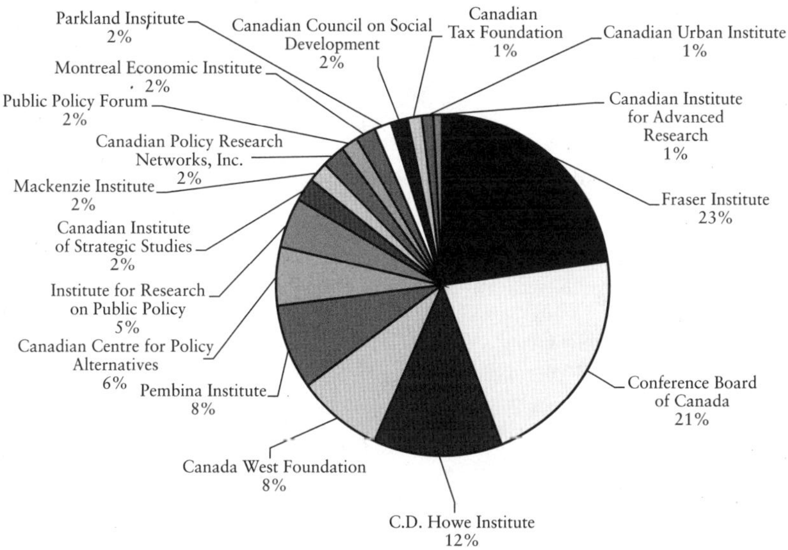

Table A4.1.1
Media Citations for Selected Canadian Think Tanks (radio, televsion, and newspaper), 2009–2016

Institute	*Radio*	*Television*	*Newspapers*	*Totals*
Fraser Institute	11	107	5,904	6,022
Conference Board of Canada	19	184	5,586	5,789
C.D. Howe Institute	14	42	4,736	4,792
Canada West Foundation	3	24	3,870	3,897
Canadian Centre for Policy Alternatives	17	64	3,104	3,185
Pembina Institute	27	79	2,213	2,319
Institute for Research on Public Policy	7	9	1,708	1,724
Public Policy Forum	7	31	1,419	1,457
Canadian Policy Research Networks	0	0	876	876
Vanier Institute of the Family	1	5	754	760
Frontier Centre for Public Policy	3	17	580	600
Montreal Economic Institute	0	3	514	517
Parkland Institute	1	1	323	325
Mackenzie Institute	0	23	265	288
Caledon Institute of Social Policy	1	0	262	263
North-South Institute	1	1	194	196
Canadian Tax Foundation	0	0	190	190
Canadian Institute for Advanced Research	0	2	181	183
Parliamentary Centre	0	0	164	164
Canadian Council on Social Development	0	1	142	143
Canadian Urban Institute	0	0	141	141
Economic Council of Canada	0	2	106	108
National Council on Welfare	0	0	40	40
Couchiching Institute on Public Affairs	0	0	9	9
Canadian Institute of International Affairs	0	0	7	7
Canadian Council for International Peace and Security	0	0	4	4
Canadian Institute for International Peace and Security	0	0	3	3
Pearson-Shoyama Institute	0	0	3	3
Canadian Institute of Strategic Studies	0	0	0	0
Quebec Institute of Advanced International Studies	0	0	0	0
Saskatchewan Institute of Public Policy	0	0	0	0

Source: Eureka.cc, LexisNexis.com, Factiva.com and Virtual News Library.

Figure A4.1.1
Media Citations for Selected Canadian Think Tanks (radio, television, and newspaper), 2009–2016

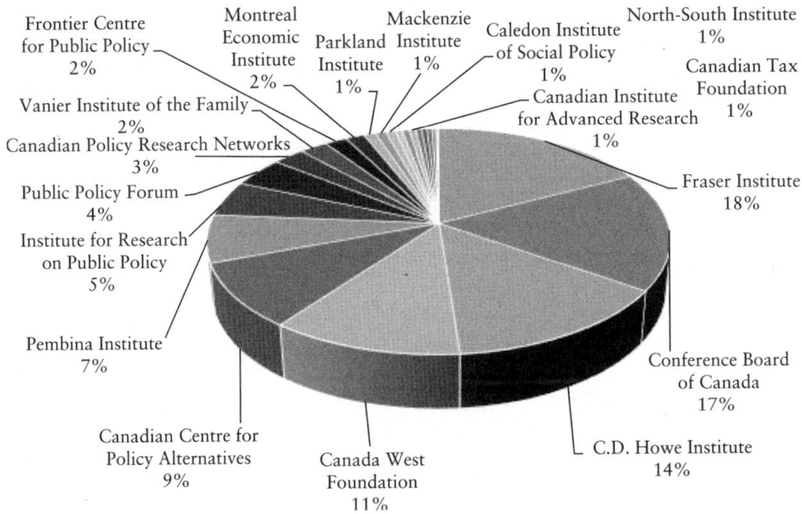

Table A4.2
Television Citations for Selected Canadian Think Tanks, 2000–2008

Institutes	*National evening news total*
Conference Board of Canada	60
Fraser Institute	44
Pembina Institute	38
Canadian Institute of Strategic Studies	37
Mackenzie Institute	35
Canada West Foundation	29
Canadian Centre for Policy Alternatives	19
C.D. Howe Institute	14
Institute for Research on Public Policy	7
Canadian Policy Research Networks, Inc.	7
Canadian Council on Social Development	6
Canadian Urban Institute	3
National Council of Welfare	3
Public Policy Forum	3
Canadian Tax Foundation	2
Canadian Institute of International Affairs	2
Parkland Institute	2
Montreal Economic Institute	2
Frontier Centre for Public Policy	1
North-South Institute	1
Canadian Institute for Advanced Research	1
Couchiching Institute on Public Affairs	1
Canadian Institute for Int'l Peace & Security	0
Canadian Council for Int'l Peace & Security	0
Caledon Institute of Social Policy	0
Pearson-Shoyama Institute	0
Parliamentary Centre	0
Quebec Institute of Advanced Int'l Studies	0
Saskatchewan Institute of Public Policy	0
Total	317

Figure A4.2
Television Citations for Selected Canadian Think Tanks, 2000–2008

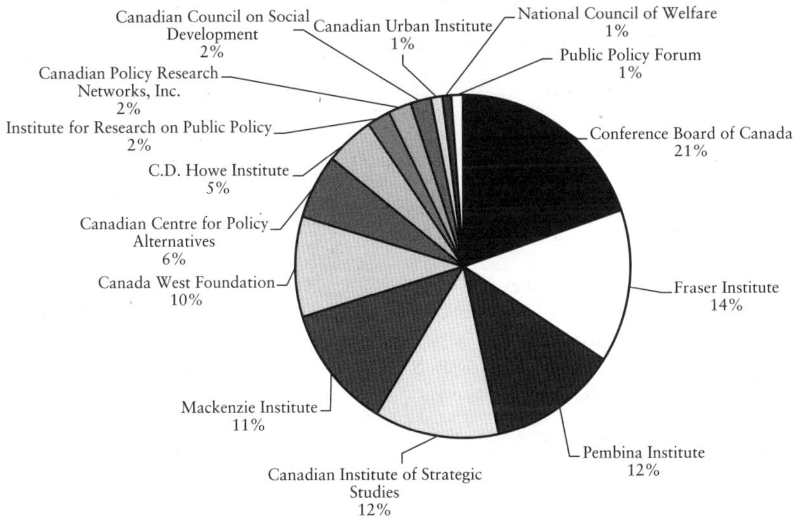

Table A4.2.1
Television Citations for Selected Canadian Think Tanks, 2009–2016

Institute	*National Evening News*
Conference Board of Canada	184
Fraser Institute	107
Pembina Institute	79
Canadian Centre for Policy Alternatives	64
C.D. Howe Institute	42
Public Policy Forum	31
Canada West Foundation	24
Mackenzie Institute	23
Frontier Centre for Public Policy	17
Institute for Research on Public Policy	9
Montreal Economic Institute	3
Canadian Institute for Advanced Research	2
Canadian Council on Social Development	1
North-South Insitute	1
Parkland Institute	1
Caledon Institute of Social Policy	0
Canadian Council for International Peace and Security	0
Canadian Institute for International Peace and Security	0
Canadian Institute of International Affairs	0
Canadian Policy Research Networks	0
Canadian Tax Foundation	0
Canadian Urban Institute	0
Canadian Institute of Strategic Studies	0
Couchiching Institute on Public Affairs	0
National Council on Welfare	0
Parliamentary Centre	0
Pearson-Shoyama Institute	0
Quebec Institute of Advanced International Studies	0
Saskatchewan Institute of Public Policy	0
Total	588

Source: Eureka.cc.

Figure A4.2.1
Television Citations for Selected Canadian Think Tanks, 2009–2016

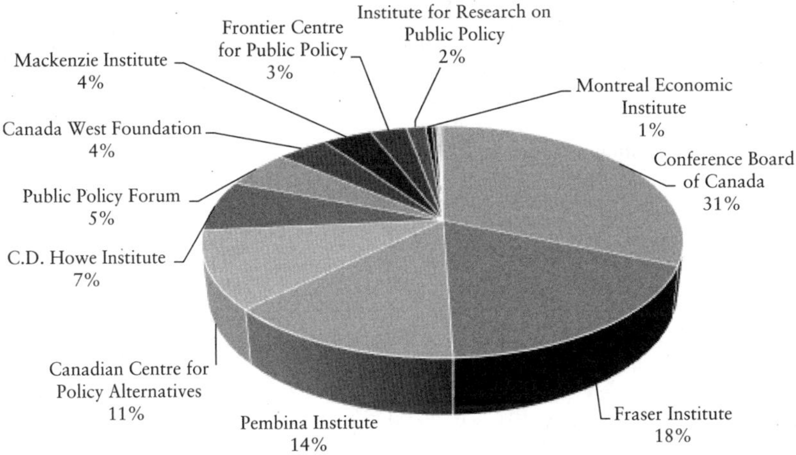

Table A4.3
CBC TV National Evening News Citations for Selected Canadian Think Tanks, 2000–2008

Institutes	*2000*	*2001*	*2002*	*2003*	*2004*	*2005*	*2006*	*2007*	*2008*	*Total*
Pembina Institute	0	0	3	1	1	2	9	11	2	29
Fraser Institute	0	0	3	3	4	5	4	3	0	22
Canada West Foundation	0	0	3	2	7	1	6	2	0	21
Canadian Institute of Strategic Studies	0	0	3	7	5	2	4	0	0	21
Mackenzie Institute	0	0	4	4	1	2	6	2	0	19
Conference Board of Canada	0	0	3	0	0	0	6	2	2	13
Canadian Centre for Policy Alternatives	0	0	3	2	0	2	1	2	2	12
C.D. Howe Institute	0	0	0	0	1	0	3	0	1	5
Institute for Research on Public Policy	0	0	0	0	2	1	0	0	0	3
Public Policy Forum	0	0	0	1	1	0	1	0	0	3
Canadian Policy Research Networks, Inc.	0	0	0	0	0	0	2	1	0	3
National Council of Welfare	0	0	1	0	0	0	1	0	0	2
Canadian Council on Social Development	0	0	1	0	1	0	0	0	0	2
Parkland Institute	0	0	0	0	1	0	1	0	0	2
Montreal Economic Institute	0	0	0	0	0	1	0	1	0	2
Canadian Tax Foundation	0	0	1	0	0	0	0	0	0	1
North-South Institute	0	0	1	0	0	0	0	0	0	1
Canadian Institute of International Affairs	0	0	0	1	0	0	0	0	0	1
Canadian Institute for Advanced Research	0	0	0	0	0	0	0	1	0	1
Couchiching Institute on Public Affairs	0	0	0	0	0	1	0	0	0	1
Canadian Institute for Int'l Peace & Security	0	0	0	0	0	0	0	0	0	0
Canadian Council for Int'l Peace & Security	0	0	0	0	0	0	0	0	0	0
Caledon Institute of Social Policy	0	0	0	0	0	0	0	0	0	0
Pearson-Shoyama Institute	0	0	0	0	0	0	0	0	0	0
Frontier Centre for Public Policy	0	0	0	0	0	0	0	0	0	0
Canadian Urban Institute	0	0	0	0	0	0	0	0	0	0
Quebec Institute of Advanced Int'l Studies	0	0	0	0	0	0	0	0	0	0
Saskatchewan Institute of Public Policy	0	0	0	0	0	0	0	0	0	0
Total	0	0	26	21	24	17	44	25	7	164

Search from: CBC TV *Saturday Report, Sunday Night, The National.*
Source: Virtual News Library.

Figure A4.3
CBC TV National Evening News Citations for Selected Canadian Think Tanks, 2000–2008

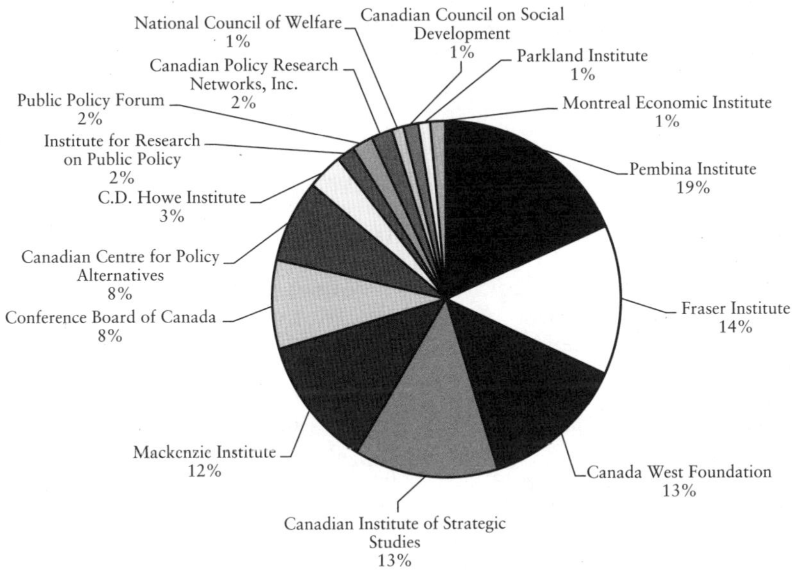

Table A4.3.1
CBC TV National Evening News Citations for Selected Canadian Think Tanks, 2009–2016

Institute	*2009*	*2010*	*2011*	*2012*	*2013*	*2014*	*2015*	*2016*	*Total*
Conference Board of Canada	4	2	14	5	3	6	12	20	66
Pembina Institute	6	11	2	2	10	7	7	4	49
Fraser Institute	8	4	4	1	3	3	4	9	36
Canadian Centre for Policy Alternatives	2	2	1	4	2	7	5	5	28
C.D. Howe Institute	2	2	2	2	2	5	6	3	24
Public Policy Forum	4	1	0	2	0	0	1	3	11
Canada West Foundation	0	0	0	0	1	2	0	3	6
Mackenzie Institute	2	2	1	0	0	0	0	0	5
Frontier Centre for Public Policy	1	0	0	0	0	0	2	0	3
Montreal Economic Institute	0	1	1	0	0	0	1	0	3
Canadian Institute for Advanced Research	0	0	0	0	2	0	0	0	2
Institute for Research on Public Policy	1	0	0	0	0	0	1	0	2
Parkland Institute	0	0	0	0	0	0	0	1	1
Caledon Institute of Social Policy	0	0	0	0	0	0	0	0	0
Canadian Council for International Peace and Security	0	0	0	0	0	0	0	0	0
Canadian Council on Social Development	0	0	0	0	0	0	0	0	0
Canadian Institute for International Peace and Security	0	0	0	0	0	0	0	0	0
Canadian Institute of International Affairs	0	0	0	0	0	0	0	0	0
Canadian Institute of Strategic Studies	0	0	0	0	0	0	0	0	0
Canadian Policy Research Networks	0	0	0	0	0	0	0	0	0
Canadian Tax Foundation	0	0	0	0	0	0	0	0	0
Canadian Urban Institute	0	0	0	0	0	0	0	0	0
Couchiching Institute on Public Affairs	0	0	0	0	0	0	0	0	0
National Council on Welfare	0	0	0	0	0	0	0	0	0
North-South Institute	0	0	0	0	0	0	0	0	0
Parliamentary Centre	0	0	0	0	0	0	0	0	0
Pearson-Shoyama Institute	0	0	0	0	0	0	0	0	0
Quebec Institute of Advanced International Studies	0	0	0	0	0	0	0	0	0
Saskatchewan Institute of Public Policy	0	0	0	0	0	0	0	0	0

Source: Eureka.cc.

Figure A4.3.1
CBC TV National Evening News Citations for Selected Canadian Think Tanks, 2009–2016

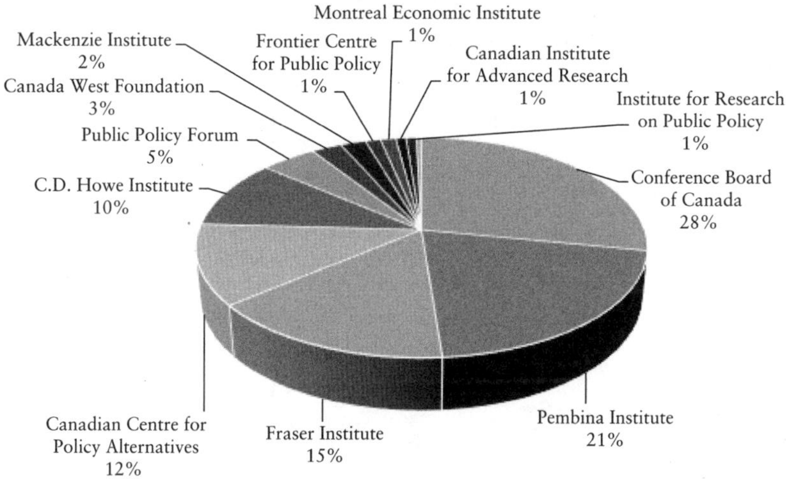

Table A4.4
CTV National Evening News Citations for Selected Canadian Think Tanks, 2000–2008

Institutes	*2000*	*2001*	*2002*	*2003*	*2004*	*2005*	*2006*	*2007*	*2008*	*Total*
Conference Board of Canada	3	13	2	5	1	5	10	4	4	47
Fraser Institute	1	3	5	5	4	2	0	2	0	22
Canadian Institute of Strategic Studies	0	5	4	3	1	2	1	0	0	16
Mackenzie Institute	0	5	2	0	3	1	2	3	0	16
C.D. Howe Institute	0	2	3	1	0	0	1	2	0	9
Pembina Institute	1	0	0	0	0	0	0	6	2	9
Canada West Foundation	1	2	2	0	0	1	0	2	0	8
Canadian Centre for Policy Alternatives	1	0	0	0	0	1	3	2	0	7
Canadian Council on Social Development	2	0	0	2	0	0	0	0	0	4
Institute for Research on Public Policy	1	2	0	0	1	0	0	0	0	4
Canadian Policy Research Networks, Inc.	0	0	0	0	1	0	0	2	1	4
Canadian Urban Institute	0	0	0	0	1	2	0	0	0	3
Canadian Tax Foundation	0	0	0	0	0	1	0	0	0	1
National Council of Welfare	0	1	0	0	0	0	0	0	0	1
Canadian Institute of International Affairs	0	1	0	0	0	0	0	0	0	1
Frontier Centre for Public Policy	0	0	0	0	0	0	0	0	1	1
Canadian Institute for Int'l Peace & Security	0	0	0	0	0	0	0	0	0	0
North-South Institute	0	0	0	0	0	0	0	0	0	0
Public Policy Forum	0	0	0	0	0	0	0	0	0	0
Canadian Council for Int'l Peace & Security	0	0	0	0	0	0	0	0	0	0
Caledon Institute of Social Policy	0	0	0	0	0	0	0	0	0	0
Pearson-Shoyama Institute	0	0	0	0	0	0	0	0	0	0
Parliamentary Centre	0	0	0	0	0	0	0	0	0	0
Parkland Institute	0	0	0	0	0	0	0	0	0	0
Canadian Institute for Advanced Research	0	0	0	0	0	0	0	0	0	0
Couchiching Institute on Public Affairs	0	0	0	0	0	0	0	0	0	0
Montreal Economic Institute	0	0	0	0	0	0	0	0	0	0
Quebec Institute of Advanced Int'l Studies	0	0	0	0	0	0	0	0	0	0
Saskatchewan Institute of Public Policy	0	0	0	0	0	0	0	0	0	0
Total	10	34	18	16	12	15	17	23	8	153

Search from: CTV *Canada AM*, CTV *News*.
Source: Virtual News Library.

Figure A4.4
CTV National Evening News Citations for Selected Canadian Think Tanks, 2000–2008

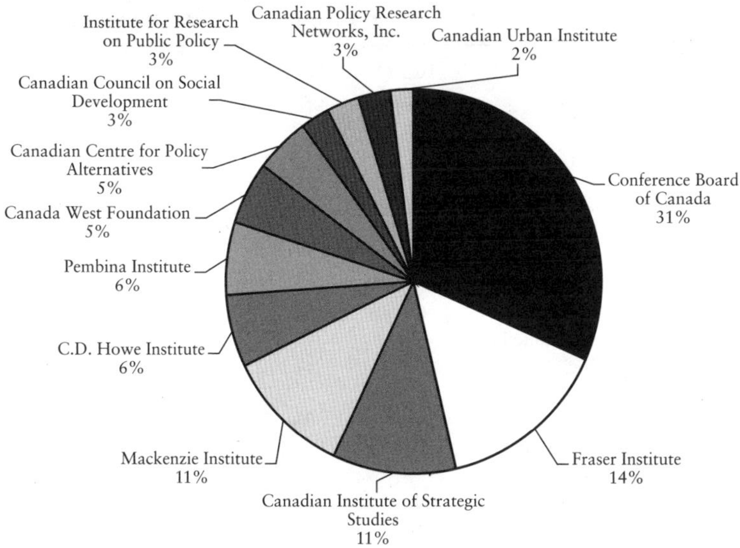

Table A4.4.1
CTV National Evening News Citations for Selected Canadian Think Tanks, 2009–2016

Institute	*2009*	*2010*	*2011*	*2012*	*2013*	*2014*	*2015*	*2016*	*Total*
Conference Board of Canada	16	8	17	9	16	11	21	20	118
Fraser Institute	5	2	9	7	11	11	12	14	71
Canadian Centre for Policy Alternatives	4	4	3	2	4	7	5	7	36
Pembina Institute	9	4	2	5	4	0	3	3	30
Public Policy Forum	2	4	5	1	0	2	2	4	20
C.D. Howe Institute	1	0	1	1	0	4	3	8	18
Mackenzie Institute	2	1	2	1	1	8	3	0	18
Canada West Foundation	0	0	0	2	2	6	2	4	16
Frontier Centre for Public Policy	0	1	0	0	0	3	8	2	14
Institute for Research on Public Policy	0	0	1	1	2	0	2	1	7
Canadian Council on Social Development	0	0	0	0	0	0	1	0	1
North-South Institute	1	0	0	0	0	0	0	0	1
Caledon Institute of Social Policy	0	0	0	0	0	0	0	0	0
Canadian Council for International Peace and Security	0	0	0	0	0	0	0	0	0
Canadian Institute for Advanced Research	0	0	0	0	0	0	0	0	0
Canadian Institute for International Peace and Security	0	0	0	0	0	0	0	0	0
Canadian Institute of International Affairs	0	0	0	0	0	0	0	0	0
Canadian Institute of Strategic Studies	0	0	0	0	0	0	0	0	0
Canadian Policy Research Networks	0	0	0	0	0	0	0	0	0
Canadian Tax Foundation	0	0	0	0	0	0	0	0	0
Canadian Urban Institute	0	0	0	0	0	0	0	0	0
Couchiching Institute on Public Affairs	0	0	0	0	0	0	0	0	0
Montreal Economic Institute	0	0	0	0	0	0	0	0	0
National Council on Welfare	0	0	0	0	0	0	0	0	0
Parkland Institute	0	0	0	0	0	0	0	0	0
Parliamentary Centre	0	0	0	0	0	0	0	0	0
Pearson-Shoyama Institute	0	0	0	0	0	0	0	0	0
Quebec Institute of Advanced International Studies	0	0	0	0	0	0	0	0	0
Saskatchewan Institute of Public Policy	0	0	0	0	0	0	0	0	0

Source: Virtual News Library.

Figure A4.4.1
CTV National Evening News Citations for Selected Canadian Think Tanks, 2009–2016

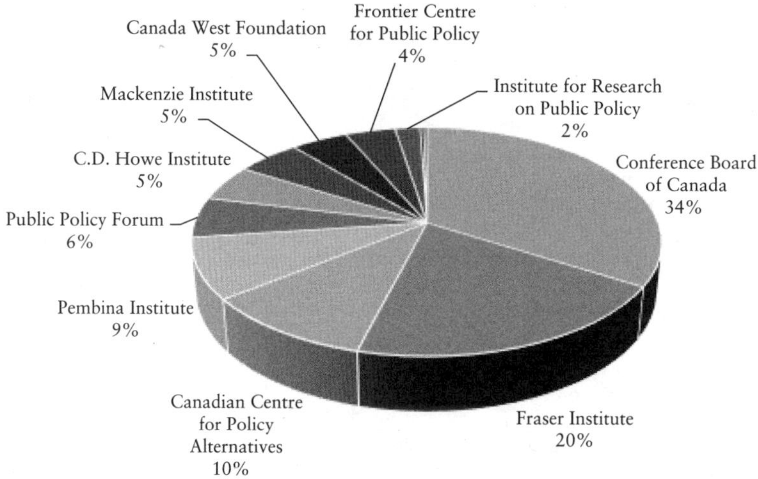

Table A4.5
References to Selected Canadian Think Tanks on CBC Radio, Oct. 2004–2008

Institutes	*Total*
Pembina Institute	49
Fraser Institute	49
Canadian Centre for Policy Alternatives	36
Conference Board of Canada	32
Canada West Foundation	22
C.D. Howe Institute	15
Mackenzie Institute	14
Canadian Policy Research Networks, Inc.	10
Parkland Institute	9
National Council of Welfare	4
Frontier Centre for Public Policy	4
Canadian Institute of Strategic Studies	3
Institute for Research on Public Policy	3
Public Policy Forum	3
Canadian Tax Foundation	2
North-South Institute	2
Canadian Institute of International Affairs	2
Canadian Council on Social Development	1
Canadian Institute for Int'l Peace & Security	1
Caledon Institute of Social Policy	1
Montreal Economic Institute	0
Canadian Council for Int'l Peace & Security	0
Pearson-Shoyama Institute	0
Parliamentary Centre	0

Source: CBC Radio Archives.

Figure A4.5
References to Selected Canadian Think Tanks on CBC Radio, Oct. 2004–2008

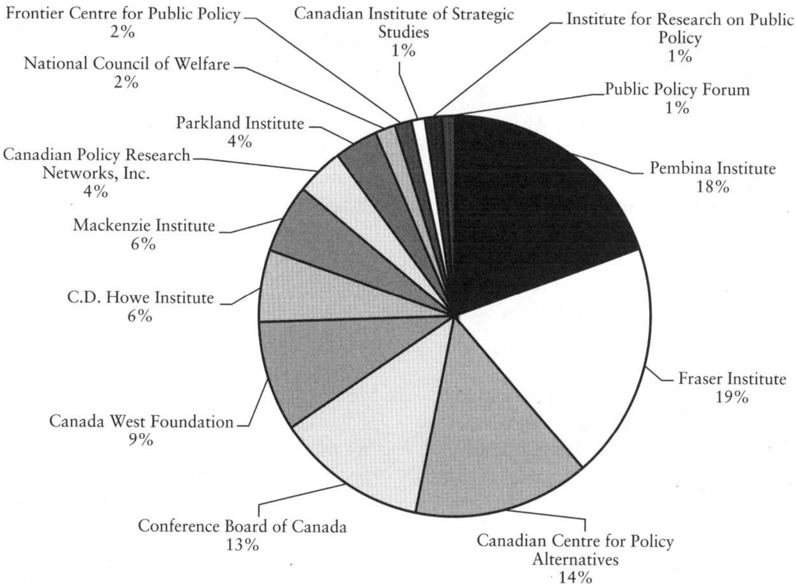

Table A4.5.1
References to Selected Canadian Think Tanks on CBC Radio, 2009–2016

Institute	*Total*
Pembina Institute	27
Conference Board of Canada	19
Canadian Centre for Policy Alternatives	17
C.D. Howe Institute	14
Fraser Institute	11
Institute for Research on Public Policy	7
Public Policy Forum	7
Canada West Foundation	3
Frontier Centre for Public Policy	3
Caledon Institute of Social Policy	1
North-South Institute	1
Parkland Institute	1
Canadian Council for International Peace and Security	0
Canadian Council on Social Development	0
Canadian Institute for International Peace and Security	0
Canadian Institute of International Affairs	0
Canadian Institute of Strategic Studies	0
Canadian Policy Research Networks	0
Canadian Tax Foundation	0
Mackenize Institute	0
Montreal Economic Institute	0
National Council of Welfare	0
Parliamentary Centre	0
Pearson-Shoyama Institute	0

Source: Eureka.cc.

Figure A4.5.1
References to Selected Canadian Think Tanks on CBC Radio, 2009–2016

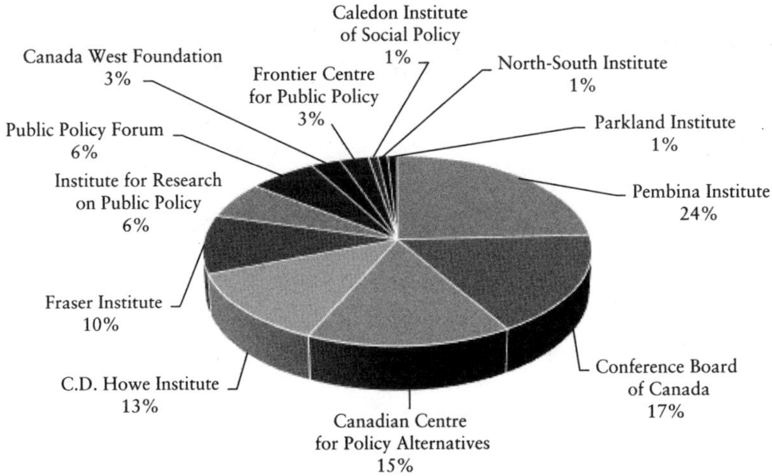

Table A4.6
Newspaper Citations for Selected Canadian Think Tanks, 2000–2008

Institute	*Globe and Mail*	*Toronto Star*	*Toronto Sun**	*Montreal Gazette*	*Vancouver Sun*	*Edmonton Journal*	*Calgary Herald*	*Halifax Daily News*	*Ottawa Citizen*	*National Post*	*Total*
Fraser Institute	423	366	330	335	881	326	999	130	488	1,176	5,454
Conference Board of Canada	830	559	176	365	499	447	623	178	559	903	5,139
C.D. Howe Institute	500	259	53	185	223	198	234	56	264	1,054	3,026
Canada West Foundation	211	63	14	39	109	415	839	16	102	186	1,994
Pembina Institute	238	172	29	52	78	572	515	26	97	106	1,885
Canadian Centre for Policy Alternatives	166	212	39	71	293	82	90	80	161	137	1,331
Institute for Research on Public Policy	133	120	13	111	71	57	70	28	150	364	1,117
Canadian Institute of Strategic Studies	67	32	16	34	24	46	33	15	124	101	492
Mackenzie Institute	43	27	43	21	37	26	43	14	108	116	478
Canadian Policy Research Networks, Inc.	91	70	18	22	29	46	34	14	96	49	469
Montreal Economic Institute	33	11	9	208	7	11	10	2	31	127	449
Public Policy Forum	55	73	6	22	9	36	17	2	144	83	447
Parkland Institute	18	9	3	7	9	240	92	1	5	22	406
Canadian Council on Social Development	46	76	13	29	20	29	30	23	58	44	368
Canadian Tax Foundation	59	37	11	24	30	26	32	15	54	68	356
Canadian Urban Institute	83	112	12	4	4	3	4	2	5	29	258
Canadian Institute for Advanced Research	40	36	5	13	28	16	7	2	17	59	223

Table A4.6
Newspaper Citations for Selected Canadian Think Tanks, 2000–2008 (*continued*)

Institute	*Globe and Mail*	*Toronto Star*	*Toronto Sun**	*Montreal Gazette*	*Vancouver Sun*	*Edmonton Journal*	*Calgary Herald*	*Halifax Daily News*	*Ottawa Citizen*	*National Post*	*Total*
Frontier Centre for Public Policy	5	1	4	11	8	18	45	1	11	83	187
Canadian Institute of International Affairs	38	17	3	17	8	10	11	1	33	45	183
Caledon Institute of Social Policy	42	41	1	4	8	10	7	5	24	21	163
North-South Institute	62	24	2	9	2	11	2	1	30	5	148
Economic Council of Canada	47	10	0	6	6	5	10	5	4	28	121
Parliamentary Centre	13	4	4	0	2	2	1	0	24	21	71
National Council of Welfare	5	14	2	3	5	5	6	5	1	4	50
Couchiching Institute on Public Affairs	7	11	2	3	0	1	0	0	5	4	33
Science Council of Canada	6	5	0	1	2	4	1	0	5	5	29
Saskatchewan Institute of Public Policy	10	1	0	3	2	4	2	1	2	3	28
Canadian Institute for Int'l Peace & Security	3	3	0	1	1	2	1	0	3	1	15
Pearson-Shoyama Institute	0	0	0	1	1	0	0	2	7	2	13
Canadian Council for Int'l Peace & Security	1	0	0	0	0	0	0	0	0	0	1
Quebec Institute of Advanced Int'l Studies	0	0	0	0	0	0	0	0	0	0	0
Total	3,275	2,365	808	1,601	2,396	2,648	3,758	625	2,612	4,846	24,934

Source: ProQuest.
* *Source*: LexisNexis.
Search parameters: 1 January 2000–4 July 2008.

Figure A4.6
Newspaper Citations for Selected Canadian Think Tanks, 2000–2008

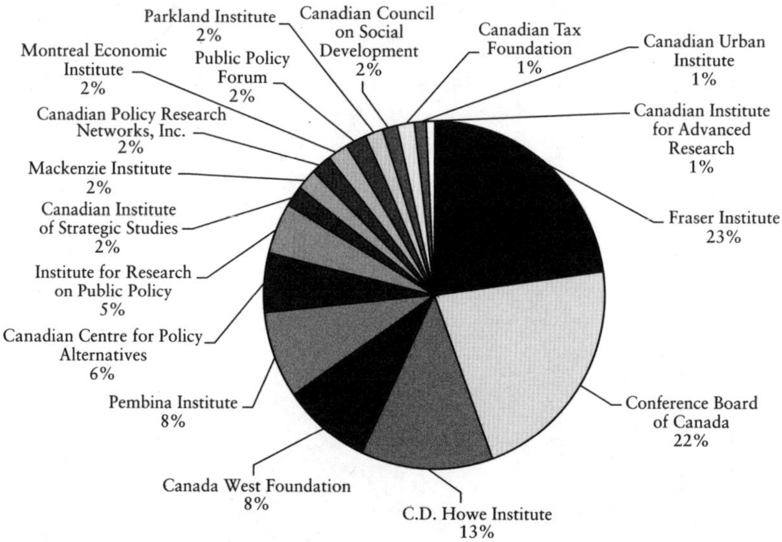

Table A4.6.1
Newspaper Citations for Selected Canadian Think Tanks, 2009–2016

Institute	*Globe and Mail*	*Toronto Star*	*Toronto Sun*	*Montreal Gazette*	*Vancouver Sun*	*Edmonton Journal*	*Calgary Herald*	*Halifax Daily News**	*Ottawa Citzen*	*National Post*	*Total*
Fraser Institute	486	299	555	239	786	282	749	1,000	273	1,235	5,904
Conference Board of Canada	1,565	585	105	448	594	455	764	0	449	621	5,586
C.D. Howe Institute	1,145	485	59	185	299	204	211	1,000	266	882	4,736
Canada West Foundation	146	35	3	19	118	155	345	2,924	31	94	3,870
Canadian Centre for Policy Alternatives	328	737	36	89	371	106	124	1,000	137	176	3,104
Pembina Institute	0	289	27	110	0	629	768	0	111	279	2,213
Institute for Research on Public Policy	218	89	6	47	73	50	69	1,000	73	83	1,708
Public Policy Forum	111	48	2	28	37	29	18	999	108	39	1,419
Canadian Policy Research Networks	9	2	0	0	1	2	0	855	7	0	876
Frontier Centre for Public Policy	74	14	16	26	68	45	136	0	25	176	580
Montreal Economic Institute	61	0	50	146	11	14	39	0	23	170	514
Parkland Institute	14	11	1	10	4	181	93	0	6	3	323
Mackenzie Institute	14	11	8	3	4	8	8	165	12	32	265
Caledon Institute of Social Policy	36	32	0	3	11	7	6	154	6	7	262
North-South Institute	19	29	0	3	4	1	1	113	17	7	194
Canadian Tax Foundation	40	3	1	6	4	1	3	117	3	12	190
Canadian Institute for Advanced Research	96	37	0	2	7	5	9	0	3	21	180
Parliamentary Centre	7	0	0	0	0	2	1	142	6	6	164
Canadian Council on Social Development	13	7	1	4	3	3	5	87	16	3	142

Table A4.6.1
Newspaper Citations for Selected Canadian Think Tanks, 2009–2016 (*continued*)

Institute	*Globe and Mail*	*Toronto Star*	*Toronto Sun*	*Montreal Gazette*	*Vancouver Sun*	*Edmonton Journal*	*Calgary Herald*	*Halifax Daily News**	*Ottawa Citzen*	*National Post*	*Total*
Canadian Urban Institute	42	53	2	1	2	3	10	0	7	21	141
Science Council of Canada	4	0	0	0	1	1	0	30	3	7	46
National Council on Welfare	2	7	0	0	0	0	1	28	0	2	40
Couchiching Institute on Public Affairs	1	8	0	0	0	0	0	0	0	0	9
Canadian Institute of International Affairs	4	0	0	0	0	0	0	0	2	1	7
Canadian Institute of Strategic Studies	1	0	0	1	1	0	0	0	1	2	6
Canadian Council for International Peace and Security	1	0	0	0	0	0	0	2	1	0	4
Quebec Institute of Advanced International Studies	0	0	0	0	0	0	0	0	0	0	0
Saskatchewan Institute of Public Policy	0	0	0	0	0	0	0	0	0	0	0
Totals	4,437	2,781	872	1,370	2,399	2,183	3,360	9,616	1,586	3,879	32,483

Source: Factiva.com.
**Souce*: LexisNexis.com.

Figure A4.6.1
Newspaper Citations for Selected Canadian Think Tanks, 2009–2016

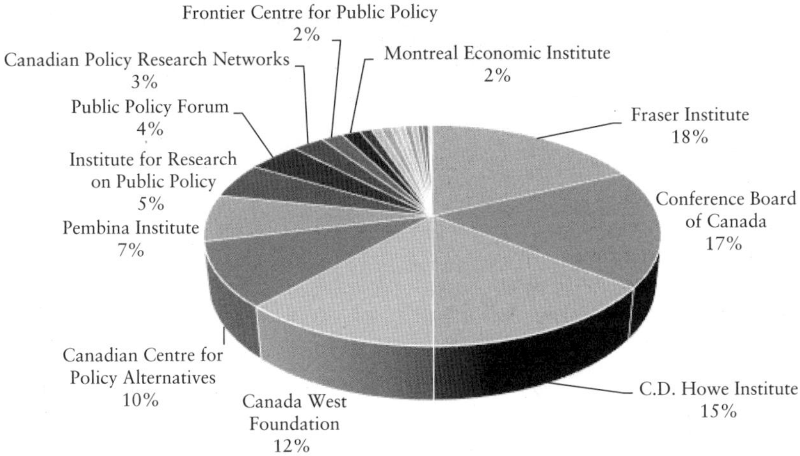

Table A4.7
References to Selected Canadian Think Tanks in American Newspapers, 1998–2008

Institute	*Washington Post* DC	*New York Times*	*Christian Science Monitor*	*Wall Street Journal*	*Boston Globe*	*Totals*
Fraser Institute	4	6	9	44	2	65
Public Policy Forum	19	6	0	1	15	41
Conference Board of Canada	3	9	2	17	1	32
Pembina Institute	2	8	1	5	1	17
C.D. Howe Institute	1	2	1	5	3	12
Mackenzie Institute	4	0	1	2	1	8
Montreal Economic Institute	0	1	0	6	0	7
Institute for Research on Public Policy	2	0	1	1	0	4
Canada West Foundation	2	2	0	0	0	4
Canadian Council on Social Development	2	0	1	0	0	3
Canadian Institute of Strategic Studies	1	2	0	0	0	3
Canadian Centre for Policy Alternatives	0	1	0	1	0	2
North-South Institute	0	0	1	0	0	1
Canadian Council for International Peace and Security	0	0	0	0	1	1
Canadian Policy Research Networks, Inc.	0	0	0	0	1	1
Canadian Tax Foundation	0	1	0	0	0	1
National Council of Welfare	0	0	0	0	0	0
Parliamentary Centre	0	0	0	0	0	0
Caledon Institute of Social Policy	0	0	0	0	0	0
Canadian Institute of International Affairs	0	0	0	0	0	0
Pearson-Shoyama Institute	0	0	0	0	0	0
Parkland Institute	0	0	0	0	0	0
Saskatchewan Institute for Public Policy	0	0	0	0	0	0

Source: Factiva.com.

Figure A4.7
References to Selected Canadian Think Tanks in American Newspapers, 1998–2008

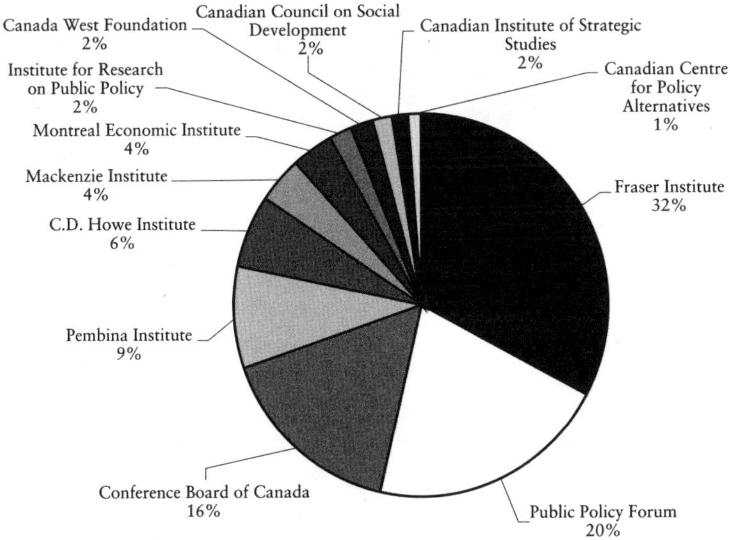

Table A4.7.1
References to Selected Canadian Think Tanks in American Newspapers, 2009–2016

Institute	*Washington Post* DC	*New York Times*	*Christian Science Monitor*	*Wall Street Journal*	*Boston Globe*	*Totals*
Fraser Institute	6	9	1	56	2	74
Pembina Institute	3	29	2	33	0	67
Conference Board of Canada	3	18	0	31	0	52
C.D. Howe Institute	0	4	0	13	0	17
Public Policy Forum	5	1	1	5	1	13
Institute for Research on Public Policy	0	1	0	8	0	9
Canada West Foundation	0	4	0	4	0	8
Canadian Centre for Policy Alternatives	2	2	0	2	0	6
Mackenzie Institute	0	0	0	2	0	2
North-South Institute	0	0	0	1	0	1
Parliamentary Centre	1	0	0	0	0	1
Montreal Economic Institute	0	0	0	1	0	1
Caledon Institute of Social Policy	0	0	0	0	0	0
Canadian Council for International Peace and Security	0	0	0	0	0	0
Canadian Council on Social Development	0	0	0	0	0	0
Canadian Institute of Strategic Studies	0	0	0	0	0	0
Canadian Policy Research Networks	0	0	0	0	0	0
Canadian Tax Foundation	0	0	0	0	0	0
National Council on Welfare	0	0	0	0	0	0
Pearson-Shoyama Institute	0	0	0	0	0	0
Canadian Institute of International Affairs	0	0	0	0	0	0
Parkland Institute	1	0	0	0	0	0
Saskatchewan Institute for Social Policy	0	0	0	0	0	0

Source: Factiva.com.

Figure A4.7.1
References to Selected Canadian Think Tanks in American Newspapers, 2009–2016

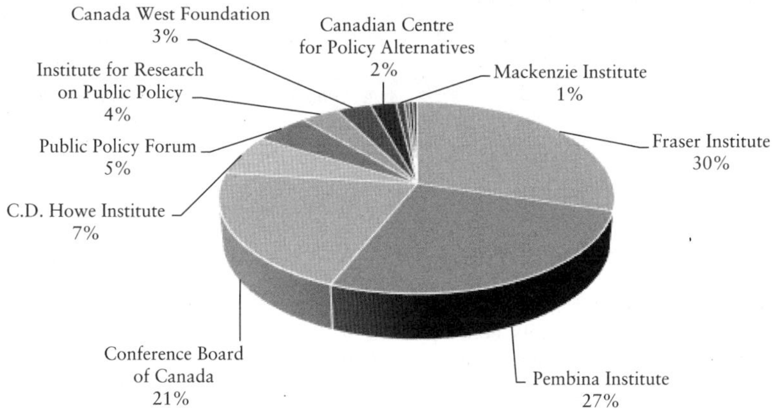

Table A4.8
Comparison of Annual Budget to Number of National Media References for Selected Canadian Think Tanks

	Annual budget (millions of dollars)	*Number of television, radio and newspaper references*
The Fraser Institute	15	5,547
Conference Board of Canada	30	5,231
C.D. Howe Institute	5	3,055
Canada West Foundation	5	2,045
Pembina Institute	5	1,972
Canadian Centre for Policy Alternatives	2	1,386
Institute for Research on Public Policy	5	1,117
Canadian Institute of Strategic Studies	0	532
Mackenzie Institute	0	527
Canadian Policy Research Networks, Inc.	5	486
Public Policy Forum	2	453
Montreal Economic Institute	2	451
Parkland Institute	0	417
Canadian Council on Social Development	2	375
Canadian Tax Foundation	5	360
Canadian Urban Institute	0	263
Canadian Institute for Advanced Research	15	224
Frontier Centre for Public Policy	0	192
Canadian Institute of International Affairs	2	187
Caledon Institute of Social Policy	2	164
The North-South Institute	5	151
Parliamentary Centre	9	71
National Council of Welfare	0	54
Couchiching Institute on Public Affairs	0	34
Saskatchewan Institute of Public Policy	0	28
Canadian Centre for Philanthropy	5	0
Canadian Centre for Foreign Policy Development	5	0
Atlantic Provinces Economic Council	2	0
Institute on Governance	2	0
Atlantic Institute for Market Studies	2	0

Figure A4.8
Comparison of Annual Budget to Number of National Media References for Selected Canadian Think Tanks

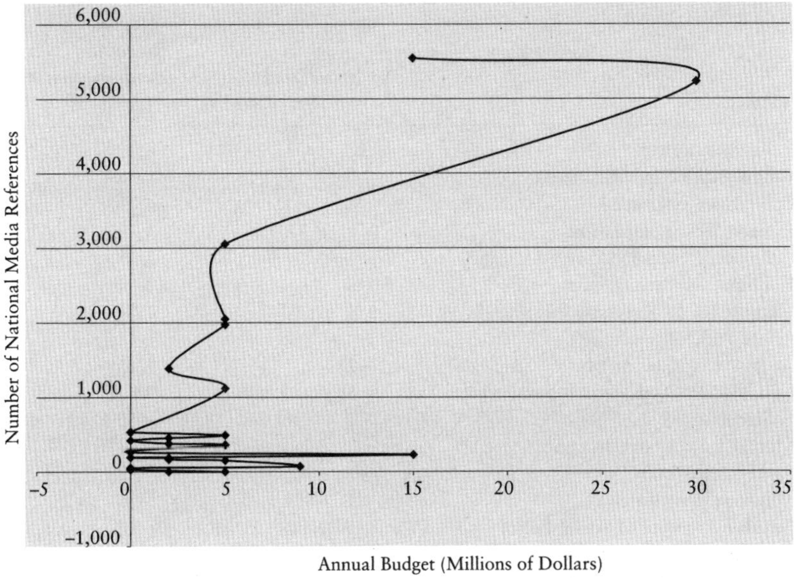

Table A4.8.1
Comparison of Annual Budget to Number of National Media References for Selected Canadian Think Tanks, 2009–2016

Institute	*Annual budgets (millions of dollars)*	*Number of television, radio and newspaper references*
Fraser Institute	10	6,022
Conference Board of Canada	40	5,789
C.D. Howe Institute	4	4,792
Canada West Foundation	3	3,897
Canadian Centre for Policy Alternatives	6	3,185
Pembina Institute	4	2,319
Institute for Research on Public Policy	3	1,724
Public Policy Forum	4	1,457
Atlantic Institute for Market Studies	2	1,159
Canadian Policy Research Networks	5	876
Frontier Centre for Public Policy	1	600
Montreal Economic Institute	2	517
Parkland Institute	1	325
Mackenzie Institute	1	288
Caledon Institute of Social Policy	1	263
The North-South Institute	5	196
Canadian Tax Foundation	6	190
Canadian Institute for Advanced Research	35	183
Parliamentary Centre	1	164
Canadian Council on Social Development	2	143
Canadian Urban Institute	2	141
Atlantic Provinces Economic Council	2	108
Institute on Governance	2	84
National Council on Welfare	1	40
Couchiching Institute on Public Affairs	1	9
Canadian Centre for Philanthropy	5	9
Canadian Institute of International Affairs	0	7
Canadian Centre for Foreign Policy Development	5	2
Canadian Institute of Strategic Studies	1	0

Figure A4.8.1
Comparison of Annual Budget to Number of National Media References for Selected Canadian Think Tanks, 2009–2016

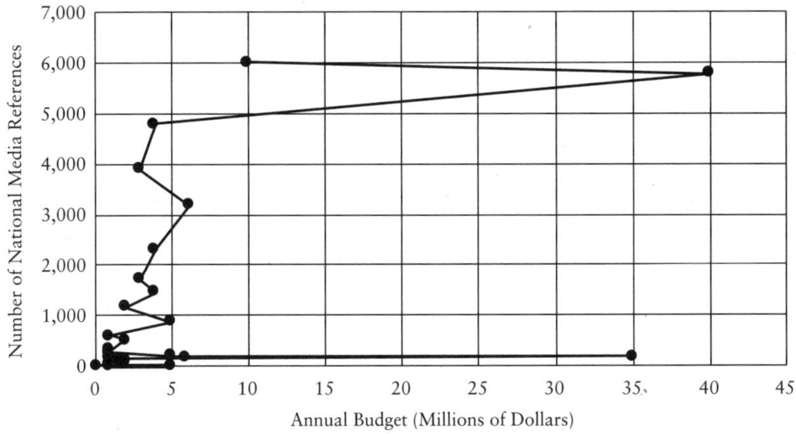

APPENDIX FIVE

References to Selected American Think Tanks in the US Congress, 1999–2008; 2009–2016

Table A5.1
Total References to Selected American Think Tanks in the US Congress (Senate, House of Representatives, *Extension of Remarks*, and *Daily Digest*), 1999–2008

Institute	*110th Congress 1st Session 1/07–12/07*	*110th Congress 2nd Session 1/08–*	*109th Congress 1st Session 1/05–12/05*	*109th Congress 2nd Session 1/06–12/06*	*108th Congress 1st Session 1/03–12/03*	*108th Congress 2nd Session 1/04–12/04*	*107th Congress 1st Session 1/01–12/01*	*107th Congress 2nd Session 1/02–11/02*	*106th Congress 1st Session 1/99–11/99*	*106th Congress 2nd Session 1/00–12/00*	*Totals*
Heritage Foundation	108	47	67	66	76	49	48	46	46	54	607
Brookings Institution	67	26	47	32	54	50	29	57	39	26	427
RAND	49	34	35	37	22	21	38	4	28	33	301
Center for Strategic and International Studies	33	16	19	30	39	30	34	21	15	19	256
Urban Institute	36	12	29	13	39	23	24	19	21	27	243
American Enterprise Institute	32	18	26	27	42	27	15	8	21	18	234
Cato Institute	18	8	26	21	16	16	22	19	23	23	192
Carnegie Endowment for International Peace	6	1	4	9	12	10	7	14	7	7	77
Hudson Institute	11	6	12	4	4	4	8	8	6	11	74
Manhattan Institute	5	2	13	5	3	4	7	1	6	3	49
Progressive Policy Institute	1	1	7	1	2	3	6	0	15	6	42
Hoover Institution	3	0	5	5	7	4	3	4	6	5	42
Institute for Policy Studies	2	1	2	0	1	0	2	11	15	5	39
Worldwatch Institute	0	1	1	0	0	0	0	0	0	3	5
Rockford Institute	0	0	0	0	0	0	0	0	0	0	0
Total	371	173	293	250	317	241	243	212	248	240	2,588

Source: Congressional Record.

Figure A5.1
Total References to Selected American Think Tanks in the US Congress (Senate, House of Representatives, *Extension of Remarks*, and *Daily Digest*), 1999–2008

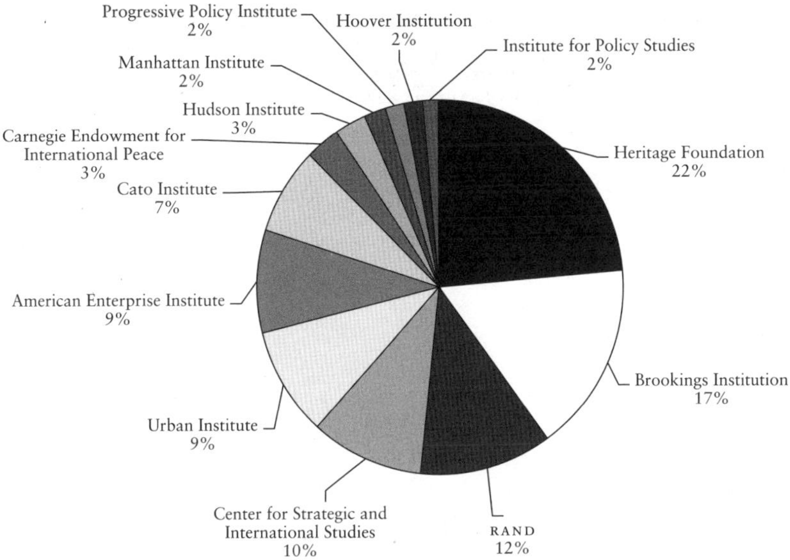

Figure A5.1.1
Total References to Selected American Think Tanks in the US Congress (Senate, House of Representatives, *Extension of Remarks*, and *Daily Digest*, 2009–2016

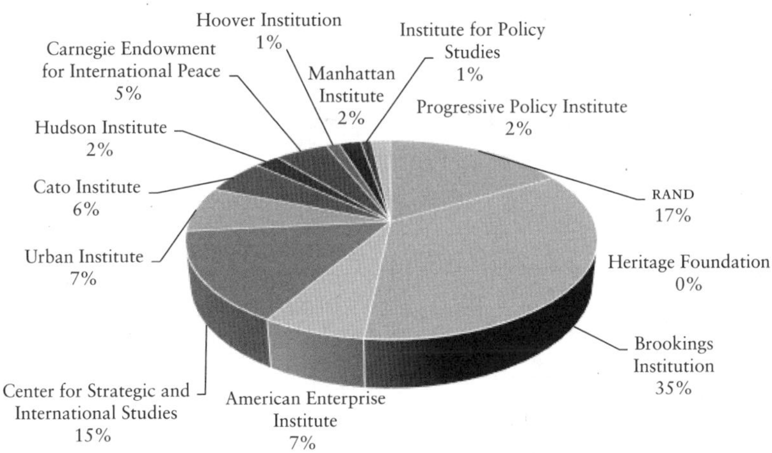

Table A5.1.1
Total References to Selected American Think Tanks in the US Congress (Senate, House of Representatives, *Extension of Remarks*, and *Daily Digest*, 2009–2016

Institute	*107th Congress 1st Session 1/01–11/02*	*107th Congress 2nd Session 1/02–12/03*	*108th Congress 1st Session 01/03–12/02*	*108th Congress 2nd Session 01/04–12/04*	*109th Congress 1st Session 01/05–12/05*	*109th Congress 2nd Session 01/06–12/06*	*110th Congress 1st Session 01/07–12/07*	*110th Congress 2nd Session 01/08–01/09*
RAND	39	52	69	50	61	65	88	60
Heritage Foundation	0	0	0	0	0	0	0	0
Brookings Institution	74	56	107	98	112	100	130	105
American Enterprise Institute	26	17	46	22	25	17	30	11
Center for Strategic and International Studies	47	67	71	55	61	54	59	52
Urban Institute	19	15	32	19	26	28	29	27
Cato Institute	21	17	27	27	12	23	23	11
Hudson Institute	6	7	8	8	8	10	3	6
Carnegie Endowment for International Peace	18	20	17	14	23	16	14	17
Hoover Institution	5	8	6	2	2	2	4	3
Manhattan Institute	10	7	5	4	12	6	4	9
Institute for Policy Studies	6	1	5	6	5	5	2	1
Progressive Policy Institute	7	3	6	5	10	5	3	3
Rockford Institute	0	0	0	0	0	0	0	0
Worldwatch Centre	2	3	1	0	2	1	0	0
Total	280	273	400	310	359	332	389	305

Source: Congressional Record.

111th Congress 1st Session 01/09–12/09	*111th Congress 2nd Session* 01/10–12/10	*112th Congress 1st Session* 01/11–01/12	*112th Congress 2nd Session* 01/12–12/13	*1113th Congress 1st Session* 01/13–12/13	*113th Congress 2nd Session* 01/14–12/14	*114th Congress 1st Session* 01/15–12/15	*114th Congress 2nd Session* 01/16–01/17	*Totals*
90	48	52	43	50	36	48	41	892
0	0	0	0	0	0	0	0	0
141	90	190	165	157	120	121	59	1825
42	30	23	15	10	17	16	13	360
54	42	47	32	30	43	47	23	784
22	30	26	25	22	30	15	23	388
15	17	24	19	10	17	19	15	297
9	12	3	9	13	9	4	7	122
14	17	19	19	11	14	18	14	265
4	2	3	3	4	6	6	5	65
8	8	5	5	5	3	7	8	106
0	0	6	3	1	6	3	1	51
5	5	5	5	5	8	8	12	95
0	0	0	0	0	0	0	0	0
2	0	4	2	4	3	5	2	31
406	301	407	345	322	312	317	223	5281

Table A5.2
References to Selected American Think Tanks in the US Senate, 1999–2008

Institute	*110th Congress 1st Session 1/07–12/07*	*110th Congress 2nd Session 1/08–*	*109th Congress 1st Session 1/05–12/05*	*109th Congress 2nd Session 1/06–12/06*	*108th Congress 1st Session 1/03–12/03*	*108th Congress 2nd Session 1/04–12/04*	*107th Congress 1st Session 1/01–12/01*	*107th Congress 2nd Session 1/02–11/02*	*106th Congress 1st Session 1/99–11/99*	*106th Congress 2nd Session 1/00–12/00*	*Totals*
Heritage Foundation	36	17	25	28	30	17	21	20	21	25	240
Brookings Institution	25	5	20	9	25	25	15	29	17	17	187
RAND	32	14	17	21	10	7	24	2	14	19	160
Urban Institute	12	2	19	2	21	10	8	7	9	10	100
Center for Strategic and International Studies	11	5	3	7	14	11	13	10	5	8	87
American Enterprise Institute	8	9	13	9	19	9	0	0	8	5	80
Cato Institute	5	6	8	8	7	4	8	6	10	12	74
Progressive Policy Institute	1	0	4	0	1	2	5	0	11	5	29
Hudson Institute	1	0	6	1	1	1	6	5	2	2	25
Carnegie Endowment for International Peace	4	0	1	1	4	0	2	7	1	1	21
Hoover Institution	0	0	2	1	4	2	2	2	2	3	18
Manhattan Institute	2	2	4	2	0	2	3	0	2	0	17
Institute for Policy Studies	1	0	0	0	1	0	1	1	1	0	5
Worldwatch Institute	0	1	0	0	0	0	0	0	0	0	1
Rockford Institute	0	0	0	0	0	0	0	0	0	0	0
Total	138	61	122	89	137	90	108	89	103	107	1,044

Source: Congressional Record.

Figure A 5.2
References to Selected American Think Tanks in the US Senate, 1999–2008

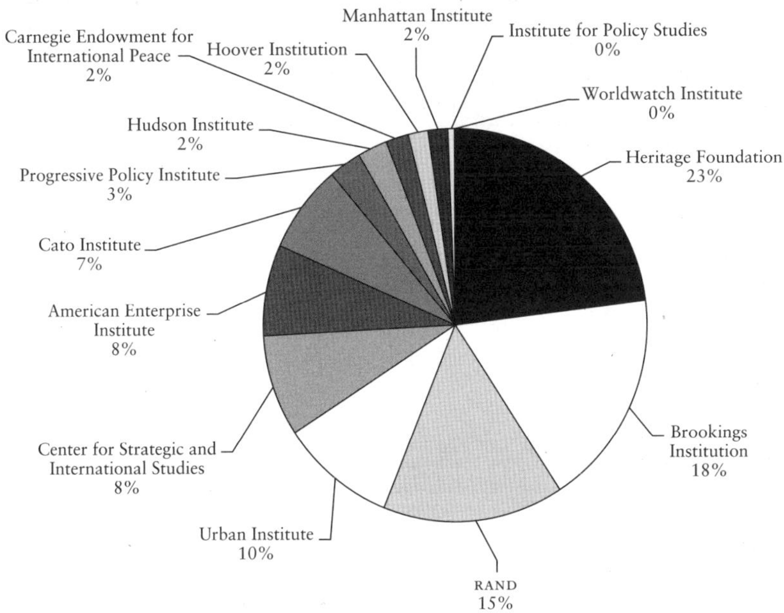

Figure A 5.2.1
References to Selected American Think Tanks in the US Senate, 2009–2016

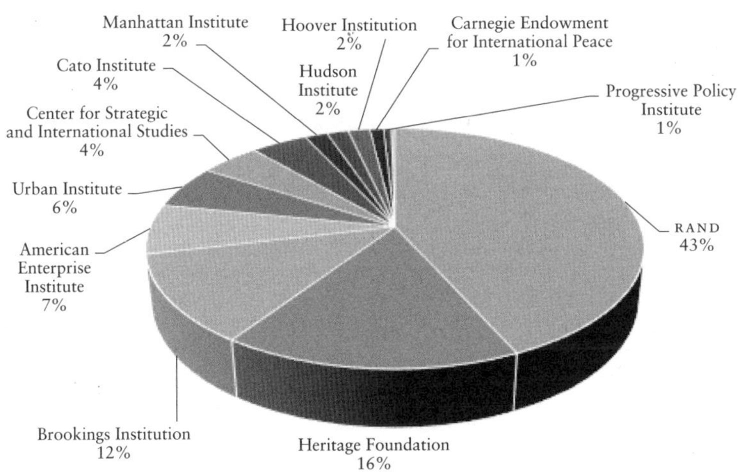

Table A 5.2.1
References to Selected American Think Tanks in the US Senate, 2009–2016

Institute	*107th Congress 1st Session 1/01–11/02*	*107th Congress 2nd Session 1/02–12/03*	*108th Congress 1st Session 01/03–12/02*	*108th Congress 2nd Session 01/04–12/04*	*109th Congress 1st Session 01/05–12/05*	*109th Congress 2nd Session 01/06–12/06*	*110th Congress 1st Session 01/07–12/07*	*110th Congress 2nd Session 01/08–01/09*
RAND	41	29	68	54	75	62	64	65
Heritage Foundation	21	23	31	17	25	28	36	26
Brookings Institution	17	34	34	30	27	13	28	8
American Enterprise Institute	12	5	19	5	13	9	8	9
Urban Institute	9	7	22	10	19	8	13	2
Center for Strategic and International Studies	14	10	14	11	3	7	10	10
Cato Institute	8	7	7	4	8	8	5	8
Manhattan Institute	3	0	0	2	4	2	2	2
Hudson Institute	6	5	1	1	7	1	1	0
Hoover Institution	2	3	4	2	2	1	0	2
Carnegie Endowment for International Peace	2	7	4	0	1	1	4	0
Progressive Policy Institute	5	0	1	2	4	0	1	0
Institute for Policy Studies	1	0	0	0	0	0	0	0
Worldwatch Centre	0	0	0	0	0	0	0	0
Rockford Institute	0	0	0	0	0	0	0	0
Total	141	130	205	138	188	140	172	132

Source: Congressional Record.

111th Congress 1st Session 01/09–12/09	111th Congress 2nd Session 01/10–12/10	112th Congress 1st Session 01/11–01/12	112th Congress 2nd Session 01/12–12/13	1113th Congress 1st Session 01/13–12/13	113th Congress 2nd Session 01/14–12/14	114th Congress 1st Session 01/15–12/15	114th Congress 2nd Session 01/16–01/17	Totals
65	46	138	118	85	77	95	33	1115
52	24	32	18	27	15	26	20	421
25	19	17	11	7	13	20	4	307
7	10	16	8	11	18	11	12	173
22	11	7	6	1	5	7	3	152
6	2	4	6	1	6	8	6	118
7	10	6	2	9	1	15	7	112
5	2	1	2	9	4	3	4	45
3	3	2	1	4	1	3	4	43
5	3	3	3	2	2	3	6	43
1	2	1	0	2	2	1	0	28
0	0	0	2	0	0	0	0	15
0	0	0	0	0	0	5	1	7
0	0	0	0	0	0	0	0	0
0	0	0	0	0	0	0	0	0
198	132	227	177	158	144	197	100	2579

Table A5.3
References to Selected American Think Tanks in the US House of Representatives, 1999–2008

Institute	*110th Congress 1st Session 1/07–12/07*	*110th Congress 2nd Session 1/08–*	*109th Congress 1st Session 1/05–12/05*	*109th Congress 2nd Session 1/06–12/06*	*108th Congress 1st Session 1/03–12/03*	*108th Congress 2nd Session 1/04–12/04*	*107th Congress 1st Session 1/01–12/01*	*107th Congress 2nd Session 1/02–11/02*	*106th Congress 1st Session 1/99–11/99*	*106th Congress 2nd Session 1/00–12/00*	*Totals*
Heritage Foundation	51	15	26	21	32	22	16	11	11	18	223
Brookings Institution	24	5	10	8	15	11	3	9	9	3	97
RAND	12	13	9	9	7	8	8	2	9	11	88
Cato Institute	5	1	9	9	6	5	7	8	8	5	63
Urban Institute	13	3	2	3	11	7	6	6	5	7	63
American Enterprise Institute	11	1	4	8	9	9	1	1	5	1	50
Center for Strategic and International Studies	10	2	3	3	4	5	2	1	2	1	33
Hudson Institute	8	1	3	0	1	2	1	0	2	6	24
Carnegie Endowment for International Peace	0	0	0	0	2	8	2	1	0	0	13
Manhattan Institute	1	0	4	0	0	2	2	0	1	1	11
Hoover Institution	0	0	1	2	2	2	0	0	1	0	8
Institute for Policy Studies	0	0	1	0	0	0	0	3	2	0	6
Progressive Policy Institute	0	0	1	0	1	0	1	0	2	0	5
Worldwatch Institute	0	0	1	0	0	0	0	0	0	2	3
Rockford Institute	0	0	0	0	0	0	0	0	0	0	0
Total	135	41	74	63	90	81	49	42	57	55	687

Source: Congressional Record.

Figure A 5.3
References to Selected American Think Tanks in the US House of Representatives, 1999–2008

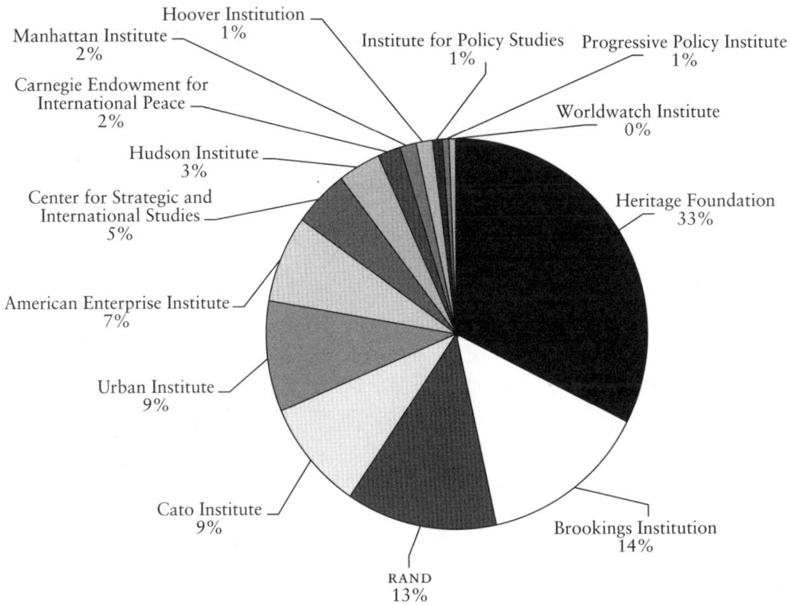

Figure A 5.3.1
References to Selected American Think Tanks in the US House of Representatives, 2009–2016

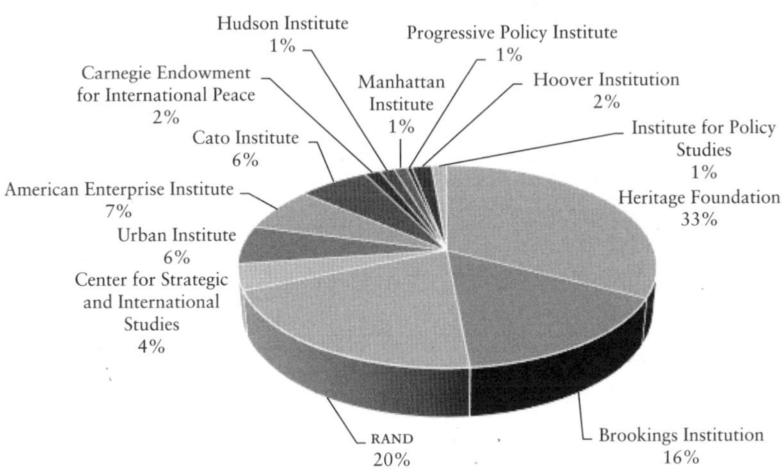

Table A5.3.1
References to Selected American Think Tanks in the US House of Representatives, 2009–2016

Institute	*107th Congress 1st Session 1/01–11/02*	*107th Congress 2nd Session 1/02–12/03*	*108th Congress 1st Session 01/03–12/02*	*108th Congress 2nd Session 01/04–12/04*	*109th Congress 1st Session 01/05–12/05*	*109th Congress 2nd Session 01/06–12/06*	*110th Congress 1st Session 01/07–12/07*	*110th Congress 2nd Session 01/08–01/09*
Heritage Foundation	16	11	32	21	26	22	49	15
Brookings Institution	5	13	20	13	16	16	34	9
RAND	17	14	18	11	17	18	14	25
Center for Strategic and International Studies	2	2	4	6	3	3	11	2
Urban Institute	4	6	10	7	2	3	11	3
American Enterprise Institute	1	1	9	10	4	8	12	2
Cato Institute	7	9	6	5	10	1	5	4
Carnegie Endowment for International Peace	1	2	8	2	0	0	0	0
Hudson Institute	1	0	1	2	3	0	2	2
Manhattan Institute	2	0	0	2	4	0	1	0
Progressive Policy Institute	1	0	1	0	1	0	0	0
Hoover Institution	0	0	3	2	1	2	1	0
Institute for Policy Studies	0	3	0	0	1	0	0	0
Worldwatch Centre	0	0	0	0	0	0	0	0
Rockford Institute	0	0	0	0	0	0	0	0
Total	57	61	112	81	88	73	140	62

Source: Congressional Record.

111th Congress 1st Session 01/09–12/09	*111th Congress 2nd Session 01/10–12/10*	*112th Congress 1st Session 01/11–01/12*	*112th Congress 2nd Session 01/12–12/13*	*1113th Congress 1st Session 01/13–12/13*	*113th Congress 2nd Session 01/14–12/14*	*114th Congress 1st Session 01/15–12/15*	*114th Congress 2nd Session 01/16–01/17*	*Totals*
51	26	37	22	49	22	12	8	419
20	7	13	6	8	10	12	4	206
18	13	20	18	16	22	14	7	262
1	1	4	6	1	2	1	4	53
8	4	5	2	4	5	4	1	79
	12	5	5	7	6	5	4	91
4	2	7	11	2	4	2	3	82
1	3	0	0	1	0	0	0	18
2	0	1	1	1	0	1	0	17
0	1	0	0	1	2	2	0	15
1	0	0	0	0	2	0	0	6
0	0	5	1	0	5	2	1	23
2	0	3	1	3	3	0	1	17
0	0	0	0	0	0	0	0	0
0	0	0	0	0	0	0	0	0
108	69	100	73	93	83	55	33	1,288

Table A5.4
References to Selected American Think Tanks in the US Congress (*Extension of Remarks*), 1999–2008

Institute	*110th Congress 1st Session 1/07–12/07*	*110th Congress 2nd Session 1/08–*	*109th Congress 1st Session 1/05–12/05*	*109th Congress 2nd Session 1/06–12/06*	*108th Congress 1st Session 1/03–12/03*	*108th Congress 2nd Session 1/04–12/04*	*107th Congress 1st Session 1/01–12/01*	*107th Congress 2nd Session 1/02–11/02*	*106th Congress 1st Session 1/99–11/99*	*106th Congress 2nd Session 1/00–12/00*	*Totals*
Heritage Foundation	13	7	5	8	7	3	6	8	5	7	69
Urban Institute	5	5	3	5	4	3	6	4	3	7	45
Brookings Institution	7	3	6	4	2	4	2	5	3	1	37
Center for Strategic and International Studies	1	0	1	4	8	2	5	1	2	3	27
RAND	2	2	6	4	2	3	1	0	2	2	24
American Enterprise Institute	2	3	2	4	1	1	0	2	1	0	16
Cato Institute	1	0	2	0	2	1	0	2	2	4	14
Manhattan Institute	2	0	2	1	2	0	2	0	0	2	11
Hoover Institution	2	0	2	1	1	0	0	1	1	2	10
Carnegie Endowment for International Peace	0	0	0	2	0	0	1	1	1	2	7
Institute for Policy Studies	1	1	0	0	0	0	0	1	3	1	7
Hudson Institute	0	2	1	0	0	0	0	0	1	0	4
Progressive Policy Institute	0	0	1	1	0	0	0	0	0	0	2
Worldwatch Institute	0	0	0	0	0	0	0	0	0	1	1
Rockford Institute	0	0	0	0	0	0	0	0	0	0	0
Total	36	23	31	34	29	17	23	25	24	32	274

Source: Congressional Record.

Figure A5.4
References to Selected American Think Tanks in the US Congress (*Extension of Remarks*), 1999–2008

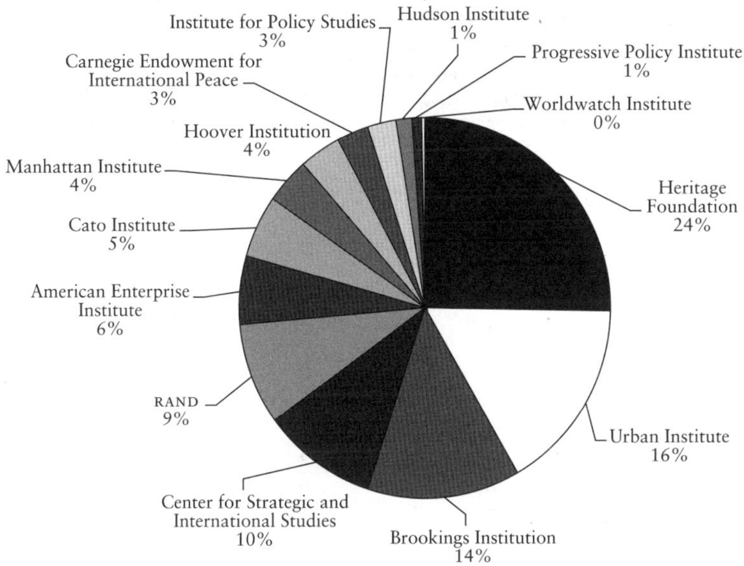

Figure A5.4.1
References to Selected American Think Tanks in the US Congress (*Extension of Remarks*), 2009–2016

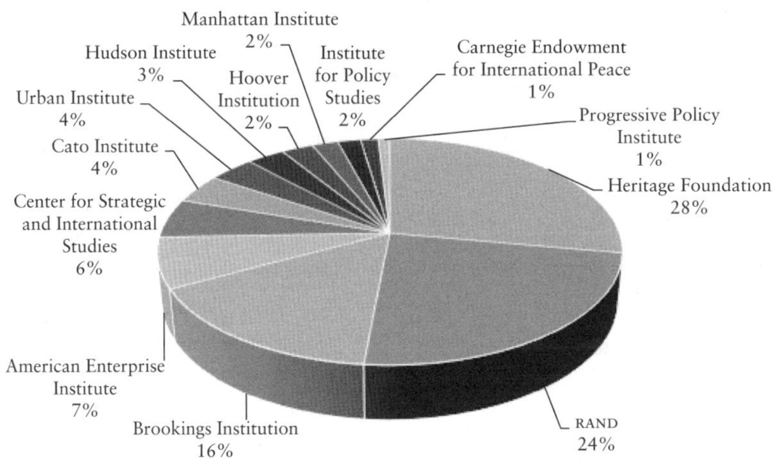

Table A5.4.1
References to Selected American Think Tanks in the US Congress (*Extension of Remarks*), 2009–2016

Institute	*107th Congress 1st Session 1/01–11/02*	*107th Congress 2nd Session 1/02–12/03*	*108th Congress 1st Session 01/03–12/02*	*108th Congress 2nd Session 01/04–12/04*	*109th Congress 1st Session 01/05–12/05*	*109th Congress 2nd Session 01/06–12/06*	*110th Congress 1st Session 01/07–12/07*	*110th Congress 2nd Session 01/08–01/09*
Heritage Foundation	6	8	5	3	5	9	13	11
RAND	2	4	8	7	10	9	6	9
Brookings Institution	3	6	5	3	7	5	7	7
American Enterprise Institute	0	2	1	1	2	4	2	5
Center for Strategic and International Studies	6	0	8	0	1	0	1	0
Cato Institute	0	2	2	1	2	0	1	0
Urban Institute	0	1	0	2	0	4	0	0
Hudson Institute	0	0	0	0	2	0	0	2
Hoover Institution	0	1	0	1	0	2	0	3
Manhattan Institute	2	0	2	0	2	1	2	0
Institute for Policy Studies	0	1	0	0	0	0	0	2
Carnegie Endowment for International Peace	1	1	0	0	0	2	0	0
Progressive Policy Institute	0	0	1	0	1	1	0	0
Worldwatch Centre	0	0	0	0	0	0	0	0
Rockford Institute	0	0	0	0	0	0	0	0
Total	20	26	32	18	32	37	32	39

Source: Congressional Record.

	111th Congress 1st Session 01/09–12/09	111th Congress 2nd Session 01/10–12/10	112th Congress 1st Session 01/11–01/12	112th Congress 2nd Session 01/12–12/13	1113th Congress 1st Session 01/13–12/13	113th Congress 2nd Session 01/14–12/14	114th Congress 1st Session 01/15–12/15	114th Congress 2nd Session 01/16–01/17	Totals
	12	3	6	10	12	8	4	4	119
	10	8	1	9	6	2	2	8	101
	6	5	4	1	2	1	3	2	67
	2	4	3	1	2	2	0	0	31
	2	0	4	0	2	0	0	0	24
	3	2	4	1	0	0	0	0	18
	0	2	0	3	0	4	0	0	16
	0	3	0	2	1	3	0	0	13
	0	1	0	2	0	1	0	0	11
	0	0	0	0	0	0	0	0	9
	1	0	1	1	1	0	1	0	8
	0	0	1	0	1	0	0	0	6
	0	0	0	1	0	0	0	0	4
	0	0	0	0	0	0	0	0	0
	0	0	0	0	0	0	0	0	0
	36	28	24	31	27	21	10	14	427

Table A5.5
References to Selected American Think Tanks in the US Congress (*Daily Digest*), 1999–2008

Institute	*110th Congress 1st Session 1/07–12/07*	*110th Congress 2nd Session 1/08–*	*109th Congress 1st Session 1/05–12/05*	*109th Congress 2nd Session 1/06–12/06*	*108th Congress 1st Session 1/03–12/03*	*108th Congress 2nd Session 1/04–12/04*	*107th Congress 1st Session 1/01–12/01*	*107th Congress 2nd Session 1/02–11/02*	*106th Congress 1st Session 1/99–11/99*	*106th Congress 2nd Session 1/00–12/00*	*Totals*
Center for Strategic and International Studies	11	9	12	16	13	12	14	9	6	7	109
Brookings Institution	11	13	11	11	12	10	9	14	10	5	106
American Enterprise Institute	11	5	7	6	13	8	14	5	7	12	88
Heritage Foundation	8	8	11	9	7	7	5	7	9	4	75
Cato Institute	7	1	7	4	1	6	7	3	3	2	41
Carnegie Endowment for International Peace	2	1	4	6	6	2	2	5	5	3	36
Urban Institute	6	2	5	3	3	3	4	2	4	3	35
RAND	3	5	3	3	3	3	5	0	3	1	29
Institute for Policy Studies	0	0	1	0	0	0	1	6	9	4	21
Hudson Institute	2	3	2	3	2	1	1	3	1	3	21
Manhattan Institute	0	0	3	2	1	0	0	1	3	0	10
Progressive Policy Institute	0	1	1	0	0	1	0	0	2	1	6
Hoover Institution	1	0	0	1	0	0	1	1	2	0	6
Worldwatch Institute	0	0	0	0	0	0	0	0	0	0	0
Rockford Institute	0	0	0	0	0	0	0	0	0	0	0
Total	62	48	67	64	61	53	63	56	64	45	583

Source: Congressional Record.

Figure A5.5
References to Selected American Think Tanks in the US Congress (*Daily Digest*), 1999–2008

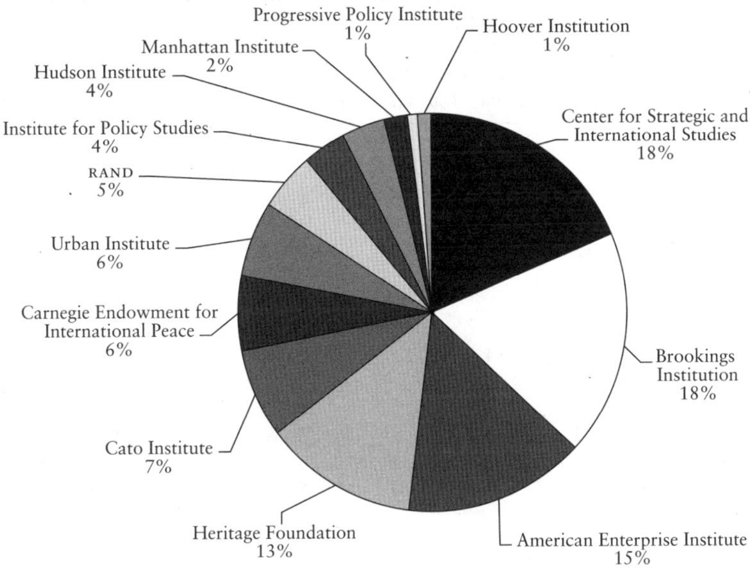

Figure A5.5.1
References to Selected American Think Tanks in the US Congress (*Daily Digest*), 2009–2016

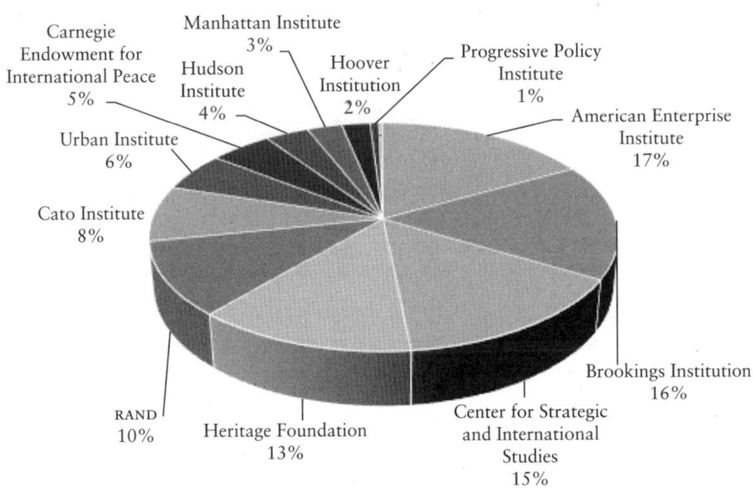

Table A5.5.1
References to Selected American Think Tanks in the US Congress (*Daily Digest*), 2009–2016

Institute	*107th Congress 1st Session 1/01–11/02*	*107th Congress 2nd Session 1/02–12/03*	*108th Congress 1st Session 01/03–12/02*	*108th Congress 2nd Session 01/04–12/04*	*109th Congress 1st Session 01/05–12/05*	*109th Congress 2nd Session 01/06–12/06*	*110th Congress 1st Session 01/07–12/07*	*110th Congress 2nd Session 01/08–01/09*
American Enterprise Institute	11	8	2	20	6	7	4	14
Brookings Institution	11	12	10	13	10	12	12	16
Center for Strategic and International Studies	10	13	14	11	10	18	10	12
Heritage Foundation	5	6	8	7	8	12	8	11
RAND	7	4	6	5	3	6	5	6
Cato Institute	6	4	2	5	3	8	0	8
Urban Institute	3	3	4	3	5	3	4	5
Carnegie Endowment for International Peace	2	5	0	8	2	8	1	2
Hudson Institute	3	1	3	0	2	3	1	4
Manhattan Institute	1	0	0	1	2	3	0	1
Hoover Institution	2	0	1	2	0	1	0	1
Progressive Policy Institute	0	0	1	2	0	1	0	1
Institute for Policy Studies	1	0	0	0	0	0	0	0
Worldwatch Centre	0	0	0	0	0	0	0	0
Rockford Institute	0	0	0	0	0	0	0	0
Total	62	56	51	77	51	82	45	81

Source: Congressional Record.

111th Congress 1st Session 01/09–12/09	111th Congress 2nd Session 01/10–12/10	112th Congress 1st Session 01/11–01/12	112th Congress 2nd Session 01/12–12/13	1113th Congress 1st Session 01/13–12/13	113th Congress 2nd Session 01/14–12/14	114th Congress 1st Session 01/15–12/15	114th Congress 2nd Session 01/16–01/17	Totals
13	15	9	15	11	13	10	14	172
8	9	6	10	9	9	8	9	164
5	5	6	2	5	7	10	10	148
12	15	3	10	8	8	3	7	131
10	15	7	7	3	7	5	9	105
6	1	11	7	2	5	6	5	79
3	3	6	3	0	5	1	4	55
3	4	2	5	2	2	1	3	50
3	4	2	1	0	1	3	4	35
0	1	2	2	2	4	3	6	28
1	0	1	2	1	2	4	5	23
0	0	0	0	0	1	1	0	7
0	0	1	0	1	0	0	0	3
0	0	0	0	0	0	0	0	0
0	0	0	0	0	0	0	0	0
64	72	56	64	44	64	55	76	1,000

Table A5.6
Comparison of Annual Budget to Number of References in the US Congress for Selected American Think Tanks

Institutes	*Annual budget (millions of dollars)*	*Number of references in the US Congress*
Heritage Foundation	30	607
Brookings Institution	30	427
RAND	200	301
Centre for Strategic and International Studies	20	256
Urban Institute	50	243
American Enterprise Institute for Public Policy Research	20	234
Cato Institute	20	192
Carnegie Endowment for International Peace	20	77
Hudson Institute	10	74
Manhattan Institute for Policy Research	15	49
Hoover Institution	30	42
Progressive Policy Institute	2	42
Institute for Policy Studies	2	39
Worldwatch Institute	5	5
Russell Sage Foundation	5	0
The Twentieth Century Fund/ Century Foundation	5	0
National Bureau of Economic Research	10	0
Council on Foreign Relations	30	0
Foreign Policy Research Institute	3	0
Northeast-Midwest Institute	5	0
The Carter Center	30	0
Citizens for a Sound Economy Foundation	20	0
United States Institute of Peace	20	0
Economic Policy Institute	5	0
Empower America	10	0
The Progress and Freedom Foundation	5	0

Figure A 5.6
Comparison of Annual Budget to Number of References in the US Congress for Selected American Think Tanks

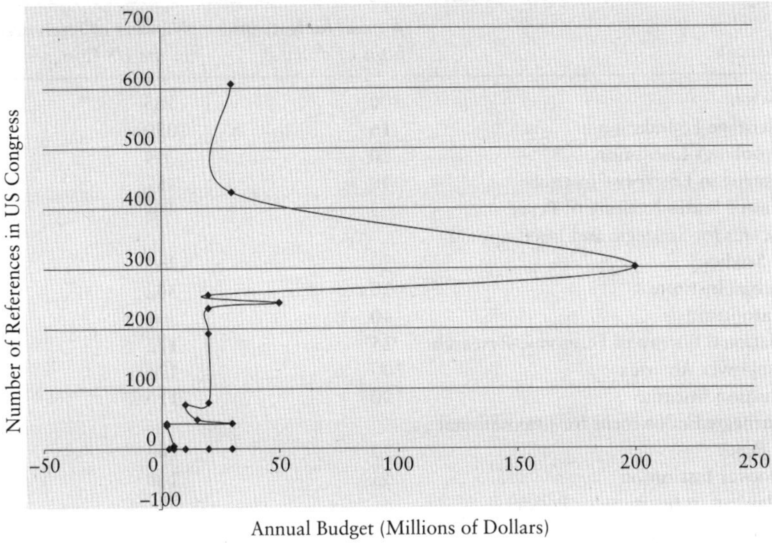

Table A5.6.1
Comparison of Annual Budget to Number of References in the US Congress for Selected American Think Tanks, 2009–2016

Institute	*Annual budgets (millions of dollars)*	*Number of references in the US Congress*
RAND	300	1583
Heritage Foundation	16	1090
Brookings Institution	70	744
American Enterprise Institute	40	487
United States Institute of Peace	5	384
Center for Strategic and International Studies	30	343
Urban Institute	20	302
Cato Institute	40	301
National Bureau of Economic Research	25	172
Empower America	200	124
Hudson Institute	100	110
Carnegie Endowment for International Peace	90	102
Hoover Institution	33	100
Manhattan Institute for Policy Research	4	97
The Twentieth Century Fund/Century Foundation	5	38
Institute for Policy Studies	12	35
Progressive Policy Institute	10	32
Northeast-Midwest Institute	2	30
The Progress and Freedom Foundation	62	21
Economic Policy Institute	6	12
Foreign Policy Research Institute	30	11
Russel Sage Foundation	2	7
Council on Foreign Relations	60	5
Citizens for Sound Economy Foundation	85	0
The Carter Centre	3	0
Worldwatch Institute	13	0

Figure A 5.6.1
Comparison of Annual Budget to Number of References in the US Congress for Selected American Think Tanks, 2009–2016

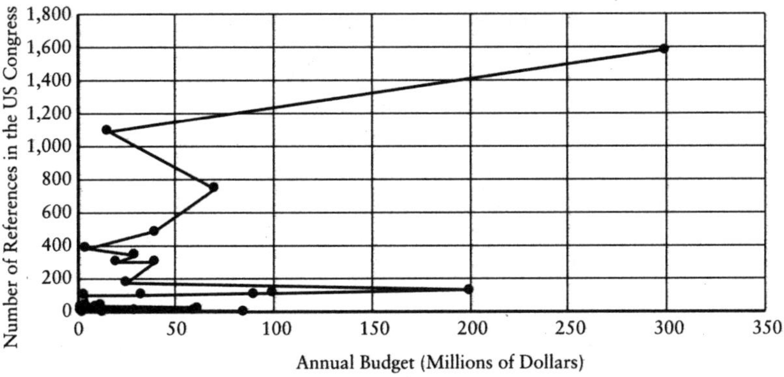

Table A5.7
Appearances by Selected American Think Tanks before Congressional Committees, 1999–2008

Institute	*1999*	*2000*	*2001*	*2002*	*2003*	*2004*	*2005*	*2006*	*2007*	*2008*	*Totals*
American Enterprise Institute	18	14	21	25	39	18	40	28	40	21	264
Center for Strategic and International Studies	15	17	21	11	23	23	32	29	32	18	221
Heritage Foundation	10	14	26	20	25	8	12	30	25	38	208
Cato Institute	5	7	13	10	21	16	24	25	27	30	178
RAND	5	7	17	6	12	19	20	18	31	17	152
Urban Institute	15	8	18	7	8	11	18	11	27	12	135
Hoover Institution	4	5	1	2	5	3	1	4	6	15	46
Brookings Institution	0	1	1	8	8	1	9	4	6	4	42
Hudson Institute	0	0	1	2	0	1	8	3	12	12	39
Carnegie Endowment for International Peace	3	4	0	1	4	2	0	3	5	14	36
Institute for Policy Studies	1	0	0	0	2	0	1	1	3	12	20
Manhattan Institute	0	0	0	0	2	0	1	1	0	0	4
Progressive Policy Institute	0	0	0	0	0	0	0	0	0	0	0
Worldwatch Institute	0	0	0	0	0	0	0	0	0	0	0
Rockford Institute	0	0	0	0	0	0	0	0	0	0	0

Information obtained from think tank websites and through email correspondence.

Figure A5.7
Appearances by Selected American Think Tanks before Congressional Committees, 1999–2008

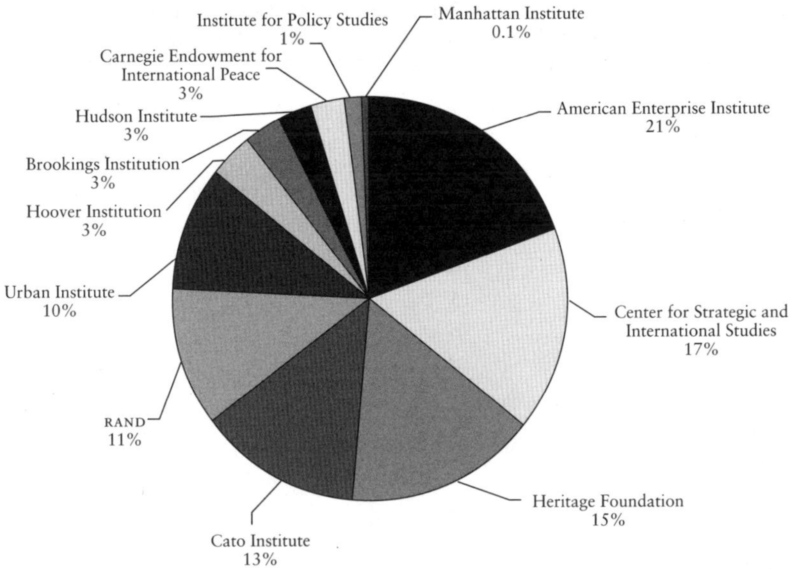

Table A5.7.1
Appearances by Selected American Think Tanks before Congressional Committees, 2009–2016

Institute	*111th Congress (2009–2010)*	*112th Congress (2011–2012)*	*113th Congress (2013–2014)*	*114th Congress (2015–2016)*	*Totals*
Heritage Foundation	111	71	113	114	294
Brookings Institution	111	112	113	114	450
RAND	43	75	63	113	294
Center for Strategic and International Studies	10	18	17	12	57
Urban Institute	19	15	25	17	76
American Enterprise Institute	19	66	31	21	137
Cato Institute	13	30	2	12	57
Carnegie Endowment for International Peace	5	9	6	2	22
Hudson Institute	4	7	5	7	23
Manhattan Institute	2	21	12	10	45
Progressive Policy Institute	1	8	1	4	14
Hoover Institution	3	19	10	6	38
Institute for Policy Studies	2	1	2	0	5
Worldwatch Centre	0	0	0	0	0
Rockford Institute	0	0	0	0	0
Total	343	452	400	432	1,512

Source: Congressional Report.

NOTE: Committee reports database amalgamates all data under pairs of years. Search results not viewable per session, nor are they viewable by year.

Figure A5.7.1
Appearances by Selected American Think Tanks before Congressional Committees, 2009–2016

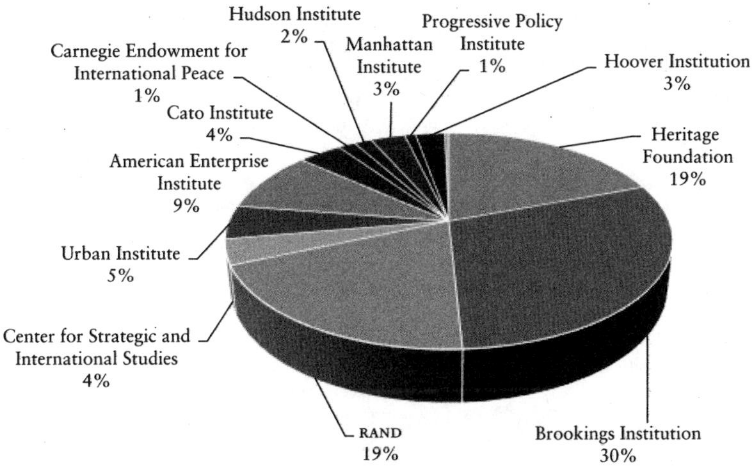

Table A5.8
Committees, United States Senate and House of Representatives

Senate	*House*
STANDING COMMITTEES	STANDING COMMITTEES
Agriculture, Nutrition, & Foresty	Agriculture
Appropriations	Appropriations
Armed Services	Armed Services
Banking, Housing, & Urban Affairs	Budget
Budget	Education & Labor
Commerce, Science, & Transportation	Energy & Commerce
Energy & Natural Resources	Financial Services
Environment & Public Works	Foreign Affairs
Finance	Homeland Security
Foreign Relations	House Administration
Health, Education, Labor, & Pensions	Judiciary
Homeland Security & Governmental Affairs	Natural Resources
	Oversight & Government Reform
Indian Affairs	Rules
Judiciary	Science & Technology
Rules & Administration	Small Business
Small Business & Entrepreneurship	Standards of Official Conduct
Veteran's Affairs	Transportation & Infrastructure
	Veteran's Affairs
SELECT, SPECIAL, & OTHER	Ways & Means
Select Committee on Ethics	
Select Committee on Intelligence	SELECT, SPECIAL, & OTHER
Special Committee on Aging	Select Bipartisan Committee to Investigate the Preparation for and Response to Hurricane Katrina
Special Committee on the Y2K Technology Problem	Permanent Select Committee on Intelligence
CAUCUSES	Select Committee on U.S. National Security & Military/Commercial Concerns with The People's Republic of China
Caucus on International Narcotics Control	Select Committee to Investigate the Voting Irregularities of August 2, 2007
JOINT COMMITTEES	
Joint Committee on Taxation	
Joint Committee of Congress on the Library	
Joint Economic Committee	
Joint Committee on Printing	

Source: US Government Printing Office.

APPENDIX SIX

References to Selected Think Tanks in Parliamentary Committees, 1999–2008; 2009–2016

Table A6.1
Appearances by Selected Canadian Think Tanks before Parliamentary Committees, 1999–2008

Institute	*Number of appearances*
Conference Board of Canada	143
C.D. Howe Institute	98
Fraser Institute	73
Canadian Council on Social Development	47
Canadian Centre for Policy Alternatives	46
Caledon Institute of Social Policy	35
North-South Institute	33
National Council of Welfare	31
Public Policy Forum	28
Parliamentary Centre	26
Canada West Foundation	26
Canadian Policy Research Networks, Inc.	22
Institute for Research on Public Policy	17
Canadian Institute of Strategic Studies	11
Canadian Institute of International Affairs	8
Mackenzie Institute	4
Canadian Tax Foundation	2
Canadian Council for International Peace and Security	1
Pearson-Shoyama Institute	0

Source: Canadian Library of Parliament, http://www.parl.gc.ca/common/Library.asp.

Figure A6.1
Appearance by Selected Canadian Think Tanks before Parliamentary Committees, 1999–2008

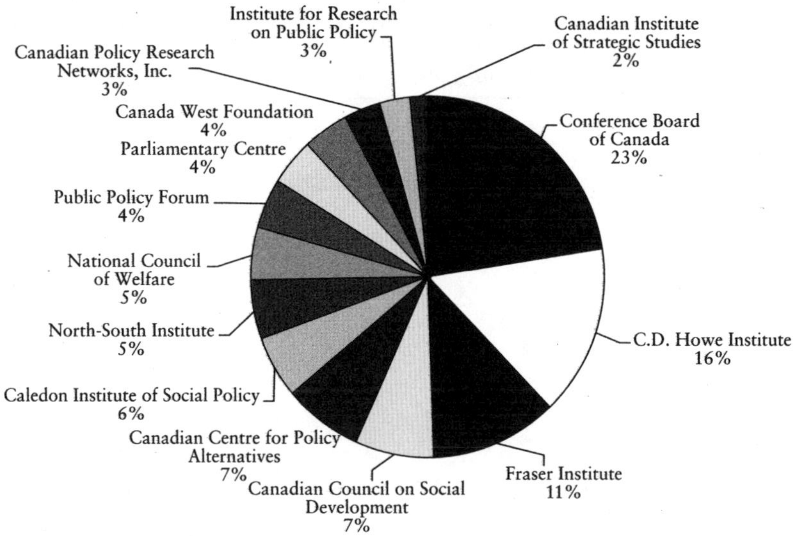

Figure A6.1.1
Appearances by Selected Canadian Think Tanks before Senate Committees, 2008–2016

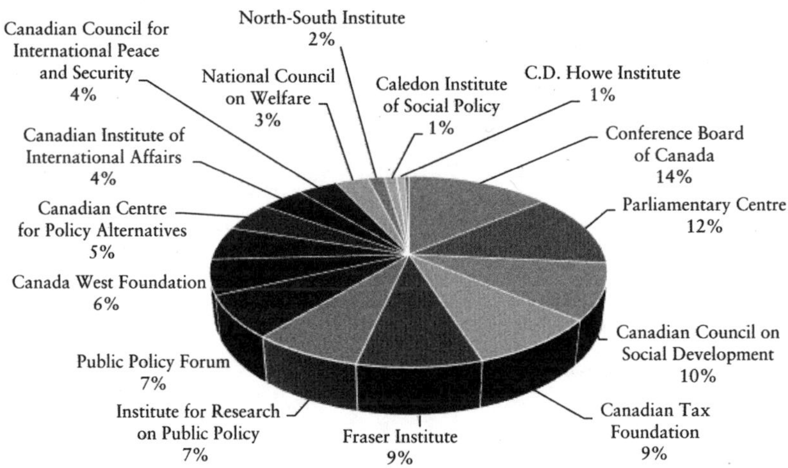

Table A6.1.1
Appearances by Selected Canadian Think Tanks before Senate Committees, 2008–2016

	37th Parliament 1st Session 01/01–09/02	*37th Parliament 2nd Session 09/02–11/03*	*37th Parliament 3rd Session 02/04–05/04*	*38th Parliament 1st Session 10/04–11/05*	*39th Parliament 1st Session 04/06–09/07*	*39th Parliament 2nd Session 10/07–09/08*
Institute	*Liberal*	*Liberal*	*Liberal*	*Liberal*	*Conservative*	*Conservative*
Conference Board of Canada	8	16	8	24	18	9
Parliamentary Centre	2	1	0	2	1	0
Canadian Council on Social Development	N/A	N/A	N/A	N/A	N/A	N/A
Canadian Tax Foundation	1	0	0	0	10	0
Fraser Institute	1	0	0	6	16	6
Institute for Research on Public Policy	2	1	1	4	8	0
Public Policy Forum	3	1	0	1	0	0
Canada West Foundation	0	2	2	0	12	2
Canadian Policy Research Networks (CLOSED)	0	1	0	0	4	0
Canadian Centre for Policy Alternatives	0	0	0	0	2	2
Canadian Institute of International Affairs	0	3	1	0	0	0
Canadian Council for International Peace and Security	0	0	0	0	0	0
National Council on Welfare	1	0	0	1	0	0
North-South Institute	0	1	0	1	0	0
Caledon Institute of Social Policy	1	0	0	0	10	0
C.D. Howe Institute	N/A	N/A	N/A	N/A	N/A	N/A
Mackenzie Institute	0	2	0	0	0	0
Canadian Institute of Strategic Studies	N/A	N/A	N/A	N/A	N/A	N/A
Pearson-Shoyama Institute	0	0	0	0	0	0
Totals	19	28	12	39	81	19

Source: Library of Parliament.
NOTE: No data for 36th Parliament session avaialble on Parliamentary database.
NOTE: Senate of Canada website database no longer offers data prior to 40th Parliament, 3rd session – existing data above is a reflection of previous research on select institutes https://sencanada.ca/en/In-The-Chamber/Debates/Search?k=%22fraser+institute%22.

40th Parliament 1st Session 11/08–12/08	*40th Parliament 2nd Session 01/09–12/09*	*40th Parliament 3rd Session 03/10–03/11*	*41st Parliament 1st Session 06/11–09/13*	*41st Parliament 2nd Session 10/13–08/15*	*42nd Parliament 1st Session 12/15–*	*Totals*
Conservative	*Conservative*	*Conservative*	*Conservative*	*Conservative*	*Liberal*	
N/A	N/A	29	53	24	24	213
N/A	N/A	27	66	60	30	189
N/A	N/A	33	55	32	25	145
N/A	N/A	20	61	26	20	138
N/A	N/A	20	35	33	14	131
N/A	N/A	25	38	20	15	114
N/A	N/A	24	37	30	14	110
N/A	N/A	13	34	17	8	90
N/A	N/A	14	37	21	9	86
N/A	N/A	9	36	16	11	76
N/A	N/A	11	30	14	5	64
N/A	N/A	9	31	9	9	58
N/A	N/A	5	19	11	11	48
N/A	N/A	5	8	6	3	24
N/A	N/A	0	1	3	3	18
N/A	N/A	1	5	4	3	13
N/A	N/A	2	2	0	0	6
N/A	N/A	0	0	0	0	0
N/A	N/A	0	0	0	0	0
N/A	N/A	247	548	326	204	1,523

Table A6.2
Appearances by Selected Canadian Think Tanks before Senate Committees, 1999–2008

Institute	*36th Parliament 2nd Session 04/99–10/00*	*37th Parliament 1st Session 01/01–09/02*	*37th Parliament 2nd Session 09/02–11/03*	*37th Parliament 3rd Session 02/04–05/04*	*38thParliament 1st Session 10/04–11/05*	*39th Parliament 1st Session 04/06–09/07*	*39th Parliament 2nd Session 10/07–09/08*	Totals
	Government majority							
Institute	*Liberal*	*Liberal*	*Liberal*	*Liberal*	*Liberal*	*Conservative*	*Conservative*	*Totals*
Conference Board of Canada	0	3	0	0	4	7	3	17
Fraser Institute	0	1	3	1	3	5	0	13
C.D. Howe Institute	2	1	0	0	4	5	1	13
Canadian Centre for Policy Alternatives	0	0	1	0	1	3	4	9
Caledon Institute of Social Policy	0	0	0	0	0	2	6	8
Institute for Research on Public Policy	0	0	0	1	0	4	1	6
Canada West Foundation	0	0	1	0	1	2	0	4
Canadian Council on Social Development	0	0	0	0	0	1	1	2
Canadian Policy Research Networks, Inc.	0	0	0	0	1	1	0	2
North-South Institute	0	1	0	0	2	0	0	1
Parliamentary Centre	0	0	0	0	0	1	0	1
Canadian Council for International Peace and Security	1	0	0	0	0	0	0	1
Mackenzie Institute	0	0	0	0	1	0	0	1
National Council of Welfare	0	0	0	0	0	0	0	0
Canadian Institute of Strategic Studies	0	0	0	0	0	0	0	0
Canadian Institute of International Affairs	0	0	0	0	0	0	0	0
Canadian Tax Foundation	0	0	0	0	0	0	0	0
Public Policy Forum	0	0	0	0	0	0	0	0
Pearson-Shoyama Institute	0	0	0	0	0	0	0	0
Total	3	6	5	2	17	31	16	80

Source: Library of Parliament, http://www.parl.gc.ca/common/Library.asp.

Figure A6.2
Appearances by Selected Canadian Think Tanks before Senate Committees, 1999–2008

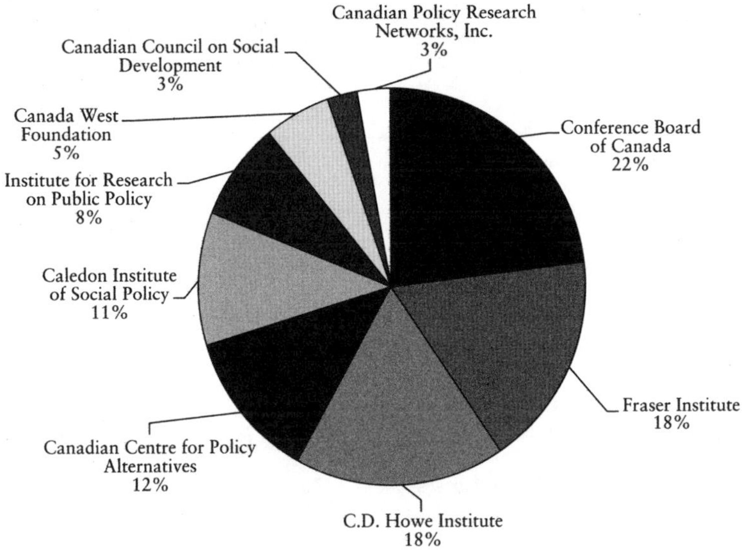

Figure A6.2.1
Appearances by Selected Canadian Think Tanks before Senate Committees, 2009–2016

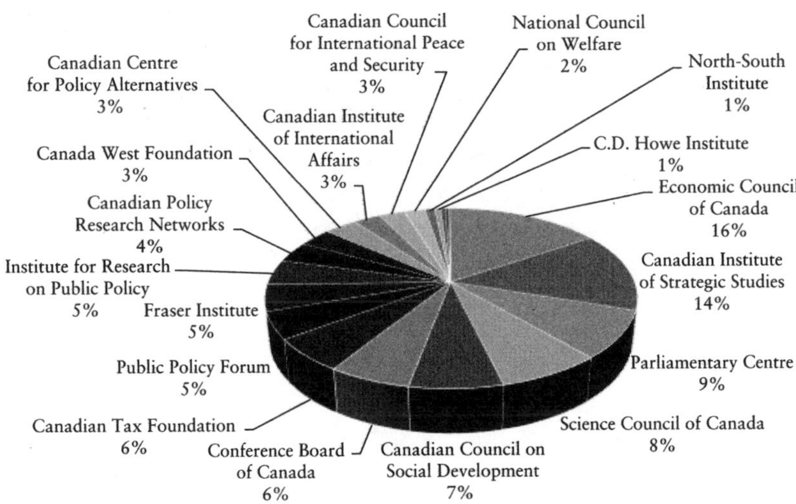

Table A6.2.1
Appearances by Selected Canadian Think Tanks before Senate Committees, 2009–2016

	40th Parliament 2nd Session 01/09–12/09	*40th Parliament 3rd Session 03/10–03/11*
Institute	*Conservative*	*Conservative*
Economic Council of Canada	N/A	65
Canadian Institute of Strategic Studies	N/A	83
Parliamentary Centre	N/A	27
Science Council of Canada	N/A	29
Canadian Council on Social Development	N/A	33
Conference Board of Canada	N/A	29
Canadian Tax Foundation	N/A	20
Public Policy Forum	N/A	24
Fraser Institute	N/A	20
Institute for Research on Public Policy	N/A	25
Canadian Policy Research Networks	N/A	14
Canada West Foundation	N/A	13
Canadian Centre for Policy Alternatives	N/A	9
Canadian Institute of International Affairs	N/A	11
Canadian Council for International Peace and Security	N/A	9
National Council on Welfare	N/A	5
North-South Institute	N/A	5
C.D. Howe Institute	N/A	1
Canadian Institute for International Peace and Security	N/A	1
Caledon Institute of Social Policy	N/A	0
Mackenzie Institute	N/A	2
Pearson-Shoyama Institute	N/A	0
Totals	0	425

Source: Library of Parliament.
NOTE: No data for 36th Parliament session avaialble on Parliamentary database.
NOTE: Senate of Canada website database no longer offers data prior to 40th Parliament, 3rd session – existing data above is a reflection of previous research on select institutes https://sencanada.ca/en/In-The-Chamber/Debates/Search.

41st Parliament 1st Session 06/11–09/13	41st Parliament 2nd Session 10/13–08/15	42nd Parliament 1st Session 12/15–	
Conservative	*Conservative*	*Liberal*	*Totals*
129	100	45	339
131	90	3	307
66	60	30	183
66	49	19	163
55	32	25	145
53	24	24	130
61	26	20	127
37	30	14	105
35	33	14	102
38	20	15	98
37	21	9	81
34	17	8	72
36	16	11	72
30	14	5	60
31	9	9	58
19	11	11	46
8	6	3	22
5	4	3	13
9	0	0	10
1	3	3	7
2	0	0	4
0	0	0	0
883	565	271	2,144

Table A6.3
Appearances by Selected Canadian Think Tanks before the House of Commons, 1999–2008

	36th Parliament 2nd Session 04/99–10/00	*37th Parliament 1st Session 01/01–09/02*
	Government majority	
Institute	*Liberal*	*Liberal*
Conference Board of Canada	18	22
C.D. Howe Institute	12	18
Fraser Institute	6	18
Canadian Council on Social Development	7	11
Canadian Centre for Policy Alternatives	7	4
North-South Institute	5	13
National Council of Welfare	5	6
Public Policy Forum	4	15
Caledon Institute of Social Policy	10	5
Parliamentary Centre	3	7
Canada West Foundation	5	7
Canadian Policy Research Networks, Inc.	6	0
Institute for Research on Public Policy	0	3
Canadian Institute of Strategic Studies	0	6
Canadian Institute of International Affairs	0	5
Mackenzie Institute	1	1
Canadian Tax Foundation	0	0
Canadian Council for International Peace and Security	0	0
Pearson-Shoyama Institute	0	0
Total	89	141

Source: Library of Parliament, http://www.parl.gc.ca/common/Library.asp.

37th Parliament 2nd Session 09/02–11/03	37th Parliament 3rd Session 02/04–05/04	38th Parliament 1st Session 10/04–11/05	39th Parliament 1st Session 04/06–09/07	39th Parliament 2nd Session 10/07–09/08	
Liberal	*Liberal*	*Liberal*	*Conservative*	*Conservative*	*Totals*
25	0	30	21	10	126
15	0	18	15	7	85
7	5	12	8	4	60
11	0	13	2	1	45
3	0	10	7	6	37
4	3	5	2	0	32
7	0	5	7	1	31
5	0	4	0	0	28
2	0	5	3	2	27
2	0	3	10	0	25
2	0	7	0	1	22
7	0	2	5	0	20
2	0	4	2	0	11
3	0	2	0	0	11
2	0	1	0	0	8
0	0	1	0	0	3
0	0	2	0	0	2
0	0	0	0	0	0
0	0	0	0	0	0
97	8	124	82	32	573

Figure A6.3
Appearances by Selected Canadian Think Tanks before the House of Commons, 1999–2008

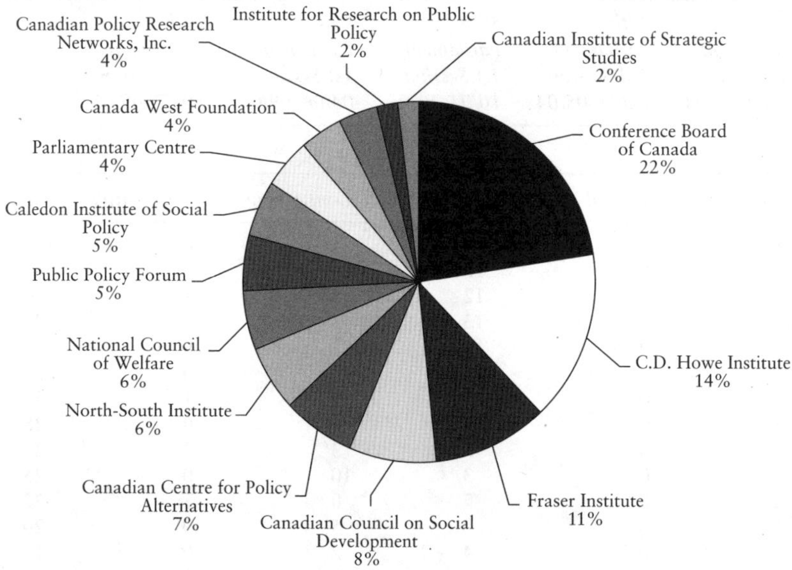

Figure A6.3.1
Appearances by Selected Canadian Think Tanks before the House of Commons, 2009–2016

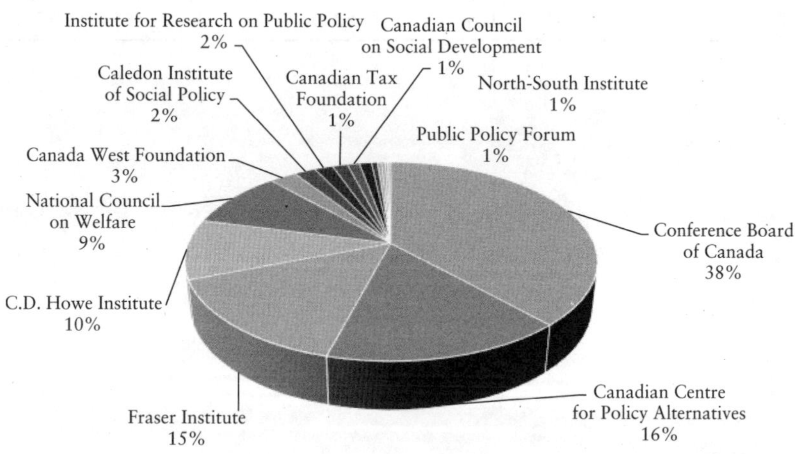

Table A6.3.1
Appearances by Selected Canadian Think Tanks before the House of Commons, 2009–2016

Institute	*40th Parliament 2nd Session 01/09–12/09*	*40th Parliament 3rd Session 03/10–03/11*	*41st Parliament 1st Session 06/11–09/13*	*41st Parliament 2nd Session 10/13–08/15*	*42nd Parliament 1st Session 12/15–*	
	Conservative	*Conservative*	*Conservative*	*Conservative*	*Liberal*	*Totals*
Conference Board of Canada	10	21	121	88	29	269
Canadian Centre for Policy Alternatives	0	26	19	44	24	113
Fraser Institute	4	17	28	23	33	105
C.D. Howe Institute	0	31	15	20	3	69
National Council on Welfare	2	1	59	4	0	66
Canada West Foundation	3	4	7	3	1	18
Caledon Institute of Social Policy	4	6	4	0	0	14
Institute for Research on Public Policy	2	1	6	0	3	12
Canadian Tax Foundation	0	0	10	0	0	10
Canadian Council on Social Development	1	3	2	2	0	8
North-South Institute	1	0	0	6	1	8
Public Policy Forum	0	1	0	1	2	4
Parliamentary Centre	0	1	0	1	1	3
Canadian Council for International Peace and Security	0	1	0	1	0	2
Canadian Institute for International Peace and Security	0	0	0	0	0	2
Economic Council of Canada	0	1	0	0	1	2
Canadian Institute of International Affairs	0	0	0	0	0	0
Canadian Institute of Strategic Studies	0	0	0	0	0	0
Canadian Policy Research Networks	0	0	0	0	0	0
Mackenzie Institute	0	0	0	0	0	0
Pearson-Shoyama Institute	0	0	0	0	0	0
Science Council of Canada	0	0	0	0	0	0
Totals	27	114	271	193	98	705

Source: Library of Parliament.
NOTE: No data for 36th Parliament session avaialble on Parliamentary database.

Table A6.4
References to Selected Think Tanks during Debates in the House of Commons, 1994–2008

	35th Parliament 1st Session 01/94–02/96	*35th Parliament 2nd Session 02/96–04/97*	*36th Parliament 1st Session 09/97–09/99*	*36th Parliament 2nd Session 04/99–10/00*
	Government majority			
Institute	*Liberal*	*Liberal*	*Liberal*	*Liberal*
Conference Board of Canada	35	6	52	32
Fraser Institute	55	60	40	14
C.D. Howe Institute	25	12	33	7
National Council of Welfare	13	12	20	15
Canadian Centre for Policy Alternatives	4	0	5	0
Canadian Council on Social Development	8	4	13	2
Public Policy Forum	7	4	6	4
Canada West Foundation	10	4	4	0
Canadian Tax Foundation	3	3	6	0
Caledon Institute of Social Policy	4	2	7	0
Mackenzie Institute	9	4	0	0
Institute for Research on Public Policy	1	2	0	2
Canadian Institute of Strategic Studies	1	0	0	0
North-South Institute	2	0	0	0
Canadian Policy Research Networks, Inc.	0	0	0	0
Parliamentary Centre	1	0	0	0
Canadian Council for International Peace and Security	0	0	0	0
Canadian Institute of International Affairs	0	0	0	0
Pearson-Shoyama Institute	0	0	0	0
Total	178	113	186	76

Source: Library of Parliament, http://www.parl.gc.ca/common/Library.asp.

37th Parliament 1st Session 01/01–09/02	*37th Parliament 2nd Session 09/02–11/03*	*37th Parliament 3rd Session 02/04–05/04*	*38th Parliament 1st Session 10/04–11/05*	*39th Parliament 1st Session 04/06–09/07*	*39th Parliament 2nd Session 10/07–09/08*	
Liberal	*Liberal*	*Liberal*	*Liberal*	*Conservative*	*Conservative*	*Totals*
34	14	6	40	26	21	266
18	19	4	21	15	13	259
8	6	4	11	14	16	136
6	6	2	5	4	9	92
4	6	1	15	19	11	65
4	9	4	6	3	2	55
5	2	1	5	3	0	37
4	1	2	0	2	2	29
1	0	0	1	8	1	23
2	0	0	0	4	3	22
7	0	0	0	0	0	20
2	2	1	0	4	0	14
4	0	0	0	2	0	7
3	0	0	0	0	0	5
1	1	0	2	1	0	5
0	1	0	1	0	0	3
0	0	0	0	0	0	0
0	0	0	0	0	0	0
0	0	0	0	0	0	0
103	67	25	107	105	78	1,038

Figure A6.4
References to Selected Think Tanks during Debates in the House of Commons, 1994–2008

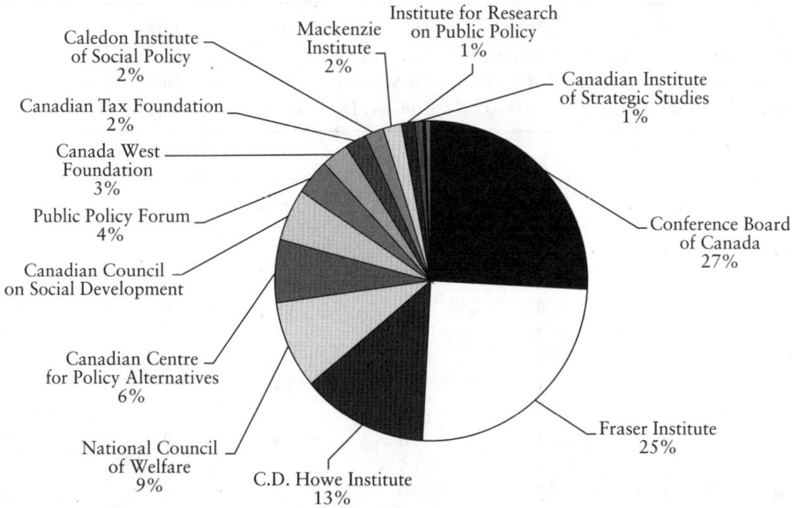

Figure A6.4.1
References to Selected Think Tanks during Debates in the House of Commons, 2009-2016

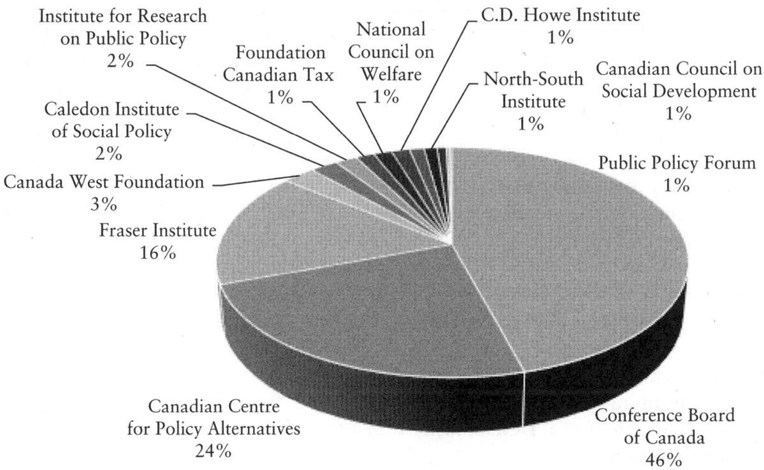

Table A6.4.1
References to Selected Think Tanks during Debates in the House of Commons, 2009–2016

	40th Parliament 1st Session 11/08–12/08	*40th Parliament 2nd Session 01/09–12/09*
Institute	*Conservative*	*Conservative*
Conference Board of Canada	10	21
Canadian Centre for Policy Alternatives	0	26
Fraser Institute	0	4
Canada West Foundation	0	3
Caledon Institute of Social Policy	1	5
Institute for Research on Public Policy	0	2
Canadian Tax Foundation	0	0
National Council on Welfare	0	0
C.D. Howe Institute	0	0
Canadian Council on Social Development	0	1
North-South Institute	0	1
Public Policy Forum	0	0
Parliamentary Centre	0	0
Mackenzie Institute	0	0
Canadian Policy Research Networks	0	0
Canadian Institute of International Affairs	0	0
Canadian Council for International Peace and Security	0	0
Canadian Institute of Strategic Studies	0	0
Pearson-Shoyama Institute	0	0
Totals	11	63

40th Parliament 3rd Session 03/10–03/11	*41st Parliament 1st Session 06/11–09/13*	*41st Parliament 2nd Session 10/13–08/15*	*42nd Parliament 1st Session 12/15–*	
Conservative	*Conservative*	*Conservative*	*Liberal*	*Totals*
40	120	88	36	315
19	43	45	30	163
17	28	24	39	112
4	7	3	1	18
4	4	1	0	15
1	6	0	3	12
0	10	0	0	10
0	10	0	0	10
0	1	6	3	10
3	2	2	0	8
0	0	6	0	7
1	0	1	3	5
1	0	1	0	2
0	0	1	0	1
0	0	0	0	0
0	0	0	0	0
0	0	0	0	0
0	0	0	0	0
0	0	0	0	0
90	231	178	115	688

Table A6.5
References to Selected Think Tanks during Debates in the Senate, 1994–2008

	35th Parliament 1st Session 01/94–02/96	*35th Parliament 2nd Session 02/96–04/97*	*36th Parliament 1st Session 09/97–09/99*	*36th Parliament 2nd Session 04/99–10/00*
	Government Majority			
Institute	*Liberal*	*Liberal*	*Liberal*	*Liberal*
Conference Board of Canada	0	4	18	10
C.D. Howe Institute	0	5	4	5
Fraser Institute	0	0	3	1
Canada West Foundation	0	0	0	6
Institute for Research on Public Policy	0	0	0	3
National Council of Welfare	0	2	11	2
Caledon Institute of Social Policy	0	2	2	0
Canadian Tax Foundation	0	0	4	0
Canadian Council on Social Development	0	2	1	0
Parliamentary Centre	0	0	1	1
Canadian Policy Research Networks, Inc.	0	2	0	1
Public Policy Forum	0	0	1	1
Canadian Centre for Policy Alternatives	0	1	0	1
Canadian Institute of International Affairs	0	0	0	1
Canadian Institute of Strategic Studies	0	1	0	1
North-South Institute	0	0	0	0
Mackenzie Institute	0	0	0	0
Canadian Council for International Peace and Security	0	0	0	0
Pearson-Shoyama Institute	0	0	0	0
Total	0	14	45	33

Source: Library of Parliament, http://www.parl.gc.ca/common/Library.asp.

37th Parliament 1st Session 01/01–09/02	37th Parliament 2nd Session 09/02–11/03	37th Parliament 3rd Session 02/04–05/04	38th Parliament 1st Session 10/04–11/05	39th Parliament 1st Session 04/06–09/07	39th Parliament 2nd Session 10/07–09/08	
Liberal	*Liberal*	*Liberal*	*Liberal*	*Conservative*	*Conservative*	Totals
8	16	8	24	18	9	115
4	2	0	8	12	8	48
1	0	0	6	16	6	33
0	2	2	0	12	2	24
2	1	1	4	8	0	19
1	0	0	1	0	0	17
1	0	0	0	10	0	15
1	0	0	2	2	1	10
2	0	0	1	2	1	9
2	1	0	2	1	0	8
0	1	0	0	4	0	8
3	1	0	1	0	0	7
0	0	0	0	2	2	6
0	3	1	0	0	0	5
2	0	0	0	0	0	4
0	1	0	1	0	0	2
0	2	0	0	0	0	2
0	0	0	0	0	0	0
0	0	0	0	0	0	0
27	30	12	50	87	29	332

Figure A6.5
References to Selected Think Tanks during Debates in the Senate, 1994–2008

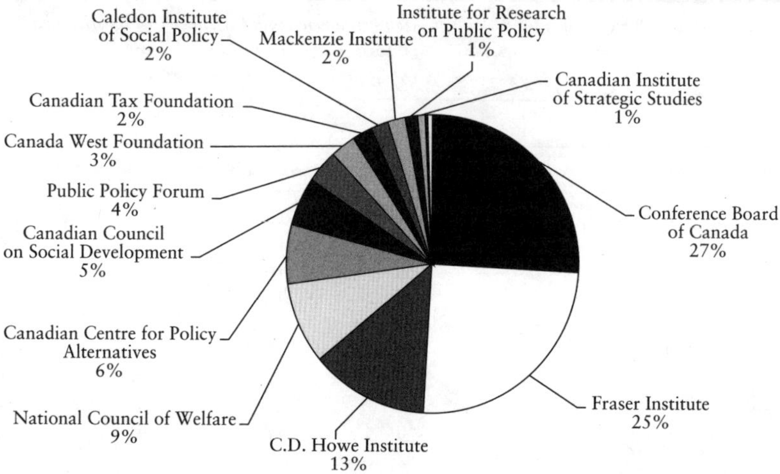

Table A6.5.1
References to Selected Think Tanks during Debates in the Senate, 2009–2016

	40th Parliament 1st Session 11/08–12/08	*40th Parliament 2nd Session 01/09–12/09*	*40th Parliament 3rd Session 03/10–03/11*	*41st Parliament 1st Session 06/11–09/13*	*41st Parliament 2nd Session 10/13–08/15*	*42nd Parliament 1st Session 12/15–*	
Institute	*Conservative*	*Conservative*	*Conservative*	*Conservative*	*Conservative*	*Liberal*	*Totals*
Conference Board of Canada	N/A	N/A	8	11	10	14	43
Fraser Institute	N/A	N/A	6	9	5	8	28
Canadian Centre for Policy Alternatives	N/A	N/A	3	9	6	4	22
C.D. Howe Institute	N/A	N/A	1	5	5	7	18
National Council on Welfare	N/A	N/A	0	12	1	1	14
Institute for Research on Public Policy	N/A	N/A	5	2	0	3	10
Canada West Foundation	N/A	N/A	3	1	2	0	6
Public Policy Forum	N/A	N/A	1	0	0	3	4
Canadian Council on Social Development	N/A	N/A	2	0	0	0	2
Caledon Institute of Social Policy	N/A	N/A	0	1	0	1	2
Parliamentary Centre	N/A	N/A	0	0	1	0	1
Canadian Tax Foundation	N/A	N/A	0	1	0	0	1
Canadian Policy Research Networks	N/A	N/A	1	0	0	0	1
Canadian Institute of International Affairs	N/A	N/A	0	0	1	0	1
Mackenzie Institute	N/A	N/A	1	0	0	0	1
Canadian Council for International Peace and Security	N/A	N/A	0	0	0	0	0
North-South Institute	N/A	N/A	0	0	0	0	0
Canadian Institute of Strategic Studies	N/A	N/A	0	0	0	0	0
Pearson-Shoyama Institute	N/A	N/A	0	0	0	0	0
Totals	N/A	N/A	31	51	31	41	154

NOTE: Senate debate information only available since the beginning of the 40th Parliament, 3rd Session (2010-03-03), nothing available prior.

Figure A6.5.1
References to Selected Think Tanks during Debates in the Senate, 2009–2016

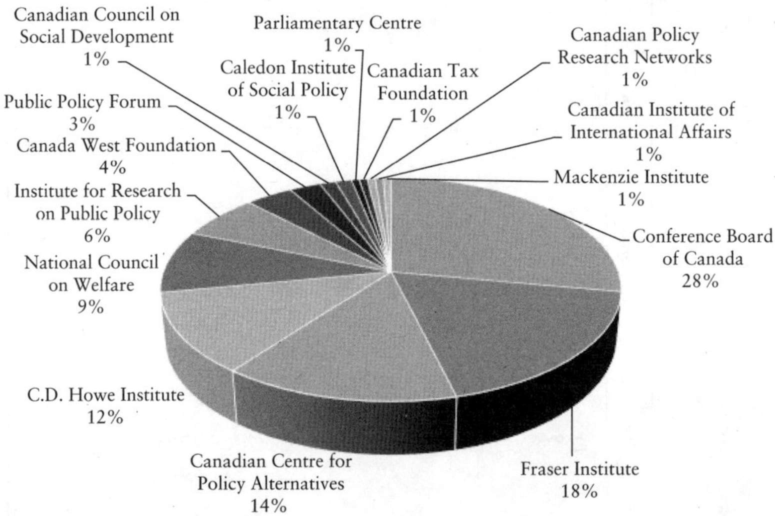

Table A6.6
Comparison of Annual Budget to Number of Appearances before Parliamentary Committees for Selected Canadian Think Tanks, 1994–2008

	Annual budget (millions of dollars)	*Number of appearances before parliamenatry committees*
Conference Board of Canada	30	143
C.D. Howe Institute	5	98
The Fraser Institute	15	73
Canadian Council on Social Development	2	47
Canadian Centre for Policy Alternatives	2	46
Caledon Institute of Social Policy	2	35
The North-South Institute	5	33
National Council of Welfare	0	31
Public Policy Forum	2	28
Parliamentary Centre	9	26
Canada West Foundation	5	26
Canadian Policy Research Networks, Inc.	5	22
Institute for Research on Public Policy	5	17
Canadian Institute of Strategic Studies	0	11
Canadian Institute of International Affairs	2	8
Mackenzie Institute	0	4
Canadian Tax Foundation	5	2
Canadian Institute for Advanced Research	15	0
Pembina Institute	5	0
Canadian Centre for Philanthropy	5	0
Canadian Centre for Foreign Policy Development	5	0
Montreal Economic Institute	2	0
Atlantic Provinces Economic Council	2	0
Institute on Governance	2	0
Atlantic Institute for Market Studies	2	0
Parkland Institute	0	0
Canadian Urban Institute	0	0
Frontier Centre for Public Policy	0	0
Couchiching Institute on Public Affairs	0	0
Saskatchewan Institute of Public Policy	0	0
Vanier Institute of the Family	0	0
Pearson-Shoyama Institute	0	0
Quebec Institute of Advanced International Studies	0	0

Figure A6.6
Comparison of Annual Budget to Number of Appearances before Parliamentary Committees for Selected Canadian Think Tanks, 1994–2008

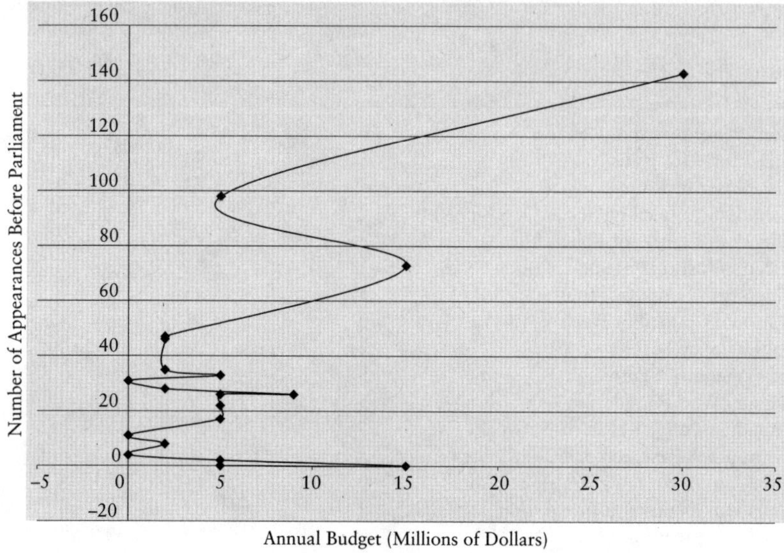

Table A 6.6.1
Comparison of Annual Budget to Number of Appearances before Parliamentary Committees for Selected Canadian Think Tanks, 2009–2016

Institute	*Annual budgets (millions of dollars)*	*Number of appearances before parliamentary committees*
Conference Board of Canada	41	399
Canadian Institute of Strategic Studies	0	307
Fraser Institute	11	207
Parliamentary Centre	7	186
Canadian Council on Social Development	0	153
Canadian Tax Foundation	5	137
National Council on Welfare	0	112
Institute for Research on Public Policy	0	110
Public Policy Forum	1	109
Canada West Foundation	2	90
Vanier Institute of the Family	0	88
C.D. Howe Institute	6	82
Canadian Policy Research Networks	5	72
Institute on Governance	2	61
Canadian Institute of International Affairs	5	60
Atlantic Provinces Economic Council	2	35
The North-South Institute	5	30
Atlantic Institute for Market Studies	1	23
Caledon Institute of Social Policy	2	21
Montreal Economic Institute	3	16
Pembina Institute	5	11
Canadian Institute for Advanced Research	9	8
Mackenzie Institute	1	4
Frontier Centre for Public Policy	1	1
Parkland Institute	0	1
Couchiching Institute on Public Affairs	0	1
Canadian Urban Institute	2	0
Canadian Centre for Philanthropy	5	0
Canadian Centre for Foreign Policy Development	5	0
Saskatchewan Institute of Public Policy	0	0
Pearson-Shoyama Institute	0	0
Quebec Institute of Advanced International Studies	0	0

NOTE: 'Appearances' amalgamated from tables 5.14.1 and 5.13.1.

Figure A6.6.1
Comparison of Annual Budget to Number of Appearances before Parliamentary Committees for Selected Canadian Think Tanks, 2009–2016

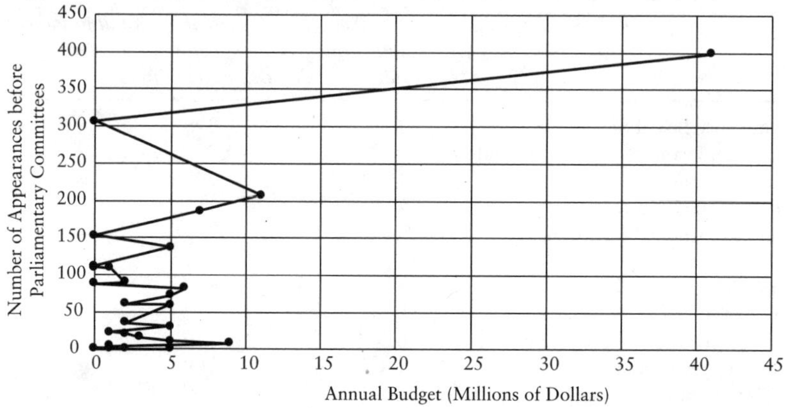

APPENDIX SEVEN

Documents Related to Keystone XL Pipeline

Table A7.1
Public Exposure of Selected American Think Tanks in Relation to Keystone XL

Think tank	*Congressional hearings*	*Newspaper articles*	*Other*
Cato Institute	Keystone XL Pipeline: Examining Scientific and Environmental Issues Paul Knappenberger 7 May 2013 US Crude Oil Export Policy: Hearing before the committee on Energy and Natural Resources, United States Senate Daniel J. Ikenson	*Washington Post* "Study: Climate Risks Growing" 7 May 2014 "Big Oil's Heirs Join Call for Action as Climate Summit Opens" 22 September 2014 *USA Today* "Clinton, Trump Show Stark Contrast on Climate Change; Dem's Warning of Major Crisis Derided by GOP Candidate as Radical" 3 August 2016 (Post-veto) *National Post* "Don't Give in on EPA Regulations" 12 February 2015 "Girling's Heroic Battle with Obama" 12 February 2015 *The Salt Lake Tribune* "Keystone Pipeline Trapped in Endless Study" 4 February 2014 *Orange County Register* "A Slow Death for the Keystone XL" 2 March 2014	"Ayesha Rascoe, TransCanada Legal Challenges over Keystone Face Long Odds," Reuters, 7 January 2016 Paul C. Knappenberger, "Keystone XL Pipeline: Enough Already!," *Cato at Liberty*, 18 November 2014 Denise Robbins, "Myths and Facts about the Koch Brothers," *Media Matters*, 27 August 2014 Michael Winship, "The President's Pain at the Pump," *Moyers & Company*, 13 March 2012 Paul C. Knappenberger, "A Slow Death for the Keystone XL Oil Pipeline?," Cato Institute, 2 March 2014 "America's Forum | Richard Rahn and Ford O'Connell," YouTube, 4 February 2015

Bipartisan Policy Center	US Energy Abundance: Exports and the Changing Global Energy Landscape: Hearing before the Subcommittee on Energy and Power of the Committee on Energy and Commerce Byron Dorgan Crude Oil Export Ban: Helpful of Hurtful: Hearing before the Subcommittee on Terrorism, Non-proliferation, and Trade of the Committee on Foreign Affairs Jason Grumet	*The New York Times* "Amid Pipeline and Climate Debate, Energy-Efficiency Bill Is Derailed" 13 May 2014 "Oil Pipeline Veto Expected to Be First in a Wave" 23 February 2015 "How We Learned Not to Guzzle" 13 September 2013 "Fuel to Burn: Now What?" 11 April 2012 *The Washington Post* "Obama, Democrats Will Tout the President's Record on Energy" 5 September 2012 "On Gas Prices, Voters Blame Obama; Experts Disagree" 13 March 2012 *The Christian Science Monitor* "On White House, Congressional Lunch Menu Friday: Compromise; The President and Republican Leaders, Who Will Have Complete Control over Congress Come January, All Say They Want to Work Together on Areas Where They Think They Can Find Agreement" 7 November 2014	"Jason Grumet: Keystone Debate Is a Sign of Progress," CNN, 10 February 2015 "Jason Grumet: A Mixed Legacy on Oil," *US News & World Report*, 4 September 2015 "How the New Congress Can Speed US Energy Independence," *Marketwatch*, 14 November 2014 "Politics, Legacy Loom over Obama Decision on Keystone XL Pipeline," Reuters, 27 January 2014 "Polls Show Energy Doesn't Spark Americans' Interest," *Politico*, 28 October 2013

Table A7.1
Public Exposure of Selected American Think Tanks in Relation to Keystone XL (*continued*)

Think tank	*Congressional hearings*	*Newspaper articles*	*Other*
Center for American Progress	Quadrennial Energy Review and Related Discussion Drafts: Hearing before the Subcommittee on Energy and Power of the Committee on Energy and Commerce Alison Cassady	*Washington Post* "Petty Politics" 14 January 2015	Kate Gordon and Daniel J. Weiss, "Keystone XL Isn't the Key," Center for American Progress, 16 December 2011
		"Keystone Copout" 20 November 2014	
		"In Senate, a New Angle on Energy" 13 February 2014	
		"On Climate, Obama Makes a Moral Case" 23 January 2013	
		"Amassing Capital for a New Climate" 18 February 2013	
		"Cory Booker as Senator: More 'Sedentary,' Less 'Agitation'" 20 November 2014	
		"Podesta Exits White House but Leaves Playbook Behind" 24 February 2015	
		"A Challenge to Obama and Romney: Deliver One Truthful Campaign Speech" 6 May 2012	

“Obama’s Strategy Confounds Allies, Foes”
4 September 2011

“Obama’s Lobbyist Edict Only Slowed the ‘Revolving Door’”
23 March 2015

“Podesta, Schiliro to Return to White House”
11 December 2013

“Is This Man Obama’s Legacy-Builder?”
5 March 2014

“In 2nd Term, Obama Adopts Bolder Tone on the Environment”
11 August 2013

“New Obama Adviser Brings Corporate Ties”
13 December 2013

“Stung by the President on Air Quality, Environmentalists Weigh Their Options”
4 September 2011

“Obama Abandons a Stricter Limit an Air Pollution”
3 September 2011

USA Today
“US Foresees Greater Energy Independence”
24 January 2012

“Keep Every Drop of Oil at Home”
5 February 2014

Table A7.1
Public Exposure of Selected American Think Tanks in Relation to Keystone XL *(continued)*

Think tank	*Congressional hearings*	*Newspaper articles*	*Other*
	US Energy Security: Enhancing Partnerships with Mexico and Canada Michael A. Levi 14 March 2013	*USA Today* "Delaying Keystone Pipeline the Right Step to Take"	
		The New York Times "Canada Prepares Plans B and C in Case Oil Sands Pipeline Hits a Roadblock" 7 June 2011	
Council on Foreign Relations	Geopolitical Potential of the US Energy Boom: Hearing before the Committee on Foreign Affairs, House of Representatives Michael A. Levi Ms Elizabeth Rosenberg, Energy, Environment and Security Programs 26 March 2014	"The Politics Of Keystone, Take 2" 11 February 2012 "Drawing the Line at Power Lines" 19 February 2012 "Obama Faces Risks in Pipeline Decision" 18 February 2013	
	The effects of Middle East events on US energy markets: hearing before the Subcommittee on Energy and Power of the Committee on Energy and Commerce	"Slow Start on Environment in Second Obama Term" 25 April 2013 "Keystone Pipeline May Be Big, but This Is Bigger" 22 April 2014 "With Veto Threat, Obama and Congress Head for Collision on Pipeline" 7 January 2015	

“A Shortsighted Victory in Delaying the Keystone Pipeline”
11 November 2011

“Mired in Canada’s Oil Sands”
19 May 2010

“In Nod to Gas Prices, Obama Talks about Energy”
24 February 2012

“Cabinet Picks Could Take On Climate Policy”
5 March 2013

“US Inches toward Goal of Energy Independence”
23 March 2012

“Obama Orders New Efficiency for Big Trucks”
19 February 2014

Washington Post
“What Keystone Won’t Do”
14 May 2012

“Keystone Report Firm Worked for Landowners”
8 February 2014

“‘Greater Diversification’”
13 November 2011

“In Coal Country, Awaiting a Future”
4 June 2012

Table A7.1
Public Exposure of Selected American Think Tanks in Relation to Keystone XL (*continued*)

Think tank	*Congressional hearings*	*Newspaper articles*	*Other*
		The Gazette (Montreal) "Harper Off to New York; Will Lobby on Behalf of Keystone Pipeline" (Video and transcript of video)	
Center for New American Security	Crude Oil Export Ban: Helpful of Hurtful: Hearing before the Subcommittee on Terrorism, Non-proliferation, and Trade of the Committee on Foreign Affairs Elizabeth Rosen		

Figure A7.1
Newspaper Coverage of Selected Canadian Think Tanks in Relation to Keystone XL

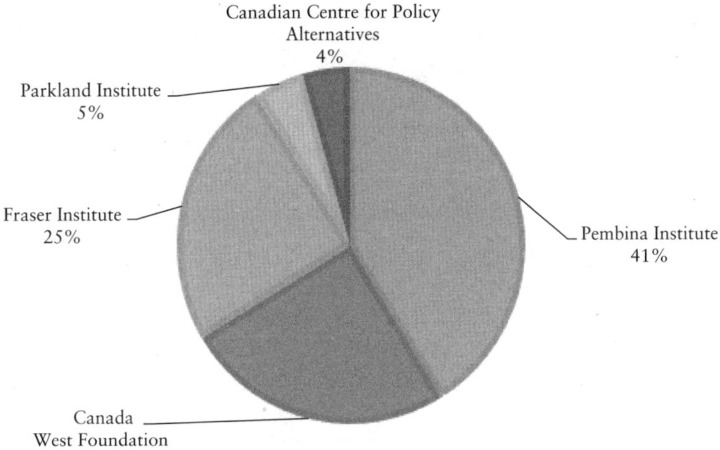

Figure A7.2
Newspaper Coverage of Selected Canadian Think Tanks in Relation to Keystone XL

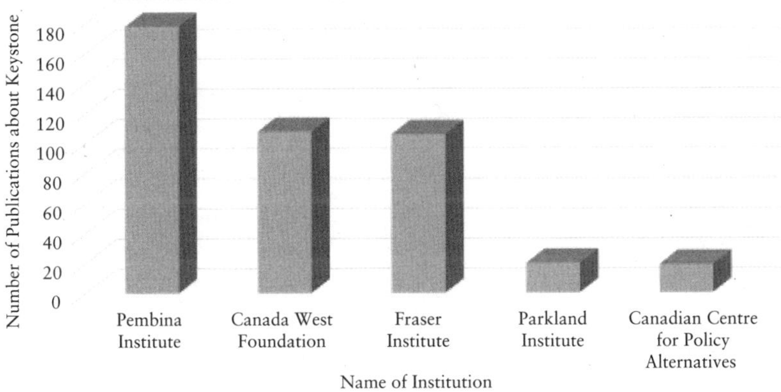

Table 7.2
Newspaper Coverage of Selected Canadian Think Tanks in Relation to Keystone XL

	Total	*National Post*	*Calgary Herald*	*Times & Transcript*	*The Spec*	*Toronto Sun*	*Canadian Press*	*The Record*	*ICIS*
Pembina Institute	178	50	8				1		
Canada West Foundation	108	20	23	4	3	1	10	2	1
Fraser Institute	106	19	9	3	1	2		2	
Parkland Institute	20	1	1						
Canadian Centre for Policy Alternatives	19	2					4		

	Natural Gas Intel	*Star Phoenix*	*Ottawa Citizen*	*Hamilton Spectator*	*Anadolu Agency*	*Prince George Citizen*	*Calgary Sun*	*The Gazette*
Pembina Institute		3	3			2		12
Canada West Foundation	1	3	3	1	1	1	1	1
Fraser Institute	1	1	4			1	3	1
Parkland Institute								3
Canadian Centre for Policy Alternatives								

	High River Times	*Fort Saskathcewan*	*World Oil*	*Winnipeg Sun*	*Ottawa Sun*	*Reuters News*	*LNG intelligence*
Pembina Institute							
Canada West Foundation							
Fraser Institute	1	2	1	1	2		
Parkland Institute							
Canadian Centre for Policy Alternatives						1	1

The Globe and Mail	*Toronto Star*	*Pincher Creek Echo*	*Telegraph-Journal*	*Leader Post*	*Vancourver Sun*	*Edmonton Journal*	*Upstream*	*Daily Gleaner*
36	29			3	7	5		
3	3	1	2	2	4	8	1	1
4	1		8	3	8	7		4
1	1		1			9		
4	1							

Windsor Star	*Postmedia new*	*Platts Oligram News*	*Inside Energy*	*Winnipeg Free Press*	*Time Colonist*	*The Guelph Mercury*	*Waterloo Region Board*	*Edmonton Sun*
1		7	1		1	1		
1	1	0	0		0	0		
1		1			2	1	2	2
				2	1			
	4			2				

Progressive Media	*Red Deer Express*	*Oil and Gas Journal*	*Engineering News-Record*	*Sherbrooke Record*	*Nanaimo Daily News*
					1
					0
1	1	3	1	1	

Notes

INTRODUCTION

1 See McGann, *2017 Global Go To Think Tank Index Report.*

2 For a detailed comparison of American and British think tanks see Stone, *Capturing the Political Imagination*, and Higgott and Stone, "The Limits of Influence." On some of the fundamental differences between Canadian and American think tanks, see Abelson and Carberry, "Following Suit?" For detailed analyses of think tanks in several different countries and regions see Abelson, Brooks and Hua, *Think Tanks, Foreign Policy and Geo-Politics*; Stone, Denham, and Garnett, *Think Tanks across Nations*; McGann and Weaver, *Think Tanks and Civil Societies*; and Langford and Brownsey, *Think Tanks.* On British and German think tanks, see Pautz, *Think Tanks, Social Democracy.*

3 Abelson and Carberry, "Following Suit?," 525–6.

4 For instance, Ernst suggests that the C.D. Howe Institute played a critical role in reinforcing and advancing the Conservative government's free trade agenda during the 1980s. See his article "Liberal Continentalism." Moreover, Brodie and Jenson have noted that several Canadian think tanks, including the Fraser Institute, C.D. Howe Institute, and the Economic Council of Canada, have contributed to the new "neoliberal" orthodoxy. See *Crisis, Challenge and Change*, 312.

5 Several scholars studying think tanks in the United States have attempted to show how think tanks shape policy issues and legislation as diverse as the Strategic Defence Initiative (SDI, or Star Wars Project) and the creation of a national budget system. For a discussion of the contribution of the Heritage Foundation to the debate over SDI, see Edwards, *The Power of Ideas.* A broader discussion about conservative think tanks and their contribution to policy debates can be found in Stahl, *Right Moves.* On the impact of the Brookings Institution in helping to create a national budget

system see Critchlow, *The Brookings Institution*, and Smith, *Brookings at Seventy-Five*. By contrast, the handful of scholars studying Canadian think tanks have provided a less than enthusiastic endorsement of the impact of policy institutes on key policy debates. See, for instance, Lindquist, *Behind the Myth*, and Tupper, "Think-Tanks."

6 Some commentators have suggested that the sheer number of think tanks, interest groups, and other organizations committed to influencing public policy in the United States may constitute a constraint. See, for example, Denham and Garnett, *British Think-Tanks*, 19. However, since not all think tanks have comparable resources, it is questionable how much constraint the think tank population imposes on these organizations. If, for instance, there were dozens of think tanks on the scale of the Brookings Institution, then perhaps this argument would be more persuasive. Yet, as this study demonstrates, the Brookings Institution and the handful of other think tanks in the United States that possess comparable resources face little competition from the majority of much smaller policy institutes.

7 In his assessment of the impact of societal groups on Canadian foreign policy, Nossal draws a distinction between influencing policy-making and the policy-making environment. See *Canadian Foreign Policy*, 117. This distinction is important when one is evaluating the impact of think tanks. As Pal notes, while think tanks in Canada "have enlarged the terms of political discourse," it is important not to exaggerate their impact on policy-making. See his *Public Policy Analysis*, 92–4.

8 See, for instance, Kitschelt, "Political Opportunity Structures," 57–85, and Kriesi et al., "New Social Movements."

9 Stone, *Capturing the Political Imagination*, 38–52.

10 For examples of how scholars have attempted to assess the impact of ideas on policy-making see Yee, "Causal Effects of Ideas"; Campbell, "Institutional Analysis"; and Goldstein and Keohane, *Ideas and Foreign Policy.*

11 The media coverage a select group of American think tanks has generated and the various factors that account for their visibility are examined by Rich and Weaver, "Think Tanks." Useful data on how often American think tanks testify before Congressional committees are provided by Rich, "Think Tanks." For a discussion of the relationship between the public visibility of a cross-section of Canadian think tanks and their relevance in policy-making, see Abelson, "Public Visibility."

12 Jérôme-Forget, "Institute for Research on Public Policy," 99.

13 Several books and articles have documented the 2016 US presidential election. See, for example, Dowd, *The Year of Voting Dangerously*, and Stone, *The Making of the President 2016*.

14 For a discussion of the events surrounding the resignation of Jim DeMint, see Dumain and Byrd, "Jim DeMint Out as President of Heritage Foundation"; Cook et al., "DeMint Set to Be Ousted"; Bolton, "DeMint

Expected to Step Down"; Peters and Haberman, "Jim DeMint Is Said to Be Out"; Hart, "The Political Assassination of the Heritage Foundation's Jim DeMint"; and Balan, "Trump Thanks Jim DeMint." An email was also sent by Thomas Saunders, chair of the Board of Trustees at Heritage on 2 May 2017 explaining the events leading up to DeMint's resignation. Kay Coles James, a senior advisor on Trump's transition team, became president of the Heritage Foundation on 1 January 2018.

15 For a discussion of the controversy surrounding Balsillie's involvement in CIGI, see Brean, "York University Teaches Jim Balsillie Hard Lesson."

16 Interview with author, 16 December 1998.

17 Smith, *The Idea Brokers*; Stone, Denham, and Garnett, *Think Tanks across Nations.* Also see Medvetz, *Think Tanks in America*; Abelson, Brooks and Hua, *Think Tanks, Foreign Policy and Geo-Politics*; and Drezner, *The Ideas Industry.*

18 For more on the controversy surrounding the NPI, see Link, "Richard Spencer's Nonprofit, Pro-hate NPI Lost Its Tax-Exempt Status," 14 March 2017.

19 McGann, *Competition for Dollars*, 9. For a detailed discussion of the defining characteristics of think tanks, see Abelson, *Northern Lights*, chap. 1.

20 For more on the role of public think tanks such as the Congressional Research Service see Robinson, "Public Think-Tanks."

21 For more on the restrictions placed on the political activities of charitable organizations in Canada see Revenue Canada, *Information Circular 87–1: Registered Charities – Ancillary and Incidental Political Activities.* A detailed examination of the many challenges facing non-profit/charitable organizations in Canada can be found in Mulé and DeSantis (eds), *The Shifting Terrain.* For information on restrictions on registered charities in the United States see *Internal Revenue Code of 1986*, 1077–96. Also see Abelson, *Northern Lights*, ch. 1. President Trump has vowed to destroy the Johnson Amendment, proposed by then Senator Lyndon B. Johnson in 1954, which places limits on the kinds of partisan activities in which religious institutions and other 501 c. 3 charitable organizations are able to take part. See Green, "Trump Wants to Make Churches the New Super PACs"; Benko, "Trump's Promise"; and Peters, "The Johnson Amendment." Some think tanks in Canada and the US are becoming more transparent about the sources of their funding. An organization called Transparify assigns ratings to think tanks based on how transparent they are regarding their funding. For more on this see Abelson, *Northern Lights.* Although think tanks registered as 501 c. 3 organizations are not required by law to disclose who makes donations and gifts to them, the US Congress requires scholars from think tanks who testify before various congressional committees to reveal who has funded the research project on which the information they are providing is based.

22 For more on Jane Addams and Hull House, see Ross, *The Origins of Social Science.*

23 Sundquist, "Research Brokerage."

24 Peschek, *Policy Planning Organizations*, 7.

25 See, for instance, McGann and Weaver, *Think Tanks and Civil Societies*; Stone, *Political Imagination*; Stone, Denham, and Garnett, *Think Tanks across Nations*; Smith, *The Idea Brokers*; and Abelson, *American Think Tanks.*

26 A somewhat dated, though extensive, directory of American think tanks is Hellebust, *Think Tank Directory.* A more up to date listing is available in the 2016 *Global Go To Think Tank Index Report* and in the database housed by the Think Tanks and Civil Societies program at the University of Pennsylvania. For a listing of conservative, or classical liberal, think tanks, see Atwood and Mead, *Directory of Public Policy Organizations.* While no comprehensive directory of Canadian think tanks has been produced (the *Global Go To Think Tank Index Reports* can be referenced), there are some international directories that should be consulted. The National Institute for Research Advancement's (NIRA) *World Directory of Think Tanks* is the most extensive. On think tanks specializing in defence and security issues see Van Der Woerd, *World Survey of Strategic Studies Centres.* For an assessment of the various global rankings of think tanks that have been undertaken in recent years, see Abelson, *Northern Lights*, chapter 7.

27 Peschek, *Policy Planning Organizations.* Also see Domhoff and Dye, *Power Elites*; and Saloma, *Ominous Politics.* Several other studies have examined think tanks from an elite theory perspective. Among them are Silk and Silk, *The American Establishment*; Shoup and Minter, *Imperial Brain Trust*; Shoup, *Wall Street's Think Tank*; and Sanders, *Peddlers of Crisis.*

28 Heclo, "Issue Networks," and Lindquist, "Think-Tanks?"

29 See Kitschelt, "Political Opportunity Structures"; Kriesi et al., "New Social Movements."

30 For a discussion on the limitations of relying on single case studies, see Baumgartner and Leech, *Basic Interests*, 146.

CHAPTER ONE

1 Smith, *Idea Brokers.*

2 See McGann, *2016 Global Go To Think Tanks Index Report.* Also see his recent study, *The Fifth Estate.*

3 Only a handful of think tanks in the US have budgets in excess of $40 million. The vast majority have operating revenue in the $1 to 5 million range.

4 For a discussion of the various think tank typologies that have been constructed, see Abelson, *Northern Lights*, chap. 1.

5 Weaver, "Changing World," 564.
6 Ibid., 567.
7 Lindquist, "Think Tanks?," 576.
8 See MacDonald and Moss, "Building a Think-and-Do Tank."
9 For more on the role of think tanks during the Progressive Era, see Smith, *The Idea Brokers*; Critchlow, *The Brookings Institution.*
10 Several scholars have argued that philanthropists often support research institutions to advance their own political and ideological interests. See, for example, Sealander, *Private Wealth*, and Culleton Colwell, *Private Foundations.*
11 For a more complete chronological listing of think tanks created during this period see McGann, "Academics to Ideologues," 739–40.
12 See Abelson, *American Think Tanks*, especially chapter 2, and "From Policy Research to Political Advocacy." For more on the political agendas of philanthropic donors see Freund, *Narcissism and Philanthropy.*
13 For more on this investigation, see Abelson, *Northern Lights*, 52, 97 and 116. In Canada, some concerns have also been raised about sizeable donations to the Mulroney Institute of Government. See Dubinsky, "New Mulroney Institute"; Bundale, "Professor Criticizes NS University"; and Cribb and Chown Oved, "Honorary Degrees for Brian Mulroney's Billionaire Friends."
14 Silverstein, "Pay for Play."
15 Abelson, *American Think Tanks*, 35.
16 Among the many factors that could account for the fact that Canada, unlike the United States, did not develop several prominent research institutions during the early 1900s is the absence of large-scale philanthropic foundations dedicated to social science research. For more on this see Richardson and Fisher, *The Development of the Social Sciences*, especially the introduction.
17 Lindquist employs the term "club" to describe the goals and functions of many Canadian policy institutes. See his "Think Tanks?"
18 For more on the early history of these organizations see Manny, "The Canadian Institute of International Affairs"; Osendarp, "A Decade of Transition"; Holmes, "The CIIA," 9–10; Demson, "Canadian Institute of International Affairs"; and Greathead, "Antecedents and Origins." The history of the CCSD is examined in Splane, *75 Years of Community Service.*
19 The RAND Corporation is now referred to simply as RAND. Several other institutes, including the Center for Naval Analyses and the Institute for Defense Analyses, advise the US government on defence issues. In recent years RAND has expanded its research program to include, among other things, health care reform. RAND also offers a joint graduate program with the University of California at Los Angeles, and it maintains a smaller office in Washington, DC. For a detailed analysis of RAND, see Kaplan, *Wizards of Armageddon*; Abella, *Soldiers of Reason*; and Samaan, *The Rand Corporation.*

20 The Hudson Institute was founded by Kahn and a handful of his former colleagues at RAND in 1961. Although originally based in Westchester County, New York, Hudson moved to Indianapolis following Kahn's death in 1984. See Ghamari-Tabrizi, *The Worlds of Herman Kahn*. It also maintains an office in Washington, DC. The Hudson Institute's major clients include the Departments of Defense (including the US Navy), Labor, State, and Commerce. Former vice president Dan Quayle and Elliot Abrams, former assistant secretary of state for human rights, took up residence at Hudson after leaving public office. The Urban Institute was created in 1968 at the request of President Lyndon B. Johnson and his domestic policy advisers. It was originally conceived as the domestic policy equivalent of RAND. From its inception, the Urban Institute has relied extensively on government contracts from the Department of Housing and Urban Development (HUD), the Department of Transportation, and several other departments and agencies at the state and federal level. It also receives financial support from various private donors and philanthropic foundations.

21 For more on CSIS see Smith, *Strategic Calling*.

22 Several studies have been written on the Institute for Policy Studies. See, for instance, Powell, *Covert Cadre*; Muravchik, "The Think-Tank of the Left"; and Yoffe, "IPS Faces Life."

23 C.D. Howe Institute, home page (www.cdhowe.org), "A History of the Institute."

24 Vanier Institute of the Family, www.familyforum.com.

25 For a discussion of how task forces and royal commissions have been used as sources of policy expertise for the Canadian government, see Bradford, *Commissioning Ideas*, and Jenson, "Commissioning Ideas."

26 The Economic Council of Canada was formerly known as the National Productivity Council, created in 1961.

27 Abelson and Lindquist, "Think Tanks in North America."

28 Ibid.

29 As noted, the Economic Council and the Science Council were disbanded following the February 1992 federal budget. Other victims of budget constraints included the Canadian Institute for International Peace and Security and the Law Reform Commission. On the demise of the Science Council of Canada, see De La Mothe, "A Dollar Short," 873–86. For budget cuts that led to the closure of the North-South Institute and the National Council of Welfare, see Abelson, *Northern Lights*.

30 For more on the PRI, see Anderson, "The New Focus."

31 On the AEI's influence on Heritage see Abelson, *American Think Tanks*, 54–5.

32 On the strategies of advocacy think tanks, see Abelson, "In Search of Policy Influence," "Policy Experts and Political Pundits," and "Think

Tanks in the United States." For a detailed analysis of the Heritage Foundation, see Edwards, *Leading the Way* and *The Power of Ideas* and Abelson, "Feulner's Pendulum."

33 For more on the involvement of the Heritage Foundation during the 1980 presidential campaign and the transition period that followed see Abelson, *American Think Tanks*.

34 See Weaver, "The Changing World," 567.

35 Abelson and Lindquist, "Think Tanks in North America." See Ritchie, *An Institute for Research on Public Policy*.

36 Ibid. The Private Planning Association of Canada was created in 1957 as the Canadian counterpart to the US National Planning Association; its creation was a condition for receiving foundation support to establish the Canadian-American Committee (CAC), a council of 100 private sector leaders and representatives who were to meet two or three times a year to discuss common problems, sponsor research, and develop consensus positions. For some additional information on the C.D. Howe Institute, see Beigie, "Economic Policy Analysis," and Ernst, "Liberal Continentalism."

37 Canadian Centre for Philanthropy, www.ccp.ca. Now part of Imagine Canada at www.imaginecanada.ca.

38 In addition to pursuing its research program, the Fraser Institute has found innovative ways to promulgate its values: the widely reported Tax Freedom Day and its blog, the *Fraser Forum*, are just some of the methods Fraser uses to convey its ideas.

39 The term vanity think tank was coined by Landers in "Think-Tanks."

40 Chisolm, "Sinking the Think Tanks Upstream."

41 As a result of a growing controversy over the legality of creating an organization that on the surface appeared to be used to circumvent campaign finance laws, Dole pulled the plug on this project. For more on this see Melton, "Closing of Dole's Think Tank."

42 On the Progress and Freedom Foundation see Regan, "A Think Tank with One Idea"; Dickerson, "Newt Inc."; Weisskopf, "New Political Landscape"; and Simpson, "New Addition." After resigning his position as speaker of the house, Newt Gingrich decided that in addition to undertaking some consulting work, he would strengthen his ties to conservative think tanks. He is currently a senior fellow at the American Enterprise Institute and a distinguished visiting fellow at the Hoover Institution.

43 For more on the Canadian Centre for Foreign Policy Development, see Lee, "Beyond Consultations."

44 See, for instance, Abelson and Lindquist, "Who's Thinking about International Affairs?"

45 Abelson and Lindquist, "Think Tanks in North America," 45.

46 For a history of the Brookings Institution see Critchlow, *The Brookings Institution*; Saunders, *The Brookings Institution*; and Smith, *Brookings at Seventy-Five.*

47 Robert S. Brookings's extraordinary life is chronicled in Hagedorn, *Brookings.*

48 Brookings Institution, *Annual Report 2016.*

49 Orlans, *The Nonprofit Research Institute*, 19.

50 On the removal of Project RAND from Douglas Aircraft, see Smith, *The RAND Corporation*, 51–74.

51 Orlans, *The Nonprofit Research Institute*, 21.

52 RAND's contribution to America's nuclear strategy is examined in Kaplan, *Wizards of Armageddon* and in Abella, *Soldiers of Reason.*

53 Budget sources are based on 2016 figures. RAND has also received funding from the Department of Health and Human Services/National Institutes of Health, other federal and government agencies, private firms, associations and international agencies, foundations, and individuals. It also draws on its sizeable endowment to support its research. See publication by RAND entitled *An Introduction to RAND.*

54 Peschek, *Policy-Planning Organizations*, 28. Also see Peschek's study, "Free the Fortune 500!," 165–80. For additional information on the history of AEI, see Ford, "American Enterprise Institute for Public Policy Research," 29–47.

55 Blumenthal, *The Rise of the Counter-Establishment*, 39.

56 Ibid., 38.

57 Ibid., 39.

58 Ibid.

59 Linden, "Powerhouses of Policy," 102.

60 Ibid.

61 Melvin Laird was secretary of defense in the Nixon administration from 1969–73.

62 Blumenthal, *The Rise of the Counter-Establishment*, 43–4.

63 For additional information on the mismanagement of the AEI under William Baroody Jr see the following: Blumenthal, "Think Tank Adrift in The Centre"; Emery, "New Troubles for an Old Think Tank"; and Goode and Hallow, "Struggling Institute Fights to Survive."

64 Linden, "Powerhouses of Policy," 102.

65 On the firing of William Baroody Jr and the appointment of Christopher C. DeMuth, see Balzano Jr, "The Sacking of a Centrist"; DeMuth, "President's Report: AEI's Mission," *Memorandum*, 1987: 2; Seabrook, "Capital Gain," 71–9 and Sussman, "Conservative Think Tank Comes Back from Brink."

66 Linden, "Powerhouses of Policy," 102.

67 Matlack, "Marketing Ideas," 1553.

68 *2015 AEI Annual Report*, 29.
69 Remarks made by Dr Jeffrey Gedmin at the Conference on Think Tanks in the USA and Germany: Democracy at Work; How and Where Do Public Decision-Makers Obtain Their Knowledge?, University of Pennsylvania, Philadelphia, PA, 18–20 November 1993.
70 See Abelson, *A Capitol Idea.*
71 Blumenthal, *The Rise of the Counter-Establishment*, 45. Pines resigned his position at the Heritage Foundation on 13 April 1992. See Hallow, "Pines Quits as Heritage Senior VP."
72 Tyman, "A Decade-Long Heritage."
73 For an interesting history of the Heritage Foundation, see Edwards, *Power of Ideas.* Also see Abelson, "Feulner's Pendulum," in Abelson et al., *Think Tanks, Foreign Policy and Geo-Politics.*
74 Taken from the Heritage Foundation's mission statement.
75 Quoted in McCombs, "Building a Heritage." For more on Heritage's goals, see Feulner, "Heritage Foundation."
76 *2016 Heritage Foundation Annual Report.*
77 Kaiser and Chinoy, "Scaife's Money," A01. For more on the financing of conservative foundations and think tanks see report by the Washington-based National Committee for Responsive Philanthropy entitled *$1 Billion for Ideas*; and Covington Colwell, *Moving a Public Policy.* In addition, see Stefancic and Delgado, *No Mercy.*
78 Incident described by Heritage Foundation president Jim DeMint in an email sent on 25 April 2017 to those on Heritage's email distribution list.
79 Interview with Gary Schmitt, 19 May 2004.
80 See Kristol and Kagan, "Toward a Neo-Reaganite Foreign Policy."
81 PNAC's Statement of Principles. View at www.newamericancentury.org.
82 See Abelson, *A Capitol Idea*, ch. 9 and Woodward, *State of Denial.*
83 Demson, *A Brief History*, 1.
84 Ibid., 2.
85 Lindquist, "Think Tanks?"
86 Conference Board of Canada, "Who We Are."
87 The Conference Board of Canada admitted to plagiarizing material from a US report in March 2009. See Abelson, *Northern Lights*, 92–3.
88 Vanier Institute of the Family, "About Us – Our History," www.vanierinstitute.ca.
89 Ibid.
90 Vanier Institute of the Family, *2013 Annual Report*, 1.
91 Ibid.
92 Ibid., 16.
93 Ibid.
94 Fraser Institute, *Challenging Perceptions*, 2.
95 Ibid., 3.

96 Ibid., 4.
97 Ibid., 8.
98 See the Fraser Institute's *2016 Annual Report.*
99 For more on Michael Walker and his impressions of the work of the Fraser Institute, see his "What's Right, Who's Left?" and Lorinc, "Hold the Fries," 11–15, 61.
100 Interview with Ken Battle, 16 December 1998.
101 Ibid.
102 Caledon Institute of Social Policy, *An Overview*, www.caledoninst.org.
103 Interview with Ken Battle.
104 Abelson, "Public Visibility and Policy Relevance."
105 Parkland Institute, home page "About the Parkland Institute," www.parklandinstitute.ca.
106 Parkland Institute, "Self-Study," www.parklandinstitute.ca.
107 Ibid., 4.
108 Ibid., 2.
109 Ibid., 15–17.

CHAPTER TWO

1 Mills, *The Power Elite.*
2 Much has been written about Eisenhower's farewell address and concerns about the military-industrial complex. See Smith, *Eisenhower.*
3 Altman, "Is Syria a Pay-to-Play Conflict?"
4 See Bentley, *The Process of Government* and Truman, *The Governmental Process.*
5 Evans et al., *Bringing the State Back In* and Krasner, *Defending the National Interest.*
6 For example, see Kingdon, *Agendas, Alternatives* and Stairs, "Public Opinion."
7 See Peschek, *Policy Planning Organizations*; Dye, *Who's Running America?*; Domhoff and Dye, *Power Elites and Organizations*; Saloma, *Ominous Politics*; and Shoup, *Wall Street's Think Tank.*
8 See Lipton, Williams and Confessore, "Foreign Powers Buy Influence at Think Tanks"; and Williams, Lipton and Parlapiano, "Foreign Government Contributions to Nine Think Tanks." For a response the findings presented in these articles, see Bruckner, "Fund a Think Tank," and Mendizabal, "Think Tank Accountability." The relationship between donors and think tanks has come under even closer scrutiny in recent months with the revelation that Google's support for the New America Foundation resulted in the termination of one of the think tank's scholars who published studies critical of the tech giant. For more on this, see Clemmitt, "Think Tanks in Transition"; Rosen, "The Do-Not-Think

Tank"; Breland, "Google Faces Blowback"; Rushe, "Google-Funded Think Tank Fired Scholar"; and Vogel, "Google Critic Ousted from Think Tank." On the funding of think tanks with interests in the Gulf states, see Grim, "Gulf Government Gave Secret $20 Million"; and Pecquet, "Gulf-Funded Think Tank."

9 A Gramscian approach to the study of think tanks is provided by Gill in *American Hegemony and the Trilateral Commission.* On the various streams of Marxism, see Kolakowski, *Main Currents of Marxism.*

10 Quoted in Lipton, Williams, and Confessore, "Foreign Powers Buy Influence at Think Tanks."

11 Mendizabal, "Think Tank Accountability."

12 Quoted in Lipton, Williams, and Confessore, "Foreign Powers Buy Influence at Think Tanks."

13 Domhoff, *The Power Elite and the State.*

14 Newsom, *The Public Dimension of Foreign Policy*, 141–62.

15 The American pluralist tradition is strongly rooted in the belief that society is composed of individual groups that compete for power and status in the policy-making community. Two studies in particular have had a major impact on shaping this perspective; Bentley, *The Process of Government*; and Truman, *The Governmental Process.*

16 Pal and Weaver (eds), *The Government Taketh Away.*

17 See Davidson, *Foreign Policy Inc.*, and Mearsheimer and Walt, *The Israel Lobby.*

18 See Evans et al., *Bringing the State Back In* and Krasner, *Defending the National Interest.*

19 Steelman, Review of *Do Think Tanks Matter?*

20 Krasner, *Defending the National Interest*, 11.

21 Steelman, Review of *Do Think Tanks Matter?*, 165.

22 For more on the relationship between Richard Nixon and the US Congress, see Schlesinger, *The Imperial Presidency.*

23 See Smith, *George Bush's War.*

24 On the relationship between the Executive and Congress in US foreign policy, see Hinckley, *Less Than Meets the Eye.*

25 See Maraniss, *First in His Class* and Abelson, "Changing Minds."

26 See Critchlow, *The Brookings Institution*; Edwards, *The Power of Ideas*; Abella, *Soldiers of Reason*; and Schulzinger, *The Wise Men of Foreign Affairs.*

27 On the rise of think tanks in the United States and around the globe, see McGann and Weaver (eds), *Think Tanks & Civil Societies*; and Stone and Denham (eds), *Think Tank Traditions.*

28 For example see Haas (ed), *Knowledge, Power.*

29 See Heclo, "Issue Networks"; Lindquist, "Think Tanks?"; and Stone, *Capturing the Political Imagination.*

30 Kingdon, *Agendas, Alternatives* and Stairs, "Public Opinion."

CHAPTER THREE

1 For more on this, see Weiss, *Organizations for Policy Analysis*; Stone, *Political Imagination*, especially chap. 3; and Weaver, "Changing World."
2 On the role of backroom strategists, see Craft, *Backrooms and Beyond.*
3 Interview with David Zussman, 14 September 1999.
4 Stone, *Political Imagination.*
5 See Kitschelt, "Political Opportunity Structures."
6 For an interesting examination of the involvement of think tanks in several government departments and agencies during the Reagan-Bush years, see Burch, *Research in Political Economy.*
7 The Rutherford Institute's support of Paula Jones in her case against President Clinton is an example of a think tank trying to influence the judicial process. The chair of the Rutherford Institute, John Whitehead, has appeared on several American talk shows and newscasts supporting Jones's legal actions. For a more detailed discussion of the ties between think tanks and the judiciary, see Burch, *Research in Political Economy.*
8 Several articles have been written on think tanks specializing in state politics. See, for instance, Scott, "Intellectuals Who Became Influential," and Moore, "Local Right Thinkers."
9 For a comprehensive discussion of the many factors that have contributed to the rise of think tanks, see Weiss, *Organizations for Policy Analysis.*
10 In addition to 100 senators and 435 elected members of the US House of Representatives, there are 3 nonvoting members representing the District of Columbia who sit in the House. The District of Columbia is currently waging a campaign to become the 51st state of the union. Should this happen, the number of representatives it would have in the House would be based on population determined by a decennial census.
11 For more on this, see Abelson, "Think Tanks in the US"
12 On the Congressional Policy Advisory Board, see the House Policy Committee, "Congressional Policy Advisory."
13 Ibid.
14 The role of think tanks and party foundations in Germany is examined in Gellner, "Think Tanks in Germany." Also see Pautz, *Think Tanks, Social Democracy, and Social Policy*; and Braml, "Germany: The Think and the Tank," in Abelson et al., *Think Tanks, Foreign Policy and Geo-Politics.*
15 The role and function of public think tanks is the focus of Robinson's paper "Public Think Tanks in the US"
16 See Abelson, *American Think Tanks.*
17 Ibid.
18 On the role of advisers in the Bush campaign, see Van Slambrouck, "California Think Tank"; Hager, "Bush Shops for Advice"; Swanson,

"Brain Power"; Schmitt, "Foreign Policy Experts"; and Abelson, "What Were They Thinking?"

19 Abelson, *American Think Tanks.*

20 See Abelson, "Changing Minds, Changing Course."

21 With the Canada Elections Act of 1996 the minimum election period was shortened from forty-seven to thirty-six days. A sitting government may run a longer election period, but politically it has rarely been in its interest to do so. A longer election period provides opposition parties with more time to criticize government policies.

22 See Abelson, *Northern Lights*, 126.

23 For more on this see Baier and Bakvis, "Think Tanks and Political Parties"; and Craft, *Backrooms and Beyond.*

24 Guy, *People, Politics and Government*, 215.

25 For more on the use of royal commissions and commissions of inquiry, see Bradford, *Commissioning Ideas*, and Jenson, "Commissioning Ideas."

26 Think tanks in Canada are registered as tax-exempt organizations under the Income Tax Act. This tax privilege is conferred by Revenue Canada on organizations that perform educational functions, but it is extended with certain limitations. Think tanks are prohibited from engaging in certain political activities, including supporting or opposing political parties and their members and furthering the political platforms of parties. See Abelson, *Northern Lights*, 20–6. Similar limitations are placed on think tanks in the United States by the Internal Revenue Service. Think tanks in the United States are also concerned about the potential political repercussions of being too closely linked to one party. Not only might such an association threaten a think tank's tax-exempt status but it would likely undermine its ability to engage in objective scholarly analysis. For more on this see Morin and Deane, "The Ideas Industry," 8 June 1999.

27 For more on the ties between the Harper government and the Fraser Institute, see Gutstein, *Harperism.*

28 Interview with author, 15 December 1998.

29 Interview with author, 17 December 1998.

30 In the fall of 1999 the PPF began a research project on managing transitions. The PPF was created in 1987 to strengthen the dialogue between government and the private and nonprofit sectors in the hope of improving public-policy decision-making. Information obtained during interview with David Zussman, president of PPF, 14 September 1999.

31 This point is reinforced by Lindquist in "Transition Teams and Government Succession," 49.

32 Guy, *People, Politics and Government*, 215.

33 The directors of the research offices of Canada's five political parties are well aware of the work being conducted by the country's leading think tanks. In interviews with the author on 14, 15, and 17 December 1998,

all the directors indicated that they regularly receive publications from Canadian policy institutes and occasionally meet with some of their staff.

34 Interview with author, 16 December 1998. Several independent sources, including Jonathan Murphy, director of the National Liberal Caucus Research Bureau (interview with author, 14 December 1998), have acknowledged Battle's access to cabinet and his significant impact in helping shape legislation on several social policy issues. For more on Battle's influence in key Liberal policy circles, see Greenspan and Wilson-Smith, *Double Vision*, especially chap. 9.
35 Ibid.
36 Interview with author, 16 December 1998.
37 Ibid.
38 Figures obtained from CME website. Information also available from *Association Canada 2017*.
39 For more on the role of the Conference Board of Canada, see Lindquist, *Behind the Myth*.
40 US data appears in US Department of Education, "Degrees and other formal awards conferred." Data on social science PhDs in Canada appears in Statistics Canada, "Earned Doctorates, by Field of Study and Sex."
41 National Science Foundation, "2014 Doctorate Recipients."
42 Interview with author, 14 September 1999. On the closure of the North-South Institute, see Abelson, *Northern Lights*.
43 For more on the role of foundations in the United States, see Berman, *Influence*, and Sealander, *Private Wealth*. On the Koch Foundation, see Mayer, *Dark Money* and Schulman, *Sons of Wichita*.
44 The AEI's financial crisis during the mid-1980s was also a result of poor management. See Abelson, *American Think Tanks*, 53–4.
45 Morgan, "Think Tank or Hired Gun?" For more on the relationship between think tanks and corporate donors, see Stefancic and Delgado, *No Mercy*.
46 Abelson and Carberry, "Following Suit?," 546–7.
47 Kingdon, *Agendas*, 129.
48 Ibid., 130.
49 Harrison and Hoberg, "Setting the Environmental Agenda."
50 Abelson and Carberry, "Following Suit?," 547. For more on theories of entrepreneurship, see Schneider and Teske, "Political Entrepreneur." On the role of institutional structures in influencing policy entrepreneurship, see Checkel, *Ideas*.
51 Ibid., 548.
52 For more on the origins of the Fraser Institute, see Lindquist, *Behind the Myth*, 377–80.
53 Drawing on their extensive service in the public sector, Kirby and Pitfield played an important role in recognizing the need for policy-makers to

draw on policy expertise both inside and outside government. Pitfield served as deputy secretary to the Cabinet (Plans) and deputy clerk of the Privy Council (1969–73). He also served as clerk of the Privy Council and secretary to Cabinet (1975–79). Kirby was assistant secretary to the prime minister (1974–76), secretary to the Cabinet for federal-provincial relations (1980–82), and deputy clerk of the Privy Council Office (1981–82). On the contribution of senior civil servants to think tank development, see Lindquist, *Behind the Myth*.

54 Abelson and Carberry, "Following Suit?," 548.

55 Ibid.

56 Gray, "Think Tanks."

57 Lipset, "Canada and the US," 110. For other treatments of US-Canadian comparisons, see Presthus, *Cross-National Perspectives*, and Merelman, *Partial Visions*.

58 Lipset, *Continental Divide*, 136.

59 The Saskatchewan Institute of Public Policy (SIPP), based in Regina, was created "to engage the academic, government, private business, and non-profit sectors in meeting the public policy challenges of our time."

60 See Abelson, *American Think Tanks*; "What Were They Thinking?"; and "Changing Minds, Changing Course."

61 For a detailed examination of the types of presidential candidates most inclined to rely on advocacy think tanks, see Abelson and Carberry, "Policy Experts in Presidential Campaigns."

62 Data on the educational and professional experience of researchers at think tanks was obtained from current annual reports. Some think tanks are able to recruit and retain more PhDs than others. Moreover, the majority of experts at C.D. Howe possess PhDs. The same, however, cannot be said of several other think tanks, including the Institute for Research on Public Policy, the Atlantic Institute for Market Studies, and the Mackenzie Institute. Not surprisingly, think tanks based at universities are heavily populated with PhDs.

63 There are some exceptions to this trend. For instance, Gordon Robertson, who held several important government positions, including clerk of the Privy Council and secretary to Cabinet (1963–75) and secretary to Cabinet for provincial-federal relations (1975–79), was president of the Institute for Research on Public Policy from 1980 to 1984 and remained as a fellow in residence until 1990. Another exception is Hugh Segal, a former staff member of Ontario Premier Bill Davis and federal Conservative leaders Robert Stanfield and Brian Mulroney, who became president of the IRPP in 1999. He went on to serve in the Canadian Senate and held the post of the fifth Master of Massey College, University of Toronto.

64 Interview with David Zussman, 14 September 1999.

65 Lindquist, *Behind the Myth*. A similar sentiment is expressed by Tupper in his assessment of the contribution of a select group of Canadian think tanks to the debate on public debt in Canada. See his "Think Tanks."

66 On the growing population of think tanks in China, see Hua, "Chinese Think Tanks' Influence," in Abelson et al. (eds), *Think Tanks, Foreign Policy and Geo-Politics*.

67 Quoted in Stone, *Political Imagination*, 43.

CHAPTER FOUR

1 For more on the increased competition among think tanks, see McGann, *Competition for Dollars*.

2 Abelson, *American Think Tanks*, 57.

3 Ibid.

4 Some presidents have relied far more heavily on scholars from think tanks to serve on presidential advisory boards than others. For instance, President Reagan invited several scholars from the Hoover Institution to sit on the President's Foreign Intelligence Advisory Board (PFIAB). Conversely, of the eleven members PFIAB appointed by President Clinton and chaired by Warren Rudman, none had permanent positions at a think tank. For more on the role of these boards, see Abelson, *American Think Tanks*, 75–9.

5 See Stewart, Chong, and Simms (eds), *Turning Parliament Inside Out*.

6 Abelson, *American Think Tanks*, 68.

7 Linden, "Powerhouses of Policy," 100.

8 Fraser Institute, *Challenging Perceptions*, 12.

9 See the *2015 Annual Reports* of the Heritage Foundation, AEI, and the Brookings Institution.

10 Heritage Foundation, *2007 Annual Report*. Also see *2015 Annual Report*.

11 Heritage Foundation, *2007 Annual Report*.

12 Crowley, "How Can Think Tanks Win Friends?"

13 Abelson, *American Think Tanks*, 88.

14 Ibid.

15 Ibid., 86.

16 Ibid.

17 Abelson, "Public Visibility and Policy Relevance," 241.

18 See Abelson, *Northern Lights*, chap. 7.

19 Quotations drawn from Fraser Institute promotional material. Before assuming office, Margaret Thatcher helped establish the Centre for Policy Studies, in London. For more on this and other British think tanks, see Stone, *Capturing the Political Imagination*, and Denham and Garnett, *British Think Tanks*.

20 See Abelson, *Northern Lights*, chap. 7.

CHAPTER FIVE

1 Some think tanks consider these and other indicators in assessing their own performance. However, for the purposes of this chapter, they will not be included.

2 Weaver and Rich, "Think Tanks."

3 Rich, "Perceptions of Think Tanks."

4 There is no consensus, nor, for that matter, are there many reliable estimates, on how many think tanks exist in Canada. Lindquist has estimated that there are likely a hundred, although this number may vary, depending on one's definition of a policy institute. This study focuses on approximately two dozen think tanks, a sizeable cross-section of the think tank population.

A think tank receives one citation per article even if several references are made to it. English-language newspapers were selected for their broad national and regional coverage of domestic and foreign policy issues. Since an index listing individuals and organizations who have appeared before various parliamentary committees and subcommittees has yet to be produced, the names of witnesses were taken from each committee report. A complete list of the committees covered in this study is included in table 5.11. Data are from the parliamentary sessions from 1980 to 1999, a period closely corresponding to the time when media data became available, were used, along with the federal government's report on policy consultants.

5 Weaver and Rich, "Think Tanks," 1.

6 Despite including twenty-two think tanks not based in the District of Columbia in their study, Weaver and Rich did not examine how much media attention regional newspapers devoted to think tanks.

7 Although the Hoover Institution generates far less media coverage than several DC-based think tanks, it received the highest overall score from the *Economist* in its ranking of think tanks. Interestingly enough, the *Economist* did not refer to Hoover's media visibility in evaluating its performance. Several other factors, including its funding, library, and high-profile staff, helped the magazine to make its assessment. See "The Good Think-Tank Guide."

8 Ibid., 23.

9 The conservative *Washington Times* quotes scholars from the Heritage Foundation, the American Enterprise Institute, CSIS, and the Cato Institute far more than any other newspaper in Rich and Weaver's study.

10 Rich and Weaver, "Advocates and Analysts," 249. See also Rich, "Think Tanks as Sources of Expertise."

11 Ibid. See also Rich, "Perceptions of Think Tanks."

12 Data on the size and budget of the Conference Board was obtained from *Associations Canada 2017*.
13 See Abelson, *Northern Lights*, Appendix One.
14 Data on the size of these institutes was obtained primarily from annual reports made available on think tank websites, from *Associations Canada 2017*, and through personal correspondence.
15 Ibid.
16 See Kingdon, *Agendas*.
17 For background information on the creation of this task force, see Anderson, "The New Focus."
18 This finding is not surprising, since six federal government departments fund CPRN, Inc.
19 Individuals not invited to testify before a parliamentary committee may request to appear by contacting the clerk of the appropriate committee. For guidelines on how individuals are selected to testify, see Dawson, *Government of Canada*, 348–51. For a more recent examination of the rules and procedures of parliamentary committees, see Docherty, *Mr. Smith*.
20 With few exceptions, majority and minority members of congressional committees and subcommittees have the authority to call witnesses to testify. However, in practice the party in power will have more input into which individuals and organizations will appear to comment.
21 Remarks made to author by staff members of the Canadian Tax Foundation, 7 April 1998.
22 A Spearman Correlation is a nonparametric correlation coefficient based on the ranks of data rather than the actual values. Values of the coefficient range from −1 to +1. The absolute correlation coefficient indicates the strength of the relationship between the variables, and the sign of the coefficient indicates the direction of the relationship. Definition obtained from *SPSS for Windows Release 6.1* (24 June 1994).
23 Pal, *Public Policy Analysis*, 92–4.

CHAPTER SIX

1 Van Slambrouck, "California Think Tank."
2 Swanson, "Brain Power."
3 Judis, "Taking Care of Business."
4 Interview with Dr Martin Anderson, 19 March 1990.
5 While presidential candidates must raise their own funds during the primaries, the nominees selected by each party can, should they elect to, draw on public funds for the general election. If presidential nominees accept public funding, they cannot draw on any private sources of money.

6 Abelson and Carberry suggest that two characteristics of presidential candidates – their status as Washington insiders or outsiders and the strength of their ideological views as approximated by voter election studies – can help to explain the recruitment patterns of think tanks by candidates. See their article "Policy Experts."

7 Swanson, "Brain Power." Think tanks have different policies for staff who advise presidential candidates. Some, such as the Cato Institute, actively discourage staff from becoming too closely associated with particular candidates, preferring them to make their advice available to any candidate who wants it. Others, like the Center for National Policy, which are more concerned about keeping the Internal Revenue Service (IRS) at bay, insist that scholars take a leave of absence if they decide to work on a campaign. The IRS expressly forbids nonprofit organizations from participating in political campaigns. For more on this, see Morin and Deane, "The Ideas Industry," 8 June 1999.

8 For an analysis of the 1976 presidential campaign, see Schram, *Running for President*, and Witcover, *Marathon*.

9 Shoup, *The Carter Presidency*, 39.

10 Ibid., 43.

11 For a detailed examination of the Trilateral Commission, see Gill, *American Hegemony*, and Sklar, *Trilateralism*. For more information on how Carter was selected to become a member of the Trilateral Commission, see Gerard Smith's Personal Files, "Memorandum from George Franklin to Gerard Smith on the Circumstances of Carter Coming with the Commission," Box 4, 1/1/76–6/3/77, Jimmy Carter Library.

12 Perloff, *The Shadows of Power*, 156.

13 Ibid.

14 Shoup, *The Carter Presidency*, 50.

15 Perloff, *The Shadows of Power*, 157.

16 Shoup, *The Carter Presidency*, 51.

17 Carter, *Why Not the Best?*, 164. Although Carter acknowledges the benefits of participating on the Trilateral Commission in his autobiography, he does not even mention the commission in his memoirs, *Keeping Faith*.

18 Contrary to Brzezinski's assertions that the Trilateral Commission did not advise Carter, Brzezinski did discuss several foreign policy issues with Carter in his capacity as director of the Commission. See, for instance, Brzezinski's Personal Files on the Trilateral Commission, Box 8, 7/1/75–8/31/75, and Box 5, 1/1/75–1/31/75, Jimmy Carter Library.

19 Interview with Dr Zbigniew Brzezinski, 30 May 1991.

20 There appears to be little agreement on the exact number of Trilateral Commission members who served in the Carter administration. Figures range from a low of eighteen to a high of twenty-five.

21 Perloff, *The Shadows of Power*, 158.

22 A majority of the trilateral commissioners who served in the Carter administration were also members of the Council on Foreign Relations. For a list of individuals who participated in both organizations, see Shoup, *The Carter Presidency*, 105.

23 Robert Pastor, Carter's Latin American specialist on the National Security Council, claims that the president's foreign policy toward Latin America was significantly influenced by two reports issued by the Commission on US-Latin American Relations; *The Americas in a Changing World* and *The US and Latin America*. The commission, chaired by Ambassador Sol Linowitz, was a bipartisan group of approximately twenty-five leaders from universities, think tanks, and corporations. Pastor, who served as executive director of the commission before joining the National Security Council, states that "The reports helped the administration define a new relationship with Latin America, and twenty-seven of the twenty-eight specific recommendations in the second report became US policy." For additional information on the background of the Linowitz Commission and its contribution to US foreign policy in Latin America, see Pastor, "The Carter Administration and Latin America," 62–5.

24 Reagan was governor of California from 1967 to 1975.

25 Anderson, *Revolution*, 47.

26 The various factors influencing Reagan's decision to leave the Democratic Party are discussed in his autobiography, *An American Life*, 132–6.

27 The term "ideas move nations" was coined by Easterbrook and is used as the title of his article on the rise of conservative think tanks, which appeared in the *Atlantic Monthly*, January 1986.

28 Anderson, *Revolution*, 8. Anderson has apparently changed his mind about universities serving as reservoirs for policy ideas. In his book *Impostors in the Temple* Anderson claims that many universities have become inundated by academic frauds and thus are unable to maintain acceptable scholarly standards.

29 Anderson, *Revolution*, 165.

30 It is not uncommon for policy task forces to be created during presidential campaigns to provide candidates with information and advice. Several presidents, including John F. Kennedy, have relied on them. For more on this see Campbell, *Managing the Presidency*, and Hess, *Organizing the Presidency*.

31 Anderson, *Revolution*, 166.

32 Seventy-four economists participated on the economic policy task forces. Six chaired issue task forces in various areas of economic policy: Arthur F. Burns (task force on international monetary policy); Alan Greenspan (task force on budget policy); Paul McCracken, former chair of the Council of Economic Advisers (task force on inflation); Charles E. Walker, former deputy secretary of the treasury (task force on tax policy); Murray L.

Weidenbaum (task force on regulatory reform); and Caspar Weinberger (task force on spending control). The other members of the coordinating committee were Milton Friedman; Michel T. Halbouty, former president of the American Association of Petroleum Geologists and chair of the task force on energy policy; Jack Kemp; James T. Lynn, former director of the Office of Management and Budget; William E. Simon, former secretary of the treasury, and Walter Wriston, chair of Citi-bank/Citicorp.

33 Interview with Mr Richard V. Allen, 29 May 1991. For a more detailed discussion of the role and function of policy task forces during the 1980 campaign, see Wood, *Whatever Possessed the President?*, 140–3.

34 Anderson, *Revolution*, 167.

35 Meese, *With Reagan*, 59.

36 Anderson, *Revolution*, 167.

37 Meese, *Transition*, 11.

38 Anderson, *Revolution*, 170.

39 The Institute for Contemporary Studies (ICS) in San Francisco was established by Caspar Weinberger and Edwin Meese III as a nonprofit organization in 1972. The ICS and its affiliated institutes publish studies on economic, social, and foreign policy issues. For an interesting analysis on the founding of the ICS, see Beers, "Buttoned-Down Bohemians."

40 Background information on these and other members of the Reagan administration can be found in Brownstein and Easton, *Reagan's Ruling Class*.

41 Since some scholars belonged to one or more think tanks before joining the Reagan administration, I have provided an approximate figure only.

42 A list of members of the Committee on the Present Danger who served in the Reagan administration can be found in Saunders, *Peddlers of Crisis*, 287–8. According to Eric Alterman, the Committee on the Present Danger eventually furnished fifty-nine members to the Reagan national security team. See his book *Sound and Fury*, 80. For additional information on the Committee on the Present Danger see Dalby, *Creating the Second Cold War*.

43 Figures for the AEI, the CSIS, and the Heritage Foundation are quoted in Blumenthal, *Counter-Establishment*, 35–8.

44 Weinraub, "Conservative Group's Blueprint for Reagan."

45 Omang, "Heritage Report."

46 Heatherly, *Mandate for Leadership*. In preparation for the 1984 and 1988 presidential campaigns, the Heritage Foundation produced similar volumes that examined a wide range of domestic and foreign policy issues. See Butler et al., *Mandate for Leadership II*, and *Mandate for Leadership III*. The Heritage Foundation also issued an interim report during the first term of the Reagan administration. See Holwill, *Agenda '83*. The Heritage Foundation was not the first think tank to produce detailed "blueprints"

for the executive and Congress. Since 1971 the Brookings Institution has published an annual series entitled *Setting National Priorities*, which provides policy-makers and scholars with in-depth analyses of domestic and foreign policy issues. Moreover, following the 1992 campaign Will Marshall and Martin Schram of the Progressive Policy Institute produced a blueprint for the Clinton administration entitled *Mandate for Change*, a title apparently borrowed from the Heritage Foundation's series *Mandate for Leadership*.

47 In an interview with the author on 29 May 1991, Richard Allen, President Reagan's first national security advisor, confirmed that Feulner presented Meese and Allen with a copy of *Mandate for Leadership* in mid-November. Allen added that the study "was immediately reproduced and distributed to our entire transition team." It is not surprising that Allen was willing to accept and reproduce Feulner's study. The two had established close ties as early as 1965 through the Intercollegiate Studies Institute, the first national conservative student organization in the United States. Eventually, through Allen, Feulner became a Hoover Institution Fellow. For a discussion on the relationship between Feulner and Allen see Blumenthal, *Counter-Establishment*, 46–8.

48 Omang, "The Heritage Report."

49 Knickerbocker, "Heritage Foundation's Ideas." Meese also acknowledged receiving studies from the National Academy of Public Administration and from the Kennedy School of Government at Harvard. When asked if he had received a study from the Hoover Institution, Meese remarked, "I don't think so. There's nobody left there; they're all here in Washington working with us, helping out." See Meese, *Transition*, 7.

50 Meese, *With Reagan*, 60.

51 Ibid. On two occasions, Edwin Feulner took leave of the Heritage Foundation to serve as a special consultant in the White House on specific strategic planning projects and throughout the two terms was an informal advisor to President Reagan and members of his cabinet.

52 Ibid. For a discussion of which policy recommendations in the Heritage study were adopted by the Reagan administration during the early 1980s, see Horwill, *Agenda '83*.

53 Duignan and Rabushka, *The US in the 1980s*. Interview with author, 2 May 1990. Campbell added that when Edwin Feulner was a public affairs fellow at the Hoover Institution, he admitted to Campbell that he was "a retailer not a wholesaler of ideas." Campbell remarked jokingly that he would "buy a used idea from Feulner anytime."

54 Richard Allen resigned as National Security Adviser in early 1981 amidst allegations of wrongdoing and was replaced by Judge William Clark. Clark left the National Security Council (NSC) in October 1983 to become secretary of the interior and was replaced by the deputy national security

adviser, Robert "Bud" McFarlane. For background information on the transfer of power in the NSC, see Menges, *National Security Council.*

55 Anderson, *Revolution*, 3.

56 Weinraub, "Conservative Group's Blueprint for Reagan."

57 Knickerbocker, "Heritage Foundation's Ideas."

58 Quoted in Wheeler, "Heritage Chiefs."

59 Interview with Dr Anderson, 19 August 1996. Richard Allen agrees that President Bush went to great lengths to distance himself from the Reaganites. Allen stated that by doing so, President Bush cut himself off from some of America's most important and influential policy experts. Interview with the author, 6 September 1996.

60 For an interesting analysis of president Bush's reaction to public opinion polls during the Gulf War, see Brace and Hinckley, *Follow the Leader*.

61 Interview with Martin Anderson, Hoover Institution, 19 March 1990.

62 Heatherly, *Mandate for Leadership*.

63 The Carnegie Endowment for International Peace, the Citizens Transition Project, and the American Enterprise Institute were among the many organizations that outlined a series of domestic and foreign policy recommendations. See Rosenbaum, "Torrent of Free Advice."

64 David Osborne, a fellow at the PPI and co-author of *Reinventing America*, helped introduce Clinton to the think tank set. See Fineman, "Clinton's Team."

65 Several books have been written on the 1992 presidential election, including Allen and Portis, *The Comeback Kid*; Brummett, *High Wire*; Germond and Witcover, *Mad As Hell*; Goldman et al., *Quest for the Presidency*; Hohenberg, *Bill Clinton Story*; and Moore and Ihde, *Clinton*.

66 Clinton resigned as chair of the DLC shortly before announcing his candidacy for the presidency. The DLC is currently chaired by Louisiana senator John Breaux. Al From is the organization's president and executive director. The DLC currently has a staff of over twenty people and an annual budget of approximately $2.5 million, which is raised from private philanthropists, corporate donors, and grass-roots organizations.

67 The DLC has approximately 3,000 members, including about 750 elected officials nationwide, with 32 US senators and 142 current and former House members. It also has chapters in twenty-eight states in every region of the country. For more on the DLC's membership, see Barnes, "Will DLC Be a Lobbying Heavyweight?"; Grove, "Steering His Party"; and Towell, "DLC Moves into Driver's Seat."

68 Achenbach, "Wonk If You Love Clinton."

69 Although Clinton appeared to draw heavily on the PPI's study *Mandate for Change*, only a few members from the PPI and the DLC received appointments in the Clinton administration. Bruce Reed and Bill Galston received positions in the domestic policy office. Reed was issues director

in the campaign and deputy director of the transition for domestic policy. He was later appointed as White House domestic policy advisor. Will Marshall, Al From, and Robert Shapiro, the PPI's vice-president (who later resigned over the Whitewater scandal), were Clinton campaign advisers. From also served in the transition. For more on Clinton's inner circle of policy advisers, see Fineman, "Clinton's Team"; Weisberg, "Clincest"; and Bandow, "New Democrats."

70 Marshall and Schram, *Mandate for Change*. In addition to providing Clinton with several policy ideas to consider during the campaign, the DLC engaged in an active lobbying campaign to support some of the president's policies. For instance, the DLC devoted considerable resources to convincing members of Congress to ratify the North American Free Trade Agreement (NAFTA). For more on this, see Barnes, "Will DLC Be a Lobbying Heavyweight?"

71 For a complete text of the Clinton-Gore Economic Conference, including the list of presenters, see *President Clinton's New Beginning*.

72 Philip Lader, a South Carolina businessman, was the founding father of the annual Renaissance Weekend, which began in 1980. The purpose of the Renaissance Weekend is to provide leaders from various careers with an opportunity to share ideas in an informal setting. Seminars are held during the retreat, and journalists are prohibited from commenting on the proceedings. Bill and Hillary Clinton have attended the Renaissance Weekends since the mid-1980s. For more on Clinton's involvement in the Renaissance Weekend, see two articles by Maraniss, "Letter from Never-Never Land" and "A Weekend With Bill and Friends." Also see Jehl, "Thinking Party," and Baer, "Network for the Nineties."

73 For more on George W. Bush's career as Texas governor, see Ivins and Dubose, *Shrub*; Mitchell, *Bush Dynasty*; and Minutaglio, *First Son*.

74 Russo, "Brain Power." Also see Daalder and Lindsay, "Bush."

75 For more on the relationship between George W. Bush and the Hoover Institution, see Hager, "Bush Shops for Advice," and Healy and Hebel, "Academics."

76 Lindsey also served as an adviser to President George Bush. For more on Lindsey's background, see Kessler, "Economic Adviser."

77 Maggs, "Tax Cuts," 2236.

78 Gorman, "Bush's Lesson Plan," 2230–2.

79 Kitfield, "Periphery Is Out," 2293.

80 For more on Rice's background see Mufson, "Daunting Challenge."

81 For more on Zoellick's appointment see Babington, "Bush Names Zoellick."

82 See Abelson, *A Capitol Idea*.

83 See two studies by Abelson: *A Capitol Idea* and "In the Line of Fire: US Think Tanks" in Richard Higgott and Ivona Malbasic (eds), *The Political Consequences of Anti-Americanism*: 44–57.

84 Kitfield, "Periphery Is Out."
85 For more on Jeb Bush's fascination with policy development, see Minutaglio, *First Son.*
86 Greenberger, "Campaign 2000."
87 The majority of think tanks in the United States are registered as chapter 501(c) tax-exempt educational institutes under the Internal Revenue Code. To qualify, they must agree not to engage in certain types of political activities. According to chapter 501(c), subsection 3 of the Internal Revenue Code of 1986, "no substantial part of the activities of [registered organizations can carry] on propaganda, or otherwise attempt, to influence legislation (except as otherwise provided in subsection (h)), and which does not participate in, or intervene in (including publishing or distributing of statements), any political campaign on behalf of (or in opposition to) any candidate for public office." It is this last statement, the inability of registered organizations to participate in political campaigns, that has resulted in IRS audits of some think tanks.

Think tanks like the Hoover Institution, which is located on a university campus, are particularly vulnerable to losing credibility by being perceived as spokespersons for a particular candidate. When several of its staff advised Reagan in the 1980 campaign, the Hoover Institution discovered that close ties with politicians can lead to serious tensions with university faculty. Tensions between Hoover and Stanford arose once again as a result of the involvement of Hoover scholars in the Bush campaign. For more on this controversy, see Manley and Rebholz, "Hoover Institution," and Abelson, *American Think Tanks*, 41–3.
88 Several articles have been written about McCain's close ties to think tanks. See, for example, *USA Today*, "Senator McCain Announces Economic Advisors," and Fred Barnes, "How Bush Decided on the Surge."
89 See Sweet, "Obama Taps Influential Foreign Policy Experts"; and Garekar, "The Gurus."
90 *The Washington Post*, "The War over the Wonks"; and Bumiller, "Research Groups Boom in Washington."
91 Nye, "Scholars on the Sidelines."
92 Bumiller, "Cast of 300."
93 *The Washington Post*, "Transition Team Profiles."
94 Crowley, "The Shadow President"; Savage, "Shepherd of a Government in Exile"; and Mann, *Rise of the Vulcans.*
95 Murray and Leonnig, "Obama Teams Are Scrutinizing Federal Agencies."
96 Dreazen, "Obama Dips into Think Tank for Talent."
97 Ackerman, "Obama's Pentagon-in-Waiting"; and Pincus, "'Experts' Report."
98 Abelson and Carberry, "Policy Experts in Presidential Campaigns."
99 Rogin, "Trump Could Cause 'the Death of Think Tanks as We Know Them.'"
100 Ibid.

101 *National Review*, "Against Trump."
102 Gunter, "Trump's 'Muslim Lockdown.'" For more on Trump and the Center for Security Policy see Colvin, "Center for Security Policy." Other think tanks, including the libertarian CATO Institute, lashed out against Trump's travel ban. See Bier, "Trump's Immigration Ban Is Illegal."
103 Ibid.
104 For more on Rubio's ties to think tanks, see Smith, "Why Marco Rubio Might Be the GOP's"; and Matthews, "Marco Rubio."
105 Much has been written about Ted Cruz and his cozy ties with the Heritage Foundation. See Deace, "Ted Cruz Gets Heritage Foundation 'Endorsement'"; and Shimshock, "Cruz, Rubio, Paul."
106 On the ties between Donald Trump and the Heritage Foundation, see Think Tank Watch, "Trump Consulting with Think Tanks"; Heritage Foundation, "Donald Trump Turns to Heritage for Policy Guidance"; Kopan, "Meet Donald Trump's Think Tank"; Shephard, "The D.C. Think Tank behind Donald Trump"; Fuller, "Donald Trump and the Heritage Foundation"; and Wegmann, "Heritage Foundation Takes Risk and Wins Big with Trump."
107 Think Tank Watch, "Has Heritage Just Released Donald Trump's Bible?" Also see the Heritage Foundation, "Blueprint for Reform."
108 See Balan, "Trump Thanks Jim DeMint"; and Wagner, "Trump Praises Jim DeMint."
109 Van Slambrouck, "California Think Tank."
110 For more on this, see Woodruff, "Donald Trump's Favorite Think Tank."

CHAPTER SEVEN

1 Lindquist, *Behind the Myth*, 227.
2 Tupper, "Think Tanks," 532.
3 Several journalists covering the constitutional conferences reported favourably on their role in stimulating public discussion. For instance, Jeffrey Simpson commented that "Against the odds, these gatherings in Halifax, Calgary, Montreal, Toronto and Vancouver worked splendidly. Indeed, they rescued constitutional reform, at least temporarily … Instead of the usual shouting and insinuation, the discussions were civil and constructive, a rediscovery of the much-ballyhooed but infrequently observed Canadian compromise and tolerance." Quoted by Milne in "Innovative Constitutional Processes," 38.
4 Kroeger, "Constitutional Conferences," 2.
5 Ibid.
6 *Shaping Canada's Future Together*, iii.
7 This was not the first attempt by the federal government to generate public discussion on constitutional reform following Meech Lake. The Spicer

Commission, formally known as the Citizens' Forum on Canada's Future, was established in November 1990 to give Canadians an opportunity to speak out on the future of Canada. For more on this, see Russell, *Constitutional Odyssey*, 154–89.

8 Kroeger, "The Constitutional Conferences," 1.

9 Milne, "Innovative Constitutional Processes," 29.

10 Russell, *Constitutional Odyssey*, 175.

11 Milne, "Innovative Constitutional Processes," 29.

12 See Russell, *Constitutional Odyssey.*

13 Harrison, *Constitutional Conferences Secretariat*, 1.

14 Ibid.

15 Kroeger, "Constitutional Conferences," 2; President of the Privy Council, *News Release.*

16 Department of Finance, *Supplementary Estimates.*

17 President of the Privy Council, *News Release*, 2.

18 A series of background papers on the various themes explored in *Shaping Canada's Future Together* were released by the Federal-Provincial Relations Office (FPRO) before the constitutional hearings began in the fall of 1991. They were edited by Ronald Watts, director of the Institute for Intergovernmental Relations at Queen's University, who had been seconded to the FPRO in April 1991, and they were intended to provide additional information and insights into the constitutional reform proposals outlined by the federal government. Among the titles released were *Responsive Institutions for a Modern Canada*, *Canadian Federalism and Economic Union*, and *Aboriginal Peoples, Self-Government, and Constitutional Reform.*

19 This observation is confirmed by Harrison, who stated that "If the conferences were to be based on openness, then it was paramount that the process used to develop them be as neutral as possible. A key decision in this regard was the decision to invite five independent institutes to sponsor the first four conferences ... It could be argued that the only way in which potential concerns about 'manipulation' could be minimized was by handing considerable authority to these outside bodies." See Constitutional Conferences Secretariat, "Constitutions Conference," 5.

20 See chapter 5.

21 Discussion with Ron Watts, 27 July 1999. David Elton, president of the Max Bell Foundation and former president of the Canada West Foundation made similar remarks to me regarding the selection criteria for think tanks (25 July 1999).

22 Information about mission statement obtained from APEC's home page at www.apec-econ.ca.

23 Correspondence with Patrick Brannon, research analyst, APEC.

24 Canada West Foundation, *Annual Report 1997*, 6.

25 Interview, 24 November 2000.
26 Niagara Institute, www.niagarainstitute.com.
27 The origins of the C.D. Howe Institute can be traced to the creation, in 1958, of the Private Planning Association of Canada (PPAC), which was established "to undertake research on educational activities and economic policy issues." In 1973 the PPAC merged with the C.D. Howe Memorial Foundation to become the C.D. Howe Research Institute (HRI). In 1981 the HRI was dissolved and the reconstituted PPAC became the C.D. Howe Institute. See the C.D. Howe Institute home page, "A History of the Institute," www.cdhowe.org.
28 See chapter 5.
29 The responsibilities varied according to each institute. See Harrison, *The Constitutional Conferences Secretariat*, figure 2, and President of the Privy Council, *News Release*.
30 Ibid., 3.
31 Ibid., 4.
32 Ibid., 5.
33 Harrison, *Constitutional Conferences Secretariat*, 16.
34 Canada West Foundation, *Renewal of Canada*, 1.
35 According to Milne, shortly after Clark invited the institutes to participate in the conferences, the heads of the institutes met and insisted that their involvement would depend on maintaining their "own independence and control over the organization, management, and final report of the Conferences, including the manner in which participants would be selected." Milne, "Innovative Constitutional Processes," 30. While the institutes developed their own models for recruiting participants, they still had to satisfy the government's selection criteria.
36 See Abelson, "New Channel of Influence," 849–72.
37 Harrison, *Constitutional Conferences Secretariat*, 8.
38 Atlantic Province's Economic Council, *Annual Report 1992*. In 1998 APEC's entire budget was $593,722.
39 Figures quoted in a press release, "Constitutional Conference Costs," issued by the Constitutional Conferences Secretariat.
40 Martha Hall Findlay is currently CEO and president of the Canada West Foundation.
41 For more on the handling of these conferences, see Lindquist, "Citizens, Experts and Budgets."
42 Ibid., 113.

CHAPTER EIGHT

1 For more on the relationship between presidents and prime ministers, see Martin, *The Presidents and the Prime Ministers*.

2 Harper's frustration with Obama over Keystone XL is covered by Ibbitson in *Stephen Harper.* Also see Harris, *Party of One.* For a full timeline of the Keystone XL Pipeline, see Global News, "A Timeline of Important Dates in Keystone XL Pipeline History," and CBC, "A Chronological History of Controversial Keystone XL Pipeline Project."
3 Several books and articles have been written on Canada-US relations. See Azzi, *Reconcilable Differences*; Bothwell, *Your Country, My Country*; Clarkson, *Canada and the Reagan Challenge*; and Anderson and Sands, *Forgotten Partnership Redux.*
4 Ibid.
5 See Alexandrov et al., "Request for Arbitration."
6 *Financial Post*, "Strong Case for US to Approve Keystone XL."
7 Egan, "Keystone XL pipeline." Also see Marsh and Isidore, "Keystone Pipeline: How Many Jobs."
8 Ibbitson, *Stephen Harper*, 336.
9 Mandel, "Obama Rejects Keystone XL."
10 McCarthy, "Harper Optimistic Keystone Pipeline Will Proceed after Obama Leaves Office."
11 For a discussion of the role of environmental groups during the NAFTA, see Abelson, "Environmental Lobbying," and Abelson and Lusztig, "The Consistency of Inconsistency."
12 Fontaine, "A Perilous Pipeline."
13 Ibid.
14 For example, the Canadian Centre for Policy Alternatives (CCPA) has maintained close ties to the NDP, while the Fraser Institute is often portrayed as a staunch ally of the Conservative Party and conservative ideology, a label to which the Fraser Institute's president, Neils Vedhuis, objects. He maintains that the institute's work is "not value-based, it's driven by data." See his comments in MacCharles, "Think-Tank Says It Was Targeted." Notwithstanding Veldhuis's remarks, Stephen Tapp of the Institute for Research on Public Policy (IRPP) has used data from Twitter to make a series of assumptions about the ideological orientation of several Canadian think tanks. See his blog, "What Can a Little Birdie (Twitter) Tell Us?"
15 On the role of think tanks in Germany, see Thunert, "Expert Policy Advice"; Braml, "Determinants of German Think Tanks"; and Pautz, *Think-Tanks, Social Democracy.*
16 For more on how the Ontario NDP government of Bob Rae relied on think tanks and other NGOs to mobilize opposition to the NAFTA, see Abelson, "Environmental Lobbying or Political Posturing?," and Abelson and Lusztig, "The Consistency of Inconsistency."
17 The phenomenon of growing apathy among voters in the United States is examined by Davidson in *Foreign Policy, Inc.* and by Putnam in *Bowling Alone.*

18 For a thorough discussion on the PATRIOT Act, see Crotty, *The Politics of Terror*; Brookings Institution, *Protecting the American Homeland: A Preliminary Analysis* and *Protecting the American Homeland: One Year On*; and Bremer and Meese, *Defending the American Homeland*. Many of the concerns raised by Americans regarding the extent to which the PATRIOT Act would encroach on civil liberties are similar to those being flagged by Canadians in reaction to the Canadian government's efforts to pass Bill C-51, commonly known as the "Anti-Terrorism Act." See an article by the Canadian Association of University Teachers (CAUT), entitled "Critics Fear Bill C-51." For a thoughtful exploration of the tension between national security and civil liberties, see Roach, *September 11: Consequences for Canada*.
19 See Abelson, *A Capitol Idea*, chapter 9.
20 See Edwards, *Leading the Way.*
21 Abelson, "Thinking Out Loud."
22 The Brookings Institution, the Heritage Foundation and CSIS, are among the handful of think tanks inside the Washington Beltway that have their own television and radio facilities.
23 Abelson, "Thinking Out Loud."
24 Abelson, "It Seemed Like a Good Idea."
25 According to the *Global Go To Think Tank Index Reports*, Chatham House consistently ranks among the world's top think tanks.
26 Personal correspondence with media relations personnel at Chatham House.
27 Comments made by Neils Veldhuis, president of the Fraser Institute at the 2014 Manning Networking Conference.
28 On the evolution of IRPP, see Ritchie, *An Institute for Research on Public Policy* and Dobell, *IRPP*. For a history of the Brookings Institution, see Critchlow, *The Brookings Institution.*
29 Parmar, *Foundations of the American Century.*
30 Lipton, Williams, and Confessore, "Foreign Powers Buy Influence at Think Tanks."
31 Talbott, "A Message from Strobe Talbott."
32 Abelson, *American Think Tanks*, 52–5.
33 McGann, *The Competition for Scholars.*
34 See Stone, *Banking on Knowledge.*
35 Krugel, "Report Says Pipeline Squeeze."
36 Ibid.
37 See Cleland et al., "A Matter of Trust."
38 See Abelson, "Environmental Lobbying and Political Posturing."
39 Green and Jackson, "Pipelines Are the Safest Way to Transport Oil and Gas"; and ""Pipelines Are Safer, Cheaper and Greener." Also see Hoberg, "The Battle Over Oil Sands Access to Tidewater."

40 Parkland Institute, home page, "About the Parkland Institute," www.parklandinstitute.ca.
41 Parkland Institute, "Self-Study," www.parklandinstitute.ca.
42 Pembina Institute, "About – Institute Story," www.pembina.org.
43 Ibid.
44 Ibid.
45 Ibid.
46 Halperin, "Keystone Pipeline Not a Big Deal."
47 McCarthy, "Influential US Think Tank."
48 Knappenberger, "Keystone XL Pipeline."
49 Most recently, Nebraska held hearings on Keystone XL beginning in August 2017 to, among other things, question representatives from TransCanada Corp about three specific concerns: the depth at which the pipeline going through Nebraska would be buried; the strategies in place to deal with potential spills and/or leaks; and whether TransCanada Corp or another entity would have the right to replace stretches of pipeline in the future, an economic benefit that could run into the billions. For a discussion of these and other concerns, as well as strategies to oppose the construction of the pipeline, see Sisson, "To Fight Keystone XL," and Slav, "Has Keystone XL Become Obsolete?"

CHAPTER NINE

1 See, for instance, Heclo, "Issue Networks."
2 Rich, "Perceptions of Think Tanks." A survey was sent to the heads of government departments in Canada as part of the Policy Research Initiative, but a more comprehensive survey has not yet been distributed.

APPENDIX ONE

1 Wall, *Andrew Carnegie*, 898.
2 Ibid.
3 For a history of the Hoover Institution see Duignan, *Hoover Institution*.
4 Mission statement of the Hoover Institution. Available on institute's home page at www.hoover.stanford.edu.
5 Quoted in "The Good Think-Tank Guide." Also see McGann, *2016 Global Go To Think Tank Index Report*.
6 Several studies have been written on the history of the Council on Foreign Relations. See, for example, Schulzinger, *Wise Men*; Shoup and Minter, *Imperial Brain Trust*; Silk and Silk, *American Establishment*; Perloff, *Shadows of Power*; Council on Foreign Relations, *Twenty-Five Years*; Grose, *The Inquiry*; Santoro, *Diffidence and Ambition*; and Wala, *Council on Foreign Relations*. For a conspiratorial interpretation of the role of the

CFR by members of the conservative John Birch Society, see Courtney and Courtney, *Council on Foreign Relations*.

7 Council on Foreign Relations home page at www.cfr.org.

8 CSIS mission statement. For a detailed history of the organization see Smith, *Strategic Calling*.

9 Abelson, *American Think Tanks*, 93.

10 Several articles have been written on the IPS. For example, see Muravchik, "Think-Tank of the Left"; Yoffe, "IPS Faces Life"; and Powell, *Covert Cadre*.

11 Dickson, *Think Tanks*, 222–3.

12 The Urban Institute, *Urban Institute*, 7.

13 Ibid., 9.

14 *Urban Institute 2015 Annual Report.*

15 The Urban Institute, *Urban Institute*, 7.

16 Ibid., 3.

17 Cato Institute home page, www.cato.org.

18 For more on the often stormy relationship between Charles Koch and the Cato Institute, see Mayer, *Dark Money*, and Schulman, *Sons of Wichita*.

19 *Cato Institute 2015 Annual Report.*

20 O'Connor and Cohn, "A Baby Boomers' Think Tank." For more on the Manhattan Institute's ties to Mayor Giuliani, see Scott, "Intellectuals."

21 Fialka, "Cato Institute's Influence Grows."

22 Friedman, "Institute Tied to Clinton."

23 Fineman, "Clinton's Team."

24 Balz, "Moderate, Conservative Democrats."

APPENDIX TWO

1 Asia-Pacific Foundation of Canada Act, R.S.C., 1985, C.A. 13.

2 Asia-Pacific Foundation of Canada home page, www.asiapacific.ca. Also see the *2014 Annual Report*.

3 Atlantic Institute for Market Studies, "Introduction," *1995–1996 Annual Report*.

4 Atlantic Institute for Market Studies, "President's Message," *1995–1996 Annual Report*.

5 Canada West Foundation, *1997 Annual Report*, 1.

6 Canada West Foundation, *2013 Annual Report*, 25.

7 Canada West Foundation, *1997 Annual Report*, 1.

8 Ibid.

9 Canada West Foundation, *2013 Annual Report*, 7.

10 Canadian Centre for Policy Alternatives, *Annual Report 2014*, 26.

11 Ibid.

12 Ibid., 42.

13 Ibid.
14 C.D. Howe home page, www.cdhowe.org.
15 Ibid.
16 Ibid. For a detailed discussion of the C.D. Howe Institute and its various incarnations, see Ernst, "From Liberal Continentalism."
17 C.D. Howe Institute, *2013 Annual Report*, 1.
18 In its *2013 Annual Report*, 33, C.D. Howe lists 7 fellows-in-residence; 49 senior fellows; 11 research fellows; and 12 international fellows.
19 Ibid.
20 C.D. Howe Institute, *2007 Annual Report.*
21 Ibid.
22 C.D. Howe Institute, *2013 Annual Report, 5.*
23 According to its *2014 Financial Statements*, CIGI had revenues in excess of $27 million and a long-term endowment valued over $55 million. Its revenues now exceed $40 million. See CIGI, *2014 Financial Statements* and its *2014 Annual Report.*
24 Valpy, "Balsillie's Disappointing Foray into Global Affairs."
25 CIGI website, www.cigionline.org.
26 Valpy, "Balsillie's Diappointing Foray into Global Affairs."
27 For more on this, see Hopper, "York University Rejects RIM Co-founder." Additional information on Balsillie's involvement in CIGI and the Balsillie School of International Affairs can be found in the Canadian Association for University Teachers, *Open for Business.*
28 Ibid.
29 Ibid.
30 Lindquist, "Behind the Myth," 347.
31 Ibid.
32 Ibid.
33 Ibid.
34 Conference Board of Canada, "About Us," home page, www.conferenceboard.ca.
35 Ibid.
36 Conference Board of Canada, *2014 Annual Report*, 4.
37 Ibid., 4–5.
38 Jérôme-Forget, "Institute for Research on Public Policy," 92. For more on the IRPP, see Dobell, *IRPP*, and Mackinnon, "The Canadian Think Tank Scene."
39 Ibid., 87.
40 Institute for Research on Public Policy, *2014 Annual Report*, 1.
41 Institute for Research on Public Policy, *2016 Annual Report.*
42 Macdonald-Laurier Institute for Public Policy, "Who We Are," home page, www.macdonaldlaurier.ca.
43 Ibid.

44 Macdonald-Laurier Institute for Public Policy, *2013 Annual Report*, 1.
45 McGann, *2017 Global Go To Think Tank Index Report.*
46 Macdonald-Laurier Institute for Public Policy, *2013 Annual Report*, 10–11.
47 Montreal Economic Institute, *2014 Annual Report*, 3.
48 Montreal Economic Institute, "About – Who We Are," home page, www.iedm.org.
49 Montreal Economic Institute, *2014 Annual Report*, 4.
50 Ibid., 5.
51 Montreal Economic Institute, *2016 Annual Report.*
52 Mowat Centre, *2014 Annual Report*, 1.
53 Ibid.
54 Mowat Centre, *2016 Annual Report.*
55 Public Policy Forum, "About" home page, www.ppforum.ca. The PPF has a second office in Toronto.
56 Ibid.
57 Ibid.
58 Abelson, *Northern Lights*, 262.
59 Ibid.
60 Ibid.

Bibliography

WORKS CITED

Abella, Alex. *Soldiers of Reason: The Rand Corporation and the Rise of the American Empire*. New York: Harcourt, Inc., 2008.

Abelson, Donald E. *American Think Tanks and their Role in US Foreign Policy*. London and New York: Macmillan and St Martin's Press, 1996.

– *A Capitol Idea: Think Tanks & US Foreign Policy*. Montreal & Kingston: McGill-Queen's University Press, 2006.

– "Changing Minds, Changing Course: Obama, Think Tanks and American Foreign Policy." In *Obama and the World: New Directions in US Foreign Policy*, 2nd ed., edited by Inderjeet Parmar, Linda B. Miller and Mark Ledwidge, 107–19. London: Routledge, 2014.

– "Do Think Tanks Matter? Opportunities, Incentives and Constraints for Think Tanks in Canada and the United States." *Global Society* 14, no. 2 (2000): 213–36.

– "Environmental Lobbying and Political Posturing: The Role of Environmental Groups in Ontario's Debate Over NAFTA." *Canadian Public Administration* 38, no. 3 (Fall 1995): 352–81.

– "From Policy Research to Political Advocacy: The Changing Role of Think Tanks in American Politics." *Canadian Review of American Studies* 25, no. 1 (1995): 93–126.

– "In Search of Policy Influence: The Strategies of American Think Tanks." *NIRA Review*, Spring 1998: 28–32.

– "It Seemed Like a Good Idea at the Time: Reflections on the Evolution of American Think Tanks." *Canadian Review of American Studies* 46, no. 1 (2016).

– "A New Channel of Influence: American Think Tanks and the News Media." *Queen's Quarterly* 99, no. 4 (1992): 849–72.

– *Northern Lights: Exploring Canada's Think Tank Landscape*. Montreal & Kingston: McGill-Queen's University Press, 2016.

– "Policy Experts and Political Pundits: American Think Tanks and the News Media." NIRA *Review*, Summer 1998: 40–3.

– "Public Visibility and Policy Relevance: Assessing the Impact and Influence of Canadian Policy Institutes." *Canadian Public Administration* 42, no. 2 (1999): 240–70.

– "Surveying the Think Tank Landscape in Canada." In *Public Administration and Policy: Governing in Challenging Times*, edited by Martin W. Westmacott and Hugh Mellon, 91–105. Scarborough, ON: Prentice-Hall, 1999.

– "Thinking Out Loud: Think Tanks and their Quest for Public Exposure." *Research Paper No. 2, The Canada-US Institute*. London, ON: The University of Western Ontario, 2012.

– "Think Tanks in the United States." In *Think Tanks across Nations: A Comparative Approach*, edited by Diane Stone, Andrew Denham, and Mark Garnett, 107–126. Manchester: Manchester University Press, 1998.

Abelson, Donald E., Stephen Brooks, and Xin Hua, eds. *Think Tanks, Foreign Policy and Geo-Politics*. London: Routledge, 2017.

Abelson, Donald E., and Christine M. Carberry. "Following Suit or Falling Behind? A Comparative Analysis of Think Tanks in Canada and the United States." *Canadian Journal of Political Science* 31, no. 3 (1998): 525–55.

– "Policy Experts in Presidential Campaigns: A Model of Think Tank Recruitment." *Presidential Studies Quarterly* 27, no. 4 (Fall 1997): 679–97.

Abelson, Donald E., and Evert A. Lindquist. "Think Tanks in North America." In *Think Tanks and Civil Societies: Catalyst for Ideas and Action*, edited by R. Kent Weaver and James G. McGann, 37–66. New Brunswick, NJ: Transaction Publishers, 2000.

– "Who's Thinking about International Affairs? The Evolution and Funding of Canada's Foreign and Defence Policy Think Tanks." Paper presented at the Annual Meetings of the Canadian Political Science Association, Ottawa, June 1998.

Abelson, Donald E., and Michael Lusztig. "The Consistency of Inconsistency: Tracing Ontario's Opposition to the North American Free Trade Agreement." *Canadian Journal of Political Science* 29, no. 4, December 1996, 681–98.

Achenbach, Joel. "Wonk If You Love Clinton." *Washington Post*, 8 November 1992.

Ackerman, S. "Obama's Pentagon-in-Waiting." *The Washington Independent*, 10 November 2008.

Alexandrov, Stanimir A., James E. Mendenhall, Jennifer Haworth McCandless, and Eric M. Solovy. "Request for Arbitration under the Convention on the Settlement of Investment Disputes Between States and Nationals of Other States and the Institution Rules and Arbitration Rules of the International

Centre for Settlement of Investment Disputes and Chapter 11 of the North American Free Trade Agreement." 24 June 2016.

Allen, Charles F., and Jonathan Portis. *The Comeback Kid: The Life and Career of Bill Clinton.* New York: Birch Lane Press, 1992.

Alterman, Eric. *Sound and Fury: The Washington Punditocracy and the Collapse of American Politics.* New York: Harper Collins, 1992.

Altman, Daniel. "Is Syria a Pay-to-Play Conflict?" *Foreign Policy*, 25 September 2014.

Anderson, George. "The New Focus on the Policy Capacity of the Federal Government." *Canadian Public Administration* 39, no. 4 (Winter 1996): 469–88.

Anderson, Greg, and Christopher Sands, eds. *Forgotten Partnership Redux: Canada-US Relations in the 21st Century.* Amherst, NY: Cambria Press, 2011.

Anderson, Martin. *Impostors in the Temple.* New York: Simon and Schuster, 1992.

– *Revolution.* New York: Harcourt Brace Jovanovich, 1988.

Associations Canada. *Associations Canada.* Toronto: Canadian Almanac and Directory Publishing Company, 1996, 1999.

– *Associations Canada 201, 38th edition.* Toronto: Grey House Publishing Canada, 2017.

Atlantic Institute for Market Studies. *1995–1996 Annual Report.* Halifax: Atlantic Institute for Market Studies, 1996.

Atlantic Province's Economic Council. *Annual Report 1992.* Halifax: Atlantic Province's Economic Council, 1992.

Atwood, Thomas C., and Thomas W. Mead. *The Directory of Public Policy Organizations 1998–1999.* Washington, DC: The Heritage Foundation, 1998.

Azzi, Stephen. *Reconcilable Differences: A History of Canada-US Relations.* Toronto: Oxford University Press, 2014.

Babington, Charles. "Bush Names Zoellick as Trade Representative." *Washington Post*, 10 January 2000.

Baer, Donald. "A Network for the Nineties: The Retreat That Spawned a Presidency." *US News & World Report*, 23 November 1992.

Baier, Gerald, and Herman Bakvis. "Think Tanks and Political Parties: Competitors or Collaborators?" *Isuma: Canadian Journal of Policy Research* 2, no. 1 (Spring 2001): 107–13.

Balan, Matthew. "Trump Thanks Jim DeMint over Gorsuch Fight amid Report He's Out at Heritage." *Mediaite*, 28 April 2017.

Balz, Dan. "Moderate, Conservative Democrats Buck 'Constraints,' Form Think Tank." *Washington Post*, 30 June 1989.

Bandow, Doug. "New Democrats Lose Think-Tank War." *Wall Street Journal*, 18 March 1993.

Barnes, Fred. "How Bush Decided on the Surge." *The Weekly Standard* 13, no. 20 (2008).

Barnes, James A. "Will DLC Be a Lobbying Heavyweight?" *National Journal*, 23 October 1993.

Baumgartner, Frank R., and Beth L. Leech. *Basic Interests: The Importance of Groups in Politics and in Political Science*. Princeton, NJ: Princeton University Press, 1998.

Beers, David. "Buttoned-Down Bohemians." *San Francisco Chronicle*, 3 August 1986.

Beigie, C.E. "Economic Policy Analysis: The Role of the C.D. Howe Research Institute." *Canadian Business Review* 39 (Summer 1974): 39–42.

Benko, Ralph. "Trump's Promise to Totally Destroy the 'Johnson Amendment' Is a Good One." *Forbes*, 20 March 2017.

Bentley, Arthur F. *The Process of Government*. Chicago: University of Chicago Press, 1908.

Berman, Edward H. *The Influence of the Carnegie, Ford and Rockefeller Foundations on American Foreign Policy: The Ideology of Philanthropy*. New York: State University of New York Press, 1983.

Bier, David. "Trump's Immigration Ban Is Illegal." *The New York Times*, 27 January 2017.

Bindman, Stephen. "Loss of a Legal Think-Tank." *Ottawa Citizen*, 11 March 1992.

Blumenthal, Sidney. *The Rise of the Counter-Establishment: From Conservative Ideology to Political Power*. New York: Harper and Row, 1988.

Bolton, Alexander. "DeMint Expected to Step Down as President of Heritage Foundation." *The Hill*, 28 April 2017.

Bothwell, Robert. *Your Country, My Country: A Unified History of the United States and Canada*. New York: Oxford University Press, 2015.

Brace, Paul, and Barbara Hinckley. *Follow the Leader: Opinion Polls and the Modern Presidents*. New York: Basic Books, 1992.

Bradford, Neil. *Commissioning Ideas: Canadian National Policy Innovation in Comparative Perspective*. Toronto: Oxford University Press, 1998.

Braml, Josef. "Determinants of German Think Tanks' Public Policy Roles." In *Policy Expertise in Contemporary Democracies*, edited by Stephen Brooks, Dorota Stasiak and Thomas Zyro. Aldershot: Ashgate, 2012.

– "Germany: The Think and the Tank." In *Think Tanks, Foreign Policy and Geo-Politics*, edited by Donald E. Abelson, Stephen Brooks, and Xin Hua, 101–18. London: Routledge, 2017.

Brean, Joseph. "York University Teaches Jim Balsillie Hard Lesson of Mixing Philanthropy with Public Academics." *National Post*, 13 April 2012.

Breland, Ali. "Google Faces Blowback after Think Tank Fires Critic." *The Hill*, 4 September 2017.

Bremmer, Robert H. *American Philanthropy.* Chicago: University of Chicago Press, 1988.

Brinkley, Douglas. "Jimmy Carter's Modest Quest for Global Peace." *Foreign Affairs* 74, no. 6 (November/December 1995): 90–100.

Brodie, Janine M., and Jane Jenson. *Crisis, Challenge, and Change: Party and Class in Canada.* Toronto: Methuen, 1980.

Brookings Institution. *Annual Report 2016.* Washington, DC: Brookings Institution, 2016.

– *2015 Annual Report.* Washington, DC: Brookings Institution, 2015.

– *Protecting the American Homeland: One Year on.* Washington, DC: Brookings Institution, 2003.

Brownstein, Ronald, and Nina Easton. *Reagan's Ruling Class: Portraits of the President's Top One Hundred Officials.* Washington, DC : Presidential Accountability Group, 1982.

Bruckner, Till. "Fund a Think Tank, Buy a Lobbyist?" *Huffington Post,* 10 September 2014.

Brummett, John. *High Wire: From the Backroads to the Beltway – The Education of Bill Clinton.* New York: Hyperion Press, 1994.

Bumiller, E. "Cast of 300 Advises Obama on Foreign Policy." *The New York Times,* 18 July 2008.

– "Research Groups Boom in Washington." *The New York Times,* 30 January 2008.

Bundale, Brett. "Professor Criticizes NS University for Awarding Billionaires Honorary Degrees." Canadian Press, 29 November 2017.

Burch, Philip H. *Research in Political Economy.* Supplement 1, *Reagan, Bush and Right-Wing Politics: Elites, Think Tanks, Power and Policy.* Greenwich, CT: Jai Press, 1997.

Butler, Stewart, M., Michael Sanera, and W. Bruce Weinrod, eds. *Mandate for Leadership II: Continuing the Conservative Revolution.* Washington, DC: Heritage Foundation, 1984.

Campbell, Colin. *Managing the Presidency: Carter, Reagan, and the Search for Executive Harmony.* Pittsburgh, PA: University of Pittsburgh Press, 1986.

Campbell, John L. "Institutional Analysis and the Role of Ideas in Political Economy." *Theory and Society* 27 (1998): 377–409.

Campbell, Murray. "Wonks." *The Globe and Mail,* 2 December 1995.

Canada West Foundation. *Annual Report 1997: 25 Years of Commitment to the West within a Strong Canada.* Calgary, AB: Canada West Foundation, 1997.

– *Conference Report: Renewal of Canada – Institutional Reform.* Calgary, AB: Canada West Foundation, 1992.

Canadian Association of University Teachers (CAUT). "Critics Fear Bill C-51 Could Limit Freedom of Speech on Campus." *CAUT Bulletin* 62, no. 3 (March 2015), 1.

– *Open for Business: On What Terms? An Analysis of 12 Collaborations between Canadian Universities and Corporations, Donors and Governments*. Ottawa: Canadian Association of University Teachers, 2013.
Canadian Centre for Philanthropy, www.ccp.ca.
Canadian Centre for Policy Alternatives, www.policyalternatives.ca.
Canadian Policy Research Networks, Inc. *Shared Responsibility: 1997–98 Annual Report*. Ottawa: CPRN, Inc., 1998.
Carter, Jimmy. *Keeping Faith: Memoirs of a President*. New York: Bantam, 1982.
– *Why Not the Best?* Nashville, TN: Broadman Press, 1975.
Cato Institute. *2015 Annual Report*. Washington, DC: Cato Institute, 2015.
CBC News. "A Chronological History of Controversial Keystone XL Pipeline Project." 24 January 2017.
C.D. Howe Institute. "A History of the Institute." C.D. Howe Institute, www.cdhowe.org.
– *2007 Annual Report*. Toronto: C.D. Howe Institute, 2007.
– *2013 Annual Report*. Toronto: C.D. Howe Institute, 2013.
– *2016 Annual Report*. Toronto: C.D Howe Institute, 2016.
Center for International Private Enterprise. "Think Tanks as Advocates of Change: An Interview with Phillip Truluck." *Economic Reform Today*, November 1996, 5–8.
Centre for International Governance Innovation. "Can Think Tanks Make a Difference?" *Conference Report*, 20 September 2011.
– *2014 Annual Report*. Waterloo: Centre for International Governance Innovation, 2014.
– *2014 Financial Statements*. Waterloo: Centre for International Governance Innovation, 2014.
Checkel, Jeffrey T. *Ideas and International Political Change*. New Haven, CT: Yale University Press, 1997.
Chisolm, Laura Brown. "Sinking the Think-Tanks Upstream: The Use and Misuse of Tax Exemption Law to Address the Use and Misuse of Tax-Exempt Organizations by Politicians." *University of Pittsburgh Law Review* 51, no. 3 (1990): 577–640.
Clarkson, Stephen. *Canada and the Reagan Challenge: Crisis and Adjustment, 1981–85*. Toronto: James Lorimer, 1985.
Cleland, Michael, Stephen Bird, Stewart Fast, Shefak Sajid, and Louis Simard. "A Matter of Trust: The Role of Communities in Energy Decision-Making." Calgary: The Canada West Foundation, 24 November 2016.
Clemmitt, Marcia. "Think Tanks in Transition: Do Their Donors Exert Too Much Influence." *CQ Researcher* 27, no. 34 (29 September 2017).
Coleman, William D., and Grace Skogstad, eds. *Public Policy and Policy Communities in Canada: A Structural Approach*. Toronto: Copp Clark Pitman, 1990.
Colvin, Jill. "Center for Security Policy, Think Tank behind Trump's Stats, Thinks Muslims Are Trying to Infiltrate US" *The Associated Press*, 9 December 2015.

Commission on US-Latin American Relations. *The Americas in a Changing World*. New York: Quadrangle and the Center for Inter-American Relations, 1975.
– *The United States and Latin America: Next Steps*. New York: Center for Inter-American Relations, 1976.
Conference Board of Canada. Home page, www.conferenceboard.ca.
–2014 *Annual Report*. Ottawa: Conference Board of Canada, 2014.
– "What's in It for You?" The Conference Board of Canada, www.conferenceboard.ca.
– "Who We Are: The Conference Board of Canada." Conference Board of Canada, www.conferenceboard.ca.
Constitutional Conferences Secretariat. "Constitutions Conference Costs." *Press Release*, 14 January 1992.
Cook, Nancy, Kenneth P. Vogel, and Eliana Johnson. "DeMint Set to Be Ousted from Heritage Foundation." *Politico*, 28 April 2017.
Council on Foreign Relations. *A Record of Twenty-Five Years*. New York: Council on Foreign Relations, 1947.
Courtney, Kent, and Phoebe Courtney. *The Council on Foreign Relations: America's Unelected Rulers*. New Orleans, LA: The Conservative Society of America, 1962.
Covington, Sally. *Moving a Public Policy: The Strategic Philanthropy of Conservative Foundations*. Washington, DC: National Committee for Responsive Philanthropy.
Craft, Jonathan. *Backrooms and Beyond: Partisan Advisers and the Politics of Policy Work in Canada*. Toronto: University of Toronto Press, 2016.
Cribb, Robert, and Marco Chown Oved. "Honorary Degrees for Brian Mulroney's Billionaire Friends Who Funded His St. F.X. Legacy Project." *Toronto Star*, 30 November 2017.
Critchlow, Donald T. *The Brookings Institution, 1916–52: Expertise and the Public Interest in a Democratic Society*. DeKalb, IL: Northern Illinois University Press, 1985.
Crotty, William J. *The Politics of Terror: The US Response to 9/11*. Boston: Northeastern University Press, 2004.
Crowley, Brian Lee. "How Can Think Tanks Win Friends and Influence People in the Media?" *Insider*, no. 264, October 1999.
Crowley, M. "The Shadow President." *The New Republic*, 19 November 2008.
Culleton Colwell, Mary Anna. *Private Foundations and Public Policy: The Political Role of Philanthropy*. New York: Garland, 1993.
Daalder, Ivo H., and James M. Lindsay. "Bush: Still Needs Work on Foreign Affairs." *Newsday*, 8 December 1999.
Dalby, Simon. *Creating the Second Cold War: The Discourse of Politics*. London: Pinter Publishers, 1990.
Davidson, Lawrence. *Foreign Policy, Inc.: Privatizing America's National Interest*. Lexington: The University Press of Kentucky, 2009.

Dawson, R. MacGregor. *The Government of Canada.* 5th ed. Toronto: University of Toronto Press, 1947.

Deace, Steve. "Ted Cruz Gets Heritage Foundation 'Endorsement." *The Washington Times*, 10 November 2015.

De La Mothe, John. "A Dollar Short and a Day Late: A Note on the Demise of the Science Council of Canada." *Queen's Quarterly* 99, no. 4 (1992): 873–86.

Demson, Sandra. *A Brief History of the Canadian Institute of International Affairs.* Toronto: Canadian Institute of International Affairs, 1995.

Denham, Andrew, and Mark Garnett. *British Think-Tanks and the Climate of Opinion.* London: UCL Press, 1998.

Department of Finance. *Supplementary Estimates (C), 1991–92, for the Fiscal Year Ending March 31, 1992.* Ottawa: Government of Canada, 1992.

– Umbrella Group on Policy Management. *Report from the Sub-group on Relations with the External Policy Research Community.* Ottawa: Department of Finance, July 1997.

Dickerson, John F. "Newt Inc." *Time*, 13 February 1995, 28.

Dickson, Paul. *Think Tanks.* New York: Atheneum, 1972.

Dobell, Peter. *IRPP: The First 30 Years.* Montreal: Institute for Research on Public Policy, 2002.

Dobuzinskis, Laurent. "Trends and Fashion in the Marketplace of Ideas." In *Policy Studies in Canada: The State of the Art*, edited by Laurent Dobuzinskis, Michael Howlett, and David Laycock, 91–124. Toronto: University of Toronto Press, 1996.

Docherty, David C. *Mr. Smith Goes to Ottawa: Life in the House of Commons.* Vancouver: UBC Press, 1997.

Dolny, Michael. "What's in a Label? Right-Wing Think Tanks Are Often Quoted, Rarely Labeled?" *Extra!* May/June 1998.

Domhoff, William G. *The Power Elite and the State: How Policy Is Made in America.* New York: Aldine de Gruyter, 1990.

Domhoff, William G., and Thomas R. Dye. *Power Elites and Organizations.* London: Sage, 1987.

Dowling, Deborah. "Closing Down the Economic Council," *Ottawa Citizen*, 10 March 1992.

Dreazen, Y.J. "Obama Dips into Think Tank for Talent." *Wall Street Journal*, 17 November 2008.

Drezner, Daniel W. *The Ideas Industry: How Pessimists, Partisans, and Plutocrats Are Transforming the Marketplace of Ideas.* New York: Oxford University Press, 2017.

Dubinsky, Zach. "New Mulroney Institute Is Bankrolled by Billionaires Steeped in Scandal." *CBC News*, 30 November 2017.

Duignan, Peter. *The Hoover Institution on War, Revolution and Peace: Seventy-Five Years of Its History.* Stanford, CA: Hoover Institution Press, 1989.

Duignan, Peter, and Alvin Rabushka, eds. *The United States in the 1980s.* Stanford, CA: Hoover Institution Press, 1980.

Dumain, Emma, and Caitlyn Byrd. "Jim DeMint Out as President of Heritage Foundation, According to Media Reports." http://www.postandcourier.com/politics/jim-demint.

Edwards, Lee. *Leading the Way: The Story of Ed Feulner and the Heritage Foundation.* New York Crown Forum, 2013.

– *The Power of Ideas: The Heritage Foundation at 25 Years.* Ottawa, IL: Jameson Books 1997.

Egan, Kelly. "Science Council Was Far Ahead of Its Time," *Ottawa Citizen,* 8 March 1992.

Egan, Matt. "Keystone XL Pipeline Would Only Create 35 Permanent Jobs." *CNN Money,* 24 March 2017.

Ernst, A. "From Liberal Continentalism to Neoconservatism: North American Free Trade and the Politics of the C.D. Howe Institute." *Studies in Political Economy* 39 (1992): 109–40.

Evans, Peter B., Dietrich Rueschemeyer, and Theda Skocpol. *Bringing the State Back In.* Cambridge: Cambridge University Press, 1985.

Federal-Provincial Relations Office. *Shaping Canada's Future Together.* Ottawa: Federal-Provincial Relations Office, 1991.

Fialka, John J. "Cato Institute's Influence Grows in Washington as Republican-Dominated Congress Sets Up Shop." *Wall Street Journal,* 14 December 1994.

Financial Post. "Strong Case for US to Approve Keystone XL: Harper." *Financial Post,* 27 June 2017.

Fineman, Howard. "Clinton's Team: The Inner Circles." *Newsweek,* 26 October 1994.

Fontaine, Tim. "'A Perilous Pipeline': Indigenous Groups Line Up Against Keystone XL." *CBC News,* 27 March 2017.

Fraser Institute. *Challenging Perceptions: Twenty-Five Years of Influential Ideas: A Retrospective, 1974–1999.* Vancouver: The Fraser Institute, 1999.

– *2007 Annual Report.* Vancouver: The Fraser Institute, 2008.

– *2015 Annual Report.* Vancouver: The Fraser Institute, 2016.

Freund, Gerald. *Narcissism and Philanthropy: Ideas and Talent Denied.* New York: Viking, 1996.

Friedman, Thomas L. "Institute Tied to Clinton Issues Policy Proposals." *The New York Times,* 7 December 1992.

Fuller, Matt. "Donald Trump and the Heritage Foundation: Friends with Benefits." *Huffington Post,* 10 August 2016.

Gairdner, William, ed. *After Liberalism: Essays in Search of Freedom, Virtue and Order.* Toronto: Stoddart, 1998.

Garekar, B. "The Gurus: With Foreign Policy Seen as a Key Campaign Issue, Barack Obama and John McCain Are Seeking Expert Advice Here." *The Strait Times,* 23 August 2008.

Gellner, Winand. "Think Tanks in Germany." In *Think Tanks across Nations*, edited by Diane Stone, Andrew Denham, and Mark Garnett, 82–106. Manchester: Manchester University Press, 1998.

– "Political Think-Tanks and Their Markets in the US: Institutional Setting." *Presidential Studies Quarterly* 25, no. 3 (Summer 1995): 497–510.

Germond, Jack W., and Jules Witcover. *Mad as Hell: Revolt at the Ballot Box, 1992*. New York: Warner Books, 1993.

Ghamari-Tabrizi, Sharon. *The Worlds of Herman Kahn: The Intuitive Science of Thermonuclear War.* Cambridge: Harvard University Press, 2005.

Gill, Stephen. *American Hegemony and the Trilateral Commission*. New York: Cambridge University Press, 1990.

Global News. "A Timeline of Important Dates in Keystone XL Pipeline History." 6 January 2016.

Goldman, Peter, Thomas M. De Frank, Mark Miller, Andrew Murr, and Tom Matthews. Quest for the Presidency, 1992. College Station, TX: Texas A&M University Press, 1994.

Goldstein, Judith, and Robert Keohane, eds. *Ideas and Foreign Policy: Beliefs, Institutions and Political Change*. Ithaca, NY: Cornell University Press, 1993.

– "The Good Think-Tank Guide." *Economist*, 21 December–3 January 1992, 49–53.

Gorman, Siobhan. "Bush's Lesson Plan." *National Journal* 31, no. 32 (7 August 1999): 2230–2.

Gray, Colin S. "Think Tanks and Public Policy." *International Journal* 33, no. 1 (Winter 1977–78): 177–94.

Greathead, E.D. "The Antecedents and Origins of the Canadian Institute of International Affairs." In *Empire and Nations: Essays in Honour of Frederic H. Soward*, edited by Harvey L. Dyck and Peter Krosby. Toronto and Vancouver: University of Toronto Press and University of British Columbia Press, 1969.

Green, Emma. "Trump Wants to Make Churches the New Super PACs." *The Atlantic*, 2 August 2016.

Green, Kenneth P., and Taylor Jackson. "Pipelines Are the Safest Way to Transport Oil and Gas." *National Post*, 7 June 2017.

– "Pipelines Are Safer, Cheaper and Greener." *Fraser Forum*, 6 October 2015.

Greenberger, Scott S. "Campaign 2000: Bush's 'Wonks' Sweat Details of His Principles: The Road to the White House." *Atlanta Journal and Constitution*, 6 August 1999.

Greenspan, Edward, and Anthony Wilson-Smith. *Double-Vision: The Inside Story of the Liberals in Power*. Toronto: Doubleday, 1996.

Grim, Ryan. "Gulf Government Gave Secret $20 Million Gift to D.C. Think Tank." *The Intercept*, 9 August 2017.

Grose, Peter. *The Inquiry: The Council on Foreign Relations from 1921 to 1996*. New York: Council on Foreign Relations, 1996.

Grove, Lloyd. "Steering His Party toward the Center." *Washington Post*, 24 July 1992.

Gunter, Joel. "Trump's 'Muslim lockdown': What Is the Center for Security Policy?" BBC *News*, 8 December 2016.

Gutstein, Donald. *Harperism: How Stephen Harper and His Think Tank Colleagues Have Transformed Canada*. Toronto: James Lorimer & Company, 2014.

Guy, John James. *People, Politics and Government*. 3d ed. Scarborough, ON: Prentice-Hall, 1995.

Haas, Peter M., ed. *Knowledge, Power and International Policy Coordination*. Columbia, SC: University of South Carolina Press, 1997.

Hagedorn, Hermann. *Brookings: A Biography*. New York: Macmillan, 1936.

Hager, George. "Bush Shops for Advice at California Think Tank: Ex-White House Stars Fill." *Washington Post*, 8 June 1999.

Halperin, David. "Keystone Pipeline Not a Big Deal – Say Interests Supported by Oil and Gas Industry." *Grist*, 13 May 2103.

Harris, Michael. *Party of One: Stephen Harper and Canada's Radical Makeover*. Toronto: Viking, 2014.

Harrison, Kathryn, and George Hoberg. "Setting the Environmental Agenda in Canada and the United States: The Cases of Dioxin and Radon." *Canadian Journal of Political Science* 24, no. 1 (1991): 3–27.

Harrison, Peter. *The Constitutional Conferences Secretariat: A Unique Response to a Public Management Challenge*. Ottawa: Canadian Centre for Management Development, 1992.

Hart, John. "The Political Assassination of the Heritage Foundation's Jim DeMint." *Forbes*, 30 April 2017.

Hay, John. "Letting CIIPS Fall Where It May Has Nothing to Do with Saving Money." *Ottawa Citizen*, 30 March 1992.

Healy, Patrick, and Sara Hebel. "Academics Start to Line Up behind Presidential Candidates." *Chronicle of Higher Education*, 28 May 1999.

Heatherly, Charles L., ed. *Mandate for Leadership: Policy Management in a Conservative Administration*. Washington, DC: The Heritage Foundation, 1981.

Heatherly, Charles L., and Burton Yale Pines, eds., *Mandate for Leadership III: Policy Strategies for the 1990s*. Washington, DC: The Heritage Foundation, 1989.

Heclo, Hugh. "Issue Networks and the Executive Establishment." In *The New American Political System*, edited by Anthony King. Washington, DC: The American Enterprise Institute, 1978.

Hellebust, Lynn, ed. *Think Tank Directory: A Guide to Nonprofit Public Policy Research Organizations*. Topeka, KS: Government Research Service, 1996.

Heritage Foundation. *1998 Annual Report*. Washington, DC: The Heritage Foundation, 1998.

– *2008 Annual Report*. Washington, DC: The Heritage Foundation, 2008.
– *2015 Annual Report*. Washington, DC: The Heritage Foundation, 2015.
– *Blueprint for Reform: A Comprehensive Policy Agenda for a New Administration in 2017*. Washington, DC: The Heritage Foundation, 2016.
– "Donald Trump Turns to Heritage for Policy Guidance," www.heritage.org, 24 March 2017.

Hess, Stephen. *Organizing the Presidency*. Washington, DC: Brookings Institution, 1988.

Higgott, Richard, and Diane Stone. "The Limits of Influence: Foreign Policy Think Tanks in Britain and the USA." *Review of International Studies* 20 (1994): 15–34.

Higgott, Richard, and Ivona Malbasic, eds. *The Political Consequences of Anti-Americanism*. London: Routledge, 2008.

Hinckley, Barbara. *Less than Meets the Eye: Foreign Policy Making and the Myth of the Assertive Congress*. Chicago: University of Chicago Press, 1994.

Hoberg, George. "The Battle over Oil Sands Access to Tidewater: A Political Risk Analysis of Pipeline Alternatives." *Canadian Public Policy* 39, no. 3 (2013): 371–91.

Hohenberg, John. *The Bill Clinton Story: Winning the Presidency*. Syracuse, NY: Syracuse University Press, 1994.

Holmes, John. "The CIIA: A Canadian Institution." *Bout de Papier* 7, no. 4 (1990): 9–10.

Holwill, Richard N. *Agenda '83: A Mandate for Leadership Report*. Washington, DC: Heritage Foundation, 1983.

Hopper, Tristin. "York University Rejects RIM Co-founder Jim Balisillie's $60 Million Deal." *National Post*, 3 April 2012.

House Policy Committee. "Congressional Policy Advisory Board Meets with House Leadership." House Policy Committee website (policy.house.gov/news/releases/1998).

Hua, Xin. "Chinese Think Tanks' Influence on Foreign-Policy-Making: A Case Study of the Role of CIIS and SIIS in the Making of China's Europe Policy." In *Think Tanks, Foreign Policy and Geo-Politics*, edited by Donald E. Abelson, Stephen Brooks, and Xin Hua, 132–53. London: Routledge, 2017.

Ibbitson, John. *Stephen Harper*. Toronto: McClelland & Stewart, 2015.

Institute for Research on Public Policy (IRPP). *2013–2014 Annual Report*. Montreal: IRPP, 2014.
– *2016 Annual Report*. Montreal: IRPP, 2016.

Internal Revenue Code of 1986: 1077–96.

Ivins, Molly, and Lou Dubose. *Shrub: The Short but Happy Political Life of George W. Bush*. New York: Random House, 2000.

Jehl, Douglas. "Clinton, Others Begin 5-Day 'Thinking Party.'" *Los Angeles Times*, 30 December 1992.

Jenson, Jane. "Commissioning Ideas: Representation and Royal Commissions." In *How Ottawa Spends: Making Change*, edited by Susan D. Phillips, 39–71. Ottawa: Carleton University Press, 1994.

Jérôme-Forget, Monique. "Institute for Research on Public Policy." In *Think Tanks and Civil Societies: Catalysts for Ideas and Actions*, edited by R. Kent Weaver and James McGann, 87–102. New Brunswick, NJ: Transaction Publishers, 2000.

Judis, John B. "The Japanese Megaphone: Foreign Influences on Foreign Policymaking." *The Domestic Sources of Foreign Policy: Insights and Evidence*, 2nd ed., edited by Eugene R. Wittkopf, 95–106. New York: St Martin's Press, 1994.

– "Taking Care of Business." *New Republic*, 19 August 1999: 24–31.

Kaiser, Robert G., and Ira Chinoy. "How Scaife's Money Powered a Movement." *Washington Post*, 2 May 1999.

Kaplan, Fred. *The Wizards of Armageddon*. New York: Simon and Schuster, 1985.

Kessler, Glenn. "Economic Adviser Has Knack for Translating Tough Issues." *Washington Post*, 4 January 2001.

Kingdon, John W. *Agendas, Alternatives and Public Policies*. New York: HarperCollins, 1984.

Kitfield, James. "Periphery Is Out: Russia and China, In." *National Journal* 31, no. 32 (7 August 1999): 2293.

Kitschelt, Herbert P. "Political Opportunity Structures and Political Protest: Anti-Nuclear Movements in Four Democracies." *British Journal of Political Science* 16 (1986): 57–85.

Knappenberger, Paul C. "Keystone XL Pipeline: Examination of Scientific and Environmental Issues." Testimony Before US House of Representatives Committee on Science, Space, and Technology Subcommittee on Energy and Subcommittee on the Environment, US House of Representatives, 7 May 2103.

Knickerbocker, Brad. "Heritage Foundation's Ideas Permeate Reagan Administration." *Christian Science Monitor*, 7 December 1984.

Kolakowski, Leszek. *Main Currents of Marxism: The Founders-The Breakdown-The Golden Age*. New York: W.W. Norton, 2007.

Kopan, Tal. "Meet Donald Trump's Think Tank." CNN *Politics*, 7 December 2016.

Krasner, Stephen D. *Defending the National Interest: Raw Material Investment and US Foreign Policy*. Princeton: Princeton University Press, 1978.

Kriesi, Hanspeter, Rudd Koopmans, Jan Willem Duyvendak, and Marco G. Guigni. "New Social Movements and Political Opportunities in Western Europe." *European Journal of Political Research* 22 (1992): 219–44.

Kristol, William, and Robert Kagan. "Toward a Neo-Reaganite Foreign Policy." *Foreign Affairs* 75, no. 4 (July/August 1996): 18–32.

Kroeger, Arthur. "The Constitutional Conferences of January-March 1992: A View from Within." Speech to the Institute of Public Administration of Canada, University of Victoria Conference, 23 April 1992.

Krugel, Lauren. "Report Says Pipeline Squeeze Could Be 'Devastating' to Canadian Economy." *The Globe and Mail*, 7 February 2013.

Landers, Robert K. "Think-Tanks: The New Partisans?" *Congressional Quarterly* 1, no. 23 (20 June 1986): 455–72.

Langford, John W., and K. Lorne Brownsey, eds. *Think Tanks and Governance in the Asia-Pacific Region*. Halifax: Institute for Research on Public Policy, 1991.

Lee, Steven. "Beyond Consultations: Public Consultations to Making Foreign Policy." In *Canada among Nations 1998: Leadership and Dialogue*, edited by Fen Osler Hampson and Maureen Appel Molot, 55–67. Toronto: Oxford University Press, 1998.

Linden, Patricia. "Powerhouses of Policy: A Guide to America's Think-Tanks." *Town and Country*, January 1987.

Lindquist, Evert A. *Behind the Myth of Think-Tanks: The Organization and Relevance of Canadian Policy Institutes*. PhD dissertation, University of California at Berkeley, 1989.

– "Transition Teams and Government Succession: Focusing on the Essentials." *Taking Power: Managing Government Transitions*, edited by Donald J. Savoie, Toronto: Institute of Public Administration of Canada, 1993.

– "Think Tanks or Clubs? Assessing the Influence and Roles of Canadian Policy Institutes." *Canadian Public Administration* 36, no. 4 (1993): 547–79.

– "Citizens, Experts and Budgets: Evaluating Ottawa's Emerging Budget Process." In *How Ottawa Spends 1994–95*, edited by Susan D. Phillips, 91–128. Ottawa: Carleton University Press, 1994.

– "A Quarter-Century of Think Tanks in Canada." In *Think Tanks across Nations: A Comparative Approach*, edited by Diane Stone, Andrew Denham, and Mark Garnett, 127–44. Manchester: Manchester University Press, 1998.

Link, Taylor. "Richard Spencer's Non-Profit, Pro-Hate NPI Lost Its Tax-Exempt Status." *Salon*, 14 March 2017.

Lipset, Seymour Martin. "Canada and the US: The Cultural Dimension." In *Canada and the United States*, edited by Charles F. Doran and John H. Sigler. Englewood Cliffs, NJ: Prentice-Hall, 1985.

– *Continental Divide*. New York: Routledge, 1990.

Lipton, Eric, Brooke Williams, and Nicholas Confessore. "Foreign Powers Buy Influence at Think Tanks." *The New York Times*, 6 September 2014.

Lorinc, John. "Hold the Fries and the Social Programmes." *Saturday Night*, March 1994, 11–15, 61.

MacCharles, Tonda. "Think-Tank Says It Was Targeted with Tax Audit Because of Its Politics." *Toronto Star*, 5 September 2014.

Macdonald-Laurier Institute. Home page, www.macdonaldlaurier.ca.
– *2013 Annual Report*. Ottawa: Macdonald-Laurier Institute, 2013.
Mackenzie Institute. "Mission and Description,"www.mackenzieinstitute.com.
Mackinnon, Janice. "The Canadian Think Tank Scene: An Insider's Perspective." In *Policy Expertise in Contemporary Democracies*, edited by Stephen Brooks, Dorota Stasiak and Thomas Zyro. Aldershot: Ashgate, 2012.
Maggs, John. "Tax Cuts, Big and Small." *National Journal* 31, no. 32 (7 August 1999): 2236.
Mandel, Charles. "Obama Rejects Keystone XL." *National Observer*, 6 November 2015.
Manley, John F., and Ronald A. Rebholz. "Questioning University's Relationship to Hoover Institution." *Standard [online] Report*, April 1999.
Mann, J. *Rise of the Vulcans: The History of Bush's War Cabinet*. New York: Viking, 2004.
Manny, Carter. "The CIIA, 1928–1939." BA thesis, Harvard University, 1971.
Maraniss, David. "A Weekend with Bill and Friends, Hilton Head's New Year's Tradition: Name Tags, Networking and Talk, Talk, Talk." *Washington Post*, 30 December 1992.
– "Letter from Never-Never Land: Epiphany and Elbow Rubbing at the Renaissance Weekend." *Washington Post*, 2 January 1993.
– *First in His Class: A Biography of Bill Clinton*. New York: Simon and Schuster, 1995.
Marsh, Rene and Chris Isidore. "Keystone Pipeline: How Many Jobs It Would Really Create." *CNN Money*, 28 January 2017.
Marshall, Will, and Martin Schram. *Mandate for Change*. New York: Berkeley Books, 1993.
Martin, Lawrence. *The Presidents and the Prime Ministers: Washington and Ottawa Face to Face: The Myth of Bilateral Bliss, 1867–1982*. Toronto; Doubleday Canada, 1982.
Matthews, Dylan. "Marco Rubio Says He'd Cut Taxes on the Poor More than the Rich. Nonesense." *Vox*, 3 November 2015.
Mayer, Jane. *Dark Money: The Hidden History of the Billionaires Behind the Rise of the Radical Right*. New York: Doubleday, 2016.
McCarthy, Shawn. "Influential US Think Tank Urges Obama to Reject Keystone XL." *The Globe and Mail*, 10 March 2014.
– "Harper Optimistic Keystone Pipeline Will Proceed after Obama Leaves Office." *The Globe and Mail*, 29 July 2015.
McCombs, Phil. "Building a Heritage in the War of Ideas." *Washington Post*, 3 October 1983.
McGann, James G. "Academics to Ideologues: A Brief History of the Public Policy Research Industry." *PS: Political Science and Politics* 24, no. 4 (December 1992): 739–40.

– *The Competition for Dollars, Scholars and Influence in the Public Policy Research Industry.* Lanham, MD: University Press of America, 1995.
– *Think Tanks, Catalysts for Ideas in Action: An International Survey.* Tokyo: National Institute for Research Advancement, 1999.
– *Think Tanks and Policy Advice in the United States.* London: Routledge, 2007.
– "The Think Tank Index." *Foreign Policy,* January/February 2009.
– *2017 Global Go To Think Tank Index Report.* Philadelphia: Think Tanks and Civil Societies Program, University of Pennsylvania, 2017.
– *2016 Global Go To Think Tank Index Report.* Philadelphia: Think Tanks and Civil Societies Program, University of Pennsylvania, 2016.
– *2014 Global Go To Think Tank Index Report.* Philadelphia: Think Tanks and Civil Societies Program, University of Pennsylvania, 2014.
– *The Fifth Estate: Think Tanks, Public Policy and Governance.* Washington, DC: Brookings Institution Press, 2016.

McGann, James G., and R. Kent Weaver. *Think Tanks and Civil Societies: Catalysts for Ideas and Action.* New Brunswick, NJ: Transaction Publishers, 2000.

MacDonald, Lawrence, and Todd Moss. "Building a Think-and-Do Tank." *Stanford Social Innovation Review,* 11 July 2014.

Mearsheimer, John J. and Stephen M. Walt. *The Israel Lobby and US Foreign Policy.* New York: Farrar, Straus and Giroux, 2007.

Medvetz, Thomas. *Think Tanks in America.* Chicago: University of Chicago Press, 2012.

Meese, Edwin III. *The Transition to a New Administration.* Stanford, CT: Hoover Institution, 1981.
– *With Reagan: The Inside Story.* Washington, DC: Regnery Gateway, 1992.

Melton, R.H. "Closing of Dole's Think Tank Raises Questions about Fund-Raising." *Washington Post,* 18 June 1995.

Menges, Constantine C. *Inside the National Security Council.* New York: Simon and Schuster, 1988.

Mendizabal, Enrique. "Think Tank Accountability: Are They Really Just Hired Guns?" *On Think Tanks,* 10 September 2014. Available at http://onthinktanks.org.

Merelman, R.M. *Partial Visions.* Madison, WI: University of Wisconsin Press, 1991.

Mills. C. Wright. *The Power Elite:* New York: Oxford University Press, 1956.

Milne, David. "Innovative Constitutional Processes: Renewal of Canada Conferences, January-March 1992." In *Canada: The State of the Federation, 1992,* edited by Douglas Brown and Robert Young, 27–51. Kingston, ON: Institute of Intergovernmental Relations, 1992.

Minutaglio, Bill. *First Son: George W. Bush and the Bush Family Dynasty.* New York: Time Books, 1999.

Mitchell, Elizabeth. *W: Revenge of the Bush Dynasty.* New York: Hyperion Press, 2000.

Montreal Economic Institute. Home page, www.iedm.org.

– *2014 Annual Report.* Montreal: Montreal Economic Institute, 2014.

– *2016 Annual Report.* Montreal: Montreal Economic Institute, 2016.

Moore, Jim, and Rick Ihde. *Clinton: Young Man in a Hurry.* Fort Worth, TX: Summit Publishing Group, 1992.

Moore, W. John. "Local Right Thinkers." *National Journal*, 1 October 1988.

Morgan, Frank B., ed. US *Department of Education, Degrees and Other Formal Awards Conferred, 1944–95.* Washington, DC: Government Printing Office, 1996.

Morin, Richard, and Claudia Deane. "The Ideas Industry," *Washington Post*, 7 December 1999.

– "The Ideas Industry," *Washington Post*, 8 June 1999.

– "The Ideas Industry: Brookings Aims to Bridge La Difference." *Washington Post,* 17 August 1999.

Mowat Centre. *2014 Annual Report.* Toronto: Mowat Centre, 2014.

– *2016 Annual Report.* Toronto: Mowat Centre, 2016.

Mulé, Nick J., and Gloria C. DeSantis, eds. *The Shifting Terrain: Non-profit Political Advocacy in Canada.* Montreal & Kingston: McGill-Queen's University Press, 2017.

Mowat Centre. *2014 Annual Report.* Toronto: Mowat Centre. *2016 Annual Report.* Toronto: Mowat Centre.

Mufson, Steven. "For Rice, a Daunting Challenge Ahead." *Washington Post*, 18 December 2000.

Muravchik, Joshua. "The Think-Tank of the Left." *The New York Times Magazine*, 27 April 1987.

Murray, S., and C.D. Leonnig. "Obama Teams are Scrutinizing Federal Agencies; Smooth Transition Is Goal." *The Washington Post*, 3 December 2008.

National Committee for Responsive Philanthropy. *$1 Billion for Ideas: Conservative Think Tanks in the 1990s.* Washington, DC: National Committee for Responsive Philanthropy, 1999.

– *Moving a Public Policy: The Strategic Philanthropy of Conservative Foundations.* Washington, DC: National Committee for Responsive Philanthropy, 1997.

National Institute for Research Advancement. *The World Directory of Think Tanks, 1998.* Tokyo: NIRA, 1998.

National Science Foundation. "2014 Doctorate Recipients for US Universities." Arlington, VA: National Science Foundation, December 2015.

Newsom, David D. *The Public Dimension of Foreign Policy.* Bloomington, IN: Indiana University Press, 1996.

Niagara Institute, www.niagarainstitute.com.

North-South Institute. *The North South Institute.* Ottawa: North-South Institute, 1997.

– *Prospectus*. Ottawa: North-South Institute, 1976.

Nossal, Kim Richard. *The Politics of Canadian Foreign Policy*. 3d ed. Scarborough, ON: Prentice-Hall, 1997.

Nye, J.S. "Scholars on the Sidelines." *The Washington Post*, 13 April 2009.

O'Connell, Brian, ed. *America's Voluntary Spirit*. New York: The Foundation Center, 1983.

O'Connor, Colleen, and Bob Cohn. "A Baby Boomer's Think Tank." *Newsweek*, 1 September 1986.

Omang, Joanne. "The Heritage Report: Getting the Government Right with Reagan." *Washington Post*, 16 November 1980.

Orlans, Harold. *The Nonprofit Research Institute: Its Origin, Operation, Problems and Prospects*. New York: McGraw-Hill, 1972.

Osendarp, J.E. "A Decade of Transition: The Canadian Institute of International Affairs, 1928–1939." MA thesis, York University, 1983.

Pal, Leslie A. *Public Policy Analysis: An Introduction*. Toronto: Methuen Press 1987.

Pal, Leslie A., and R. Kent Weaver (eds). *The Government Taketh Away: The Politics of Pain in the United States and Canada*. Washington, DC: Georgetown University Press, 2003.

Parkland Institute. Homepage (ww.parklandinstitute.ca).

Parmar, Inderjeet. *Foundations of the American Century: The Ford, Carnegie, and Rockefeller Foundations in the rise of American power*. New York: Columbia University Press, 2012.

Pastor, Robert A. "The Carter Administration and Latin America: A Test of Principle." In *United States Policy in Latin America: A Quarter Century of Crisis and Challenge*, edited by John D. Martz, 62–5. Lincoln, NE: University of Nebraska Press, 1988.

Pautz, Hartwig. *Think Tanks, Social Democracy and Social Policy*. Basingstoke: Palgrave Macmillan, 2012.

Pecquet, Julian. "Gulf-Funded Think Tank to Make Capitol Hill Debut." *Al-Monitor*, 5 October 2015.

Pembina Institute. Homepage, www.pembina.org.

Perloff, James. *The Shadows of Power: The Council on Foreign Relations and the American Decline*. Appleton, WI: Western Islands, 1988.

Peschek, Joseph G. *Policy Planning Organizations: Elite Agendas and America's Rightward Turn*. Philadelphia, PA: Temple University Press, 1987.

Peters, Jeremy W. "The Johnson Amendment Which Trump Vows to 'Destroy' Explained." *The New York Times*, 2 February 2017.

Peters, Jeremy W., and Maggie Haberman. "Jim DeMint Is Said to Be Out at Heritage Foundation." *The New York Times*, 28 April 2017.

Pincus, W. "'Experts' Report Urges Changes in National Security System." *The Washington Post*, 4 December 2008.

Powell, S. Steven. *Covert Cadre: Inside the Institute for Policy Studies.* Ottawa, IL: Green Hill Publishers, 1988.

President Clinton's New Beginning. New York: Donald I. Fine Inc., 1992.

President of the Privy Council and Minister Responsible for Constitutional Affairs. *News Release*, 2 December 1991.

Presthus, Robert, ed. *Cross-National Perspectives.* Leiden: E.J. Brill, 1977.

Pross, A. Paul. *Group Politics and Public Policy.* Toronto: Oxford University Press, 1992.

Public Policy Forum. Home page, www.ppforum.com.

– "History of the Forum," www.ppforum.com.

Putnam, Robert D. *Bowling Alone: The Collapse and Revival of American Community.* New York: Simon and Schuster, 2001.

RAND. *An Introduction to RAND: The Reach of Reason.* Santa Monica, CA: RAND, 1999.

Reagan, Ronald. *An American Life.* New York: Simon and Schuster, 1990.

Redburn, Tom. "Conservative Thinkers Are Insiders." *The New York Times*, 31 December 1993.

Regan, Mary Beth. "A Think Tank with One Idea: The Newt World Order." *Business Week*, 3 July 1995.

Rich, Andrew. "Perceptions of Think Tanks in American Politics: A Survey of Congressional Staff and Journalists." *Burson-Marstellar Worldwide Report*, December 1997.

– "Think Tanks as Sources of Expertise for Congress and the Media." Paper presented at the annual meetings of the American Political Science Association, Boston, September 1998.

Rich, Andrew, and R. Kent Weaver. "Think Tanks, the Media and the Policy Process." Paper presented at the 1997 annual meetings of the American Political Science Association, Washington, DC, August 1997.

– "Advocates and Analysts: Think Tanks and the Politicization of Expertise." In *Interest Groups Politics*, 3rd ed., edited by Allan J. Cigler and Burdett A. Loomis. Washington, DC: CQ Press, 1998.

Richardson, Theresa, and Donald Fisher, eds. *The Development of the Social Sciences in the United States and Canada: The Role of Philanthropy.* Stanford, CA: Ablex Publishing Corporation, 1999.

Ritchie, R.S. *An Institute for Research on Public Policy: A Study of Recommendations.* Ottawa: Information Canada, 1971.

Roach, Kent. *September 11; Consequences for Canada.* Montreal & Kingston: McGill-Queens University Press, 2003.

Robinson, William H. "Public Think-Tanks in the United States: The Special Case of Legislative Support Agencies." Paper presented at the conference Think Tanks in the USA and Germany, University of Pennsylvania, Philadelphia, 1993.

Rogin, Josh. "Trump Could Cause 'The Death of Think Tanks as We Know Them.'" *Jewish World Review*, 17 January 2017.

Rosen, Christine. "The Do-Not-Think Tank: Google and Other Big Tech Companies Are a Growing Threat to Open Discourse." *The Weekly Standard*, 18 September 2017.

Rosenbaum, David E. "Torrent of Free Advice Flows into Little Rock." *The New York Times*, 15 November 1992.

Ross, Dorothy. *The Origins of American Social Science*. New York: Cambridge University Press, 1992.

Rushe, Dominic. "Google-Funded Think Tank Fired Scholar over Criticism of Tech Firm." *Guardian*, 30 August 2017.

Russell, Peter H. *Constitutional Odyssey: Can Canadians Become Sovereign People?* Toronto: University of Toronto Press, 1993.

Russo, Robert. "Bush Battling Questions of Brain Power." *London Free Press*, 13 December 1999.

Saloma, John S. *Ominous Politics: The New Conservative Labyrinth*. New York: Hill and Wang, 1984.

Samaan, Jean-Loup. *The Rand Corporation (1989–2009): The Reconfiguration of Strategic Studies in the United States*. Basingstoke: Palgrave Macmillan, 2012.

Sanders, Jerry W. *Peddlers of Crisis: The Committee on the Present Danger and the Politics of Containment*. Boston: South End Press, 1983.

Santoro, Carlo Maria. *Diffidence and Ambition: The Intellectual Sources of US Foreign Policy*. Boulder, CO: Westview Press, 1992.

Saunders, Charles B. *The Brookings Institution: A Fifty Year History*. Washington, DC: Brookings Institution, 1966.

Saunders, Thomas A. "Leadership Changes at Heritage." Email sent to Heritage subscribers, 2 May 2017.

Savage, C. "Shepherd of a Government in Exile." *The New York Times*, 7 November 2008.

Schlesinger, Arthur Meier. *The Imperial Presidency*. Boston: Houghton Mifflin, 1989.

Schmitt, Eric. "A Cadre of Familiar Foreign Policy Experts Is Putting Its Imprint on Bush." *The New York Times*, 23 December 1999.

Schneider, Mark, and Paul Teske. "Toward a Theory of the Political Entrepreneur: Evidence from Local Government." *American Political Science Review* 86 (1992): 737–47.

Schram, Martin. *Running for President: A Journal of the Carter Campaign*. New York: Pocket Books, 1978.

Schulman, Daniel. *Sons of Wichita: How the Koch Brothers Became America's Most Powerful and Private Dynasty*. New York: Grand Central Publishing, 2014.

Schulzinger, Robert D. *The Wise Men of Foreign Affairs: The History of the Council on Foreign Relations*. New York: Columbia University Press, 1984.

Scott, Janny. "Intellectuals Who Became Influential: The Manhattan Institute Has Nudged New York to the Right." *The New York Times*, 12 May 1997.

Sealander, Judith. *Private Wealth and Public Life: Foundation Philanthropy and the Reshaping of American Social Policy From the Progressive Era to the New Deal*. Baltimore, MD: Johns Hopkins University Press, 1997.

Shephard, Alex. "The D.C. Think Tank Behind Donald Trump." *New Republic*, 22 February 2017.

Shimshock, Rob. "Cruz, Rubio, Paul Team Up to Save Heritage Foundation Head." *Daily Caller*, 1 May 2017.

Shoup, Laurence H. *The Carter Presidency and Beyond: Power and Politics in the 1980s*. Palo Alto, CA: Ramparts Press, 1980.

– *Wall Street's Think Tank: The Council on Foreign Relations and the Empire of Neoliberal Geopolitics, 1976–2014*. New York: Monthly Review Press, 2015.

Shoup, Laurence H., and William Minter. *Imperial Brain Trust: The Council of Foreign Relations and the United States Foreign Policy*. New York: Monthly Review Press, 1977.

Silk, Leonard, and Mark Silk. *The American Establishment*. New York: Basic Books, 1980.

Silverstein, Ken. "Pay to Play Think Tanks: Institutional Corruption and the Industry of Ideas." 15 June 2014. www.ethics.harvard.edu.

Simpson, Glenn R. "New Addition to Gingrich Family Tree: The Progress and Freedom Foundation." *Roll Call*, 12 September 1994.

Sisson, Patrick. "To Fight Keystone XL Pipeline, Activists Placing Solar Panels in Its Path." *Curbed*, 11 July 2017.

Sklar, Holly, ed. *Trilateralism: The Trilateral Commission and Elite Planning for World Management*. Boston: South End Press, 1980.

Slav, Irina. "Has Keystone XL Become Obsolete?" *Oil Price*, 3 July 2017.

Smith, Andrew. "Why Marco Rubio Might Be the GOP's Long Awaited Candidate of Ideas." *National Review*, 4 February 2015.

Smith, Bruce L.R. *The RAND Corporation: Case Study of a Nonprofit Advisory Corporation*. Cambridge, MA: Harvard University Press, 1966.

Smith, James A. *Brookings at Seventy-Five*. Washington, DC: The Brookings Institution, 1991.

– *The Idea Brokers: Think Tanks and the Rise of the New Policy Elite*. New York: The Free Press, 1991.

– *Strategic Calling: The Center for Strategic and International Studies 1962–92*. Washington, DC: Center for Strategic and International Studies, 1993.

Smith, Jean Edward. *George Bush's War*. New York: H. Holt, 1992.

– *Eisenhower in War and Peace*. New York: Random House, 2012.

Splane, Richard. *75 Years of Community Service to Canada: Canadian Council on Social Development, 1920–1995*. Ottawa: Canadian Council on Social Development, 1996.

Stahl, Jason. *Right Moves: The Conservative Think Tank in American Political Culture since 1945*. Chapel Hill, NC: University of North Carolina Press, 2016.

Stairs, Denis. "Public Opinion and External Affairs: Reflections on the Domestication of Canadian Foreign Policy." *International Journal* 33, no. 1 (Winter 1977–78): 128–49.

Statistics Canada. "Earned Doctorates, by Field of Study and Sex, Canada, 2005." In *Education in Canada*. Ottawa: Supply and Services, 2005.

Steelman, Aaron. Review of *Do Think Tanks Matter? Assessing the Impact of Public Policy Institutes. Cato Journal* 23, no. 1 (Spring/Summer 2003).

Stewart, Kennedy, Chong, Michael and Scott Simms, eds. *Turning Parliament Inside Out: Practical Ideas for Reforming Canada's Democracy.* Vancouver: Douglas and McIntyre, 2017.

Stone, Diane. *Banking on Knowledge: The Genesis of the Global Development Network*. London: Routledge, 2003.

– *Capturing the Political Imagination: Think Tanks and the Policy Process.* London: Frank Cass, 1996.

Stone, Diane, Andrew Denham, and Mark Garnett, eds. *Think Tanks across Nations: A Comparative Approach*. Manchester: Manchester University Press, 1998.

Sundquist, James L. "Research Brokerage: The Weak Line." In *Knowledge and Policy: The Uncertain Connection*, edited by Laurence E. Lynn. Washington, DC: The National Academy of Sciences, 1978.

Swanson, J. "Brain Power: Bush Aligns with Hoover Think Tank." *Dallas Morning News*, 11 August 1999.

Sweet, L. "Obama Taps Influential Foreign Policy Experts." *The Chicago-Sun Times*, 10 May 2007.

Talbott, Strobe. "A Message from Strobe Talbott, President of the Brookings Institution." *Brookings Institution News Release*, 7 September 2014.

Tapp, Stephen. "What Can a Little Birdie (Twitter) Tell Us about Think Tank Ideology?" *Blog Post-IRPP*, 19 November 2014.

Taylor, Peter Shawn. "The Idea Peddlers." *National Post Business*, December 2000, 86–90, 92, 94, 96.

Think Tank Watch. "Has Heritage Just Released Donald Trump's Bible?" *Think Tank Watch*, 27 July 2016.

– "Trump Consulting with Think Tanks." *Think Tank Watch*, 17 August 2016.

Thunert, Martin W. "Expert Policy in Advice in Germany." In *Policy Expertise in Contemporary Democracies*, edited by Stephen Brooks, Dorota Stasiak and Tomasz Zyro. Aldershot: Ashgate, 2012.

Towell, Pat. "DLC Moves into Driver's Seat." *National Convention News: The Daily Newspaper for the 1992 Democratic National Convention*, 13 July 1992.

Troester, Rod. *Jimmy Carter as Peacemaker: A Post-Presidential Biography.* New York: Praeger Publishers, 1996.

Truman, David B. *The Governmental Process: Political Interests and Public Opinion.* New York: Alfred A. Knopf, 1951.

Tupper, Allan. "Think-Tanks, Public Debt, and the Politics of Expertise in Canada." *Canadian Public Administration* 36, no. 4 (1993): 530–46.

Tyman, Kathleen. "A Decade-Long Heritage of Conservative Thought." *Washington Post*, 4 October 1983.

The Urban Institute. *30: The Urban Institute 1968–1998.* Washington, DC: The Urban Institute, 1998.

– *2015 Annual Report.*

US Department of Education. *Degrees and Other Awards Conferred by Institutions of Higher Education.* Washington, DC: National Center for Education Statistics, 2006.

USA Today. "Senator McCain Announces Economic Advisors." *USA Today*, 12 July 2007.

Valpy, Michael. "Balsillie's Disappointing Foray into Global Affairs." *The Globe and Mail*, 16 December 2009.

Van Der Woerd, Nicoline. *World Survey of Strategic Studies Centres.* London: International Institute of Strategic Studies, 1992.

Vanier Institute of the Family Home Page, www.familyforum.com.

Van Slambrouck, Paul. "California Think Tank Acts as Bush 'Brain Trust.'" *Christian Science Monitor*, 2 July 1999.

Vogel, Kenneth P. "Google Critic Ousted from Think Tank Funded by the Tech Giant." *The New York Times*, 30 August 2017.

Wagner, John. "Trump Praises Jim Demint Who Soon Might Be Ousted from Heritage." 28 April 2017.

Wala, Michael. *The Council on Foreign Relations and American Foreign Policy in the Early Cold War.* Providence, RI: Berghahn Books, 1994.

Walker, Michael. "What's Right, Who's Left, and What's Leftover?" In *After Liberalism: Essays in Search of Freedom, Virtue, and Order*, edited by William D. Gairdner. Toronto: Stoddart, 1998.

Wall, John Frazier. *Andrew Carnegie.* Pittsburgh: University of Pittsburgh Press, 1989.

Wallace, William. "Between Two Worlds: Think-Tanks and Foreign Policy." *Two Worlds of International Relations: Academics, Practitioners and the Trade in Ideas*, edited by Christopher Hill and Pamela Beshoff, 139–63. London: Routledge, 1994.

Washington Post. "The War Over the Wonks." 2 October 2007.

– "Transition Team Profiles." 7 November 2008.

Weaver, R. Kent. "The Changing World of Think Tanks." *PS: Political Science and Politics* 22, no. 2 (September 1989): 563–78.

Wegmann, Philip. "Heritage Foundation Takes Risk and Wins Big with Trump." *Washington Examiner*, 10 November 2016.

Weinraub, Bernard. "Conservative Group's Blueprint for Reagan." *San Francisco Chronicle*, 11 December 1980.

Weisberg, Jacob. "Clincest: Washington's New Ruling Class." *New Republic*, 26 April 1993.

Weiss, Carol H. *Organizations for Policy Analysis: Helping Government Think*. Newbury Park, CA: Sage Publications, 1992.

Weisskopf, Michael. "New Political Landscape Bountiful for Think Tank with Gingrich Ties." *Washington Post*, 5 February 1995.

Wheeler, Charles. "Heritage Chiefs Recall Decade of Growth, Power." *Washington Times*, 29 April 1987.

Whitaker, Ben. *The Foundations: An Anatomy of Philanthropy and Society*. London: Eyre Methuen, 1974.

Wiarda, Howard J. *Universities, Think Tanks and War Colleges: The Main Institutions of American Educational Life: A Memoir*. Philadelphia: Xlibris Corporation, 1999.

Witcover, Jules. *Marathon: The Pursuit of the Presidency 1972–1976*. New York: Viking, 1977.

Wood, Robert C. *Whatever Possessed the President? Academic Experts and Presidential Policy, 1960–1968*. Amherst, MA: University of Massachusetts Press, 1993.

Woodruff, Betsy. "Donald Trump's Favorite Think Tank Wants Him to Stop Talking about It." *The Daily Beast*, 9 August 2016.

Woodward, Bob. *State of Denial: Bush at War Part III*. New York: Simon and Schuster, 2006.

Yee, Albert S. "The Causal Effects of Ideas on Policies." *International Organization* 50, no. 1 (1996): 69–108.

Yoffe, Emily. "IPS Faces Life." *New Republic*, 6–13 August 1977, 16–18.

SELECTED PUBLICATIONS OF THINK TANKS

American Think Tanks

THE AMERICAN ENTERPRISE INSTITUTE

Antos, Joseph, James C. Capretta, Lanhee J. Chen, Scott Gottlieb, Yuval Levin, Thomas P. Miller, Ramesh Ponnuru, Avik Roy, Gail R. Wilensky, and David Wilson. *Improving Health and Health Care: An Agenda for Reform*. Washington, DC: American Enterprise Institute, 2015.

Aron, Leon. *Putin's Agenda and Medvedev's Dilemma*. Washington, DC: American Enterprise Institute, 2010.

Bate, Robert. *The Market for Inferior Medicines: Comparing The Price of Falsified and Substandard Products With the Legitimate Medicines in Emerging Markets.* Washington, DC: American Enterprise Institute, 2011.

– *Phake: The Deadly World of Falsified and Substandard Medicines.* Washington, DC: American Enterprise Institute Press, 2012.

Bauer, Katherine. *Beyond Syria and Iraq: Examining Islamic State Provinces.* Washington, DC: Washington Institute for Near East Policy, 2016.

Biggs, Andrew G. *The Multiplying Risks of Public Employee Pensions to State and Local Government Budgets.* Washington, DC: American Enterprise Institute, 2013.

Bolton, John R. *The Key to Changing the United Nations System.* Washington, DC: American Enterprise Institute, 2010.

Bowen, Daniel H. *Politics and the Scoring of Race to the Top Applications.* Washington, DC: American Enterprise Institute, 2010.

Bowman, Karlyn, and Andrew Rugg. *Attitudes toward the Tea Party over Time: An American Enterprise Institute Compilation.* Washington, DC: American Enterprise Institute, 2013.

Broda, Christian and David E. Weinstein. *Prices, Poverty and Inequality: Why Americans are Better off than You Think.* Washington, DC: American Enterprise Press, 2008.

Calfee, John E. *Prices, Markets, and the Pharmaceutical Revolution.* Washington, DC: American Enterprise Institute Press, 2000.

Cheney, Lynne V. *We the People: The Story of the Constitution.* New York, NY: Simon and Schuster, 2008.

Columbus, Rooney. Report and Disclose: *State Oversight of Institutional Performance in Higher Education.* Washington, DC: Center on Higher Education Reform – American Enterprise Institute, 2016.

Eaglen, Mackenzie, and Douglas A. Birkey. *Nearing Coffin Corner: US Air Power on the Edge.* Washington, DC: American Enterprise Institute, 2012.

– *Trends in Military Compensation: A Chartbook.* Washington, DC: American Enterprise Institute, 2014.

Eberstadt, Nicholas. *China's New 'Two-Child Policy': Still Coercive.* Washington, DC: American Enterprise Institute – Testimony before the US Congressional-Executive Commission on China, 2015.

– *The Poverty of "The Poverty Rate": Measure and Mismeasure of Want in Modern America.* Washington, DC: American Enterprise Press, 2008.

Gingrich, Newt, and Vince Haley. *Drill Here, Drill Now, Pay Less: A Handbook for Slashing Gas Prices and Solving Our Energy Crisis.* Washington, DC: Regnery, 2008.

Glaeser, Edward L., and Joseph Gyourko. *Rethinking Federal Housing Policy: How to Make Housing Plentiful and Affordable.* Washington, DC: American Enterprise Press, 2008.

Gottlieb, Scott. *Will Regulation Thwart the Personalization of Medicine? Molecular Diagnostics and the Expanding Role of the FDA*. Washington, DC: American Enterprise Institute, 2010.

Green, Kenneth P. *Managing Flood Risk*. Washington, DC: American Enterprise Institute, 2011.

Hess, Frederick M. *The Future Of Educational Entrepreneurship: Possibilities Of School Reform*. Cambridge, MA: Harvard Education Press, 2008.

Hess, Frederick M., and Taryn Hochleitner. *College Rankings Inflation: Are You Overpaying for Prestige?* Washington, DC: American Enterprise Institute, 2012.

Kelly, Andrew P., K.C. Deane, and Taryn Hochleitner. *Staying on Target for College: How Innovation Can Improve the Pipeline to Higher Education*. Washington, DC: American Enterprise Institute, 2014.

Lohaus, Phillip. *Special Operations Forces in the Gray Zone: An Operational Framework for Employing Special Operations Forces in the Space Between War and Peace*. Washington, DC: American Enterprise Institute, 2016.

Makin, John H. *Is China Slowing Down?* Washington, DC: American Enterprise Institute, 2012.

Meyer, Bruce D., and James X. Sullivan. *The Material Well-Being of the Poor and Middle Class Since 1980*. Washington, DC: American Enterprise Institute, 2011.

Miller, Thomas P. *Beyond Makers and Takers: Retargeting Entitlement Reform*. Washington, DC: American Enterprise Institute, 2015.

Noriega, Roger F., and José Javier Lanza. *Honduras Under Siege*. Washington, DC: American Enterprise Institute, 2013.

Parente, Stephen T. *Harnessing Health Information in Real Time: Back to The Future for a More Practical and Effective Infrastructure*. Washington, DC: American Enterprise Institute, 2010.

Philipson, Tomas J., and Anupam B. Jena. *Innovation and Technology Adoption in Health Care Markets*. Washington, DC: American Enterprise Press, 2008.

Russo, Alexander. *How 'Waiting for Superman' (Almost) Changed the World*. Washington, DC: American Enterprise Institute, 2014.

Satel, Sally, ed. *When Altruism Isn't Enough: The Case for Compensating Kidney Donors*. Washington, DC: American Enterprise Press, 2009.

Schmitt, Gary J. *Poland, Hungary, and the Czech Republic: The Security Record of "New Europe."* Washington, DC: American Enterprise Institute, 2016.

Shearer, Andrew. *Australian Defense in the Era of Austerity: Mind the Expectation Gap*. Washington, DC: American Enterprise Institute, 2013.

Shober, Arnold F. *From Teacher Education to Student Progress: Teacher Quality since NCLB*. Washington, DC: American Enterprise Institute, 2012.

Smith, Vincent H., and Barry K. Goodwin. *The ACRE Program: A Disaster in Waiting*. Washington, DC: American Enterprise Institute, 2011.

Strain, Michael R., and Douglas A. Webber. *High School Experiences, the Gender Wage Gap, and the Selection of Occupation*. Bonn, Germany: IZA – Institute of Labor Economics, 2015.

Valant, Jon. *Better Data, Better Decisions: Informing School Choosers to Improve Education Markets*. Washington, DC: American Enterprise Institute, 2014.

Viard, Alan D., and Ryan Lirette. *State Taxation of Interstate Commerce and Income Flows: The Economics of Neutrality*. Washington, DC: American Enterprise Institute, 2014.

Wallison, Peter J., Alex J. Pollock, and Edward J. Pinto. *Taking the Government out of Housing Finance: Principles for Reforming the Housing Finance Market*. Washington, DC: American Enterprise Institute, 2016.

Wilcox, W. Bradford, Joseph Price, and Robert I. Lerman. *Strong Families, Prosperous States: Do Healthy Families Affect the Wealth of States?* Washington, DC: American Enterprise Institute, 2015.

Zimmerman, Katherine. *Al-Shabaab and the Challenges of Providing Humanitarian Assistance in Somalia*. Washington, DC: American Enterprise Institute – Critical Threats, 2011.

– *AQAP's Role in the al Qaeda Network*. Washington, DC: American Enterprise Institute, 2013.

THE BROOKINGS INSTITUTION

Aaron, Henry J. *How to Think About the US Budget Challenge*. Washington, DC: The Brookings Institution, 2010.

Alinikoff, Emily, and Ted Piccone. *Rising Democracies and the Arab Awakening: Implications for Global Democracy and Human Rights*. Washington, DC: Report, The Brookings Institution, 2012.

Bradley, Megan. *Rethinking Return: Defining Success in Refugee Repatriation*. Washington, DC: Article, The Brookings Institution, 2013.

Chingos, Matthew M., and Kristin Blagg. *Making College Earnings Data Work for Students*. Washington, DC: Report, The Brookings Institution, 2016.

Danchenko, Igor, Erica Downs, and Fiona Hill. *One Step Forward, Two Steps Back? The Realities of a Rising China and Implications for Russia's Energy Ambitions. Policy Paper*. Washington, DC: The Brookings Institution, 2010.

Daniel, Gregory W., Derek Griffing, and Sophie Mayer. *Antimicrobial Resistance: Antibiotics Stewardship and Innovation*. Washington, DC: Article, The Brookings Institution, 2014.

Elliott, Douglas J. *The Significance of the Bank Stress Tests in Europe*. Washington, DC: The Brookings Institution, 2010.

Friedman, Allan A., Patrick Crowley, and Darrell M. West. *Online Identity and Consumer Trust: Assessing Online Risk*. Washington, DC: The Brookings Institution, 2011.

Galston, *William A. Thoughts on a Center-Left Entitlements Strategy: How We Might Shape Social Security and Medicare for the Future*. Washington, DC: Article, The Brookings Institution, 2014.

Goodby, James E., and Markku Heiskanen. *A New Day in Northeast Asia?* Washington, DC: Article, The Brookings Institution, 2013.

Hamilton, James, Ethan Harris, Jan Hatzius, and Kenneth West. *The Equilibrium Real Funds Rate: Past, Present, and Future*. Washington, DC: Working Paper #16, Hutchins Center on Fiscal & Monetary Policy at Brookings, 2015.

Gustafsson-Wright, Emily, Sophie Gardiner, and Katie Smith. *Ensuring Effective Outcome-Based Financing in Early Childhood Development: Recommendations to the International Commission on Financing Global Education Opportunity*. Washington, DC: Background Paper, The Center for Universal Education at the Brookings Institution, 2016.

Hill, Fiona, and Clifford G. Gaddy. *Putin and the Uses of History in Russia*. Washington, DC: Article, The Brookings Institution, 2012.

Hrdinová, Jana, and Natalie Helbig. *Designing Social Media Policy for Government*. Washington, DC: Report, The Brookings Institution, 2011.

Kocot, S. Lawrence, and Mark B. McClellan. *Achieving Better Chronic Care at Lower Costs across the Health Care Continuum for Older Americans*. Washington, DC: Engelberg Center for Health Care Reform at The Brookings Institution, 2010.

Kohn, Donald. *Comments on "The Most Dangerous Idea in Federal Reserve History: Monetary Policy Doesn't Matter."* Washington, DC: The Brookings Institution, 2013.

Levy, Santiago. *Good Intentions, Bad Outcomes: Social Policy, Informality and Economic Growth in Mexico*. Washington, DC: Brookings Institution Press, 2008.

Loveless, Tom. *The 2010 Brown Center Report on American Education: How Well Are American Students Learning? An Early Release of Part III*. Washington, DC: The Brookings Institution, 2011.

Mathur, Aparna, and Adele Morris. *A US Carbon Tax and the Earned Income Tax Credit: An Analysis of Potential Linkages*. Washington, DC: Climate and Energy Economics Discussion Paper, Brookings Institution, 2016.

Nivola, Pietro S. *Presidential Leadership, Then and Now: Woodrow Wilson and Barack Obama*. Washington, DC: Report, The Brookings Institution, 2012.

Pfiffner, James P. *Power Play: The Bush Presidency and the Constitution*. Washington, DC: Brookings Institution Press, 2008.

Reynolds, Molly E., and Philip A. Wallach. *The Fiscal Fights of the Obama Administration: An Interactive Timeline*. Washington, DC: The Brookings Institution, 2016.

Rhee, Changyong, Guanghua Wan, John McArthur, Douglas H. Brooks, and Kaushal Joshi. *A ZEN Approach to Post-2015: Addressing the Range of Perspectives across Asia.* Metro Manila, Philippines: Asian Development Bank, 2013.

Rogers, Melissa. *Assessing Decision-making on the NYC Islamic Center: Continuing Our Tradition of Religious Liberty.* Washington, DC: The Brookings Institution, 2010.

Shapiro, Jeremy and Samuel Charap. "How to Avoid a New Cold War." *Current History Magazine* 113, no. 765 (October 2014).

Telxelra, Ru, ed. *Red, Blue and Purple America.* Washington, DC: Brookings Institution Press, 2008.

Thurber, James A., and Canice J. Nelson, eds. *Campaign Warriors: Political Consultants in Elections.* Washington, DC: Brookings Institution Press, 2000.

Vey, Jennifer S., Mark Muro, Matthew Murray, and Sue Clark-Johnson. *Structurally Unbalanced: Cyclical and Structural Deficits in California and the Intermountain West.* Washington, DC: The Brookings Institution, 2011.

Winship, Scott. *Bogeyman Economics: Has Economic Insecurity Been Overstated?* Washington, DC: Article, The Brookings Institution, 2012.

Winston, Clifford, and Gines de Rus, eds. *Aviation Infrastructure Performance: A Study in Comparative Political Economy.* Washington, DC: Brookings Institution Press, 2008.

Winthrop, Rebecca and Marshall S. Smith. *A New Face of Education: Bringing Technology into the Classroom in the Developing World.* Washington, DC: Report, The Brookings Institution, 2012.

THE CATO INSTITUTE

Anklesaria Aiyar, Swaminathan S. *Capitalism's Assault on the Indian Caste System: How Economic Liberalization Spawned Low-Caste Dalit Millionaires.* Washington, DC: Cato Institute Policy Analysis No. 776, 2015.

Armor, David J. *The Evidence on Universal Preschool.* Washington, DC: Cato Institute Policy Analysis No. 760, 2014.

Atkin, David, Benjamin Faber, and Marco Gonzalez-Navarro. *Retail Globalization and Household Welfare: Evidence from Mexico.* Washington, DC: Cato Institute Economic Bulletin No. 30, 2015.

Autor, David H., Christopher J. Palmer, and Parag A. Pathak. *Housing Market Spillover: Evidence from the End of Rent Control in Cambridge, Massachusetts.* Washington, DC: Cato Institute Research Briefs in Economic Policy No. 9, 2014. Brannon, Ike, and Mark A. Calabria. *The Paths to*

Mortgage Finance Reform and Their Budgetary Implications. Washington, DC: Cato Institute Working Paper No. 18, 2014.

Brøns-Petersen, Otto. *The Danish Model – Don't Try This at Home*. Washington, DC: Cato Institute Economic Bulletin No. 24, 2015.

Davis, Morris A. *Questioning Homeownership as a Public Policy Goal*. Washington, DC: Cato Institute Policy Analysis No. 696, 2012.

Doherty, Brian. *Gun Control on Trial: Inside the Supreme Court Battle Over the Second Amendment*. Washington, DC: Cato Institute, 2008.

Dorn, James A. *The Genesis and Evolution of China's Economic Liberalization*. Washington, DC: Cato Institute Working Paper No. 38, 2016.

Duanjie Chen and Jack M. Mintz. *Corporate Tax Competitiveness Rankings for 2012*. Washington, DC: Cato Institute Tax and Budget Bulletin No. 65, 2012.

Griswold, Daniel. *The Trade-Balance Creed: Debunking the Belief that Imports and Trade Deficits Are a "Drag on Growth."* Washington, DC: Cato Institute Trade Policy Analysis No. 45, 2010.

Holland, Stephen P., Erin T. Mansur, Nicholas Z. Muller, and Andrew J. Yates. *Public Policy Evaluation in the Face of Strong Prior Beliefs: The Case of Electric Cars*. Washington, DC: Cato Institute Research Briefs in Economic Policy No. 34, 2015.

Horwitz, Steven. *Herbert Hoover: Father of the New Deal*. Washington, DC: Cato Institute Briefing Paper No. 122, 2011.

Kling, Arnold. *Crisis of Abundance: Rethinking How We Pay for Health Care*. Washington, DC: Cato Institute, 2008.

Kuznicki, Jason. *Marriage against the State: Toward a New View of Civil Marriage*. Washington, DC: Cato Institute Policy Analysis No. 671, 2010.

Lee, Lavina. *Beyond Symbolism? The US Nuclear Disarmament Agenda and Its Implications for Chinese and Indian Nuclear Policy*. Washington, DC: Cato Institute Foreign Policy Briefing No. 91, 2010.

Lester, Simon. *Is the Doha Round Over? The WTO's Negotiating Agenda for 2016 and Beyond*. Washington, DC: Cato Institute Free Trade Bulletin No. 64, 2016.

– *One Year into the TTIP Negotiations: Getting to Yes*. Washington, DC: Cato Institute Free Trade Bulletin No. 59, 2014.

Levy, Robert A. *The Case against President Obama's Health Care Reform: A Primer for Nonlawyers*. Washington, DC: Cato Institute White Paper, 2010.

Lindsey, Brink. *Why Growth Is Getting Harder*. Washington, DC: Cato Institute Policy Analysis No. 737, 2013.

Michaels, Patrick J., and Robert C. Balling Jr. *Climate of Extremes: Global Warming Science They Don't Want You to Know*. Washington, DC: Cato Institute, 2009.

Murphy, Ryan, and Alex Nowrasteh. *US Immigration Levels, Urban Housing Values, and Their Implications for Capital Share*. Washington, DC: Cato Institute Working Paper No. 37, 2016.

Nowrasteh, Alex, and Sophie Cole. *Building a Wall around the Welfare State, Instead of the Country.* Washington, DC: Cato Institute Policy Analysis No. 732, 2013.

Nowrasteh, Alex. *How to Make Guest Worker Visas Work.* Washington, DC: Cato Institute Policy Analysis No. 719, 2013.

O'Toole, Randy. *The Best Laid Plans: How Government Planning Harms Your Quality of Life, Your Pocketbook and Your Future.* Washington, DC: Cato Institute, 2007.

Pearson, Daniel R. *Global Steel Overcapacity: Trade Remedy "Cure" Is Worse than the "Disease."* Washington, DC: Cato Institute Free Trade Bulletin No. 66, 2016.

Rappaport, Michael B. *Renewing Federalism by Reforming Article V: Defects in the Constitutional Amendment Process and a Reform Proposal.* Washington, DC: Cato Institute Policy Analysis No. 691, 2012.

Sally, Razeen. *Asia's Story of Growing Economic Freedom.* Washington, DC: Cato Institute Policy Analysis No. 725, 2013.

– *New Frontiers in Free Trade: Globalization's Future and Asia's Rising Role.* Washington, DC: Cato Institute, 2008.

Sanchez, Julian. *Leashing the Surveillance State: How to Reform Patriot Act Surveillance Authorities.* Washington, DC: Cato Institute Trade Policy Analysis No. 75, 2011.

Selgin, George. *New York's Bank: The National Monetary Commission and the Founding of the Fed.* Washington, DC: Cato Institute Policy Analysis No. 793, 2016.

Shapiro, Ilya. *Cato Supreme Court Review: 2007–2008.* Washington, DC: Cato Institute, 2008.

Tanner, Michael D. *Social Security, Ponzi Schemes, and the Need for Reform.* Washington, DC: Cato Institute Policy Analysis No. 689, 2011.

Tanner, Michael D., and Charles Hughes. *The Work versus Welfare Trade-Off: Europe.* Washington, DC: Cato Institute Policy Analysis No. 779, 2015.

Watson, K. William. *Antidumping Fowls Out: US–South Africa Chicken Dispute Highlights the Need for Global Reform.* Washington, DC: Cato Institute Free Trade Bulletin No. 62, 2015.

– *Will Nonmarket Economy Methodology Go Quietly into the Night? US Antidumping Policy toward China after 2016.* Washington, DC: Cato Institute Policy Analysis No. 763, 2014.

Wilson, Mark. *The Negative Effects of Minimum Wage Laws.* Washington, DC: Cato Institute Policy Analysis No. 701, 2012.

THE CARNEGIE ENDOWMENT FOR INTERNATIONAL PEACE

Abdel-Latif, Omayma. *In the Shadow of the Brothers: The Women of the Egyptian Muslim Brotherhood.* Washington, DC: Carnegie Paper, Carnegie Endowment for International Peace, 2008.

Achy, Lahcen. *The Price of Stability in Algeria*. Washington, DC: Carnegie Paper, Carnegie Endowment for International Peace, 2013.

Acton, James M. *Deterrence During Disarmament: Deep Nuclear Reductions and International Security*. Washington, DC: Carnegie Book, Carnegie Endowment for International Peace, 2011.

– *Low Numbers: A Practical Path to Deep Nuclear Reductions*. Washington, DC: Carnegie Report, Carnegie Endowment for International Peace, 2011.

Arbatov, Alexei, and Vladimir Dvorkin. *The Great Strategic Triangle*. Washington, DC: Carnegie Paper, Carnegie Endowment for International Peace, 2013.

Boukhars, Anouar. *In The Crossfire: Islamists' Travails in Tunisia*. Washington, DC: Carnegie Brief, Carnegie Endowment for International Peace, 2014.

Brown, Nathan J., and Amr Hamzawy. *Between Religion and Politics*. Washington, DC: Carnegie Endowment for International Peace, 2010.

Brown, Nathan J., and Michele Dunne. *Unprecedented Pressures, Uncharted Course for Egypt's Muslim Brotherhood*. Washington, DC: Carnegie Paper, Carnegie Endowment for International Peace, 2015.

Carothers, Thomas, and Oren Samet-Marram. *The New Global Marketplace of Political Change*. Washington, DC: Carnegie Brief, Carnegie Endowment for International Peace, 2015.

Choubey, Deepti. *Are New Nuclear Bargains Attainable?* Washington, DC: Carnegie Endowment for International Peace, 2008.

Dadush, Uri, Sergey Aleksashenko, Shimelse Ali, Vera Eidelman, Moisés Naím, Bennett Stancil, and Paola Subacchi. *Paradigm Lost: The Euro in Crisis*. Washington, DC: Carnegie Endowment for International Peace, 2010.

Dadush, Uri, Shimelse Ali, and Rachel Esplin Odell. *Is Protectionism Dying?* Washington, DC: Carnegie Endowment for International Peace, 2011.

Dempsey, Judy. *Why Defense Matters: A New Narrative for NATO*. Washington, DC: Carnegie Endowment for International Peace, 2014.

Dorronsoro, Gilles. *Afghanistan: At The Breaking Point*. Washington, DC: Carnegie Endowment for International Peace, 2010.

El-Issawi, Fatima. *Tunisian Media in Transition*. Washington, DC: Carnegie Endowment for International Peace, 2012.

El-Sherif, Ashraf. *Egypt's Salafists at a Crossroads: Part 3 of a Series on Political Islam in Egypt*. Washington, DC: Carnegie Endowment for International Peace, 2015.

Gabuev, Alexander. *Friends with Benefits? Russian-Chinese Relations After the Ukraine Crisis*. Moscow, RUS: Carnegie Paper, Carnegie Moscow Center, 2015.

Gengler, Justin. *The Political Economy of Sectarianism in the Gulf*. Washington, DC: Carnegie Endowment for International Peace, 2016.

Gogolashvili, Kakha, Tengiz Pkhaladze, Nikolay Silaev, Tornike Sharashendize, Ivan Sukhov, Vladimer Papava, Boris Frumkin, George Tarkhan-Mouravi,

Andrei Zagorski, Ivlian Haindrava, and Alexander Skakov. *Russia and Georgia: Searching the Way Out*. Washington, DC: Carnegie Endowment for International Peace, 2011.

Hamzawy, Amr, and Farah Choucair. *Obama's Middle East Policy: What the Arab World Expects*. Washington, DC: Web Commentary, Carnegie Endowment for International Peace, 2008.

Henley, Alexander D. M. *Religious Authority and Sectarianism in Lebanon*. Washington, DC: Carnegie Endowment for International Peace, 2016.

Jacob, Happymon. *Putting the Periphery at The Center: Indian States' Role in Foreign Policy*. Washington, DC: Carnegie Endowment for International Peace, 2016.

Mikulova, Kristina, and Benedetta Berti. *Converts to Missionaries: Central and Eastern European Democracy Assistance in the Arab World*. Washington, DC: Carnegie Endowment for International Peace, 2013.

Nehru, Vikram. *Myanmar's Economic Policy Priorities*. Washington, DC: Carnegie Endowment for International Peace, 2012.

Ottaway, Marina, and Amr Hamzawy. *Islamists in Politics: The Dynamics of Participation*. Washington, DC: Carnegie Paper, Carnegie Endowment for International Peace, 2008.

Perkovich, George. *Toward Realistic US–India Relations*. Washington, DC: Carnegie Endowment for International Peace, 2010.

Pierini, Marc, and Sinan Ülgen. *A Moment of Opportunity In The EU-Turkey Relationship*. Washington, DC: Carnegie Endowment for International Peace, 2014.

Reddy, R. Shashank. *India and the Challenge of Autonomous Weapons*. Washington, DC: Carnegie Endowment for International Peace, 2016.

Saif, Ibrahim, and Ahmed Ghoneim. *The Private Sector in Postrevolution Egypt*. Washington, DC: Carnegie Endowment for International Peace, 2013.

Salem, Paul. *Iraq's Tangled Foreign Interests and Relations*. Beirut, Leb: Carnegie Middle East Center, 2013.

Sayigh, Yezid. *Policing the People, Building the State: Authoritarian Transformation in The West Bank and Gaza*. Washington, DC: Carnegie Endowment for International Peace, 2011.

Siegel, Alexandra. *Sectarian Twitter Wars: Sunni-Shia Conflict and Cooperation in the Digital Age*. Washington, DC: Carnegie Endowment for International Peace, 2015.

Techau, Jan. *The Politics of 2 Percent: NATO and The Security Vacuum In Europe*. Washington, DC: Carnegie Endowment for International Peace, 2015.

Trenin, Dmitri, Alexei Arbatov, Maria Lipman, Alexey Malashenko, Nikolay Petrov, Andrei Ryabov, and Lilia Shevtsova. *The Russian Awakening*. Moscow, RUS: Carnegie Moscow Centre and Carnegie Endowment for International Peace, 2012.

Trenin, Dmitri, and Pavel K. Baev. *The Arctic: A View from Moscow.* Washington, DC: Carnegie Endowment for International Peace, 2010.

Trenin, Dmitri. *Russia's Breakout from the Post-Cold War System: The Drivers of Putin's Course.* Moscow, RUS: Carnegie Moscow Center, 2014.

Ülgen, Sinan. *Locked in or Left Out? Transatlantic Trade Beyond Brussels and Washington.* Washington, DC: Carnegie Endowment for International Peace, 2014.

Wehrey, Frederic. *The Struggle for Security in Eastern Libya.* Washington, DC: Carnegie Endowment for International Peace, 2012.

CENTRE FOR A NEW AMERICAN SECURITY

Brimley, Shawn. *While We Can: Arresting the Erosion of America's Military Edge.* Washington, DC: Centre for a New American Security, 2016.

Chang, Amy. *Warring State: China's Cybersecurity Strategy.* Washington, DC: Centre for a New American Security, 2014.

Chow, Eugene, and Richard Weitz. *Rebuilding Diplomacy: A Survey of Past Calls for State Department Transformation.* Washington, DC: Centre for a New American Security, 2010.

Colby, Elbridge. *A Nuclear Strategy and Posture for 2030.* Washington, DC: Centre for a New American Security, 2015.

Cronin, Patrick M., and Brian M. Burton. *Extreme Crises: Reassessing US Preparedness after Japan.* Washington, DC: Centre for a New American Security, 2011.

Danzig, Richard, Marc Sageman, Terrance Leighton, Lloyd Hough, Hidemi Yuki, Rui Kotani, and Zachary M. Hosford. *Aum Shinrikyo: Insights into How Terrorists Develop Biological and Chemical Weapons.* Washington, DC: Centre for a New American Security, 2011.

Denmark, Abraham M., and Zachary M. Hosford. *Securing South Korea: A Strategic Alliance for the 21st Century.* Washington, DC: Centre for a New American Security, 2010.

Ellis, Jason D. *Directed-Energy Weapons: Promise and Prospects.* Washington, DC: Centre for a New American Security, 2015.

Eunpyoung Jee, David, Elbridge Colby, Hannah Suh, Patrick M. Cronin, Richard Fontaine and Van Jackson. *Solving Long Division: The Geopolitical Implications of Korean Unification.* Washington, DC: Centre for a New American Security, 2015.

Exum, Andrew M., and Zachary M. Hosford. *Forging a Libya Strategy: Policy Recommendations for the Obama Administration.* Washington, DC: Centre for a New American Security, 2011.

Fisher, Richard D. Jr. *Defending the Philippines: Military Modernization and the Challenges Ahead.* Washington, DC: Centre for a New American Security, 2012.

FitzGerald, Ben, and Parker Wright. *Digital Theaters: Decentralizing Cyber Command and Control.* Washington, DC: Centre for a New American Security, 2014.

Fontaine, Richard, and Will Rogers. *Unleashing US-India Defense Trade.* Washington, DC: Centre for a New American Security, 2010.

– *Internet Freedom: A Foreign Policy Imperative in the Digital Age.* Washington, DC: Centre for a New American Security, 2011.

Holmes, James. *A Competitive Turn: How Increased Chinese Maritime Actions Complicate US Partnerships.* Washington, DC: Centre for a New American Security, 2012.

Kidder, Katherine, and Phillip Carter. *Needs Assessment: Veterans in the Western United States.* Washington, DC: Centre for a New American Security, 2013.

– *Charting the Sea of Goodwill.* Washington, DC: Centre for a New American Security, 2015.

Klein, Adam, Michele Flournoy and Richard Fontaine. *Surveillance Policy: A Pragmatic Agenda for 2017 and Beyond.* Washington, DC: Centre for a New American Security, 2016.

Martin, Aaron, and Ben FitzGerald. *Process Over Platforms: A Paradigm Shift in Acquisition Through Advanced Manufacturing.* Washington, DC: Centre for a New American Security, 2013.

Mastro, Oriana Skylar. *The Sansha Garrison: China's Deliberate Escalation in the South China Sea.* Washington, DC: Centre for a New American Security, 2012.

Miller, Gordon, Katherine Kidder, Nora Bensahel, Patrick M. Cronin, Phillip Carter, Richard Fontaine, Richard Williamson, and David W. Barno. *CNAS Commentaries: The Way Forward in Syria.* Washington, DC: Centre for a New American Security, 2013.

O'Hanlon, Michael, Michele Flournoy, and John R. Allen. *Toward a Successful Outcome in Afghanistan.* Washington, DC: Centre for a New American Security, 2013.

Parthemore, Christine. *Elements of Security: Mitigating the Risks of US Dependence on Critical Minerals.* Washington, DC: Centre for a New American Security, 2011.

Parthemore, Christine, and John Nagl. *Fueling the Future Force: Preparing the Department of Defense for a Post-Petroleum Era.* Washington, DC: Centre for a New American Security, 2010.

Rand, Dafna, and Stephen Tankel. *Security Cooperation and Assistance: Rethinking the Return on Investment.* Washington, DC: Centre for a New American Security, 2015.

Ratner, Ely. *The Obama-Xi Summit: Three Essential Messages from Washington.* Washington, DC: Centre for a New American Security, 2014.

Saidel, Andrew M., Richard Danzig, and Zachary Hosford. *Beyond Fukushima: A Joint Agenda for US-Japanese Disaster Management*. Washington, DC: Centre for a New American Security, 2012.

Schneider, Jacquelyn. *Digitally-Enabled Warfare: The Capability-Vulnerability Paradox*. Washington, DC: Centre for a New American Security, 2016.

Securing US Interests in Afghanistan Beyond 2011. Washington, DC: Centre for a New American Security, 2010.

Shevin-Coetzee, Michelle. *The Labyrinth Within: Reforming the Pentagon's Budgeting Process*. Washington, DC: Centre for a New American Security, 2016.

Shevin-Coetzee, Michelle, and Jerry Hendrix. *From Blue to Black: Applying the Concepts of Sea Power to the Ocean of Space*. Washington, DC: Centre for a New American Security, 2016.

Stokes, Jacob, and Nora Bensahel. *NATO Matters: Ensuring the Value of the Alliance for the United States*. Washington, DC: Centre for a New American Security, 2013.

Sturgis, Linda A. *Port Recovery in the Aftermath of Hurricane Sandy: Improving Port Resiliency in the Era of Climate Change*. Washington, DC: Centre for a New American Security, 2014.

Sullivan, Alexander. *Advancing US-Malaysia Security Cooperation in a Changing Environment*. Washington, DC: Centre for a New American Security, 2014.

CENTER FOR AMERICAN PROGRESS

Alexander-Kearns, Myriam, Miranda Peterson, and Alison Cassady. *The Impact of Vehicle Automation on Carbon Emissions: Where Uncertainty Lies*. Washington, DC: Center for American Progress, Report, 2016.

Arons, Jessica. *The Adoption Option: Adoption Won't Reduce Abortion but It Will Expand Women's Choices*. Washington, DC: Center for American Progress, Report, 2010.

Boadi, Kwame. *Sequestering American Innovation*. Washington, DC: Center for American Progress, Issue Brief, 2013.

Boser, Ulrich. *Teacher Diversity Matters: A State-by-State Analysis of Teachers of Color*. Washington, DC: Center for American Progress, Report, 2011.

Burns, Crosby, and Jeff Krehely. *The Freedom to Work, the Freedom to Worship: The Employment Non-Discrimination Act Advances Workplace Equality and Protects Religious Liberty*. Washington, DC: Center for American Progress, Issue Brief, 2012.

Cookman, Colin, and Bill French. *The Pakistan Aid Dilemma: Historical Efforts at Conditionality and Current Disputes Converge in the US Congress*. Washington, DC: Center for American Progress, Issue Brief, 2011.

Cray, Andrew, Crosby Burns, and Erin Fitzgerald. *Caught in the Budget Battle: How the 'Fiscal Showdown' Impacts Gay and Transgender Americans.* Washington, DC: Center for American Progress, Report, 2012.

Davenport, Karen, Renée Markus Hodin, and Judy Feder. *The 'Dual Eligible' Opportunity: Improving Care and Reducing Costs for Individuals Eligible for Medicare and Medicaid.* Washington, DC: Center for American Progress, Report, 2010.

DeGood, Kevin. *Public-Private Partnerships: Understanding the Difference Between Procurement and Finance.* Washington, DC: Center for American Progress, Report, 2014.

DeMonte, Jenny. *High-Quality Professional Development for Teachers: Supporting Teacher Training to Improve Student Learning.* Washington, DC: Center for American Progress, Report, 2013.

Dewan, Sabina. *Social Protection Is a Necessity, Not a Privilege: From the Just Jobs Report Series.* Washington, DC: Center for American Progress, Report, 2010.

Emanuel, Zeke, Topher Spiro, and Maura Calsyn. "Reducing the Cost of Defensive Medicine." *Issue Brief.* Washington, DC: Center for American Progress, 2013.

Goad, Jessica, Christy Goldfuss, and Tom Kenworthy. *Using Public Lands for the Public Good: Rebalancing Coal and Renewable Electricity with a Clean Resources Standard.* Washington, DC: Center for American Progress, Report, 2012.

Jealous, Ben. *Toward Trust: Grassroots Recommendations for Police Reform in Baltimore.* Washington, DC: Center for American Progress, Report, 2015.

Konoske-Graf, Annette, Lisette Partelow, and Meg Benner. *To Attract Great Teachers, School Districts Must Improve Their Human Capital Systems.* Washington, DC: Center for American Progress, Report, 2016.

Korb, Lawrence J., Alex Rothman, and Max Hoffman. *Reforming Military Compensation: Addressing Runaway Personnel Costs Is a National Imperative.* Washington, DC: Center for American Progress, Report, 2012.

Lazarín, Melissa. *Federal Investment in Charter Schools: A Proposal for Reauthorizing the Elementary and Secondary Education Act.* Washington, DC: Center for American Progress, Report, 2011.

Lefton, Rebecca. *Time to Update 1980s Air Quality Standards for Drilling in the Arctic.* Washington, DC: Center for American Progress, Issue Brief, 2014.

Mirza, Shabab, Ahmed, Steven Soto, and Caitlin Rooney. *State ID Card Policies for LGBTQ Youths Experiencing Homelessness.* Washington, DC: Center for American Progress, 2016.

Pastor, Manuel, Tom Jawetz, and Lizet Ocampo. *DAPA Matters: The Growing Electorate Directly Affected by Executive Action on Immigration.* Washington, DC: Center for American Progress, Report, 2015.

Podesta, John, Brian Katulis, and Caroline Wadhams. *The Need for a Political and Economic Transition Strategy in Afghanistan: Report from July 2011 Trip to Kabul, Afghanistan.* Washington, DC: Center for American Progress, Report, 2011.

Public Impact. *Giving Every Student Access to Excellent Teachers: A Vision for Focusing Federal Investments in Education.* Washington, DC: Center for American Progress, Report, 2013.

Robbins, Katherine Gallagher, and Shawn Fremstad. *4 Progressive Policies that Make Families Stronger.* Washington, DC: Center for American Progress, Issue Brief, 2016.

Sargrad, Scott, Max Marchitello, and Robert Hanna. *Invisible by Design: How Congress Risks Hiding the Performance of Disadvantaged Students.* Washington, DC: Center for American Progress, Issue Brief, 2015.

Spiro, Topher, Maura Calsyn, and Thomas Huelskoetter. *Enough Is Enough: The Time Has Come to Address Sky-High Drug Prices.* Washington, DC: Center for American Progress, Report, 2015.

Tusiray, Melis, Peter Juul, and Michael Werz. *The IHH Riddle: Why It Doesn't Make Sense to List the Turkish Humanitarian Group as a Foreign Terrorist Organization.* Washington, DC: Center for American Progress, Report, 2010.

Warner, Judith. *For Women to Lead, They Have to Stay in the Game: Why We Need Public Policy to Level the Playing Field.* Washington, DC: Center for American Progress, Report, 2014.

Weiss, Daniel J., Jackie Weidman, and Stephanie Pinkalla. *States of Denial: States with the Most Federal Disaster Aid Sent Climate-Science Deniers to Congress.* Washington, DC: Center for American Progress, Policy Report, 2013.

Weller, Christian E., and Jackie Odum. "Economic Snapshot: September 2015 – Christian E. Weller on the State of the US Economy." *Issue Brief.* Washington, DC: Center for American Progress, 2015.

THE CENTER FOR STRATEGIC AND INTERNATIONAL STUDIES

Aras, Bulent, and Bulent Aliriza. *US-Turkish Relations: A Review at the Beginning of the Third Decade of the Post–Cold War Era.* Washington, DC: CSIS, 2012.

Ben-Ari, Guy, and Pierre A. Chao. *Organizing for a Complex World: Developing Tomorrow's Defense and Net-Centric Systems.* Washington; DC, CSIS Press, 2009

Bergsten, C. Fred, Charles Freeman, Nicholas R. Lardy, and Derek J. Mitchell. *China's Rise: Challenge and Opportunities.* Washington, DC: Pie/CSIS, 2008.

Bliss, Katherine E., and Katey Peck. *Transitioning from Gavi Support in Lower-Middle-Income Countries: Options for US Engagement in Central America.* Washington, DC: CSIS Report, 2016.

Boynton, Xiaoqing Lu, Olivia Ma, and Molly Claire Schmalzbach. *Key Issues in China's Health Care: Payment System Reform and Health Technology Assessment.* Washington, DC: CSIS Report, 2012.

Bryden, Matt. *The Reinvention of Al-Shabaab: A Strategy of Choice or Necessity?* Washington, DC: CSIS Report, 2014.

Bugajski, Janusz. *Expanding Eurasia: Russia's European Ambitions.* Washington, DC: CSIS Press, 2008.

Cooke, Jennifer G., Derek Schlickeisen. *Africa's Wildlife Poaching and Trafficking Crisis: The Need for Urgent Action.* Washington, DC: CSIS Report, 2015.

Cordesman, Anthony H. *US and Iranian Strategic Competition: Competition Involving the EU, EU3, and non-EU European States.* Washington, DC: CSIS Report, 2011.

– *Changing US Security Strategy: The Search for Stability and the "Non-War" against "Non-Terrorism."* Washington, DC: CSIS Analysis Paper, 2013.

– *Constructing a New Syria: Dealing with the Real Outcome of the "ISIS War."* Washington, DC: CSIS Report, 2015.

– *Iran's Rocket and Missile Forces and Strategic Options.* Washington, DC: CSIS Report, 2014.

Cordesman, Anthony H., and Marrisa Allison. *The US Air War in Iraq, Afghanistan, and Pakistan.* Washington, DC: CSIS Report, 2010.

Cordesman, Anthony H., Jordan D'Amato, and Robert Hammond. *"Unplanning" for Uncertainty: Reshaping Future Defense Plans.* Washington, DC: CSIS Report, 2010.

Cordesman, Anthony H., and Abdullah Toukan. *Analyzing the Impact of Preventive Strikes Against Iran's Nuclear Facilities.* Washington, DC: CSIS Report, 2012.

Daniel, J. Christopher. *Drug-Resistant Malaria: A Generation of Progress in Jeopardy.* Washington, DC: CSIS Report, 2013.

De Galbert, Simond. *Transatlantic Economic Statecraft: The Challenge to Building a Balanced Transatlantic Sanctions Policy between the United States and the European Union.* Washington, DC: CSIS Gulf Analysis Paper, 2016.

Downie, Richard (ed.). *Global Health as a Bridge to Security: Interviews with US Leaders.* Washington, DC: CSIS Report, 2012.

Fleischman, Janet. *Political Tensions Threaten HIV Programs in Malawi.* Washington, DC: CSIS Blog Post, 2011.

Green, Shannon N., Keith Proctor, Juan C. Zarate, Farah Pandith, Tony Blair, and Leon Panetta. *Turning Point: A New Comprehensive Strategy for Countering Violent Extremism.* Washington, DC: CSIS Interactive Report, 2016.

Hall, Aaron. *Why US Leadership Is Critical to Reforming the Mineral Trade in Eastern Congo.* Washington, DC: CSIS commentary, 2010.

Hertzberg, Michael. *Shining a Brighter Light on Dark Places: Improving the IAEA's Use of Intelligence through Cooperation with NATO*. Washington, DC: CSIS Report, 2010.

Hyman, Gerald F. *Bringing Realism to Paris in Busan: The Paris Declaration on Aid Effectiveness*. Washington, DC: CSIS Report, 2011.

Jun, Jenny, Scott LaFoy, Ethan Sohn, Victor D. Cha, and James A. Lewis. *North Korea's Cyber Operations: Strategy and Responses*. Washington, DC: CSIS Report, 2015.

Lamb, Robert D. *Africa in the Wider World: State Building Challenges in Africa*. Washington, DC: CSIS Report, 2014.

Leonard, William. *"Closing the Gap": The Euromissiles and President Carter's Nuclear Weapons Strategy for Western Europe (1977–1979)*. Washington, DC: CSIS Report, 2010.

Malka, Haim, and William Lawrence. *Jihadi-Salafism's Next Generation*. Washington, DC: CSIS Analysis Paper, 2013.

McGiffert, Carola, and James T.H. Tang, eds. *Hong Kong on the Move: 10 Years as the Hksar*. Washington, DC: CSIS Press, 2008.

Murdock, Clark A. *Defense in an Age of Austerity: Conference Proceedings, Presentations, and Key Takeaways*. Washington, DC: CSIS Report, 2011.

Peschard-Sverdrup, Armand B. *The Future of North American, 2025: Outlook and Recommendations*. Washington, DC: CSIS, 2008.

Pourchot, Georgeta. *Eurasia Rising: Democracy and Independence in the Post-Soviet Space*. Westport, CN: Praeger Publishers/CSIS, 2008.

Rosen, Daniel H., and Beibei Bao. *Broken Abacus? A More Accurate Gauge of China's Economy*. Washington, DC: CSIS Report, 2015.

Sachdeva, Gulshan. *India in a Reconnecting Eurasia: Foreign Economic and Security Interests*. Washington, DC: CSIS Report, 2016.

Santoro, David, and Brad Glosserman. *Building Toward Trilateral Cooperation on Extended Deterrence in Northeast Asia: The First US-ROK-Japan Extended Deterrence Trilateral Dialogue*. Washington, DC: CSIS Issues & Insights vol. 13 - No. 14 Report, 2013.

Stash, Sharon, Jennifer Cooke, Matt Fisher, and Alisha Kramer. *Competing Pressures for US PEPFAR in Botswana: Rising Ambitions, Declining Resources*. Washington, DC: CSIS Report, 2012.

Todman, Will. *Gulf States' Policies on Syria*. Washington, DC: CSIS Gulf Analysis Paper, 2016.

Twigg, Judith. *US-Russia Health Engagement: Still on the Agenda*. Washington, DC: CSIS Report, 2014.

Zikibayeva, Aigerim, Serge Korepin, and Shalini Sharan. *What Does the Arab Spring Mean for Russia, Central Asia, and the Caucasus?* Washington, DC: CSIS Report, 2011.

FOREIGN POLICY RESEARCH INSTITUTE

Amend, Kurt. *Counterinsurgency Principles for the Diplomat*. Philadelphia, PA: Foreign Policy Research Institute, *Orbis* vol. 54, Issue 2, 215–31, 2010.

Berti, Benedetta. *How Does the Syrian Civil War End for Hezbollah?* Philadelphia, PA: Foreign Policy Research Institute, E-Notes, 2016.

– *Why Humanitarian Aid Workers Are Under Attack*. Philadelphia, PA: Foreign Policy Research Institute, Outside Publications, Originally Published by The National Interest, 2016.

Bolgiano, David G. *A Nationalist's View of Lawfare*. Philadelphia, PA: Foreign Policy Research Institute, *Orbis* vol. 54, Issue 3, 387–99, 2010.

Caldwell, William B., Derek S. Reveron. *Beyond the Tenth Year in Afghanistan: Security Force Assistance and International Security.* Philadelphia, PA: Foreign Policy Research Institute E-Notes, 2011.

Chang, Felix K. *A Salutation to Arms: Asia's Military Buildup, Its Reasons, and Its Implications*. Philadelphia, PA: Foreign Policy Research Institute, E-Notes, 2013.

Charai, Ahmed. *Soft Power, Hard Results in North Africa*. Philadelphia, PA: Foreign Policy Research Institute, E-Notes, 2013.

– *Is Political Islam Compatible with Democracy?* Philadelphia, PA: Foreign Policy Research Institute, Outside Publications, originally published by The National Interest, 2016.

Cook, James L. *Military Alliances in the 21st Century: Still Relevant after all These Years?* Philadelphia, PA: Foreign Policy Research Institute, *Orbis* vol. 57, Issue 4, 559–73, 2013.

DeLise, Jacques. *Taiwan's Quest for International Space: Ma's Legacy, Tsai's Options, China's Choices, and US Policy*. Philadelphia, PA: Foreign Policy Research Institute, *Orbis* vol. 60, Issue 4, 550–74, 2016.

Dueck, Colin. *Nuclear Nonproliferation and Obama*. Philadelphia, PA: Foreign Policy Research Institute, *Orbis* vol. 56, Issue 3, 503–12, 2012.

Foust, Joshua. *What It's Like to Be Gay in the Ultra-Masculine NatSec Community.* Philadelphia, PA: Foreign Policy Research Institute, Outside Publications, 2015.

Garfield, Andrew. *The Afghan Elections: Is Abdullah Right That He Was Wronged (Twice)?* Philadelphia, PA: Foreign Policy Research Institute, E-Notes, 2014.

Garfinkle, Adam. *US Influence Drip-Dripping Away*. Philadelphia, PA: Foreign Policy Research Institute, E-Notes, 2014.

Granieri, Ronald J. *More Faith, Less Fear: Islam, Islamism, and the Future of the West*. Philadelphia, PA: Foreign Policy Research Institute, E-Notes, 2014.

Green, Michael. *China's Periphery: Implications for US Policy and Interests*. Philadelphia, PA: Foreign Policy Research Institute, *Orbis* vol. 56, Issue 3, 357–69, 2012.

Grygiel, Jakub. *Emperor Nero's Lesson on Ukraine*, Philadelphia, PA: Foreign Policy Research Institute, Outside Publications, Originally Published by The American Interest, 2015.

Hodge, Carl C. *The Pivot in Perspective: American Naval Power, Then and Now.* Philadelphia, PA: Foreign Policy Research Institute, *Orbis* vol. 58, Issue 4, 392–412, 2014.

Hoffman, Frank G., and Evan Kalikow. *To Drone or Not to Drone.* Philadelphia, PA: Foreign Policy Research Institute, E-Notes, 2013.

Horowitz, Irving Louis. *Quo Vadis Fidel? Where are You Going?* Philadelphia, PA: Foreign Policy Research Institute E-Note, 2010.

Jones, David T. *The Summer of Canadian Content – 2011.* Philadelphia, PA: Foreign Policy Research Institute E-Note, 2011.

Masse, Todd. *Nuclear Terrorism Redux: Conventionalists, Skeptics, and the Margin of Safety.* Philadelphia, PA: Foreign Policy Research Institute, *Orbis* vol. 54, Issue 2, 302–19, 2010.

Noonan, Michael P. *American Geostrategy in a Disordered World.* Philadelphia, PA: Foreign Policy Research Institute, *Orbis* vol. 59, Issue 4, 600–12, 2015.

Rubel, Robert C. *Getting a Grip on Tailored Deterrence: The World of Conflict Management.* Philadelphia, PA: Foreign Policy Research Institute, *Orbis* vol. 56, Issue 4, 676 – 91, 2012.

Sicherman, Harvey. *Saddam Hussein, Stalin on the Tigris.* Philadelphia, PA: Foreign Policy Research Institute, *Orbis* vol. 55, Issue 3, 489–97, 2011.

Siddiqi, Toufiq. *Pakistan, India, China, and the United States: Energy, Climate Change, and National Security.* Philadelphia, PA: Foreign Policy Research Institute, *Orbis* vol. 57, Issue 4, 615–26, 2013.

Simons, Anna. *Sovereignty – The Ultimate States' Rights Argument.* Philadelphia, PA: Foreign Policy Research Institute Telegram, Temple University, 2011.

Spechler, Martin C., and Dina R. Spechler. *Is Russia Succeeding in Central Asia?* Philadelphia, PA: Foreign Policy Research Institute, *Orbis* vol. 54, Issue 4, 615–29, 2010.

Sucherman, Harvey. *Hafez Al-Assad: The Man Who Waited Too Long.* Philadelphia, PA: Foreign Policy Research Institute, *Orbis* vol. 55, Issue 3, 46 –71, 2011.

Tadros, Samuel. *The Muslim Brotherhood and Washington: Courtship and Its Discontents.* Philadelphia, PA: Foreign Policy Research Institute, E-Notes Middle East Media Monitor, 2012.

Zakheim, The Hon. Dov S. *Did Donald Trump's Presidential Luck Just Run Out?* Philadelphia, PA: Foreign Policy Research Institute, Outside Publications, 2015.

THE HOOVER INSTITUTION ON WAR, REVOLUTION, AND PEACE

Anderson, Terry L., and Laura E. Huggins. *Greener than You: Are You Really an Environmentalist?* Stanford, CA: The Hoover Institution, 2008.

– *If Hayek and Coase Were Environmentalists: Linking Economics and Ecology*. Stanford, CA: The Hoover Institution Economic Working Papers, 2015.

– *Why It's Safer to Drill in the Backyard*. Stanford, CA: The Hoover Institution, The Hoover Digest, 2010.

Atlas, Scott W. *In Excellent Health: Setting the Record Straight on America's Health Care*. Stanford, CA: The Hoover Institution Press, 2012.

Becker, Gary S. *You're Hired! Eventually…* Stanford, CA: The Hoover Institution, The Hoover Digest, 2010.

Carl, Jeremy, ed. *Distributed Power in the United States: Prospects and Policies*. Stanford, CA: The Hoover Institution Press, 2013.

Carl, Jeremy, and David Fedor. *For California's AB 32: Cap-and-Trade-and-Cash Back, Not Cap-and-Trade-and-Tax*. Stanford, CA: The Hoover Institution Analysis, 2014.

– *More Simplicity, Less Charisma: Improving the Effectiveness, Cost, and Fairness of California's Climate Agenda*. Stanford, CA: The Hoover Institution Analysis, 2014.

Carl, Jeremy, Dian Grueneich, and Cara Goldenberg. *Renewable and Distributed Power in California: Simplifying the Regulatory Maze – Making the Path for the Future*. Stanford, CA: The Hoover Institution Analysis, 2012.

Chen, Lanhee J. *Hearing on the Impact of the Affordable Care Act (ACA) Employer Mandate's Definition of Full-Time Employee on Jobs and Opportunities*. Stanford, CA: The Hoover Institution Economic Working Papers, 2014.

Cobbs, Elizabeth. *American Umpire*. Stanford, CA: The Hoover Institution Press, 2013.

Cogan, John F., R. Glenn Hubbard, and Daniel P. Kessler. *The Effect of Massachusetts' Health Reform on Employer-sponsored Insurance Premiums*. Stanford, CA: The Hoover Institution Economic Working Papers, 2010.

– *The Effect of Tax Preferences on Health Spending*. Stanford, CA: The Hoover Institution Economic Working Papers, 2011.

– *Healthy, Wealthy, and Wise: Five Steps to a Better Health Care System, Second Edition*. Stanford, CA: The Hoover Institution Press, 2012.

Epstein, Richard A. *The Blue State Model Has Failed*. Stanford, CA: The Hoover Institution, Defining Ideas, 2016.

Gregory, Paul R. *Lenin's Brain and Other Tales from the Secret Soviet Archives*. Stanford, CA: The Hoover Institution, 2009.

Jackson, Thomas, Kenneth E. Scott, Kimberly Anne Summe, and Mark Moyar. *The White House's Seven Deadly Errors*. Stanford, CA: The Hoover Institution Analysis, 2015.

Nash, George H. *Freedom Betrayed: Herbert Hoover's Secret History of the Second World War and Its Aftermath*. Stanford, CA: The Hoover Institution Press, 2011.

Rauh, Joshua D. *Why City Pension Problems Have Not Improved, and a Roadmap Forward*. Stanford, CA: The Hoover Institution Economic Working Papers, 2015.

Roberts, Rus. *The Human Side of Trade*. Stanford, CA: The Hoover Institution, 2016.

Schake, Kori. *Managing American Hegemony: Essays on Power in a Time of Dominance*. Stanford, CA: The Hoover Institution, 2009.

Scott, Kenneth E. *Designing a Better Bankruptcy Resolution*. Stanford, CA: The Hoover Institution Economic Working Papers, 2013.

– *Designing a Better Bankruptcy Resolution*. Stanford, CA: The Hoover Institution Economic Working Papers, 2015.

Shultz, George P., Jeremy Carl, and David Fedor. *The State Clean Energy Cookbook: A Dozen Recipes for State Action on Energy Efficiency and Renewable Energy*. Stanford, CA: The Hoover Institution Analysis, 2014.

Shultz, George P., Steven P. Andreasen, Sidney D. Drell, and James E. Goodby, eds. *Reykjavik Revisited: Steps Toward a World Free of Nuclear Weapons: Complete Report of 2007 Hoover Institution Conference*. Stanford, CA: The Hoover Institution, 2008.

Sowell, Thomas. *"Trickle Down Theory" and "Tax Cuts for the Rich."* Stanford, CA: The Hoover Institution Analysis, 2012.

Sweeney, James L. *The Energy Revolution*. Stanford, CA: The Hoover Institution, Defining Ideas, 2016.

Taylor, John B. *Getting Off Track: How Government Actions and Interventions Caused, Prolonged and Worsened the Financial Crisis*. Stanford, CA: The Hoover Institution, 2009.

– *Resolution of Failed Financial Institutions: Orderly Liquidation Authority and a New Chapter 14*. Stanford, CA: The Hoover Institution Analysis, 2011.

Thornton, Bruce. *NATO, Brexit, And America's Security*. Stanford, CA: The Hoover Institution Analysis, 2016.

– *Obama Wants to Create More Victims of White Privilege: More Phony Racial "Identities" – For More Racial Conflict*. Stanford, CA: The Hoover Institution, Front-page Mag, 2016.

– *The Wages of Appeasement: Ancient Athens, Munich, and Obama's America*. Stanford, CA: The Hoover Institution Press, 2011.

Warsh, Kevin. *The Conduct of Monetary Policy*. Stanford, CA: The Hoover Institution Analysis, 2013.

West, Bing. *How We Fight in the Twenty-First Century: Winning Battles While Losing Wars*. Stanford, CA: The Hoover Institution Analysis, 2015.

Whitehurst, Grover J. *American Education in 2030: Curriculum Then and Now*. Stanford, CA: The Hoover Institution Analysis, 2010.

Williams, Walter. *Liberty versus the Tyranny of Socialism: Controversial Essays*. Stanford, CA: The Hoover Institution, 2008.

THE HERITAGE FOUNDATION

Abbott, Alden, and John Malcolm. *A Measured Approach to Patent Reform Legislation*. Washington, DC: The Heritage Foundation, 2015.

Addington, David. *What Is the Proper Role of the Courts?* Washington, DC: The Heritage Foundation, 2012.

Bradley, Gerard V. *Religious Liberty in the American Republic*. Washington, DC: The Heritage Foundation, 2008.

Chen, Lanhee. *How Obamacare Burdens Already Strained State Budgets*. Washington, DC: The Heritage Foundation, 2010.

Dodge, Michaela, Lisa Curtis, and Jessica Zuckerman. *Eleven Years Later: US Should Not Lose Momentum in the War on Terrorism*. Washington, DC: The Heritage Foundation, 2012.

Enos, Olivia. *US Counternarcotics Efforts in Afghanistan Fail to Deliver*. Washington, DC: The Heritage Foundation, 2014.

Feulner, Edwin J., and Doug Wilson. *Getting America Right: The True Conservative Values Our Nation Needs Today*. Washington, DC: The Heritage Foundation, 2008.

Florance, Charlotte, James Phillips, James Carafano, Steven Bucci, and Peter Brookes. *Kenya Attack: Vigilance Required to Combat al-Shabaab's Resurgence*. Washington, DC: The Heritage Foundation, 2014.

Gattuso, James. *Adjusting the Picture: Television Regulation for the 21st Century*. Washington, DC: The Heritage Foundation, 2012.

– *Can the Postal Service Have a Future?* Washington, DC: The Heritage Foundation, 2013.

– *Joblessness and Regulation: The "Mass Layoff" Fallacy*. Washington, DC: The Heritage Foundation, 2011.

Gattuso, James, Stephen Keen, and Diane Katz. *Red Tape Rising: Obama's Torrent of New Regulation*. Washington, DC: The Heritage Foundation, 2010.

Grossman, Andrew. *Evenwel v. Abbott: What Does One Person, One Vote Really Mean?* Washington, DC: The Heritage Foundation, 2015.

Groves, Steven, James Roberts, and Brett Schaefer. *Why the US Should Oppose the Creation of an International Anti-Corruption Court*. Washington, DC: The Heritage Foundation, 2014.

Haislmaier, Edmund. *2015 Health Insurance Enrollment: Net Increase of 4.8 Million, Trends Slowing*. Washington, DC: The Heritage Foundation, 2016.

Hayden, General Michael. *Protecting America and Winning the Intelligence War*. Washington, DC: The Heritage Foundation, 2010.

Holmes, Kim R. *Liberty's Best Hope: American Leadership for the 21st Century*. Washington, DC: The Heritage Foundation, 2009.

Inserra, David. *A Dangerous Executive Precedent on Immigration*. Washington, DC: The Heritage Foundation, 2015.

Katz, Diane. *CAFE Standards: Fleet-Wide Regulations Costly and Unwarranted.* Washington, DC: The Heritage Foundation, 2011.

– *Obama's Regulatory Agenda: Calm Before the Superstorm.* Washington, DC: The Heritage Foundation, 2012.

Kronquist, Amanda. *The Prescription Drug User Fee Act: History and Reauthorization Issues for 2012.* Washington, DC: The Heritage Foundation, 2011.

Larkin, Paul. *Reasonably Construing the Computer Fraud and Abuse Act to Avoid Overcriminalization.* Washington, DC: The Heritage Foundation, 2013.

Larkin, Paul, David Bernstein, Randy Barnett, and Clark Neily. *Economic Liberty and the Constitution: An Introduction.* Washington, DC: The Heritage Foundation, 2014.

Meese, Edwin, Matthew Spalding, and David F. Forte. *The Heritage Guide to the Constitution.* Washington, DC: The Heritage Foundation, 2009.

Miller, Terry, and Kim R. Holmes. *The 2009 Index of Economic Freedom: The Link Between Economic Opportunity and Prosperity.* Washington, DC: The Heritage Foundation, 2009.

O'Shea, John. *Reforming Veterans Health Care: Now and for the Future.* Washington, DC: The Heritage Foundation, 2016.

Phillips, James. *Gaza Crisis: US Should Press Egypt to Rein in Hamas.* Washington, DC: The Heritage Foundation, 2012.

Phillips, James, and Ladan Archin. *More International Pressure Needed to Advance Freedom in Iran.* Washington, DC: The Heritage Foundation, 2011.

Policy Experts. *The Insider Guide to Public Policy Experts and Organizations 2008–2009.* Washington, DC: The Heritage Foundation, 2009.

Rector, Robert, and Jamie Hall. *National Academy of Sciences Report Indicates Amnesty for Unlawful Immigrants Would Cost Trillions of Dollars.* Washington, DC: The Heritage Foundation, 2016.

Rosenzweig, Paul. *Government Cyber Failures Reveal Weaknesses of Regulatory Approach to Cybersecurity.* Washington, DC: The Heritage Foundation, 2013.

Rosenzweig, Paul, James Carafano and Jena Baker McNeill. *Using the SAFETY Act to Build a Stronger US–Israeli Terrorism-Fighting Partnership.* Washington, DC: The Heritage Foundation, 2010.

Schreiber, Mark, and Elizabeth Fender. *Majority Say ISIS Strategy Unsuccessful, US at Risk of Attack.* Washington, DC: The Heritage Foundation, 2016.

Slattery, Elizabeth, Stephanos Bibas, Richard Garnett, and Josh Blackman. *The Legacy of Justice Antonin Scalia: Remembering a Conservative Legal Titan's Impact on the Law.* Washington, DC: The Heritage Foundation, 2016.

Von Spakovsky, Hans A. *Sanctuary Cities Put Law-Abiding Citizens at Risk.* Washington, DC: The Heritage Foundation, 2015.

Wainstein, Kenneth. *The Changing Nature of Terror: Law and Policies to Protect America*. Washington, DC: The Heritage Foundation, 2013.

Walters, Riley. *The 75th Terrorist Plot on the United States*. Washington, DC: The Heritage Foundation, 2015.

HUDSON INSTITUTE

Adelman, Carol. *Emerging Economies Bring New Life to Philanthropy*. Washington, DC: The Hudson Institute, 2013.

Adelman, Carol, Jeremiah Norris, Yulya Spantchak, and Kacie Marano. *The Index of Global Philanthropy and Remittances 2010*. Washington, DC: The Hudson Institute, 2010.

Avery, Dennis T. *What Really Triggers a Resource Crisis?* Washington, DC: The Hudson Institute, 2012.

Cardello, Hank. *We're Going Back to Counting Calories … And Here's Why That's a Good Thing*.

– *Why the AMA's Obesity Ruling Is Bad Medicine*. Washington, DC: The Hudson Institute, 2013.

Cardello, Hank, and Jeffrey Wolfson. *Lower-Calorie Foods and Beverages Fuel Growth at Healthy Weight Commitment Foundation Companies*. Washington, DC: The Hudson Institute, 2014.

Cardello, Hank, Jeffrey Wolfson, and Lauren Warren. *How Supermarkets Are Shaping Up and Growing Their Lower-Calorie Products: An Analysis of the Fence Sitter Consumer Segment*. Washington, DC: The Hudson Institute, 2016.

Cropsey, Seth, and Eric B. Brown. Energy: *The West's Strategic Opportunity in the Eastern Mediterranean*. Washington, DC: The Hudson Institute, 2014.

Feith, Douglas J. *A Responsibility to Explain Why Iraq Matters*. Washington, DC: The Hudson Institute, 2010.

Haqqani, Husain. *A Doomed Strategy for Afghanistan and Pakistan*. Washington, DC: The Hudson Institute, 2012.

– *Inclusive Security for the Muslim World*. Washington, DC: The Hudson Institute, 2016.

Herman, Arthur. *From GI Joe to Trader Joe's*. Washington, DC: The Hudson Institute, 2015.

Hudson Institute. *Stuffed at Thanksgiving: A New Corporate Solution to the Obesity Crisis*. Washington, DC: The Hudson Institute, 2011.

Marlowe, Ann. *Pets Later!* Washington, DC: The Hudson Institute, 2010.

Marshall, Paul. *Kenya, Pakistan, Egypt – It Is Now Open Season on Christians*. Washington, DC: The Hudson Institute, 2013.

Mead, Walter Russell. *Why the EU Is in Trouble: The EU's Trade Deal with Canada is on life Support*. Washington, DC: The Hudson Institute, Wall Street Journal, 2016.

Murray, David W. *Mexican Heroin Surge Revealed by the White House.* Washington, DC: The Hudson Institute, 2015.

Natsios, Andrew. *Foreign Aid Programs are Important for American National Security.* Washington, DC: The Hudson Institute, 2011.

Polin, Justin. *Toward a Smarter Power: Moving Beyond the Rhetoric.* Washington, DC: The Hudson Institute, 2011.

Poole, Robert W., Jr. *Organization and Innovation in Air Traffic Control.* Washington, DC: The Hudson Institute, 2013.

Sands, Christopher. *Like Father, Like Son.* Washington, DC: The Hudson Institute, 2015.

– *Mexico: Nice Place to Visit but Wouldn't Want to Trade There.* Washington, DC: The Hudson Institute, 2011.

– *What Prevented the Detroit Bridge? Stubborn Waters.* Washington, DC: The Hudson Institute, 2012.

– *Will Khadr Come Between Canada and the United States?* Washington, DC: The Hudson Institute, 2012.

Sands, Christopher, and Jesse N. Barnett. *The Problem with One Customer.* Washington, DC: The Hudson Institute, 2015.

Sands, Christopher, and Thomas Klier. *The Federal Role in Supporting Auto Sector Innovation.* Washington, DC: The Hudson Institute, 2010.

Simcox, Robin. *AQAP's Ideological Battles at Home and Abroad.* Washington, DC: The Hudson Institute, 2015.

Stelzer, Irwin M. *The Times and the Post Take a Peculiar Line on Israel.* Washington, DC: The Hudson Institute, 2016.

Tadros, Samuel. *Mapping Egyptian Islamism.* Washington, DC: The Hudson Institute, 2014.

THE INSTITUTE FOR CONTEMPORARY STUDIES

Gilder, George. *Recapturing the Spirit of Enterprise.* Richmond, CA: The Institute for Contemporary Studies Press, 2008.

Glenn, Charles L. Jr. *The Myth of the Common School.* Richmond, CA: The Institute for Contemporary Studies Press, 2008.

Hickell, Walter J. *Crisis in The Common: The Alaska Solution.* Richmond, CA: The Institute for Contemporary Studies Press, 2008.

Nisbet, Robert. *The Quest for Community: A Study in Ethics in Order and Freedom.* Richmond, CA: The Institute for Contemporary Studies Press, 2008.

Richards, John F. *Land, Property, and the Environment.* Richmond, CA: The Institute for Contemporary Studies Press, 2008.

Wilson, James Q., and Joan Petersilia, eds. Crime: *Public Policies for Crime Control.* Richmond, CA: The Institute for Contemporary Studies Press, 2008.

THE INSTITUTE FOR POLICY STUDIES

Alperstein, Olivia. *When Children Hurt, Schools Can Help: Nobody Should Lose Out on a Good Education Because of a Bad Experience.* Washington, DC: Institute for Policy Studies, 2015.

Anderson, Sarah. *Memo to US: Only Fools Rush In.* Washington, DC: Institute for Policy Studies, 2010.

– *Retirement Divide: 100 CEOs v. the Rest of Us.* Washington, DC: Institute for Policy Studies, 2016.

– *The Trojan Horse in the Debt Debate.* Washington, DC: Institute for Policy Studies, 2012.

Anderson, Sarah, Marjorie Wood, Sam Pizzigati, and Leslie Garvey. *Infographic: The Obamacare Benefit You've Never Heard of.* Washington, DC: Institute for Policy Studies, 2014.

Asante-Muhammed, Dedrick, Karen Dolan, Daphne Wysham, Phyllis Bennis, Sarah Anderson, and John Feffer. *Barely Making the Grade: Obama's First Year.* Washington, DC: Institute for Policy Studies, 2010.

Baraka, Ajamu. *The Assassination of Sandra Bland and the Struggle against State Repression.* Washington, DC: Institute for Policy Studies, 2015.

Bennis, Phyllis. *Understanding the US-Iran Crisis: A Primer.* Washington, DC: Institute for Policy Studies, 2008.

Broad, Robin, and Chuck Cavanagh. *Development Redefined: How the Market Met Its Match.* Washington, DC: Institute for Policy Studies, 2008.

Broad, Robin, and John Cavanagh. *The Age of Vulnerability: How the 2008 Financial Crash Redefined What It Means to be Economically Vulnerable.* Washington, DC: Institute for Policy Studies, 2011.

Bruun, Jonas, Lauren Gifford, and Robbie Watt. *What's Hot and What's Not at COP19 in Warsaw.* Washington, DC: Institute for Policy Studies, 2013.

Cavanagh, John. *Heroes Fighting to Save the Middle Class: Wisconsin's Progressives.* Washington, DC: Institute for Policy Studies, 2010.

Collins, Chuck. *Racial Wealth Inequality and the Dream Deferred.* Washington, DC: Institute for Policy Studies, 2014.

Collins, Chuck, and Nick Thorkelson. *The Economic Meltdown Funnies.* Washington, DC: Institute for Policy Studies, 2008.

Dolan, Karen. *Beyond the Jobs Report: A Call for a Transformational Economy.* Washington, DC: Institute for Policy Studies, 2012.

Feffer, John. *Recognizing Palestine: As More European Governments Line Up to Recognize a Palestinian state, Israel (and the US) Look More Isolated Than Ever.* Washington, DC: Institute for Policy Studies, 2014.

Glover, Danny. *Danny Glover's Letelier-Moffitt Award Speech.* Washington, DC: Institute for Policy Studies, 2012.

Hartman, Chester. *Mandate for Change: Policies and Leadership for 2009 and Beyond.* Washington, DC: Institute for Policy Studies, 2009.

Hartung, William D., and Miriam Pemberton. *Lessons from Iraq: Avoiding the Next War*. Washington, DC: Institute for Policy Studies, 2008.

Klinger, Scott. *Five Taxpayer-Supported Corporations that Paid Their CEOs More than Uncle Sam*. Washington, DC: Institute for Policy Studies, 2016.

Klinger, Scott, Sam Pizzigati, Chuck Collins, and Sarah Anderson. *A Response to Disputes by Corporations over Our Methodology*. Washington, DC: Institute for Policy Studies, 2011.

Klinger, Scott, Sarah Anderson, and Brent Soloway. *A Pension Deficit Disorder: The Massive CEO Retirement Funds and Underfunded Worker Pensions at Firms Pushing Social Security Cuts*. Washington, DC: Institute for Policy Studies, 2012.

Perez-Rocha, Manuel. *Peoples Sovereignty vs. Impunity Inc.: Counterpower and Struggles for Justice*. Washington, DC: Institute for Policy Studies, 2015.

– *Urging Presidents Obama and Calderon to Address Human and Workers' Rights Issues*. Washington, DC: Institute for Policy Studies, 2010.

Pizzigati, Sam. *Paying for Poor Performance*. Washington, DC: Institute for Policy Studies, 2013.

Redman, Janet, and Oscar Reyes. *Gates Funding Welcome, but No Substitute for Finance Commitments in Paris Climate Agreement*. Washington, DC: Institute for Policy Studies, 2015.

Redman, Janet, and Sarah Anderson. *Activists in More than 20 Countries Urge G20 Leaders to Tax Speculators*. Washington, DC: Institute for Policy Studies, 2011.

Reyes, Oscar. *California's Cap and Trade Policy Is Actually Working against Its Climate Action Targets*. Washington, DC: Institute for Policy Studies, 2016.

Shih, Kevin, and Sarah Anderson. *Tax Wall Street to Pay for Jobs*. Washington, DC: Institute for Policy Studies, 2010.

Slaughter-Johnson, Ebony. *Mother's Day Is Another Day to Struggle for Justice When Your Child Is behind Bars*. Washington, DC: Institute for Policy Studies, 2016.

Villeda, Krysta. *World Bank Energy Lending Still Veering in Wrong Direction*. Washington, DC: Institute for Policy Studies, 2014.

Williams. Tiffany. *Domestic Workers Deserve Protection: Hold Diplomats Like Khobragade to Account*. Washington, DC: Institute for Policy Studies, 2013.

– *What Immigration Reform Means for Women*. Washington, DC: Institute for Policy Studies, 2013.

Woods, Emira. *New Policy Statement: A New Direction for US Policy on Africa*. Washington, DC: Institute for Policy Studies, 2013.

Canadian Think Tanks

ATLANTIC INSTITUTE FOR MARKET STUDIES

Amir Attaran, Rosario, and Taylor Andree Cartagena. *The Effectiveness of the Common Drug Review in Canada's National Drug Strategy.* Halifax, NS: Atlantic Institute for Market Studies, 2011.

Audas, Rick, Charles Cirtwill, and Jaime Newman. *2nd Annual Report Card on Western Canadian High Schools.* Halifax, NS: Atlantic Institute for Market Studies, 2012.

Bennett, Paul W. *Building a Bigger Tent: Serving All Special Needs Students in New Brunswick's Inclusive Education System.* Halifax, NS: Atlantic Institute for Market Studies, 2012.

– *Reclaiming At-Risk Children and Youth: A Review of Nova Scotia's SchoolsPlus (ISD) Initiative.* Halifax, NS: Atlantic Institute for Market Studies, 2013.

– *E-Learning in K-12 Schools.* Halifax, NS: Atlantic Institute for Market Studies, 2016.

Bennett, Paul W., and Derek M. Gillis. *Education on Wheels, Seizing Cost and Energy Efficiency Opportunities in Student Transportation.* Halifax, NS: Atlantic Institute for Market Studies, 2015.

Bennett, Paul W., and Karen Mitchell. *Maintaining "Spotless Records:" Professional Standards, Teacher Misconduct and the Teaching Profession.* Halifax, NS: Atlantic Institute for Market Studies, 2014.

Eisen, Ben, and Shaun Fantauzzo. *The Size and Cost of Atlantic Canada's Public Sector.* Halifax, NS: Atlantic Institute for Market Studies, 2014.

Fantauzzo, Shaun. *Reforming Atlantic Fisheries, Lessons from Iceland.* Halifax, NS: Atlantic Institute for Market Studies and Frontier Centre for Public Policy, 2014.

Flanagan, Tom, and Lee Harding. *Seven Habits of Highly Effective First Nations.* Halifax, NS: Atlantic Institute for Markey Studies, 2016.

Freehan, James. *Electricity Market Integration, Newfoundland Chooses Monopoly and Protectionism.* Halifax, NS: Atlantic Institute for Market Studies, 2013.

Hebb, Barrie B.F., and Charles Cirtwill. *What You Don't Know Can Hurt You: Where Does All the Money Go?* Halifax, NS: Atlantic Institute for Market Studies, 2010.

Lucani, Patrick. *Is the Obesity-Industry-Complex Making Us Fat?* Halifax, NS: Atlantic Institute for Market Studies, 2013.

Mansur, Salim. *The Muddle of Multiculturalism: A Liberal Critique.* Halifax, NS: Atlantic Institute for Market Studies, 2010.

McDonald, Meredith. *The Road Ahead, Options for Reforming Registry Service Delivery.* Halifax, NS: Atlantic Institute for Market Studies, 2015.

McIver, Don. *Who Could Have Seen* THAT *Coming? The History and Consequences of a Global Crisis.* Halifax, NS: Atlantic Institute for Market Studies, 2010.
– *Nova Scotians without Borders: Why Economic and Industrial Development Strategies Should Refocus on People Rather Than Regions.* Halifax, NS: Atlantic Institute for Market Studies, 2011.
Munro, Ian. *Signal Strength: Setting the Stage for Canada's Wireless Industry in the Next Decade.* Halifax, NS: Atlantic Institute for Market Studies, 2010.
– *Crisis? What Crisis? Understanding Child Care Shortages in Nova Scotia.* Halifax, NS: Atlantic Institute for Market Studies, 2013.
– *Radio Free Canada, Ending Protectionism in Canada's Communications Industries.* Halifax, NS: Atlantic Institute for Market Studies, 2013.
– *Checking the Math on Childcare.* Halifax, NS: Atlantic Institute for Market Studies, 2015.
Murrell, David, and Shaun Fantauzzo. *New Brunswick's Debt and Deficit, A Historical Look.* Halifax, NS: Atlantic Institute for Market Studies, 2014.
Pavel, Jan. *E-Government in the Atlantic Provinces: Review on Future Trends.* Halifax, NS: Atlantic Institute for Market Studies, 2016.
Pickford, Andrew. *Gas Opportunities for Atlantic Canada.* Halifax, NS: Atlantic Institute for Market Studies, 2016.
Roach, Robert, Jeff Collins, and Marco Navarro-Génie. *A Good Problem to Have, Lessons for Atlantic Canada from Alberta's Experience with Natural Resource Revenue.* Halifax, NS: Atlantic Institute for Market Studies, 2015.
Spencer, Juanita. *Putting our Money Where Our Mouths Are: Why Local Governments Should Support Equalization of People, Not Provinces.* Halifax, NS: Atlantic Institute for Market Studies, 2012.
– *This Rose, by Any Other Name, Stinks: Property Taxes Are Just a Badly Designed Income Tax and Should Be Replaced with a Better One.* Halifax, NS: Atlantic Institute for Market Studies, 2012.
Weil, Gordon L. *Atlantic Canada and the US Electricity Market: Projects and Perspectives.* Halifax, NS: Atlantic Institute for Market Studies, 2015.
Weil, Gordon L., Ed Martin, and Ben Eisen. *Muskrat Falls, Opportunities to Reduce Risk and Enhance Benefits.* Halifax, NS: Atlantic Institute for Market Studies, 2014.
Zawai, Ma'n, Brian Van Ness, and Bartha Maria Knoppers. *Incidental Findings in Genomic Research: A Review of International Norms.* Halifax, NS: Atlantic Institute for Market Studies, 2012.
Zitnet, David, and Dianne Kelderman. *A Third Option for the Health Care Debate: Think Community and Courage.* Halifax, NS: Atlantic Institute for Market Studies, 2010.

THE CALEDON INSTITUTE OF SOCIAL POLICY
Battle, Ken. *Caring for Caregivers.* Ottawa: The Caledon Institute, 2009.

– *Child Benefits and the 2015 Federal Budget.* Ottawa: The Caledon Institute, 2015.
– *Community Roles in Policy.* Ottawa: The Caledon Institute, 2009.
– *Restoring Minimum Wage in Canada.* Ottawa: The Caledon Institute, 2011.
– *Trends in Canada's Payroll Taxes.* Ottawa: The Caledon Institute, 2011.
Battle, Ken, and Sherri Torjman. *If You Don't Pay, You Can't Play: The Children's Fitness Tax Credit.* Ottawa: The Caledon Institute, 2014.
Battle, Ken, Sherri Torjman, and Michael Mendelson. *As the Fiscal Chill Thaws: Social Policy Ideas for the Medium Term.* Ottawa: The Caledon Institute, 2013.
– *The Forgotten Fundamental.* Ottawa: The Caledon Institute, 2008.
– *The No-Budge Budget.* Ottawa: The Caledon Institute, 2012.
– *Old Age Insecurity?* Ottawa: The Caledon Institute, 2012.
– *Policy Agenda in Search of a Budget.* Ottawa: The Caledon Institute, 2011.
– *The Skilled Budget.* Ottawa: The Caledon Institute, 2013.
– *The 2015 Deficit-of-Ideas Budget.* Ottawa: The Caledon Institute, 2015.
Hayes, Brigid. *What You Need to Know about the Canada Job Fund.* Ottawa: The Caledon Institute, 2014.
Jai, Julie. *The Journey of Reconciliation: Understanding our Treaty Past, Present and Future.* Ottawa: The Caledon Institute, 2014.
Kent, Tom. *Immigration: For Young Citizens.* Ottawa: The Caledon Institute, 2010.
Loewen, Garry, and Anne Makhoul. *When Collaboration Stumbles: The Opportunities Niagara Story.* Ottawa: The Caledon Institute, 2009.
Makhoul, Anne. *Bold Solutions for Tackling Poverty in Waterloo Region.* Ottawa: The Caledon Institute, 2008.
– *Effecting Policy Change: Lessons from the Canadian Caregiver Coalition.* Ottawa: The Caledon Institute, 2011.
– *New Brunswick's "Overcoming Poverty Together" Plan Earns Praise and Creates Hope.* Ottawa: The Caledon Institute, 2010.
Makhoul, Anne, and Sherry Torjman. *Assessing the Benefits of Community Human Services.* Ottawa: The Caledon Institute, 2012.
Makhoul, Anne, Jean-François Aubin, Caroline Lachance, and Dal Brodhead. LaDémarche: *Revitalizing Neighbourhoods in Trois-Rivières.* Ottawa: The Caledon Institute, 2008.
Mendelson, Michael. *Federal Election – Politicians Refuse to Admit that Deficits Are Inevitable.* Ottawa: The Caledon Institute, 2008.
– *Options for a Refundable Disability Tax Credit for 'working age' persons.* Ottawa: The Caledon Institute, 2015.
Mendelson, Michael, and Ken Battle. *Fixing the Hole in EI: Temporary Income Assistance for the Unemployed.* Ottawa: The Caledon Institute, 2011.
Mendelson, Michael, Ken Battle, Sherri Torjman, and Ernie Lightman. *A Basic Income Plan for Canadian with Severe Disabilities.* Ottawa: The Caledon Institute, 2010.

Mendelson, Michael, Sherri Torjman, and Ken Battle. *Canada Pension Plan: The New Deal*. Ottawa: The Caledon Institute, 2016.

Metallic, Naiomi, and Sébastian Grammond. *Ensuring Real Accountability on First Nation Reserves*. Ottawa: The Caledon Institute, 2016.

Notten, Geranda, and Michael Mendelson. *Using Low Income and Material Deprivation to Monitor Poverty Reduction*. Ottawa: The Caledon Institute, 2016.

Torjman, Sherri. *Disability Policy Highlights*. Ottawa: The Caledon Institute, 2014.

Torjman, Sherri, and Anne Makhoul. *Knowledge Exchange for Mental Health*. Ottawa: The Caledon Institute, 2013.

Torjman, Sherri, Ken Battle, and Michael Mendelson. *Counsel for the Council*. Ottawa: The Caledon Institute, 2012.

– *Disability Supports: Missing on the Policy Radar.* Ottawa: The Caledon Institute, 2015.

– *Ensuring the Welfare of 'Welfare Incomes.'* Ottawa: The Caledon Institute, 2013.

– *Financing Long-Term Care: More Money in the Mix*. Ottawa: The Caledon Institute, 2013.

– *How Did the Just Society Become Just Don't Care?* Ottawa: The Caledon Institute, 2010.

– *Poverty Reduction in Québec: The First Five Years*. Ottawa: The Caledon Institute, 2010.

– *Recreation and Resilience*. Ottawa: The Caledon Institute, 2012.

Tweddle, Anne, Ken Battle, and Sherri Torjman. *Welfare in Canada*. Ottawa: The Caledon Institute, 2014.

– *Welfare in Canada, 2014*. Ottawa: The Caledon Institute, 2015.

Wood, Donna E. *Strengthening Canada's Public Employment Service Post-Devolution*. Ottawa: The Caledon Institute, 2016.

Zuker, Richard. *Some Implications of the Liberal Government's Tax Changes*. Ottawa: The Caledon Institute, 2016.

CANADIAN GLOBAL AFFAIRS INSTITUTE (FORMERLY CANADIAN DEFENCE & FOREIGN AFFAIRS INSTITUTE)

Boudreau, Brett. Preparing for Contemporary Operations in a Strategic Communications World. Calgary, AB: Canadian Global Affairs Institute, 2016.

Bow, Brian. *Getting Past the Bilateral-Trilateral Debate: A Pragmatic Functionalist Approach to North America*. Calgary, AB: Canadian Global Affairs Institute, 2011.

Brodie, Ian. *After America, Canada's Moment?* Calgary, AB: Canadian Global Affairs Institute, 2015.

Cooper, Barry. *What makes the Middle East Such a Difficult Place?* Calgary, AB: Canadian Global Affairs Institute, 2014.

Coulon, Jocelyn. *Whatever Happened to Peacekeeping? The Future of a Tradition*. Calgary, AB: Canadian Global Affairs Institute, 2010.

D'Aquino, Thomas. *Security and Prosperity in the Canada-United States Relationship Two Sides of the Same Coin: An Address to the Conference of Defence Associations and the CDA Institute 2011 Conference on Defence and Security*. Calgary, AB: Canadian Global Affairs Institute, 2011.

De Kerckhove, Ferry. *Canada and International Organizations: Time for a Review*. Calgary, AB: Canadian Global Affairs Institute, 2013.

Diebert, Robert. *Distributed Security as Cyber Strategy: Outlining a Comprehensive Approach for Canada in Cyberspace*. Calgary, AB: Canadian Global Affairs Institute, 2012.

Ferris, John. *Personal Privacy and Communications Security from the Telegraph to the Internet*. Calgary, AB: Canadian Global Affairs Institute, 2014.

Godefroy, Andrew. *The Ghost of General Otter: Putting the Canadian Forces Report on Transformation 2011 in Context*. Calgary, AB: Canadian Global Affairs Institute, 2012.

Granatstein, J.L. *Is NATO Still Necessary for Canada?* Calgary, AB: Canadian Global Affairs Institute, 2013.

Grinius, Marius. *Canada and Asia: Prosperity and Security*. Calgary, AB: Canadian Global Affairs Institute, 2015.

Hage, Robert. *Canada-EU Free Trade: The End or Future of Trade Liberalization*. Calgary, AB: Canadian Global Affairs Institute, 2016.

Lindley-French, Julian. *NATO: Countering Strategic Maskirovka*. Calgary, AB: Canadian Global Affairs Institute, 2015.

Matthews, Kyle. *Jihad versus R2P: The Future of Atrocity Prevention*. Calgary, AB: Canadian Global Affairs Institute, 2014.

Morese, Eric, and Stéfanie von Hlatky. *Sovereignty Collapse: Daesh and the Return of Bandit Kings*. Calgary, AB: Canadian Global Affairs Institute, 2016.

Perry, David. *2015 Status Report on Major Defense Equipment Procurements*. Calgary, AB: Canadian Global Affairs Institute, 2015.

Plouffe, Joël. Towards a North American Arctic Region. Calgary, AB: Canadian Global Affairs Institute, 2013.

Rebien, Sven Tommi. *Canada's New Defense Procurement Strategy: Has the Pendulum Swung Too Far?* Calgary, AB: Canadian Global Affairs Institute, 2014.

Robertson, Colin. *'Now for the Hard Part': A User's Guide to Renewing the Canadian-American Partnership*. Calgary, AB: Canadian Global Affairs Institute, 2011.

– *A Canadian Primer to the G20 Summit in Los Cabos, Mexico*. Calgary, AB: Canadian Global Affairs Institute, 2012.

– *A Canadian Agenda for the USA: Obama and Beyond*. Calgary, AB: Canadian Global Affairs Institute, 2016.

Segal, Hugh, and Jessica McLean. *Exigencies of Future Deployments: What Canada Must Exact from its Military Partners*. Calgary, AB: Canadian Global Affairs Institute, 2013.

Soroka, Gary. *Crisis – Order – Europe: Germany Steps Up*. Calgary, AB: Canadian Global Affairs Institute, 2015.

Stairs, Denis. *Being Rejected in the United Nations: The Causes and Implications of Canada's Failure to Win a Seat in the UN Security Council.* Calgary, AB: Canadian Global Affairs Institute, 2011.

Sutherland, Peter. *Philippines.* Calgary, AB: Canadian Global Affairs Institute, 2012.

Wallace, Ron. *Redefining Security in the Post- Afghanistan Era: The Future of Canadian Military Policy in an Uncertain World.* Calgary, AB: Canadian Global Affairs Institute, 2010.

– *Unstoppable Momentum: The Real Meaning and Value Behind Operation Nunavilut 10*. Calgary, AB: Canadian Global Affairs Institute, 2010.

Westdal, Christopher. *A Way Ahead With Russia.* Calgary, AB: Canadian Global Affairs Institute, 2016.

– *NATO Summit: Making Peace with Russia, Canada Notwithstanding.* Calgary, AB: Canadian Global Affairs Institute, 2010.

THE CANADA WEST FOUNDATION

Ascah, Bob, Ted Chambers, Satya Das, John Kolkman, Dan Holinda, Mel McMillan, and Robert Roach. *Becoming Alberta's Next Premier: Policy Ideas for Leadership Candidates*. Calgary, AB: Canada West Foundation, 2011.

Bandali, Farahnaz. *Shedding Light on the TFW Program.* Calgary, AB: Canada West Foundation, 2014.

Berdhal, Loleen. *Whither Western Alienation?: Shifting Patterns of Western Canadian Discontent with the Federal Government.* Calgary, AB: Canada West Foundation, 2010.

Berdahl, Loleen, and Brett Gartner. *Competitive Mindset: Are Western Canadians Ready to "Go for Gold?"* Calgary, AB: Canada West Foundation, 2008.

Cameron, Anna, and Trevor McLeod. *Patchwork Pollution Solution: Stitching Together a Canadian Climate Plan.* Calgary, AB: Canada West Foundation, 2015.

Chendong Li, and Naomi Christensen. *Canada – Korea Free Trade Agreement.* Calgary, AB: Canada West Foundation, 2015.

Cleland, Michael. *From the Ground Up: Earning Public Support for Resource Development.* Calgary, AB: Canada West Foundation, 2014.

– *Let's Talk Energy: A Continuing Dialogue.* Calgary, AB: Canada West Foundation, 2012.

– *Unpacking Social License: Toward Framework for Addressing the Social License Challenge Facing the Natural Resource Sector.* Calgary, AB: Canada West Foundation, 2013.

Cleland, Michael F., and Len Coad. *Engine of Growth: A Western Canadian Energy Policy Framework*. Calgary, AB: Canada West Foundation, 2013.

Cleland, Michael F., Anastasia Comumbos, and Him Hume. *Seismic Shifts: The Changing World of Natural Gas*. Calgary, AB: Canada West Foundation, 2011.

Cleland, Michael, and Roger Gibbins. *Western Leadership for a Canadian Energy Strategy*. Calgary, AB: Canada West Foundation, 2010.

Cleland, Michael, Roger Gibbins, and Robbie Rolfe. *Climate Change? Reflections on the 20th Anniversary of the 1992 Rio Conference*. Calgary, AB: Canada West Foundation, 2012.

Coad, Len. *Managing Expectations: Assessing the Potential of BC's Liquid Natural Gas Industry*. Calgary, AB: Canada West Foundation, 2013.

Coffin, Victoria, David W. Poulton, and Casey Vander Ploeg. *Our Water and NAFTA: Implications for the Use of Market-Based Instruments for Water Resource Management*. Calgary, AB: Canada West Foundation, 2011.

Dade, Carlo. *The Business Case for an Alberta International Development Office*. Calgary, AB: Canada West Foundation, 2014.

– *The Pacific Alliance: Why It's Important for Western Canada*. Calgary, AB: Canada West Foundation, 2014.

Dade, Carlo, and Shafka Sajid. *The TPP: The West Wants In*. Calgary, AB: Canada West Foundation, 2016.

Gibbins, Roger. *An Extraordinary Future: A Strategic Vision for Western Canada*. Calgary, AB: Canada West Foundation, 2010.

Gibbins, Roger, Jacques Marcil, and Robert Roach. *Taking Action on the Economy*. Calgary, AB: Canada West Foundation, 2008.

Gibbins, Roger, and Robert Roach. *Taking Stock of the Federation*. Calgary, AB: Canada West Foundation, 2012.

Harder, Catherine, Geoff Jackson, and Janet Lane. *Talent Is Not Enough: Closing the Skills Gap*. Calgary, AB: Canada West Foundation, 2014.

Holden, Michael. *Pipe or Perish: Saving an Oil Industry at Risk*. Calgary, AB: Canada West Foundation, 2013.

Lane, Janet, and Jeff Griffiths. *Building Block: Modular Credentials for Canada's Trades*. Calgary, AB: Canada West Foundation, 2016.

Lane, Janet, and Naomi Christensen. *Competence is the Best Credential*. Calgary, AB: Canada West Foundation, 2015.

– *Know, Do, Understand: Development of Competencies in Canada's Schoolchildren*. Calgary, AB: Canada West Foundation, 2016.

Lane, Janet, and T. Scott Murray. *Smarten Up: It's Time to Build Essential Skills*. Calgary, AB: Canada West Foundation, 2015.

Marcil, Jacques. *Well Balanced: Manitoba Economic Profile and Forecast*. Calgary, AB: Canada West Foundation, 2008.

McKenzie, Kenneth. *Business Taxation in Western Canada: Settling for a Personal Best?* Calgary, AB: Canada West Foundation, 2009.

McLeod, Trevor. *Walkin' The Walk: Five Steps Toward Efficient Cities.* Calgary, AB: Canada West Foundation, 2015.

Miris, Rolf, and Chris Ryan. *Western Canada's Exports: Causes and Implications of Changing Competiveness in Key Markets.* Calgary, AB: Canada West Foundation, 2008.

Nourallah, Laura, and Stewart Fast. *Fair Enough: Assessing Community Confidence in Energy Authorities.* Calgary, AB: Canada West Foundation, 2016.

Roach, Robert. *State of the West 2010: Western Canadian Demographic and Economic Trends.* Calgary, AB: Canada West Foundation, 2010.

Sommerfeld, Larissa. *Stress Points: An Overview of Water & Economic Growth in Western Canada.* Calgary, AB: Canada West Foundation, 2012.

Sommerfeld, Larissa, and Dave Hume. *Northern Voices, Southern Choices: Water Policy Lessons for Alberta.* Calgary, AB: Canada West Foundation, 2011.

St. Louis, Liam, and Janet Lane. *Start 'Em Up: Incubating NextGen Innovators.* Calgary, AB: Canada West Foundation, 2016.

Stirrett, Shawna. *The Missing Link: Constructive Ideas for Improving Urban Environmental Performance in Western Canada.* Calgary, AB: Canada West Foundation, 2013.

Stirrett, Shawna, and Stephanie Shewchuck. *Bright Spots: Urban Development Initiatives in Western Canada.* Calgary, AB: Canada West Foundation, 2012.

Vander Ploeg, Casey. *Problematic Property Tax: Why the Property Tax Fails to Measure Up and What to Do about It.* Calgary, AB: Canada West Foundation, 2008.

– *From H_2O: Turning Alberta's Water Headache into Opportunity.* Calgary, AB: Canada West Foundation, 2010.

Vander Ploeg, Casey G., and Larissa Sommerfeld. *Charging for Water Use in Canada: A Workbook of the Central Principles, Key Questions, and Initial Steps.* Calgary, AB: Canada West Foundation, 2011.

THE CANADIAN CENTRE FOR POLICY ALTERNATIVES

A Network of NGOs, Trade Unions and Independent Experts. *Progress on Women's Rights: Missing in Action – A Shadow Report on Canada's Implementation of the Beijing Declaration and Platform for Action.* Ottawa: CCPA, 2014.

Adekunle, Bamidele, Jaime Cidro, and Glen Filson. *The Political Economy of Culturally Appropriate Foods in Winnipeg: A Case of Refugee Path Immigrants (RPIs).* Winnipeg: CCPA, 2015.

Angus, Murray, and Morley Hanson. *The New "Three R's": An Award-Winning College Program for Inuit Youth Shows the Benefits of a Small Learning Environment and Culturally-Relevant Curriculum.* Ottawa: CCPA, 2011.

Baines, Donna, and Pat Armstrong. *Promising Practices in Long Term Care: Ideas Worth Sharing*. Ottawa: CCPA, 2015.

Bigland-Pritchard, Mark. *Plugging the Gap: Sustainable Power Options to Complement Wind and Solar.* Regina: CCPA, 2011.

Brodsky, Gwen, and Shelagh Day. *Strengthening Human Rights: Why British Columbia Needs a Human Rights Commission*. Vancouver: CCPA, 2014.

Canadian Centre for Policy Alternatives: BC Office – BC Commentary: A Review of Provincial Social and Economic Trends. Ottawa: CCPA, 2009.

Canadian Centre for Policy Alternatives: National Office. *Quel type de mesures: Des critères pour évaluer le budget fédéral.* Ottawa: CCPA, 2009.

– *What Kind of Stimulus: Tests for Assessing the Federal Budget*. Ottawa: CCPA, 2009.

– *Alternative Federal Budget 2009: Beyond the Crisis: A Budget for a Strong and Sustainable Future*. Ottawa: CCPA, 2009.

– *Leadership des temps difficiles: Alternative budgétaire pour le gouvernement fédéral: Programme de stimulation fiscal*. Ottawa: CCPA, 2009.

Canadian Centre for Policy Alternatives: Ont Office – ON. *Maps You'll Never Find at the Gas Station: Ontario's Working Poor.* Toronto: CCPA, 2016.

Curran, Amelia, Evan Bowness, and Elizabeth Cormack. *Meeting the Needs of Youth: Perspectives from Youth – Serving Agencies*. Winnipeg: CCPA, 2010.

Daub, Shannon, and Heather Whiteside. *Election Chill Effect: The Impact on BC's New Third Party Advertising Rules on Social Movement Groups.* Vancouver: CCPA, 2010.

Dutt, Monika. *Affordable Access to Medicines: A Prescription for Canada.* Ottawa: CCPA, 2014.

Erdmann, Jen. *Lived Experiences and Perspectives: Women, Mental Health, and Housing in Winnipeg*. Winnipeg: CCPA, 2015.

Fairey, David, John Calvert, and Wayne Peppard. *Building a Safer Work Environment for BC Construction Workers*. Ottawa: CCPA, 2009.

Fernandez, Lynne. *It's Time to Give Back to Manitoba's North*. Winnipeg: CCPA, 2016.

Foster, Karen. *Youth Employment and Un(der) Employment in Canada: More Than a Temporary Problem?* Ottawa: CCPA, 2012.

Frank, Lesley. *The Nova Scotia Child Poverty Report Card 2010: 1989 – 2008*. Halifax: CCPA, 2010.

Himelfarb, Alex, and Trish Hennessey. *Basic Income: Rethinking Social Policy.* Ottawa: CCPA, 2016.

Ivanova, Igilka. *The Cost of Poverty in BC*. Vancouver: CCPA, 2011.

Jamasi, Zohra, and Trish Hennessey. *Nobody's Business: Airbnb in Toronto.* Ontario: CCPA, 2016.

Jarosiewicz, Scott. *A Family Living Wage for Manitoba: 2013 Update.* Winnipeg: CCPA, 2013.

Lee, Marc, and Amanda Card. *Who Occupies the Sky? The Distribution of GHGs in Canada.* Ottawa | Vancouver: CCPA, 2011.

Lee, Marc, and John Calver. *Clean Electricity, Conservation and Climate Justice in BC: Meeting Our Energy Needs in a Zero – Carbon Future.* Vancouver: CCPA, 2012.

Lee, Marc, Herb Barbolet, Tegan Adams, and Matt Thomson. *Every Bite Counts: Climate Justice and BC's Food System.* Vancouver: CCPA, 2010.

Lexchin, Joel. *Canada and Access to Medicines in Developing Countries: Intellectual Property Rights First.* Ottawa: CCPA, 2013.

Macdonald, David, and Erika Shaker. *Eduflation and the High Cost of Learning.* Ottawa: CCPA, 2012.

Macdonald, David, and Kayle Hatt. *At What Cost? The Impacts of Rushing to Balance the Budget.* Ottawa: CCPA, 2014.

McInturff, Kate. *The Gap in the Gender Gap: Violence Against Women in Canada.* Ottawa: CCPA, 2013.

Ontario's Gender Gap: Women and Jobs Post – Recession. Toronto: CCPA, 2014.

McInturff, Kate, with The Canadian Research Institute for the Advancement of Women. *The Best and Worst Places to be a Woman in Canada 2016: The Gender Gap in Canada's 25 Biggest Cities.* Ottawa: CCPA, 2016.

Partiff, Ben. *Counting Every Drop: The Case for Water Use Reporting in BC.* Vancouver: CCPA, 2013. Posen, Andrew, Arjumand Siddiqi, and Clyde Hertzman. *Nurturing Early Childhood Development in Times of Austerity in BC.* Vancouver: CCPA, 2015.

Prebble, Peter, and Ann Coxworth. *SaskNotes: The Government of Canada's Legacy of Contamination in Northern Saskatchewan Watersheds.* Regina: CCPA, 2013.

Rao, Govind C. *The Great Equalizer: The Case for Investing in the Toronto Public Library.* Toronto: CCPA, 2012.

Smith, Charles C. *Pluralism in the Arts in Canada: A Change Is Gonna Come.* Ottawa: CCPA, 2012.

Social Research and Planning Council Living Wage Advisory Committee. *Calculating a Living Wage for Perth and Huron Counties.* Toronto: CCPA, 2015.

Townson, Monica. *Pension Breakdown: How the Finance Ministers Bungled Pension Reform.* Ottawa: CCPA, 2011.

White, Robert G. *Corporate Social Responsibility and a Living Wage.* Toronto: CCPA, 2012.

Yalnizyan, Armine. *The Rise of Canada's Richest 1%.* Ottawa: CCPA, 2010.

THE C.D. HOWE INSTITUTE

Ambler, Steve. *Ripple Effects: Oil Prices Shocks and Monetary Policy.* Toronto: C.D Howe Institute e-brief, 30 August 2016.

– *Putting Money to Work: Monetary Policy in a Low Interest Rate Environment*. Toronto: C.D. Howe Institute e-brief, 3 November 2016.

Ambler, Steve, and Craig Alexander. *One Percent? For Real? Insights from Modern Growth Theory about Future Investment Returns*. Toronto: C.D. Howe Institute e-brief, 7 October 2015.

Bergevin, Phillippe, and Colin Busby. *Core, What Is It Good For? Why the Bank of Canada Should Focus on Headline Inflation*. Toronto: C.D. How Institute E-Brief, 29 September 2011.

Bergevin, Phillippe, and William B.P. Robson. *More RRBs, Please! Why Ottawa Should Issue More Inflation – Indexed Bonds*. Toronto: C.D. How Institute Commentary 363, September 2012.

Blomqvist, Åke, and Colin Busby. *Better Value for Money in Healthcare: European Lessons for Canada*. Toronto: C.D. Howe Institute Commentary 339. January 2012.

– *Paying Hospital-Based Doctors: Fee for Whose Service?* Toronto: C.D. How Institute Commentary 392, October 2013.

Busby, Colin, William B.P. Robson, and Aaron Jacobs. *Delivering Healthcare to an Aging Population: Nova Scotia's Fiscal Glacier*. Toronto: C.D. Howe Institute e-brief, 7 January 2016.

Busby, Colin, and Alexandre Laurin. *The 8 Percent Solution: A Sensible Tax Compromise for Albertans*. Toronto: C.D. How Institute E-Brief, 4 July 2013.

Busby, Colin, and William B.P. Robson. *A Social Insurance Model for Pharmacare: Ontario's Options for a More Sustainable, Cost Effective Drug Program*. Toronto: C.D. Howe Institute Commentary 326, April 2011.

Busby, Colin, William B.P. Robson, and Aaron Jacobs. *Managing the Costs of Healthcare for an Aging Population: How Alberta Can Confront its Fiscal Glacier*. Toronto: C.D. Howe Institute e-brief, 18 December 2014.

Dachis, Ben, Gilles Duranton, and Matthew A. Turner. *Sand in the Gears: Evaluating the Effects of Toronto's Land Transfer Tax*. Toronto: C.D. Howe Institute Commentary no. 277, December 2008.

Dachis, Benjamin, and William B.P. Robson. *Holding Canada's Cities to Account: An Assessment of Municipal Fiscal Management*. Toronto: C.D. Howe Institute Backgrounder 145, November 2011.

Dachis, Benjamin, William B.P. Robson, and Aaron Jacobs. *A Crisis of Capital: Canadian Workers Need More Tools, Buildings and Equipment*. Toronto: C.D. Howe Institute e-brief, 16 December 2015.

Dachis, Benjamin, William B.P. Robson, and Nicholas Chesterley. *Capital Needed: Canada Needs More Robust Business Investment*. Toronto: C.D. Howe Institute e-brief, 17 July 2014.

Dachis, Benjamin. *Picking Up Savings: The Benefits of Competition in Municipal Waste Services*. Toronto: C.D. Howe Institute Commentary 308, September 2010.

– *Full Throttle: Reforming Canada's Aviation Policy*. Toronto: C.D. Howe Institute Commentary 398, January 2014.

Freehan, James P. *Newfoundland's Electricity Options: Making the Right Choice Requires an Efficient Pricing Regime*. Toronto: C.D. How Institute E-Brief, 11 January 2012.

Goulding, A.J. *A New Blueprint for Ontario's Electricity Market*. Toronto: C.D. Howe Institute Commentary 389, September 2013.

Gray, David, and Colin Busby. *Making Sense of EI Eligibility Rules and How to Improve Them*. Toronto: C.D. Howe Institute Commentary 450, May 2016.

Gros, Barry. *Ontario Pension Policy 2013: Key Challenges Ahead*. Toronto: C.D. Howe Institute Commentary 386. August 2013.

Hale, Geoffrey, and Yale Belanger. *From "Social License" to "Social Partnership": Promoting Shared Interests for Resource and Infrastructure Development*. Toronto: C.D. Howe Institute Commentary 440, December 2015.

Herman, Lawrence L. *Trend Spotting: NATA Disputes After Fifteen Years*. Toronto: C.D. Howe Institute Backgrounder 133, July 2010.

– *Who Else Benefits from CETA? Some Implications of "Most Favoured Nation" Treatment*. Toronto: C.D. Howe Institute e-brief, 19 December 2013.

Krzepkowski, Matt, and Jack Mintz. *Squeaky Hinges: Widening the Door to Canadian Cross-border Investment*. Toronto: C.D. Howe Institute e-brief, 27 November 2008.

Laidler, David, and Robin Banerjee. *Unstable Foundations: Asset Markets, Inflation Targets, and Canada's 2011 Policy Choices*. Toronto: C.D. Howe Institute Commentary No. 278, December 2008.

Longworth, David. *Combatting the Ganders Lurking in the Shadows: The Macroprudential Regulation of Shadow Banking*. Toronto: C.D. Howe Institute Commentary 361, September 2012.

Melino, Angelo, and Michael Parkin. *Greater Transparency Needed*. Toronto: C.D. Howe Institute E-Brief, 14 July 2010.

Mysicka, Robert. *Who Watches the Watchmen? The Role of the Self-Regulator*. Toronto: C.D. Howe Institute Commentary 416, October 2014.

Parkin, Andrew. *Underperforming Adults? The Paradox of Skills Development in Canada*. Toronto: C.D. Howe Institute e-brief, 16 September 2015.

Parkin, Michael. *What Is the Ideal Monetary Policy Regime? Improving the Bank of Canada's Inflation-targeting Program*. Toronto: C.D. Howe Institute Commentary No. 279, January 2009.

Pedde, Richard, and Al Loyns. *Pulling the Plug on Monopoly Power: Reform for the Canadian Wheat Board*. Toronto: C.D. Howe Institute E-Brief. 23 June 2011.

Richards, John, Jennifer Hove, and Kemi Afolabi. *Understanding the Aboriginal/Non-Aboriginal Gap in Student Performance: Lessons from British Columbia*. Toronto: C.D. Howe Institute Commentary 276, December 2008.

Robson, William B.P. *Bending Canada's Healthcare Cost Curve: Watch Not What Governments Say, But What They Do*. Toronto: C.D. Howe Institute e-brief, 2 October 2014.

– *Boomer Bulge: Dealing with the Stress of Demographic Change on Government Budgets in Canada:* Toronto: C.D. Howe Institute e-brief, 13 January 2009.

– *What to do About Seniors' Benefits in Canada: The Case for Letting Recipients Take Richer Payments Later.* Toronto: C.D. Howe Institute E-Brief, 13 March 2012.

Spicer, Zachary, and Adam Found. *Thinking Regionally: How to Improve Service Delivery in Canada's Cities.* Toronto: C.D Howe Institutue Commentary 458, October 2016.

Stabile, Mark, and Sevil N-Marandi. *Fatal Flaws: Assessing Quebec's Failed Health Deductible Proposal.* Toronto: C.D. Howe Institute Social Policy, September 2010.

VanDuzer, Tony. *Investor–State Dispute Settlement in CETAL: Is it the Gold Standard?* Toronto: C.D. Howe Institute Commentary 459, October 2016.

THE CENTRE FOR INTERNATIONAL GOVERNANCE INNOVATION

Alexandroff, Alan S. *China the Part-Time Global Leader.* Waterloo: Centre for International Governance Innovation, June 2010.

Bernes, Thomas A. *IMF Legitimacy and Governance Reform: Will the G20 Help or Hinder?* Waterloo: Centre for International Governance Innovation, October 2010.

Blustein, Paul. *Off Balance: The Travails of Institutions that Govern the Global Financial System.* Waterloo: Centre for International Governance Innovation, October 2013.

Burch, Sarah. *Will Ontario's Climate Change Action Plan Trap Communities?* Waterloo: Centre for International Governance Innovation Policy Brief No. 90, October 2016.

Centre for International Governance Innovation. *Can Think Tanks Make a Difference? Conference Report.* Waterloo: Centre for International Governance Innovation, September 2011.

Chertoff, Michael, and Tobby Simon. *The Impact of the Dark Web on Internet Governance and Cyber Security.* Waterloo: Centre for International Governance Innovation Paper Series No. 6, February 2015.

Curtis, John M. *Intellectual Property Rights and International Trade: An Overview.* Waterloo: Centre for International Governance Innovation Paper Series No. 3, May 2012.

DeNardis, Laura. *Internet Points of Control as Global Governance.* Waterloo: Centre for International Governance Innovation Internet Governance Papers No. 2, August 2013.

Findlay, Trevor. *Unleashing the Nuclear Watchdog: Strengthening and Reform of the IAEA.* Waterloo: Centre for International Governance Innovation, June 2012.

Giustozzi, Antonio. *The Taliban Beyond the Pashtuns*. Waterloo: Centre for International Governance Innovation Afghanistan Paper No. 5, July 2010.

Haley, James A. *The Short View: The Global Conjuncture and the Need for Cooperation*. Waterloo: Centre for International Governance Innovation Papers No. 14, March 2013.

Hochstetler, Kathryn. *Infrastructure and Sustainable Development Goals in the BRICS-Led New Development Bank*. Waterloo: Centre for International Governance Innovation Policy Brief No. 46, 2014.

Ibbitson, John. *Bootstrap Immigrants: Assessing the Conservative Transformation of Canada's Immigration Policy*. Waterloo: Centre for International Governance Innovation Policy Brief No. 52, December 2014.

Jardine, Eric. *The Dark Web Dilemma: Tor, Anonymity, and Online Policing*. Waterloo: Centre for International Governance Innovation Paper Series No. 21, September 2015.

Jepsen, Henrik. *Policy Options Could Increase Ambition in the 2015 Climate Agreement*. Waterloo: Centre for International Governance Innovation, Fixing Climate Governance Series 1, April 2015.

Lawrence, Michael. *Towards a Non-State Security Sector Reform Strategy*. Waterloo: Centre for International Governance Innovation SSR Issue Paper No. 8, May 2012.

Lebond, Patrick. *A Transatlantic Perspective on CETA*. Waterloo: Centre for International Governance Innovation Policy Brief No. 89, October 2016.

Maclean, Jesse, Andrew Mccauley, and Emily Newcombe. *Disasters and Dividends: An Asia-Pacific Strategy for Canada*. Waterloo: Centre for International Governance Innovation Policy Brief No. 17, October 2014.

Medhora, Rohinton P. *The G20's "Development" Agenda: Fundamental, Not A Sidebar*. Waterloo: Centre for International Governance Innovation Policy Brief No. 80, June 2016.

Momani, Bessma. *Where Was the Fight for IMF Leadership?* Waterloo: Centre for International Governance Innovation, June 2011.

Rustomjee, Cyrus. *Vulnerability and Debt in Small States*. Waterloo: Centre for International Governance Innovation Policy Brief No. 83, July 2016.

Schadler, Susan. *Ukraine: Stress at the IMF*. Waterloo: Centre for International Governance Innovation Policy Brief No. 49, October 2014.

– *Ukraine and the IMF's Evolving Debt Crisis Narrative*. Waterloo: Centre for International Governance Innovation Policy Brief No. 68, November 2015.

Schwanen, Daniel. *The G20 Battens Down the Hatches*. Waterloo: Centre for International Governance Innovation, November 2011.

Siklos, Pierre. *Another Fine Mess: Repairing the Governance of International Financial Regulation*. Waterloo: Centre for International Governance Innovation CIGI Papers No. 12, January 2013.

Tesi. Moses. *Global Warming and Health: The Issue of Malaria in Eastern Africa's Highlands.* Waterloo: Centre for International Governance Innovation African Initiative Discussion paper Series No. 2, August 2011.

Thompson, Andrew S., and David A. Welch. *Responding to Disaster: Neglecting Dimensions of Preparedness and Their Consequences.* Waterloo: Centre for International Governance Innovation Policy Brief No. 1, July 2012.

Whalley, John, Manmohan Agarwal, and Yao Li. *Approaches to Fostering Productivity Growth in Brazil, China, and India.* Waterloo: Centre for International Governance Innovation Working Paper No. 47, April 2010.

THE CONFERENCE BOARD OF CANADA

Bostjancic, Kathy. *United States: A Need to Bridge the Political Divide.* Ottawa, ON: The Conference Board of Canada. August 2013.

Brender, Natalie. *Across the Sea with CETA: What New Labour Mobility Might Mean for Canadian Business.* Ottawa, ON: The Conference Board of Canada. July 2014.

Brichta, Jessica, and Michelle Parkouda. *Developing Partnership Capacity: The Rewards of Effective Business-Aboriginal Partnerships.* Ottawa, ON: The Conference Board of Canada. October 2015.

Chenier, Louise. *Disability Management in Practice – Ottawa-Carleton District School Board: Unleashing Employee Potential.* Ottawa, ON: The Conference Board of Canada. December 2013.

Chenier, Louise, and Elise Wohlbold. *Women in Senior Management: Where Are They?* Ottawa, ON: The Conference Board of Canada. August 2011.

Chenier, Louise, et Karla Thorpe. *Créer des milieux de travail propices à la santé mentale: points de vue des employés et des gestionnaires.* Ottawa, ON: The Conference Board of Canada. October 2011.

Coad, Len. *Finding the Mix: The Choice of Generation Technologies in Canada.* Ottawa, ON: The Conference Board of Canada. September 2015.

Crawford, Todd A. *Index of Consumer Confidence: December 2010.* Ottawa, ON: The Conference Board of Canada. December 2010.

Edge, Jessica. *Public Affairs Reputation Management: Benchmarking Report.* Ottawa, ON: The Conference Board of Canada. October 2015.

Grant, Michael. *Learning in the Digital Age.* Ottawa, ON: The Conference Board of Canada. October 2016.

Grant, Michael, James Knowles, and Vijay Gill. *Seeds for Success: The Value of Seed Treatments for Ontario Growers.* Ottawa, ON: The Conference Board of Canada. July 2014.

Hallock, Kevin, and Judit Torok. *Top Executive Compensation in 2008.* Ottawa, ON: The Conference Board of Canada, January 2009.

Hawkins, Naoko. *Overcoming Barriers to Leadership for Young Women.* Ottawa, ON: The Conference Board of Canada. December 2013.

Hodgson, Glen. *The Endgame for the Euro: Fresh Insights, but the Options Remain the Same.* Ottawa, ON: The Conference Board of Canada. October 2012.

Iacobacci, Mario. *Shared Corridors, Strange Bedfellows: Understanding the Interface Between Freight and Passenger Rail.* Ottawa, ON: The Conference Board of Canada. September 2010.

Kabilan, Satyamoorthy. *Evolving Skills Needs for Emergency Management.* Ottawa, ON: The Conference Board of Canada. August 2014.

Martin, Heidi, and Katie O'Brien. *Helping CEOs Drive Value: The Role of the Chief Operating Officer.* Ottawa, ON: The Conference Board of Canada. August 2014.

McIntyre, Jane. *Metropolitan Monthly Monitors: Metropolitan Housing Starts November 2012.* Ottawa, ON: November 2012.

McKean, Matthew. *Beyond Citations: Knowledge Mobilization, Research Impact, and the Changing Nature of Academic Work.* Ottawa, ON. The Conference Board of Canada. October 2016.

O'Byrne, Stephen. *Achieving Pay for Performance.* Ottawa, ON: The Conference Board of Canada. December 2012.

Robins, Allison, James Knowles, Len Coad. *A Long, Hard Road: Reducing GHG Emissions in Canada's Road Transportation Sector by 2050.* Ottawa, ON: The Conference Board of Canada. November 2015.

Robins, Allison, Prince Owusu, Dan Munro, and Len Coad. *A Changing Tide: British Columbia's Emerging Liquefied Natural Gas Industry.* Ottawa, ON. The Conference Board of Canada. February 2016.

Rosner, Laura, and Mary B. Young. *The Strategic Workforce Planning Leader's Bookshelf.* Ottawa, ON: The Conference Board of Canada. November 2011.

Stewart, Nicole. *Disability Management in Practice – Encana: Fitness for Work.* Ottawa, ON: The Conference Board of Canada. October 2013.

The Canadian Tourism Research Institute. *Travel Exclusive: Key trends for the Travel Industry July – August 2012.* Ottawa, ON: The Conference Board of Canada. August 2012.

Conference Board of Canada. *Canadian Outlook Economic Forecast: Winter 2009.* Ottawa, ON: The Conference Board of Canada, January 2009.

– *Public Sector Transformation: Leading, Managing and Sustaining Change.* Ottawa, ON: The Conference Board of Canada: Conference e-proceedings, January 2009.

– *2008 Workplace Diversity and Inclusiveness Forum.* Ottawa, ON: The Conference Board of Canada: Conference e-proceedings, January 2009.

– *Private Ordering and Proxy Access Rules: The Case for Prompt Attention.* Ottawa, ON: The Conference Board of Canada. December 2010.

– *Risk Watch: Thought Leadership in Risk and Governance – December 2010.* Ottawa, ON: The Conference Board of Canada. December 2010.
– *Air Transportation Industry: Industrial Outlook*, Summer 2011. Ottawa, ON: The Conference Board of Canada. September 2011.
– *Whose Job is Diversity Anyway? Transforming Diversity Through Co-Accountability.* Ottawa, ON: The Conference Board of Canada. August 2012.
– *Canadian Outlook Long-Term Economic Forecast: 2016 Mid-Year Update.* Ottawa, ON. The Conference Board of Canada. September 2016.
Zarnowitz, Victor. *A Crisis of Confidence.* Ottawa, ON: The Conference Board of Canada, January 2009.

THE FRASER INSTITUTE
Barua, Bacchis, Nadeem Esmail, and Taylor Jackson. *The Effect of Wait Times on Mortality in Canada.* Vancouver: The Fraser Institute, 2013.
Barua, Bacchus, and Feixue Ren. *The Private Cost of Public Queues for Medically Necessary Care, 2015 Edition.* Vancouver: The Fraser Institute, 2015.
– *Waiting Your Turn: Wait Times for Health Care in Canada, 2016 Report.* Vancouver: The Fraser Institute, 2016.
Barua, Bacchus, and Nadeem Esmail. *For-Profit Hospitals and Insurers In Universal Health Care Countries.* Vancouver: The Fraser Institute, 2015.
Barua, Bacchus, Ingrid Timmermans, Matthew Lau, and Feixue Ren. *Leaving Canada for Medical Care, 2016.* Vancouver: The Fraser Institute, 2016.
Clemens, Jason. *Wait Lists for Independent Schools in British Columbia's Lower Mainland.* Vancouver: The Fraser Institute, 2012.
Clemens, Jason, Charles Lammam, and Matthew Lo. *The Economic Costs of Capital Gains Taxes in Canada.* Vancouver: The Fraser Institute, 2014.
Cross, Phillip. *Evaluating the Proposed Ontario Pension Plan.* Vancouver: The Fraser Institute, 2013.
Dawson, Laura. *Toward Free Trade in Canada: Five Things the Federal Government Can Do to Open our Market.* Vancouver: The Fraser Institute, 2015.
Esmail, Nadeem. *Health Care Lessons from the Netherlands: Lessons from Abroad A Series on Health Care Reform.* Vancouver: The Fraser Institute, 2013.
Gibson, Gordon. *A New Look at Canadian Indian Policy.* Vancouver: The Fraser Institute, 2009.
Globerman, Steven, and Kristina M. Lybecker. *The Benefits of Incremental Innovation: Focus on the Pharmaceutical Industry.* Vancouver: The Fraser Institute, 2014.
Globerman, Steven, Kristina Lybecker, Christopher Sands, and Izumi, Lance, Fraxier Fathers, and Jason Clemens. *Technology and Education: A Primer.* Vancouver: The Fraser Institute, 2013.

Lammam, Charles, Milagros Palacios, Amela Karabegović, and Niels Veldhuis. *Measuring the Fiscal Performance of Canada's Premieres*. Vancouver: The Fraser Institute, 2010.

Lammam, Charles, and High MacIntyre. *The Practical Challenges of Creating a Gurainteed Annual Income in Canada*. Vancouver: The Fraser Institute, 2014.

Miljan, Lydia, John Pepall, Jason Clemens Taylor Jackson, Steve LaFleur, Joel Emes, and Patrice Dutil. *Counting Votes: Essays on Electoral Reform*. Vancouver: The Fraser Institute, 2016.

Milke, Mark. *Corporate Welfare: Now a $182 Billion Addiction*. Vancouver: The Fraser Institute, 2008.

– *Corporate Welfare Bargains at Industry Canada*. Vancouver: The Fraser Institute, 2012.

– *Ontario's Corporate Welfare Bill: $27.7 billion*. Vancouver: The Fraser Institute, 2011.

Moens, Alexander, and Nachum Gabler. *Measuring the Costs of the Canada – US Border*. Vancouver: The Fraser Institute, 2012.

– *What Congress Thinks of Canada: Studies in Canada – US Relations*. Vancouver: The Fraser Institute, 2011.

Mohindra, Neil. *Should the Canada Pension Plan Be Enhanced?* Vancouver: The Fraser Institute, 2011.

Murphy, Robert P., Jason Clemens, Joel Emes, and Niels Veldhuis. *Ontario vs. the US "Rust Belt": Coping with a Changing Economic World*. Vancouver: The Fraser Institute, 2015.

Palacios, Milagros, and Niels Veldhuis. *Taxes versus the Necessities of Life: The Canadian Consumer Tax Index*. Vancouver: The Fraser Institute, 2012.

Philipson, Tomas J. *Intellectual Property Rights and the Promotion of Biologics, Medical Devices, and Trade in Pharmaceuticals*. Vancouver: The Fraser Institute, 2016.

Rawson, Dr. Nigel. *Has PCODR Improved Access to Oncology Drugs? Timeliness and Provincial Acceptance of Pan-Canadian Oncology Drug Review Recommendations*. Vancouver: The Fraser Institute, 2014.

Skiner, Brett J., and Mark Rovere. *Access Delayed, Access Denied: Waiting for New Medicines in Canada 2010*. Vancouver: The Fraser Institute, 2010.

– *Canada's Drug Price Paradox, 2010*. Vancouver: The Fraser Institute, 2010.

– *Value for Money from Health Insurance Systems in Canada and the OECD*. Vancouver: The Fraser Institute, 2010.

– *The Misguided War Against Medicines 2011*. Vancouver: The Fraser Institute, 2011.

Vaillancourt, François. *The Cost to Canadians of Complying with Personal Income Taxes*. Vancouver: The Fraser Institute, 2010.

Vaillancourt, François, Marylène Roy, and Charles Lammam. *Measuring Tax Complexity in Canada*. Vancouver: The Fraser Institute, 2015.

Veldhuis, Niels, Milagros Palacious, and Keith Godin. *Canadian Provincial Investment Climate: 2008 Report*. Vancouver: The Fraser Institute, 2008.

Veldhuis, Niels, and Keith Godin. *The Economic Effects of Increasing British Columbia's Minimum Wage*. Vancouver: The Fraser Institute, 2009.

Veldhuis, Niels, Charles Lamman, and Alex Gainer. *Generosity in Canada and the United States: The 2008 Generosity Index*. Vancouver: The Fraser Institute, 2009.

Veldhuis, Niels, Jason Clemens, and Milagros Palacios. *Budget Blueprint: How Lessons from Canada's 1995 Budget Can Be Applied Today*. Vancouver: The Fraser Institute, 2011.

Walker, Michael, and Nadeem Esmail. *How Good is Canadian Health Care: 2008 Report?* Vancouver: The Fraser Institute, 2008.

Wood, Karina, and Niels Veldhuis. *The 2008 Non-Profit Performance Report*. Vancouver: The Fraser Institute, 2009.

THE INSTITUTE FOR RESEARCH ON PUBLIC POLICY

Assache, Ari Van, with commentary by Todd Evans. *Global Value Chains and Canada's Trade Policy*. Montreal: The Institute for Research on Public Policy, 2012.

Assaf, Dany H., and Rory A. McGillis. *Foreign Direct Investment and the National Interest: A Way Forward*. Montreal: The Institute for Research on Public Policy, 2013.

Atanackovic, Jelena, and Ivy Lynn Bourgeault. *Economic and Social Integration of Immigrant Live-in Caregivers in Canada*. Montreal: The Institute for Research on Public Policy, 2014.

Bédard, Michel, et Pierre Fortin. *Onze propositions pour un meilleur régime d'assurance – emploi*. Montreal: The Institute for Research on Public Policy, 2015.

Brown, Robert L., and Tyler Meredith. *Pooled Target-Benefit Pension Plans: Building on PRPPs*. Montreal: The Institute for Research on Public Policy, 2011.

Charters, David. *The (Un) Peaceable Kingdom: Terrorism and Canada before 9/11*. Montreal: The Institute for Research on Public Policy, 2008.

Cleveland, Gordon. *New Evidence about Child Care in Canada: Use Patterns, Affordability and Quality*. Montreal: The Institute for Research on Public Policy, 2008.

Corak, Miles. *Immigration in the Long Run: The Education and Earnings Mobility of Second Generation Canadians*. Montreal: The Institute for Research on Public Policy, 2008.

Côté-Boucher, Karine. *Round Table on EU-Canada Cooperation on Anti-Terrorism and Human Rights*. Montreal: The Institute for Research on Public Policy and University of Toronto, 2008.

Deeper Continental Integration or Diversification? Montreal: The Institute for Research on Public Policy, 2010.

Derwing, Tracey M., and Erin Waugh. *Language Skills and the Social Integration of Canada's Adult Immigrants.* Montreal: The Institute for Research on Public Policy, 2012.

Drewes, Torben, and Tyler Meredith. *If at First You Don't Succeed: Toward an Adult Education and Training Strategy for Canada.* Montreal: The Institute for Research on Public Policy, 2016.

Drummond, Don. *Wanted: Good Canadian Labour Market Information.* Montreal: The Institute for Research on Public Policy, 2014.

Finnie, Ross, and David Gray. *Labour Force Participation of Older Displaced Workers in Canada: Should I Stay or Should I Go?* Montreal: The Institute for Research on Public Policy, 2011.

Georges, Patrick, and Michael Mérrette. *Canada's Strategic Trade Policy Options.* Montreal: The Institute for Research on Public Policy, 2010.

Golant, Stephen M. *Age-Friendly Communities: Are We Expecting Too Much?* Montreal: The Institute for Research on Public Policy, 2014.

Goldring, Luin and Patricia Landolt. *The Impact of Precarious Legal Status on Immigrants' Economic Outcomes.* Montreal: The Institute for Research on Public Policy, 2012.

Halliwell, Cliff. *No Shortage of Opportunity: Policy Ideas to Strengthen Canada's Labour Market in the Coming Decade.* Montreal: The Institute for Research on Public Policy, 2013.

Hejazi, Walid. *Dispelling Canadian Myths about Foreign Direct Investment.* Montreal: The Institute for Research on Public Policy, 2010.

Hicks, Bruce, and Andre Blais. *Restructuring the Canadian Senate through Elections.* Montreal: Institute for Research on Public Policy, 2008.

Hicks, Peter. *The Enabling Society.* Montreal: The Institute for Research on Public Policy, 2015.

– *The Next Boomer Shift? Our Policy Assumptions.* Montreal: The Institute for Research on Public Policy, 2015.

Japel, Christa. *Factors of Risk, Vulnerability and School Readiness among Preschoolers: Evidence from Quebec.* Montreal: The Institute for Research on Public Policy, 2008.

Keefe, Janice M. *Supporting Caregivers and Caregiving in an Aging Canada.* Montreal: The Institute for Research on Public Policy, 2011.

Kukucha, Christopher J. *Provincial / Territorial Governments and the Negotiation of International Trade Agreements.* Montreal: The Institute for Research on Public Policy, 2016.

Lazar, Harvey. *Many Degrees of Policy Freedom: The Federal Government's Role in Care for Seniors?* Montreal: The Institute for Research on Public Policy, 2011.

Lewis Steven, and Terrence Sullivan. *How to Bend the Cost Curve in Health Care.* Montreal: The Institute for Research on Public Policy, 2013.

Macklin, Audrey and François Crépeau. *Multiple Citizenship, Identity and Entitlement in Canada*. Montreal: The Institute for Research on Public Policy, 2010.

Meredith, Tyler. *The Risk We All Face But Aren't Talking About*. Montreal: The Institute for Research on Public Policy, 2015.

Morgan, Steven G., Jamie R. Daw and Michael R. Law. *Are Income-Based Public Drug Benefit Programs Fit for an Aging Population?* Montreal: The Institute for Research on Public Policy, 2014.

Nakache, Delphine, and Paula J. Kinoshita. *The Canadian Temporary Foreign Worker Program: Do Short-Term Economic Needs Prevail over Human Rights Concerns?* Montreal: The Institute for Research on Public Policy, 2010.

Newhouse, David. *Indigenous Peoples, Canada and the Possibility of Reconciliation*. Montreal: The Institute for Research on Public Policy, 2016.

Picot, Garnett and Arthur Sweetman. *Making It in Canada: Immigration Outcomes and Policies*. Montreal: The Institute for Research on Public Policy, 2012.

Prince, Michael J. *Inclusive Employment for Canadians with Disabilities*. Montreal: The Institute for Research on Public Policy, 2016.

Snoddon, Tracy, and Debora Van Nijnatten. *Carbon Pricing and Intergovernmental Relations in Canada*. Montreal: The Institute for Research on Public Policy, 2016.

Wolfson, Michael. *Not-So-Modest Options for Expanding the CPP/QPP*. Montreal: The Institute for Research on Public Policy, 2013.

MACDONALD-LAURIER INSTITUTE

Ajzenstat, Janet. *Canada's Founding Ideas: Confederation and Individual Liberty*. Ottawa, ON: Macdonald-Laurier Institute, 2010.

Blue, Ian A. *Free Trade within Canada: Say Goodbye to Gold Seal*. Ottawa, ON: Macdonald-Laurier Institute, 2011.

Chapin, Paul H. *To Stand on Guard*. Ottawa, ON: Macdonald-Laurier Institute, 2010.

Clemens, Jason, and Brian Lee Crowley. *Canada's Looming Fiscal Squeeze: Collected Essays on Solutions*. Ottawa, ON: Macdonald-Laurier Institute, 2012.

Clemens, Jason, and Nadeem Esmail. *First, Do No Harm: How the Canada Health Act Obstructs Reform and Innovation*. Ottawa, ON: Macdonald-Laurier Institute, 2012.

Coates, Ken S., Greg Finnegan, Craig J. Hall, And Kelly J. Lendsay. *Unearthing Human Resources: Aboriginal Skills Development and Employment in the Natural Resource Sector*. Ottawa, ON: Macdonald-Laurier Institute, 2015.

Cross, Philip. *Six Myths Surrounding the Development of Canada's Natural Resources*. Ottawa, ON: Macdonald-Laurier Institute, 2013.

Crowley, Brian Lee, and Sean Speer. *A Home for Canada's Middle Class: A Plan for Housing Affordability and Opportunity in Canada.* Ottawa, ON: Macdonald-Laurier Institute, 2016.

Crowley, Brian Lee, Robert Knox, and John Robson. *Citizen of One, Citizen of the Whole: How Ottawa Can Strengthen Our Nation by Eliminating Provincial Trade Barriers with a Charter of Economic Rights.* Ottawa, ON: Macdonald-Laurier Institute, 2010.

Daudelin, Jean, Stephanie Soiffer, and Jeff Willows. *Border Integrity, Illicit Tobacco, And Canada's Security.* Ottawa, ON: Macdonald-Laurier Institute, 2013.

Favel, Blaine, and Ken S. Coates. *Understanding Undrip: Choosing Action on Priorities over Sweeping Claims about the United Nations 'Declaration on the Rights of Indigenous Peoples.'* Ottawa, ON: Macdonald-Laurier Institute, 2016.

Graham, Andrew. *Canada's Critical Infrastructure: When Is Safe Enough Safe Enough?* Ottawa, ON: Macdonald-Laurier Institute, 2011.

Hataley, Todd, and Christian Leuprecht. *Organized Crime Beyond the Border.* Ottawa, ON: Macdonald-Laurier Institute, 2013.

Laporte, Audrey. *How Markets Can Put Patients First: Economics Before Politics in Canadian Health Care Delivery.* Ottawa, ON: Macdonald-Laurier Institute, 2014.

Leuprecht, Christian. *The Blue Line or the Bottom Line of Police Services in Canada? Arresting Runaway Growth in Costs.* Ottawa, ON: Macdonald-Laurier Institute, 2014.

– *Smoking Gun: Strategic Containment of Contraband Tobacco and Cigarette Trafficking in Canada.* Ottawa, ON: Macdonald – Laurier Institute, 2016.

Leuprecht, Christian, and Conrad Winn. *What Do Muslim Canadians Want? The Clash of Interpretations and Opinion Research.* Ottawa, ON: Macdonald-Laurier Institute, 2011.

Londerville, Jane. *Mortgage Insurance in Canada: Basically Sound but Room for Improvement.* Ottawa, ON: Macdonald-Laurier Institute, 2010.

Lundbäck, Mattias. *A European Flavour for Medicare: Learning from Experiments in Switzerland and Sweden.* Ottawa, ON: Macdonald-Laurier Institute, 2013.

Murphy, Robert P. *The Carbon Tax Win-Win: Too Good to Be True? The Tax Interaction Effect and Political Realities.* Ottawa, ON: Macdonald-Laurier Institute, 2014.

Newark, Scott. *Why Canadian Crime Statistics Don't Add Up: Not the Whole Truth.* Ottawa, ON: Macdonald-Laurier Institute, 2011.

Newman, Dwight. *Is the Sky the Limit? Following the Trajectory of Aboriginal Legal Rights in Resource Development.* Ottawa, ON: Macdonald-Laurier Institute, 2015.

Noble, Bram. *Learning to Listen: Snapshots of Aboriginal Participation in Environmental Assessment*. Ottawa, ON: Macdonald-Laurier Institute, 2016.

Noble, Bram, and Aniekan Udofia. *Protectors of the Land Toward an EA Process That Works for Aboriginal Communities and Developers*. Ottawa, ON: Macdonald-Laurier Institute, 2015.

Peng, Ito, and James Tiessen. *An Asian Flavour for Medicare: Learning from Experiments in Japan, Korea, and Taiwan*. Ottawa, ON: Macdonald-Laurier Institute, 2015.

Perrin, Benjamin. *The Supreme Court of Canada: Policy-Maker of the Year*. Ottawa, ON: Macdonald-Laurier Institute, 2014.

Perry, Dave. *Putting The 'Armed' Back into the Canadian Armed Forces: Improving Defence Procurement in Canada*. Ottawa, ON: CDA Institute Vimy Paper in cooperation with Macdonald-Laurier Institute, 2015.

Schmidt, Claudia, Al Mussell, Janalee Sweetland, and Bob Seguin. *The Greening of Canadian Agriculture: Policies to Assist Farmers as Stewards of the Environment*. Ottawa, ON: Macdonald-Laurier Institute, 2012.

Sheikh, Munir A. *Estimating the True Size of Government: Adjusting for Tax Expenditures*. Ottawa, ON: Macdonald-Laurier Institute, 2014.

Thayer Scott, Jacquelyn. *An Atlantic Fishing Tale 1999–2011*. Ottawa, ON: Macdonald-Laurier Institute, 2012.

Watts, Michael. *Debunking the Myths: A Broader Perspective of the Canada Health Act*. Ottawa, ON: Macdonald-Laurier Institute, 2013.

Wilner, Alex. *From Rehabilitation to Recruitment*. Ottawa, ON: Macdonald-Laurier Institute, 2010.

MOWAT CENTRE FOR PUBLIC POLICY

Bednar, Vass, and John Stapleton. *Trading Places: Single Adults Replace Lone Parents as The New Face of Social Assistance in Canada*. Toronto, ON: Mowat Centre, 2011.

Bitran, Maurice, and Serene Tan. *Diaspora Nation: An Inquiry into the Economic Potential of Diaspora Networks in Canada*. Toronto, ON: Mowat Centre, 2013.

Canada West Foundation – The Federal Idea, The Mowat Centre, The Atlantic Provinces Economic Council. *Canada and Its Natural Resources*. Toronto, ON: Mowat Centre, 2013.

Carlson, Richard, and Eric Martin. *Re-energizing the Conversation: Engaging the Ontario Public on Energy Issues*. Toronto, ON: Mowat Centre, 2014.

Carlson, Richard, Rob Dorling, Peter Spiro, and Mike Moffatt. *A Review of the Economic Impact of Energy East on Ontario*. Toronto, ON: Mowat Centre, 2015.

Choudhry, Sujit, and Michael Pal. *The Impact of Regionally Differentiated Entitlement to EI on Charter-Protected Canadians*. Toronto, ON: Mowat Centre, 2011.

Dorling, Rob, and Kyle Hanniman. *Restoring Water Levels on Lake Michigan – Huron: A Cost-Benefit Analysis*. Toronto, ON: Mowat Centre, 2016.

Galley, Andrew. *Employment Skills Training*. Toronto, ON: Mowat Centre, 2015.

Galley, Andrew, and Jill Shirey. *Brokering Success: Improving Skilled Immigrant Employment Outcomes through Strengthened Government-Employer Engagement*. Toronto, ON: Mowat Centre, 2014.

Gold, Jennifer. *Integrating Human Services in an Age of Fiscal Restraint: A Shifting Gears Report*. Toronto, ON: Mowat Centre, 2012.

– *International Delivery: Centres of Government and the Drive for Better Policy Implementation*. Toronto, ON: Mowat Centre, 2014.

Gold, Jennifer, Josh Hjartarson, and Matthew Mendelsohn. *Fiscal Sustainability and the Future of Public Spending: A Shifting Gears Progress Report*. Toronto, ON: Mowat Centre, 2011.

Hering, Martin and Thomas R. Klassen. *Is 70 the New 65? Raising the Eligibility Age in the Canada Pension Plan*. Toronto, ON: Mowat Centre, 2010.

Hughes, James. *Homelessness: Closing the Gap Between Capacity and Performance*. Toronto, ON: Mowat Centre, 2012.

Jarvis, Mark. *Creating a High-Performing Canadian Civil Service against a Backdrop of Disruptive Change*. Toronto, ON: Mowat Centre, 2016.

Johal, Sunil, Andrew Galley, and Melissa Molson. *Reprogramming Government for the Digital Era*. Toronto, ON: Report, Mowat Centre, 2014.

Johal, Sunil, Matthew Mendelsohn, and Noah Zon. *Let's Talk: Coordinating Economic Development Spending in Canada*. Toronto, ON: Book Chapter, Mowat Centre, 2013.

Johal, Sunil, Noah Zon, Jordann Thirgood, and Jane Stacey. *Policies for the Tourism Sharing Economy*. Toronto, ON: Book Chapter, Mowat Centre, 2016.

Keller, Tony, and Neville McGuire. *The New Economics of the NHL: Why Canada Can Support 12 Teams*. Toronto, ON: Report, Mowat Centre, 2011.

Lalande, Lisa, Joanne Cave, and Rajesh Sankat. *Unpacking Impact: Exploring Impact Measurement for Social Enterprises in Ontario*. Toronto, ON: Report, Mowat Centre, 2016.

Lecours, André, and Daniel Béland. *Equalization at Arm's Length*. Toronto, ON: Report, Mowat Centre, 2012.

Matthews, J. Scott, and Matthew Mendelsohn. *The New Ontario: The Shifting Attitudes of Ontarians toward the Federation*. Toronto, ON: Report, Mowat Centre, 2010.

Mendelsohn, Matthew, and Richard Carlson. *The Politics of Pipelines: Ontario's Stake in Canada's Pipeline Debate*. Toronto, ON: Report, Mowat Centre, 2013.

Pal, Michael, and Melissa Molson. *Moving Toward Voter Equality: Mowat Centre Report on the Proposed Federal Electoral Boundaries for Ontario*. Toronto, ON: Report, Mowat Centre, 2012.

Sancton, Andrew. *The Principle of Representation by Population in Canadian Federal Politics*. Toronto, ON: Report, Mowat Centre, 2010.

Seidle, F. Leslie. *The Canada-Ontario Immigration Agreement: Assessment and Options for Renewal*. Toronto, ON: Report, Mowat Centre, 2010.

Van Ymeren, Jamie. *An Open Future: Data Priorities for the Not-For-Profit Sector*. Toronto, ON: Report, Mowat Centre, 2015.

Vosko, Leah F. *The Challenge of Expanding EI Coverage: Charting Exclusions and Partial Exclusions on the Bases of Gender, Immigration Status, Age, and Place of Residence and Exploring Avenues for Inclusive Policy Redesign*. Toronto, ON: Report, Mowat Centre, 2011.

Zon, Noah. *Access to Affordable Housing*. Toronto, ON: Report, Mowat Centre, 2015.

PARKLAND INSTITUTE

Barnetson, Bob. *Illegal and Injurious: How Alberta Has Failed Teen Workers*. Edmonton, AB: Report, Parkland Institute, 2015.

Boychuk, Regan. *Misplaced Generosity: Extraordinary Profits in Alberta's Oil and Gas Industry*. Edmonton, AB: Report, Parkland Institute, 2010.

Campanella, David. *A Profitable Brew: A Financial Analysis of the SLGA and Its Potential Privatization*. Edmonton, AB: Report, Parkland Institute, 2014.

– *Losing Ground: Alberta's Residential Elder Care Crisis*. Edmonton, AB: Report, Parkland Institute, 2016.

Campanella, David, and Greg Flanagan. *Impaired Judgement: The Economic and Social Consequences of Liquor Privatization in Western Canada*. Edmonton, AB: Report, Parkland Institute, 2012.

Campanella, David, and Shannon Stunden Bower. *From Bad to Worse: Residential Elder Care in Alberta*. Edmonton, AB: Report, Parkland Institute, 2013.

Clements, Jill, and Diana Gibson. *Delivery Matters: The High Costs of For-Profit Health Services in Alberta*. Edmonton, AB: Report, Parkland Institute, 2012.

– *Delivery Matters: Cyber Charter Schools and K-12 Education in Alberta*. Edmonton, AB: Report, Parkland Institute, 2013.

Evan, Bowness, and Mark Hudson. *Directly and Adversely Affected: Public Participation in Tar Sands Development 2005–2014*. Edmonton, AB: Fact Sheet, Parkland Institute, 2014.

Foster, Jason, and Bob Barnetson. *Buried and Forgotten: Newspaper Coverage of Workplace Injury and Death in Alberta*. Edmonton, AB: Report, Parkland Institute, 2016.

Gibson, Diana. *Delivery Matters: Infrastructure Privatization and Accountability.* Edmonton, AB: Fact Sheet, Parkland Institute, 2012.

– *A Social Policy Framework for Alberta: Fairness and Justice for All.* Edmonton, AB: Report, Parkland Institute, 2012.

Gibson, Diana, and Colleen Fuller. *Fixing What's Broken: Fair and Sustainable Solutions to Alberta's Revenue Problems.* Edmonton, AB: Report, Parkland Institute, 2011.

– *The New Alberta Health Act: Risks and Opportunities Report 1.* Edmonton, AB: Parkland Institute, 2010.

– *The New Alberta Health Act: Risks and Opportunities Report 2.* Edmonton, AB: Parkland Institute, 2010.

Hughes, David J. *Can Canada Expand Oil and Gas Production, Build Pipelines and Keep Its Climate Change Commitments?* Edmonton, AB: Report, Parkland Institute, 2016.

Krahn, Harvey, and Trevor Harrison. *Less Exclusion, More Engagement: Addressing Declining Voter Turnout in Alberta.* Edmonton, AB: Report, Parkland Institute, 2014.

Lahey, Kathleen. *Equal Worth: Designing Effective Pay Equity Laws for Alberta.* Edmonton, AB: Report, Parkland Institute, 2016.

Loxley, John. *Wrong Turn: Is a P3 the Best Way to Expand Edmonton's LRT?* Edmonton, AB: Report, Parkland Institute, 2013.

Mcmillan, Melville. *Hard Math, Harder Choices: Alberta's Budget Reality.* Edmonton, AB: Report, Parkland Institute, 2015.

Parkland Institute. *As Long as the Rivers Flow: Athabasca River Knowledge, Use and Change.* Edmonton, AB: Report, Parkland Institute, 2010.

Parkland Institute. *Unpacking Alberta's Infrastructure Spending: Real Increases Have Been Moderate.* Edmonton, AB: Fact Sheet, Parkland Institute, 2011.

Roy, Jim. *Billions Forgone: The Decline in Alberta Oil and Gas Royalties.* Edmonton, AB: Fact Sheet, Parkland Institute, 2015.

Schmidt, Jeremy. *Alternative Water Futures in Alberta.* Edmonton, AB: Report, Parkland Institute, 2011.

Stunden Bower, Shannon. *Sick of Inequality: The Case for Action by the Government of Alberta on the Social Determinants of Health.* Edmonton, AB: Report, Parkland Institute, 2014.

– *Smoke Screen: Results-based Budgeting, Privatization, and Public Sector Cuts in Alberta.* Edmonton, AB: Report, Parkland Institute, 2013.

Thompson, David. *No Free Lunch: Financing the Priorities of Calgarians.* Edmonton, AB: Report, Parkland Institute, 2010.

Weber, Barret. *Ending Pay to Play: The Need for Political Reform in Alberta.* Edmonton, AB: Fact Sheet, Parkland Institute, 2015.

Weber, Barret, and Trevor Harrison. *Neoliberalism and the Non-Profit Social Services Sector in Alberta.* Edmonton, AB: Report, Parkland Institute, 2015.

PEMBINA INSTITUTE

Anderson, Kristi, Arne Jungjohann, and Tim Weis. *Harvesting Clean Energy on Ontario Farms: A Transatlantic Comparison*. Washington, DC: Report, Heinrich Böll Stiftung, Climate Action Network Canada, and Pembina Institute, 2011.

Bramley, Matthew. *Evaluation of the Government of Canada's Greenhouse Gas Reduction Policies: Prepared for the Climate Change Performance Index 2011*. Drayton Valley, AB: The Pembina Institute, 2010.

Burda, Cherise. *Priced Out: Understanding the Factors Affecting Home Prices in the GTA*. Toronto, ON: Report, RBC and The Pembina Institute, 2013.

Burda, Cherise, Travis Allan, Burgandy Dunn, Anastasia Lintner, Theresa McClenaghan and Laura Zizzo. *Live Where You Go: Encouraging Location-Efficient Development in Ontario*. Drayton Valley, AB: Report, The Pembina Institute, 2012.

Demerse, Clare. *Fighting Climate Change in Mexico: Facing the Climate Challenge: Mexico Opportunities Fact Sheet*. Drayton Valley, AB: Fact Sheet, The Pembina Institute, 2010.

– *Getting on Track for Canada's Climate Target: Designing a Technology Fund That Works for 2020: Part of the Green Budget Coalition Recommendations for Federal Budget 2014*. Vancouver, BC: Fact Sheet, The Pembina Institute, 2013.

Dyer, Simon, Matthew Bramley, Marc Huot, and Matt Horn. *Responsible Action? An Assessment of Alberta's Greenhouse Gas Policies*. Vancouver, BC: Report, The Pembina Institute, 2015.

Flanagan, Erin, Dianne Zimmerman, Matt Horne and Tom-Pierre Frappé-Sénéclauze. *Race to the front: Tracking pan-Canadian climate progress and where we go from here*. Vancouver, BC: Report, The Pembina Institute, 2015.

Frappé-Sénéclauze, Tom-Pierre, and Josha MacNab. *Evolution of Energy Efficiency Requirements in the BC Building Code*. Victoria, BC: Report, Pacific Institute for Climate Solutions and The Pembina Institute.

Frappé-Sénéclauze, Tom-Pierre, and Karen Tam Wu. *Pathways to Net-Zero Buildings in B.C.: Policy Proposal: Getting New Part 3 Buildings Net-Zero Ready*. Vancouver, BC: Policy Proposal, The Pembina Institute, 2015.

Frappé-Sénéclauze, Tom-Pierre, Dylan Heerema, and Karen Tam Wu. *Accelerating Market Transformation for High-Performance Building Enclosures State of Market, Policy Developments, and Lessons Learned from the Passive House Movement*. Calgary, AB: Report, The Pembina Institute, 2016.

Frappé-Sénéclauze, Tom-Pierre, Josha MacNab, Ellen Pond, Claire Beckstead, Benjamin Thibault. *Home Energy Labelling Requirement at Point of Sale: Pilot Program Design*. Drayton Valley, AB: Report, The Pembina Institute, 2012.

Grant, Jennifer, Simon Dyer, Marc Huot, and Danielle Droitsch. *Solving the Puzzle: Environmental Responsibility in Oilsands Development*. Drayton Valley, AB: Report, The Pembina Institute, 2011.

Guilbeault, Steven, Sarah Dobson, and Nathan Lemphers. *Booms, Busts and Bitumen: The Economic Implications of Canadian Oilsands Development*. Calgary, AB: Report, The Pembina Institute, 2013.

Horne, Matt, and Josha MacNab. *Liquefied Natural Gas and Climate Change the Global Context*. Victoria, BC: Report, Pacific Institute for Climate Solutions and The Pembina Institute.

Horne, Matt, EMRG, and P.J. Partington. *British Columbia's Carbon Tax: Exploring Perspectives and Seeking Common Ground*. Drayton Valley, AB: Report, The Pembina Institute, 2012.

Israel, Benjamin, and Erin Flanagan. *Out with the Coal, in with the New: National Benefits of an Accelerated Phase-Out of Coal-Fired Power*. Calgary, AB: Report, The Pembina Institute, 2016.

Jeyakumar, Binnu, Bora Plumptre, Erin Flanagan. *Canada and Coal at COP22: Tracking Global Momentum to End Coal-Fired Power — and Why Canada Should Lead the Way*. Vancouver, BC: Backgrounder, The Pembina Institute, 2016.

Laufenberg, Katie, Graham Haines, Cherise Burda, and Alison Bailie. *Behind the Wheel: Opportunities for Canadians to Drive Less, Reduce Pollution and Save Money*. Drayton Valley, Alberta: Report, The Pembina Institute, 2012.

Pembina Institute. *Pembina Institute Annual Financial Report 2013*. The Pembina Institute, 2014.

Read, Andrew. *Climate Change Policy in Alberta*. Calgary, AB: Backgrounder, The Pembina Institute, 2014.

Sauve, Josha, Josha MacNab, Steven Cretney, Matt Horne. *Is B.C. LNG Really a Climate Change Solution?* Vancouver, BC: Infographic, The Pembina Institute, 2014.

Srivastava, Lorie, and Cherise Burda. *Fare Driving: Exploring the Benefits of Traffic Pricing in Toronto and the GTA*. Toronto, ON: Report, The Pembina Institute, 2015.

Tam Wu, Karen. *Vancouver's Zero Emissions Building Plan Will Take Key Step Forward with Rezoning Policy Updates: Letter to Mayor Gregor Robertson on Green Buildings Policy for Rezonings*. Vancouver, BC: Letter, The Pembina Institute, 2016.

Vijayakumar, Nithya and Cherise Burda. *Cycle Cities Supporting Cycling in Canadian Cities*. Vancouver, BC: Report, The Pembina Institute, 2015.

Weis, Tim, Kristi Anderson, and Alex Doukas. *Landowners' Guide to Wind Energy in Alberta*. Drayton Valley, AB: Report, The Pembina Institute, 2010.

Weis, Tim, Paul Gipe, Shine Ontario, and Green Energy Act Alliance. *Ontario Feed-in-Tariff 2011 Review*. Drayton Valley, AB: Report, The Pembina Institute, 2011.

Weis, Tim, Shawn-Patrick Stensil, and Jeff Harti. *Renewable is Doable: Affordable and Flexible Options for Ontario's Long-Term Energy Plan*. Toronto, ON: Report, The Pembina Institute, 2013.

Index

Abelson, Donald E., 33, 83, 175
Allan MacEachen Institute, 25, 38
Allen, Richard, 76; and Ronald Reagan, 159, 161, 438n47, 438n54, 439n59
American Enterprise Institute (AEI), 3–4, 13, 15, 49, 63, 76, 83, 92, 97, 150, 161, 164, 167–70, 172, 177, 208, 214, 423n42, 430n44, 439n63; and congressional testimony, 114, 139; history of, 43–7; and media visibility, 109, 122, 232–4, 433n9
Anderson, Martin, 75; and Ronald Reagan, 76, 150, 159–61
Armacost, Michael, 42
Arnold, H.H., 42
Atlantic Institute for Market Studies (AIMS), 15, 38–9, 262, 431n62; and media visibility, 100; profile of, 253–5
Atlantic Provinces Economic Council (APEC), 33, 254; and 1994 budget consultations, 195; and constitutional conferences, 182, 187–9

Balsillie, Jim, 9, 39, 258–9
Bannon, Steve, 9, 176
Barnett, Richard, 32, 246
Baroody, William, Jr, 45–6, 83
Battle, Ken, 38, 54, 80, 87–8, 196, 234, 430n34
Beaudoin-Dobbie Committee, 186–9
Bennett, William, 38
Better America, 38
Bipartisan Policy Center, and Keystone XL, 200, 217, 221, 223
Boskin, Michael, 150
Boyle, T. Patrick, 53, 84
British Institute of International Affairs (BIIA), 28
Broadbent, Alan, 55
Broadbent Institute, 24, 38, 208
Brodie, Bernard, 43
Brookings, Robert, 13, 27, 41, 44
Brookings Institution, 3–4, 6, 11, 21, 23, 26, 28, 35, 79, 81, 86, 96, 153, 205, 212–14, 220–1, 261, 418n6, 437n46; congressional testimony, 91, 114–15; history of, 27, 41–2, 68; media visibility, 62, 91–2, 99, 101, 109–10, 112, 122, 232–4, 446n22; and Barack Obama, 170–1
Brzezinski, Zbigniew, 96, 171; and Jimmy Carter, 32, 154–6, 435n18
Buchanan, Pat, 35
Budget and Accounting Act (1921), 28

Bush, George, 67, 126, 164, 167–8
Bush, George W., 14, 47, 68, 175, 199; and Hoover Institution, 76, 150, 167; and think tanks, 4, 95, 151–2, 167–9, 179

Caledon Institute of Social Policy, 4, 9, 15, 40, 82, 87, 196, 234; and consultations with government, 98, 135, 231; history of, 38, 54–5; media exposure, 80, 89, 107, 122–3, 145
Campbell, Bruce, 78
Campney, Alan F., 99
Canada 2020, 9, 15, 39
Canada West Foundation, 36; and constitutional conferences, 182, 185, 188–9, 192–3; and Keystone XL, 200, 217–18; media exposure, 116–17, 123; and 1994 budget consultations, 195; research mandate, 123; profile of, 255–6
Canadian Alliance (Party), 78
Canadian Centre for Arms Control and Disarmament (CCACD), 38
Canadian Centre for Foreign Policy Development (CCFPD), 38
Canadian Centre for Global Security, 38
Canadian Centre for Management and Development (CCMD), 132
Canadian Centre for Philanthropy, 36, 235
Canadian Centre for Policy Alternatives (CCPA), 4, 36, 63, 78, 254, 445n14; contributions to public policy, 181, 185, 206, 231–2; and Keystone XL, 200, 217–19; media exposure, 116, 230; profile of, 256–7
Canadian Council for International Peace and Security (CCIPS), 38
Canadian Council on Social Development (CCSD), 29, 35, 55, 78; consultations with government, 78, 91, 135; media exposure, 116–7, 145; parliamentary testimony, 136, 231
Canadian Institute for Economic Policy, 36, 38
Canadian Institute for International Peace and Security (CIIPS), 34, 36; budget of, 40, 422n29
Canadian Institute of International Affairs (CIIA), 92; budget of, 235; history of, 28, 36
Canadian Institute of Strategic Studies (CISS), 35, 235; consultations with government, 135; media exposure, 116–17, 126; policy expertise, 135–6, 231
Canadian International Council (CIC), 36, 92, 117, 119, 135, 231–2, 258
Canadian International Development Agency (CIDA), 24, 35
Canadian Manufacturers & Exporters (CME), 81
Canadian Policy Research Networks, Inc. (CPRN), 10, 38, 40, 80; budget of, 24, 434n18; consultations with government, 87, 107, 135
Canadian Tax Foundation (CTF), 32, 35, 119; media exposure, 116–17; parliamentary testimony, 141
Canadian Welfare Council, 35
Carberry, Christine, 83, 175
Carnegie, Andrew, 13, 27, 44, 84, 241, 244
Carnegie Endowment for International Peace (CEIP), 3, 13, 27, 46, 97, 244, 439n63; and media visibility, 62, 109, 112, 233; profile of, 241–2

Carnegie Foundations, 82, 212
Carter, Jimmy, 153–4; and Brookings Institution, 157; and the Council on Foreign Relations, 156–7; and think tanks, 151–2, 154, 179; and Trilateral Commission, 154–7
Carter Center, 24, 37
Castonguay-Dobbie Committee, 186–9
Cato Institute, 35, 145, 249, 435n7, 442n102; and congressional testimony, 114, 139, 224, 234; and media exposure, 112, 233, 248, 433n9; and Keystone XL, 200, 217, 221, 223; profile of, 247–8
C.D. Howe Institute, 4, 15, 35, 38, 115, 215, 219, 254, 256, 262, 431n62, 444n27; budget of, 119, 231; and consultations with government, 135; and constitutional conferences, 182, 185, 188, 190, 193; and contributions to public policy, 63, 79, 88, 181, 196, 417n4; media exposure, 56–7, 101, 107, 116–17, 122–3, 230; and parliamentary testimony, 136, 231–2; profile of, 257–8
Center for American Progress (CAP), 9, 40, 170–1, 173; and Keystone XL, 200, 217, 221
Center for Global Development, 25, 61
Center for a New American Security (CNAS), 39–40, 86, 171, 173–4
Center for Strategic and International Studies (CSIS), 32, 100–1, 150, 161, 163, 168, 171, 173, 176; and media exposure, 126, 233–4, 433n9, 446n22; and presidential elections, 153, 170; profile of, 245–6
Centre for International Governance Innovation (CIGI), 9, 11, 23, 39, 82; profile of, 258–9
Centre for the Study of Living Standards, 38
Charlottetown Accord, 19, 182, 185
Cheney, Dick, 50, 168
Chrétien, Jean, 34, 139, 199
Citizens for a Sound Economy Foundation (CSE), 38, 83
Clark, Joe, and constitutional conferences, 182, 188, 193
Climate Institute, 21
Clinton, Bill, 167, 171, 173–4, 199, 439n66, 440n72, 440n70; and think tanks, 151–2, 164–6, 179, 249, 428n7, 432n4, 437n46, 439n69
Clinton, Hillary, 8, 40, 172, 174–5, 207, 440n72; and think tanks, 170
Collbohm, Frank, 42–3
Committee on the Present Danger, 161, 163, 437n42
Competitive Enterprise Institute (CEI), 8–9, 177; and Keystone XL, 177, 200, 217, 222; and Paris Climate Agreement, 9, 177
Conference Board (US), 27, 32, 35, 51, 259–60
Conference Board of Canada, 11, 23, 25–6, 81, 425n87; and budget of, 51; and history of, 32, 51–2; and media exposure, 107, 116–17, 230–2; and Niagara Institute, 190; and parliamentary testimony, 91, 136, 140
Congressional Budget Office, 12, 161
Congressional Policy Advisory Board, 75
Congressional Research Service, 12, 76
Coors, Joseph, 47, 49
Council of Canadians, 37
Council on Foreign Relations, 27, 68, 92, 97, 153–5, 157, 170, 436n22; and Keystone XL, 200, 202, 217,

222–4; profile of, 244–5
Crowe, William, 32
Crowley, Brian Lee, 39, 100–1, 234, 254, 262
Culpeper, Roy, 82

DeMint, Jim, 8, 94, 177
Democratic Leadership Council (DLC), 165–6, 249, 439n66–7, 439n69, 440n70
Domhoff, William, 16, 61, 63
Donaldson, Sam, 101–2
Donovan, Hedley, 154
Douglas Aircraft Company, 42
Dye, Thomas, 16, 61

Ebell, Myron, 8–9, 177
Economic Council of Canada, 24, 33, 38, 85, 417n4, 422n26, 422n29; budget of, 34, 40; media exposure, 116–17; parliamentary testimony, 136, 231
elite theory, 17, 58–9, 71
Empower America, 38
Executive Office of the President (EOP), 76, 205

Federal-Provincial Relations Office (FPRO), 183, 191, 443n18
Feulner, Edwin, 8, 47–8, 84, 161–3, 177–8, 438n47, 438n53; and Ronald Reagan, 93, 102–3, 162, 438n51
Fisher, Sir Antony, 53, 84
Foreign Policy Initiative, 49
Fraser Institute, 4, 13, 15, 25–6, 63, 77–8, 84, 105, 145, 254, 256, 417n4, 445n14; budget of, 119; consultations with government, 103, 135, 185; history of, 36, 53–4; Keystone XL, 200, 217–19, 223; media exposure, 56–7, 79, 88–9, 92, 98–9, 101, 107, 116–17, 122–3, 126–7, 212, 230; parliamentary testimony, 136, 139–40, 231; and Tax Freedom Day, 123, 423n38
Friedman, Milton, 44, 103, 159, 436n32

General Accounting Office (GAO), 76
Gingrich, Newt, 14, 38, 47, 92, 423n42
Goldwater, Barry, 155
Gorbachev, Mikhail, 163
Gordon, Walter, 36
Gorsuch, Neil, 8, 175, 177
Gray, Colin, 85, 88

Haddad, Tammy, 102
Hajdú, Csaba, 53
Harper, Stephen, 40, 77, 82, 140; and Keystone XL, 197–9, 200–2, 208, 222–3
Harrison, Kathryn, 84
Harrison, Peter, 191, 443n19
Heclo, Hugh, 17, 69
Heritage Foundation, 3–4, 13–15, 21, 25–6, 28, 47, 49, 54, 78, 97, 122, 173, 437n46; congressional testimony, 114–15, 139, 234; history of, 139; media visibility, 89, 91–3, 99, 101, 109–10, 126, 232–3, 433n9, 446n22; perceived influence of, 63, 72, 76, 87, 94–6, 98, 105, 205, 208, 213; and Ronald Reagan, 102–3, 151, 161–3; and Donald Trump, 8, 77, 175, 177
Hess, Stephen, 157
Hoberg, George, 84
Hoover, Herbert, 13, 27, 242–3
Hoover Institution on War, Revolution and Peace, 4, 14, 21, 23, 27, 75, 86, 212, 423n42, 441n87; and congressional testimony, 234; and George Bush, 164, 167–8; and media exposure, 62, 81, 99, 109, 122, 433n7; and presidential elections, 76, 78, 150, 172, 178; profile of, 242–4; and Reagan administration, 151, 159–61, 163, 432n4; and Trump administration,

176; and Washington seminars, 96–7
Hudson Institute, 29, 32, 220, 243, 422n20

Income Tax Act, 12, 62, 429n26
Institute for Government Research, 27–8, 41
Institute for International Economics, 11, 40
Institute for Policy Studies (IPS), 32, 63; profile of, 246
Institute for Research on Public Policy (IRPP), 7, 35–6, 39, 82, 84–5, 184, 212, 215, 254, 431n62–3; 1994 budget consultations, 195; and constitutional conferences, 182, 188, 190, 193; consultations with government, 135; and media exposure, 91–2, 117, 122, 230; and parliamentary testimony, 136; profile of, 260–2
Institute of Economic Affairs, 53
Institute of Economics, 27, 41
Institute of Pacific Relations, 28
Institute on Governance, 36
interest groups, 11, 14–16, 64–6, 72, 134, 165, 169, 202, 204, 206, 216, 418n6; and Keystone XL, 224
Internal Revenue Code, 12, 49, 62, 178, 419n21, 441n87
Internal Revenue Service, 11, 178, 235, 429n26, 435n7

Jérôme-Forget, Monique, 7
Johnson, Lyndon B., 29, 32, 199, 246–7, 419n21, 422n20

Kagan, Robert, 50
Kahn, Herman, 29, 43, 422n20
Kansas Policy Institute, 92, 210
Kemp, Jack, 38, 436n32
Keystone XL Pipeline, 8, 197; and First Nations, 203, 218; and Harper government, 8, 197–9, 200, 222; history of, 201–3; and Obama administration, 8, 197–9, 200, 222; and think tanks, 19, 149, 196, 200, 203–7, 217–24; and Trudeau government, 199, 201, 222; and Trump administration, 8, 177, 201, 207, 222
Kingdon, John, 70–1, 84
Kirby, Michael, 85, 430n53
Kirkpatrick, Jeane, 38, 44, 95, 164
Kissinger, Henry, 86
Koch, Charles, 248
Koch brothers, 92, 221
Koch Foundation, 82
Krasner, Stephen, 66–7, 71–2
Kristol, William, 49–50
Kroeger, Arthur, 183, 186–7
Kurtz, Howard, 100

Law Reform Commission of Canada, 33–4, 40, 422n29
Libby, Lewis "Scooter," 50
Linden, Patricia, 44, 98
Lindquist, Evert, 17, 25, 33, 51, 69, 87, 180–1, 195–6, 260, 433n4
Lindsey, Lawrence, 47, 95, 440n76; and George W. Bush, 150, 167
Lipset, Seymour Martin, 85

MacDonald-Laurier Institute, 39, 100, 235, 254; profile of, 262–3
Mackenzie Institute, 12, 36, 431n62; and media exposure, 116; and parliamentary testimony, 140
Manhattan Institute, 75, 168; profile of, 248–9
Manning, Preston, 24, 37
Manning Centre, 24, 37–8, 84–5, 208
Manning Foundation, 24, 37–8, 84–5
Martin, Paul, 80, 195
Maxwell, Judith, 9, 38, 80, 87, 257
Maytree Foundation, 38, 55

McCain, John, 170–1, 173
McGann, James G., 3, 11–12, 22
Meech Lake Accord, 185–6, 193–4, 442n7
Meese, Edwin, 93, 160, 162, 437n39, 438n47, 438n49
Mendelson, Michael, 56
Milne, David, 186
Mondale, Walter, 156, 165
Montreal Economic Institute (MEI), 15, 39–40; profile of, 263–4
Mowat Centre, 23, 39; profile of, 264–5
Mullins, Mark, 54
Mulroney, Brian, 34, 40, 55, 126, 139, 199, 431n63; and constitutional conferences, 182, 184–7
Mulroney Institute of Government, 25, 38

National Anti-Poverty Organization, 78
National Bureau of Economic Research, 11, 27
National Center for Charitable Statistics, 93
National Council of Welfare, 24, 33, 38, 40, 55, 78, 83, 422n29; media exposure, 116; parliamentary testimony, 136, 140
National Institute for Public Policy, 85
National Planning Association (NPA), 33, 423n36
National Policy Institute, 11, 175
National Rifle Association (NRA), 14
National Security Council, 76, 168, 436n23, 438n54
New Democratic Party (NDP), 25, 37, 53, 78, 206, 445n14, 445n16
Newsom, David, 64
Niagara Institute: and constitutional conferences, 182, 187–90, 193
Nixon, Richard, 45, 67, 153, 159, 199
Nixon Center for Peace and Freedom, 24, 37
North American Free Trade Agreement (NAFTA), 183, 197, 203, 206, 218, 220, 440n70
North-South Institute (NSI), 35, 82, 212, 422n29; and budget of, 24; and media exposure, 119; and parliamentary testimony, 136

Obama, Barack, 40, 68, 72, 151; and Keystone XL, 8, 198–203, 218, 221–3; and think tanks, 4, 39, 77, 86, 95, 170–4
Obamacare, 8, 49, 69; as Affordable Care Act, 8
Office of Management and Budget (OMB), 42, 76, 161, 436n32
Olin Foundation, 46, 83
Ontario Federation of Labour, 81

Paris Climate Agreement, 8–9, 175, 177, 222
Paris Peace Conference, 244
Parkland Institute, 39, 56–7, 63; and Keystone XL, 200, 217, 219, 223
Parliamentary Centre for Foreign Affairs, 33, 123; budget of, 119; media exposure, 117
Pearson-Shoyama Institute, 38, 123; media exposure, 118–21
Pembina Institute, 36; and budget of, 231; and Keystone XL, 200, 217, 219–20; and media exposure, 117, 230
Perot, Ross, 38
Peschek, Joseph, 16, 61
philanthropic foundations, 41, 61–2, 82–3, 212–13, 235, 421n16, 422n20
Pipes, Sally, 53, 84
Pitfield, Michael, 85, 430n53
pluralism, 16–17, 58, 60, 64–5, 69, 71, 427n15
Podesta, John D., 40, 173
policy communities, 17, 48, 68–70, 77, 229

policy cycles, 4, 6–7, 10, 17–18, 57, 63, 70–3, 79, 116, 145, 182, 195, 201, 225, 227, 229
policy entrepreneurship, 37, 44, 83–5, 208, 236
policy research capacity, 15, 17
Policy Research Initiative (PRI), 34
President's Economic Policy Advisory Board (PEPAB), 95
President's Foreign Intelligence Advisory Board (PFIAB), 95, 432n4
Prime Minister's Office (PMO), 77, 205, 227
Private Planning Association of Canada (PPAC), 33, 35, 257, 423n36, 444n27
Privy Council Office (PCO), 34, 79, 205, 227, 430n53
Progress and Freedom Foundation, 38
Progressive Policy Institute (PPI), 164–5, 437n46; profile of, 249
Project for a New American Century (PNAC), 49–51, 168–9, 208
Pruitt, Scott, 9
Public Policy Forum, 9, 15, 36, 74, 78, 87, 145; 1994 budget consultations, 195; consultations with government, 98, 135; and media exposure, 89, 122, 231; profile of, 265–6

RAND, 6, 11–12, 21, 23, 32, 47, 63, 68, 81, 97, 108–9, 112, 145, 153, 161, 234, 243, 421n19, 422n20, 424n53; history of, 29, 42–3; and media exposure, 232–3
Raisian, John, 178
Randall, Judy, 78
Raskin, Marcus, 32, 246
Rawson, Garry, 189–90
Raybould, John, 53
Raymond, Arthur, 42
Reader's Digest Foundation, 83
Reagan, Ronald, 46, 48, 76, 126, 150, 167, 169, 199, 248; and Heritage Foundation, 93–4, 102–3, 162–3, 208; and think tanks, 86, 151–2, 158–61, 164, 166, 179, 432n4, 441n87
Renewal of Canada initiative, 149, 182–3, 185, 189, 193–4
Rice, Condoleezza, 14, 168
Rice, Susan, 170–2, 174
Rich, Andrew, 106, 108–9, 114–15, 117, 234, 238
Ritchie, Ronald, 35, 261
Rivlin, Alice, 42
Robert S. Brookings Graduate School of Economics and Government, 27, 41
Rockefeller, David, 154–5
Rockefeller Foundation, 82, 212
Round Table Movement, 28
Royal Commission on Taxation, 35
Royal Institute of International Affairs (RIIA), 28, 211
Rumsfeld, Donald, 14, 50
Russell, Peter, 186
Russell Sage Foundation, 27

Sage, Margaret Olivia, 27
Saloma, John, 16, 61
Saskatchewan Institute of Public Policy, 39–40, 431n59
Scaife, Richard Mellon, 49
Schlesinger, James, 32
Schmitt, Gary, 50
Schultze, Charles, 42
Science Council of Canada, 24, 33–4, 40, 85, 422n29; and media exposure, 116; parliamentary testimony, 136
Scowcroft, Brent, 86
Shoup, Laurence, 154–5
Shultz, George, 14, 86, 150, 161, 163, 168
Skocpol, Theda, 66
Smith, James, 10, 21
Spencer, Richard, 11
Stairs, Denis, 70

state theory, 58, 60, 65–8, 71–2, 85
Steelman, Aaron, 66
Stone, Diane, 69, 74
Strategic Defence Forum (SDF), 12

Talbott, Strobe, 28, 42, 86, 213–14
Taylor, William J., Jr, 100
Thatcher, Margaret, 103, 432n19
think tanks: appearances before legislative committees, 137–44, 146–8; assessing influence of, 94–5, 102–4, 418n7; barriers to policy-making process, 74, 81–6; and Bush administration, 14, 47, 49, 95, 168–9, 208; and Carter administration, 151–2, 154, 436n22; and channels of influence, 90–6; and Clinton administration, 42, 151–2, 166, 437n46, 439n69; conceptual frameworks for, 17–18, 58–72; concerns of Internal Revenue Service, 11, 429n26; and donors, 91, 93–4, 102, 153, 178, 210–14, 217, 223, 235; evolution of, 27–41; and government consultations, 133–8; involvement in policy-making, 86–8, 105, 132; involvement in policy research initiative, 203–4; and the media, 98–102, 110–16, 118–31, 209–12; participation in constitutional conferences, 182–4, 187–96; and presidential candidates, 150–3, 179; and Obama administration, 8, 39, 72, 86, 95, 173–4, 218, 221; and Reagan administration, 46, 102, 151–2, 161–4, 166, 437n46; role of, 14–16; selected profiles of, 41–57, 241–9, 251–66; and ties to policymakers, 17, 89, 204–7, 229; and Trump administration, 8, 19, 49, 175–6, 179, 246; typologies of, 22–6; and World Bank, 47, 168
Torjman, Sherri, 55
Trudeau, Justin, 39, 80, 208, 222; and Keystone XL, 199, 201
Trudeau, Pierre Elliott, 35, 53, 199, 261
Truluck, Phillip, 48
Trump, Donald, 7, 37, 69, 174, 207–8, 220, 419n21; and Heritage Foundation, 101, 151–2, 175, 177; and Keystone XL, 8, 199, 201, 203, 222; and Paris Climate Agreement, 8–9, 222; and think tanks, 4, 8, 11, 19, 49, 77, 95, 98, 151, 175–7, 179, 246
Tupper, Allan, 180–1, 195–6, 432n65

Urban Institute, 11, 23, 29, 32, 93, 109, 234, 422n20; profile of, 246–7
US Department of State, 42, 66–7, 97, 159, 168, 171–2, 174; and Keystone XL, 202, 222, 225

Vanier Institute of the Family, 33, 52–3, 122
Veldhuis, Niels, 54, 103
Volcker, Paul, 156

Walker, Michael, 53–4, 84, 103
Warnke, Paul, 156
Watts, Ron, 188, 193, 443n18
Weaver, R. Kent, 11, 22, 24, 76, 106, 108–9, 114–15, 117, 234
Western Centre for Economic Research, 181
Weyrich, Paul, 47, 84
Williams, Brooke, 28, 94, 213
Wilson, Paul, 78
Wolfowitz, Paul, 47, 50, 168
World Bank, 47, 168

Zoellick, Robert, 95; and George W. Bush, 150, 168
Zussman, David, 74, 80, 265